Financial Reporting and Advanced Financial Reporting

Pearson

Financial Reporting and Advanced Financial Reporting

Selected chapters from:

Financial Accounting and Reporting
Nineteenth Edition
Barry Elliott and Jamie Elliott

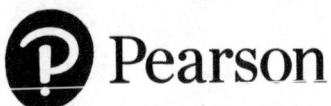

P Pearson

Harlow, England • London • New York • Boston • San Francisco • Toronto • Sydney • Dubai • Singapore • Hong Kong
Tokyo • Seoul • Taipei • New Dehli • Cape Town • São Paulo • Mexico City • Madrid • Amsterdam • Munich • Paris • Milan

Pearson
KAO Two
KAO Park
Harlow
Essex CM17 9NA

And associated companies throughout the world

Visit us on the World Wide Web at:
www.pearson.com/uk

© Pearson Education Limited 2019

Compiled from:

Financial Accounting and Reporting
Nineteenth Edition
Barry Elliott and Jamie Elliott
ISBN 978-1-292-25599-6
© Pearson Education Limited 2012, 2013, 2015, 2017, 2019

ISBN 978-1-78764-505-9

Printed and bound in Great Britain by CPI Group.

CONTENTS

CHAPTER 1

Review of financial ratio analysis

1.1 Introduction

The key objective of financial statements is to provide useful financial information to the stakeholders, or 'users' – those with legitimate rights to such information. Different users have different information needs, for example:

- Existing and potential equity investors will be primarily interested in the profitability of an entity but will also require reassurance that the entity's liquidity (ability to generate cash) is such that it can continue in operational existence for the foreseeable future as a going concern.

- Lenders (both short- and long-term) will be primarily interested in the ability of the entity to generate the cash that is required to repay them and will focus on liquidity issues.

- Management will be concerned with both profitability (to satisfy the legitimate needs of the investors to whom they are accountable) and liquidity (to satisfy the legitimate needs of the lenders and suppliers to receive repayment of the amounts owed to them).

A financial analyst needs to be able to extract useful information from financial data, whether this is produced internally as detailed statements for the benefit of management or published externally for the benefit of external stakeholders, primarily the equity investors. The purpose of this chapter is to provide a framework for the analysis of financial data in order to write a report.

Objectives

By the end of this chapter, you should be able to:

- appreciate the potential of ratio analysis as an analytical tool;
- carry out an initial overview of financial statements;
- discuss the relationship between the return on capital employed and supporting accounting ratios through the 'pyramid of ratios';
- analyse the financial statements of a single entity;
- draft a report based on an inter-period and inter-firm comparison;
- explain the limitations of comparisons based on ratios.

1.2 Overview of techniques for the analysis of financial data

1.2.1 The 'golden rule of analysis'

This might be described as 'identify your yardstick of comparison'. Analysis without comparison is meaningless. For example, if you were simply told that an entity generated revenue of £10 million and made a profit of £900,000 it would be difficult or impossible to assess whether that was 'good' or 'bad' without reference to factors such as:

- the previous year's revenues and profits;
- the budgeted revenues and profits;
- the revenues and profits of competitors in the same industry; and
- the underlying expectations of the analyst based on their knowledge of relevant internal and external factors.

If we are making an inter-firm comparison for management purposes care has to be taken to select a company that is in the same industry.

While it is possible to compare the return on investment that is obtainable in different industries when deciding whether to invest, it would be extremely difficult to compare management ratios in different industries looking at, say, how well managers are controlling the cash cycle. For example, the cash cycle of a retail company where customers generally pay on receipt of goods is completely different from that of a construction company. We need to be sure, as far as possible, that we are making a valid comparison.

1.2.2 The benefits of ratio analysis

The use of accounting ratios for analysis purposes has a number of important benefits for analysts:

- Ratios allow comparison with peers through inter-firm comparison schemes and comparison with industry averages so that possible strengths and weaknesses can be identified.
- Through the pyramid approach it is possible to carry out a structured analysis of financial performance and financial position by drilling down to identify ratios in ever greater detail, building up to the return on capital employed.
- It enables, for certain ratios, the comparison of entities of different sizes. For example, it is very difficult to compare the absolute profits of two entities without an appreciation of how 'large' one entity is relative to another. However, it might be perfectly legitimate to compare the ratio of profit to revenue of two entities of very different sizes in the same industry.

1.2.3 Ratio analysis – some notes of caution

In order to evaluate a ratio, it is customary to make a comparison with that of the previous year or with the industry average. However, remember to check if:

- The same accounting policies have been applied; for example, have non-current assets been reported using the same measurement bases (i.e. at depreciated cost or revalued amounts in both cases)?
  Inter-firm comparison schemes overcome this problem by requiring all member companies to report using uniform defined ratios.

● Note has been taken of different commercial practices. For example, some retail entities lease their properties on operating leases whilst others purchase them. *Accounting ratios that use assets as their denominator will be affected.*

● The ratios have been defined in the same way. This is important when comparing ratios from different companies' Annual Reports – check to see if the company has defined its ratios.

1.3 Ratio analysis – a case study

Vertigo plc is a family company which deals in building materials and garden supplies. It has been managed by non-family members since the principal shareholder/managing director retired from active management at the end of 20X6 on health grounds. Let us assume that you are a trainee in an accounting firm that has been approached by a client who is a family member for a report on the company's financial position and financial performance following a fall in profit available for dividend and a request by the management for an injection of more capital.

We will use the financial statements of Vertigo (see below) to illustrate the technique.

1.3.1 Financial statements for the case study

Vertigo plc: statement of income for year ended 31 December

	20X9		*20X8*	
	£000	*£000*	*£000*	*£000*
Revenues		3,461		3,296
Opening inventory	398		253	
Purchases	2,623		2,385	
Closing inventory	(563)		(398)	
Cost of goods sold		(2,458)		(2,240)
Gross profit		1,003		1,056
Distribution costs:				
Depreciation	187		239	
Irrecoverable debts	17		32	
Advertising	24		94	
		(228)		(365)
Administrative expenses:				
Rent	60		60	
Salaries and wages	362		316	
Miscellaneous expenses	177		159	
		(599)		(535)
Operating profit		176		156
Dividend received		—		51
Finance costs		(60)		(53)
Profit before tax		116		154
Income tax expense		(25)		(39)
Profit after taxation		91		115

Vertigo plc: statement of financial position at 31 December

	20X9 £000	20X8 £000
ASSETS		
Non-current assets:		
Machinery	2,100	2,240
Motor vehicles	394	441
Investments	340	340
	2,834	3,021
Current assets:		
Inventory	563	398
Trade receivables	1,181	912
Cash and cash equivalents	9	11
	1,753	1,321
	4,587	4,342
EQUITY AND LIABILITIES		
Equity:		
Ordinary shares of 50p each	3,000	3,000
Retained earnings	353	262
	3,353	3,262
Non-current liabilities:		
Long-term borrowings (repayable in 8 years)	600	600
Current liabilities:		
Trade payables	498	398
Accrued expenses	15	12
Taxation	24	29
Short-term borrowings	97	41
	634	480
	4,587	4,342

1.4 Introductory review

Before embarking on detailed ratio analysis, an analyst (whether an internal or an external user of the financial statements) would carry out a review to gain an overall impression of:

(a) the external trading conditions for the building materials sector, for example, refer to subscription sources such as the Markit/CIPS Purchasing Managers' Index (PMI) indices; and

(b) the financial statements as a whole.

We will illustrate one approach using common-sized statements for Vertigo before proceeding to consider more detailed ratios and the preparation of a report.

Overall impressions from initial review

Common-sized statements are a useful aid when making an initial review of a company's financial structure, such as seeing the percentage of cash to current assets, and cost structures such as the percentage of sales revenue that goes on administration.

1.4.1 The company's financial structure

Our first thought might be to gain an impression of the financial structure of a company.

Vertical analysis – common-sized statement

The vertical analysis approach highlights the structure of the statement of financial position by presenting non-current assets, working capital, debt and equity as a percentage of debt plus equity. It allows us to form a view on the financing of the business, in particular the extent to which a business is reliant on debt to finance its non-current assets. In times of recession this is of particular interest and is described as indicating the strength of the financial position.

	20X8 £000	20X8 %	20X9 £000	20X9 %
Non-current assets	3,021	69.6	2,834	61.8
Current assets	1,321	30.4	1,753	38.2
Total	4,342	100	4,587	100
Equity	3,262	75.1	3,353	73.1
Debt	600	13.8	600	13.1
Current liabilities	480	11.1	634	13.8
Total	4,342	100	4,587	100

This indicates that the financial strength is maintained in terms of the amount of debt compared to the amount of capital put in by the shareholders.

However, the non-current assets have fallen and the fall appears to be due to the depreciation charge. We need to assess whether this lack of investment in non-current assets is likely to be a concern for the future and to check if the management has identified and quantified future capital expenditure commitments.

Horizontal analysis – common-sized statement

A horizontal analysis looks at the percentage change that has occurred. We could calculate the percentage change for every asset and liability, but it is more helpful in Vertigo to concentrate on the area that seems to require closer investigation, i.e. current assets and liabilities. The analysis is as follows:

	20X8 £000	20X9 £000	Percentage change
Current assets:			
Inventory	398	563	+41.5
Trade receivables	912	1,181	+29.5
Cash and cash equivalents	11	9	−18.2
Trade payables	398	498	+25.1
Accrued expenses	12	15	+25.0
Taxation	29	24	−17.2
Bank overdraft	41	97	+136.6

Inventories and (to a lesser extent) trade receivables have risen significantly when we consider that sales have increased by only 5%.

This raises questions in our mind. For example, is it possibly because greater quantities of inventory are expected to be required in anticipation of growth in future sales? Alternatively, is the inventory slow-moving with the possibility that net realisable value is lower than cost?

Trade payables have increased significantly. This could be due to poor cash flow putting pressure on liquidity (short-term borrowings have increased by around £50,000 and there has been no additional long-term equity or loan finance).

The common-sized analysis of the financial position has given us questions to have in our minds when carrying out a more detailed analysis. The next step would be to extract detailed turnover ratios for inventory, trade receivables and payables and ascertain the terms and limit of the overdraft. Before doing that, we carry out a similar common-sized exercise to form a view of a company's cost structure.

1.4.2 The company's cost structure

Again, both a vertical and horizontal analysis is helpful.

Vertical analysis – common-sized statement

An overview is obtained by restating by function into a vertical common-sized statement format as follows:

	20X8 £000	20X8 %	20X9 £000	20X9 %
Sales	3,296	100.0	3,461	100.0
Cost of sales	2,240	68.0	2,458	71.0
Total gross profit	1,056	32.0	1,003	29.0
Distribution costs	365	11.1	228	6.6
Administration expenses	588	17.8	659	19.0
Net profit before tax	103	3.1	116	3.4

We can see that there has been a change in the cost structure with a fall in the gross profit from 32% to 29% compensated for by a significant fall in the distribution costs.

Horizontal analysis – common-sized statement

An overview is obtained by calculating the percentage change as follows:

	20X8 £000	20X9 £000	Percentage change
Sales	3,296	3,461	+5.0
Cost of sales	2,240	2,458	+9.7
Total gross profit	1,056	1,003	−5.0
Distribution costs	365	228	−37.5
Administration expenses	588	659	+12.1
Net profit before tax and dividend income	103	116	+12.6

Our initial observations are as follows:

- Revenues have risen slightly but gross profits have fallen. We need to establish the reasons for this.
- Other operating expenses (distribution costs and administrative expenses) have fallen significantly. This appears in the main to be caused by the reduction in depreciation charges and advertising expenditure.
- No income has been received from the financial asset in the period. This may be due to timing issues (given that dividend income is basically recognised only when received). However, we would need to carry out further investigations here.

We can now go on to a more detailed analysis.

1.5 Financial statement analysis, part 1 – financial performance

Return on investment

If the analysis is being performed exclusively for the shareholders then an appropriate ROI measure might be 'Return on equity (ROE)'. This ratio would be calculated as:

$$\frac{\text{Profit attributable to the shareholders}}{\text{Equity}}$$

For Vertigo, ROE would be

	20X9	20X8
Profit after tax	91	115
Equity	3,353	3,262
So ROE equals	2.7%	3.5%

This shows a fall of more than 20%.

Return on capital employed

If the analysis is of the overall performance of the entity (however it is financed) then the appropriate ratio is 'Return on Capital Employed (ROCE)'. Management would be likely to consider this to be the best measure of ROI, as it shows the return on the assets under their control without any effect from the rates of tax and interest which operational management might regard as outside their control.

This ratio would be calculated as:

$$\frac{\text{Profit before interest and tax (PBIT)}}{\text{Capital employed (CE) (equity + borrowings)}}$$

Definitions of ratios vary
It should be remembered that there is no 'accounting standard' that governs the exact composition of this ratio and care needs to be taken when making inter-firm comparisons. For example, capital employed might be defined as:

(a) total assets, also expressed as equity plus long-term loans plus current liabilities; or

(b) net assets, also expressed as equity plus long-term loans. Even here, though, care is needed – if a company maintains a high level of relatively permanent overdraft it might be added to the long-term loans.

For the purposes of this analysis, we will take 'borrowings' to be long-term borrowings only. Therefore our ROCE would be as follows:

	20X9	20X8
Profit before interest and tax	116 + 60	154 + 53
Capital employed	3,353 + 600	3,262 + 600
So ROCE equals	4.4%	5.4%

Our initial conclusion would be that Vertigo is less profitable in 20X9 than it was in 20X8. We would need to investigate further to establish the reasons for this. In looking for a reason for the fall from 5.4% to 4.4% we propose to follow the pyramid approach.

Figure 1.1 Pyramid for return on capital employed

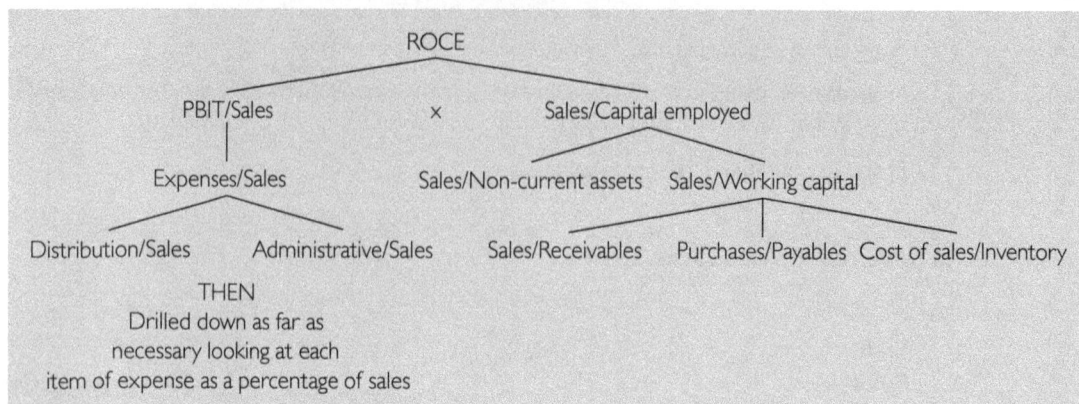

ROCE

PBIT/Sales × Sales/Capital employed

Expenses/Sales   Sales/Non-current assets   Sales/Working capital

Distribution/Sales   Administrative/Sales   Sales/Receivables   Purchases/Payables   Cost of sales/Inventory

THEN
Drilled down as far as
necessary looking at each
item of expense as a percentage of sales

1.5.1 The Du Pont pyramid approach

In this approach we start at the top of the pyramid with the return on capital employed and systematically analyse those ratios that impact on the profit and those that impact on the assets employed in the business. This approach is also the basis for a number of inter-firm comparison schemes.

Diagrammatically the pyramid is shown in Figure 1.1. We can see the pyramid starts with the following relationship:

$$\frac{\text{Profit before interest and tax}}{\text{Capital employed}} = \frac{\text{Profit before interest and tax}}{\text{Revenue}} = \frac{\text{Revenue}}{\text{Capital employed}}$$

This is often expressed as:

$$\text{ROCE} = \text{Profit margin} \times \text{Asset turnover}$$

This shows us that the two key components of the return on capital employed are '**margin**' (PBIT/Revenue) and '**volume**' (Revenue/Capital employed). It is to these two aspects that we now turn.

1.5.2 Margin and expense analysis

The first 'margin ratio' we compute is the 'net profit margin'. This is simply:

$$\frac{\text{'Profit' (PBIT as used the ROCE ratio)}}{\text{Revenue}}$$

For Vertigo, the profit margins for 20X9 and 20X8 are:

	20X9	20X8
Profit	176	207
Revenue	3,461	3,296
So profit margin equals	5.1%	6.3%

This shows us that one of the reasons for the decline in ROCE is a decline in the profit margin. For our report we 'drill down' into the detail and investigate further why the margin has reduced. Is it because the gross profit has fallen or is it due to expenses?

Gross profit

One possibility is that the relationship between our revenues and our cost of sales has altered, so it is instructive to compute the gross profit margin. This ratio is computed as:

$$\frac{\text{Gross profit}}{\text{Revenue}}$$

For Vertigo, the gross profit margins for 20X9 and 20X8 are:

	20X9	20X8
Gross profit	1,003	1,056
Revenue	3,461	3,296
So profit margin equals	29.0%	32.0%

Clearly the reduction in gross margin is not a good thing and internal analysts would almost certainly call for further investigation. We do not have the data here to perform more detailed checks.

Remember, however, that in answering any interpretation question it is always important to identify the further questions you would ask and the further information you would request, giving your reasons. For example, questions would be asked as to whether there has been:

- a change in the sales mix, with a greater proportion of lower-margin items being sold this year than last year;
- a change to maintain sales volume at the expense of the profit margin;
- discounting or longer-running sales;
- a rise in raw material costs that could not be passed on to customers in the form of increased sales prices; or
- a rise in the employment costs of production workers that could not be passed on to customers in the form of increased sales prices. This is unlikely to be the reason for the change in the gross margin here, given that cost of sales appears to include purchases, rather than production costs. Apparently Vertigo is a retail organisation rather than a manufacturing organisation – unless, perhaps, it is involved in also constructing any of the building products such as conservatories and garden studios.

Operating expenses – administrative expenses

We could also compute:

	20X9	20X8
Administrative expenses	599	535
Revenues	3,461	3,296
Ratio	17.3%	16.2%

This ratio reveals a slightly less satisfactory position in 20X9 compared with 20X8. The information we have shows us that a key factor behind the increase is the rise in salary costs of approximately 15%. This seems excessive given that revenues have grown by only 5%.

Operating expenses – distribution costs

A further part of the analysis of the profit margin is to investigate the relationship between other operating expenses and revenues. For Vertigo, this would involve computing:

	20X9	20X8
Distribution costs	228	365
Revenues	3,461	3,296
Ratio	6.6%	11.1%

Clearly, for Vertigo, the adverse movement in the gross profit margin is at least partly mitigated by a reduction of the percentage of distribution costs to revenues. Given the information we have for Vertigo (not necessarily available to an external analyst), we can see that there has been a significant reduction in depreciation (all of which has been charged to this expense heading) and advertising costs.

We would at this stage drill down further, in the same way as when designing audit tests, to target areas of significant change.

	20X8 £000	20X9 £000	Percentage change
Sales revenue	3,296	3,461	+5.0
Inventory – opening	253	398	
Purchases	2,385	2,623	+10.0
Inventory – closing	(398)	(563)	+41.5
Cost of goods sold	(2,240)	(2,458)	+9.7
Gross profit	1,056	1,003	−5.0
Distribution costs:			
Depreciation	239	187	−21.8
Bad debts	32	17	−46.9
Advertising	94	24	−74.5
Administrative expenses:			
Rent	60	60	—
Salaries and wages	316	362	+14.6
Miscellaneous expenses	159	177	+11.3
Operating profit	156	176	+12.8

It is interesting to see that discretionary costs in the form of advertising have been reduced by 74.5%. However, if the advertising had been maintained at 20X8 levels the operating profit would be reduced by £70,000 to £106,000, which would have shown a fall from the previous year of 32% rather than an increase of 12.8%.

This is where it is important to look at trends, in particular from 1 January 20X6 which was the last year when the previous Managing Director had been in control. There should be further enquiry to establish (a) the normal level over the previous three years – whether there was heavier advertising in 20X8 to achieve the 5% increase in sales in the light of the company's intention to attempt to obtain further investment in 20X9; (b) whether the reduction is likely to have an adverse effect on future sales; (c) what the company's reason was for reduced spending; and (d) the necessity or otherwise to return to a higher level in future years. This is more of commercial relevance to the client who is already concerned about the fall in profits than audit relevance.

1.5.3 Volume analysis – asset turnover

The basic 'volume ratio' is:

$$\frac{\text{Revenue}}{\text{Capital employed}}$$

This ratio is commonly referred to as the *asset turnover ratio*. For Vertigo, this ratio is:

	20X9	*20X8*
Revenue	3,461	3,296
Capital employed	3,953	3,862
Asset turnover	87.6%	85.3%
Turnover expressed as a multiple	0.876×	0.853×

This shows us that the asset turnover has in fact slightly improved in 20X9 compared with 20X8. Therefore an overall conclusion we can make is that the decline in ROCE is due to a declining margin rather than a decline in the utilisation of assets. Using our formula, we can now see that:

ROCE (4.4%) = profit margin (5.1%) × asset turnover (0.876)

Although the asset turnover rate has improved, we still need to analyse the reasons for the change, because the change can have resulted from changes in sales or any of the non-current and current assets.

Non-current asset turnover

The non-current asset turnover is:

$$\frac{\text{Revenue}}{\text{Non-current assets}}$$

For Vertigo, this ratio is:

	20X9	*20X8*
Revenue	3,461	3,296
Non-current assets	2,834	3,021
Non-current asset turnover	122.1%	109.1%
Turnover expressed as a multiple	1.22×	1.09×

From a profitability point of view, this is an improvement. However, we should remember that there has been no investment in non-current assets this year and, after depreciation, the asset turnover would appear to have improved simply because the written-down value of the non-current assets is lower.

An increasing ratio is not always an improving ratio and might not always be good for the long-term health of the business. For example, if we had made an investment in non-current assets this year we would have quite possibly replaced older, fully depreciated, assets with newer assets that have higher net book values. This might be good for the long term but in the short term the fall in the rate of turnover of non-current assets would have a negative impact on the ROCE.

New, growth companies are likely to have a fall in the rate of non-current asset turnover as they expand. We must take care that our use of ratios does not take us into 'short-term thinking'.

Asset turnover – working capital

When we analyse net current assets (or 'working capital') we generally do this by an individual focus on the three key components of inventory, trade receivables and trade payables.

Inventory turnover

The ratio we use to assess the effectiveness of our inventory management is the 'inventory days ratio'. This would normally be computed as:

$$\frac{\text{Closing inventory} \times 365}{\text{Cost of sales}}$$

The rationale behind the ratio is that we are effectively dividing closing inventory by 'one day's usage' to give us a hypothetical period for how long it will take us to sell the inventory. Whilst this analysis can be useful, we need to sound two notes of caution:

- We are relating the closing inventory to the average 'usage' in the previous year. The closing inventory will of course be used next year and so a more 'realistic' figure would be to base it on next year's projected usage, but of course this often is not available to the analyst.
- With this (and other) ratios we are comparing a 'point of time' figure (closing inventory) with a 'period' figure (cost of sales).

To a certain extent, both of the above factors are at least partly mitigated by the fact that, when using ratio analysis, we are comparing one ratio with another, and if the above factors apply to both the ratio and its comparative, to a certain extent the above 'defects' can cancel each other out.

That said, our inventory days ratio will be:

	20X9	20X8
Closing inventory × 365	563 × 365	398 × 365
Cost of sales	2,458	2,240
Inventory days	84 days	65 days
Turnover expressed as a multiple	4.4×	5.6×

Inventory is not being turned over as quickly in 20X9. This is not a positive sign. Not only does it affect the profitability of Vertigo but it also affects its liquidity, as we will see in the next section.

Trade receivables

The second key component of working capital is trade receivables. The equivalent ratio for trade receivables is:

$$\frac{\text{Trade receivable} \times 365}{\text{Revenue}}$$

For Vertigo, this ratio would be

	20X9	20X8
Trade receivables × 365	1,181 × 365	912 × 365
Sales	3,461	3,296
Trade receivables days	125 days	101 days
Turnover expressed as a multiple	2.9×	3.6×

It appears that Vertigo is collecting its cash from its customers less quickly in 20X9 than was the case in 20X8. This has a negative impact on profitability as the working capital cycle is lengthened when customers take longer to pay. This in turn has a negative impact on liquidity.

Late payment is a serious problem and a study in 2012 by the Clydesdale Bank and Yorkshire Bank in the UK reported that 10% of businesses say closing or seriously scaling back operations would have to be looked at if customers took more than 90 days to pay invoices. This poses a problem for management who need to tighten up their systems and controls and introduce procedures such as agreeing payment terms and conditions upfront or using incentives for early payment. Vertigo's management need to review their current procedures.

Trade payables

The third key component of working capital is trade payables. The equivalent ratio for trade payables is:

$$\frac{\text{Trade payables} \times 365}{\text{Credit purchases}}$$

For Vertigo, this ratio would be

	20X9	20X8
$\dfrac{\text{Trade payables} \times 365}{\text{Credit purchases}}$	$\dfrac{498 \times 365}{2,623}$	$\dfrac{398 \times 365}{2,385}$
Trade payables days	69 days	61 days
Turnover expressed as a multiple	5.3×	6.0×

It appears that Vertigo is taking slightly longer to pay its suppliers in 20X9 than in 20X8. Given the way we have computed the profitability ratios (capital employed is total assets less current liabilities) this will actually improve the asset turnover and hence the ROCE. Given that our suppliers effectively provide us with interest-free finance there is, in a sense, a liquidity benefit in extending the credit we take from our suppliers.

However, this can also be indicative of liquidity problems that make it difficult for us to settle our debts as they fall due and, if we allow the level of our trade payables to get too high, it could lead to problems with future supplies and ultimately could lead to the entity being wound up. Overall the 'real' level of trade payables of Vertigo is probably not a major concern but management will need to monitor this going forward.

It should be noted that, whilst the trade payables ratio can be calculated from the accounts of Vertigo, those accounts are more detailed than the information available in the published financial statements. Credit purchases would not normally be available from the published financial statements. In practice external analysts would use cost of sales as a 'proxy' for credit purchases. As stated before, while this practice clearly isn't strictly correct, the fact that interpretation involves a comparison of ratios means that, if used consistently, this slightly contrived ratio can be used as a means of comparing the payment policies of a single entity over time or two comparable entities over a corresponding period.

The cash cycle

The cash cycle, also referred to as the cash conversion cycle, measures the number of days it takes to acquire and sell inventory and convert sales into cash. It measures how effective managers are in managing this process.

For Vertigo the cash cycle is:

$$\text{Accounts Receivable days} + \text{Inventory days} - \text{Accounts Payable days} = \text{Cash Cycle}$$
$$125 \quad + \quad 84 \quad - \quad 69 \quad = \quad 140 \text{ days}$$

This means it takes Vertigo 140 days from the time the company acquires inventory from its suppliers, completes the sale of the inventory to its customers and collects the cash from accounts receivable.

The 140 days can be regarded as the length of time the company needs to have cash to cover the cash cycle or, thinking defensively, to cover its operating expenses. The means that the management of the cash cycle is critical to the cash flow and profitability of the company.

High working capital turnover rate

As with all ratios, a high rate does not always indicate that it is acceptable. For example, a high turnover rate can indicate overtrading, i.e. the sales volume is excessive in relation to the equity investment in the business. A high turnover might be an indication that the business relies too much on credit granted by suppliers or the bank instead of providing an adequate margin of operating funds.

1.6 Financial statement analysis, part 2 – liquidity

Liquidity is the lifeblood of any business. The ultimate price for poor liquidity is insolvency and therefore internal managers cannot ignore it. External users who have lent or who are thinking about lending money to the entity, whether on a short-term or a long-term basis, will almost certainly be more concerned with liquidity than with profitability.

Analysts can consider the liquidity of an entity in two ways. The first is through ratio analysis. We discussed in the previous section the fact that investment in working capital, as revealed when calculating changes in inventory days, trade receivables days and trade payables days, had an impact on liquidity.

However, there are also other ratios that are commonly used to assess liquidity. These include the current ratio, the quick ratio and cash flow ratios.

1.6.1 The current ratio

This ratio is simply the ratio of current assets to current liabilities. In the case of Vertigo, this ratio would be:

	20X9	20X8
Current assets	1,753	1,321
Current liabilities	634	480
So current ratio equals	2.76	2.75

The rationale behind the ratio is that the current assets are a short-term source of cash for the entity, whilst the current liabilities are the amounts that need settling reasonably quickly.

It is very difficult to give a general level for this ratio which analysts would regard as 'satisfactory' because different entities vary so much in their working capital cycles. In most cases you would expect this ratio to be well in excess of 1 for analysts to feel comfortable. However, entities that can generate cash easily are often able to operate with current ratios well below 1.

Consider a food retailer: food retailers have little if any trade receivables, since they sell to their customers for cash. Their inventory levels necessarily have to be quite low, since their products are often perishable. However, their trade payables days would be just as large as for any manufacturing entity and, if they reinvest the cash they generate quickly, their current ratios are often less than 1/2:1. This does not mean they have liquidity problems, however!

Rather, therefore, than identifying an absolute level at which the current ratio should be, it is probably better to monitor whether or not there has been a significant change from one period to another and compare with the industry average or peer group. Comparing it with the previous year we can see that it is virtually unchanged – this does not mean, however, that it is acceptable. We would need to look further at the trend over the past four years and also at competitors' current ratios.

An increase in the current ratio beyond the company's own normal range may arise for a number of reasons, some beneficial, others unwelcome.

Beneficial reasons

These include:

- A build-up of inventory in order to support increased sales following an advertising campaign or increasing popular demand as for, say, a PlayStation. Management action will be to establish from a cash budget that the company will not experience liquidity problems from holding such inventory, e.g. there may be sufficient cash in hand or from operations, short-term loans, extended credit or bank overdraft facilities.

- A permanent expansion of the business which will require continuing higher levels of inventory. Management action will be to consider existing cash resources or future cash flows from operations or arrange additional long-term finance, e.g. equity or long-term borrowings to finance the increased working capital.

Unwelcome reasons

These include:

- Operating losses may have eroded the working capital base. Management action will vary according to the underlying problem, e.g. disposing of underperforming segments, arranging a sale of non-current assets or inviting a takeover.

- Inefficient control over working capital, e.g. poor inventory or accounts receivable control allowing a build-up of slow-moving inventories or doubtful trade receivables.

- Adverse trading conditions, e.g. inventory becoming obsolete or introduction of new models by competitors.

1.6.2 The quick ratio

Another ratio that is used for liquidity assessment purposes is the quick ratio (also known as the acid test ratio). This ratio is:

$$\frac{\text{Current assets} - \text{inventory}}{\text{Current liablities}}$$

The rationale for using the quick ratio is that entities cannot regard their inventory as a short-term source of cash because of the time it takes to realise cash through its sale. Whether this is true depends on the nature of the entity. This would certainly be true for entities in the construction sector, but for many entities in the retail sector, particularly those entities that sell their goods directly to the general public for cash, the current ratio would be a better measure of liquidity.

For Vertigo, the quick ratio would be:

	20X9	*20X8*
Current assets − inventory	1,753 − 563	1,321 − 398
Current liabilities	634	480
So quick ratio equals	1.88	1.92

There has been a small decline in this ratio given the higher trade payables levels but the decline is not significant.

1.6.3 Cash flow ratios

Even if a statement of cash flows is not provided in a question it is worth preparing and analysing one. If we prepared such a statement for Vertigo for the year ended 31 December 20X9 we would get the following:

	£000	*£000*
Profit before tax	116	
Finance costs	60	
Depreciation	187	
Increase in inventory	(165)	
Increase in trade receivables	(269)	
Increase in trade payables	100	
Increase in accrued expenses	3	
Cash generated from operations		32
Interest paid		(60)
Tax paid		(30)
Reduction in cash and cash equivalents		(58)
Cash and cash equivalents, 1 January 20X9 (11 − 41)		(30)
Cash and cash equivalents, 31 December 20X9 (9 − 97)		(88)

This statement shows that the entity is struggling to generate cash from its operations. This is mainly due to the increased levels of working capital; all three components have increased in real terms as we have already seen.

This increase has absorbed significant amounts of cash such that cash from operating activities is negative. There has been no investment in non-current assets or additional equity or loan capital raised, and cash flow fails to cover the current year's interest and any dividend payments.

Interest cover

The lenders would be interested in their interest cover, i.e. the number of times that their interest could be paid out of cash generated by the operations. In this case, the interest cover is $32/60 = 0.53$ times. Notice that this is far worse than the interest cover based on the statement of income which indicates that there is adequate cover at 2.93 times ($176/60$).

Servicing future debt

As we have already seen, the entity has not purchased any non-current assets this year but sooner or later they may have to. Their borrowing levels are not currently excessive (see Section 1.7 below) but their ability to service additional debt is questionable. Based on this, it would appear that consideration may need to be given to raising further long-term finance if future expansion of the business is envisaged.

1.6.4 The cash ratio

This is a more conservative ratio than the quick ratio as it shows the ratio of cash and cash equivalents to current liabilities. Suppliers are able to see whether these are enough to settle the amount owed to them. In this case, of course, it is a negative figure.

It is certainly not a problem that faces Vertigo but there are companies sitting on hoards of cash to meet cyclical demands or because they are nervous about investing in the uncertain economic climate or they are unable to find investment opportunities. We see major companies like Apple, therefore, setting aside US$10 billion for stock buybacks.

1.7 Financial statement analysis, part 3 – financing

One of the key issues for analysts is the way a business is financed. Of particular concern is the relationship between borrowings (debt finance) and equity finance. Because most equity investors are risk-averse, the return required by the providers of debt finance is lower than that required by equity investors as they would normally have fixed or floating security. However, management must balance the benefit of 'cheaper' debt finance against the fact that the greater the proportion of finance provided through borrowings the greater the risk for both as measured by the gearing ratio.

1.7.1 The gearing ratio

There are a number of ways in which the gearing ratio can be computed but the two most common are:

$$\frac{\text{Debt finance}}{\text{Debt finance} + \text{equity finance}}$$

and

$$\frac{\text{Debt finance}}{\text{Equity finance}}$$

Both these ratios will increase as the proportion of debt finance gets greater. We will use the former ratio to illustrate the gearing of Vertigo:

	20X9	20X8
Debt finance (long-term only)	600	600
Debt finance + equity finance	600 + 3,353	600 + 3,262
So gearing ratio equals	15.2%	15.5%

Gearing is relatively stable, the only fluctuation being caused by the retention of 20X9 profits increasing equity while long-term borrowings stay static. It is difficult to generalise, but this is a relatively low gearing ratio – ratios of less than one-third would normally be regarded as 'low' and gearing would normally only be regarded as 'high' when it exceeded 50%. There would appear to be plenty of scope for Vertigo to obtain more debt finance subject to being able to produce forecasts showing its ability to service the debt.

1.7.2 How should a potential investor decide on an acceptable level of gearing?

This is initially influenced by the political and economic climate of the time. We have seen that prior to the credit crisis arising in 2007 high gearing was not seen by many as risky and there was a general feeling that borrowing was good, leverage was respectable, and capital gains were inevitable. This might have reduced the importance of questions that would normally have been asked, such as the following.

Asset values
- Are the values in the statement of financial position reasonably current? If much lower than current then the gearing ratio may be significantly overstated.

Gearing ratios
- Is the gearing ratio constant or has it increased over time with heavier borrowing? If higher:
  - further borrowing might be difficult;
  - it might indicate that there has been investment that will lead to higher profits, so details are needed as to how the funds borrowed have been used.
- What covenants are in place and what is the risk that they might be breached? A breach could lead to a company having to renegotiate finance at a higher interest rate or even go into administration or liquidation.
- How does the gearing compare to other companies in the same sector?

Use of funds
- If gearing has increased, what were the funds used for? Was it to:

  - restructure debt following inability to meet current repayment terms?
  - finance new maintenance/expansion capital expenditure?
  - improve liquid ratios?

Interest commitment
- How variable is the rate of interest that is being charged on the borrowings? If rates are falling then equity shareholders benefit, but if rates rise then expenses are higher.
- How many times does the earnings before tax cover the interest? A highly geared company is more at risk if the business cycle moves into recession because the company has to continue to service the debts even if sales fall substantially.
- How many times does the cash flow from operations currently cover the interest? This is a useful ratio if profits are not converted into cash, e.g. they might be reinvested in working capital.

Cash flows
- How variable is the company's cash flow from operations? A company with a stable cash flow is less at risk, so the trend is important.
- What is the likely effect of contingent liabilities if they crystallise on the cash flows and debt ratio? Could it have a significant adverse impact?

A company's attitude to leverage may vary over time

This is often dependent on the availability of finance and the possibility of profitable capital investment. If there is uncertainty about either then there will an unwillingness to lend and an unwillingness to borrow.

1.8 Peer comparison

We have so far prepared internal ratios for two years making our comparison with 20X8. We have now selected comparative ratios from a competitor and set out some comparative ratios where Vertigo's ratios seem too high or too low:

	20X9	20X8	20X7	20X6	20X5
Asset turnover ratio:					
Vertigo	0.88	0.85			
Competitor*	2.77	2.10	1.96	1.59	1.43
Inventory turnover:					
Vertigo	84 days	65 days			
Competitor	58 days	70 days	62 days	80 days	87 days

* For illustration, the competitor comparisons were ratios reported in the Everest Industries 2012 Annual Report.

	20X9	20X8	20X7	20X6	20X5
Profit before interest and tax margin:					
Vertigo	5.1%	6.3%			
Competitor	7.9%	6.41%	7.2%	6.9%	4.38%
Debt/equity ratio:					
Vertigo	0.15	0.15			
Competitor	0.28	0.53	0.69	1.13	0.94
Current ratio:					
Vertigo	2.76	2.75			
Competitor	0.86	1.33	1.07	0.90	0.89
Quick ratio:					
Vertigo	1.88	1.92			
Competitor	0.66	0.63	0.70	0.67	0.70

Looking at the profit before interest and tax, it is interesting to see that the competitor has had a rising trend over the five years with alternating positive and negative changes but the overall trend is up. An examination of the past five years' figures for Vertigo would be helpful in identifying its trend.

The inventory turnover has risen in 20X9 for Vertigo but it is interesting to see that again the trend with the competitor is falling with uneven positive and negative changes over the five years. The competitor has clearly addressed the level of inventory held in the last year. This could well indicate that a target of 70 days for Vertigo should be achievable.

The debt/equity ratio is steady at 0.15 in Vertigo. This is almost half of the gearing in the competitor where the gearing has fallen year on year to less threatening levels.

The asset turnover, however, paints a different picture with the competitor turning over its assets three times faster than Vertigo. This would seem to indicate that Vertigo needs to work its assets more effectively and aim at increasing its sales. A 5% increase in sales compares with a 22% increase in the competitor's sales.

The current ratio and quick ratio are more than double those of the competitor whose trend figures show that it is operating on levels of less than 1:1 for both ratios.

Note that it is important to obtain a comparator from the same industry and size, as far as possible.

1.9 Report based on the analysis

A report based on the above analysis might read as follows:

Report:

From:

To:

Date:

Subject: Financial Performance of Vertigo Ltd

Profitability

Vertigo's profitability has declined compared with 20X8, with the ROCE declining from 5.4% in 20X8 to 4.4% in 20X9. This decline is mainly due to a reduction in the profit margin (see Appendix). The reduction is a combination of three factors:

- A reduction in the gross margin. Reasons for this need to be investigated further.
- An increase in administrative expenses. This is mainly caused by a 15% rise in salary costs which is a little surprising given the rise in revenue is only 5%.
- The reduction in the profit margin is slightly mitigated by a fall in distribution costs. The key reason for this is a significant reduction (almost 75%) in advertising expenditure. This reduction might be beneficial for profitability in the short term, but as a long-term measure this may be unwise.

Liquidity

Liquidity ratios are conservative but seem excessive when compared to the current and quick ratios of the competitor (see Appendix).

The cash generated from operations is very low given the level of profits and this amount does not cover the interest and tax payments made in the year. During 20X9 the cash balances declined by £88,000. A key reason for the disappointing cash flow is the significant increase in working capital, particularly inventory and trade receivables.

The reason for the increase in the inventory turnover needs to be discussed further with management. As far as the impact on cash is concerned, if inventory is brought back to the 65 days turnover level, the increase of £165,000 would be reduced by more than £120,000 – more than enough to pay off the existing short-term borrowings. An improvement to 70 days would be sufficient to clear all short-term borrowings.

Further investigation of the management of receivables is required, particularly in the present credit climate.

The overall rise in working capital is mitigated to a certain extent by a rise in trade payables. This needs to be carefully monitored to ensure that the credit status of Vertigo is not compromised.

Financial position

As stated above, overall liquidity ratios are unchanged in both years but the management of the working capital needs to be addressed. There has been no investment in non-current assets during 20X9 and the shareholders have not received a dividend. Both these factors may be due to a cash shortage and Vertigo would appear to require additional long-term finance. Compared to the competitor the gearing is low which, on the basis of the current level of borrowing, would allow Vertigo to seek additional debt finance.

Conclusion

Profits are under pressure. Although revenues are continuing to rise there appears to be a decline in the gross margin which needs investigating further.

As far as the possibility of an improvement in profitability is concerned, there is concern that the asset turnover is low and sales are increasing but at a slower rate than the competitor's. There has at the same time been a significant reduction in advertising spend, which seems strange in a competitive environment and with the slow rate of sales growth.

It is noted that there has been no investment in non-current assets in 20X9. It is not clear without further enquiry whether the current level of non-current assets can sustain an increase in sales. If not, the need for further capital expenditure could not be provided by the current level of operating cash-flow.

Further attention urgently needs to be paid to working capital management.

As far as obtaining additional loan or equity capital, profitability needs to be addressed. The ROE is low at 2.7% and operating cash is insufficient to fully cover interest payments. The more positive aspect is that, given an improvement in profitability, it would appear possible to obtain this through issuing more debt as gearing levels are fairly low.

To support a request for additional funding a feasible three-year forecast would be required and we would be pleased to assist with this if so instructed.

Appendix – detailed ratios (not reproduced here as computed earlier)

Subscription sources are available for inter-firm ratios such as *RMA Annual Statement Studies* (Risk Management Association).[1]

1.10 Caution when using ratios for prediction

At the beginning of the chapter we mentioned the importance of taking an overview which influenced your expectations as to, say, the level of sales or profits that could be expected.

The same approach has to be taken when interpreting the ratios. This involves considering external and internal factors that could help explain current ratios and what might be predicted from them.

1.10.1 External factors

There are a number of external factors that need to be considered when interpreting ratios bearing in mind the economic context within which a business has been and will be operating. Consider, for example, assuming that Vertigo is a retail company:

- Have the retail sales been adversely or positively affected by growth of Internet sales?
- Has there been a change in fashion or downturn in the market?
- Will this mean inventory write-downs? Discounted sales?

- Have wage costs gone up (or will they be going up) following legislation for equal pay for women, fairer pay for part-time staff and legislation for maternity and paternity leave?
- Have credit sales been affected by less being spent on non-essential items?
- Has the company had to respond to pressure to pay small suppliers on time?
- Has there been a change in the sales mix that has impacted (or will impact) on sales or profits?
- Is property leased and, if so, are any rent reviews due? Are there any onerous covenants on the leases?

1.10.2 Internal factors

There are internal factors to consider:

- Ratios need to be interpreted in conjunction with reading the narrative and notes in the annual reports. The narrative could be helpful in explaining changes in the ratios, e.g. whether an inventory build-up is in anticipation of sales or a fall in demand. The notes could be helpful in corroborating the narrative, e.g. if the narrative explains that the increase in inventory is due to anticipated further production and sales, check whether the non-current assets have increased or whether there is a note about future capital expenditure.
- Ratios might be distorted because they are based on period-end figures. The end-of-year figures are static and might not be a fair reflection of normal relationships such as when a business is seasonal, e.g. an arable farm might have no inventory until the harvest and a toy manufacturer might have little inventory after supplying wholesalers in the lead-up to Christmas. Any ratios based on the inventory figure such as inventory turnover could be misleading if calculated at, say, a 31 December year-end.
- The use of norms can be misleading, e.g. the current ratio of 2:1 might be totally inappropriate for an entity like Asda which does not have long inventory turnover periods and, as its sales are for cash, it would not produce trade receivable collection period ratios.
- Factors that could invalidate inter-firm comparisons, such as:
  - use of different measurement bases with non-current assets reported at historical cost or revaluation and revaluations carried out at different dates;
  - use of different commercial practices, e.g. factoring trade receivables so that cash is increased – a perfectly normal transaction but one that could cause the comparative ratio of days' credit allowed to be significantly reduced;
  - applying different accounting practice, e.g. adopting different depreciation methods such as straight-line and reducing balance; adopting different inventory valuation methods such as FIFO and weighted average; or assuming different degrees of optimism or pessimism when making judgement-based adjustments to non-current and current assets;
  - having different definitions for ratios, e.g. the numerator for ROCE could be operating profit, profit before interest, profit before interest and tax (PBIT), earnings before interest, tax, depreciation and amortisation (EBITDA), profit after tax, etc.; the denominator for ROCE could be total assets, total assets less intangibles, net assets, average total assets, etc.

1.10.3 Degree of scepticism

This depends on the role of the person using the ratios. For example, a financial controller/ FD preparing a report to the Board would have local knowledge of the company's business activities. In the Vertigo circumstances a reporting accountant, and to a lesser extent an external auditor, might not have this local knowledge and their starting point would be to form an overall impression followed by a more detailed analysis.

In expressing an opinion, they might need to be more investigative and consider:

- Whether there is a risk of window dressing to improve sales, e.g. dispatching goods at the end of the period knowing them to be defective so that they appear in the current year's sales and accepting that they will be returned later in the next period.

- Whether liabilities have been omitted to improve the quick ratio, e.g. simply by suppressing purchase invoices at the year-end.

- Whether liabilities have been omitted to improve gearing, e.g. by the use of off-balance-sheet finance such as structuring the terms of a lease to ensure that it is treated as an operating lease and not a finance lease and special-purpose enterprises to keep debts off the statement of financial position.

- Whether there has been full disclosure in the notes of, say, contingent liabilities, which could result in ratios not being accurate predictors of future earnings and solvency.

Summary

Ratios are an aid in interpreting financial performance and liquidity. Comparison with prior periods and competitor/industry averages can provide a business with an indication of its relative performance – has it improved and how does it compare to its competitors? In this chapter we have followed a common-sized approach to the initial overview and the pyramid approach to calculating the ratios for two years to provide a basis for a report.

A comparison was made with a competitor's ratios for those areas that required further investigation. In practice it would be helpful to have data for 3–5 years in order to review trends. Reference was then made to the need to be cautious when using the ratios for prediction – remembering that at all times there needs to be a degree of scepticism when interpreting the ratios.

REVIEW QUESTIONS

1 State and express two ratios that can be used to analyse each of the following:

   (i) profitability;

   (ii) liquidity;

   (iii) management control.

2 Discuss the importance of the disclosure of exceptional items to the users of the annual report in addition to the operating profit.

3 Explain how a reader of the accounts might be able to assess whether the non-current asset base is being maintained.

4 Explain in what circumstances an increase in the revenue to current assets might be an indication of a possible problem.

5 Explain in what circumstances a decrease in the rate of non-current asset turnover might be a positive indicator.

6 Discuss why an increasing current ratio might not be an indicator of better working capital management.

7 The management of Alpha Ltd calculates ROCE using profit before interest and tax as a percentage of net closing assets. Discuss how this definition might be improved.

8 The asset turnover rate has increased by 50% over the previous year. Explain the questions you would have in mind and what other ratios you would review.

9 The current ratio has doubled since the previous year. Explain the questions that you would have in mind when reviewing the accounts.

10 Explain the problems a creditor might have when assessing the creditworthiness of a subsidiary entity.

11 You ascertain that inventories and (to a lesser extent) trade receivables have risen significantly when you consider that sales have increased by only 5%. Discuss the questions that you ask and the possible impact of each answer on the ratios.

12 Access the annual reports of two companies in the same industry and identify (a) the ratios that they report in common, (b) how these have been defined, and (c) why some ratios are not common to both.

13 A company has a very high rate of inventory turnover. Discuss circumstances when this might be of concern to management.

14 The ratio of current liabilities to net worth (equity + retained earnings) was 75%. Discuss how this would be viewed by suppliers and management.

15 The ratio of non-current assets to net worth was 75%. Discuss the risk that this poses for a company.

EXERCISES

* **Question 1**

Flash Fashions plc has had a difficult nine months and the management team is discussing strategy for the final quarter.

In the last nine months the company has survived by cutting production, reducing staff and reducing overheads wherever possible. However, the share market, whilst recognising that sales across the industry have been poor, has worried about the financial strength of the business and as a result the share price has fallen 40%.

The company is desperate to increase sales. It has been recognised that the high fixed costs of the factory are not being fully absorbed by the lower volumes which are costed at standard cost. If sales and production can be increased then more factory costs will be absorbed and increased sales volume will raise staff morale and make analysts think the firm is entering a turnaround phase.

The company decides to drop prices by 15% for the next two months and to change the terms of sale so that property does not pass until the clothes are paid for. This is purely a reflection of the tough economic conditions and the need to protect the firm against customer insolvency. Further, it is decided that if sales have not increased enough by the end of the two months, the company representatives will be advised to ship goods to customers on the understanding that they will be invoiced but if they don't sell the goods in two months they can return them. Volume discounts will be stressed to keep the stock moving.

These actions are intended to increase sales, increase profitability, justify higher stocks, and ensure that more overheads are transferred out of the profit statement into stocks.

For the purposes of annual reporting it was decided not to spell out sales growth in financial figure terms in the managing director's report but rather to focus on units shipped in graphs using scales (possibly log scales) designed to make the fall look less dramatic. Also comparisons will be made against industry volumes as the fashion industry has been more affected by economic conditions than the economy as a whole.

To make the ratios look better, the company will enter into an agreement on the last week of the year with a so-called 'two-dollar company' called Upstart Ltd owned by Colleen Livingston, friend of the managing director of Flash Fashions, Sue Cotton. Upstart Ltd will sign a contract to buy a property for £30 million from Flash Fashions and will also sign promissory notes payable over the next three quarters for £10 million each. The auditors will not be told, but Flash Fashions will enter into an agreement to buy back the property for £31 million any time after the start of the third month in the new financial year.

Required:
Critically discuss each of the proposed strategies.

* Question 2

Relationships plc
You are informed that the non-current assets totalled €350,000, current liabilities €156,000, the opening retained earnings totalled €103,000, the administration expenses totalled €92,680 and that the available ratios were the current ratio 1.5, the acid test ratio 0.75, the trade receivables collection period was six weeks, the gross profit was 20% and the net assets turned over 1.4 times.

Required:
Prepare the Relationships plc statement of financial position from the above information.

* Question 3

The major shareholder/director of Esrever Ltd has obtained average data for the industry as a whole. He wishes to see what the forecast results and position of Esrever Ltd would be if in the ensuing year its performance were to match the industry averages.

At 1 July 20X0, actual figures for Esrever Ltd included:

	£
Land and buildings (at written-down value)	132,000
Fixtures, fittings and equipment (at written-down value)	96,750
Inventory	22,040
12% loan (repayable in 20X5)	50,000
Ordinary share capital (50p shares)	100,000

For the year ended 30 June 20X1 the following forecast information is available:

1   Depreciation of non-current assets (on reducing balance)

Land and buildings	2%
Fixtures, fittings and equipment	20%

2   Net current assets will be financed by a bank overdraft to the extent necessary.

3   At 30 June 20X0 total assets minus current liabilities will be £231,808.

4   Profit after tax for the year will be 23.32% of gross profit and 11.16% of total assets minus all external liabilities, both long-term and short-term.

5   Tax will be at an effective rate of 20% of profit before tax.

6   Cost of sales will be 68% of turnover (excluding VAT).

7   Closing inventory will represent 61.9 days' average cost of sales (excluding VAT).

8   Any difference between total expenses and the aggregate of expenses ascertained from this given information will represent credit purchases and other credit expenses, in each case excluding VAT input tax.

9   A dividend of 2.5p per share will be proposed.

10 The collection period for the VAT-exclusive amount of trade receivables will be an average of 42.6 days of the annual turnover. All the company's supplies are subject to VAT output tax at 15%.

11 The payment period for the VAT-exclusive amount of trade payables (purchases and other credit expenses) will be an average of 29.7 days. All these items are subject to (reclaimable) VAT input tax at 15%. This VAT rate has been increased to 17.5% and may be subject to future changes, but for the purpose of this question the theory and workings remain the same irrespective of the rate.

12 Payables, other than trade payables, will comprise tax due, proposed dividends and VAT payable equal to one-quarter of the net amount due for the year.

13 Calculations are based on a year of 365 days.

Required:
Construct a forecast statement of comprehensive income for Esrever Ltd for the year ended 30 June 20X1 and a forecast statement of financial position at that date in as much detail as possible. (All calculations should be made to the nearest £1.)

* Question 4

Saddam Ltd is considering the possibility of diversifying its operations and has identified three firms in the same industrial sector as potential takeover targets. The following information in respect of the companies has been extracted from their most recent financial statements.

	Ali Ltd	Baba Ltd	Camel Ltd
ROCE before tax %	22.1	23.7	25.0
Net profit %	12.0	12.5	3.75
Asset turnover ratio	1.45	1.16	3.73
Gross profit %	20.0	25.0	10.0
Sales/non-current assets	4.8	2.2	11.6
Sales/current assets	2.1	5.2	5.5
Current ratio	3.75	1.4	1.5
Acid test ratio	2.25	0.4	0.9
Average number of weeks' receivables outstanding	5.6	6.0	4.8
Average number of weeks' inventory held	12.0	19.2	4.0
Ordinary dividend %	10.0	15.0	30.0
Dividend cover	4.3	5.0	1.0

Required:

(a) Prepare a report for the directors of Saddam Ltd, assessing the performance of the three companies from the information provided and identifying areas which you consider require further investigation before a final decision is made.

(b) Discuss briefly why a firm's statement of financial position is unlikely to show the true market value of the business.

* Question 5

You work for Euroc, a limited liability company, which seeks growth through acquisitions. You are a member of a team that is investigating the possible purchase of Choggerell, a limited liability company that manufactures a product complementary to the products currently being sold by Euroc.

Your team leader wants you to prepare a report for the team evaluating the recent performance of Choggerell and the quality of its management, and has given you the following financial information which has been derived from the financial statements of Choggerell for the three years ended 31 March 2006, 2007 and 2008.

Financial year ended 31 March	2006	2007	2008
Revenue (€ million)	2,243	2,355	2,237
Cash and cash equivalents (€ million)	−50	81	−97
Return on equity	13%	22%	19%
Sales revenue to total assets	2.66	2.66	2.01
Cost of sales to sales revenue	85%	82%	79%
Operating expenses to sales revenue	11%	12%	15%
Net income to sales revenue	2.6%	4.3%	4.2%
Current/Working capital ratio (to 1)	1.12	1.44	1.06
Acid test ratio (to 1)	0.80	1.03	0.74
Inventory turnover (months)	0.6	0.7	1.0
Credit to customers (months)	1.3	1.5	1.7
Credit from suppliers (months)	1.5	1.5	2.0
Net assets per share (cents per share)	0.86	0.2	0.97
Dividend per share (cents per share)	10.0	14.0	14.0
Earnings per share (cents per share)	11.5	20.1	18.7

Required:

Use the above information to prepare a report for your team leader which:

(a) reviews the performance of Choggerell as evidenced by the above ratios;

(b) makes recommendations as to how the overall performance of Choggerell could be improved; and

(c) indicates any limitations in your analysis.

(The Association of International Accountants)

* Question 6

Liz Collier runs a small delicatessen. Her profits in recent years have remained steady at around £21,000 per annum. This type of business generally earns a uniform rate of net profit on sales of 20%.

Recently, Liz has found that this level of profitability is insufficient to enable her to maintain her desired lifestyle. She is considering three options to improve her profitability.

Option 1   Liz will borrow £10,000 from her bank at an interest rate of 10% per annum, payable at the end of each financial year. The whole capital sum will be repaid to the bank at the end of the second year. The money will be used to hire the services of a marketing agency for two years. It is anticipated that turnover will increase by 40% as a result of the additional advertising.

Option 2   Liz will form a partnership with Joan Mercer, who also runs a local delicatessen. Joan's net profits have remained at £12,000 per annum since she started in business five years ago. The sales of each shop in the combined business are expected to increase by 20% in the first year and then remain steady. The costs of the amalgamation will amount to £6,870, which will be written off in the first year. The partnership agreement will allow each partner a partnership salary of 2% of the revised turnover of their own shop. Remaining profits will be shared in the ratio of Liz 3/5, Joan 2/5.

Option 3   Liz will reduce her present sales by 80% and take up a franchise to sell Nickson's Munchy Sausage. The franchise will cost £80,000. This amount will be borrowed from her bank. The annual interest rate will be 10% flat rate based on the amount borrowed. Sales of Munchy Sausage yield a net profit to sales percentage of 30%. Sales are expected to be £50,000 in the first year, but should increase annually at a rate of 15% for the following three years then remain constant.

Required:

(a) Prepare a financial statement for Liz comparing the results of each option for each of the next two years.

(b) Advise Liz which option may be the best to choose.

(c) Discuss any other factors that Liz should consider under each of the options.

* Question 7

Chelsea plc has embarked on a programme of growth through acquisitions and has identified Kensington Ltd and Wimbledon Ltd as companies in the same industrial sector, as potential targets.

Using recent financial statements of both Kensington and Wimbledon and further information obtained from a trade association, Chelsea plc has managed to build up the following comparability table:

	Kensington	Wimbledon	Industrial average
Profitability ratios			
ROCE before tax %	22	28	20
Return on equity %	18	22	15
Net profit margin %	11	5	7
Gross profit ratio %	25	12	20
Activity ratios			
Total assets turnover = times	1.5	4.0	2.5
Non-current asset turnover = times	2.3	12.0	5.1
Receivables collection period in weeks	8.0	5.1	6.5
Inventory holding period in weeks	21.0	4.0	13.0
Liquidity ratios			
Current ratio	1.8	1.7	2.8
Acid test	0.5	0.9	1.3
Debt–equity ratio %	80.0	20.0	65.0

Required:

(a) **Prepare a performance report for the two companies for consideration by the directors of Chelsea plc indicating which of the two companies you consider to be a better acquisition.**

(b) **Indicate what further information is needed before a final decision can be made.**

* Question 8

The Housing Department of Chaldon District Council has invited tenders for re-roofing 80 houses on an estate. Chaldon Direct Services (CDS) is one of the Council's direct services organisations and it has submitted a tender for this contract, as have several contractors from the private sector.

The Council has been able to narrow the choice of contractor to the four tenderers who have submitted the lowest bids, as follows:

	£
Nutfield & Sons	398,600
Chaldon Direct Services	401,850
Tandridge Tilers Ltd	402,300
Redhill Roofing Contractors plc	406,500

The tender evaluation process requires that the three private tenderers be appraised on the basis of financial soundness and quality of work. These tenderers were required to provide their latest final accounts (year ended 31 March 20X4) for this appraisal; details are as follows:

	Nutfield & Sons	Tandridge Tilers Ltd	Redhill Roofing Contractors plc
Profit and loss account for year ended 31 March 20X4			
	£	£	£
Revenue	611,600	1,741,200	3,080,400
Direct costs	(410,000)	(1,190,600)	(1,734,800)
Other operating costs	(165,000)	(211,800)	(811,200)
Interest	—	(85,000)	(96,000)
Net profit before taxation	36,600	253,800	438,400
Statement of financial position as at 31 March 20X4			
	£	£	£
Non-current assets (net book value)	55,400	1,542,400	2,906,800
Inventories and work in progress	26,700	149,000	449,200
Receivables	69,300	130,800	240,600
Bank	(11,000)	10,400	(6,200)
Payables	(92,600)	(140,600)	(279,600)
Dividend declared	—	(91,800)	(70,000)
Loan	—	(800,000)	(1,200,000)
	47,800	800,200	2,040,800
Capital	47,800	—	—
Ordinary shares @ £1 each	—	250,000	1,000,000
Reserves	—	550,200	1,040,800
	47,800	800,200	2,040,800

Nutfield & Sons employ a workforce of six operatives and have been used by the Council for four small maintenance contracts worth between £60,000 and £75,000 which they have completed to an appropriate standard. Tandridge Tilers Ltd have been employed by the Council on a contract for the replacement of flat roofs on a block of flats, but there have been numerous complaints about the standard of the work. Redhill Roofing Contractors plc is a company which has not been employed by the Council in the past and, as much of its work has been carried out elsewhere, its quality of work is not known.

CDS has been suffering from the effects of increasing competition in recent years and achieved a return on capital employed of only 3.5% in the previous financial year. CDS's manager has successfully renegotiated more beneficial service-level agreements with the Council's central support departments with effect from 1 April 20X4. CDS has also reviewed its non-current asset base which has resulted in the disposal of a depot which was surplus to requirements and in the rationalisation of vehicles and plant. The consequence of this is that CDS's average capital employed for 20X4/X5 is likely to be some 15% lower than in 20X3/X4.

A further analysis of the tender bids is provided below:

	Nutfield & Sons	Chaldon Direct Services	Tandridge Tilers Ltd
	£	£	£
Labour		234,000	251,400
Materials	140,000	100,000	80,000
Overheads (including profit)	24,600	50,450	18,700

The Council's Client Services Committee can reject tenders on financial and/or quality grounds. However, each tender has to be appraised on these criteria and reasons for acceptance or rejection must be justified in the appraisal process.

Required:

In your capacity as accountant responsible for reporting to the Client Services Committee, draft a report to the Committee evaluating the tender bids and recommending to whom the contract should be awarded.

* Question 9

The statements of financial position, cash flows, income and movements of non-current assets of Dragon plc for the year ended 30 September 20X6 are set out below:

(i) *Statement of financial position*

	20X5		20X6	
	£000	£000	£000	£000
Tangible non-current assets		1,200		1,160
Freehold land and buildings, at cost		700		1,700
Plant and equipment, at net book value		1,900		2,860
Current assets:				
Inventory	715		1,020	
Trade receivables	590		826	
Short-term investments	52		—	
Cash at bank and in hand	15		47	
	1,372		1,893	
Current liabilities:				
Trade payables	520		940	
Taxation payable	130		45	
Dividends payable	90		105	
	740		1,090	
Net current assets		632		803
		2,532		3,663
Long-term liability and provisions:				
8% debentures, 20X9		500		1,500
Provisions for deferred tax		100		180
		1,932		1,983
Capital and reserves		1,400		1,400
Ordinary shares of £1 each				
Share premium account		250		250
Retained earnings		282		333
		1,932		1,983

(ii) *Statement of income (extract) for the year ended 30 September 20X6*

EBITDA		1,161
Depreciation		660
Operating profit		501
Interest payable: debentures		150
Profit before taxation		351
Income tax		125
Profit attributable to shareholders		226
Dividends: paid	70	
: proposed	105	175
Retained earnings for year		51
Retained earnings brought forward		282
Retained earnings carried forward		333

(iii) *Statement of cash flows*

Net cash flow from operating activities		1,033
Interest paid	(150)	
Income taxes paid	(130)	(280)
Net cash from operating activities:		753
Cash flows from investing activities		
Purchase of property, plant and equipment	(1,620)	
Net cash used in investing activities:		(1,620)
Cash flows from financing activities		
Proceeds from sale of short-term investments	59	
Proceeds from long-term borrowings	1,000	
Dividends paid	(160)	
Net cash from financing activities:		899
Net increase in cash and cash equivalents		32
Cash and cash equivalents at the beginning of the period		15
Cash and cash equivalents at the end of the period		47

(iv) *Tangible non-current assets (or PPE)*

The movements in the year were as follows:

	Freehold land and buildings £000	Plant and machinery £000	Total £000
Cost:			
At 1 October 20X5	2,000	1,600	3,600
Additions	—	1,620	1,620
At 30 September 20X6	2,000	3,220	5,220
Depreciation:			
At 1 October 20X5	800	900	1,700
Charge during the year	40	620	660
At 30 September 20X6	840	1,520	2,360
Net book value:			
Beginning of year	1,200	700	1,900
End of year	**1,160**	**1,700**	**2,860**

You are also provided with the following information:

(i)   There was a debenture issue on 1 October 20X5 with interest payable on 30 September each year.

(ii) An interim dividend of £70,000 was paid on 1 July 20X6.

(iii) The short-term investment was sold for £59,000 on 1 October 20X5.

(iv) Business activity increased significantly to meet increased consumer demand.

Required:
(a) **Prepare a reconciliation of operating profit to net cash inflow from operating activities.**
(b) **Discuss the financial developments at Dragon plc during the financial year ended 30 September 20X6 with particular regard to its financial position at the year-end and prospects for the following financial year, supported by appropriate financial ratios.**

* Question 10

Drucker plc is a public listed wholesaler. Its summarised financial statements for the year ended 31 December 2013 (and 2012 comparatives) are as follows:

Statements of profit or loss and other comprehensive income
for the years ended 31 December

	2013	2012
	€ million	€ million
Revenue	275	200
Cost of sales	(200)	(100)
Gross profit	75	100
Operating costs	(36)	(30)
Investment income	—	2
Gains on revaluation of investments held at fair value through P/L	(5)	10
Finance costs	(5)	(5)
Profit (loss) before taxation	29	77
Income tax expense	(4)	(15)
Profit for the year	25	62
Other comprehensive income		
(Amounts that will not be reclassified to profit or loss)		
Revaluation losses on property plant & equipment	(45)	—
Total comprehensive income (loss) for the year	(20)	62

Statements of Financial Position as at 31 December:

	2013	2012
	€ million	€ million
Assets		
Non-current assets:		
Property, plant and equipment	215	245
Investments at fair value through profit or loss	35	40
	250	285

	2013 € million	2012 € million
Current assets		
Inventory	40	19
Trade receivables	52	28
Bank	—	10
	92	57
Total assets	342	342
Equity and liabilities		
Equity:		
Equity shares of €1 each	120	120
Revaluation reserve	10	55
Retained earnings	90	65
	220	240
Non-current liabilities:		
Bank loan	50	50
Current liabilities:		
Trade payables	50	39
Bank overdraft	20	—
Current tax payable	2	13
	72	52
Total equity and liabilities	342	342

You are a newly recruited accountant working for Drucker plc. The draft financial statements for year ended 31 December 2013 have just been produced. Your managing director, Tom Kirby, has asked you to explain to him what the above financial statements mean for the company's performance for the year 2013 and its financial position at 31 December 2013. He makes you aware of the following points and opinions:

(i) Drucker plc has traditionally been very profitable, but in recent years has been finding it difficult to keep up its sales level due to the effects of internet sales. Basically it finds more customers are buying directly online from suppliers and cutting out the middleman, which includes Drucker as a wholesaler. To counteract this, on 1 January 2013, Drucker launched a strategy of cutting its prices in the hope that this would generate additional sales volume and profits.

(ii) To support the new strategy and allow faster movement of goods, a new product movement and control system was commissioned and installed on 1 January 2013 at a cost of €40 million. This is being depreciated over a five-year useful economic life. The old system was disposed of for nil consideration on the same date, but had been carried at €15 million at the date of disposal. The loss was taken to Cost of Sales, as is depreciation. No other non-current assets were acquired or disposed of in either of the two years.

(iii) Tom expresses the opinion that this strategy has not failed so far, as the total on the statement of financial position has remained the same from year to year. This proves (he claims) the company has retained its book value and therefore has not suffered any deterioration in performance from 2012 to 2013.

(iv) The share price has declined from €2.80 per share on 31 December 2012 to €1.60 per share on 31 December 2013. Tom does not understand the reasons for this.

(v) Tom is aware that there are valuable tools for analysing profitability, liquidity and efficiency. However, he has no knowledge of how to calculate or interpret these.

Required:
(a) Calculate at least eight suitable ratios for each financial year in order to assist in addressing the issues raised by the managing director.
(b) Discuss Tom's assertion in point (iii) above that the new strategy has not failed because the company has retained its book value.
(c) Analyse and discuss the financial performance and position of Drucker plc as portrayed by the financial statements above and the additional information provided. Pay particular attention to the issues raised by Tom and their impact on the performance and position of the company.
(d) Identify the limitations of your analysis.

(Institute of Certified Public Accountants (CPA) Professional Stage 1
Corporate Reporting Examination, August 2017)

Note

1 www.rmahq.org/

CHAPTER 2

Statements of cash flows

2.1 Introduction

The main purpose of this chapter is to explain the reasons for preparing a statement of cash flows and how to prepare a statement applying IAS 7.

Objectives

By the end of this chapter, you should be able to:

- prepare a statement of cash flows in accordance with IAS 7;
- analyse a statement of cash flows;
- critically discuss their strengths and weaknesses.

2.2 Development of statements of cash flows

We saw in Chapter 7 that, at the end of an accounting period, a statement of income is prepared which explains the change in the retained earnings at the beginning and end of an accounting period. In this chapter we prepare a statement of cash flows in accordance with IAS 7 *Statements of Cash Flows*.

IAS 7 explains the changes that have occurred in the amount of liquid assets easily accessible – these are defined as cash + cash equivalents.

2.2.1 Statements of cash flows – their benefits

As far back as 1991 Professor John Arnold wrote in a report by the ICAEW Research Board and ICAS Research Advisory Committee *The Future Shape of Financial Reports:*[1]

> little attention is paid to the reporting entity's cash or liquidity position. Cash is the lifeblood of every business entity. The report . . . advocates that companies should provide a cash flow statement . . . preferably using the direct method.

Statements of cash flows are now primary financial statements and as important as statements of comprehensive income:

> The emphasis on cash flows, and the emergence of the statement of cash flows as an important financial report, does not mean that operating cash flows are a substitute for, or are more important than, net income. In order to analyse financial statements correctly we need to consider *both* operating cash flows and net income.[2]

They are now primary financial statements because the financial viability and survival prospects of any organisation rest on the ability to generate positive operating cash flows. These are necessary in order to be able to pay the interest on loans and repay the loans, finance capital expenditure to maintain or expand operating capacity, and reward the investors with an acceptable dividend policy. If there is still a positive cash flow after this, it will help to reduce the need for additional external loans or equity funding.

The message is that, independent of reported profits, if an organisation is unable to generate sufficient cash, it will eventually become insolvent and fail.

The following extract from Heath and Rosenfield's article on solvency[3] is a useful conclusion to our analysis of the benefits of cash flow statements, emphasising that they also provide a basis for predicting future performance:

> Solvency is a money or cash phenomenon. A solvent company is one with adequate cash to pay its debts; an insolvent company is one with inadequate cash . . . Any information that provides insight into the amounts, timings and certainty of a company's future cash receipts and payments is useful in evaluating solvency. Statements of past cash receipts and payments are useful for the same basic reason that statements of comprehensive income are useful in evaluating profitability: both provide a basis for predicting future performance.

2.3 Applying IAS 7 (revised) Statements of Cash Flows

2.3.1 IAS 7 format

The cash flows are analysed under three standard headings to explain the net increase/decrease in cash and cash equivalents and the effect on the opening amount of cash and cash equivalents. The headings are:

- Net cash generated by operating activities;
- Cash flows from investing activities;
- Cash flows from financing activities.

2.3.2 The two methods of presenting cash flows from operating activities

In the quote from *The Future Shape of Financial Reports* above, reference was made to the direct method. This preference was expressed because there are two methods, both of which are permitted by IAS 7. These are the direct method and the indirect method.

- The *direct* method reports cash inflows and outflows directly, starting with the major categories of gross cash receipts and payments. This means that cash flows such as receipts from customers and payments to suppliers are stated separately within the operating activities.

- The *indirect* method starts with the profit before tax and then adjusts this figure for non-cash items such as depreciation and changes in working capital.

2.3.3 Statement of cash flows illustrated using the direct method

The following shows the statement of cash flows for Tyro Bruce for the period ended 31.3.20X4.

Cash flows from operating activities	£000	£000
Cash received from customers (note (a))	11,740	
Cash paid to suppliers and employees (note (b))	(11,431)	
Cash generated from operations	309	
Interest paid (expense + (closing accrual − opening accrual))	(20)	
Income taxes paid (expense + (closing accrual − opening accrual))	(220)	
Net cash (used in) generated by operating activities		69
Cash flows from investing activities		
Purchase of property, plant and equipment	(560)	
Proceeds from sale of equipment	241	
Net cash used in investing activities		(319)
Cash flows from financing activities		
Proceeds from issue of shares at a premium	300	
Redemption of loan	(50)	
Dividends paid	(120)	
Net cash from financing activities		130
Net increase in cash and cash equivalents		(120)
Cash and cash equivalents at beginning of period		72
Cash and cash equivalents at end of period		(48)

Notes:

(a) Cash received from customers

	£000
Sales	12,000
Receivables increase	(260)
	11,740

(b) Cash paid to suppliers and employees

	£000
Cost of sales	10,000
Payables decreased	140
Inventory increased	900
Depreciation	(102)
Profit on sale	13
Distribution costs	300
Administration expenses	180
	11,431

2.3.4 Statement of cash flows illustrated using the indirect method

The two methods provide different types of information to the users. The indirect method applies changes in working capital to net income. In our illustration, for example, the cash generated from operations would be calculated as follows:

Cash flows from operating activities	£000
Profit before tax	1,500
Adjustments for non-cash items:	
Depreciation	102
Profit on sale of plant	(13)
Adjustments for changes in working capital:	
Increase in trade receivables	(260)
Increase in inventories	(900)
Decrease in trade payables	(140)
Interest expense (added back)	20
Cash generated from operations	309

2.3.5 Appraising the use of the direct method

The direct method demonstrates more of the qualities of a true cash flow statement because it provides more information about the sources and uses of cash. This information is not available elsewhere and helps in the estimation of future cash flows.

The principal advantage of the direct method is that it shows operating cash receipts and payments. Knowledge of the specific sources of cash receipts and the purposes for which cash payments were made in past periods may be useful in assessing future cash flows. Disclosure of *cash from customers* could provide additional information about an entity's ability to convert revenues to cash.

When is the direct method beneficial?

One such time is when the user is attempting to predict bankruptcy or future liquidation of the company. A research study looking at the cash flow differences between failed and non-failed companies[4] established that seven cash flow variables and suggested ratios captured statistically significant differences between failed and non-failed firms as much as five years prior to failure. The study further showed that the research findings supported the use of a direct cash flow statement, and the authors commented:

An indirect cash flow statement will not provide a number of the cash flow variables for which we found significant differences between bankrupt and non-bankrupt companies. Thus, using an indirect cash flow statement could lead to ignoring important information about creditworthiness.

The direct method is the method preferred by the standard but preparers have a choice. In the UK the indirect method is often used; in other regions (e.g. Australia) the direct method is more common. It has been proposed in a review of IAS 7 that the direct method should be mandated and the alternative removed and this is the likely requirement in a new standard to eventually replace IAS 7.

2.3.6 Appraising the use of the indirect method

The principal advantage of the indirect method is that it highlights the differences between operating profit and net cash flow from operating activities to provide a measure of the quality of income. Many users of financial statements believe that such reconciliation is essential to give an indication of the quality of the reporting entity's earnings. Some investors and creditors assess future cash flows by estimating future income and then allowing for accruals adjustments; thus information about past accruals adjustments may be useful to help estimate future adjustments.

Preparer and user response

The IASB indicates that the responses to the discussion paper were mixed with the preparers tending to prefer the indirect method and the users having a mixed response. There was a view that the direct method would be improved if the movements on working capital were disclosed as supplementary information, and the indirect method would be improved if the cash from customers and payments to suppliers was disclosed as supplementary information; i.e. both are found useful.

2.3.7 Cash equivalents

IAS 7 recognised that companies' cash management practices vary in the amount of cash and range of short- to medium-term deposits that are held. The standard standardised the treatment of near-cash items by applying the following definition when determining whether items should be aggregated with cash in the statement of cash flows:

> Cash equivalents are short-term, highly liquid investments which are readily convertible into known amounts of cash and which are subject to an insignificant risk of changes in value.

Near-cash items are normally those that are within three months of maturity at the date of acquisition. Investments falling outside this definition are reported under the heading of 'investing activities'. In view of the variety of cash management practices and banking arrangements around the world and in order to comply with IAS 1 *Presentation of Financial Statements,* an entity discloses the policy which it adopts in determining the composition of cash and cash equivalents. The following is an extract from the Tesco 2016 Annual Report:

Cash and cash equivalents

> Cash and cash equivalents in the Group Balance Sheet consist of cash at bank, in hand, demand deposits with banks, loans and advances to banks, certificates of deposits and other receivables together with short-term deposits with an original maturity of three months or less.

2.4 Step approach to preparation of a statement of cash flows – indirect method

We will now explain how to prepare a statement of cash flows for Tyro Bruce (Section 2.3.3) taking a step approach. We have shown our workings on the face of the statements of financial position and income.

Step 1: Calculate the differences in the statements of financial position and decide whether to report under operating, investing or financing activities or as a cash equivalent.

Statements of financial position of Tyro Bruce as at 31.3.20X3 and 31.3.20X4

	20X3		20X4		Calculate the	Decide which activities
	£000	£000	£000	£000	differences	to report under
Non-current assets at cost	2,520		2,760		See PPE note	Investing/financing
Accumulated depreciation	452	2,068	462	2,298	for acquisitions or disposals	
Current assets						
Inventory	800		1,700		900	Operating
Trade receivables	640		900		260	Operating
Securities maturing less than 3 months at acquisition	—		20		20	Cash equivalent
Cash	80		10		70	Cash equivalent
	1,520		2,630			
Current liabilities						
Trade payables	540		400		140	Operating
Taxation	190		170		20	Operating
Overdraft	8		78		70	Cash equivalent
	738		648			
Net current assets		782		1,982		
		2,850		4,280		
Share capital	1,300		1,400		100	Financing
Share premium a/c	200		400		200	Financing
Retained earnings	1,150	2,650	1,150	2,950		
Profit for year		—		1,180		
10% loan 20 × 7		200		150	50	Financing
		2,850		4,280		

Step 2: Identify any items in the statement of income for the year ended 31.3.20X4 after profit before interest and tax (PBIT) to be entered under operating, investing or financing activities.

	£000	£000	
Sales		12,000	
Cost of sales		10,000	
Gross profit		2,000	
Distribution costs	300		
Administrative expenses	180	480	
PBIT		1,520	
Interest expense		(20)	Operating
Profit before tax		1,500	Operating
Income tax expense		(200)	Operating
Profit after tax		1,300	
Dividend paid		(120)	Financing
Retained earnings for year		1,180	

Step 3: Refer to the PPE schedule to identify any acquisitions, disposals and depreciation charges that affect the cash flows. The Tyro Bruce schedule showed:

Cost	£000
As at 31 March 20X3	2,520
(i) Additions	560
(iii) Disposal	(320)
As at 31.3.20X4	2,760
Accumulated depreciation	
As at 31.3.20X3	452
(ii) Charge for year	102
(iii) Disposal	(92)
As at 31.3.20X4	462
NBV as at 31.3.20X4	2,298
NBV as at 31.3.20X3	2,068

Note: Disposal proceeds were £241,000.

From Step 3 we can see that there are four impacts:

(i) Additions: The cash of £560,000 paid out on additions will appear under Investing.

(ii) The depreciation charge: This is a non-cash item and the £102,000 will be added back as a non-cash item to the profit before tax in the operating activities section.

(iii) Disposal proceeds: The cash received of £241,000 from the disposal was given in the Note and will appear under Investing activities. *If the Note had provided you with the profit instead of the proceeds, then you would need to calculate the proceeds by taking the NBV and adjusting for any profit or loss. In this case it would be calculated as NBV of £228,000 (320,000 − 92,000) + the profit figure of £13,000 = £241,000.*

(iv) Profit on disposal: As the full proceeds of £241,000 are included under Investing activities there would be double counting to leave the profit of £13,000 within the profit before tax figure. It is therefore deducted as a non-cash item from PBT in the Operating activities section.

2.4.1 The statement of cash flows

The cash flow items can then be entered into the statement of cash flows in accordance with IAS 7.

		£000
Cash flows from operating activities		
Profit before tax		1,500
Adjustments for non-cash items:		
Depreciation	From Step 3 (ii)	102
Profit on sale of plant	From Step 3 (iv)	(13)
Adjustments for changes in working capital:		
Increase in trade receivables		(260)
Increase in inventories		(900)
Decrease in trade payables		(140)
Interest expense		20
Cash generated from operations		309
Interest paid (there are no closing or opening accruals)		(20)
Income taxes paid	$200 + (190 - 170)$	(220)
(expense + (opening accrual − closing accrual))		
Net cash (used in)/generated by operating activities		69
Cash flows from investing activities		
Purchase of property, plant and equipment	From Step 3 (i)	(560)
Proceeds from sale of equipment	From Step 3 (iii)	241
Net cash used in investing activities		(319)
Cash flows from financing activities		
Proceeds from issue of shares at a premium		300
Redemption of loan		(50)
Dividends paid		(120)
Net cash from financing activities		130
Net increase in cash and cash equivalents		(120)
Cash and cash equivalents at beginning of period	$80 - 8$	72
Cash and cash equivalents at end of period	$(10 + 20) - 78$	(48)

Note that interest paid and interest and dividends received could be classified either as operating cash flows or as financing (for interest paid) and investing cash flows (for receipts). Dividends paid could be presented either as financing cash flows or as operating cash flows. However, it is a requirement that whichever presentation is adopted by an enterprise should be consistently applied from year to year.

2.5 Additional notes required by IAS 7

As well as the presentation on the face of the cash flow statement, IAS 7 requires notes to the cash flow statement to help the user understand the information. The notes that are required are as follows.

Major non-cash transactions

If the entity has entered into major non-cash transactions that are therefore not represented on the face of the statement of cash flows, sufficient further information to understand the transactions should be provided in a note to the financial statements. Examples of major non-cash transactions might be:

- the acquisition of assets by way of finance leases;
- the conversion of debt to equity.

Components of cash and cash equivalents

An enterprise must disclose the components of cash and cash equivalents and reconcile these into the totals in the statement of financial position. An example of a suitable disclosure in the case of Tyro Bruce is:

	20X4	20X3
Cash	10	80
Securities	20	
Overdraft	(78)	(8)
Cash and cash equivalents	(48)	72

Disclosure must also be given on restrictions on the use by the group of any cash and cash equivalents held by the enterprise. These restrictions might apply if, for example, cash was held in foreign countries and could not be remitted back to the parent company.

Segmental information

IAS 7 encourages enterprises to disclose information about operating, investing and financing cash flows for each business and geographical segment. This disclosure may be relevant. IFRS 8 does not require a cash flow by segment.

Evaluating changes in liabilities

Under *Disclosure Initiative Amendment to IAS 7 issued in 2016* entities are required to provide disclosures that enable users of financial statements to evaluate changes in liabilities arising from financing activities, including both changes arising from cash flows and non-cash changes.

One way to fulfil the disclosure requirement is by providing a reconciliation between the opening and closing balances in the statement of financial position for liabilities arising from financing activities. The following is an illustration adapted from the *Disclosure Initiative:*

	20X1	Cash flows	Non-cash changes Foreign exchange movement	20X2
Long-term borrowings	22,000	(1,000)		21,000
Short-term borrowings	10,000	(500)	200	9,700
Total liabilities from financing activities	32,000	(1,500)	200	30,700

In practice there might be other disclosures relating to items such as lease liabilities and acquisitions.

2.6 Analysing statements of cash flows

Arranging cash flows into specific classes provides users with relevant and decision-useful information by classifying cash flows as cash generated from operations, net cash from operating activities, net cash flows from investing activities and net cash flows from financing activities.

Lack of a clear definition

However, this does not mean that companies will necessarily report the same transaction in the same way. Although IAS 7 requires cash flows to be reported under these headings, it does not define operating activities except to say that it includes all transactions and other events that are not defined as investing or financing activities.

Alternative treatments

Alternative treatments for interest and dividends paid could be presented as either operating or financing cash flows. Whilst most companies choose to report the dividends as financing cash flows, when making inter-firm comparisons we need to see which alternative has been chosen. The choice can have a significant impact. If, for example, in the Tyro Bruce illustration the dividends of £120,000 were reported as an operating cash flow, then the net cash (used in)/generated by operating activities would change from an inflow of £69,000 to an outflow of £51,000.

The classifications assist users in making informed predictions about future cash flows or raising questions for further enquiry which would be difficult to make using traditional accrual-based techniques.[5]

We will briefly comment on the implication of each classification.

2.6.1 Cash generated from operations

Cash flow generated by operations is one of the most significant numbers calculated after taking account of any investment in working capital. It shows the cash available from ongoing operations to service loans, pay tax, reinvest in the business, repay loans and pay a dividend to shareholders.

Lenders look to the cash generated from operations to pay interest and the revenue authorities to satisfy the company's tax liability. Both of these are unavoidable – it is an indication of the safety margin, i.e. how long a business could continue to pay unavoidable costs.

There are a number of examples where the failure to meet their tax liability has led to organisations being forced into administration or liquidation. Examples include football clubs: with Portsmouth FC having been put into administration; and Bolton Wanderers threatened with administration in 2016.

In the Tyro Bruce example (Section 2.3.3) we can see that there has been a significant increase in working capital of £1,300,000 (£260,000 + £900,000 + £140,000).

The effect is to reduce the profit before tax from £1,500,000 to the £309,000 reported as cash flow from operations.

Lenders in Tyro Bruce concerned with interest cover could see that there is sufficient cash available to meet their interest charges in the current year even though there has been a significant impact from the investment in working capital.

Interest cover

Interest cover is normally defined as the number of times the profit before interest and tax covers the interest charge: in the Tyro Bruce example this is 76 times (1,520/20). The position as disclosed in the statement of cash flows is a little weaker although, even so, the interest is still covered more than 15 times (309,000/20,000).

Current cash debt coverage ratio

This is a liquidity ratio which shows a company's ability to meet its current debt obligations. The ratio is the result of dividing *the net cash generated by operating activities* by *the average current liabilities*.

In the Tyro example the net cash generated by operations is £69,000 and the average current liabilities are £693,000[(738,000 + 648,000)/2] giving a ratio of 0.1:1.

Cash debt coverage ratio

In addition to interest cover, lenders also have a longer-term view and want to be satisfied that their loan will be repaid on maturity. Failure to do so could lead to a going-concern problem for the company. One measure used is to calculate the ratio of *cash flow generated by operating activities* to *total debt* and, of more immediate interest, to *loans that are about to mature*.

The ratio can be adjusted to reflect the company's current position. For example, if there is a significant cash balance, it might be appropriate to add this on the basis that it would be available to meet the loan repayment.

In the Tyro example, the ratio is £69,000/(£693,000 + £150,000) giving a ratio of 0.08:1, which is low due to the heavy investment in working capital and payment of a dividend. If the company continued to achieve profits of £1,500,000 without a further significant investment in working capital, then the ratio is in excess of 1.5:1.

Cash dividend coverage ratio

The ratio of cash flow from operating activities less interest paid to dividends paid indicates the ability to meet the current dividend. If the dividend rate shows a rising trend, dividends declared might be used rather than the cash flow dividend paid figure. This would give a better indication of the coverage ratio for future dividends. In our example coverage is again reduced by the heavy working capital investment.

2.6.2 Future cash flows from operations

We need to consider trends, the discretionary costs and the investment in working capital.

Trends

We need to look at previous periods to identify the trend. Trends are important with investors naturally hoping to invest in a company with a rising trend. If there is a loss or a downward trend, this is a cause for concern and investors should make further enquiries to identify any proposed steps to improve the position.

This is where narrative may be helpful, such as that proposed in the IFRS Practice Statement *Management Commentary,* in the Strategic Review in the UK and in a Chairman's Statement. Reading these may give some indication as to how the company will be addressing the situation. For example, is the company planning a cost reduction programme or disposing of loss-making activities? If it is not possible to improve the trend or reverse the negative cash flow, then there could be future liquidity difficulties.

Discretionary costs

The implication for future cash flow is that such difficulties could have an impact on future discretionary costs, e.g. the curtailment of research, marketing or advertising expenditure; on investment decisions, e.g. postponing capital expenditure; and on financing decisions, e.g. the need to raise additional equity or loan capital.

Working capital

We can see the cash implication but would need to make further enquiries to establish the reasons for the change and the likelihood of similar cash outflow movements recurring in future years. If, for example, the increased investment in inventory resulted from an increase in turnover, then a similar increase could recur if the forecast turnover continued to increase.

If, on the other hand, the increase was due to poor inventory control, then it is less likely that the increase will recur once management addresses the problem.

The cash flow statement indicates the cash **extent** of the change; additional ratios (see Chapter 1) and enquiries are required to allow us to **evaluate** the change.

2.6.3 Evaluating the investing activities cash flows

These arise from the acquisition and disposal of non-current assets and investments.

It is useful to consider how much of the expenditure is to replace existing non-current assets and how much is to increase capacity. One way is to relate the cash expenditure to the depreciation charge; this indicates that the cash expenditure is more than five times greater than the depreciation charge, calculated as £540,000/£102,000. This seems to indicate a possible increase in productive capacity. However, the cash flow statement does not itemise the expenditure, as the extract from the non-current asset schedule does not reveal how much was spent on plant – this information would be available in practice.

How to inform investors how much of the capital expenditure relates to replacing existing non-current assets

There has been a criticism that it is not possible to assess how much of the investing activities cash outflow related to simply maintaining operations by replacing non-current assets that were worn out rather than to increasing existing capacity with a potential for an increase in turnover and profits. The solution proposed was that investment that is merely maintained should be shown as an operating cash flow and that the investing cash flow should be restricted to increasing capacity. The IASB doubted the reliability of such a distinction but there is a view that such an analysis provides additional information, provided the breakdown between the two types of expenditure can be reliably ascertained.

Capital expenditure ratio

This is a ratio where the numerator is *net cash flow generated by operating activities* and the denominator is *capital expenditures.* This ratio measures the capital available for internal re-investment and for meeting existing debt. We look for a ratio that exceeds 1.0, showing that the company has funds to maintain its operational capability and has cash towards meeting its debt repayments and dividends.

It is important to remember that this ratio is industry-specific and any comparator should be with another company that has similar capital expenditure ratio (CAPEX) requirements. The ratio would be expected to be lower for companies in growth industries as opposed to those in mature industries and more variable in cyclical industries, such as housing.

It should be recognised, however, that there is a risk if a company has significant free cash flow that its managers may be too optimistic about future performance. When they are not reliant on satisfying external funders there could be less constraint on their investment decisions. If there is negative free cash flow then the opposite applies and the business would require external finance which then means that it would be subject to any conditions imposed by the new source of finance.

2.6.4 Free cash flow (FCF)

This is a performance measure showing how much cash a company has for further investment after deducting from net cash generated by operating capital the amount spent on capital expenditure to maintain or expand its asset base. Many companies refer to it in their annual report with possible slight variations in definition.

For example, Colt SA in its 2015 Annual Report states:

Free cash flow is net cash generated from operating activities less net cash used to purchase non-current assets *and net finance costs paid.*

Reasons for reporting FCF

It is emphasised by companies for different reasons – some emphasising its use as the way that the company manages its capital. For example, the following is an extract from the Kingfisher Group's 2013 Annual Report:

The Group manages its capital by:
Continued focus on free cash flow generation; Setting the level of capital expenditure and dividend in the context of current year and *forecast free cash flow* generation; Rigorous review of capital investments and post investment reviews to drive better returns; and Monitoring the level of the Group's financial and leasehold debt in the context of Group performance and its credit rating.

The company recognises the importance of free cash flow in maintaining its credit rating:

The Group will maintain a high focus on free cash flow generation going forward to maintain its solid investment grade balance sheet, fund investment where economic returns are attractive and pay healthy dividends to shareholders.

Other companies might place their emphasis on liquidity. For example, the following is an extract from the Merck Group 2011 Annual Report:

Free cash flow and underlying free cash flow are indicators that we use internally to measure the contribution of our divisions to liquidity.

Also there might be an emphasis on operational control as illustrated in this extract from the Merck Group 2013 Annual Report:

Business free cash flow (BFCF)
Apart from EBITDA pre and sales, business free cash flow (BFCF) is the third important Group and division KPI and therefore also used for internal target agreements and individual incentive plans. It comprises the major cash-relevant items that the individual businesses can influence. . . . The introduction of business free cash flow has led to considerable improvements in cash awareness as well as reduced working capital requirements.

The amount of free cash flow will be normally positive for a mature company and negative for a younger company. It will be impacted by the investment in working capital and capital expenditure and will depend on the industry. For example, free cash flow might be high in the tobacco industry and its products industry where there is low investment in either working capital or CAPEX and low in an industry such as petroleum and gas where, although the investment in working capital is low, CAPEX is high.

Ratios based on FCF

These include the cash conversion ratio (CCR) and cash dividend coverage ratio (CDCR).
     The CCR is calculated as free cash flow divided by earnings before interest, tax, depreciation and amortisation (EBITDA). It indicates the rate at which profits are being turned into cash. From the point of view of the shareholders it indicates how much of the profit could be distributed as dividends without causing liquidity or cash flow problems for the company.
     The CDCR is calculated as free cash flow divided by dividends. It indicates that the company is able to generate earnings beyond maintaining its current operational capacity.

2.6.5 Evaluating the financing cash flows

Additional capital of £300,000 has been raised. After repaying a loan of £50,000 and payment of a dividend of £120,000, only £130,000 was left towards a negative free cash flow with a net outflow of £250,000 (£319,000 − £69,000).

This does not allow us to assess the financing policy of the company, e.g. whether the capital was raised the optimum way. Nor does it allow us to assess whether the company would have done better to provide finance by improved control over its assets, e.g. working capital reduction.[6]

The indications are healthy in that the company is relying on earnings and equity capital to finance growth. It is low-geared and further funds could be sought, possibly from the bank or private equity, particularly if it is required for capacity building purposes.

2.6.6 Reconciliation of net cash flows to net debt

A net debt reconciliation is useful in that it allows investors to see how business financing has changed over the year, identifying, for example, if a significant increase in cash has been achieved only by taking on increased debt.

It is not required by IFRS but is often sought by investors. The following illustrates the notes that would be prepared for Tyro Bruce (see Section 2.4 above) if the company decided to publish a reconciliation:

		20X4		20X3
1 Borrowings		(150)		(200)
Overdraft	(78)		(8)	
Securities	20			
Cash	10		80	
		(48)		72
		(198)		(128)

2 Reconcile net cash flow to movement in net debt

Decrease in cash	(48 + 72)	(120)
Change in net debt resulting from cash	(200 − 150)	50
Movement in net debt	(198 − 128)	(70)
Net debt at beginning of period		(128)
Net debt at end of period		(198)

3 Analysis of net debt

	20X3	Cash flow	20X4
Cash at bank	80	(120)	10
Government securities			20
Overdraft	(8)		(78)
Debt outstanding	(200)	50	(150)
Net debt	(128)	(70)	(198)

2.6.7 Voluntary disclosures

IAS 7 (paragraphs 50–52) lists additional information, supported by a management commentary that may be relevant to understanding:

- liquidity, e.g. the amount of undrawn borrowing facilities;
- future profitability, e.g. cash flow representing increases in operating capacity separate from cash flow maintaining operating capacity; and
- risk, e.g. cash flows for each reportable segment, to better understand the relationship between the entity's cash flows and each segment's cash flows.

2.7 Approach to answering questions with time constraints

We have explained the step approach with the explanatory detail on the statements of financial position and income. In an examination it is preferable to show the workings on the statement of cash flows itself as shown in the examination question for Riddle worked below.

The following are the statements of financial position and income for Riddle plc.

Statements of financial position as at 31 March

	20X8		20X9	
	$000	$000	$000	$000
Non-current assets:				
Property, plant and equipment, at cost	540		720	
Less accumulated depreciation	(145)		(190)	
		395		530
Investments		115		140
Current assets:				
Inventory	315		418	
Trade receivables	412		438	
Bank	48	775	51	907
Total assets		1,285		1,577
Capital and reserves:				
Ordinary shares	600		800	
Share premium	40		55	
Retained earnings	217	857	311	1,166
Non-current liabilities:				
12% debentures		250		200
Current liabilities:				
Trade payables	139		166	
Taxation	39	178	45	211
Total equity and liabilities		1,285		1,577

Statement of income for the year ended 31 March 20X9

	$000	$000
Revenue		2,460
Cost of sales		1,780
Gross profit		680
Distribution costs	(124)	
Administration expenses	(300)	(424)
Operating profit		256
Interest on debentures		(24)
Profit before tax		232
Tax		(48)
Profit after tax		184

Note: The statement of changes in equity disclosed a dividend of $90,000.

Teaching note: Take an initial look at the statement of financial position and notes to check whether or not there has been any disposal of non-current assets which would give rise to a profit or loss adjustment as a non-cash adjustment to the profit after tax figure in the statement of income. In the case of Riddle there have only been acquisitions.

Required

(a) Prepare the statement of cash flows for Riddle plc for the year ended 31 March 20X9 and show the operating cash flows using the 'indirect method'.

(b) Calculate the cash generated from operations using the 'direct method'.

Solution

(a) Using indirect method

Statement of cash flows for the year ended 31 March 20X9

		$000	$000
Cash from operating activities			
Profit before tax	Income statement		232
Adjustments for:			
Depreciation	190 − 145	45	
Interest expense		24	69
Operating profit before working capital changes			301
Increase in inventory	418 − 315	(103)	
Increase in trade receivables	438 − 412	(26)	
Increase in trade payables	166 − 139	27	(102)
Cash generated from operations			199
Interest paid		(24)	
Tax paid	39 + 48 − 45	(42)	(66)
Net cash used in operating activities			133
Cash flows from investing activities:			
Purchase of PPE	720 − 540	(180)	
Disposal proceeds of PPE	None in question		
Investments	140 − 115	(25)	(205)
Cash flows from financing activities:			
Share capital	800 − 600	200	
Share premium	55 − 40	15	
Debentures	200 − 250	(50)	
Dividends paid	Given in note	(90)	75
Net increase in cash and cash equivalents			3
Cash and cash equivalents at beginning of year			48
Cash and cash equivalents at end of year			51

(b) Cash generated from operations using the direct method

	$000	$000
(i) Received from customers		2,434
(ii) Paid to suppliers	1,856	
(iii) Paid expenses (124 + 300 − depreciation 45)	379	2,235
Cash generated from operations		199

(i) Received from customers	$000
Trade receivables at beginning of year	412
Sales	2,460
	2,872
Less: Trade receivables at end of year	438
Cash received from customers	2,434

(ii) Paid to suppliers

	$000	$000
Trade payables at beginning of year		139
Cost of sales	1,780	
Closing inventory	418	
	2,198	
Less: Opening inventory	315	1,883
		2,022
Less: Trade payables at end of year		166
Cash paid to trade payables		1,856

Teaching note: Interest on the debentures is added back when preparing the statement using the indirect method. When using the direct method there is no need to include it within the payables calculation.

2.8 Preparing a statement of cash flows when no statement of income is available

Questions might be met where the statements of financial position are provided and figures have to be derived.

2.8.1 Flow Ltd + – an example

As an example, the following statements of financial position have been provided for Flow Ltd for the years ended 31 December 20X5 and 20X6:

	20X5		20X6	
	€	€	€	€
Non-current assets				
Tangible assets				
PPE at cost	1,743,750		1,983,750	
Accumulated depreciation	551,250	1,192,500	619,125	1,364,625
Current assets				
Inventory		101,250		85,500
Trade receivables		252,000		274,500
		1,545,750		1,724,625

	20X5		20X6	
	€	€	€	€
Capital and reserves				
Common shares of €1 each		900,000		1,350,000
Share premium				30,000
Retained earnings		387,000		176,625
Current liabilities				
Trade payables		183,750		159,750
Bank overdraft		75,000		8,250
		1,545,750		1,724,625

Notes stated that during the year ended 31 December 20X6:

1 Equipment that had cost €25,500 and with a net book value of €9,375 was sold for €6,225.

2 The company paid a dividend of €45,000.

3 A bonus issue was made at the beginning of the year of one bonus share for every three shares.

4 A new issue of 150,000 shares was made on 1 July 20X6 at a price of €1.20 for each share.

5 A dividend of €60,000 was declared but no entries had been made in the books of the company.

The requirement is to prepare a statement of cash flows for the year ended 31 December 20X6 that complies with IAS 7.

2.8.2 Solution to Flow Ltd

Step 1. Calculate the profit by working back from the end-of-period retained earnings.

Retained earnings	176,625
Less opening retained earnings	387,000
	(210,375)
Add back the dividend already paid	45,000
Add back amount transferred to Capital on issue of bonus shares	300,000
	134,625

Step 2. Calculate the cash flow from operating activities.

Profit	134,625
Depreciation	
619,125 − 551,250 = 67,875	83,500
25,500 − 9,375 = 15,625	
Loss on sale of plant	3,150
9,375 − 6,225	
Decrease in inventory	15,750
101,250 − 85,500	
Increase in receivables	(22,500)
252,000 − 274,500	
Decrease in payables	(24,000)
183,750 − 159,750	
Cash flow from operating activities	190,525

Step 3. Statement of cash flows for the year ended 31 December 20X6 for Flow Ltd.

Net cash inflow from operating activities		190,025
Cash flows from investing activities		
Purchase of non-current assets	(265,500)	
(1,983,750 + 25,500 − 1,743,750)		
Receipts from sale of non-current assets	6,225	
Net cash paid on investing activities		(259,275)
Cash flows from financing activities		
Proceeds from issue of common shares	180,000	
Dividends paid	(45,000)	
(could be shown as operating cash flow)		
Net cash inflow from financing activities		135,000
Net increase in cash and cash equivalents		66,250
(75,000 − 8,250)		

2.9 Disclosure Initiative (Amendments to IAS 7)

The amendments effective from 1 January 2017 require disclosures that enable users of financial statements to evaluate changes in liabilities arising from financing activities including both changes arising from cash flow and non-cash changes.

The changes relate to:

(a) changes from financing cash flows;

(b) changes arising from obtaining or losing control of subsidiaries or other businesses;

(c) the effect of changes in foreign exchange rates;

(d) changes in fair values; and

(e) other changes.

Items (b) to (e) are non-cash changes.

The requirement is satisfied by providing a reconciliation between opening and closing balances for liabilities with changes arising from financing activities.

For example, considering changes from financing cash flows, a reconciliation for a long-term loan might be as follows:

	$000
Opening balance in the statement of financial position	1,000
Interest expense from the income statement	50
Interest paid from the cash flow statement	
(whether classified as operating or financing)	(40)
Capital repayment	(400)
Closing balance in statement of financial position	610

We have not yet dealt with items (b) to (e) in the text – that comes in later chapters – but to illustrate treatment of non-cash changes in principle, consider the acquisition of a subsidiary with existing loans in the subsidiary.

Say the subsidiary had been acquired during the year with an existing loan of $300,000. On consolidation, the reconciliation would show this separately as a non-cash change reconciling to the new consolidated closing balance of $610,000

This disclosure gives the user a full explanation for the movement in the opening balance in the statement of financial position of $1,000,000 and the closing balance of $610,000.

2.10 Critique of cash flow accounting

IAS 7 (revised) applies uniform requirements to the format and presentation of cash flow statements. It still, however, allows companies to choose between the direct and the indirect methods, and the presentation of interest and dividend cash flows. It can be argued, therefore, that it has failed to rectify the problem of a lack of comparability between statements.

An important point is that, in its search for improved comparability, IAS 7 (revised) reduced the scope for innovation. It might be argued that standard setters should not be reducing innovation, but that there should be concerted effort to increase innovation and improve the information available to user groups. The acceptability of innovation is a fundamental issue in a climate that is becoming increasingly prescriptive.

Summary

IAS 7 (revised) defines the format and treatment of individual items within the cash flow statement. This leads to uniformity and greater comparability between companies. However, there is still some criticism of the current IAS 7:

- There are options within IAS 7 for presentation, since either the direct or the indirect method can be used; and there are choices about the presentation of dividends and interest.

- The cash flow statement does not distinguish between discretionary and non-discretionary cash flows, which would be valuable information to users.

- There is no separate disclosure of cash flows for expansion from cash flows to maintain current capital levels. This distinction would be useful when assessing the position and performance of companies, and is not always easy to identify in the current presentation.

- The definition of cash and cash equivalents can cause problems in that companies may interpret which investments are cash equivalents differently, leading to a lack of comparability. Statements of cash flows could be improved by removing cash equivalents and concentrating solely on the movement in cash, which is the current UK practice.

REVIEW QUESTIONS

1 Explain the entries in the statement of cash flows when a non-current asset is sold (a) at a loss and (b) at a profit.

2 Explain the two ways in which dividends received might be classified and discuss which provides the more relevant information.

3 Discuss if long-term debts are ever included with cash equivalents.

4 Discuss three ways in which free cash flow might be improved.

5   Discuss the significance of a ratio relating free cash flow to EBITDA.

6   Explain why depreciation appears in a statement of cash flows prepared applying the indirect method but not in that applying the direct method.

7   Explain the information that a user can obtain from a statement of cash flows that cannot be obtained from the current or comparative statements of financial position.

8   It is suggested that a reconciliation of net cash flows to net debt should be required by IFRS. Discuss the relevance of such a reconciliation and the suggestion that it should be a mandatory requirement.

9   Discuss the limitations of a statement of cash flows when evaluating a company's control over its working capital.

10 Discuss why the financing section of a statement of cash flows does not allow a user to assess a company's financing policy.

11 Access http://scheller.gatech.edu/centers-initiatives/financial-analysis-lab/index.html and discuss what accounts for the difference in free cash flow between the top three and bottom three industries.

EXERCISES

* Question 1

Direct plc provided the following information from its records for the year ended 30 September 20X9:

	€000	
Sales	316,000	
Cost of goods sold	110,400	
Other expenses	72,000	
Rent expense	14,400	
Dividends	10,000	
Amortisation expense – PPE	8,000	
Advertising expense	4,800	
Gain on sale of equipment	2,520	
Interest expense	320	
	20X9	20X8
Accounts receivable	13,200	15,200
Unearned revenue	8,000	9,600
Inventory	18,400	19,200
Prepaid advertising	0	400
Accounts payable	11,200	8,800
Rent payable	0	1,200
Interest payable	40	0

Required:
Using the direct method of presentation, prepare the cash flows from the operating activities section of the statement of cash flows for the year ended 30 September 20X9.

* Question 2

Marwell plc reported a profit after tax of €14.04m for 20X2 as follows:

	€m	€m
Revenue		118.82
Materials	29.70	
Wages	30.80	
Depreciation	22.68	
Loss on disposal of plant	3.78	
Profit on sale of buildings	(6.48)	
		80.48
Operating profit		38.34
Interest payable		16.20
Profit before tax		22.14
Income tax expense		8.10
Profit after tax		14.04

The statements of financial position and changes in equity showed:

(i)   Inventories at the year end were €5.94m higher than the previous year.

(ii) Trade receivables were €10.26m higher.

(iii) Trade payables were €4.86m lower.

(iv) Tax payable had increased by €2.7m.

(v) Dividends totalling €18.36m had been paid during the year.

Required:
(a) **Calculate the net cash flow from operating activities.**
(b) **Explain why depreciation and a loss made on disposal of a non-current asset are both treated as a source of cash.**

* Question 3

The statements of financial position of Radar plc at 30 September were as follows:

	20X8		20X9	
	$000	$000	$000	$000
Non-current assets:				
Property, plant and equipment, at cost	760		920	
Less accumulated depreciation	(288)		(318)	
		472		602
Investments		186		214

	20X8		20X9	
	$000	$000	$000	$000
Current assets:				
Inventory	596		397	
Trade receivables	332		392	
Bank	5	933	—	789
Total assets		1,591		1,605
Capital and reserves:				
Ordinary shares	350		500	
Share premium	75		125	
Retained earnings	137	562	294	919
Non-current liabilities:				
12% debentures		400		100
Current liabilities:				
Trade payables	478		396	
Accrued expenses	64		72	
Taxation	87		96	
Overdraft	—		22	
		629		586
Total equity and liabilities		1,591		1,605

The following information is available:

(i)   An impairment review of the investments disclosed that there had been an impairment of $20,000.

(ii)   The depreciation charge made in the statement of comprehensive income was $64,000.

(iii)   Equipment costing $72,000 was sold for $54,000 which gave a profit of $16,000.

(iv)   The debentures redeemed in the year were redeemed at a premium of 25%.

(v)   The premium paid on the debentures was written off to the share premium account.

(vi)   The income tax expense was $92,000.

(vii)   A dividend of $25,000 had been paid and dividends of $17,000 had been received.

Required:
Prepare a statement of cash flows for the year ended 30 September using the indirect method.

* Question 4

Shown below are the summarised final accounts of Martel plc for the last two financial years:

Statements of financial position as at 31 December

	20X1		20X0	
	£000	£000	£000	£000
Non-current assets				
Tangible				
Land and buildings	1,464		1,098	

	20X1		20X0	
	£000	£000	£000	£000
Plant and machinery	520		194	
Motor vehicles	140		62	
		2,124		1,354
Current assets				
Inventory	504		330	
Trade receivables	264		132	
Government securities	40		—	
Bank	—		22	
	808		484	
Current liabilities				
Trade payables	266		220	
Taxation	120		50	
Proposed dividend	72		40	
Bank overdraft	184		—	
	642		310	
Net current assets		166		174
Total assets less current liabilities		2,290		1,528
Non-current liabilities				
9% debentures		(432)		(350)
		1,858		1,178
Capital and reserves				
Ordinary shares of 50p each fully paid		900		800
Share premium account	120		70	
Revaluation reserve	360		—	
General reserve	100		50	
Retained earnings	378		258	
		958		378
		1,858		1,178

Summarised statement of comprehensive income for the year ending 31 December

	20X1	20X0
	£000	£000
Operating profit	479	215
Interest paid	52	30
Profit before taxation	427	185
Tax	149	65
Profit after taxation	278	120

Additional information:

1 The movement in non-current assets during the year ended 31 December 20X1 was as follows:

	Land and buildings £000	Plant, etc. £000	Motor vehicles £000
Cost at 1 January 20X1	3,309	470	231
Revaluation	360	—	—
Additions	81	470	163
Disposals	—	(60)	—
Cost at 31 December 20X1	3,750	880	394
Depreciation at 1 January 20X1	2,211	276	169
Disposals	—	(48)	—
Added for year	75	132	85
Depreciation at 31 December 20X1	2,286	360	254

The plant and machinery disposed of during the year was sold for £20,000.

2 During 20X1, a rights issue was made of one new ordinary share for every eight held at a price of £1.50.

3 A dividend of £36,000 (20X0 £30,000) was paid in 20X1. A dividend of £72,000 (20X0 £40,000) was proposed for 20X1. A transfer of £50,000 was made to the general reserve.

Required:
(a) **Prepare a statement of cash flows for the year ended 31 December 20X1, in accordance with IAS 7.**
(b) **Prepare a report on the liquidity position of Martel plc for a shareholder who is concerned about the lack of liquid resources in the company.**

* Question 5

The following information has been taken from the financial statements for Payne plc (Payne) for the year ended 31 March 2013.

*Statement of Profit or Loss and Other Comprehensive Income (extracts) for year ended 31 March 2013:

	€000
Profit before interest and tax	981
Finance costs	(108)
Profit before tax	873
Income tax expense	(305)
Profit for the year	568
Other comprehensive income	
Revaluation surplus on property, plant and equipment	418
Total comprehensive income	986

Statements of Financial Position as at 31 March

	2013 €000	2012 €000
ASSETS		
Non-current assets:		
Property, plant and equipment	11,250	10,500
Intangibles	500	452
	11,750	10,952
Current assets:		
Inventories	840	1,125
Trade and other receivables	260	210
Investments	38	18
Cash and cash equivalents	5	30
	1,143	1,383
Total assets	12,893	12,335
EQUITY AND LIABILITIES		
Equity:		
Ordinary share capital	6,000	5,250
Share premium account	1,800	1,425
Revaluation surplus	750	356
Retained earnings	2,011	3,369
	10,561	10,400
Non-current liabilities:		
Preference share capital (redeemable)	760	600
Current liabilities:		
Trade and other payables	222	210
Taxation	600	525
Ordinary dividend payable	750	600
	1,572	1,335
Total equity and liabilities	12,893	12,335

Statement of Changes in Equity for the year ended 31 March 2013 (extract)

	Retained Earnings €'000	Revaluation Surplus €'000
Balance at 1 April 2012	3,369	356
Dividends declared	(1,950)	
Total comprehensive income for the year	568	418
Transfer from revaluation surplus to retained earnings	24	(24)
Balance at 31 March 2013	2,011	750

*In June 2011, the IASB issued amendments to *IAS 1 Presentation of Financial Statements*. One of these proposed the adoption of the title *Statement of Profit or Loss and Other Comprehensive Income* for the performance statement. The title *Statement of Comprehensive Income* could have been used above.

The following additional information is relevant:

(i)   During the year Payne issued both ordinary shares and redeemable preference shares for cash. The latter were issued at par.

(ii) Investments classified as current assets are held for the short term and are readily convertible into the stated amounts of cash on demand.

(iii) During the year, Payne sold plant and equipment with a carrying amount of €840,500 for €900,000. Total depreciation charges for the year amounted to €1,100,000. Plant costing €50,000 was purchased on credit. The amount is included within trade and other payables.

(iv) Trade and other payables include accrued interest of €5,000 as at 31 March 2013 (2012: €10,000).

(v) Intangibles relate to development costs capitalised in accordance with IAS 38 *Intangible Assets*. Costs amounting to €70,000 were capitalised during the year.

Required:

(a) Prepare a Statement of Cash Flows for Payne for the year to 31 March 2013 in accordance with IAS 7 Statement of Cash Flows.

(b) You have been provided with the following additional information in relation to Payne's trading performance for the years ended on the stated dates:

	31/3/2013	31/3/2012
	€000	*€000*
Revenue	3,400	2,800
Cost of sales	(2,040)	(1,400)
Operating expenses	(379)	(357)

Write a report concisely analysing the cash flow, profitability and working capital management of Payne Ltd during the year ended 31 March 2013. Your report should be supported by appropriate ratios.

(Institute of Certified Public Accountants (CPA) Professional Stage 1
Corporate Reporting Examination, April 2013)

* Question 6

Ridgeway Ltd is a company that has manufactured steel shelving systems for sale to retail customers. In 2017 the directors decided following the Brexit vote to expand into the industrial market.

On 1 April 2018 it raised a five year loan of £6.4m at 8% interest +with repayments starting on 1 April 2019, invested £8m in new plant which became fully operational on that date and undertook an advertising campaign in trade journals. Sales increased and the company paid a dividend of £524,000 on 1 October 2018.

Draft statements of financial performance and position are as follows:

Statement of financial performance for the year ended 31 March	2019	2018
	£000	£000
Revenue	54,000	36,000
Operating profit	3,376	1,800
Finance costs	892	—
Profit before tax	2,484	1,800
Taxation expense	828	616
Profit after tax	1,656	1,184

Statement of financial position at 31 March	2019	2018
	£000	£000
Non-current assets		
Property, plant and equipment at cost	24,000	16,000
Accumulated depreciation	8,800	6,400
	15,200	9,600
Current assets		
Inventories	3,520	2,400
Trade receivables	9,304	4,800
Cash	—	280
	12,824	7,480
Total assets	28,024	17,080
Equity and liabilities		
Share capital	8,000	8,000
Retained earnings	7,836	6,704
Total equity	15,836	14,704
Non-current liabilities		
Loan	6,400	
Current liabilities		
Trade payables	2,616	1,760
Overdraft	2,344	—
Taxes payable	828	616
Total current liabilities	5,788	2,376
Total liabilities	12,188	2,376
Total equity and liabilities	28,024	17,080

Required

(a) **Prepare a statement of cash flows for the year ended 31 March 2019.**

(b) **Explain the points you would raise when approaching the bank seeking to maintain the bank overdraft at its current level.**

Notes

1 J. Arnold et al., *The Future Shape of Financial Reports*, ICAEW and ICAS, 1991.
2 G.H. Sorter, M.J. Ingberman and H.M. Maximon, *Financial Accounting: An Events and Cash Flow Approach*, McGraw-Hill, 1990.
3 L.J. Heath and P. Rosenfield, 'Solvency: the forgotten half of financial reporting', in R. Bloom and P.T. Elgers (eds), *Accounting Theory and Practice*, Harcourt Brace Jovanovich, 1987, p. 586.
4 J.M. Gahlon and R.L. Vigeland, 'Early warning signs of bankruptcy using cash flow analysis', *Journal of Commercial Lending*, December 1988, pp. 4–15.
5 J.W. Henderson and T.S. Maness, *The Financial Analyst's Deskbook*, Van Nostrand Reinhold, 1989, p. 72.
6 G. Holmes and A. Sugden, *Interpreting Company Reports and Accounts* (5th edition), Woodhead-Faulkner, 1995, p. 134.

CHAPTER 3

Property, plant and equipment (PPE)

3.1 Introduction

The main purpose of this chapter is to explain how to determine the initial carrying value of PPE and to explain and account for the normal movements in PPE that occur during an accounting period.

Objectives

By the end of this chapter, you should be able to:

- explain the meaning of PPE and determine its initial carrying value;
- account for subsequent expenditure on PPE that has already been recognised;
- explain the meaning of depreciation and compute the depreciation charge for a period;
- account for PPE measured under the revaluation model;
- explain the meaning of impairment;
- compute and account for an impairment loss;
- explain the criteria that must be satisfied before an asset is classified as held for sale and account for such assets;
- explain the accounting treatment of government grants for the purchase of PPE;
- identify an investment property and explain the alternative accounting treatment of such properties;
- explain the impact of alternative methods of accounting for PPE on key accounting ratios.

3.2 PPE – concepts and the relevant IASs and IFRSs

For PPE the accounting treatment is based on the accruals or matching concepts, under which expenditure is capitalised until it is charged as depreciation against revenue in the periods in which benefit is gained from its use. Thus, if an item is purchased that has an economic life of two years, so that it will be used over two accounting periods to help earn profit for the entity, then the cost of that asset should be apportioned in some way between the two accounting periods.

However, this does not take into account the problems surrounding PPE accounting and depreciation, which have so far given rise to six relevant international accounting standards. We will consider these problems in this chapter and cover the following questions.

- What is PPE (IAS 16)?
- How is the cost of PPE determined (IAS 16 and IAS 23)?
- How is depreciation of PPE computed (IAS 16)?
- What are the regulations regarding carrying PPE at revalued amounts (IAS 16)?

Other relevant international accounting standards and pronouncements

- How should grants receivable towards the purchase of PPE be dealt with (IAS 20)?
- Are there ever circumstances in which PPE should not be depreciated (IAS 40)?
- What is impairment and how does this affect the carrying value of PPE (IAS 36)?
- What are the key changes made by the IASB concerning the disposal of non-current assets (IFRS 5)?

3.3 What is PPE?

IAS 16 *Property, Plant and Equipment*[1] defines PPE as tangible assets that are:

(a) held by an entity for use in the production or supply of goods and services, for rental to others, or for administrative purposes; and

(b) expected to be used during more than one period.

It is clear from the definition that PPE will normally be included in the non-current assets section of the statement of financial position.

3.3.1 Problems that may arise

Problems may arise in relation to the interpretation of the definition and in relation to the application of the materiality concept.

The definitions give rise to some areas of practical difficulty. For example, an asset that has previously been held for use in the production or supply of goods or services but is now going to be sold should, under the provisions of IFRS 5, be classified separately on the statement of financial position as an asset 'held for sale'.

Differing accounting treatments arise if there are different assessments of materiality. This may result in the same expenditure being reported as an asset in the statement of financial position of one company and as an expense in the statement of comprehensive income of another company. In the accounts of a self-employed carpenter, a kit of hand tools that, with careful maintenance, will last many years will, quite rightly, be shown as PPE. Similar assets used by the maintenance department in a large factory will, in all probability, be treated as 'loose tools' and written off as acquired.

Many entities have *de minimis* policies, whereby only items exceeding a certain value are treated as PPE; items below the cut-off amount will be expensed through the statement of comprehensive income.

For example, the Volkswagen AG 2015 Annual Report stated in its accounting policies:

Low-value assets are written off and derecognized in full in the year they are acquired. In addition, certain items of operating and office equipment with individual purchase costs of up to €1,500 are treated as disposals when their standard useful life has expired.

3.4 How is the cost of PPE determined?

3.4.1 Components of cost[2]

According to IAS 16, the cost of an item of PPE comprises its purchase price, including import duties and non-refundable purchase taxes, plus any directly attributable costs of bringing the asset to working condition for its intended use. Examples of such directly attributable costs include:

(a) the costs of site preparation;

(b) initial delivery and handling costs;

(c) installation costs;

(d) professional fees such as for architects and engineers;

(e) the estimated cost of dismantling and removing the asset and restoring the site, to the extent that it is recognised as a provision under IAS 37 *Provisions, Contingent Liabilities and Contingent Assets.*

Administration and other general overhead costs are not a component of the cost of PPE unless they can be directly attributed to the acquisition of the asset or bringing it to its working condition. Similarly, start-up and similar pre-production costs do not form part of the cost of an asset unless they are necessary to bring the asset to its working condition.

3.4.2 Self-constructed assets[3]

The cost of a self-constructed asset is determined using the same principles as for an acquired asset. If the asset is made available for sale by the entity in the normal course of business then the cost of the asset is usually the same as the cost of producing the asset for sale. This cost would usually be determined under the principles set out in IAS 2 *Inventories.*

The normal profit that an enterprise would make if selling the self-constructed asset would not be recognised in 'cost' if the asset were retained within the entity. Following similar principles, where one group company constructs an asset that is used as PPE by another group company, any profit on sale is eliminated in determining the initial carrying value of the asset in the consolidated accounts (this will also clearly affect the calculation of depreciation).

If an item of PPE is exchanged in whole or in part for a dissimilar item of PPE then the cost of such an item is the fair value of the asset received. This is equivalent to the fair value of the asset given up, adjusted for any cash or cash equivalents transferred or received.

3.4.3 Capitalisation of borrowing costs

Where an asset takes a substantial period of time to get ready for its intended use or sale then the entity may incur significant borrowing costs in the preparation period. Under the accruals basis of accounting there is an argument that such costs should be included as a directly attributable cost of construction. IAS 23 *Borrowing Costs* was issued to deal with this issue.

IAS 23 states that borrowing costs that are directly attributable to the acquisition, construction or production of a 'qualifying asset' should be included in the cost of that asset.[4] A 'qualifying asset' is one that necessarily takes a substantial period of time to get ready for its intended use or sale.

Borrowing costs that would have been avoided if the expenditure on the qualifying asset had not been undertaken are eligible for capitalisation under IAS 23. Where the funds are borrowed specifically for the purpose of obtaining a qualifying asset, the borrowing costs that are eligible for capitalisation are those incurred on the borrowing during the period less any investment income on the temporary investment of those borrowings. Where the funds are borrowed generally and used for the purpose of obtaining a qualifying asset, the entity should use a capitalisation rate to determine the borrowing costs that may be capitalised. This rate should be the weighted average of the borrowing costs applicable to the entity, other than borrowings made specifically for the purpose of obtaining a qualifying asset. Capitalisation should commence when:

- expenditures for the asset are being incurred;
- borrowing costs are being incurred;
- activities that are necessary to prepare the asset for its intended use or sale are in progress.

When substantially all the activities necessary to prepare the qualifying asset for its intended use or sale are complete, capitalisation should cease.

Borrowing costs for SMEs

IAS 23 *Borrowing Costs* requires borrowing costs directly attributable to the acquisition, construction or production of a qualifying asset (including some inventories) to be capitalised as part of the cost of the asset. For cost–benefit reasons, the IFRS for SMEs requires such costs to be charged to expense.

IFRS for SMEs

All borrowing costs are charged to expense when incurred. Borrowing costs are not capitalised.

3.4.4 Subsequent expenditure

Subsequent expenditure relating to an item of PPE that has already been recognised should normally be recognised as an expense in the period in which it is incurred. The exception to this general rule is where it is probable that future economic benefits in excess of the originally assessed standard of performance of the existing asset will, as a result of the expenditure, flow to the entity. In these circumstances, the expenditure should be added to the carrying value of the existing asset. Examples of expenditure that might fall to be treated in this way include:

- modification of an item of plant to extend its useful life, including an increase in its capacity;
- upgrading machine parts to achieve a substantial improvement in the quality of output;
- adoption of new production processes enabling a substantial reduction in previously assessed operating costs.

Conversely, expenditure that restores, rather than increases, the originally assessed standard of performance of an asset is written off as an expense in the period incurred.

Some assets have components that require replacement at regular intervals. Two examples of such components would be the lining of a furnace and the roof of a building. IAS 16 states[5] that, provided such components have readily ascertainable costs, they should be accounted for as separate assets because they have useful lives different from the items of PPE to which they relate. This means that when such components are replaced they are accounted for as an asset disposal and acquisition of a new asset.

3.5 What is depreciation?

IAS 16 defines depreciation as the systematic allocation of the depreciable amount of an asset over its life. The depreciable amount is the cost of an asset or other amount substituted for cost in the financial statements, less its residual value.

Note that this definition places an emphasis on the consumption in a particular accounting period rather than an average over the asset's life. We will consider two aspects of the definition: the measure of wearing out; and the useful economic life.

3.5.1 Allocation of depreciable amount

Depreciation is a measure of wearing out that is calculated annually and charged as an expense against profits. Under the 'matching concept', the depreciable amount of the asset is allocated over its productive life.

It is important to make clear what depreciation is *not*:

● It is not 'saving up for a new one'; it is not setting funds aside for the replacement of the existing asset at the end of its life; it is the matching of cost to revenue. The effect is to reduce the profit available for distribution, but this is not accompanied by the setting aside of cash of an equal amount to ensure that liquid funds are available at the end of the asset's life.

● It is not 'a way of showing the real value of assets on the statement of financial position' by reducing the cost figure to a realisable value.

We emphasise what depreciation is *not* because both of these ideas are commonly held by non-accountant users of accounts; it is as well to realise these possible misconceptions when interpreting accounts for non-accountants.

Depreciation is currently conceived as a charge for funds **already expended,** and thus it cannot be considered as the setting aside of funds to meet future expenditure. If we consider it in terms of capital maintenance, then we can see that it results in the maintenance of the initial invested monetary capital of the company. It is concerned with the allocation of that expenditure over a period of time, without having regard for the **value** of the asset at any intermediate period of its life.

Where an asset has been revalued the depreciation is based on the revalued amount. This is because the revalued amount has replaced cost (less residual value) as the depreciable amount.

3.5.2 Useful life

IAS 16 defines this as:

(a) the period of time over which an asset is expected to be used by an entity; or

(b) the number of production or similar units expected to be obtained from the asset by an entity.[1]

The IAS 16 definition is based on the premise that almost all assets have a finite useful economic life. This may be true in principle, but it is incredibly difficult in real life to arrive at an average economic life that can be applied to even a single class of assets, e.g. plant. This is evidenced by the accounting policy in the AkzoNobel 2017 Annual Report which states:

> Depreciation is calculated using the straight-line method, based on the estimated useful life of the asset components. The useful life of plant equipment and machinery generally ranges from ten to 25 years, and for buildings ranges from 20 to 50 years. Land is not depreciated. In the majority of cases residual value is assumed to be insignificant. Depreciation methods, useful lives and residual values are reassessed annually

In addition to the practical difficulty of estimating economic lives, there are also exceptions where nil depreciation is charged. Two common exceptions found in the accounts of UK companies relate to freehold land and certain types of property.

3.5.3 Freehold land

Freehold land (but not the buildings thereon) is considered to have an infinite life unless it is held simply for the extraction of minerals, etc. Thus land held for the purpose of, say, mining coal or quarrying gravel will be dealt with for accounting purposes as a coal or gravel deposit. Consequently, although the land may have an infinite life, the deposits will have an economic life only as long as they can be profitably extracted. If the cost of extraction exceeds the potential profit from extraction and sale, the economic life of the quarry has ended. When assessing depreciation for a commercial company, we are concerned only with these private costs and benefits, and not with public costs and benefits which might lead to the quarry being kept open.

The following extract from the Goldfields 2017 Annual Report illustrates accounting policies for land and mining assets.

Land
Land is shown at cost and is not depreciated.

Amortisation and depreciation of mining assets
Amortisation is determined to give a fair and systematic to profit or loss taking into account the nature of a particular ore body and the method of mining that ore body. To achieve this the following calculation methods are used:

Mining assets, including mine development and infrastructure costs, mine plant facilities and evaluation costs, are amortised over the lives of the mines using the units-of-production method, based on estimated proved and probable ore reserves.

Few jurisdictions have comprehensive accounting standards for extractive activities. IFRS 6 *Exploration for and Evaluation of Mineral Resources* is an interim measure pending a more comprehensive view by the IASB in future. IFRS 6 allows an entity to develop an accounting policy for exploration and evaluation assets without considering the consistency of the policy with the IASB framework. This may mean that for an interim period accounting policies might permit the recognition of both current and non-current assets that do not meet the criteria laid down in the IASB *Framework*. This is considered by some commentators to be unduly permissive. Indeed, about the only firm requirement IFRS 6 can be said to contain is the requirement to test exploration and evaluation assets for impairment whenever a change in facts and circumstances suggests that impairment exists.

3.6 What are the constituents in the depreciation formula?

In order to calculate depreciation it is necessary to determine three factors:

1   Cost (or revalued amount if the company is following a revaluation policy)
2   Economic life
3   Residual value.

A simple example is the calculation of the depreciation charge for a company that has acquired an asset on 1 January 20X1 for £1,000 with an estimated economic life of four years and an estimated residual value of £200. Applying a straight-line depreciation policy, the charge would be £200 per year using the formula of:

$$\frac{\text{Cost } - \text{ estimated residual value}}{\text{Estimated economic life}} = \frac{£1{,}000 - £200}{4} = £200 \text{ per annum}$$

We can see that the charge of £200 is influenced in all cases by the definition of cost, the estimate of the residual value, the estimate of the economic life and the management decision on depreciation policy.

In addition, if the asset were to be revalued at the end of the second year to £900, then the depreciation for 20X3 and 20X4 would be recalculated using the revised valuation figure. Assuming that the residual value remained unchanged, the depreciation for 20X3 would be:

$$\frac{\text{Revalued asset } - \text{ estimated residual value}}{\text{Estimated economic life}} = \frac{£900 - £200}{2} = £350 \text{ per annum}$$

3.6.1 How is the useful life of an asset determined?

The IAS 16 definition of useful life is given in Section 3.5.2 above. This is not necessarily the total life expectancy of the asset. Most assets become less economically and technologically efficient as they grow older. For this reason, assets may well cease to have an economic life long before their working life is over. It is the responsibility of the preparers of accounts to estimate the economic life of all assets.

It is conventional for entities to consider the economic lives of assets by class or category, e.g. buildings, plant, office equipment, or motor vehicles. However, this is not necessarily appropriate, since the level of activity demanded by different users may differ. For example, compare two motor cars owned by a business: one is used by the national sales manager, covering 100,000 miles per annum visiting clients; the other is used by the accountant to drive from home to work and occasionally the bank, covering perhaps one-tenth of the mileage.

In practice, the useful economic life would be determined by reference to factors such as repair costs, the cost and availability of replacements, and the comparative cash flows of existing and alternative assets. The problem of optimal replacement lives is a normal financial management problem; its significance in financial reporting is that the assumptions used within the financial management decision may provide evidence of the expected economic life.

3.6.2 Other factors affecting the useful life figure

We can see that there are technical factors affecting the estimated economic life figure. In addition, other factors have prompted companies to set estimated lives that have no relationship to the active productive life of the asset. One such factor is the wish of management to take into account the effect of inflation. This led some companies to reduce the estimated economic life, so that a higher charge was made against profits during the early period of the asset's life to compensate for the inflationary effect on the cost of replacement. The total charge will be the same, but the timing is advanced. This does not result in the retention of funds necessary to replace; but it does reflect the fact that there is at present no coherent policy for dealing with inflation in the published accounts – consequently, companies resort to *ad hoc* measures that frustrate efforts to make accounts uniform and comparable. *Ad hoc* measures such as these have prompted changes in the standards.

3.6.3 Residual value

IAS 16 defines residual value as the net amount which an entity expects to obtain for an asset at the end of its useful life after deducting the expected costs of disposal. Where PPE is carried at cost, the residual value is initially estimated at the date of acquisition. In subsequent periods the estimate of residual value is revised, the revision being based on conditions prevailing at each statement of financial position date. Such revisions have an effect on future depreciation charges.

Besides inflation, residual values can be affected by changes in technology and market conditions. For example, during the period 1980–90 the cost of small business computers fell dramatically in both real and monetary terms, with a considerable impact on the residual (or second-hand) value of existing equipment.

3.7 Calculation of depreciation

Having determined the key factors in the computation, we are left with the problem of how to allocate that cost between accounting periods. For example, with an asset having an economic life of five years:

	£
Asset cost	11,000
Estimated residual value (no significant change anticipated over useful economic life)	1,000
Depreciable amount	10,000

How should the depreciable amount be charged to the statement of comprehensive income over the five years? IAS 16 tells us that it should be allocated on a systematic basis and the depreciation method used should reflect as fairly as possible the pattern in which the asset's economic benefits are consumed. The two most popular methods are **straight-line,** in which the depreciation is charged evenly over the useful life, and **diminishing balance,** where depreciation is calculated annually on the net written-down amount. In the case above, the calculations would be as in Figure 3.1.

Note that, although the diminishing balance is generally expressed in terms of a percentage, this percentage is arrived at by inserting the economic life into the formula as n; the 38% reflects the expected economic life of five years. As we change the life, so we change the percentage that is applied. The normal rate applied to vehicles is 25% diminishing balance; if we apply that to the cost and residual value in our example, we can see that we would be assuming an economic life of eight years. It is a useful test when using reducing balance percentages to refer back to the underlying assumptions.

We can see that the end result is the same. Thus, £10,000 has been charged against income, but with a dramatically different pattern of statement of comprehensive income charges. The charge for straight-line depreciation in the first year is less than half that for reducing balance.

3.7.1 Arguments in favour of the straight-line method

The method is simple to calculate. However, in these days of calculators and computers this seems a particularly facile argument, particularly when one considers the materiality of the figures.

Figure 3.1 Effect of different depreciation methods

	Straight-line (£2,000) £	Diminishing balance (38%) £	Difference £
Cost	11,000	11,000	
Depreciation for year 1	2,000	4,180	2,180
Net book value (NBV)	9,000	6,820	
Depreciation for year 2	2,000	2,592	592
NBV	7,000	4,228	
Depreciation for year 3	2,000	1,606	(394)
NBV	5,000	2,622	
Depreciation for year 4	2,000	996	(1,004)
NBV	3,000	1,626	
Depreciation for year 5	2,000	618	(1,382)
Residual value	1,000	1,008	

The diminishing balance formula was $1 - \sqrt[n]{(\text{Residual value}/\text{Cost})}$

3.7.2 Arguments in favour of the diminishing balance method

First, the charge reflects the efficiency and maintenance costs of the asset. When new, an asset is operating at its maximum efficiency, which falls as it nears the end of its life. This may be countered by the comment that in year 1 there may be 'teething troubles' with new equipment, which, while probably covered by a supplier's guarantee, will hamper efficiency.

Secondly, the pattern of diminishing balance depreciation gives a net book amount that approximates to second-hand values. For example, with motor cars the initial fall in value is very high.

3.7.3 Other methods of depreciating

Besides straight-line and diminishing balance, there are a number of other methods of depreciating, such as the sum of the units method, the machine-hour method and the annuity method. We will consider these briefly.

Sum of the units method

A compromise between straight-line and reducing balance that is popular in the USA is the sum of the units method. The calculation based on the information in Figure 3.1 is now shown in Figure 3.2. This has the advantage that, unlike diminishing balance, it is simple to obtain the exact residual amount (zero if appropriate), while giving the pattern of high initial charge shown by the diminishing balance approach.

Machine-hour method

The machine-hour system is based on an estimate of the asset's service potential. The economic life is measured not in accounting periods but in working hours, and the depreciation is allocated in the proportion of the actual hours worked to the potential total hours available.

Figure 3.2 Sum of the units method

		£
Cost		11,000
Depreciation for year 1	£.10,000 × 5/15	3,333
Net book value (NBV)		7,667
Depreciation for year 2	£.10,000 × 4/15	2,667
NBV		5,000
Depreciation for year 3	£.10,000 × 3/15	2,000
NBV		3,000
Depreciation for year 4	£.10,000 × 2/15	1,333
NBV		1,667
Depreciation for year 5	£.10,000 × 1/15	667
Residual value		1,000

This method is commonly employed in aviation, where aircraft are depreciated on the basis of flying hours.

Annuity method

With the annuity method, the asset, or rather the amount of capital representing the asset, is regarded as being capable of earning a fixed rate of interest. The sacrifice incurred in using the asset within the business is therefore twofold: the loss arising from the exhaustion of the service potential of the asset; and the interest forgone by using the funds invested in the business to purchase the non-current asset. With the help of annuity tables, a calculation shows what equal amounts of depreciation, written off over the estimated life of the asset, will reduce the book value to nil, after debiting interest to the asset account on the diminishing amount of funds that are assumed to be invested in the business at that time, as represented by the value of the asset.

Figure 3.3 contains an illustration based on the treatment of a five-year lease which cost the company a premium of £10,000 on 1 January year 1. It shows how the total depreciation charge is computed. Each year the charge for depreciation in the statement of comprehensive income is the equivalent annual amount that is required to repay the investment over the

Figure 3.3 Annuity method

Year	Opening written-down value £	Notional interest (10%) £	Annual payment £	Net movement £	Closing written-down value £
1	10,000	1,000	(2,638)	(1,638)	8,362
2	8,362	836	(2,638)	(1,802)	6,560
3	6,560	656	(2,638)	(1,982)	4,578
4	4,578	458	(2,638)	(2,180)	2,398
5	2,398	240	(2,638)	(2,398)	Nil

five-year period at a rate of interest of 10% less the notional interest available on the remainder of the invested funds.

An extract from the annuity tables to obtain the annual equivalent factor for year 5 and assuming a rate of interest of 10% would show:

Year	Annuity A_n^{-1}
1	1.1000
2	0.5762
3	0.4021
4	0.3155
5	0.2638

Therefore, at a rate of interest of 10% five annual payments to repay an investor of £10,000 would each be £2,638.

A variation of this system involves the investment of a sum equal to the net charge in fixed interest securities or an endowment policy, so as to build up a fund that will generate cash to replace the asset at the end of its life.

This last system has significant weaknesses. It is based on the misconception that depreciation is 'saving up for a new one', whereas in reality depreciation is charging against profits funds already expended. It is also dangerous in a time of inflation, since it may lead management not to maintain the capital of the entity adequately, in which case they may not be able to replace the assets at their new (inflated) prices.

The annuity method, with its increasing net charge to income, does tend to take inflationary factors into account, but it must be noted that the *total* net profit and loss charge only adds up to the cost of the asset.

3.7.4 Which method should be used?

The answer to this seemingly simple question is 'it depends'. On the matter of depreciation IAS 16 is designed primarily to force a fair charge for the use of assets into the statement of comprehensive income each year, so that the earnings reflect a true and fair view.

Straight-line is most suitable for assets such as leases which have a definite fixed life. It is also considered most appropriate for assets with a short working life, although with motor cars the diminishing balance method is sometimes employed to match second-hand values. Extraction industries (mining, oil wells, quarries, etc.) sometimes employ a variation on the machine-hour system, where depreciation is based on the amount extracted as a proportion of the estimated reserves.

Despite the theoretical attractiveness of other methods the straight-line method is, by a long way, the one in most common use by entities that prepare financial statements in accordance with IFRSs. Reasons for this are essentially pragmatic:

- It is the most straightforward to compute.
- In the light of the three additional subjective factors – cost (or revalued amount), residual value and useful life – that need to be estimated, any imperfections in the charge for depreciation caused by the choice of the straight-line method are not likely to be significant.
- It conforms to the accounting treatment adopted by peers. For example, one group reported that it currently used the reducing balance method but, as peer companies used the straight-line method, it decided to change and adopt that policy.

3.8 Measurement subsequent to initial recognition

3.8.1 Choice of models

An entity needs to choose either the cost or the revaluation model as its accounting policy for an entire class of PPE. The cost model (definitely the most common) results in an asset being carried at cost less accumulated depreciation and any accumulated impairment losses.

3.8.2 The revaluation model

Under the revaluation model the asset is carried at revalued amount, being its fair value at the date of the revaluation less any subsequent accumulated depreciation and subsequent accumulated impairment losses. The fair value of an asset is defined in IAS 16 as 'the amount for which an asset could be exchanged between knowledgeable and willing parties in an arm's length transaction'. Thus fair value is basically market value. If a market value is not available, perhaps in the case of partly used specialised plant and equipment that is rarely bought and sold other than as new, then IAS 16 requires that revaluation be based on depreciated replacement cost. Note that the fair value falls within the scope of IFRS 13.

EXAMPLE ● An entity purchased an item of plant for £12,000 on 1 January 20X1. The plant was depreciated on a straight-line basis over its useful economic life, which was estimated at six years. On 1 January 20X3 the entity decided to revalue its plant. No fair value was available for the item of plant that had been purchased for £12,000 on 1 January 20X1 but the replacement cost of the plant at 1 January 20X3 was £21,000.

The carrying value of the plant immediately before the revaluation would have been:

● Cost £12,000
● Accumulated depreciation £4,000 $[(£12,000/6) \times 2]$
● Written-down value £8,000.

Under the principles of IAS 16 the revalued amount would be £14,000 (£21,000 $\times$ 4/6). This amount would be reflected in the financial statements by either:

● showing a revised gross figure of £14,000 and reversing out all the accumulated depreciation charged to date so as to give a carrying value of £14,000; or
● restating both the gross figure and the accumulated depreciation by the proportionate change in replacement cost. This would give a gross figure of £21,000, with accumulated depreciation restated at £7,000 to once again give a net carrying value of £14,000.

3.8.3 Detailed requirements regarding revaluations

The frequency of revaluations depends upon the movements in the fair values of those items of PPE being revalued. In jurisdictions where the rate of price changes is very significant revaluations may be necessary on an annual basis. In other jurisdictions revaluations every three or five years may well be sufficient.

Where an item of PPE is revalued, the entire class of PPE to which that asset belongs should be revalued.[6] A class of PPE is a grouping of assets of a similar nature and use in an entity's operations. Examples would include:

● land;
● land and buildings;
● machinery.

This is an important provision because without it entities would be able to select which assets they revalued on the basis of best advantage to the financial statements. Revaluations will usually increase the carrying values of assets and equity and leave borrowings unchanged. Therefore gearing (or leverage) ratios will be reduced. It is important that, if the revaluation route is chosen, assets are revalued on a rational basis.

The following is an extract from the financial statements of Coil SA, a company incorporated in Belgium that prepares financial statements in euros in accordance with international accounting standards: 'Items of PPE are stated at historical cost modified by revaluation and are depreciated using the straight-line method over their estimated useful lives.'

3.8.4 Accounting for revaluations

When the carrying amount of an asset is increased as a result of a revaluation, the increase should be credited directly to other comprehensive income, being shown in equity under the heading of revaluation surplus. The only exception is where the gain reverses a revaluation decrease previously recognised as an expense **relating to the same asset.**

This means that, in the example we considered under Section 3.8.2 above, the revaluation would lead to a credit of £6,000 (£14,000 − £8,000) to other comprehensive income.

If, however, the carrying amount of an asset is decreased as a result of a revaluation, the decrease should be recognised as an expense. The only exception is where that asset had previously been revalued. In those circumstances the loss on revaluation is charged against the revaluation surplus to the extent that the revaluation surplus contains an amount **relating to the same asset.**

EXAMPLE 1 ● REVALUED BUT NOT SOLD An entity buys freehold land for £100,000 in year 1. The land is revalued to £150,000 in year 3 and £90,000 in year 5. The land is not depreciated.

- In year 3 a surplus of £50,000 (£150,000 − £100,000) is reported as other comprehensive income and included in equity under the heading 'revaluation surplus'.

- In year 5 a deficit of £60,000 (£90,000 − £150,000) arises on the second revaluation. £50,000 of this deficit is deducted from the revaluation surplus and £10,000 is charged as an expense.

- It is worth noting that £10,000 is the amount by which the year 5 carrying amount is lower than the original cost of the land.

EXAMPLE 2 ● REVALUED AND THEN SOLD WITH THE REVALUATION SURPLUS REALISED AT TIME OF SALE Where an asset that has been revalued is sold, the revaluation surplus becomes realised.[7] It may be transferred to retained earnings when this happens but this transfer is not made through the statement of comprehensive income.

Continuing with our example in Section 3.8.2, let us assume that:

- the plant was sold on 1 January 20X5 for £5,000; and

- the carrying amount of the asset in the financial statements immediately before the sale was £7,000 [£14,000 − (2 × £3,500)].

This means that a loss on sale of £2,000 would be taken to the statement of comprehensive income, and the revaluation surplus of £6,000 would be transferred to retained earnings.

EXAMPLE 3 ● REVALUED AND THEN SOLD WITH THE EXCESS DEPRECIATION RECOGNISED EACH YEAR IAS 16 allows for the possibility that the revaluation surplus is transferred to retained earnings as the asset is depreciated. To turn once again to our example, we see that:

- the revaluation on 1 January 20X3 increased the annual depreciation charge from £2,000 (£12,000/6) to £3,500 (£21,000/6);
- following revaluation an amount equivalent to the 'excess depreciation' may be transferred from the revaluation surplus to retained earnings as the asset is depreciated. This would lead in our example to a transfer of £1,500 each year; and
- if this occurs then the revaluation surplus that is transferred to retained earnings on sale is £3,000 [£6,000 − (2 × £1,500)].

3.8.5 IFRS for SMEs

The IFRS for SMEs was amended in 2015 to allow the use of the revaluation model.

3.9 IAS 36 *Impairment of Assets*

3.9.1 IAS 36 approach

IAS 36 sets out the principles and methodology for accounting for impairments of non-current assets and goodwill. Where possible, individual non-current assets should be individually tested for impairment. However, where cash flows do not arise from the use of a single non-current asset, impairment is measured for the smallest group of assets which generates income that is largely independent of the company's other income streams. This smallest group is referred to as a cash-generating unit (CGU).

Impairment of an asset, or CGU (if assets are grouped), occurs when the carrying amount of an asset or CGU is greater than its recoverable amount, where:

- the carrying amount is the depreciated historical cost (or depreciated revalued amount);
- the recoverable amount is the higher of the net selling price and the value in use, where:

  - the net selling price is the amount at which an asset could be disposed of, less any direct selling costs;
  - and the value in use is the present value of the future cash flows obtainable as a result of an asset's continued use, including those resulting from its ultimate disposal.

When impairment occurs, a **revised carrying amount** is calculated for the statement of financial position as follows:

Revised carrying amount = The lower of

Carrying amount OR Higher of

Net selling price Value in use (VIU)

It is not always necessary to go through the potentially time-consuming process of computing the value in use of an asset. If the net selling price can be shown to be higher than the existing carrying value then the asset cannot possibly be impaired and no further action is necessary. However, this is not always the case for non-current assets and a number of assets (e.g. goodwill) cannot be sold, so several value in use computations are inevitable.

The revised carrying amount is then depreciated over the remaining useful economic life.

3.9.2 Dividing activities into CGUs

In order to carry out an impairment review it is necessary to decide how to divide activities into CGUs. There is no single answer to this – it is extremely judgemental, e.g. if the company has multi-retail sites, the cost of preparing detailed cash flow forecasts for each site could favour grouping.

The risk of grouping is that poorly performing operations might be concealed within a CGU and it would be necessary to consider whether there were any commercial reasons for breaking a CGU into smaller constituents, e.g. if a location was experiencing its own unique difficulties such as local competition or inability to obtain planning permission to expand to a more profitable size.

3.9.3 Indications of impairment

A review for impairment is required when there is an indication that an impairment has actually occurred. The following are indicators of impairment:

- External indicators:
  - a fall in the market value of the asset;
  - material adverse changes in regulatory environment;
  - material adverse changes in markets;
  - material long-term increases in market rates of return used for discounting.

- Internal indicators:
  - material changes in operations;
  - major reorganisation;
  - loss of key personnel;
  - loss or net cash outflow from operating activities if this is expected to continue or is a continuation of a loss-making situation.

If there is such an indication, it is necessary to determine the depreciated historical cost of a single asset, or the net assets employed if a CGU, and compare this with the net realisable value and value in use.

AkzoNobel stated in its 2015 Annual Report:

We assess the carrying value of intangible assets and property, plant and equipment whenever events or changes in circumstances indicate that the carrying value of an asset may not be recoverable. In addition, for goodwill and other intangible assets with an indefinite useful life, the carrying value is reviewed annually in the fourth quarter. If the carrying value of an asset or its cash-generating unit exceeds its estimated recoverable amount, an impairment loss is recognized in the statement of income.

The assessment for impairment is performed at the lowest level of assets generating largely independent cash inflows. For goodwill and other intangible assets with an indefinite life, we have determined this to be at business unit level (one level below segment).

Except for goodwill, we reverse impairment losses in the statement of income if and to the extent we have identified a change in estimates used to determine the recoverable amount.

3.9.4 Value in use calculation

Value in use is arrived at by estimating and discounting the income stream. The **income streams:**

- are likely to follow the way in which management monitors and makes decisions about continuing or closing the different lines of business;
- may often be identified by reference to major products or services;
- should be based on reasonable and supportable assumptions;
- should be consistent with the most up-to-date budgets and plans that have been formally approved by management, or if they are for a period beyond that covered by formal budgets and plans should, unless there are exceptional circumstances, assume a steady or declining growth rate;[8]
- should be projected cash flows unadjusted for risk, discounted at a rate of return expected from a similarly risky investment, or should be projected risk-adjusted pre-tax cash flows discounted at a risk-free rate.

The **discount rate** should be:

- calculated on a pre-tax basis;
- an estimate of the rate that the market would expect on an equally risky investment excluding the effects of any risk for which the cash flows have been adjusted:[9]
  - increased to reflect the way the market would assess the specific risks associated with the projected cash flows;
  - reduced to a risk-free rate if the cash flows have been adjusted for risk.

The following illustration is from the Roche Holdings, Inc. 2014 Annual Report:

> When the recoverable amount of an asset, being the higher of its net selling price and its value in use, is less than the carrying amount, then the carrying amount is reduced to its recoverable amount. This reduction is reported in the income statement as an impairment loss. Value in use is calculated using estimated cash flows, generally over a five-year period, with extrapolating projections for subsequent years. These are discounted using an appropriate long-term pre-tax interest rate. When an impairment arises, the useful life of the asset in question is reviewed and, if necessary, the future depreciation/amortisation charge is accelerated.

3.9.5 Treatment of impairment losses

If the carrying value exceeds the higher of net selling price and value in use, then an impairment loss has occurred. The accounting treatment of such a loss is as follows.

Asset not previously revalued

An impairment loss should be recognised in the statement of comprehensive income in the year in which the impairment arises.

Asset previously revalued

An impairment loss on a revalued asset is effectively treated as a revaluation deficit. As we have already seen, this means that the decrease should be recognised as an expense. The only exception is where that asset had previously been revalued. In those circumstances the loss on revaluation is charged against the revaluation surplus to the extent that the revaluation surplus contains an amount **relating to the same asset.**

Allocation of impairment losses

Where an impairment loss arises, the loss should ideally be set against the specific asset to which it relates. Where the loss cannot be identified as relating to a specific asset, it should be apportioned within the CGU to reduce the most subjective values first, as follows:

- first, to reduce any goodwill within the CGU;
- then to the unit's other assets, allocated on a *pro rata* basis;
- with the proviso that no individual asset should be reduced below the higher of:
- its net selling price (if determinable);
- its value in use (if determinable);
- zero.

The following is an example showing the allocation of an impairment loss.

EXAMPLE • A cash-generating unit contains the following assets:

	£
Goodwill	70,000
Intangible assets	10,000
PPE	100,000
Inventory	40,000
Receivables	30,000
	250,000

The unit is reviewed for impairment due to the existence of indicators and the recoverable amount is estimated at £150,000. The PPE includes a property with a carrying amount of £60,000 and a market value of £75,000. The net realisable value of the inventory is greater than its carrying values and none of the receivables is considered doubtful.

The table below shows the allocation of the impairment loss:

	Pre-impairment £	Impairment £	Post-impairment £
Goodwill	70,000	(70,000)	Nil
Intangible assets	10,000	(6,000)	4,000
PPE	100,000	(24,000)	76,000
Inventory	40,000	Nil	40,000
Receivables	30,000	Nil	30,000
	250,000	(100,000)	150,000

Notes to table:

1 The impairment loss is first allocated against goodwill. After this has been done £30,000 (£100,000 − £70,000) remains to be allocated.

2 No impairment loss can be allocated to the property, inventory or receivables because these assets have a recoverable amount that is higher than their carrying value.

3 The remaining impairment loss is allocated pro rata to the intangible assets (carrying amount £10,000) and the plant (carrying amount £40,000 (£100,000 − £60,000)).

Restoration of past impairment losses

Past impairment losses in respect of an asset other than goodwill may be restored where the recoverable amount increases due to an improvement in economic conditions or a change in use of the asset. Such a restoration should be reflected in the statement of comprehensive income to the extent of the original impairment previously charged to the statement of comprehensive income, adjusting for depreciation which would have been charged otherwise in the intervening period.

3.9.6 Illustration of data required for an impairment review

Pronto SA has a product line producing wooden models of athletes for export. The carrying amount of the net assets employed on the line as at 31 December 20X3 was £114,500. The scrap value of the net assets at 31 December 20X6 is estimated to be £5,000.

There is an indication that the export market will be adversely affected in 20X6 by competition from plastic toy manufacturers. This means that the net assets employed to produce this product might have been impaired.

The finance director estimated the net realisable value of the net assets at 31 December 20X3 to be £70,000. The value in use is now calculated to check if it is higher or lower than £70,000. If it is higher it will be compared with the carrying amount to see if impairment has occurred; if it is lower the net realisable value will be compared with the carrying amount.

Pronto SA has prepared budgets for the years ended 31 December 20X4, 20X5 and 20X6. The assumptions underlying the budgets are as follows:

Unit costs and revenue:

	£
Selling price	10.00
Buying-in cost	(4.00)
Production cost: material, labour, overhead	(0.75)
Head office overheads apportioned	(0.25)
Cash inflow per model	5.00

Estimated sales volumes:

	20X3	20X4	20X5	20X6
Estimated at 31 December 20X2	6,000	8,000	11,000	14,000
Revised estimate at 31 December 20X3	—	8,000	11,000	4,000

Determining the discount rate to be used:

	20X4	20X5	20X6
Rate obtainable elsewhere at same level of risk	10%	10%	10%

The discount factors to be applied to each year are then calculated using cost of capital discount rates as follows:

20X4	$1/1.1$	$= 0.909$
20X5	$1/(1.1)^2$	$= 0.826$
20X6	$1/(1.1)^3$	$= 0.751$

3.9.7 Illustrating calculation of value in use

Before calculating value in use, it is necessary to ensure that the assumptions underlying the budgets are reasonable, e.g. is the selling price likely to be affected by competition in 20X6 in addition to loss of market? Is the selling price in 20X5 likely to be affected? Is the estimate of scrap value reasonably accurate? How sensitive is value in use to the scrap value? Is it valid to assume that the cash flows will occur at year-ends? How accurate is the cost of capital? Will components making up the income stream, e.g. sales, materials, labour, be subject to different rates of inflation?

Assuming that no adjustment is required to the budgeted figures provided above, the estimated income streams are discounted using the normal DCF approach as follows:

	20X4	20X5	20X6
Sales (models)	8,000	11,000	4,000
Income per model	£5	£5	£5
Income stream (£)	40,000	55,000	20,000
Estimated scrap proceeds			5,000
Cash flows to be discounted	40,000	55,000	25,000
Discounted (using cost of capital factors)	0.909	0.826	0.751
Present value	36,360	45,430	18,775

Value in use = £100,565

3.9.8 Illustration determining the *revised* carrying amount

If the carrying amount at the statement of financial position date exceeds net realisable value and value in use, it is revised to an amount which is the higher of net realisable value and value in use. For Pronto SA:

	£
Carrying amount as at 31 December 20X3	114,500
Net realisable value	70,000
Value in use	100,565
Revised carrying amount	**100,565**

3.10 IFRS 5 *Non-current Assets Held for Sale and Discontinued Operations*

IFRS 5 sets out requirements for the classification, measurement and presentation of non-current assets held for sale. The requirements which replaced IAS 35 *Discontinuing Operations* were discussed in Chapter 8. The IFRS is the result of the joint short-term project to resolve differences between IFRSs and US GAAP.

Classification as 'held for sale'

The IFRS (paragraph 6) classifies a non-current asset as 'held for sale' if its carrying amount will be recovered principally through a sale transaction rather than through continuing use. The criteria for classification as 'held for sale' are:

● the asset must be available for immediate sale in its present condition; and
● its sale must be *highly probable*.

The criteria for a sale to be highly probable are:

● the appropriate level of management must be committed to a plan to sell the asset;
● an active programme to locate a buyer and complete the plan must have been initiated;
● the asset must be actively marketed for sale at a price that is reasonable in relation to its current fair value;
● the sale should be expected to qualify for recognition as a completed sale within one year from the date of classification unless the delay is caused by events or circumstances beyond

the entity's control and there is sufficient evidence that the entity remains committed to its plan to sell the asset; and

● actions required to complete the plan should indicate that it is unlikely that significant changes to the plan will be made or that the plan will be withdrawn.

Measurement and presentation of assets held for sale

The IFRS requires that assets 'held for sale' should:

● be measured at the lower of carrying amount and *fair value* less costs to sell;
● not continue to be depreciated; and
● be presented separately on the face of the statement of financial position.

The following additional disclosures are required in the notes in the period in which a non-current asset has been either classified as held for sale or sold:

● a description of the non-current asset;
● a description of the facts and circumstances of the sale;
● the expected manner and timing of that disposal;
● the gain or loss if not separately presented on the face of the statement of comprehensive income; and
● the caption in the statement of comprehensive income that includes that gain or loss.

· 3.10.1 IFRS for SMEs

The IFRS does not require separate presentation in the statement of financial position of 'non-current assets held for sale'. However, if an entity has plans to discontinue or restructure the operation to which an asset belongs and has plans to dispose of an asset before the previously expected date, then this is to be treated as an indication that an asset may be impaired and in such a case an impairment test is required.

3.11 Disclosure requirements

For each class of PPE the financial statements need to disclose:

● the measurement bases used for determining the gross carrying amount;
● the depreciation methods used;
● the useful lives or the depreciation rates used;
● the gross carrying amount and the accumulated depreciation (aggregated with accumulated impairment losses) at the beginning and end of the period;
● a reconciliation of the carrying amount at the beginning and end of the period.

The style employed by J Sainsbury plc in its 2015 accounts is almost universally employed for this:

Property, plant and equipment

	Group Land and buildings £m	Group Fixtures and equipment £m	Group Total £m
Cost			
At 16 March 2014	9,652	5,049	14,701
Acquisition of subsidiary	5		5
Additions	475	485	960
Disposals	(110)	(608)	(718)
Transfer to assets held for sale	(90)	(4)	(94)
At 14 March 2015	9,932	4,922	14,854
Accumulated depreciation and impairment			
At 16 March 2014	1,774	3,047	4,821
Depreciation expense for the year	158	387	545
Impairment	412	128	540
Disposals	(86)	(604)	(690)
Transfer to assets held for sale	(9)	(1)	(10)
At 14 March 2015	2,249	2,957	5,206
Net book value at 14 March 2015	7,683	1,965	9,648

Additionally the financial statements should disclose:

- the existence and amounts of restrictions on title, and PPE pledged as security for liabilities;
- the accounting policy for the estimated costs of restoring the site of items of PPE;
- the amount of expenditures on account of PPE in the course of construction; and
- the amount of commitments for the acquisition of PPE.

3.12 Government grants towards the cost of PPE

The accounting treatment of government grants is covered by IAS 20. The basis of the standard is the accruals concept, which requires the matching of cost and revenue so as to recognise both in the statements of comprehensive income of the periods to which they relate. This should, of course, be tempered with the prudence concept, which requires that revenue is not anticipated. Therefore, in the light of the complex conditions usually attached to grants, credit should not be taken until receipt is assured.

Similarly, there may be a right to recover the grant wholly or partially in the event of a breach of conditions, and on that basis these conditions should be regularly reviewed and, if necessary, provision made.

Should the tax treatment of a grant differ from the accounting treatment, the effect of this would be accounted for in accordance with IAS 12 *Income Taxes*.

IAS 20

Government grants should be recognised in the statement of comprehensive income so as to match the expenditure towards which they are intended to contribute. If this is retrospective, they should be recognised in the period in which they became receivable.

Grants in respect of PPE should be recognised over the useful economic lives of those assets, thus matching the depreciation or amortisation.

IAS 20 outlines two acceptable methods of presenting grants relating to assets in the statement of financial position:

(a) The first method sets up the grant as deferred income, which is recognised as income on a systematic and rational basis over the useful life of the asset.

> EXAMPLE ● An entity purchased a machine for £60,000 and received a grant of £20,000 towards its purchase. The machine is depreciated over four years.
>
> The 'deferred income method' would result in an initial carrying amount for the machine of £60,000 and a deferred income credit of £20,000. In the first year of use of the plant the depreciation charge would be £15,000. £5,000 of the deferred income would be recognised as a credit in the statement of comprehensive income, making the net charge £10,000. At the end of the first year the carrying amount of the plant would be £45,000 and the deferred income included in the statement of financial position would be £15,000.
>
> The following is an extract from the 2015 Go-Ahead Annual Report:
>
> **Government grants**
> Government grants are recognised at their fair value where there is reasonable assurance that the grant will be received and all attaching conditions will be complied with. When the grant relates to an expense item, it is recognised in the income statement over the period necessary to match on a systematic basis to the costs that it is intended to compensate. *Where the grant relates to a non-current asset, value is credited to a deferred income account and is released to the income statement over the expected useful life of the relevant asset.*

(b) The second method deducts the grant in arriving at the carrying amount of the relevant asset. If we were to apply this method to the above example then the initial carrying amount of the asset would be £40,000. The depreciation charged in the first year would be £10,000. This is the same as the net charge to income under the 'deferred credit' method. The closing carrying amount of the plant would be £30,000. This is of course the carrying amount under the 'deferred income method' (£45,000) less the closing deferred income under the 'deferred income method' (£15,000).

The following extract is from the 2015 Annual Report of A & J Muklow plc:

> **Capital grants**
> Capital grants received relating to the building or refurbishing of investment properties are deducted from the cost of the relevant property. Revenue grants are deducted from the related expenditure.

3.12.1 Arguments in favour of each approach

The capital approach

Supporters of the capital approach argue that (a) government grants are a means of financing and should therefore be reported as such in the statement of financial position rather than be recognised in profit or loss to offset the items of expense which they finance, and (b) it is inappropriate to recognise government grants in profit or loss, because they are not earned but represent an incentive provided by government without related costs.

The income approach

Supporters of this approach argue that (a) government grants are receipts from a source other than shareholders which should not, therefore, be recognised directly in equity but should be recognised in profit or loss in appropriate periods, and (b) they are not without cost in that the entity earns them through its compliance with their conditions. Their preferred treatment is, therefore, to recognise in profit or loss over the periods in which the entity recognises as expenses the related costs for which the grant was intended to compensate.

3.12.2 IASB future action

The IASB is currently considering drafting an amended standard on government grants. Among the reasons for the Board amending IAS 20 were the following:

- The recognition requirements of IAS 20 often result in accounting that is inconsistent with the *Framework,* in particular the recognition of a deferred credit when the entity has no liability, e.g. the following is an extract from the Annual Report of SSL International plc (now part of Reckitt Benckiser):

    Grant income
    Capital grants are shown in other creditors within the statement of financial position and released to match the depreciation charge on associated assets.

- IAS 20 contains numerous options. Apart from reducing the comparability of financial statements, the options in IAS 20 can result in understatement of the assets controlled by the entity and do not provide the most relevant information to users of financial statements.

In due course there is the prospect of the IASB issuing a revised standard which requires entities to recognise grants as income as soon as their receipt becomes unconditional. This is consistent with the specific requirements for the recognition of grants relating to agricultural activity laid down in IAS 41 *Agriculture.*

IFRS for SMEs

Government grants are measured at the fair value of the asset received or receivable and treated as income when the proceeds are receivable if there are no future performance conditions attached. If there are performance conditions, the grant is recognised in profit or loss when the conditions are satisfied.

3.13 Investment properties

While IAS 16 requires all PPE to be subjected to a systematic depreciation charge, this may be considered inappropriate for properties held as assets but not employed in the normal activities of the entity, rather being held as investments. For such properties a more relevant treatment is to take account of the current market value of the property. The accounting treatment is set out in IAS 40 *Investment Property.*

Such properties may be held either as a main activity (e.g. by a property investment company) or by a company whose main activity is not the holding of such properties. In each case the accounting treatment is similar.

Definition of an investment property[10]

For the purposes of the statement, an investment property is property held (by the owner or by the lessee under a finance lease) to earn rentals or capital appreciation or both.

Investment property does **not** include:

(a) property held for use in the production or supply of goods or services or for administrative purposes (dealt with in IAS 16);

(b) property held for sale in the ordinary course of business (dealt with in IAS 2);

(c) an interest held by a lessee under an operating lease, even if the interest was a long-term interest acquired in exchange for a large upfront payment (dealt with in IAS 17);

(d) forests and similar regenerative natural resources (dealt with in IAS 41 *Agriculture*); and

(e) mineral rights, the exploration for and development of minerals, oil, natural gas and similar non-regenerative natural resources (dealt with in IFRS 6).

Accounting models

Under IAS 40, an entity must choose either:

● a fair value model: investment property should be measured at fair value and changes in fair value should be recognised in the statement of comprehensive income; or

● a cost model (the same as the benchmark treatment in IAS 16 *Property, Plant and Equipment*): investment property should be measured at depreciated cost (less any accumulated impairment losses). An entity that chooses the cost model should disclose the fair value of its investment property.

An entity should apply the model chosen to all its investment property. A change from one model to the other model should be made only if the change will result in a more appropriate presentation. The standard states that this is highly unlikely to be the case for a change from the fair value model to the cost model.

In exceptional cases, there is clear evidence when an entity that has chosen the fair value model first acquires an investment property (or when an existing property first becomes investment property following the completion of construction or development, or after a change in use) that the entity will not be able to determine the fair value of the investment property reliably on a continuing basis. In such cases, the entity measures that investment property using the benchmark treatment in IAS 16 until the disposal of the investment property. The residual value of the investment property should be assumed to be zero. The entity measures all its other investment property at fair value.

3.14 Effect of accounting policy for PPE on the interpretation of the financial statements

A number of difficulties exist when we attempt to carry out inter-firm comparisons using the external information that is available to a shareholder.

3.14.1 Effect of inflation on the carrying value of the asset

The most serious difficulty is the effect of inflation, which makes the charges based on historical cost inadequate. Companies have followed various practices to take account of inflation. None of these is as effective as an acceptable surrogate for index adjustment using specific asset indices on a systematic annual basis: this is the only way to ensure uniformity and comparability of the cost/valuation figure upon which the depreciation charge is based.

The method that is currently allowable under IAS 16 is to revalue the assets. This is a partial answer, but it results in lack of comparability of ratios such as gearing or leverage.

3.14.2 Effect of revaluation on ratios

The rules of double entry require that when an asset is revalued the 'profit' (or, exceptionally, 'loss') must be credited somewhere. As it is not a 'realised' profit, it would not be appropriate to credit the statement of comprehensive income, so a 'revaluation reserve' must be created. As the asset is depreciated, this reserve may be realised to income; similarly, when an asset is ultimately disposed of, any residue relevant to that asset may be taken into income.

One significant by-product of revaluing assets is the effect on gearing. The revaluation reserve, while not distributable, forms part of the shareholders' funds and thus improves the debt/equity ratio. Care must therefore be taken in looking at the revaluation policies and reserves when comparing the gearing or leverage of companies.

The problem is compounded because the carrying value may be amended at random periods and on a selective category of asset.

3.14.3 Choice of depreciation method

There are a number of acceptable depreciation methods that may give rise to very different patterns of debits against the profits of individual years.

3.14.4 Inherent imprecision in estimating economic life

One of the greatest difficulties with depreciation is that it is inherently imprecise. The amount of depreciation depends on the estimate of the economic life of assets, which is affected not only by the durability and workload of the asset, but also by external factors beyond the control of management. Such factors may be technological, commercial or economic. Here are some examples:

● the production by a competitor of a new product rendering yours obsolete, e.g. watches with battery-powered movements replacing those with mechanical movements;

● the production by a competitor of a product at a price lower than your production costs, e.g. imported goods from countries where costs are lower;

● changes in the economic climate which reduce demand for your product.

This means that the interpreter of accounts must pay particular attention to depreciation policies, looking closely at the market where the entity's business operates. However, this understanding is not helped by the lack of requirement to disclose specific rates of depreciation and the basis of computation of residual values. Without such information, the potential effects of differences between policies adopted by competing entities cannot be accurately assessed.

3.14.5 Mixed values in the statement of financial position

The effect of depreciation on the statement of financial position is also some cause for concern. The net book amount shown for non-current assets is the result of deducting accumulated depreciation from cost (or valuation); it is not intended to be (although many non-accountants assume it is) an estimate of the value of the underlying assets. The valuation of a business based on the statement of financial position is extremely difficult.

3.14.6 IFRS for SMEs

This IFRS differs from IAS 16 in that:

- PPE is reported at historical cost less depreciation and less any impairment of the carrying amount. The revaluation model is now permitted.
- A review of the useful life, residual value or depreciation rate is only carried out if there is a significant change in the asset or how it is used. Any adjustment is a change in estimate.
- Assets held for sale are not reported separately, although the fact that an asset is held for sale might be an indication that there has been an impairment.
- Most investment property is treated in the same way as PPE. However, if the fair value of investment property can be measured reliably without excessive cost then the fair value model applies with changes being through profit or loss.
- Separate significant components should be depreciated separately if there are significantly different patterns of consumption of economic benefits.

3.14.7 Different policies may be applied within the same sector

Inter-company comparisons are even more difficult. Two entities following the historical cost convention may own identical assets, which, as they were purchased at different times, may well appear as dramatically different figures in the accounts. This is particularly true of interests in land and buildings.

3.14.8 Effect on the return on capital employed

There is an effect not only on the net asset value, but also on the return on capital employed. To make a fair assessment of return on capital it is necessary to know the current replacement cost of the underlying assets, but, under present conventions, up-to-date valuations are required only for investment properties.

3.14.9 Effect on EPS

IAS 16 is concerned to ensure that the earnings of an entity reflect a fair charge for the use of the assets by the enterprise. This should ensure an accurate calculation of earnings per share. But there is a weakness here. If assets have increased in value without revaluations, then depreciation will be based on the historical cost.

Summary

Before IAS 16 there were significant problems in relation to the accounting treatment of PPE such as the determination of a cost figure and the adjustment for inflation; companies providing nil depreciation on certain types of asset; and revaluations being made selectively and not kept current.

With IAS 16 the IASB has made the accounts more consistent and comparable. This standard has resolved some of these problems, principally requiring companies to provide for depreciation and if they have a policy of revaluation to keep such valuations reasonably current and applied to all assets within a class, i.e. removing the ability to cherry-pick which assets to revalue.

However, certain difficulties remain for the user of the accounts in that there are different management policies on the method of depreciation, which can have a major impact on the profit for the year; subjective assessments of economic life that may be reviewed each year with an impact on profits; and inconsistencies such as the presence of modified historical costs and historical costs in the same statement of financial position. In addition, with pure historical cost accounting, where non-current asset carrying values are based on original cost, no pretence is made that non-current asset net book amounts have any relevance to current values. The investor is expected to know that the depreciation charge is arithmetical in character and will not wholly provide the finance for tomorrow's assets or ensure maintenance of the business's operational base. To give recognition to these factors requires the investor to grapple with the effects of lost purchasing power through inflation; the effect of changes in supply and demand on replacement prices; technological change and its implication for the company's competitiveness; and external factors such as exchange rates. To calculate the effect of these variables necessitates not only considerable mental agility, but also far more information than is contained in a set of accounts. This is an area that needs to be revisited by the standard setters.

REVIEW QUESTIONS

1 Define PPE and explain how materiality affects the concept of PPE.

2 Define depreciation. Explain what assets need not be depreciated and list the main methods of calculating depreciation.

3 What is meant by the phrases 'useful life' and 'residual value'?

4 Define 'cost' in connection with PPE.

5 What effect does revaluing assets have on gearing (or leverage)?

6 How should grants received towards expenditure on PPE be treated?

7 Define an investment property and explain its treatment in financial statements.

8 'Depreciation should mean that a company has sufficient resources to replace assets at the end of their economic lives.' Discuss.

EXERCISES

* Question I

Simple SA has just purchased a roasting/salting machine to produce roasted walnuts. The finance director asks for your advice on how the company should calculate the depreciation on this machine. Details are as follows:

Cost of machine	SF800,000
Residual value	SF104,000
Estimated life	4 years
Annual profits	SF2,000,000
Annual turnover from machine	SF850,000

Required:
(a) Calculate the annual depreciation charge using the straight-line method and the reducing balance method. Assume that an annual rate of 40% is applicable for the reducing balance method.
(b) Comment upon the validity of each method, taking into account the type of business and the effect each method has on annual profits. Are there any other methods which would be more applicable?

* Question 2

(a) Discuss why IAS 40 *Investment Property* was produced.

(b) Universal Entrepreneurs plc has the following items on its PPE list:

(i)   £1,000,000 – the right to extract sandstone from a particular quarry. Geologists predict that extraction at the present rate may be continued for 10 years.
(ii) £5,000,000 – a freehold property, let to a subsidiary on a full repairing lease negotiated on arm's-length terms for 15 years. The building is a new one, erected on a greenfield site at a cost of £4,000,000.
(iii) A fleet of motor cars used by company employees. These have been purchased under a contract which provides a guaranteed part exchange value of 60% of cost after two years' use.
(iv) A company helicopter with an estimated life of 150,000 flying hours.
(v)   A 19-year lease on a property let out at arm's-length rent to another company.

Required:
Advise the company on the depreciation policy it ought to adopt for each of the above assets.

(c) The company is considering revaluing its interests in land and buildings, which comprise freehold and leasehold properties, all used by the company or its subsidiaries.

Required:
Discuss the consequences of this on the depreciation policy of the company and any special instructions that need to be given to the valuer.

* Question 3

You have been given the task, by one of the partners of the firm of accountants for which you work, of assisting in the preparation of a trend statement for a client, Mercury.

Mercury has been in existence for four years. Figures for the three preceding years are known but those for the fourth year need to be calculated. Unfortunately, the supporting workings for the preceding years' figures cannot be found and the client's own ledger accounts and workings are not available.

One item in particular, plant, is causing difficulty and the following figures have been given to you:

12 months ended 31 March	20X6	20X7	20X8	20X9
	£	£	£	£
(A) Plant at cost	80,000	80,000	90,000	?
(B) Accumulated depreciation	(16,000)	(28,800)	(28,080)	?
(C) Net (written down) value	64,000	51,200	61,920	?

The only other information available is that disposals have taken place at the beginning of the financial years concerned:

	Date of		Original	Sales
	Disposal	Original acquisition	cost	Proceeds
	12 months ended 31 March		£	£
First disposal	20X8	20X6	15,000	8,000
Second disposal	20X8	20X6	30,000	21,000

Plant sold was replaced on the same day by new plant. The cost of the plant which replaced the first disposal is not known but the replacement for the second disposal is known to have cost £50,000.

Required:
(a) Identify the method of providing for depreciation on plant employed by the client, stating how you have arrived at your conclusion.
(b) Show how the figures shown at line (B) for each of the years ended 31 March 20X6, 20X7 and 20X8 were calculated. Extend your workings to cover the year ended 31 March 20X9.
(c) Produce the figures that should be included in the blank spaces on the trend statement at lines (A), (B) and (C) for the year ended 31 March 20X9.
(d) Calculate the profit or loss arising on each of the two disposals.

* Question 4

IAS 20 Accounting for Government Grants and Disclosure of Government Assistance sets out the requirements for recognising as income any grants received from government agencies, together with any repayments of such grants.

On 1 January 2014, Gilmartin plc (Gilmartin) applied to a government agency for a grant to assist with the construction of a factory in Portlaoise. The proposed construction cost of the factory was €52 million and the company projected that 350 people would be employed on its completion. The land was already owned by Gilmartin.

On 1 March 2014, the government agency offered to grant a sum amounting to 25% of the factory's construction cost to a maximum of €13 million. The grant aid was to be payable on completion, and would be repayable on demand if total employment at the factory fell below 300 people within 5 years of completion. at the financial year end, 31 March 2014, Gilmartin had accepted the offer of grant aid, and had signed contracts for the construction of the factory at a total cost of €52 million.

Construction work was due to commence on 1 April 2014. By 31 March 2015, the factory had been completed on budget, 400 people were employed ready to commence manufacturing activities, and the government agency agreed that the conditions necessary for the drawdown of the grant had been met.

On 1 April 2015, the factory was brought into use. It was estimated that it would have a ten-year useful economic life.

On 1 June 2015, the government agency paid over the agreed €13 million. In addition, the company sought and was paid an employment grant of €1.2 million as employment exceeded original projections. This is expected to be payable annually for 5 years in total, at a rate of €12,000 per additional person employed over 300 in each year. There are no repayment provisions attached to the employment grant. The directors of Gilmartin expect employment levels to exceed 350 people for at least 4 further years from 31 March 2016.

Required:
(a) Detail the requirements of IAS 20 Accounting for Government Grants and Disclosure of Government Assistance with respect to government grants to aid capital expenditure. Your answer should cover the initial recognition and subsequent treatment of these grants.
(b) Discuss, showing calculations and journal entries where relevant, how Gilmartin plc should record the above transactions and events in its financial statements for years ended 31 March 2014, 2015 and 2016.
(c) Advise what accounting adjustments which would be necessary should it become apparent at 31 March 2017, that employment at the factory would soon drop below 300 people.

(Institute of Certified Public Accountants (CPA), Professional Stage 1 Corporate Reporting Examination, April 2016)

* Question 5 CSC

CSC is a furniture retailer which operates in out of town retail parks. The following information is relevant for the year ended 30 April 2016:

During the year CSC commissioned the construction of a new retail store which cost $5 million to build.

On 1 May 2015 CSC issued 50,000 $100 5% loan notes at par to fund the construction. The loan notes are redeemable on 30 April 2020 at a 10% premium. Issue costs of $100,000 were incurred and the effective rate of interest is 7.2%.

The construction commenced on 1 June 2015 and the store was completed and was ready for use on 31 March 2016. However, the construction was suspended for two months from 1 August to 30 September 2015 due to industrial action.

The store has an estimated useful life of thirty years and the company charges depreciation on a monthly basis.

The store was opened on 30 April 2016 and on the first day of trade sold furniture with a value of $200,000 on a one-year interest-free credit basis. The market rate of interest is 5%.

Required
Explain the accounting treatment of the above items in the financial statements for the year ended 30 April 2016. You should include all relevant calculations.

(Association of International Accountants)

* **Question 6**

(a) IAS 16 *Property, Plant and Equipment* requires that where there has been a permanent diminution in the value of property, plant and equipment, the carrying amount should be written down to the recoverable amount. The phrase 'recoverable amount' is defined in IAS 16 as 'the amount which the entity expects to recover from the future use of an asset, including its residual value on disposal'. The issues of how one identifies an impaired asset, the measurement of an asset when impairment has occurred and the recognition of impairment losses were not adequately dealt with by the standard. As a result the International Accounting Standards Committee issued IAS 36 *Impairment of Assets* in order to address the above issues.

Required:
(i)   Describe the circumstances which indicate that an impairment loss relating to an asset may have occurred.
(ii) Explain how IAS 36 deals with the recognition and measurement of the impairment of assets.

(b) AB, a public limited company, has decided to comply with IAS 36 *Impairment of Assets*. The following information is relevant to the impairment review:

(i)   Certain items of machinery appeared to have suffered a permanent diminution in value. The inventory produced by the machines was being sold below its cost and this occurrence had affected the value of the productive machinery. The carrying value at historical cost of these machines is $290,000 and their net selling price is estimated at $120,000. The anticipated net cash inflows from the machines are now $100,000 per annum for the next three years. A market discount rate of 10% per annum is to be used in any present value computations.

(ii) AB acquired a car taxi business on 1 January 20X1 for $230,000. The values of the assets of the business at that date based on net selling prices were as follows:

	$000
Vehicles (12 vehicles)	120
Intangible assets (taxi licence)	30
Trade receivables	10
Cash	50
Trade payables	(20)
	190

On 1 February 20X1, the taxi company had three of its vehicles stolen. The net selling value of these vehicles was $30,000 and because of non-disclosure of certain risks to the insurance company, the vehicles were uninsured. As a result of this event, AB wishes to recognise an impairment loss of $45,000 (inclusive of the loss of the stolen vehicles) due to the decline in the value in use of the cash generating unit, that is the taxi business. On 1 March 20X1 a rival taxi company commenced business in the same area. It is anticipated that the business revenue of AB will be reduced by 25%, leading to a decline in the present value in use of the business, which is calculated at $150,000. The net selling value of the taxi licence has fallen to $25,000 as a result of the rival taxi operator. The net selling values of the other assets have remained the same as at 1 January 20X1 throughout the period.

Required:
Describe how AB should treat the above impairments of assets in its financial statements.
(In part (b) (ii) you should show the treatment of the impairment loss at 1 February 20X1 and 1 March 20X1.)

(ACCA)

* Question 7

Aspers is a long-established manufacturer and retailer of children's safety equipment. Due to difficult trading conditions and increased competition, the directors decided to sell off its loss-making manufacturing division and focus on its retail operations. The sale was completed on 1 April 2016 which generated a loss on disposal of $5 million which is included in the trial balance below for the year ended 30 April 2016:

	$000	$000
Revenue		51,000
Cost of sales	30,000	
Distribution costs	8,000	
Administrative expenses	7,000	
Loss on disposal of manufacturing division	5,000	
Interim dividend paid	400	
Land and buildings – carrying value at 30.4.16	20,000	
Plant and machinery – carrying value at 30.4.16	5,000	
Investment property – market value at 30.4.15	3,000	
Investment in equity shares – cost	600	
Inventories	10,000	
Trade and other receivables	7,000	
Cash and cash equivalents	5,500	
Share capital - $1 equity shares		10,000
Share premium		5,000
Retained earnings		16,500
Revaluation surplus		2,000
5% convertible loan stock (2019)		10,000
Deferred tax liability at 30.4.15		500
Trade and other payables		6,000
Income tax payable		500
	101,500	101,500

The following items require attention:

1   The sale of the manufacturing division on 1 April 2016 qualifies as a discontinued operation. The following balances relating to the manufacturing division are included in the relevant trial balance figures above:

	$000
Revenue	10,000
Cost of sales	(8,000)
Distribution costs	(3,000)
Administrative expenses	(2,000)

2   The balance on the income tax payable account represents the under/over provision from the previous year. An income tax liability for the year of $1.7 million needs to be provided for and this has been analysed as follows:

	$000
Income tax due on profits from retail operations	2,000
Income tax credit on loss from manufacturing division	(300)
Tax liability for the year ended 30 April 2016	1,700

The deferred tax liability has been calculated at $650,000 as at 30 April 2016.

3 Depreciation has already been correctly provided for in the year ended 30 April 2016. On 30 April 2016 Aspers conducted an impairment review of its remaining property, plant and equipment and the following information is relevant:

	Carrying value	Fair value less costs to sell	Value in use
	$000	$000	$000
Land and buildings	20,000	16,500	17,000
Plant and equipment	5,000	4,500	4,000

The land and buildings had previously been revalued and a balance of $2,000,000 remained on the revaluation surplus at 30 April 2016. Impairment losses should be recognised in administrative expenses. (Ignore deferred tax on the revaluation).

4 Aspers has adopted the fair value model for its investment property in accordance with IAS40 *Investment Properties*. An external valuation of $3.5 million was obtained on 30 April 2016.

5 During the year Aspers acquired a 1% shareholding in Harwick, a quoted company for $600,000. Aspers made the irrevocable election to hold these shares at fair value through other comprehensive income. As at 30 April 2015 the shares were quoted at $750,000. The investment is included in the trial balance at cost.

6 On 1 May 2015 Aspers signed a five-year operating lease on a retail unit in a new shopping outlet. As an inducement to sign the agreement, Aspers was given the right to occupy the unit rent free until 30 April 2016 and then will be required to pay four annual instalments of $250,000 per annum commencing on 1 May 2016. No entries have been made in respect of the lease as at the year end.

7 On 30 April 2016 Aspers issued 10,000 $1,000 5% convertible loan stock. Each loan note may be converted into 100 equity shares on 30 April 2019. The effective rate of interest for similar three-year loan notes with no rights of conversion is 8%. Aspers credited the $10 million raised to '5% convertible loan stock – 2019' liability account as shown in the trial balance.

The relevant discount rates are as follows:

Year	5%	8%
1	0.952	0.926
2	0.907	0.857
3	0.864	0.794

8 An interim dividend of 4c per share was paid during the year. At the year end the directors propose a final dividend of 5c per share.

Required

(a) **Prepare the statement of profit or loss and other comprehensive income for Aspers for the year ended 30 April 2016.**

(b) **Prepare the statement of changes in equity for the year ended 30 April 2016.**

(c) **Prepare the statement of financial position for Aspers as at 30 April 2016.**

Notes to the financial statements are not required. All workings should be shown.

(Association of International Accountants)

* Question 8

The Blissopia Leisure Group consists of three divisions: Blissopia 1, which operates mainstream bars; Blissopia 2, which operates large restaurants; and Blissopia 3, which operates one hotel – the Eden.

Divisions 1 and 2 have been trading very successfully and there are no indications of any potential impairment. It is a different matter with the Eden, however. The Eden is a 'boutique' hotel and was acquired on 1 November 2006 for $6.90m. The fair value (using net selling price) of the hotel's net assets at that date and their carrying value at the year-end were as follows:

	Fair value 1.11.06 $m	Carrying value 31.10.07 $m
Land and buildings	3.61	3.18
Plant and equipment	0.90	0.81
Cash	1.40	1.12
Vehicles	0.10	0.09
Trade receivables	0.34	0.37
Trade payables	(0.60)	(0.74)
	5.75	4.83

The following facts were discovered following an impairment review as at 31 October 2007:

(i)   During August 2007, a rival hotel commenced trading in the same location as the Eden. The Blissopia Leisure Group expects hotel revenues to be significantly affected and has calculated the value-in-use of the Eden to be $3.52m.

(ii)   The company owning the rival hotel has offered to buy the Eden (including all of the above net assets) for $4m. Selling costs would be approximately $50,000.

(iii)   One of the hotel vehicles was severely damaged in an accident whilst being used by an employee to carry shopping home from a supermarket. The vehicle's carrying value at 31 October 2007 was $30,000 and insurers have indicated that as it was being used for an uninsured purpose the loss is not covered by insurance. The vehicle was subsequently scrapped.

(iv)   A corporate client, owing $40,000, has recently gone into liquidation. Lawyers have estimated that the company will receive only 25% of the amount outstanding.

Required:
Prepare a memo for the directors of the Blissopia Leisure Group explaining how the group should account for the impairment to the Eden Hotel's assets as at 31 October 2007.

(Association of International Accountants)

* Question 9

International Financial Reporting Standards (IFRS) support the use of fair values when reporting the values of assets wherever practical. This involves periodic remeasurements of assets and the consequent recognition of gains and losses in the financial statements. There are several methods of recognising gains and losses on remeasurement of assets required by IFRS.

Required:
(a) Advise how IFRS require gains or losses on remeasurement to be dealt with in the financial statements in the case of each of the following assets. The calculation of such gains or losses is not necessary, merely their accounting treatment. Your answer should indicate clearly where in the performance statement each component of gain or loss should appear.
   (i)   Property, plant & equipment held under the revaluation model of IAS 16.
   (ii)   Investment property held under the fair value model of IAS 40.
   (iii)   Financial assets held at fair value under IFRS 9. (4 marks)
(b) In each case (i) and (ii) below, outline briefly the appropriate accounting treatment and show the journal entries in the financial statements of Williamson plc (Williamson) for year ended 31

March 2015, resulting from recording the events described. Any entry affecting the performance statement must be clearly classified as either 'profit or loss' or 'other comprehensive income'. Williamson adopts the revaluation model of IAS 16 *Property, Plant & Equipment* and the fair value model of IAS 40 Investment Property. Williamson chooses to recognise any fair value gains or losses arising on its equity investments in 'other comprehensive income' as permitted by IFRS 9 Financial Instruments.

(i)   Williamson owns a piece of property it purchased on 1 April 2012 for €3.5 million. The land component of the property was estimated to be €1 million at the date of purchase. The useful economic life of the building on this land was estimated to be 25 years on 1 April 2012. The property was used as the corporate headquarters for two years from that date. On 1 April 2014, the company moved its headquarters to another building and leased the entire property for five years to an unrelated tenant on an arms' length basis in order to benefit from the rental income and future capital appreciation. The fair value of the property on 1 April 2014 was €4.1 million (land component €1.9 million), and on 31 March 2015, €4.8 million (land component €2.1 million). The estimate of useful economic life remained unchanged throughout the period. Land and buildings are considered to be two separate assets by the directors of Williamson.

(ii) Williamson holds a portfolio of equity investments the value of which was correctly recorded at €12 million on 1 April 2014. During the year ended 31 March 2015, the company received dividends of €0.75 million. Further equity investments were purchased at a cost of €1.6 million. Shares were disposed of during the year for proceeds of €1.1 million. These shares had cost €0.4 million a number of years earlier but had been valued at €0.9 million on 1 April 2014. The fair value of the financial assets held on 31 March 2015 was €14 million.

*(Institute of Certified Public Accountants (CPA), Professional Stage 1
Corporate Reporting Examination, April 2015)*

* Question 10

Why was Rio Tinto fined £27m by the Financial Conduct Authority (FCA) for breaching Disclosure and Transparency Rules?
Access https://www.fca.org.uk/publication/final-notices/rio-tinto-plc-2017.pdf

Notes

1   IAS 16 *Property, Plant and Equipment*, IASB, revised 2004, para. 6.
2   Ibid., para. 16.
3   Ibid., para. 22.
4   IAS 23 *Borrowing Costs*, IASB, revised 2007, para. 8.
5   IAS 16 *Property, Plant and Equipment*, IASB, revised 2004, para. 18.
6   Ibid., para. 29.
7   Ibid., para. 41.
8   IAS 36 *Impairment of Assets*, IASB, 2004, para. 33.
9   Ibid., paras 55–56.
10 IAS 40 *Investment Property*, IASB, 2004.

CHAPTER 4

Intangible assets

4.1 Introduction

Intangible assets are those identifiable non-monetary assets that cannot be seen, touched or physically measured but are identifiable as separate assets.

Accounting can, consistent with the treatment of tangible assets, recognise **some** intangible assets which result from a payment and are also protected by legal rights such as patents or copyrights or trademarks, However, accounting is struggling to identify the best way to account for all intangibles. One approach is to provide additional information relevant to their valuation outside the financial reports. In that way, interested parties can make their own assessment of the value of such assets. (See the chapter on integrated reporting.)

Important issues also arise in regard to the recorded intangibles particularly in relation to changes in their market values (e.g. brandnames[1]) or the value to company in their use in its operations (customer databases), and the timing of such recognition (e.g. impairment). Management may use their discretion in relation to estimates to delay recognising impairments.

Also, the potential volatile nature of valuations of these types of assets as reflected in the surge in valuations of high-tech companies in the period from about 1997 to 1999 followed by substantial revaluations (mostly downward) between 2000 and 2002. During the period of reassessment, some innovative firms which were consuming a lot of cash without generating profits found it difficult to refinance and went out of existence.

This raises important issues about what degree of inaccuracy is acceptable in accounting.

The above issues are particularly relevant in the current commercial environment where intangibles have in some firms become the most critical elements of the business. Examples include Facebook, Amazon, Apple. To the extent that operating outlays to enhance some intangible assets are treated as expenses rather than assets, the profit is under stated and the assets are under stated. A hedge fund (GMO) which manages 70 billion dollars of investment tries to correct such perceived errors when considering whether to invest in companies.[2]

The main purpose of this chapter is to consider the approach taken by IAS 38 *Intangible Assets*[3] and IFRS 3 *Business Combinations*[4] to the accounting treatment of intangible assets.

Objectives

By the end of this chapter, you should be able to:

- define and explain how to account for:
  - legally enforceable intangibles and internally generated intangibles;
  - research and development (R&D);
  - goodwill; and
  - brands.
- account for development costs;
- comment critically on the IASB requirements in IAS 38 and IFRS 3.

4.2 Intangible assets defined

An intangible asset is defined in IAS 38 as 'an identifiable non-monetary asset without physical substance.' Thus, in addition to the other criteria which it has to meet, it must satisfy the normal definition of an asset namely:

'An asset is a resource: (a) controlled by an entity as a result of past events and (b) from which future economic benefits are expected.' From 2020 that will change in the conceptual framework to 'A present economic resource controlled by the entity as a result of past events. An economic resource is a right that has the potential to produce economic benefits.'[5] This second definition presumably will only apply if and when the standard is revised.

IAS 38 *Intangible Assets* states that an asset is recognised in respect of an intangible item if the asset is characterised by the following properties:

- The asset is identifiable.

- The standard states that for an intangible asset to exist (or be identifiable) it must either be separable or arise from contractual or other legal rights (such as a patent), whether or not the asset can be separately disposed of (such as goodwill).

- The asset is controlled by the entity.

  Control is one of the central features of the *Framework* definition of an asset. Control is said to exist if the entity has the power to obtain the future economic benefits flowing from the underlying resource and to restrict the access of others to those benefits. *It is failing to satisfy the control criterion that prevents the skills of the workforce being recognised as an asset in the statement of financial position. Staff can leave a company and take their unique skills and knowledge with them.*

- The asset gives future economic benefits.

  Again, it is inherent in the *Framework* definition of an asset that the potential future economic benefits can be identified with reasonable certainty.

If the identifiability and control tests are satisfied then IAS 38 allows recognition of an intangible asset if:

- it is **probable** that the expected future economic benefits that are attributable to the asset will flow to the entity; and

- the cost of the asset can be **measured reliably.**

Application of these criteria means that the costs associated with most internally generated intangible assets are expensed to the statement of income. An exception is development costs, **provided** these meet additional recognition criteria required by the standard.

4.2.1 Examples of intangible assets to be recognised and reported

Examples of intangible assets that should be recognised and reported in the statement of financial position are set out in IAS 38.[6] They include:

- **Marketing-related** intangible assets which provide an advantage in the marketing or promotion of products or services such as trademarks, newspaper mastheads, Internet domain names and non-compete agreements.
- **Technology-related** intangible assets which arise from contractual rights to use technology (patented and unpatented), databases, formulae, designs, software, processes and recipes.
- **Customer- or supplier-related** intangible assets which arise from relationships with or knowledge of customers or suppliers such as licensing, royalty and standstill agreements, servicing contracts and use rights such as airport landing slots and customer lists.
- **Artistic-related** intangible assets which arise from the right to benefits such as royalties from artistic works such as plays, books, films and music, and from non-contractual copyright protection.

4.2.2 Recognition criteria illustrated

Devon Cheeses Ltd decided to diversify into the production of vegetarian organic sausages. The project team produced a list of cost headings for the acquisition of:

(a) recipes from an international chef;

(b) a licence to use a specialised computer-controlled oven;

(c) registration of a trade name 'The Organo One'; and

(d) training courses for management in sausage making.

Their auditors were asked for advice on the possibility of capitalising all costs arising in respect of the above. The advice received was that the cost of recipes, the licence and the trade name registration could be capitalised, since:

- they were identifiable arising from contractual rights;
- Devon Cheeses Ltd controlled the future economic benefits;
- the costs could be measured reliably;
- it was probable that there would be future economic benefits; and
- the trade name was a defensive intangible that protected the receipt of the future economic benefits.

The training courses would improve management expertise but failed the control criterion and should be expensed.

4.2.3 Accounting treatment of recognised intangible assets at year-ends

The accounting treatment depends on whether the asset has a finite or an indefinite life.

Recognising intangible assets with a finite life

IAS 38 states that recognised intangible non-current assets should be reported at cost less accumulated amortisation or, as when a parent acquires a subsidiary with intangible assets, fair value less accumulated amortisation.

Amortisation of intangible assets with a finite life

The asset should be amortised on a systematic basis over its estimated useful economic life. This is very similar to the treatment of property, plant and equipment under IAS 16 in that it is frequently on a straight-line basis as for patents with a finite legal life. The following extract is from the Bayer Group 2017 Annual Report:[7]

> Other intangible assets are recognised at the cost of acquisition or generation. Those with a determinable useful life are amortised accordingly on a straight-line basis over a period of up to 30 years, except where their actual depletion demands a different amortisation pattern.

An acceptable basis for amortisation

Amortisation is to be based on the expected pattern of consumption of the future economic benefits of an asset. A clarification[8] issued by the IASB in 2014 advised that the use of revenue-based methods to calculate the depreciation of an asset is not appropriate because revenue generated by an activity that includes the use of an asset generally reflects factors other than the consumption of the economic benefits embodied in the asset.

Impairment of intangible assets with a finite life

Intangible assets are also tested for impairment where there is a triggering event. The following Accounting Policy extract from the SABMiller 2016 Annual Report explains the amortisation and impairment policy for intangibles with finite lives:

> Intangible assets are stated at cost less accumulated amortisation on a straight-line basis (if applicable) and impairment losses . . . Amortisation is included within net operating expenses in the income statement . . . Intangible assets with finite lives are amortised over their estimated useful economic lives, and only tested for impairment where there is a triggering event.

Amortisation of intangible assets with an indefinite life

Where the estimated useful economic life is indefinite there is no amortisation but the asset is subject to annual impairment reviews under IAS 36.

Other

An unusual case:

Emission rights provides an unusual example. BlueScope Group says in its 2017 Annual Report in note 8a; 'Emission unit (EU) permits which are not held for trading are classified as intangible assets and are carried at cost. Intangible EU assets are not amortised or subject to impairment as the economic benefits are realized from surrendering the rights to settle obligations arising from the ETS.' Thus units would be expensed at their cost when used. Similarly, the Bridon Ropes Group in their 2017 Annual Report record emission rights at cost. Other companies which trade rights would account applying the rules for financial instruments.

4.2.4 Disclosure of intangible assets under IAS 38

IAS 38 requires the disclosure of the following for each type of intangible asset:[9]

- whether useful lives are indefinite or finite;
- the amortisation methods used for intangible assets with finite useful lives;
- the gross carrying amount and accumulated amortisation at the beginning and end of the period;
- increases or decreases resulting from revaluations and from impairment losses recognised or reversed directly in equity (IAS 36 *Impairment of Assets*); and
- for R&D, disclosure in the financial statements of the expenses for research and development in the period.[10]

Where an intangible asset is assessed as having an indefinite useful life, the carrying value of the asset must be stated[11] along with the reasons for supporting the assessment of an indefinite life.

4.3 Accounting treatment for research and development

Under IAS 38 *Intangible Assets*, research expenditure **must be expensed** whereas development expenditure **must be capitalised** provided a strict set of criteria is met. In this section we will consider R&D activities, why research expenditure is written off and the tests for capitalising development expenditure.

4.3.1 Research activities

IAS 38 states[12] 'expenditure on research shall not give rise to an asset but rather must be expensed. The standard gives examples of research activities[13] as:

- activities aimed at obtaining new knowledge;
- the search for, evaluation and final selection of, applications of research findings or other knowledge;
- the search for alternatives for materials, devices, products, processes, systems and services; and
- the formulation, design, evaluation and final selection of possible alternatives for new or improved materials, devices, products, processes, systems or services.

Normally, research expenditure is not related directly to any of the company's products or processes. For instance, development of a high-temperature material which could be used in any aero engine would be 'research', but development of a honeycomb for a particular engine would be 'development'.

While it is in the research phase, the IAS position[14] is that an entity cannot demonstrate that an intangible asset exists that will generate probable future economic benefits. It is this inability that justifies the IAS requirement for research expenditure not to be capitalised but to be charged as an expense when it is incurred.

4.3.2 Development activities

Expenditure on development is recognised[15] as an asset if the entity can demonstrate that the expenditure will generate probable future economic benefits. The standard gives examples of development activities:[16]

(a) the design, construction and testing of pre-production and pre-use prototypes and models;

(b) the design of tools, jigs, moulds and dies involving new technology;

(c) the design, construction and operation of a pilot plant that is not of a scale economically feasible for commercial production; and

(d) the design, construction and testing of a chosen alternative for new or improved materials, devices, products, processes, systems or services.

4.4 Why is research expenditure not capitalised?

Many readers will think of research not as a cost but as a strategic investment which is essential to remain competitive in world markets. Indeed, this was the view[17] taken by Martin, O'Brien & Proctor of the Office for National Statistics who re-estimated the intangibles which are not currently reflected in the National Accounts and accordingly distorts the measures of productivity. They do not give estimates separately for research assets but overall the figures show non-capitalised intangibles at 88.3 billion pounds compared to capitalised intangibles of 45.9 billion pounds.

It is reported[18] that global R&D spending is in excess of 1.7% of GDP, taking place particularly in the advanced technical industries such as pharmaceuticals, where a sustained high level of R&D investment is required. The regulators, however, do not consider that the expenditure can be classified as an asset for financial reporting purposes.

Why do the regulators not regard research expenditure as an asset?

The IASC in its *Framework for the Preparation and Presentation of Financial Statements*[19] defines an asset as a resource that is controlled by the enterprise, as a result of past events and from which future economic benefits are expected to flow.

Research is controlled by the enterprise and results from past events but there is no reasonable certainty that the intended economic benefits will be achieved. Because by definition research is exploring new knowledge without knowing whether it will lead to new or improved products or services and because of the high level of uncertainty, the accounting profession has traditionally considered it more appropriate to write off the investment in research as a cost rather than report it as an asset in the statement of financial position.

The importance to investors of disclosure

It might be thought that this is concealing an asset from investors, but in research on the reactions of both analysts[20] and accountants[21] to R&D expenditure, B. Nixon found that: 'Two important dimensions of the corporate reporting accountants' perspective emerge: first, disclosure is seen as more important than the accounting treatment of R&D expenditure and, second, the financial statements are not viewed as the primary channel of communication for information on R&D.'

This highlights the importance of reading carefully the narrative in financial reports. An interesting study in Singapore[22] examined the impact of annual report disclosures on analysts' forecasts for a sample of firms listed on the Stock Exchange of Singapore (SES) and showed that the level of disclosure affected the accuracy of earnings forecasts among analysts and also led to greater analyst interest in the firm.

Management attitudes to capitalising research expenditure

Management might prefer in general to be able to capitalise research expenditure but there could be circumstances where writing off might be preferred. For example, directors might be pleased to take the expense in a year when they know its impact rather than carry it forward. They are aware of profit levels in the year in which the expenditure arises and could, perhaps, find it embarrassing to take the charge in a subsequent year when profits were lower or the company even reported a trading loss. There is a considerable body of literature that demonstrates that management under pressure will employ reported earnings management.[23]

Development expenditure, on the other hand, has more probability of achieving future economic benefits and the regulators, therefore, require such expenditure to be capitalised.

4.5 Capitalising development costs

4.5.1 Conditions to be satisfied

The relevant paragraph of IAS 38[19] says an intangible asset for development expenditure must be recognised if and only if an entity can demonstrate **all** of the following:

(a) the technical feasibility of completing the intangible asset so that it will be available for use or sale;

(b) the intention to complete the intangible asset and use or sell it;

(c) its ability to use or sell the intangible asset;

(d) how the intangible asset will generate probable future economic benefits;

(e) the availability of adequate technical, financial and other resources to complete the development and to use or sell the intangible asset;

(f) its ability to measure reliably the expenditure attributable to the intangible asset during its development.

It is important to note that if the answers to all the conditions (a) to (f) above are 'Yes' then the entity *must* capitalise the development expenditure subject to reviewing for impairment.

4.5.2 What costs can be included?

The costs that can be included in development expenditure are similar to those used in determining the cost of inventory (IAS 2 *Inventories*).

It is important to note that only expenditure incurred after the project satisfies the IAS 38 criteria can be capitalised – all expenditure incurred prior to this date must be written off as an expense in the statement of income. Experience tends to indicate that people who develop products are notoriously optimistic. In practice, they encounter many more problems than they imagined and the cost is much greater than estimates. This means that the development project may well be approaching completion before future development costs can be estimated reliably.

At the year-ends development costs are usually amortised over the sales of the product (i.e. the charge in 20X5 would be: 20X5 sales/total estimated sales $\times$ capitalised development expenditure) with straight-line as the default.

While development cost can be capitalised, there is a requirement in the EU Accounting Directive that, where the costs of development have not been completely written off, there can be no distribution of profits unless the amount of the reserves available for distribution and profits brought forward is at least equal to that of the costs not written off.

4.6 Disclosure of R&D

R&D is important to many manufacturing companies, such as pharmaceutical companies and car and defence manufacturers. Disclosure is required of the aggregate amount of research and development expenditure recognised as an expense during the period.[24] Normally, this total expenditure will be:

(a) research expenditure;

(b) development expenditure amortised;

(c) development expenditure not capitalised; and

(d) impairment of capitalised development expenditure.

Under IAS 38 more companies may capitalise development expenditure. Management view of the probability of making future profits from the sale of the product is a critical element in making a decision. The following is the R&D policy extract from the Rolls-Royce Holdings plc Annual Report for the year ended 31 December 2017:

> Research and development
>
> In accordance with IAS 38 Intangible Assets, expenditure incurred on research and development is distinguished as relating either to a research phase or to a development phase.
>
> All research phase expenditure is charged to the income statement. Development expenditure . . . is capitalised as an internally generated intangible asset (programme asset) only if it meets strict criteria, relating in particular to technical feasibility and generation of future economic benefits. . . . .
>
> Development expenditure capitalised is amortised on a straight-line basis up to a maximum of 15 years from the entry into service of the programme asset. In accordance with IAS 38, we assess the basis on which we amortise programme assets annually. At the end of 2017, we confirmed that we will commence amortization of programme assets on a 15 year straight line basis pro rata over the estimated number of units produced. We will apply this approach prospectively from 1 January 2018.

4.7 IFRS for SMEs' treatment of intangible assets

Internally generated intangible assets

The IFRS provides that internally generated intangible assets are not recognised. This means that both research and development costs are expensed.

Separately purchased intangible assets

The IFRS provides the following:

- Such assets should be amortised over the asset's useful life; and if the useful life cannot be estimated, then a 10-year useful life is presumed.
- If there is a significant change in the asset or how it is used, then the useful life, residual value and depreciation rate are reviewed.
- Impairment testing is carried out where there are impairment indications.
- The revaluation of intangible assets is prohibited.

4.8 Internally generated and purchased goodwill

IFRS 3 *Business Combinations* defines goodwill[25] as: 'future economic benefits arising from assets that are not capable of being individually identified and separately recognised'. The definition effectively affirms that the value of a business as a whole is more than the sum of the accountable and identifiable net assets. Goodwill can be internally generated through the normal operations of an existing business or purchased as a result of a business combination.

4.8.1 Internally generated goodwill

Internally generated goodwill falls within the scope of IAS 38 *Intangible Assets* which states that 'Internally Generated Goodwill (or "self-generated goodwill") shall not be recognised as an asset'. If companies were allowed to include internally generated goodwill as an asset in the statement of financial position, it would boost total assets and produce a more favourable view of the statement of financial position, for example by reducing the gearing ratio.

4.8.2 Purchased goodwill

How goodwill is calculated

The key distinction between internally generated goodwill and purchased goodwill is that purchased goodwill has an identifiable 'cost', being the difference between the fair value of the total consideration that was paid to acquire a business and the fair value of the identifiable net assets acquired.[26] This is the initial cost reported in the statement of financial position.

Companies reporting under IFRS are required to disclose the nature of the intangible assets comprising goodwill and explain why they cannot be valued separately. Examples of separate assets which they are referring to here might be separately identifying trademarks or patents.

4.9 The accounting treatment of goodwill

Now that we have a definition of goodwill, we need to consider how to account for it in subsequent years. One might have reasonably thought that a simple requirement to amortise the cost over its estimated useful life would have been sufficient. This has been far from the case. Over the past 40 years, there have been a number of approaches to accounting for purchased goodwill, including:

(a) writing off the cost of the goodwill directly to reserves in the year of acquisition;

(b) reporting goodwill at cost in the statement of financial position (this was attractive to management as there was no charge against profits in any year);

(c) reporting goodwill at cost, amortising over its expected life with or without an upper time limit; and

(d) reporting goodwill at cost, but checking it annually for impairment (now required by IFRS 3);

(e) another method that has been discussed is to write off over a short period of time, the difference between the implied goodwill as reflected in share prices prior to the market becoming aware of a takeover and the goodwill implied by the takeover price. The justification for this would be that it is possible that the companies may have paid too much as experience shows the risk associated with the premium may be greater than the uncertainty associated with the pre-takeover goodwill.[27]

4.9.1 The current IFRS 3 treatment

IFRS 3 prohibits the amortisation of purchased goodwill. It treats goodwill as if it has an indefinite life with the amount reviewed annually for impairment. If the carrying value is greater than the recoverable value of the goodwill, the difference is written off.

Whereas goodwill amortisation gave rise to an annual charge, impairment losses will arise at irregular intervals. This means that the profit for the year will become more volatile. This is why companies and analysts rely more on the EBITDA (earnings before interest, tax, depreciation and amortisation) when assessing a company's performance, assuming that this is a better indication of maintainable profits.

This volatility is illustrated by the following percentages of impairment losses relative to sales based on Vodafone Annual Reports:

Impairments as a percentage of revenue

2017	0%
2016	1.1%
2015	0%
2014	17.2%
2013	20.2%

This illustrates the volatility when impairment charges are included when calculating operating profit or loss.

4.9.2 Identifying intangible assets to reduce the amount of goodwill

Because goodwill is reviewed annually for impairment under IFRS 3 and other intangible assets are mainly amortised annually under IAS 38, standard setters wanted companies to identify any intangible assets that were acquired on an acquisition of another company (IFRS 3) and not to include them within a global figure of goodwill.

It is well known that businesses are often slow to impair assets.[28] If the payment is identified with very specific assets which are subject to amortization rather to a very general asset called goodwill the problem is less severe. Firstly, the asset is more clearly identified with specific products or activities and can therefore be more readily checked for decreases in value. Secondly, as they are amortised annually they are more likely to be below the current valuation than if they were at the initial valuation. Thirdly, annual amortization means the unusual impairments are smaller and less frequent and hence reported income is less volatile.

The following is an extract from the Intel 2016 Annual Report relating to intangible assets:

(In millions)	Gross Assets	Accumulated Amortisation	Net
Acquisition-related developed technology	$7,405	$(1,836)	$5,569
Acquisition-related customer relationships	1,449	(260)	1,189
Acquisition-related trade names	87	(21)	66
Licensed technology and patents	3,285	(1,423)	1,862
Identified intangible assets subject to amortization	12,226	(3,540)	8,686
In-process research & development	808	—	808
Identified intangible assets not subject to amortization	808	—	808
Total identified intangible assets	$13,034	($3,540)	$9,494

During the year research and development expenses were $12,740 million.

4.10 Critical comment on the various methods that have been used to account for goodwill

Let us consider briefly the alternative accounting treatments.

(a) Reporting goodwill unchanged at cost

It is (probably) wrong to keep purchased goodwill unchanged in the statement of financial position, as its value will decline with time. Its value may be *maintained* by further expenditure, e.g. continued advertising, but this expenditure is essentially creating 'internally generated goodwill' which is not allowed to be capitalised. Sales of most manufactured products often decline during their life and their selling price falls. Eventually, the products are replaced by a technically superior product. An example is computer microprocessors, which initially command a high price and high sales. The selling price and sales quantities declined as faster microprocessors were produced. Much of the goodwill of businesses is represented by the products they sell. Hence, it is wrong to not amortise the goodwill. In addition, management has purchased earnings for the immediate future (the number of years being dependent on the discount rate used to value goodwill) and it could be argued such earnings have not been generated by management.

(b) Writing off the cost of the goodwill directly to reserves in the year of acquisition

A buyer pays for goodwill on the basis that future profits will be improved. It is wrong, therefore, to write it off in the year of acquisition against previous years in the reserves. The loss in value of the goodwill should not occur at the time of acquisition but occurs over a longer period. The goodwill is losing value over its life, and this loss in value should be charged to the statement of comprehensive income each year. Making the charge direct to reserves stops this charge from appearing in the future income statements.

(c) Amortising the goodwill over its expected useful life

Amortising goodwill over its life could achieve a matching under the accrual concept with a charge in the statement of comprehensive income. However, there are problems (i) in determining the life of the goodwill and (ii) in choosing an appropriate method for amortising.

(i) What is the life of the goodwill?

Companies wishing to minimise the amortisation charge could make a high estimate of the economic life of the goodwill and auditors have to be vigilant in checking the company's justification. The range of lives can vary widely. For example, goodwill paid to acquire a business in the fashion industry could reflect a short goodwill life compared to that paid to acquire an established business with a loyal customer base.

(ii) The method for amortising

Straight-line amortisation is the simplest method. However, as the benefits are likely to be greater in earlier years than in later ones, amortisation could use the reducing balance method. One might think intuitively that amortisation based on the percentage of actual sales to expected total sales would reasonably match the cost consumed with the revenue – however, it is not an acceptable method under IFRS.

It could be argued that amortising goodwill is equivalent to depreciating tangible fixed assets as prescribed by IAS 16 *Property, Plant and Equipment* and that the amortisation approach appears to be the best way of treating goodwill in the statement of financial position and statement of comprehensive income.

There are difficulties, but these should not prevent us from using this method. After all, accountants have to make many judgements when 'valuing' items in the statement of financial position, such as assessing the life of property, plant and equipment, the value of inventory and bad debt provisions.

(d) An annual impairment check

IFRS 3 introduced a new treatment for purchased goodwill when it arises from a business combination (i.e. the purchase of a company which becomes a subsidiary). It assumes that goodwill has an indefinite economic life, which means that it is not possible to make a realistic estimate of its economic life and a charge should be made to the statement of income only when it becomes impaired.

This is called a 'statement of financial position' approach to accounting, as the charge is made only when the value (in the statement of financial position) falls below its original cost.

The IFRS 3 treatment is consistent with the *Framework*,[29] which says: 'Expenses are recognised in the statement of comprehensive income when a decrease in future economic benefits related to a decrease in an asset or an increase of a liability has arisen that can be measured reliably.'

Criticism of the 'statement of financial position' approach

However, there has been much criticism of the 'statement of financial position' approach of the *Framework*.

For example, if a company purchased specialised plant which had an immediate resale value of 5% of its cost as scrap metal, then it could be argued that the depreciation charge should be 95% of its cost immediately after it comes into use. This is not sensible, as the purpose of buying the plant is to produce a product, so the depreciation charge should be over the life of the product.

Alternatively, if the 'future economic benefit' approach was used to value the plant, there would be no depreciation until the future economic benefit was less than its original cost. So, initial sales would incur no depreciation charge, but later sales would have an increased charge.

This example shows the weakness of using impairment and the 'statement of financial position' approach for charging goodwill to the statement of comprehensive income – the charge occurs at the wrong time. The charge should be made earlier when sales, selling prices and profits are high, not when the product becomes out of date and sales and profits are falling.

Why the impairment charge occurs at the wrong time

Although the IFRS 3 treatment of impairment appears to be correct according to the *Framework,* it could be argued that the impairment approach is not correct, as the charge occurs at the wrong time (i.e. when there is a loss in value, rather than when profits are being made), it is very difficult to estimate the future economic benefit of the goodwill and those estimates are likely to be over-optimistic.

In addition, it means that the treatment of goodwill for IFRS 3 transactions is different from the treatment in IAS 38 *Intangible Assets.* This shows the inconsistency of the standards – they should use a single treatment, either IAS 38 amortisation or IFRS 3 impairment.

(e) Takeover specific goodwill

The additional payment in a takeover should reflect the premium for control and/or the synergies which the acquirer expects to achieve such as combining marketing efforts or better utilisation of assets or staff redundancies or elimination of competition. Due to cultural conflicts or overestimation of benefits often the synergies do not materialise or not to the degree forecast. In that case the premium paid is not justified and should be written off.

4.10.1 Why has the IFRS 3 treatment of goodwill differed from the treatment of intangible assets in IAS 38?

The answer is probably related to the convergence of International Accounting Standards to US accounting standards, and pressure from listed companies.

Convergence pressure

In issuing recent International Standards, the IASB has not only aimed to produce 'world-wide' standards but also standards which are acceptable to US standard setters. The IASB wanted their standards to be acceptable for listing on the New York Stock Exchange (NYSE), so there was strong pressure on the IASB to make their standards similar to US standards. The equivalent US standard to IFRS 3 uses impairment of goodwill as the charge against profits (rather than amortisation). Thus, IFRS 3 uses the same method and it prohibits amortisation.

Commercial pressure

A further pressure for impairment rather than amortisation comes from listed companies. Essentially, listed companies want to maximise their reported profit, and amortisation reduces profit. For most of the time, companies can argue that the future economic benefit of the goodwill is greater than its original cost (or carrying value if it has been previously impaired), and thus avoid a charge to the statement of comprehensive income. Also, companies could argue that the 'impairment charge' is an unexpected event and charge it as an exceptional item.

In the UK, many companies publicise their profit before exceptional items and impairment to highlight maintainable profits.

The EU Accounting Directive provides that in exceptional cases where the useful life of goodwill and development costs cannot be reliably estimated, such assets shall be written off within a maximum period set by the member state – that maximum period to be not shorter than five years and not longer than 10 years. IFRS takes precedence over the Directive.

4.11 Negative goodwill/Badwill

Negative goodwill/badwill arises when the amount paid is less than the fair value of the net assets acquired. IFRS 3 says the acquirer should:

(a) reassess the identification and measurement of the acquiree's identifiable assets, liabilities and contingent liabilities and the measurement of the cost of the combination in case the assets have been undervalued or the liabilities overstated; and

(b) recognise immediately in the statement of comprehensive income any excess remaining after that reassessment.

The immediate crediting of badwill to the statement of comprehensive income seems difficult to justify when, as in many situations, the reason why the consideration is less than the value of the net identifiable assets is that there are expected to be future losses or redundancy payments. Redundancy payment forecasts in anticipation of the new management undertaking a reorganisation are not a liability at the time of the takeover and cannot give rise to a liability at that date. Standard setters are very reluctant to allow a provision to be made for future losses (this has been prohibited in recent accounting standards). This means that the only option is to say the badwill should be credited to the statement of comprehensive income at the date of acquisition. This results in the group profit being inflated when a subsidiary with badwill is acquired.

In some ways, it would be better to credit the badwill to the statement of comprehensive income over the years the losses are expected. However, the 'provision for future losses' (i.e. the badwill) does not fit in very well with the *Framework*'s definition of a liability as being recognised 'when it is probable that an outflow of resources embodying economic benefits will result from the settlement of a present obligation and the amount at which the settlement will take place can be measured reliably'. It is questionable whether future losses are a 'present obligation' and whether they can be 'measured reliably', so it is very unlikely that future losses can be included as a liability in the statement of financial position.[30]

4.12 Brands

We have discussed intangible assets and goodwill above but brands deserve a separate consideration because of their major significance in some companies. For example, the following information appears in the 2017 Diageo annual report:

	£m	£m
Total equity (i.e. net assets)		12,028
Intangible assets:		
Brands	8,229	

We can see that brands alone are 68% of total equity. It is interesting to take a look at the global importance of brands within sectors.

4.12.1 The importance of brands to particular sectors

It is interesting to note that certain sectors have high global brand valuations. For example, the Best Global Brands Report 2017[31] showed electronics (Apple $184,154m), Internet services (Google $141,703m), e-services (Amazon $64,796m) and beverages (Coca-Cola $69,733m) and business services (Microsoft $67,670m). Even the hundredth exceeded $4,000 million (Lenovo $4,004m).

This indicates the importance of investors having as much information as possible to assess management's stewardship of brands. If this cannot be reported on the face of the statement of financial position then there is an argument for having an additional statement to assist shareholders, including the information that the directors consider when managing brands.

4.12.2 Justifications for reporting all brands as assets

We now consider some other justifications that have been put forward for the inclusion of brands as a separate asset in the statement of financial position.[32]

Reduce equity depletion

For acquisitive companies it could be attributed to the accounting treatment previously required for measuring and reporting goodwill. The London Business School carried out research into the 'brands phenomenon' and found that 'a major aim of brand valuation has been to repair or pre-empt equity depletion caused by UK goodwill accounting rules'.[33]

Strengthen the statement of financial position

Non-acquisitive companies do not incur costs for acquiring goodwill, so their reserves are not eroded by writing off purchased goodwill. However, these companies may have incurred promotional costs in creating home-grown brands and it would strengthen the statement of financial position if they were permitted to include a valuation of these brands.

Effect on equity shareholders' funds

Immediate goodwill write-off results in a fall in net tangible assets as disclosed by the statement of financial position, even though the market capitalisation of the company increases. One way to maintain the asset base and avoid such a depletion of companies' reserves was to divide the purchased goodwill into two parts: the amount attributable to brands and the remaining amount attributable to pure goodwill.

Effect on borrowing powers

The borrowing powers of public companies may be expressed in terms of multiples of net assets. In Articles of Association there may be strict rules regarding the multiple that a company must not exceed. In addition, borrowing agreements and Stock Exchange listing agreements are generally dependent on net assets.

Effect on ratios

Immediate goodwill write-off distorted the gearing ratios, but the inclusion of brands as intangible assets minimises this distortion by providing a more realistic value for shareholders' funds.

Effect on management decisions

Including brands on the statement of financial position should lead to more informed and improved management decision making. As brands represent one of the most important assets of a company, management should be aware of the success or failure of each individual brand. Knowledge about the performance of brands ensures that management reacts accordingly to maintain or improve competitive advantage.

Effect on management decisions where brands are not capitalised

Whether or not a brand is capitalised, management does take its existence into account when making decisions affecting a company's gearing ratios. For example, in 2007 the Hugo Boss management in explaining its thinking about the advisability of making a Special Dividend payment[34] recognised that one effect was to reduce the book value of equity and increase the gearing ratio, but commented:

> The book value of the equity capital of the HUGO BOSS Group will be reduced by the special dividend. However this perception does not take into consideration that the originally created market value 'HUGO BOSS' is not reflected in the book value of the equity capital. This does not therefore mirror the strong economic position of HUGO BOSS fully.

The implication is that the existence of brand value is recognised by the market and leads to a more sustainable market valuation.

There is also evidence[35] that companies with valuable brand names are not including these in their statements of financial position and are not, therefore, taking account of the assets for insurance purposes.

The above are the justifications for recognising internally generated brands as assets. However, IAS 38 prohibits[36] this by saying: 'Internally generated brands, mastheads, publishing titles, customer lists and items similar in substance shall not be recognised as intangible assets.'

4.13 Accounting for acquired brands

Acquired brands require to be valued. In 2017, the International Valuation Standards Council[37] issued, *The International Valuation Standard 2017* which includes a section on valuation of intangibles for both IFRS and other purposes.

Under IFRS normally the asset has to be classified as having an indefinite life (i.e. no foreseeable limit to the period of future cashflows and thus is not subject to amortization but rather subject to impairment reviews annually and when an impairment event occurs) **or** as having a finite life when amortization is required over its useful life.

An example is the 31December 2017 accounting policy in the Annual Report of WPP:

Corporate brand names . . . acquired as part of acquisitions of businesses are capitalised separately from goodwill as intangible assets if their value can be measured reliably on initial recognition and it is probable that the expected future economic benefits that are attributed to the asset will flow to the Group.

Certain corporate brands of the Group are considered to have an indefinite economic life because of the institutional nature of the corporate brand names, their proven ability to maintain market leadership and profitable operations over long periods of time and the Group's commitment to develop and enhance their value. The carrying value of these intangible assets are reviewed at least annually for impairment and adjusted to the recoverable amount if required.

Amortisation is provided at rates calculated to write off the cost less estimated residual value of each asset on a straight-line basis over its estimated useful life as follows:

Brand names (with finite lives) – 10–20 years; Customer-related intangibles – 3–10 years; Other proprietary tools – 3–10 years; Other (including capitalised computer software) – 3–5 years.[38]

4.13.1 How effective have IFRS 3 and IAS 38 been?

There is still a temptation for companies to treat the excess paid on acquiring a subsidiary as goodwill. If it is treated as goodwill, then there has been no requirement to make an annual amortisation charge. If any part of the excess is attributed to an intangible, then this has to be amortised.

The position in the UK is that the Financial Reporting Review Panel of the Financial Reporting Council will be policing the allocation of any excess on acquisitions to ensure that there is appropriate effort to attribute to intangible asset categories if that is the economic reality.

However, even so, the information is limited in that only acquired brands can be reported on the statement of financial position, which gives an incomplete picture of an entity's value. Even with acquired brands, their value can only remain the same or be revised downward following an impairment review. This means that there is no record of any added value that might have been achieved by the new owners to allow shareholders to assess the current stewardship.

4.14 Intellectual capital disclosures (ICDs) in the annual report

The problem of valuing for financial reporting purposes has meant that investors need to look outside the annual report for information which tends to be predominately narrative. This is highlighted in an ICAEW Research Report[39] which comments:

A wide range of media were used to report ICDs, with the annual report accounting for less than a third of total ICDs across all reporting media . . . examination of ICDs in annual reports was not a good proxy for overall ICD practices in the sample studied . . . disclosures are overwhelmingly narrative. Previous studies have tended to indicate that monetary expression of IC elements in corporate reports is a relatively rare practice (see, for example, Beattie and Thompson, 2010).[40] This current study of UK ICR practices reinforces this observation.

The report also referred to the fact that preparers of reports did not see that the annual report was the appropriate place to be providing stakeholders with new information on intellectual capital – the annual report being seen as having a confirmatory role in relation to information that was already in the public domain.

Recent research has focused on subdividing intellectual capital into subcomponents such as human capital, organisational capital and external capital (brands, customer and supplier relationships),[41] and another paper relates financial contributions to expenditure on the components of intellectual costs (human, structural and relational) to predict probabilities of bankruptcy.[42] The second paper would justify disclosure of the components of intellectual capital expenses in the accounts of companies with high dependence on intellectual property.

4.14.1 The downside of not recognising ICDs in the statement of financial position

There is a common saying 'out of sight – out of mind' which could well be applied to ICDs that are not quantified and reported in the financial statements.

The focus of management's attention may be the physical assets that are reported with a concentration on return on total assets, return on capital employed and return on equity – all of which fail to include the ICDs within the denominator.

The focus of investors' attention may be on assessing the risks attached to achieving maintainable profits. This risk might well be overestimated if there is not an observable asset 'ICD' reported in the financial statements which leads to an increase in the cost of capital.

Investors may be unaware of a failure to achieve the optimum return on ICDs if they are not reported. For example, is the company commercially exploiting its ICDs by, for example, licensing its intellectual property?[43]

Lenders have tended to lend against assets with longer-term debts secured on non-current assets and short-term finance secured by factoring and invoice discounting. There is less confidence and more scepticism in lending against intellectual property. This is seen in SMEs where lenders tend to look for a guarantee supported by a tangible asset in addition to lending on the basis of ICDs. In an increasingly technological world, this is a severe disadvantage to SMEs.

Recognising and reporting ICDs remains an unsolved challenge.

4.14.2 Can internally generated intangibles continue to be unseen?

When a company acquires net assets in another company and pays more than their fair value the difference is treated as goodwill. This is a figure that is evidenced by a payment in the open market, so we know this is an arm's length valuation.

This total figure for goodwill is, for financial report purposes, disaggregated if possible into identifiable intangibles. The IASB view is that if they can be recognised they can be valued as a subset of the total market evidenced figure.

It would seem that companies do not consider that their market value is undervalued by the omission of an 'intellectual property' asset provided they keep investors and analysts up-to-date with developments. A contrary approach could be taken by companies that see an economic value in valuing and reporting in acquisition situations, e.g. payment to acquire customer lists. Also when the chapter on integrated reporting is read you may like to come back to this question and consider whether a separate reporting on intangibles outside the financial accounts but subject to attestation is or is not a viable alternative.

4.15 Review of implementation of IFRS 3

In 2014 the IASB started a post-implementation review seeking comments from stakeholders to identify whether IFRS 3 *Business Combinations* provides information that is useful to users of financial statements, in particular identifying separate intangible assets and badwill; whether there are areas of IFRS 3 that are difficult to implement and may prevent the consistent implementation of the standard; and whether unexpected costs have arisen in connection with applying or enforcing the standard.

Report and Feedback Statement

In June 2015 there was a *Report and Feedback Statement*[44] which reported opposing views as to the separate recognition of intangible assets. Some investors support the current practice of identifying additional intangible assets (for example, brands, customer relationships, etc.) separately from goodwill because it provides an insight on why an entity purchased another entity and provides critical information on the fundamental drivers of value in an acquired business. Other investors do not agree because they think it is highly subjective and their view is that these intangible assets should only be recognised if there is a market for them.

The report raised, but did not resolve, the issue of whether some intangibles such as customer lists should not be separately recognised or should have greater guidance relating to measurement.

4.16 Review of the implementation of identified intangibles under IAS 38

We saw in Section 4.9.2 the following in the Intel 2016 Annual Report relating to identified intangible assets subject to amortisation:

Acquisition–related customer relationships   1,449   (260)   1,189

This item appears in the balance sheet of Intel but not in the balance sheet of the company from which the customer relationships had been purchased. On acquisition intangibles are valued at fair value using one of three IFRS 13 approaches. These are:

- the **market** approach using observable market prices or market transactions – this might be difficult to apply to many of the intangible assets such as brands which are company-specific; or
- the **income** approach which is based on relief from cost (say of a trademark) or the present value of excess earnings over an agreed number of years or the present value of incremental cash flows – this is the most appropriate approach for the majority of intangible assets; or
- the **cost** approach which attaches a value which is no higher than replacement cost.

Treatment of unrealised profits/gains

It is clear that the relationships are capable of being valued and the principal reason for omitting them from the balance sheet is the fact that they have been unrealised.

This is now at odds with the treatment of other assets which have been revalued and the difference between their carrying value and fair value being included in Other comprehensive income and carried through into Total equity.

Is it time that the balance sheet reported *Other comprehensive equity* and *Other comprehensive asset* entries with each class of asset disclosed at carrying value and fair value?

Taking human capital as an example, this value would have been built up over time and the expenditure charged against profits – not as an identified charge but subsumed within the cost of recruitment and training.

It would be useful for users to have the asset and equity identified and revalued each year. If human capital improved the asset would increase – if it deteriorated then the asset would be reduced.

4.16.1 How might human resources be valued each year?

One approach might be that taken by Infosys Technologies (www.infosys.com) which became the first software company to value its human resources in India. The company stated in its 2011 Annual Report:

A fundamental dichotomy in accounting practices is between human and non-human capital. As a standard practice, non-human capital is considered as assets and reported in the financial statements, whereas human capital is mostly ignored by accountants. The definition of wealth as a source of income inevitably leads to the recognition of human capital as one of the several forms of wealth such as money, securities and physical capital.

We have used the Lev & Schwartz model to compute the value of human resources. The evaluation is based on the present value of future earnings of employees and on the following assumptions:

(a) Employee compensation includes all direct and indirect benefits earned both in India and overseas

(b) The incremental earnings based on group/age have been considered

(c) The future earnings have been discounted at the cost of capital of 11.21% (previous year 10.60%).

It produced the following analysis:

	2011	2010
Total income[1]	27,501	22,742
Total employee cost[1]	14,856	12,093
Value-added	25,031	20,935
Net profit[1]	6,823	6,219
Ratios		
Value of human resources per employee	1.03	1.00
Total income / human resources value (ratio)	0.20	0.20
Employee cost / human resources value (%)	11.0	10.7
Value-added / human resources value (ratio)	0.19	0.18
Return on human resources value (%)	5.1	5.5

[1]*As per IFRS (audited) financial statements*

Research has shown a link between human resource information disclosure and share prices.[45]

Summary

Intangible assets have grown in importance with the rise of the new economy. This has been principally driven by information and knowledge. It has been identified by the Organisation for Economic Co-operation and Development (OECD) as explaining the increased prominence of intellectual capital as a business and research topic.[46] A review of the of the major companies today shows that the majority have achieved their position by utilising new technical knowledge, or envisioning new ways of providing goods and services, or applying new marketing methods, or a combination of these. Business has been very dynamic and their future is dependent on continual renewal of knowledge and processes and evolving visions of the future. This has made reporting on the current status of these intangible attributes very difficult for at least three reasons, namely a reluctance of companies to disclose information which is of strategic importance, value uncertainty because it depends on what competitors achieve, and these assets are often internally generated rather than purchased so their value is difficult to assess. The problem is that the current partial information provides insufficient guidance to investors. Intangible assets have at the same time have become the most significant determinants of value of companies in many industries. Are accounting standards which preclude the recognition of some important internally generated intangible assets (e.g. human capital and customer relations) decreasing the usefulness of accounting reports? Do we need additional disclosure of both quantitative and qualitative information to keep investors fully informed? Would fuller disclosure generate greater trust in business in this period of greater scepticism.[47]

REVIEW QUESTIONS

1 Why do standard setters consider it necessary to distinguish between research and development expenditure, and how does this distinction affect the accounting treatment?

2 Discuss the suggestion that the requirement for companies to write off research investment rather than showing it as an asset encourages short term perspectives from management who feel under pressure to be seen to perform. Are such actions contrary to the interests of the company, the majority of shareholders and employees?

3 Discuss why the market value of a business may increase to reflect the analysts' assessment of future growth but the asset(s) responsible for the growth may not appear in the statement of financial position.

4 Discuss the advantages and disadvantages of the proposal that there should be a separate category of asset in the statement of financial position clearly identified as 'research investment – outcome uncertain'.

5 IFRS 3 has introduced a new concept into accounting for purchased goodwill – annual impairment testing, rather than amortisation. Consider the effect of a change from amortisation of goodwill (in IAS 22) to impairment testing and no amortisation in IFRS 3, and in particular:
   ● the effect on the financial statements;
   ● the effect on financial performance ratios;
   ● the effect on the annual impairment or amortisation charge and its timing;
   ● which method gives the fairest charge over time for the value of the goodwill when a business is acquired;

- whether impairment testing with no amortisation complies with the IASB's Conceptual Framework for Financial Reporting issued in March 2018;

- why there has been a change from amortisation to impairment testing – is this pandering to pressure from the US FASB and/or listed companies? (How would we evaluate these possibilities?)

6 Discuss reasons for the undervaluing of intangibles and subsuming them within goodwill.

7 One goodwill impairment indicator is the loss of key personnel. Discuss two further possible indicators.

8 There has been a requirement for companies to disaggregate the amount paid for goodwill into other intangible assets. This has led to the valuation of certain of the relational intellectual capital items such as customer lists. Research[48] indicates that there is a variety of structural, human and relational capital components which are considered by a representative cross-section of preparers to be significantly more important than others and these key components should be a focus for future research. The researchers raise the need to investigate whether a set of industry-specific standardised metrics can be developed and their disclosure regulated and recommend that IASB include the intangibles project on its active agenda.

Discuss the argument that potentially the future of the accounting profession and its role as the key reporting function could depend on addressing this issue effectively.

9 Critically evaluate the basis of the following assertion: 'I am sceptical that the impairment test will work reliably in practice, given the complexity and subjectivity that lie within the calculations.'[49]

10 Access the annual report of a company (such as BlackBerry Group) in which there is a large amount of goodwill and discuss the effect on earnings if goodwill is required to be amortised over a period of between 5 and 10 years. Discuss how this would affect headline profit.

11 Prior to IFRS 3 some countries permitted goodwill to be written off to equity. Discuss the reason why this was a permitted option and consider whether it is preferable to the estimated amortisation approach.

12 Discuss, after considering the approach taken by Infosys in valuing, whether investors would benefit from having human capital included as an asset in the statement of financial position.

13 Identify a listed Block Technology company and identify the recording of goodwill and intangible assets and their book values. Then ascertain the market value and the amount of goodwill and intangibles implied by that figures. What implications can you draw from the comparison of book and market values?

14 Identify a listed company which has failed and identify the difference between book values of goodwill and intangibles, and either the actual or anticipated recovery in relation to those items.

EXERCISES

* **Question 1**

IAS 38 *Intangible Assets* was issued primarily in order to identify the criteria that need to be present before expenditure on intangible items can be recognised as an asset. The standard also prescribes the subsequent accounting treatment of intangible assets that satisfy the recognition criteria and are recognised in the statement of financial position.

Required:
(a) Explain the criteria that need to be satisfied before expenditure on intangible items can be recognised in the statement of financial position as intangible assets.
(b) Explain how the criteria outlined in (a) are applied to the recognition of separately purchased intangible assets, intangible assets acquired in a business combination, and internally generated intangible assets. You should give an example of each category discussed.
(c) Explain the subsequent accounting treatment of intangible assets that satisfy the recognition criteria of IAS 38.

Iota prepares financial statements to 30 September each year. During the year ended 30 September 20X6 Iota (which has a number of subsidiaries) engaged in the following transactions:

1   On 1 April 20X6 Iota purchased all the equity capital of Kappa, and Kappa became a subsidiary from that date. Kappa sells a branded product that has a well-known name and the directors of Iota have obtained evidence that the fair value of this name is $20 million and that it has a useful economic life that is expected to be indefinite. The value of the brand name is not included in the statement of financial position of Kappa, as the directors of Kappa do not consider that it satisfies the recognition criteria of IAS 38 for internally developed intangible assets. However, the directors of Kappa have taken legal steps to ensure that no other entities can use the brand name.

2   On 1 October 20X4 Iota began a project that sought to develop a more efficient method of organising its production. Costs of $10 million were incurred in the year to 30 September 20X5 and debited to the statement of comprehensive income in that year. In the current year the results of the project were extremely encouraging and on 1 April 20X6 the directors of Iota were able to demonstrate that the project would generate substantial economic benefits for the group from 31 March 20X7 onwards as its technical feasibility and commercial viability were clearly evident. Throughout the year to 30 September 20X6 Iota spent $500,000 per month on the project.

Required:
(d) Explain how both of the above transactions should be recognised in the financial statements of Iota for the year ending 30 September 20X6. You should quantify the amounts recognised and make reference to relevant provisions of IAS 38 wherever possible.

* Question 2

Environmental Engineering plc is engaged in the development of an environmentally friendly personal transport vehicle. This will run on an electric motor powered by solar cells, supplemented by passenger effort in the form of pedal assistance.

At the end of the current accounting period, the following costs have been attributed to the project:

(a) A grant of £500,000 to the Polytechnic of the South Coast Faculty of Solar Engineering to encourage research.
(b) Costs of £1,200,000 expended on the development of the necessary solar cells prior to the decision to incorporate them in a vehicle.
(c) Costs of £5,000,000 expended on designing the vehicle and its motors, and the planned promotional and advertising campaign for its launch on the market in 12 months' time.

Required:
(i) Explain, with reasons, which of the above items could be considered for treatment as deferred development expenditure, quoting any relevant International Accounting Standard.
(ii) Set out the criteria under which any items can be so treated.
(iii) Advise on the accounting treatment that will be afforded to any such items after the product has been launched.

* Question 3

As chief accountant at Italin NV, you have been given the following information by the director of research:

Project Luca

	£000
Costs to date (pure research 25%, applied research 75%)	200
Costs to develop product (to be incurred in the year to 30 September 20X1)	300
Expected future sales per annum for 20X2–20X7	1,000
Fixed assets purchased in 20X1 for the project:	
Cost	2,500
Estimated useful life	7 years
Residual value	400
(These assets will be disposed of at their residual value at the end of their estimated useful lives.)	

The board of directors considers that this project is similar to the other projects that the company undertakes, and is confident of a successful outcome. The company has enough finances to complete the development and enough capacity to produce the new product.

Required:

(a) **Prepare a report for the board outlining the principles involved in accounting for research and development and showing what accounting entries will be made in the company's accounts for each of the years ending 30 September 20X1–20X7 inclusive.**

(b) **Indicate what factors need to be taken into account when assessing each research and development project for accounting purposes, and what disclosure is needed for research and development in the company's published accounts.**

* Question 4

Oxlag plc, a manufacturer of pharmaceutical products, has the following research and development projects on hand at 31 January 20X2:

(A) A general survey into the long-term effects of its sleeping pill Chalcedon upon human resistance to infections. At the year-end the research is still at a basic stage and no worthwhile results with any particular applications have been obtained.

(B) A development for Meebach NV in which the company will produce market research data relating to Meebach's range of drugs. Meebach is an unrelated company and that company has not yet been charged for the work done and the consulting is expected to be ongoing.

(C) An enhancement of an existing drug, Euboia, which will enable additional uses to be made of the drug and which will consequently boost sales. This project was completed successfully on 30 April 20X2, with the expectation that all future sales of the enhanced drug would greatly exceed the costs of the new development.

(D) A scientific enquiry with the aim of identifying new strains of antibiotics for future use. Several possible substances have been identified, but research is not sufficiently advanced to permit patents and copyrights to be obtained at the present time.

The following costs have been brought forward at 1 February 20X1:

Project	A £000	B £000	C £000	D £000
Specialised laboratory				
Cost	—	—	500	—
Depreciation	—	—	25	—
Specialised equipment				
Cost	—	—	75	50
Depreciation	—	—	15	10
Capitalised development costs	—	—	200	—
Market research costs	—	250	—	—

The following costs were incurred during the year:

Project	A £000	B £000	C £000	D £000
Research costs	25	—	265	78
Market research costs	—	75	—	—
Specialised equipment cost	50	—	—	50

Depreciation on specialised laboratories and special equipment is provided by the straight-line method and the assets have an estimated useful life of 25 and five years respectively. A full year's depreciation is provided on assets purchased during the year.

Required:
(a) Write up the research and development, fixed asset and market research accounts to reflect the above transactions in the year ended 31 January 20X2.
(b) Calculate the amount to be charged as research costs in the statement of comprehensive income of Oxlag plc for the year ended 31 January 20X2.
(c) State on what basis the company should amortise any capitalised development costs and what disclosures the company should make in respect of amounts written off in the year to 31 January 20X3.
(d) Calculate the amounts to be disclosed in the statement of financial position in respect of fixed assets, deferred development costs and work in progress as at 31 January, 20X2.
(e) State what disclosures you would make in the accounts for the year ended 31 January 20X2 in respect of the new improved drug developed under project C, assuming sales begin on 1 May 20X2, and show strong growth to the date of signing the accounts, 14 July 20X2, with the expectation that the new drug will provide 25% of the company's pre-tax profits in the year to 31 January 20X3.

* Question 5

Ross Neale is the divisional accountant for the Research and Development division of Critical Pharmaceuticals PLC. He is discussing the third-quarter results with Tina Snedden who is the manager of the division. The conversation focuses on the fact that while they have already fully committed the development capital expenditure budget for the year, the annual expense budget for research is well underspent because of the staff shortages which occurred in the last quarter. Tina mentions that she is under pressure to meet or exceed her expense budgets this year as the industry is renegotiating prescription costs this year and doesn't want to be seen to be too profitable.

Ross suggests that there are several strategies they could employ, namely:

(a) Several of the subcontractors have us as their largest customer and so we could ask them to describe the services in the fourth quarter, which are essentially development cost, as research costs.

(b) We could ask them to charge us in advance for research work that will be required in the first quarter of next year without mentioning that it is an advance in documentation. That would be good for them as it would improve their cash flow and it would guarantee that they would get the work next year.

(c) We could ask some of the subcontractors on development projects to charge us in the first quarter of next year and we could hold out to them that we would give them some better-priced projects next year to compensate them for the interest incurred as a result of the delayed payment.

Required:
Discuss the advantages and disadvantages of adopting these strategies.

* Question 6

The brands debate

Under IAS 22, which was superseded by IFRS 3 in March 2004, the depletion of equity reserves caused by the accounting treatment for purchased goodwill resulted in some companies capitalising brands on their statements of financial position. This practice was started by Rank Hovis McDougall (RHM) – a company which has since been taken over. Martin Moorhouse, the group chief accountant at RHM, claimed that putting brands on the statement of financial position forced a company to look to their value as well as to profits. It served as a reminder to management of the value of the assets for which they were responsible and that at the end of the day those companies which were prepared to recognise brands on the statement of financial position could be better and stronger for it.[50]

There were many opponents to the capitalisation of brands. A London Business School research study found that brand accounting involves too many risks and uncertainties and too much subjective judgement. In short, the conclusion was that 'the present flexible position, far from being neutral, is potentially corrosive to the whole basis of financial reporting and that to allow brands – whether acquired or homegrown – to continue to be included in the statement of financial position would be highly unwise'.[51]

Required:
Consider the arguments for and against brand accounting. In particular, consider the issues of brand valuation; the separability of brands; purchased versus home-grown brands; and the maintenance/substitution argument.

* Question 7

Brands plc is preparing its accounts for the year ended 31 October 20X8 and the following information is available relating to various intangible assets acquired on the acquisition of Countrywide plc:

(a) A milk quota of 2,000,000 litres at 30p per litre. There is an active market trading in milk and other quotas.

(b) A government licence to experiment with the use of hormones to increase the cream content of milk had been granted to Countrywide shortly before the acquisition by Brands plc. No fee had been required. This is the first licence to be granted by the government and was one of the reasons why Brands acquired Countrywide. The licence is not transferable but the directors estimate that it has a value to the company based on discounted cash flows for a five-year period of £1 million.

(c) A full-cream yoghurt sold under the brand name 'Naughty but Nice' was valued by the directors at £2 million. Further enquiry established that a similar brand name had been recently sold for £1.5 million.

Required:
Explain how each of the above items would be treated in the consolidated financial statements using IAS 38.

* Question 8

James Bright has just taken up the position of managing director following the unsatisfactory achievements of the previous incumbent. James arrives as the accounts for the previous year are being finalised. James wants the previous performance to look poor so that whatever he achieves will look good in comparison. He knows that if he can write off more expenses in the previous year, he will have lower expenses in his first year and possibly a lower asset base. He gives directions to the accountants to write off as many bad debts as possible and to make sure accruals can be as high as they can get past the auditors. Further, he wants all brand name assets reviewed using assumptions that the sales levels achieved during the economic downturn are only going to improve slightly over the foreseeable future. Also he mentions that the cost of capital has risen over the period of the financial crisis so the projected benefits are to be discounted at a higher rate, preferably at a much higher rate than that used in the previous reviews!

Required:
Discuss the accountant's professional responsibility and any ethical questions arising in this case.

* Question 9

Rustled has just completed its financial year and has produced the following balances from its books at 31 October 20x6.

	£
Draft profit for the year	4,584
Cash at bank and in hand	348
Bank loans repayable within 1 year	204
Allowance for receivables, as at 1 November 2016	48
Corporation tax (credit balance)	132
Debentures, repayable in October 20x9	600
Debentures, repayable in October 20x7	360
Land at valuation	960
Deferred tax	288
Development expenditure	564
Dividends paid	288
Goodwill, at cost	576
Inventory, as at 31 October 20x6	624
Buildings, at valuation	2,640
Equipment, at cost	1,692
Accumulated depreciation, as at 1 November 20x5	
Buildings	480
Equipment	936
Revaluation reserve	288
Proceeds from sale of non-current assets	528
Investment properties	1,596
Ordinary shares of 25 pence	1,200
Retained earnings, as at 1 November 20x5	288
Share premium	768
Other receivables	336
Trade and Other Payables	816
Trade and Other Receivables	1,896

Additional information is available as follows:

1   An impairment review of receivables was carried out as at 31 October 20x5 and it was judged that invoices totalling €384,000 are to be written off. It was decided that no allowance for doubtful debts is required to be made on trade receivables as at 31 October 20x6.

2   There has been an over provision for corporation tax when providing for corporation tax for the year ended 31 October 20x5. Corporation tax payable for the year ended 31 October 20x6 has been estimated at €720,000.

3   Taxable temporary differences have arisen during the current year. The effect is that the deferred tax account is to be adjusted for corporation tax of €162,000.

    There were no reversing temporary differences during the year.

4   Development expenditure as at 31 October 20x6 comprises:

    ● €144,000 has been spent during the year on training of staff for a proposed automated warehouse in anticipation of increased need following Brexit negotiations. The company set up a team to keep the situation under review and their advice in October 20x6 was not to proceed any further with the project.

    ● €420,000 was spent during the year to improve the automated processes at their current warehouses. This would make product selection and packaging more efficient and reduce the labour costs. The finance director has reported that the budgeted further development costs of €128,400 are expected to be sufficient, the new processes will be in operation by February 20x7 and the company will recover all its development costs.

5   Rustled paid a final dividend of 3c during the year ended 31 October 20x6 for the year ended 31 October 20x5. It has paid an interim dividend of 3c per share for the year ended 31 October 20x6. The company has achieved a growth in its sales and profit and the directors will be proposing a final dividend of 4c pence per share at its annual general meeting in January 20x7. The shareholders are expected to approve the proposal.

6   Consultants have carried out a strategic review of the company following the takeover of another business on 1 November 20x5 to determine how well the business has been integrated into the group as a whole. They reported that it did not appear that the expected profits arising from synergy would be achieved and the fair value of goodwill was €420,000.

7   Non-current assets have been sold during the year. The proceeds from the sale totalled €528,000 have now ben banked but no entries have yet been made in the non-current asset accounts.

    The carrying values of the assets sold during the year were:

Land	€120,000
Buildings	€348,000 (€432,000 revaluation and €84,000 accumulated depreciation)
Equipment	€168,000 (€348,000 cost and €180,000 accumulated depreciation)

    Rustled uses the revaluation model for land and buildings and the revaluation reserve includes €108,000 of revaluation surpluses relating to the land and buildings sold during the year.

    Rustled's depreciation policies are:

Land	no depreciation
Buildings	5% straight line, full year basis
Equipment	30% reducing balance, full year basis

Depreciation for the year ended 31 October 20x6 is still to be charged on all assets in use at the end of the financial year.

8 Investment properties are valued at fair value. As at 31 October 20x6 the market value of the investment properties was estimated at €1,680,000.

9 A bonus issue of 1 for 4 shares was made on 31 October 20x6 with transfer out of the share premium account and this has yet to be recorded in the accounts. The bonus shares will qualify for all dividends paid after 31 October 20x6.

10 Other receivables includes the sales tax that is recoverable.

11 Following the strategic review the directors have decided that the two head offices should be merged. As Rustled owns the freehold of its head office and the head office of the company acquired during the year is currently being leased it was decided to terminate the lease which was due to expire on 31 July 20x7.

Under the lease agreement the company was committed as at 31 October 20x6 to make further payments totalling €129,600. Rustled engaged agents to seek to sublet for the balance of the lease and managed to obtain a tenant who would pay €26,400. The lease is an operating lease.

Requirement

(a) **Prepare Rustled's Statement of Financial Position as at 31 October 20x6.**

(b) **Prepare a calculation of retained earnings as at 31 October 20x6 starting with the draft profit before tax of €4,584,000 for the year ended 31 October 20x6.**

Notes

1 Wall Street Journal, *Accounting's 21st Century Challenge: How to Value Intangible Assets*, accessed 22 March 2016.
2 J. Shapiro, 'GMO on mission to revalue listed firms', *The Australian Financial Review*, 26 March, 2018, pp. 15,23.
3 IAS 38 *Intangible Assets*, IASB, revised January, 2012.
4 IFRS 3 *Business Combinations*, IASB, revised January, 2012
5 Conceptual Framework for Financial Reporting, IFRS Conceptual Framework Project Summary, March 2018.
6 IAS 38, para. 119.
7 This statement is in the section titled Basic Principles, Methods and Critical Accounting Estimates.
8 Clarification of Acceptable Methods of Depreciation and Amortisation (Amendments to IAS 16 and IAS 38), IASB, 2014.
9 IAS 38, Intangible Assets, IASB, revised 2012, para. 118.
10 Ibid., para. 126.
11 Ibid., para. 122.
12 Para. 54.
13 Ibid., para. 56.
14 Ibid., para. 55.
15 Ibid., para. 58.
16 Ibid., para. 59.
17 Office of National Statistics, Experimental estimates of investment in intangible assets in the UK: 2015, released 7 February 2018.
18 http://www.rdmag.com/Featured-Articles/2011/12/2012-Global-RD-Funding-Forecast-RD-Spending-Growth-Continues-While-Globalization-Accelerates/

19 IASC, *Framework for the Preparation and Presentation of Financial Statements*, IASB, April 2001, para. 49. While there is a new conceptual framework, the standard is based on the framework when it was developed.

20 A. Goodacre and J. McGrath, 'An experimental study of analysts' reactions to corporate R&D expenditure', *British Accounting Review*, vol. 29, 1997, pp. 155–179.

21 B. Nixon, 'The accounting treatment of research and development expenditure: views of UK company accountants', *European Accounting Review*, vol. 6(2), 1997, pp. 265–277.

22 Li Li Eng and Hong Kiat Teo, 'The relation between annual report disclosures, analysts' earnings forecast and analysts following: evidence from Singapore', *Pacific Accounting Review*, vol. 11(1/2), 1999, pp. 219–239. Interestingly in 2018 FEI comment on analyst response to the report that many US companies were behind in preparing for the introduction of the new leasing standard responded that based on the relevant disclosures they would make their own calculations of lease liabilities. It appears that where management has discretion in arriving at figures then some analysts tend to prefer disclosure to allow them to make their own estimates. (C. Westfall, Lease Accounting Faces Analyst Ambivalence, *FEI Daily*, 20 May 2018.)

23 An example is P.K. Ozili, 'Banks earnings management and income smoothing using commission and fee income: A European context', *International Journal of Managerial Finance*, vol. 14(4), 2017, pp. 419–439.

24 Clarification of Acceptable Methods of Depreciation and Amortisation (Amendments to IAS 16 and IAS 38) IASB, 2014.

25 IFRS 3 Business Combinations, IASB, 2004, para. 51.

26 Where less than 100% of shares are owned when it becomes a subsidiary then the consideration given is compared to the holding company's share of the fair value of net assets.

27 A more sophisticated version of this was successfully tested by S.L. Henning, B.L. Lewis and W. H. Shaw, 'Valuation of the components of purchased goodwill', *Journal of Accounting Research*, vol. 38(2), Autumn 2000, pp. 375–386.

28 An example of this, whilst not relating to goodwill, is the action being taken against a past CEO and a past CFO of Rio Tinto who are facing court action because they were slow in recognising a loss on a mine they had acquired (reported in May 2018).

29 IASC, *Framework for the Preparation and Presentation of Financial Statements*, IASB, April 2001, para. 94.

30 The new conceptual framework expands the definition of liability and recognises additional items where there is 'no practical ability to avoid' an obligation. However, it is unlikely that anticipation of future losses or redundancies would fall within the scope of the new element.

31 www.interbrand.com/best-brands/best-global-brands/2017/ranking/

32 A discussion of the issue of not recognising internally generated intangibles and only considering impairment and not increments is discussed in R.N. Sinclair and K.L. Keller, 'A case for brands as assets: Acquired and internally developed', *Journal of Brand Management*, vol. 21(4), 2014, pp. 286–302.

33 P. Barwise, C. Higson, A. Likierman and P. Marsh, *Accounting for Brands*, ICAEW, June 1989; M. Cooper and A. Carey, 'Brand valuation in the balance', *Accountancy*, June 1989.

34 http://group.hugoboss.com/en/faq_special_dividend.htm

35 M. Gerry, 'Companies ignore value of brands', *Accountancy Age*, March 2000, p. 4.

36 IAS 38, para. 63.

37 www.ivsc.org

38 WPP 2017 Annual Report, p. 114.

39 J. Unerman, J. Guthrie and M. Striukova, *UK Reporting of Intellectual Capital*, ICAEW, 2007, www.icaew.co.uk

40 V. Beattie and S.J. Thompson, *Intellectual Capital: Academic Utopia or Corporate Reality in a Brave New World?*, 2010, www.icas.org.uk

41 Terminology differs across studies. One example is T. De Silva, M.Stafford and C. Murray, 'Intellectual Capital Reporting. A longitudinal study of New Zealand companies, *Journal of Intellectual Capital*, vol. 15(1), 2014, pp. 157–172.

42 V.G. Cenciarelli and G. Greco, 'Does intellectual capital help predict bankruptcy?, *Journal of Intellectual Capital* , vol. 19(2), 2018, pp. 321–337.

43 http://www.ipo.gov.uk/ipresearch-bankingip.pdf

44 http://www.ifrs.org/Current-Projects/IASB-Projects/PIR/PIR-IFRS-3/Documents/PIR_
    IFRS%203-Business-Combinations_FBS_WEBSITE.pdf

45 R. Gamerschlag, 'Value relevance of human capital information', *Journal of Intellectual Capital*, vol.
    14(2), 2013, pp. 325–345 but a different result was found in Japan and it was suggested cultural
    differences or uniformly good human resource management could explain the different results
    (Katsuhiro Motokawa, 'Human capital disclosure, accounting numbers, and share price', *Journal
    of Financial Reporting and Accounting*, vol. 13(2), 2015, pp. 159–178.

46 OECD, *Final Report: Measuring and Reporting Intellectual Capital: Experience, Issues and Prospects*,
    OECD 2000.

47 In the future the standard for intangibles may or may not be revised in light of the new conceptual
    framework with new definitions for assets, and relevance and faithful representation (covering meas-
    urement uncertainty and recognition inconsistency).

48 V. Beattie and S.J. Thomson, *Intellectual Capital Reporting: Academic Utopia or Corporate Reality
    in a Brave New World?*, ICAS, 2010, http://www.icas.org.uk/site/cms/contentviewarticle.
    asp?article=6837

49 Ibid.

50 M. Moorhouse, 'Brands debate: wake up to the real world', *Accountancy*, July 1990, p. 30.

51 P. Barwise, C. Higson, A. Likierman and P. Marsh, *Accounting for Brands*, ICAEW, June 1989; M.
    Cooper and A. Carey, 'Brand valuation in the balance', *Accountancy*, June 1989.

CHAPTER 5

Liabilities

5.1 Introduction

In order for financial statements to show a true and fair view, it is essential that reporting entities recognise all the liabilities that satisfy the *Framework* criteria, but **only** those liabilities that satisfy the criteria. Given that the recognition of a liability often involves a charge against profits, and the derecognition of a liability sometimes involves a credit to profits, there is the possibility that, unless this area of financial reporting is appropriately regulated, there is scope for manipulation of reporting profits when liabilities are recognised or derecognised inappropriately.

There are a number of financial reporting standards dealing with the recognition and measurement of specific liabilities that are dealt with elsewhere in this book:

- Financial liabilities (including, *inter alia,* trade payables and loans) are dealt with in IAS 39 *Financial Instruments: Recognition and Measurement* and, in the future, in IFRS 9 *Financial Instruments.*
- Pension liabilities are dealt with in IAS 19 *Employee Benefits.*
- Income tax liabilities are dealt with in IAS 12 *Income Taxes.*
- Lease liabilities are dealt with in IFRS 16 *Leases* (see Chapter 6).

The above financial reporting standards deal with many types of liability but not with all liabilities. Examples of liabilities, or potential liabilities, not dealt with by the above financial reporting standards include:

- liabilities arising from legal disputes;
- liabilities arising due to corporate restructurings;
- environmental and decommissioning obligations;
- liabilities arising under contracts that have become onerous.

IAS 37 *Provisions, Contingent Liabilities and Contingent Assets* deals with the recognition, measurement and disclosure of these liabilities or potential liabilities.

Objectives

By the end of this chapter, you should be able to:

- account for provisions, contingent liabilities and contingent assets under IAS 37;
- explain the potential change the IASB is considering in relation to provisions.

5.2 Provisions – a decision tree approach to their impact on the statement of financial position

The IASC (now the IASB) approved IAS 37 *Provisions, Contingent Liabilities and Contingent Assets*[1] in July 1998. The key objective of IAS 37 is to ensure that appropriate recognition criteria and measurement bases are applied and that sufficient information is disclosed in the notes to enable users to understand their nature, timing and amount.

The IAS sets out a useful decision tree, shown in Figure 5.1, for determining whether an event requires the creation of a provision, the disclosure of a contingent liability or no action.

Figure 5.1 Decision tree

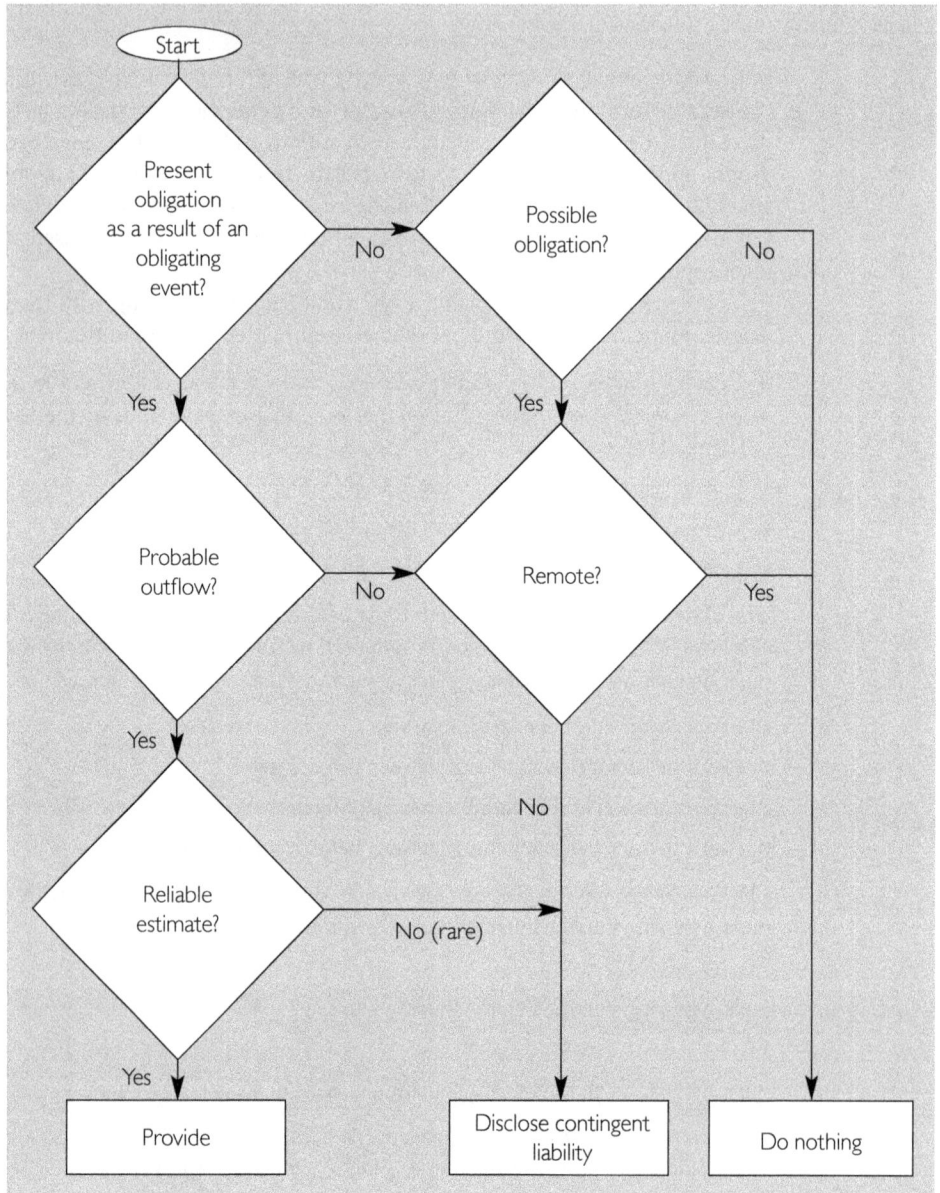

In June 2005 the IASB issued an exposure draft, IAS 37 *Non-financial Liabilities,* to revise IAS 37. A further exposure draft clarifying the proposed amendments was issued in January 2010. However, the current IASB timetable does not envisage a new accounting standard on liabilities very soon. We will now consider the current IAS 37 treatment of provisions, contingent liabilities and contingent assets.

5.3 Treatment of provisions

IAS 37 is mainly concerned with provisions and the distorting effect they can have on profit trends, income and capital gearing. It defines a provision as 'a liability of uncertain timing or amount'.

In particular it targets 'big-bath' provisions that companies historically have been able to make. This is a type of creative accounting that it has been tempting for directors to make in order to smooth profits without any reasonable certainty that the provision would actually be required in subsequent periods. Sir David Tweedie, the former chairman of the IASB, has said:

> A main focus [of IAS 37] is 'big-bath' provisions. Those who use them sometimes pray in aid of the concept of prudence. All too often however the provision is wildly excessive and conveniently finds its way back to the statement of comprehensive income in a later period. The misleading practice needed to be stopped and [IAS 37] proposed that in future provisions should only be allowed when the company has an unavoidable obligation – an **intention** which may or may not be fulfilled will **not be enough.** Users of accounts can't be expected to be mind readers.

5.4 The general principles that IAS 37 applies to the recognition of a provision

The general principles are that a provision should be recognised when:[2]

(a) an entity has a present obligation (legal or constructive) as a result of past events;

(b) it is probable that a transfer of economic benefits will be required to settle the obligation;

(c) a reliable estimate can be made of the amount of the obligation.

Provisions by their nature relate to the future. This means that there is a need for estimation, and IAS 37 comments[3] that the use of estimates is an essential part of the preparation of financial statements and does not undermine their reliability. The IAS addresses the uncertainties arising in respect of present obligation, past event, probable transfer of economic benefits and reliable estimates when deciding whether to recognise a provision.

Present obligation

Provisions can arise under law or because the entity has created an expectation due to its past actions that it cannot realistically avoid.

The test to be applied is whether it is more likely than not, i.e. has more than a 50% chance of occurring. For example, if involved in a disputed lawsuit, the company is required to take account of all available evidence including that of experts and of events after the reporting period to decide if there is a greater than 50% chance that the lawsuit will be decided against the company.

Where it is more likely that no present obligation exists at the period-end date, the company discloses a contingent liability, unless the possibility of a transfer of economic resources is remote.

Past event[4]

A past event that leads to a present obligation is called an 'obligating event'. This is a new term with which to become familiar. It means that the company has no realistic alternative to settling the obligation. The IAS defines 'no alternative' as being only where the settlement of the obligation can be enforced by law or, in the case of a constructive obligation, where the event creates valid expectations in other parties that the company will discharge the obligation.

The IAS stresses that it is only those obligations arising from past events existing independently of a company's future actions that are recognised as provisions, e.g. clean-up costs for unlawful environmental damage that has occurred require a provision; environmental damage that is not unlawful but is likely to become so and involve clean-up costs will not be provided for until legislation is virtually certain to be enacted as drafted.

Probable transfer of economic benefits[5]

The IAS defines probable as meaning that the event is more likely than not to occur. Where it is not probable, the company discloses a contingent liability unless the possibility is remote.

5.5 Management approach to measuring the amount of a provision

IAS 37 states[6] that the amount recognised as a provision should be the *best estimate* of the expenditure required to settle the present obligation at the period-end date.

'Best estimate' is defined as the amount that a company would rationally pay to settle the obligation or to transfer it to a third party. The estimates of outcome and financial effect are determined by the judgement of management supplemented by experience of similar transactions and reports from independent experts. Management deal with the uncertainties as to the amount to be provided in a number of ways:

- A class obligation exists:
  - where the provision involves a large population of items as with a warranty provision – statistical analysis of expected values should be used to determine the amount of the provision.
- A single obligation exists but a number of outcomes may be possible:
  - where a single obligation is measured, the individual most likely outcome may be the best estimate;
  - more than one outcome exists or the outcome is anywhere within a range; or
  - expected values may be most appropriate.

For example, a company had been using unlicensed parts in the manufacture of its products and, at the year-end, no decision had been reached by the court. The plaintiff was seeking damages of $10 million.

In the draft accounts a provision had been made of $5.85 million using expected values. This had been based on the estimate by the entity's lawyers that there was a 20% chance that the plaintiff would be unsuccessful and a 25% chance that the entity would be required to pay $10 million and a 55% chance of $7 million becoming payable to the plaintiff. The provision had been calculated as 25% of $0 + 55% of $7 million + 20% of $10 million.

The finance director, however, disagreed with this on the grounds that it was a single obligation and more likely than not there would be an outflow of funds of $7 million, and required an additional $1.15 million to be provided.

Avoiding excessive provisions

Management must avoid creating excessive provisions based on a prudent view. Uncertainty does not justify the creation of excessive provisions.[7] If the projected costs of a particular adverse outcome are estimated on a prudent basis, that outcome should not then be deliberately treated as more probable than is realistically the case.

The measurement requirements of the current IAS 37 are somewhat imprecise and can be interpreted in more than one way. Therefore there is consideration being given to ways of removing the imprecision in the current standard. We will discuss this matter further in Section 5.10.

Approach when time value of money is material

The IAS states[8] that 'where the effect of the time value of money is material, the amount of a provision should be the present value of the expenditures expected to be required to settle the obligation'.

Present value is arrived at by discounting the future obligation at 'a pre-tax rate (or rates) that reflect(s) current market assessments of the time value of money and the risks specific to the liability. The discount rate(s) should not reflect risks for which future cash flow estimates have been adjusted.'

If provisions are recognised at present value, a company will have to account for the unwinding of the discounting. As a simple example, assume a company is making a provision at 31 December 2017 for an expected cash outflow of €1 million on 31 December 2019. The relevant discount factor is estimated at 10%. Assume the estimated cash flows do not change and the provision is still required at 31 December 2018.

	€000
Provision recognised at 31 December 2017 (€1m × 1/1.121)	826
Provision recognised at 31 December 2018 (€1m × 1/1.1)	909
Increase in the provision	83

This increase in the provision is purely due to discounting for one year in 2018 as opposed to two years in 2017. This increase in the provision must be recognised as an expense in profit or loss, usually as a finance cost, although IAS 37 does not make this mandatory.

The following is an extract from the Minefinders Corporation Ltd 2011 Annual Report:

A provision for site closure and reclamation is recorded when the Company incurs liability for costs associated with the eventual retirement of tangible long-lived assets (for example, reclamation costs). The liability for such costs exists from the time the legal or constructive obligation first arises, not when the actual expenditures are made.

Such obligations are based on estimated future cash flows discounted at a rate specific to the liability. . . . The amount added to the asset is amortized in the same manner as the asset.

The liability is increased in each accounting period by the amount of the implied interest inherent in the use of discounted present value methodology. . . .

5.6 Application of criteria illustrated

Scenario I

An offshore oil exploration company is required by its licence to remove the rig and restore the seabed. Management has estimated that 85% of the eventual cost will be incurred in removing the rig and 15% through the extraction of oil. The company's practice on similar projects has been to account for the decommissioning costs using the 'unit of production' method whereby the amount required for decommissioning was built up year by year, in line with production levels, to reach the amount of the expected costs by the time production ceased.

Decision process

1 **Is there a present obligation as a result of a past event?**
   The construction of the rig has created a legal obligation under the licence to remove the rig and restore the seabed.

2 **Is there a probable transfer of economic benefits?**
   This is probable.

3 **Can the amount of the outflow be reasonably estimated?**
   A best estimate can be made by management based on past experience and expert advice.

4 **Conclusion**
   A provision should be created of 85% of the eventual future costs of removal and restoration. This provision should be discounted if the effect of the time value of money is material. A provision for the 15% relating to restoration should be created when oil production commences.

The unit of production method is not acceptable in that the decommissioning costs relate to damage already done.

Scenario 2

A company has a private jet costing £24 million. Air regulations required it to be overhauled every four years. An overhaul costs £1.6 million. The company policy has been to create a provision for depreciation of £2 million on a straight-line basis over 12 years and an annual provision of £400,000 to meet the cost of the required overhaul every four years.

Decision process

1 **Is there a present obligation as a result of a past obligating event?**
   There is no present obligation. The company could avoid the cost of the overhaul by, for example, selling the aircraft.

2 **Conclusion**
   No provision for cost of overhaul can be recognised. Instead of a provision being recognised, the depreciation of the aircraft takes account of the future incidence of maintenance costs, i.e. an amount equivalent to the expected maintenance costs is depreciated over four years.

5.7 Provisions for specific purposes

Specific purposes could include considering the treatment of future operating losses, onerous contracts, restructuring and environmental liabilities. Let us consider each of these.

5.7.1 A provision for future operating losses

Such losses should not be recognised if there is no obligation at the reporting date on the basis that the entity could decide to discontinue that particular business activity. However, if it is contractually unable to discontinue then it classifies the contract as an onerous contract and makes provision.

5.7.2 Onerous contracts

A provision should be recognised if there is an onerous contract. An onerous contract is one entered into with another party under which the unavoidable costs of fulfilling the contract exceed the revenues to be received and where the entity would have to pay compensation to the other party if the contract was not fulfilled. A typical example in times of recession is the requirement to make a payment to secure the early termination of a lease where it has been impossible to sublet the premises. This situation could arise where there has been a downturn in business and an entity seeks to reduce its annual lease payments on premises that are no longer required.

The following is an extract from the 2011 Preliminary Results of the Spirit Pub Company plc:

Onerous lease provisions
The Group provides for its onerous obligations under leases where the property is closed or vacant and for properties where rental expense is in excess of income. The estimated timings and amounts of cash flows are determined using the experience of internal and external property experts; however, any changes to the estimated method of exiting from the property could lead to changes to the level of the provision recorded.

5.7.3 Restructuring provisions

- **A provision for restructuring** should only be recognised when there is a commitment supported by:
  (a) a detailed formal plan for the restructuring identifying at least:
      (i) the business or part of the business concerned;
      (ii) the principal locations affected;
      (iii) details of the approximate number of employees who will receive compensation payments;
      (iv) the expenditure that will be undertaken; and
      (v) when the plan will be implemented; and
  (b) a valid expectation in those affected that the business will carry out the restructuring by implementing its restructuring plans or announcing its main features to those affected by it.

- **A provision for restructuring should not be created merely on the intention to restructure.** For example, a management or board decision to restructure taken before the reporting date does not give rise to a constructive obligation at the reporting date unless the company has, before the reporting date:
  - started to implement the restructuring plan, e.g. by dismantling plant or selling assets; or
  - announced the main features of the plan with sufficient detail to raise the valid expectation of those affected that the restructuring will actually take place.

- **A provision for restructuring** should only include the direct expenditures arising from the restructuring which are necessarily entailed and not associated with the ongoing activities of the company. For example, redundancy costs would be included, but note that the following costs which relate to the future conduct of the business are not included: retraining costs, relocation costs, marketing costs and investment in new systems and distribution networks.

5.7.4 Environmental liabilities and decommissioning costs

- **A provision for environmental liabilities** should be recognised at the time and to the extent that the entity becomes obliged, legally or constructively, to rectify environmental damage or to perform restorative work on the environment. This means that a provision should be set up only for the entity's costs to meet its *legal* or *constructive* obligations. It could be argued that any provision for any additional expenditure on environmental issues is a public relations decision and should be written off.

- **A provision for decommissioning costs** should be recognised to the extent that decommissioning costs relate to damage already done or goods and services already received.

Provisions for decommissioning costs often relate to non-current assets, e.g. power stations. Where a liability for decommissioning exists at the date of construction, it is recognised, normally at the present value of the expected future outflow of cash, and added to the cost of the non-current asset.

EXAMPLE • An entity constructs a nuclear power station at a cost of €20 million. The estimated useful life of the power station is 25 years. The entity has a legal obligation to decommission the power station at the end of its useful life and the estimated costs of this are €15 million in 25 years' time. A relevant annual discount factor is 5% and the present value of a payment of €15 million in 25 years' time is approximately €4.43 million.

In these circumstances a liability of €4.43 million is recognised at the completion of the construction of the facility. The debit side of this accounting entry is to property, plant and equipment, giving a total carrying amount for the power station of €24.43 million. This amount is then depreciated over 25 years which gives an annual charge (assuming straight-line depreciation with no residual value) of approximately €977,200.

The discounting of the liability is 'unwound' over the 25-year life of the power station, the annual unwinding being shown as a finance cost. The unwinding in the first year of operation is approximately €221,500 (€4.43 million × 5%).

5.7.5 Disclosures required by IAS 37 for provisions

Specific disclosures,[9] for each material class of provision, should be given as to the amount recognised at the year-end and about any movements in the year, e.g.:

- **Increases in provisions** – any new provisions; any increases to existing provisions; and, where provisions are carried at present value, any change in value arising from the passage of time or from any movement in the discount rate.

- **Reductions in provisions** – any amounts utilised during the period. Management are required to review provisions at each reporting date and adjust to reflect the current best estimates. If it is no longer probable that a transfer of economic benefits will be required to settle the obligation, the provision should be reversed. Note, however, that only expenditure that relates to the original provision may be set against that provision.

Disclosures need not be given in cases where to do so would be seriously prejudicial to the company's interests. For example, an extract from the Technotrans 2002 Annual Report states:

A competitor filed patent proceedings in 2000, . . . the court found in favour of the plaintiff . . . paves the way for a claim for compensation which may have to be determined in further legal proceedings . . . the particulars pursuant to IAS 37.85 are not disclosed, in accordance with IAS 37.92, in order not to undermine the company's situation substantially in the ongoing legal dispute.

5.8 Contingent liabilities

IAS 37 deals with provisions and contingent liabilities within the same IAS because the IASB regarded all provisions as contingent as they are uncertain in timing and amount. For the purposes of the accounts, it distinguishes between provisions and contingent liabilities in that:

- Provisions are a present obligation requiring a probable transfer of economic benefits that can be reliably estimated – a provision can therefore be recognised as a liability.
- Contingent liabilities fail to satisfy these criteria, e.g. lack of a reliable estimate of the amount; not probable that there will be a transfer of economic benefits; yet to be confirmed that there is actually an obligation. A contingent liability cannot therefore be recognised in the accounts but may be disclosed by way of note to the accounts or not disclosed if an outflow of economic benefits is remote.

Where the occurrence of a contingent liability becomes sufficiently probable, it falls within the criteria for recognition as a provision as detailed above and should be accounted for accordingly and recognised as a liability in the accounts.

Where the likelihood of a contingent liability is possible but not probable and not remote, disclosure should be made, for each class of contingent liability, where practicable, of:

(a) an estimate of its financial effect, taking into account the inherent risks and uncertainties and, where material, the time value of money;

(b) an indication of the uncertainties relating to the amount or timing of any outflow; and

(c) the possibility of any reimbursement.

For example, an extract from the 2015 Manchester City financial statements informs us that:

20 - Contingent liabilities
Additional transfer fees, signing on fees and loyalty bonuses of £112,918,000 (2014: £100,563,000) that will become payable upon the achievement of certain conditions contained within player and transfer contracts if they are still in the service of the Club on specific future dates are accounted for in the year in which they fall due for payment.

5.9 Contingent assets

A contingent asset is a possible asset that arises from past events whose existence will be confirmed only by the occurrence of one or more uncertain future events not wholly within the entity's control.

Recognition as an asset is only allowed if the asset is *virtually certain,* and therefore by definition no longer contingent.

Disclosure by way of note is required if an inflow of economic benefits is *probable.* The disclosure would include a brief description of the nature of the contingent assets at the reporting date and, where practicable, an estimate of their financial effect taking into account the inherent risks and uncertainties and, where material, the time value of money.

The following is an extract from The Watford Association Football Club Limited Report and financial statements For the year ended 30 June 2015:

> At 30th June 2015 the Club had sums receivable from other clubs in respect of players, dependent upon the number of first team appearances or percentage sell-on clauses. Due to the uncertainty of receipt of these contingent assets, it is not practical to disclose the amount likely to be received. Since the year end, £30,000 has become due.

> No disclosure is required where the chance of occurrence is anything less than probable. For the purposes of IAS 37, probable is defined as more likely than not, i.e. with more than a 50% chance.

5.10 ED IAS 37 *Non-financial Liabilities*

In June 2005, the International Accounting Standards Board (IASB) proposed amendments to IAS 37 *Provisions, Contingent Liabilities and Contingent Assets*. These strip IAS 37 of the words 'Provisions', 'Contingent' and 'Assets' and add the term 'Non-financial' to create the new title IAS 37 *Non-financial Liabilities*.[10] It is interesting to see that the new standard has been developed around the *Framework*'s definitions of an asset and a liability.

It appears that the word 'non-financial' has been added to distinguish the subject from 'financial liabilities' which are covered by IAS 32 and IAS 39. It should be noted that whilst the exposure draft remains in issue a new standard based on these proposals is not in the current IASB work-plan.

5.10.1 The 'old' IAS 37 *Provisions, Contingent Liabilities and Contingent Assets*

To understand the 'new' approach in ED IAS 37 *Non-financial Liabilities*, it is necessary first to look at the 'old' IAS 37. The old treatment can be represented by the following table:

Probability	Contingent liabilities	Contingent assets
Virtually certain	Liability	Asset
Probable ($p > 50\%$)	Provide	Disclose
Possible ($p < 50\%$)	Disclose	No disclosure
Remote	No disclosure	No disclosure

Note that contingent liabilities are those items where the probability is less than 50% ($p < 50\%$). Where, however, the liability is probable, i.e. the probability is $p > 50\%$, the item is classified as a provision and not a contingent liability. Normally, such a provision will be reported as the product of the value of the potential liability and its probability.

Note that the approach to contingent assets is different in that the 'prudence' concept is used which means that only virtually certain assets are reported as assets. If the probability is probable, i.e. $p > 50\%$, then contingent assets are disclosed by way of a note to the accounts, and if the probability is $p < 50\%$ then there is no disclosure.

Criticisms of the 'old' IAS 37

The criticisms included the following:

- The 'old' IAS 37 was not even-handed in its treatment of contingent assets and liabilities. In ED IAS 37 the treatment of contingent assets is similar to that of contingent liabilities, and provisions are merged into the treatment of contingent liabilities.

- The division between 'probable' and 'possible' was too strict or crude (at the $p = 50\%$ level) rather than being proportional. For instance, if a television manufacturer was considering the need to provide for guarantee claims (e.g. on televisions sold with a three-year warranty), then it is probable that each television sold would have a less than 50% chance of being subject to a warranty claim and so no provision would need to be made. However, if the company sold 10,000 televisions, it is almost certain that there would be some claims which would indicate that a provision should be made. A company could validly take either treatment, but the effect on the financial statements would be different.

- If there was a single possible legal claim, then the company could decide it was 'possible' and just disclose it in the financial statements. However, a more reasonable treatment would be to assess the claim as the product of the amount likely to be paid and its probability. This latter treatment is used in the new ED IAS 37.

5.10.2 Approach taken by ED IAS 37 *Non-financial Liabilities*

The new proposed standard uses the term 'non-financial liabilities' which it defines as 'a liability other than a financial liability as defined in IAS 32 *Financial Instruments: Presentation*'. In considering ED IAS 37, we will look at the proposed treatment of contingent liabilities/provisions and contingent assets, starting from the *Framework*'s definitions of a liability and an asset.

The *Framework's* definition

At the time of publication of the exposure draft the *Framework*, paragraph 91, required a liability to be recognised as follows:

> A liability is recognised in the statement of financial position when it is probable that an outflow of resources embodying economic benefits will result from the settlement of a present obligation and the amount at which the settlement will take place can be measured reliably.

The ED IAS 37 approach to provisions

Considering a provision first, the old IAS 37 (paragraph 10) defines it as follows:

> A provision is distinguished from other liabilities because there is uncertainty about the timing or amount of the future expenditure required in settlement.

ED IAS 37 argues that a provision should be reported as a liability, as it satisfies the *Framework*'s definition of a liability. It makes the point that there is no reference in the *Framework* to 'uncertainty about the timing or amount of the future expenditure required in settlement'. It considers a provision to be just one form of liability which should be treated as a liability in the financial statements.

Will the item 'provision' no longer appear in financial statements?

One would expect that to be the result of the ED (exposure draft) classification. However, the proposed standard does not take the step of prohibiting the use of the term, as seen in the following extract (paragraph 9):

> In some jurisdictions, some classes of liabilities are described as provisions, for example those liabilities that can be measured only by using a substantial degree of estimation. Although this [draft] Standard does not use the term 'provision', it does not prescribe how entities should describe their non-financial liabilities. Therefore, entities may describe some classes of non-financial liabilities as provisions in their financial statements.

The ED IAS 37 approach to contingent liabilities

Now considering contingent liabilities, the old IAS 37 (paragraph 10) defines these as:

(a) a possible obligation that arises from past events and whose existence will be confirmed only by the occurrence or non-occurrence of one or more uncertain future events not wholly within the control of the entity; or

(b) a present obligation that arises from past events, but is not recognised because:

  (i) it is not probable that an outflow of resources embodying economic benefits will be required to settle the obligation; or

  (ii) the amount of the obligation cannot be measured with sufficient reliability.

This definition means that the old IAS 37 has taken the strict approach of using the term 'possible' ($p < 50\%$) when it required no liability to be recognised.

ED IAS 37 is different in that it takes a two-stage approach in considering whether 'contingent liabilities' are 'liabilities'. To illustrate this, we will take the example of a restaurant where some customers have suffered food poisoning.

First determine whether there is a present obligation

The restaurant's year-end is 30 June 20X6. If the food poisoning took place after 30 June 20X6, then this is not a 'present obligation' at the year-end, so it is not a liability. If the food poisoning occurred up to 30 June, then it is a 'present obligation' at the year-end, as there are possible future costs arising from the food poisoning. This is the first stage in considering whether the liability exists.

Then determine whether a liability exists

The second stage is to consider whether a 'liability' exists. The *Framework*'s definition of a liability says it is a liability if 'it is probable that an outflow of resources will result from the settlement of the present obligation'. So, there is a need to consider whether any payments (or other expenses) will be incurred as a result of the food poisoning. This may involve settling legal claims, other compensation or giving 'free' meals. The estimated cost of these items will be the liability (and expense) included in the financial statements.

The rationale

ED IAS 37 explains this process as:

● the unconditional obligation (stage 1) establishes the liability; and

● the conditional obligation (stage 2) affects the amount that will be required to settle the liability.

The liability is the amount that the entity would rationally pay to settle the present obligation or to transfer it to a third party on the statement of financial position date. Often, the liability will be estimated as the product of the maximum liability and the probability of it occurring, or a decision tree will be used with a number of possible outcomes (costs) and their probability.

In many cases, the new ED IAS 37 will cover the 'possible' category for contingent liabilities and include the item as a liability (rather than as a note to the financial statements). This gives a more 'proportional' result than the previously strict line between 'probable' ($p > 50\%$) (when a liability is included in the financial statements) and 'possible' ($p < 50\%$) (when only a note is included in the financial statements and no charge is included for the liability).

What if they cannot be measured reliably?

For other 'possible' contingent liabilities, which have not been recognised because they cannot be measured reliably, the following disclosure should be made:

● a description of the nature of the obligation;

● an explanation of why it cannot be measured reliably;

● an indication of the uncertainties relating to the amount or timing of any outflow of economic benefits; and

● the existence of any rights to reimbursement.

ED IAS 37 does not require disclosure of the maximum potential liability, e.g. the maximum damages if the entity loses the legal case.

5.10.3 Measured reliably

The *Framework*'s definition of a liability includes the condition 'and the amount at which the settlement will take place can be measured reliably'. This posed a problem when drafting ED IAS 37 because of the concern that an entity could argue that the amount of a contingent liability could not be measured reliably and that there was therefore no need to include it as a liability in the financial statements – i.e. to use this as a 'cop out' to give a 'rosier' picture in the financial statements. While acknowledging that in many cases a non-financial liability cannot be measured exactly, it considered that it could (and should) be estimated. It then says that cases where the liability cannot be measured reliably are 'extremely rare'. We can see from this that the ED approach is that 'measured reliably' does not mean 'measured exactly' and that cases where the liability 'cannot be measured reliably' will be 'extremely rare'.

5.10.4 Contingent asset

The *Framework*, paragraph 89, requires recognition of an asset as follows:

> An Asset is recognised in the statement of financial position when it is probable that the future economic benefits will flow to the entity and the asset has a cost or value that can be measured reliably.

Note that under the old IAS 37, contingent assets included items where they were 'probable' (unlike liabilities, when this was called a 'provision'). However, probable contingent assets are not included as assets but only included in the notes to the financial statements.

The ED IAS 37 approach

ED IAS 37 takes a similar approach to 'contingent assets' as it does to 'provisions/contingent liabilities'. It abolishes the term 'contingent asset' and replaces it with the term 'contingency'. The term contingency refers to uncertainty about the amount of the future economic benefits embodied in an asset, rather than uncertainty about whether an asset exists.

Essentially, the treatment of contingent assets is the same as that of contingent liabilities. The first stage is to consider whether an asset exists and the second stage is concerned with valuing the asset (i.e. the product of the value of the asset and its probability). A major change is to move contingent assets to IAS 38 *Intangible Assets* (and not include them in IAS 37).

The treatment of 'contingent assets' under IAS 38 is now similar to that for 'contingent liabilities/provisions'. This seems more appropriate than the former 'prudent approach' used by the old IAS 37.

5.10.5 Reimbursements

Under the old IAS 37 an asset could be damaged or destroyed, when the expense would be included in profit or loss (and any future costs included as a provision). If the insurance claim relating to this loss was made after the year-end, it is likely that no asset could be included in the financial statements as compensation for the loss, as the insurance claim was 'not virtually certain'. In reality, this did not reflect the true situation when the insurance claim would compensate for the loss, and there would be little or no net cost.

With the new rules under ED IAS 37, the treatment of contingent assets and contingent liabilities is the same, so an asset would be included in the statement of financial position as the insurance claim, which would offset the loss on damage or destruction of the asset. The ED position is that an asset exists because there is an unconditional right to reimbursement – the only uncertainty is to the amount that will be received. But ED IAS 37 says the liability relating to the loss (e.g. the costs of repair) must be stated separately from the asset for the reimbursement (i.e. the insurance claim) – they cannot be netted off (although they will be in profit or loss).

5.10.6 Constructive and legal obligations

The term 'constructive obligation' is important in determining whether a liability exists. ED IAS 37 (paragraph 10) defines it as follows:

A constructive obligation is a present obligation that arises from an entity's past actions when:

(a) by an established pattern of past practice, published policies or a sufficiently specific current statement, the entity has indicated to other parties that it will accept particular responsibilities, and

(b) as a result, the entity has created a valid expectation in those parties, that they can reasonably rely on it to discharge those responsibilities.

It also defines a legal obligation as follows:

A legal obligation is a present obligation that arises from the following:

(a) a contract (through its explicit or implicit terms)

(b) legislation, or

(c) other operating law.

A contingent liability/provision is a liability only if it is either a constructive and/or a legal obligation. Thus, an entity would not normally make a provision (recognise a liability) for the potential costs of rectifying faulty products outside their guarantee period.

5.10.7 Present value

ED IAS 37 says that future cash flows relating to the liability should be discounted at the pre-tax discount rate. Unwinding of the discount would still need to be recognised as an interest cost.

5.10.8 Subsequent measurement and derecognition

On subsequent measurement, ED IAS 37 says the carrying value of the non-financial liability should be reviewed at each reporting date. The non-financial liability should be derecognised when the obligation is settled, cancelled or expires.

5.10.9 Onerous contracts

If a contract becomes onerous, the entity is required to recognise a liability as the present obligation under the contract. However, if the contract becomes onerous as a result of the entity's own actions, the liability should not be recognised until it has taken the action. For example, let us assume that an entity has a non-cancellable 10-year lease on a warehouse and decides during year 7 to vacate the property. Under the old IAS 37 the present obligation arises when the entity communicates this to the lessor, whereas under ED IAS 37 the present obligation does not arise until the property is actually vacated. The contract is still onerous but there may be a later recognition.

5.10.10 Restructurings

ED IAS 37 says:

> An entity shall recognise a non-financial liability for a cost associated with a restructuring only when the definition of a liability has been satisfied.

There are situations where management has made a decision to restructure and the ED provides that in these cases a decision by the management of an entity to undertake a restructuring is not the requisite past event for recognition of a liability. The ED position is that an announcement is insufficient, even if there is a detailed plan, if the entity continues to be able to modify the plan. A cost associated with a restructuring is recognised as a liability on the same basis as if that cost arose independently of the restructuring. This change would, if implemented, align IAS 37 with the equivalent US standard in this area.

5.10.11 Other items

These include the treatment of termination costs and future operating losses where the approach is still to assess whether a liability exists. The changes to termination costs will require an amendment to IAS 19 *Employee Benefits*. In the case of termination costs, these are only recognised when a liability is incurred: e.g. the costs of closure of a factory become a liability only when the expense is incurred, and redundancy costs become a liability only when employees are informed of their redundancy. In the case of future operating losses, these are not recognised as they do not relate to a past event.

Under the new ED IAS 37, the liability arises no earlier than under the old IAS 37 and sometimes later.

5.10.12 Disclosure

ED IAS 37 requires the following disclosure of non-financial liabilities:

> For each class of non-financial liability, the carrying amount of the liability at the period-end together with a description of the nature of the obligation.
> For any class of non-financial liability with uncertainty about its estimation:

(a) a reconciliation of the carrying amounts at the beginning and end of the period showing:

   (i) liabilities incurred;

   (ii) liabilities derecognised;

   (iii) changes in the discounted amount resulting from the passage of time and the effect of any change in the discount rate; and

   (iv) other adjustments to the amount of the liability (e.g. revisions in the estimated cash flows that will be required to settle it);

(b) the expected timing of any resulting outflows of economic benefits;

(c) an indication of the uncertainties about the amount or timing of those outflows. If necessary, to provide adequate information on the major assumptions made about future events;

(d) the amount of any right to reimbursement, stating the amount of any asset that has been recognised.

If a non-financial liability is not recognised because it cannot be measured reliably, that fact should be disclosed together with:

(a) a description of the nature of the obligation;

(b) an explanation of why it cannot be measured reliably;

(c) an indication of the uncertainties relating to the amount or timing of any outflow of economic benefits; and

(d) the existence of any right to reimbursement.

5.10.13 Conclusion on ED IAS 37 *Non-financial Liabilities*

This proposed standard makes significant changes to the subject of 'Provisions, Contingent Liabilities and Contingent Assets', which are derived from the general principles of accounting. Its good features include:

(a) It is conceptually sound by basing changes on the *Framework*'s definitions of an asset and a liability.

(b) It is more appropriate that the treatment of provisions/contingent liabilities and contingent assets should be more 'even-handed'.

(c) It avoids the 'strict' breaks at 50% probability between 'probable' and 'possible'. It uses probability in estimating the liability down (effectively) to 0%.

(d) The definition of a constructive obligation has been more clearly defined.

(e) It overcomes the previous anomaly of not allowing reimbursements after the year-end (e.g. where there is an unsettled insurance claim at the year-end).

However, in some ways it could be argued that the proposed standard goes too far, particularly in its new terminology:

(a) The abolition of the term 'contingent liability' and not defining 'provision'. The new term 'non-financial liability' does not seem as meaningful as 'contingent liability'. It would seem better (more meaningful) to continue to use the term 'contingent liability' and make this encompass provisions (as it does for contingent assets).

(b) It would seem more appropriate to continue to include 'contingent assets' in this standard, rather than move them to 'intangible assets', as the treatment of these items is similar to that of 'contingent liabilities'.

ED IAS 37 has proved to be a controversial exposure draft where there have been significant discussions surrounding the potential changes. In addition this project could be influenced by other projects that the IASB has in development, such as on leasing and revenue recognition.

5.11 ED/2010/1 *Measurement of Liabilities in IAS 37*[11]

This ED is a limited re-exposure of a proposed amendment to IAS 37. It deals with only one of the measurement requirements for liabilities. The ED proposes that the non-financial liability should be measured at the amount that the entity would rationally pay to be relieved of the liability.

If the liability cannot be cancelled or transferred, the liability is measured as the present value of the resources required to fulfil the obligation. It may be that the resources required are uncertain. If so, the expected value is estimated based on the probability-weighted average of the outflows. The expected value is then increased to take into account the risk that the actual outcome might be higher, estimating the amount a third party would require to take over this risk. Where there is an obligation to undertake a service at a future date such as decommissioning plant and there is no market for such a service, it is proposed that the amount of any provision should be the cost that the entity would itself charge another party to carry out the work, including a profit margin.

If the liability can be cancelled or transferred, there is a choice available – to fulfil the obligation, to cancel the obligation or to transfer the liability. The logical choice is to choose the lower of the present value of fulfilling the obligation and the amount that would have to be paid to either cancel or transfer.

Potential impact on ratios and transparency

A new standard that applies this measurement approach will not have an identical impact on all entities – some will have to include higher non-financial liabilities on their statement of financial position, others will have to reduce the non-financial liabilities. This means that there will be different impacts on returns on equity, gearing and debt covenants.

Given the process of establishing expected values and risk adjustments, it might be that additional narrative explanation will be required in the annual report, particularly if the non-financial liabilities are material.

Future progress

In July 2015 the IASB issued a staff paper on a Research Project—provisions, contingent liabilities and contingent assets (IAS 37). It stated that more evidence was being gathered about the nature and extent of practical problems with IAS 37, and views on possible solutions to the problems identified. The staff paper focused particularly on six topics:

1 **Identifying liabilities.** This matter is likely to be revisited following the publication of the revised *Conceptual Framework* in March 2018 and the consequential refinement of the definition of a liability – see Chapter 10 for more details.

2 **Recognition criteria.** IAS 37 was unique in that it has three recognition criteria for liabilities, and in particular, it was unusual because it required that it was probable, which is defined as more likely than not that there will be an outflow of resources required to settle the present obligation. The last time the IASB had looked at IAS 37; the IASB members had raised a concern about the lack of completeness this criterion resulted in, especially when other Standards that were being written at the time did not have the probable outflows criterion.

3 **Measurement.** With respect to risk adjustments, one IASB member pointed out that the guidance in IAS 37 in this area was old and that it had been discussed in more recent Standards, and suggested that it would make sense to update to reflect the best/most recent thinking if the IASB was to do something on measurement. He also noted that paragraph 43 of IAS 37 contained a reference to the word 'prudence', which was inconsistent with where the IASB was going as regards the new *Conceptual Framework* (see Chapter 10 for more details), and noted that it was dangerous to allow it to stay there. He noted that prudence and risk adjustments were completely different things and that they were being confused here.

4 **Onerous contracts.** These will be re-examined both from a recognition and from a measurement perspective.

5 **Reimbursement rights and contingent assets.** More clarity is needed regarding the different thresholds for contingent assets and contingent liabilities, and how this would be impacted by the symmetrical Conceptual Framework definitions of assets and liabilities. No one has suggested the threshold for contingent assets should be lowered to be symmetrical with contingent liabilities, and it is important to consider the concept of relevance – and whether relevant information would be provided, noting that in the Basis for Conclusions it was not explicit that the IASB proposed either to systematically require symmetry or systematically require asymmetry.

6 **Other issues.** With respect to scope, one IASB member noted that there was a signifcant gap in IFRS regarding the disclosure of contractual commitments, noting that it was a very material area of interest for any investor in any company, and that he believed it should be part of the scope. He observed that in the Conceptual Framework, where the IASB talked about relevance and measurement uncertainty as one of the considerations in determining whether something was capable of making a difference, the IASB had said that there would be situations where disclosure was an important substitute, and noted that there was a nexus between that concept and what the IASB was trying to achieve here.

The IASB member agreed that the terminology section needed some work, and noted specifically that the term 'contingent liability' was difficult to understand as an entity either had a liability or it did not. He noted that an entity could have loss contingencies, but not contingent liabilities – and noted that this should be made clearer. He also noted that the proposed section in the Conceptual Framework on executory contracts needed a lot more clarity, and noted that the lack of required disclosure of these arrangements was a gaping hole in IFRS.

Another IASB member noted that in the analysis in agenda paper 14C with respect to the *Conceptual Framework* versus IAS 37, the agenda paper appeared to equate 'economic compulsion' with 'no realistic alternative' and cautioned against viewing the concepts as equivalent. She noted that if the IASB was to do a project on IAS 37, it might be a good idea to look at how the Conceptual Framework discussion of 'no realistic alternative' related to the concept of economic compulsion.

Summary

The *Framework* defines a liability as a present obligation to transfer an economic resource arising from a past event. The treatment of provisions has been the subject of an ED IAS 37 which considers that a provision should be reported as a liability.

The chapter considers the approach to be taken when accounting for a variety of scenarios including the treatment of onerous contracts, future operating losses, restructuring and environmental liabilities and decommissioning costs.

Further consideration will be given by the IASB prior to a revised standard being issued.

REVIEW QUESTIONS

1 The Notes in the BG Group 2015 Annual Report included the following extract:

Provisions for liabilities

Decommissioning

	2011 £m	2010 £m
As at 1 January	4,605	3,662
Unwinding of discount	131	146

Decommissioning costs

The estimated cost of decommissioning at the end of the producing lives of fields is reviewed at least annually and engineering estimates and reports are updated periodically. Provision is made for the estimated cost of decommissioning at the statement of financial position date, to the extent that current circumstances indicate BG Group will ultimately bear this cost.

Explain why the provision has been increased in 2014 and 2015 by the unwinding of discount and why these increases are for different amounts.

2 Mining, nuclear and oil companies historically provided an amount each year over the life of an enterprise to provide for decommissioning costs. Explain why the IASB considered this to be an inappropriate treatment and how these companies would be affected by IAS 37 *Provisions, Contingent Liabilities and Contingent Assets* and ED IAS 37 *Non-financial Liabilities*.

3 The following note appeared in the Compass-Group Annual Report:

> Provisions for onerous contracts represent the liabilities in respect of short and long term leases on unoccupied properties and other contracts lasting under five years.

Discuss the criteria for assessing whether a provision may be created in these circumstances under both IAS 37 and ED IAS 37. Discuss the criteria for assessing whether a contract is onerous.

4 One of the reasons why the IASB considered in its EDs an amendment to IAS 37 is that the criteria within that standard for the recognition of provisions are allegedly inconsistent with those in other international financial reporting standards. Discuss the extent to which you believe this statement to be true, and the improvements proposed in the 2005 and 2010 exposure drafts.

5 Given the uncertainty inherent in the recognition of provisions or contingent liabilities, financial statements would be much more reliable if the existence of potential liabilities were disclosed, rather than being recognised under conditions of potential uncertainty. Discuss this statement.

EXERCISES

* Question 1

(a) Provisions are particular kinds of liabilities. It therefore follows that provisions should be recognised when the definition of a liability has been met. The key requirement of a liability is a present obligation and thus this requirement is critical also in the context of the recognition of a provision. IAS 37 *Provisions, Contingent Liabilities and Contingent Assets* deals with this area.

Required:
(i) **Explain why there was a need for detailed guidance on accounting for provisions.**
(ii) **Explain the circumstances under which a provision should be recognised in the financial statements according to IAS 37** *Provisions, Contingent Liabilities and Contingent Assets.*

(b) World Wide Nuclear Fuels, a public limited company, disclosed the following information in its financial statements for the year ending 30 November 20X9:

> The company purchased an oil company during the year. As part of the sale agreement, oil has to be supplied to the company's former holding company at an uneconomic rate for a period of five years. As a result, a provision for future operating losses has been set up of $135m, which relates solely to the uneconomic supply of oil. Additionally the oil company is exposed to environmental liabilities arising out of its past obligations, principally in respect of soil and ground water restoration costs, although currently there is no legal obligation to carry out the work. Liabilities for environmental costs are provided for when the group determines a formal plan of action on the closure of an inactive site. It has been decided to provide for $120m in respect of the environmental liability on the acquisition of the oil company. World Wide Nuclear Fuels has a reputation for ensuring the preservation of the environment in its business activities. The company is also facing a legal claim for $200 million from a competitor who claims they have breached a patent in one of their processes. World Wide Nuclear Fuels has obtained legal advice that the claim has little chance of success and the insurance advisers have indicated that to insure against losing the case would cost $20 million as a premium.

Required:
Discuss whether the provision has been accounted for correctly under IAS 37 *Provisions, Contingent Liabilities and Contingent Assets*, and whether any changes are likely to be needed under ED IAS 37.

* Question 2

On 20 December 20X6 one of Incident plc's lorries was involved in an accident with a car. The lorry driver was responsible for the accident and the company agreed to pay for the repair to the car. The company put in a claim to its insurers on 17 January 20X7 for the cost of the claim. The company expected the claim to be settled by the insurance company except for a £250 excess on the insurance policy. The insurance company may dispute the claim and not pay out; however, the company believes that the chance of this occurring is low. The cost of repairing the car was estimated as £5,000, all of which was incurred after the year-end.

Required:
Explain how this item should be treated in the financial statements for the year ended 31 December 20X6 according to both IAS 37 and ED IAS 37 *Non-financial Liabilities*.

* Question 3

Plasma Ltd, a manufacturer of electrical goods, guarantees them for 12 months from the date of purchase by the customer. If a fault occurs after the guarantee period but is due to faulty manufacture or design of the product, the company repairs or replaces the product. However, the company does not make this practice widely known.

Required:
Explain how repairs after the guarantee period should be treated in the financial statements.

* Question 4

In 20X6 Alpha AS made the decision to close a loss-making department in 20X7. The company proposed to make a provision for the future costs of termination in the 20X6 profit or loss. Its argument was that a liability existed in 20X6 which should be recognised in 20X6. The auditor objected to recognising a liability, but agreed to recognition if it could be shown that the management decision was irrevocable.

Required:
Discuss whether a liability exists and should be recognised in the 20X6 statement of financial position.

* Question 5

Easy View Ltd had started business publishing training resource material in ring binder format for use in primary schools. Later it diversified into the hiring out of videos and had opened a chain of video hire shops. With the growing popularity of a mail order video/DVD supplier the video hire shops had become loss-making.

The company's year-end was 31 March and in February the financial director (FD) was asked to prepare a report for the board on the implications of closing this segment of the business.

The position at the board meeting on 10 March was as follows:

1   It was agreed that the closure should take place from 1 April 2010 to be completed by 31 May 2010.

2   The premises were freehold except for one that was on a lease with six years to run. It was in an inner-city shopping complex where many properties were empty and there was little chance of sub-letting. The annual rent was £20,000 per annum. Early termination of the lease could be negotiated for a figure of £100,000. An appropriate discount rate is 8%.

3   The office equipment and vans had a book value of £125,000 and were expected to realise £90,000, a figure tentatively suggested by a dealer who indicated that he might be able to complete by the end of April.

4   The staff had been mainly part-time and casual employees. There were 45 managers, however, who had been with the company for a number of years. These were happy to retrain to work with the training resources operation. The cost of retraining to use publishing software was estimated at £225,000.

5   Losses of £300,000 were estimated for the current year and £75,000 for the period until the closure was complete.

A week before the meeting the managing director made it clear to the FD that he wanted the segment to be treated as a discontinued operation so that the continuing operations could reflect the profitable training segment's performance.

Required:
Draft the finance director's report to present to the MD before the meeting to clarify the financial reporting implications.

* Question 6

Suktor is an entity that prepares financial statements to 30 June each year.

On 30 April 20X1 the directors decided to discontinue the business of one of Suktor's operating divisions. They decided to cease production on 31 July 20X1, with a view to disposing of the property, plant and equipment soon after 31 August 20X1.

On 15 May 20X1 the directors made a public announcement of their intentions and offered the employees affected by the closure termination payments or alternative employment opportunities elsewhere in the group. Relevant financial details are as follows:

(a)   On 30 April 20X1 the directors estimated that termination payments to employees would total $12 million and the costs of retraining employees who would remain employed by other group companies would total $1.2 million. Actual termination costs paid out on 31 May 20X1 were $12.6 million and the latest estimate of total retraining costs is $960,000.

(b)   Suktor was leasing a property under an operating lease that expires on 30 September 20Y0. On 30 June 20X1 the present value of the future lease rentals (using an appropriate discount rate) was $4.56 million. On 31 August 20X1 Suktor made a payment to the lessor of $4.56 million in return for early termination of the lease. There were no rental payments made in July or August 20X1.

(c)   The loss after tax of Suktor for the year ended 30 June 20X1 was $14.4 million. Suktor made further operating losses totalling $6 million for the two-month period 1 July 20X1 to 31 August 20X1.

Required:
Compute the provision that is required in the financial statements of Suktor at 30 June 20X1 in respect of the decision to close.

* Question 7

On 1 April 20W9 Kroner began to lease an office block on a 20-year lease. The useful economic life of the office buildings was estimated at 40 years on 1 April 20W9. The supply of leasehold properties exceeded the demand on 1 April 2009 so as an incentive the lessor paid Kroner $1 million on 1 April 20W9 and allowed Kroner a rent-free period for the first two years of the lease, followed by 36 payments of $250,000, the first being due on 1 April 20X1.

Between 1 April 20W9 and 30 September 20W9 Kroner carried out alterations to the office block at a total cost of $3 million. The terms of the lease require Kroner to vacate the office block on 31 March 20Y9 and leave it in exactly the same condition as it was at the start of the lease. The directors of Kroner have consistently estimated that the cost of restoring the office block to its original condition on 31 March 20Y9 will be $2.5 million at 31 March 20Y9 prices.

An appropriately risk-adjusted discount rate for use in any discounting calculations is 6% per annum. The present value of $1 payable in $19\frac{1}{2}$ years at an annual discount rate of 6% is 32 cents.

Required:
Prepare extracts from the financial statements of Kroner that show the depreciation of leasehold improvements and unwinding of discount on the restoration liability in the statement of comprehensive income for *both* of the years ended 31 March 20X0 and 20X1.

* Question 8

Epsilon is a listed entity. You are the financial controller of the entity and its consolidated financial statements for the year ended 31 March 2009 are being prepared. The board of directors is responsible for all key financial and operating decisions, including the allocation of resources.

Your assistant is preparing the first draft of the statements. He has a reasonable general accounting knowledge but is not familiar with the detailed requirements of all relevant financial reporting standards. There is one issue on which he requires your advice and he has sent you a note as shown below:

I note that on 31 January 2009 the board of directors decided to discontinue the activities of a number of our subsidiaries. This decision was made, I believe, because these subsidiaries did not fit into the long-term plans of the group and the board did not consider it likely that the sub-sidiaries could be sold. This decision was communicated to the employees on 28 February 2009 and the activities of the subsidiaries affected were gradually curtailed starting on 1 May 2009, with an expected completion date of 30 September 2009. I have the following information regarding the closure programme:

(a) All the employees in affected subsidiaries were offered redundancy packages and some of the employees were offered employment in other parts of the group. These offers had to be accepted or rejected by 30 April 2009. On 31 March 2009 the directors estimated that the cost of redundancies would be $20 million and the cost of relocation of employees who accepted alternative employment would be $10 million. Following 30 April 2009 these estimates were revised to $22 million and $9 million respectively.

(b) Latest estimates are that the operating losses of the affected subsidiaries for the six months to 30 September 2009 will total $15 million.

(c) A number of the subsidiaries are leasing properties under non-cancellable operating leases. I believe that at 31 March 2009 the present value of the future lease payments relating to these properties totalled $6 million. The cost of immediate termination of these lease obligations would be $5 million.

(d) The carrying values of the freehold properties owned by the affected subsidiaries at 31 March 2008 totalled $25 million. The estimated net disposal proceeds of the properties are $29 million and all properties should realise a profit.

(e) The carrying value of the plant and equipment owned by the affected subsidiaries at 31 March 2008 was $18 million. The estimated current disposal proceeds of this plant and equipment is $2 million and its estimated value in use (including the proceeds from ultimate disposal) is $8 million.

I am unsure regarding a number of aspects of accounting for this decision by the board. Please tell me how the decision to curtail the activities of the three subsidiaries affects the financial statements.

Required:
Draft a reply to the questions raised by your assistant.

* Question 9

Epsilon is a listed entity. You are the financial controller of the entity and its consolidated financial statements for the year ended 30 September 2008 are being prepared. Your assistant, who has prepared the first draft of the statements, is unsure about the correct treatment of a transaction and has asked for your advice. Details of the transaction are given below.

On 31 August 2008 the directors decided to close down a business segment which did not fit into its future strategy. The closure commenced on 5 October 2008 and was due to be completed on 31 December 2008. On 6 September 2008 letters were sent to relevant employees offering voluntary redundancy or redeployment in other sectors of the business. On 13 September 2008 negotiations commenced with relevant parties with a view to terminating existing contracts of the business segment and arranging sales of its assets. Latest estimates of the financial implications of the closure are as follows:

(i)   Redundancy costs will total $30 million, excluding the payment referred to in (ii) below.

(ii)   The pension plan (a defined benefit plan) will make a lump sum payment totalling $8 million to the employees who accept voluntary redundancy in termination of their rights under the plan. Epsilon will pay this amount into the plan on 31 January 2009. The actuaries have advised that the accumulated pension rights that this payment will extinguish have a present value of $7 million and this sum is unlikely to alter significantly before 31 January 2009.

(iii) The cost of redeploying and retraining staff who do not accept redundancy will total $6 million.

(iv)   The business segment operates out of a leasehold property that has an unexpired lease term of 10 years from 30 September 2008. The annual lease rentals on this property are $1 million, payable on 30 September in arrears. Negotiations with the owner of the freehold indicate that the owner would accept a single payment of $5.5 million in return for early termination of the lease. There are no realistic opportunities for Epsilon to sublet this property. An appropriate rate to use in any discounting calculations is 10% per annum. The present value of an annuity of $1 receivable annually at the end of years 1 to 10 inclusive using a discount rate of 10% is $6.14.

(v)   Plant having a net book value of $11 million at 30 September 2008 will be sold for $2 million.

(vi)   The operating losses of the business segment for October, November and December 2008 are estimated at $10 million.

Your assistant is unsure of the extent to which the above transactions create liabilities that should be recognised as a closure provision in the financial statements. He is also unsure as to whether or not the results of the business segment that is being closed need to be shown separately.

Required:
Explain how the decision to close down the business segment should be reported in the financial statements of Epsilon for the year ended 30 September 2008.

References

1 IAS 37 *Provisions, Contingent Liabilities and Contingent Assets*, IASC, 1998.
2 Ibid., para. 2.
3 Ibid., para. 25.
4 Ibid., para. 17.
5 Ibid., para. 23.
6 Ibid., para. 36.
7 Ibid., para. 43.
8 Ibid., para. 45.
9 Ibid., para. 84.
10 ED IAS 37 *Non-financial Liabilities*, IASB, 2005.
11 ED/2010/1 *Measurement of Liabilities in IAS 37*, IASB, 2010.

CHAPTER 6

Leasing

6.1 Introduction

A *lease* is an agreement whereby the lessor (the legal owner or controller of an asset) conveys to the lessee (the user of the asset) the right to use an asset for an agreed period of time in return for a payment or a series of payments.

An alternative method of obtaining the use of an asset is to purchase the asset outright. In the case of a purchase the new owner records the cost of the physical asset and either the payment of cash, or a liability, or the issue of shares.

In the case of leasing, no physical asset is owned by the lessee (the user) but rather the lessee only has a valuable right, namely the right to use the asset for a specified period, and an obligation to pay for that right of use. Initially accountants were reluctant to record an asset (the right of use) and the liability (the payment obligations under the lease) as the two sides of the contract were substantially unperformed (that is most of the right of use has not yet been provided and the majority of obligations to pay for the use is contingent on the provision of the access to the asset for use). (Some people would argue that as most leases are non-cancellable, or the major component of them is non-cancellable, then a liability arises as defined in the *Conceptual Framework*.)

One of the fundamental characteristics of useful financial information is that it faithfully represents the transactions reported within it. Another way of saying this is that useful financial information should reflect the economic substance of transactions. Where this 'economic substance' differs from the legal form then the economic substance will prevail. We will see in this chapter that the issue of 'substance over form' is a key factor when we consider the financial reporting of leasing transactions in the financial statements of both lessor and lessee.

Objectives

By the end of this chapter, you should be able to:

- evaluate the 'substance over form' issue and so identify why an accounting standard on leasing is necessary
- know the broad thrust of the history of accounting for leases and the considerable effort to develop a leasing accounting standard IFRS16 – *Leases*
- explain how a lease is identified in IFRS 16 – *Leases* – issued in January 2016
- account for leases in the financial statements of lessees under IFRS 16
- account for leases in the financial statements of lessors under IFRS 16
- account for sale and leaseback transactions in the financial statements of both the seller/lessee and the buyer/lessor
- discuss the economic impact of IFRS 16 on the extent to which leasing is used as a means of asset procurement

6.2 Need for an accounting standard on leasing

In the introduction we explained that initially accountants were reluctant to record the lease as an asset and liability in the books of the **lessee (the user)**. Instead the amount payable by the lessee for the use of the asset was recorded as an expense in the period in which it was used and no liability was recorded for use in future periods of the contract. Being consistent with that there was no asset recorded for future rights of use in the books of the lessee (user).

However, this resulted in financial statements which looked substantially different for companies which were similar in all respects except that one purchased an asset with a loan whereas the other acquired the use of the asset through a lease agreement. How that distorts financial comparisons will be illustrated by the following example.

EXAMPLE ● The summarised statement of financial position of an entity at the start of its accounting period (all accounting periods in this example are of one year's duration) is as follows:

	$000
Non-current assets	60,000
Current assets	40,000
	100,000
Equity	40,000
Non-current liabilities (loans)	41,000
Current liabilities (no loans included)	19,000
	100,000

Suppose the entity needs to obtain the use of an item of plant that would cost $40 million to purchase outright. The estimated useful economic life of the plant is five years, with no estimated residual value. The entity has no surplus cash to finance the purchase and it has two options available:

● To finance the purchase with a five-year loan carrying an annual finance cost of 5%. The loan is repayable in five annual amounts of $9,240,000, payable at the end of each of the next five years

● To lease the asset on a five-year lease with annual rentals of $9,240,000, payable in arrears. The lease has no escape clauses.

In order to help us with some of the figures we are going to demonstrate, it would be good to show the profile of the additional loan over the five-year term assuming the asset is purchased on the first of January and annual payments are on 31 December:

Period	Opening balance $000	Finance cost (5%) $000	Annual Payment $000	Closing balance $000
1	40,000	2,000	(9,240)	32,760
2	32,760	1,638	(9,240)	25,158
3	25,158	1,258	(9,240)	17,176
4	17,176	859	(9,240)	8,795
5	8,795	440	(9,240)	(5)
				(a rounding difference)

This means that the loan balances at the beginning and end of period 1 will be as follows:

	Start of period $000	End of period $000	Comment
Current	7,240	7,602	The amount by which the overall loan balance reduces in the following period (32,760–25,158) or alternatively the annual payment 9,240 less the interest component of 1,638 which has not yet been incurred.
Non-current	32,760	25,158	
Total	40,000	32,760	The overall loan balance

Impact on gearing ratio

Let's compare the impact on the statement of financial position on 1 January under the purchase option and the lease option, assuming the lease option is accounted for according to its legal form – i.e. no asset or liability recognised:

	Lease option $000	Purchase option $000	Comment
Non-current assets	60,000	100,000	
Current assets	40,000	40,000	
	100,000	140,000	
Equity	40,000	40,000	
Non-current liabilities (loans)	41,000	73,760	Including the non-current portion of the loan (32,760)
Current liabilities	19,000	26,240	Including the current portion of the loan (7,240)
	100,000	140,000	
Gearing ratio Loans/(Loans + Equity)	51%	67%	

The two options show a significantly different gearing ratio – the 'purchase option' showing a significantly higher (and probably less acceptable) ratio.

Statements of financial performance and position assuming asset was leased

Let's further assume that the summarised statement of profit or loss of the entity (there is no other comprehensive income) for the period immediately following the acquisition of the asset (and assuming for the moment the asset is leased and the associated asset and any associated liability is not recognised) is as follows:

	$000	
Revenue	80,000	
Operating costs	(68,000)	Includes the lease payment of $9.24m
Operating profit	12,000	
Finance costs	(2,000)	
Pre-tax profit	10,000	
Tax	(2,000)	
Post-tax profit	8,000	

Assuming also that no additional shares had been issued, then the statement of financial position at the end of the period could appear as:

	$000	
Non-current assets	66,000	
Current assets	44,000	
	110,000	
Equity	48,000	
Non-current liabilities (loans)	40,000	
Current liabilities	22,000	Includes $2m tax
	110,000	

Compare financial statements under both lease and purchase options

Let's compare the profit or loss for the period and the closing statement of financial position under the leasing option and the purchase option. We'll start with the statements of profit or loss:

	Lease option $000	Purchase Option $000	Comment
Revenue	80,000	80,000	
Operating costs	(68,000)	(66,760)	Rental of $9.24 million not included but depreciation of $8 million added in
Operating profit	12,000	13,240	
Finance costs	(2,000)	(4,000)	Includes interest of 5% on additional $40 million loan
Pre-tax profit	10,000	9,240	
Tax	(2,000)	(1,848)	Assumes changed treatment is allowed for tax purposes
Post-tax profit	8,000	7,392	

We now proceed to a comparison of the statements of financial position:

	Lease option $000	Purchase Option $000	Comment
Non-current assets	66,000	98,000	Includes asset purchased for $40m at the **start** of the year less 20% depreciation of $8m (66,000 + 40,000 − 8,000)
Current assets	44,000	44,000	
	110,000	142,000	
Equity	48,000	47,392	
Non-current liabilities (loans)	40,000	65,158	Includes the non-current portion of the loan (25,158)
Current liabilities	22,000	29,450	Reduced by the slightly lower tax charge (152) but includes the current portion of the loan (7,602)(22,000 + 7,602 − 152)
	110,000	142,000	

Impact on return on capital employed

As a final step, let's compare some accounting ratios under the two options for the period immediately following the acquisition of the asset. This is done in the following table:

	Lease option	*Purchase Option*	*Comment*
Closing equity ($000)	48,000	47,392	
Closing loans ($000)	40,000	72,760	Includes both current and non-current elements of the loan (32,760)
Closing capital employed ($000)	88,000	120,152	
Closing gearing ratio	45%	61%	Measuring gearing as loans expressed as a percentage of capital employed (Loans plus equity)
Operating profit ($000)	12,000	13,240	
Return on capital employed	14%	11%	Measuring return on capital employed as operating profit expressed as a percentage of capital employed

This example shows that under the leasing option we report lower borrowing ratios (gearing) and higher returns on capital employed. Both those factors would be regarded as indicating a superior performance when compared to the purchase option.

The argument could of course be made that the two scenarios are different. However, when you analyse the underlying commercial effect of the two options they are basically identical; under both options the entity is given the use of an asset for its entire useful economic life and under both options identical payments are made at the end of each accounting period. It would, therefore, be misleading to users for the two options to be reported differently under scenarios such as the one we have illustrated in the above example. This is particularly important for those companies who make extensive use of leases given the big differences it can make on apparent economic performance.

Before there were any standards on accounting for leases financial analysts and sophisticated investors tried to estimate what the financial position and profitability of lessees would have been if they had borrowed and purchased the assets they had leased. Of course, these estimates varied because they were based on partial information. This, in itself, led to requirements that there be more disclosure in the notes to the accounts regarding the nature of the leases used and the amount and timing of payments.

The example that we have just been through assumed that the lease was for an asset which was held for essentially the life of the asset so as to be comparable to an outright purchase of the asset. Then the situations were as close as possible to being equivalent and so the differences in the comparisons were a good indicator of the differences caused by the different accounting treatments.

However, not all leases are equivalent, or close to equivalent, to a purchase such as when they are for a much shorter period than the life of an asset. This led to the introduction of an accounting standard with different accounting treatments depending on whether the lease was equivalent to a sale or whether they represent the use of assets for a shorter period.

Those leases which were not equivalent to purchases were called operating leases. In that event they **were under the previous accounting standard** treated in the traditional way in the **lessee's** books with the cost being recognised as expense in the current period and most future obligations not appearing. The lease example above reflected that method. Once again, the sophisticated investors tried to quantify the amount of such leases and their implications for leverage ratios.

Thus, we then had an accounting standard which treated **the equivalent of purchases** as the purchase of an asset which was the right of use of the physical asset rather than the physical asset itself, and a corresponding (primarily longer term) liability. These were called finance leases.

This induced some companies to modify their leases to make them satisfy the conditions to be classified as operating leases so that they would not appear as an asset and liability in the balance sheet of the lessee.

In 2005 the SEC estimated that $1.25 trillion of obligations were off balance sheet. (This paragraph is based on IFRS 16 Leases, Effects Analysis, 2016. www.ifrs.orgCurrent-Projects/IASB-Projects/Leases/Documents/IFRS_16_effects_analysis.pdf (January 2016).) Some industries use leases more than others with airlines, retailers, leisure and travel, and transport being the heaviest user groups. Other industries use leases but to a lesser extent. Also the use of leases varies across regions, with the North America and Europe being heavy users of leases. Because of the widespread use of leases, and the major consequences for financial reporting for some companies, any change to the system involves long periods of consultation and learning of the practical issues involved. In the latest revision of the standard the Financial Accounting Standards Board (FASB) and the International Accounting Standards Board set out to develop a new joint standard. In 2009 the IASB issued a discussion paper outlining the issues followed by an exposure draft in 2010. In 2013 a revised draft was issued. As a result of feedback including advisory bodies, 1,700 comment letters received, public roundtables and outreach activities and interaction with the FASB (USA) with their own feedback on practical issues, a new standard (IFRS 16) was issued in January 2016 with operation from January 2019. Note that while the two boards agreed on the broad principles they made different trade-offs in relation to practical issues as well as transitional arrangements. (Ernst and Young has a US GAAP/IFRS accounting differences identifier.)

While the IASB did not say so this illustrates how difficult it is to change standards which have major implications for accounting for important companies. This also reflects the wide variety of lease terms and conditions, the work involved in reworking the financial information to meet the new definitions and procedures, and the size of the impacts on the reports of many companies.

2017 Examples of lease accounting under the previous rules

To give some actual examples of the size and varieties of leases some details extracted from the 2017 financial reports of selected European companies will be presented. One large listed company was identified from each of the top three industries said to be high users of leases. Note that these will have been reported under the older rules for lessee accounting and in the 2019 or 2020 accounts the lessee will show all leases as rights of use assets unless they satisfy the exemptions which should only account for a small proportion (value wise) of leases.

The International Airlines Group which owns British Airways mentioned under both finance and operating leases planes, property, plant and equipment. The present value of financial leases was €5,507 million. These would be reflected in assets and liabilities. The operating leases covered aircraft (up to 14 years in length), property, plant and equipment up to 21 years. Mention was also made of a ground lease which runs for 128 years. Under the life of the existing operating leases it was disclosed that operating lease payments in the next year will be €992 million followed in subsequent years by payments in aggregate of a further €6,650 million. These operating leases would not have been reported in the assets and liabilities of the company under the rules in effect in 2017. In addition, in a discussion of the future impact of the new lease accounting standard they said they would have to make judgements as to what extent agreements relating to terminal capacity fall within the definition of a lease.

Tesco plc shows in note 34 finance leases where the present value of the minimum lease payments is £114 million. On the other hand, operating lease payments, which are not discounted, amount to payments of £1,199 million in the next year and £11,162 million in total in the years beyond one year.

Thomas Cook Group plc discloses financial leases in note 20 and operating leases in note 27. Finance leases primarily relate to leases of aircraft and aircraft parts and have a present value in the balance sheet of £39 million for items payable with one year and £115 million for payments beyond one year. In the note on operating leases, which of course are not included in their balance sheet, they identify two categories: property and other covering retail shops and hotels, and aircrafts and spares. Cashflows within one year for operating leases were £227 million and a further £1,242 million for future periods combined. Thus the uncapitalised lease payments were significant compared to the financial leases which were included in the balance sheet. This demonstrates why the accounting bodies thought it was necessary to revise the accounting standard to require the lessees record assets and liabilities reflecting the existence of the right of use and the ongoing obligations under the lease. There are some exceptions which will be discussed shortly.

Example of a company in distress

Another example of the importance of capitalising operating leases is the case of Borders Group Inc., a major book shop chain which collapsed in 2011. It had a large number of operating leases that could not be cancelled or sublet. Most of those liabilities did not appear in the statement of financial position in accordance with the standard at that time. This illustrates the need for a standard which required all significant lease obligations to be incorporated in the body of the financial statements.

6.3 Terms and conditions of a lease

A lease is defined in IFRS 16 as 'a contract, or part of a contract, that conveys the right to use an asset (the **underlying asset**) for a period of time in exchange for consideration'.

Leasing a car

A lease which you might be aware of is a lease of a car. Under the contract, the owner of the car (either a car dealer or more likely a financier) might agree that the lessee can have use of the car for a fixed period, say five years, and in return the lessee agrees to pay a monthly payment over the five-year period to cover the use of the vehicle and the cost of the insurance taken out by the lessor (financier).

Also, to protect the lessor, the agreement might have conditions such as the lessee will regularly service the car and keep it clean and in good condition. Further, if the lessee fails to make payments on time, the lessor (financier) has the right to repossess the car and sue for outstanding amounts owing and losses incurred as a result of the failure to honour the contract. At the end of the lease the car must be returned to the financier in good condition for its age.

Obviously terms and conditions can vary depending on the agreement of the parties and local laws. An example might be that there could be an option to extend the contract for a further five years or the right to purchase the car at an agreed price at the end of the contract. That agreed price could be the market value of the car at the end of the lease or a lower price designed to induce the lessee to purchase the car outright. Alternatively, the lessee could be required to guarantee the value of the car at the end of the lease, and in the event that the car is worth less at the end of the contract the lessee will have to pay the shortfall.

Leasing a shop

Another type of lease that you may have heard of is a lease of a shop in a shopping centre. A hypothetical example might be as follows:

Extraordinary Coffee and Cake shop agrees to occupancy of a specified shop for three years on the payment of a base amount of £2,000 a week. The occupier is responsible for internal fittings at their own expense and must restore the shop to its original condition at the end of the lease. At the end of the lease the lessee has the right to nominate a desire to extend the lease and the shopping centre may accept or reject that proposal. In addition to the base amount of the weekly payment there will be increased payments each quarter based on the rate of increase in the turnover of the major tenant in the shopping centre.

6.3.1 Determining whether a contract is a lease under IFRS 16

The new standard requires that **the lessee** must have **control** over the **use of an identified asset** for it to fall within the scope of the standard.

So in the lease of the car example above there is a right to a specific car namely the one the customer identified in the show room and they have freedom to use the car as they like within the restriction of the protective clause that the car must be kept in reasonable condition for its age. Thus reasonable restrictions to protect the interests of the owner of the vehicle does not undermine the concept of control. The standard specifies in B9 to have the right of control 'throughout the *period of use,* the customer has both of the following:

(a) The right to obtain substantially all of the economic benefits from use of the identified asset and

(b) The right to direct the use of the identified asset . . . '

The additional guide lines cover guidance on borderline cases. Normally the supplier cannot have the right to substitute alternative assets but there is an exception under very restrictive circumstances outlined in the guidance.

Also the customer (potential lessee) has to have the right to decide on the use of the asset, or alternatively the asset has been designed for a specific purpose by the customer, and the customer must make the operational decisions in relation to the asset. Only then does it qualify as a lease under the standard. For example, a contract to ship goods overseas would not constitute a lease because the customer would not normally control the ship. The goods would be transported with other goods and the ship would be under the control of the shipping company and not the customer. So long as the ship remains under the control of the shipping company it is not a lease.

What would not fall within this definition?

A lease is not accounted for under IFRS 16 if it falls within the scope of the following:

(a) Biological assets under IAS 41 Agriculture

(b) Service concession arrangements under IFRIC 12 Service Concession Arrangements

(c) Licences of intellectual property covered by IFRS 15 Revenue from Contracts with Customers

(d) Rights held by lessees under licensing agreements under IAS38 Intangible Assets (e.g. films, videos, plays, manuscripts, patents and copyrights)

(e) Leases to explore for or use minerals, oil, natural gas or similar are not covered by IFRS 16.

Electing not to recognise

A lessee may elect not to recognise right of use assets and associated liabilities under IFRS 16 for assets where the lease is for less than 12 months at the commencement of the lease and does not contain an option to purchase) or for leases of low value (i.e. the asset new is of low value). (Note the FASB does not have an exemption for low value leases.)

6.3.2 Separating out the lease component

Often a contract is for the supply of both equipment under a lease and a number of related services. An example of this is the lease of pleasure boat plus the provision of the insurance through annual payments in arrears. However, it may be much more complicated than this. To account for the lease it is first necessary to divide the contract into two components, namely the lease contract and the non-lease component. If there is a clearly identifiable market prices (preferably from the lessor) for both the non-lease component and for the lease of the asset alone, then it is possible to separate the cost of the contract into its two components for accounting purposes. This is done on a proportionate basis.

Example:
If individual standalone components costs are:

Non-lease component   2,000 per annum
Lease component   12,000 per annum

And

The   Combined contract   13,580 per annum

Calculate the lease component in the combined package:

Lease component × Combined contract cost
(Non-lease component + lease component)

$$\frac{12,000 \times 13,580}{(2,000 + 12,000)}$$

$$= 11,640$$

For lease accounting purpose the annual lease payment is 11,640

6.4 Leases in the financial statements of lessees under IFRS 16

Lessees recognise a **right of use asset** and **an associated liability** at the inception of the lease.

At the commencement date, a lessee shall measure the lease liability at the present value of lease payments that are not paid at that date. The lease payments shall be discounted using the interest rate implicit in the lease, if that rate can be readily determined. If that rate cannot be readily determined, the lessee shall use the lessee's incremental borrowing rate (paragraph 26)

This means the forecast future payments have to be (a) identified and (b) estimated and discounted. Items that would be include are:

(a) Scheduled fixed payments under the lease.
(b) Expected variable lease payments. (In the shop lease example the additional payments expected because of the increase in the turnover of the major tenant would have to be included.)

(c) The expected amount payable because of the guaranteed residual value. You would have to forecast what you think the asset will be worth at the termination of the lease and if it is lower than the guaranteed residual, the difference will have to be paid at the end of the lease.

(d) If the lease contract includes an option to extend the lease an assessment has to be made whether the extension of the lease term is so favourable as to make it likely that the lease will be extended. IF the assessment is that at the commencement of the lease it appears reasonably certain that the lease will be extended then the forward schedule of payments must include the payments under the extension.

(e) If the lease contains a termination penalty and the lessee anticipates a termination then that payment must be included.

The lease liability will be treated like a liability bearing a rate of interest equal to the discount rate and being reduced by payments under the terms of the lease.

Having determined the present value of the lease liability, it is then possible to calculate the amount of the right-of-use asset. Its measurement will consist of:

(a) The present value of the lease liability

PLUS:

(b) Any lease payments made before or at the commencement of the lease less any incentives received. If a landlord agreed to advertise your relocation to the shopping centre as an inducement to change locations then the cost of such advertising could be offset against the cost of the asset.

(c) Any initial direct cost. In the coffee shop and café example that would include the installation of fittings and fixtures, sign writing etc.

(d) Estimated costs at the termination of the lease such as removal of fixtures and fittings and restoring the shop to its original state at the end of the lease. (See IAS 37 *Provisions, Contingent Liabilities and Contingent Assets.*)

The right of use asset will be identified with the appropriate asset class and treated in the same way as that class is normally accounted for. If the asset class is normally recorded at cost and amortised over its useful life then that the equivalent right of use asset will be treated in the same way. If the class is normally accounted for using fair value (e.g. IAS 40 *Investment Property*) then the associated right of use asset will be accounted for in the same manner.

6.4.1 A numerical example (based on one of the IFRS 16 Illustrative examples)

A lessee enters into a 10-year lease of a floor of a building, with an option to extend for a further five years. Lease payments are £50,000 per year during the initial term and £55,000 per year during the optional period, all payable at the beginning of each year.

To obtain the lease, the *lessee* incurred initial direct costs of £20,000 of which £15,000 relates to a payment to a former tenant occupying that floor of the building and £5,000 relates to a commission paid to the property agent that arranged the lease. As an incentive to the lessee for entering into the lease, the lessor agreed to reimburse to the lessee the agent's commission of £5,000.

At the commencement date the lessee:

● concluded that it is not reasonably certain to exercise the option to extend the lease and, therefore, determined that the lease term is 10 years;

- calculates the interest rate implicit in the lease at 5% per annum;
- makes the lease payment for the first year, incurs initial direct costs, receives lease incentives from the lessor;
- calculates the lease liability to be £355,400 being the present value of the remaining nine payments of £50,000, discounted at the interest rate of 5 per cent per annum; and
- makes the following accounting entries:

	DR £	CR £
Cash (up front rental payment)		50,000
Lease liability (present value of future lease payments		355,400
Right of use asset	405,400	
Cash (initial direct costs)		20,000
Right of use asset	20,000	
Cash (lease incentive)	5,000	
Right of use asset		5,000

The carrying amount of the right of use asset after these entries is £420,400 (£405,400 + £20,000 − £5,000) and consequently the annual depreciation charge will be £42,040 (£420,400 × 1/10).

The lease liability will be measured using amortised cost principles. In order to help us with the example in the following section, we will measure the lease liability up to and including the end of year 6. This is done in the following table (note that in the case of year 1 the opening liability includes the up-front payment and so it is £405,400 (£355,400 + £50,000).

Year	Balance b/fwd £	Rental £	Balance in period £	Finance Cost (5%) £	Balance c/fwd £
1	405,400	(50,000)	355,400	17,770	373,170
2	373,170	(50,000)	323,170	16,159	339,329
3	339,329	(50,000)	289,329	14,466	303,795
4	303,795	(50,000)	253,795	12,690	266,485
5	266,485	(50,000)	216,485	10,824	227,309
6	227,309	(50,000)	177,309	8,865	186,174

The carrying value of the right of use asset at the end of year 6 will be £168,160 (£420,400 − 6 × £42,040).

The lease liability at the end of year 6 is £186,174.

6.4.2 Lease modifications

A lessee should re-measure the lease liability by discounting the revised lease payments using a revised discount rate, if either:

(a) there is a change in the lease term, or

(b) there is a change in the assessment of an option to purchase the underlying asset, assessed considering relevant events and circumstances in the context of a purchase option.

In both cases, the lessee should:

- revise its estimate of the present value of the future lease payments using the revised implicit interest rate (or if that is not identifiable then use the firm's incremental borrowing rate at the date of the reassessment);
- adjust the lease liability; and
- make a corresponding adjustment to the right of use asset.

The only exception here is if the adjustment would reduce the right of use asset to a negative carrying amount. In such circumstances, the right of use asset would be reduced to a carrying amount of nil and any further adjustment would be recognised in profit or loss.

Illustration where option to extend is exercised

Let us continue the example we started in 18.4.1 above with the addition of the following information at the end of year 6 of the original lease:

- At the end of year 6 the business of the lessee is prospering and the cost of leasing comparable space has risen by 20%. This creates an incentive for the lessee to exercise its option to extend the lease for a further five years after the end of the primary lease term at the revised rental of £55,000.

The impact of this reassessment is to increase the remaining lease term to nine years (four years left of the primary lease term plus the five-year option term). The revised rate of interest implicit in the lease is 6% per annum.

Lease liability is re-measured

The lease liability at the end of year 6 will now be the present value of four annual payments in advance of £50,000 plus the present value of five subsequent annual payments in advance of £55,000.

The present value of the four annual payments of £50,000 using an annual discount rate of 6% would be £183,650 [£50,000 + (£50,000 × 2.673)] (remember the lease payments are made in advance at the start of the year).

Similarly, the present value of the five annual payments of £55,000 starting in four years, would be £194,495 [£55,000 + (£55,000 × 3.465) (the present value of four payments of £1 in arrears at an annual discount rate of 6%)] × 0.792 (the present value of £1 payable in four years' time at an annual discount rate of 6%).

So the total revised lease liability would be re-measured to £378,145 (£183,650 + £194,495).

As the liability at the end of year six was £186,174, the increase will be £191,971 (£378,145 − £186,174).

The right of use asset (420,400 less 6 × 42040 being the amortisation = 168,160) will be increased by the same amount and so will be carried at a revised amount of £360,131 (£168,160 + £191,971). Assuming an even consumption of economic benefits future deprecation charges will be on a straight-line basis over a nine-year period and will be £40,015 (£360,131 × 1/9).

The change in the revised lease liability going forward will be as follows:

Year	Balance b/fwd £	Rental £	Balance in period £	Finance Cost (6%) £	Balance c/fwd £
7	378,145	(50,000)	328,145	19,689	347,834
8	347,834	(50,000)	297,834	17,870	315,704
9	315,704	(50,000)	265,704	15,942	281,646
10	281,646	(50,000)	231,646	13,899	245,545
11	245,545	(55,000)	190,545	11,433	201,978
12	201,978	(55,000)	146,978	8,819	155,797
13	155,797	(55,000)	100,797	6,048	106,845
14	106,845	(55,000)	51,845	3,111	54,956
15	54,956	(55,000)	(44)	44	Nil

The amount of 44 is a rounding difference.

6.4.3 A simplified approach for short-term or low-value leases

A short-term lease is a lease that, at the date of commencement, has a term of 12 months or less. Lessees can elect to treat short-term leases by recognising the lease rentals as an expense over the lease term rather than recognising a 'right of use asset' and a lease liability. The election needs to be made for relevant leased assets on a 'class-by-class' basis. For this purpose, a class of underlying asset is a grouping of underlying assets of a similar nature and use in an entity's operations.

This effectively allows lessees to continue to treat short-term leases as they would have treated operating leases under the old IAS 17 leasing standard. Note that a lease that contains a purchase option cannot be a short-term lease.

A similar election – *on a lease-by-lease basis* – can be made in respect of 'low value assets'. The assessment of whether an underlying asset is of low value is performed on an absolute basis. Leases of low-value assets qualify for the simplified accounting treatment explained above regardless of whether those leases are material to the lessee. The assessment is not affected by the size, nature or circumstances of the lessee. Accordingly, different lessees are expected to reach the same conclusions about whether a particular underlying asset is of low value.

An underlying asset can be of low value only if:

(a) the lessee can benefit from use of the underlying asset on its own or together with other resources that are readily available to the lessee; and

(b) the underlying asset is not highly dependent on, or highly interrelated with, other assets.

A lease of an underlying asset does not qualify as a lease of a low-value asset if the nature of the asset is such that, when new, the asset is typically not of low value. For example, leases of cars would not qualify as leases of low-value assets because a new car would typically not be of low value.

Examples of low-value underlying assets can include tablets and personal computers, small items of office furniture and telephones.

6.4.4 Presentation and disclosures in the lessee financial reports

The lessee is required to show separately right-of-use assets (other than investment properties) and lease liabilities either in the financial statements or in the notes to the financial statements. If disclosure is in the notes there must be details of the line item to which it relates. The statement of profit and loss and other comprehensive income shall show the depreciation related to the right of use asset separately from interest on the lease liability which has to be classified as a finance cost. Also for the short-term leases, and those of low value, which did not give rise to a right of use asset then the expense for the period should be disclosed.

Other disclosure items include:

(a) variable lease payments not included in the calculation of the lease liabilities;

(b) total cash outflows for leases;

(c) additions to right-of-use assets;

(d) subleases (that is where a leased asset is leased on to another party);

(e) gains or losses from the sale and lease back transactions;

(f) a separate maturity analysis of lease liabilities.

The nature of the leasing activities of the company and the future exposures related to leasing (e.g. variable payments, guarantees, termination costs, future commitments to additional leases) also have to be disclosed.

6.5 Leases in the financial statements of lessors

6.5.1 Introduction

Accounting for leases in the financial statements of lessors is essentially unchanged from IAS 17 and the distinction between finance and operating leases is still highly relevant.

A **finance lease** is 'a lease that transfers substantially all the risks and rewards incidental to ownership of an **underlying asset**' and an **operating lease** is 'a **lease** that does not transfer substantially all the risks and rewards incidental to ownership of an **underlying asset.**'

Examples of leases which would probably be finance leases include leases which include the transfer of the title to the asset by the end of the lease, or contain an attractive purchase option (where the option price is expected to be sufficiently lower than the fair market value when the option can be exercised so as to make it reasonably certain that the option will be exercised).

Another type of finance lease is where the lease is for the major part of the economic life of the lease asset or the present value of the lease payments calculated at the inception of the lease represents substantially all of the fair value of the underlying asset. Also where the asset subject to the lease is of a specialised nature designed to fit the needs of the lessee with the result that it would need major modifications to suit the needs of other users then the transaction is treated as a financial lease. Other situations may also fit the definition of a finance lease.

6.5.2 Finance leases in the books of the lessor

The lessor does not recognise the leased asset as property, plant and equipment but instead recognises a lease receivable equal to the cost of entering into the lease. Then the present value of the amounts expected under the lease is deemed equal to the lease receivable. The rate of implicit interest in the lease is the discount rate which makes the two equal. The expected amount amounts to be received under the lease will depend upon the circumstances of each case. It could include the minimum lease payments if the purchase option is not expected to be attractive, and the expected resale price at the end of the lease, or if the amount which has been guaranteed is expected to be higher than that amount then the guaranteed is included instead of the expected resale price.

Example where the lessor purchases the assets that is then leased

Assume a lessor has purchased an item of plant for £60,000 and leased it to a lessee on a five-year finance lease. Annual lease rentals, payable in arrears, were £15,000. The life of the plant was estimated at five years and there was no estimated residual value at the end of the five-year period. The lessor incurred direct cost of £2,000 in arranging the lease.

The rate of interest implicit in the lease is the discount rate that must be applied to the lease payments to make their present value equal to the costs (£60,000 + £2,000). By trial and error, this percentage can be computed as approximately 6.7%. The reader may wish to confirm that, at a discount rate of 6.7%, the present value of five payments of £15,000 in arrears is approximately £62,000 (the fair value of the asset plus the initial direct costs of the lessor). Therefore, assuming the lessor has purchased the asset for leasing on to the lessee, the lessor makes the following accounting entry:

Credit: Cash £62,000 (£60,000 + £2,000).

Debit: Net investment in finance leases (shown as a lease receivable).

Over the five-year lease term, the net investment in the finance lease is increased by the finance lease income (which is taken to the profit or loss) and reduced by the lease rentals received, as shown in the following table:

Year	Balance b/fwd £	Finance income (6.7%) £	Rental £	Balance c/fwd £
1	62,000	4,154	(15,000)	51,154
2	51,154	3,427	(15,000)	39,581
3	39,581	2,652	(15,000)	27,233
4	27,233	1,825	(15,000)	14,058
5	14,058	942	(15,000)	Nil

At the end of year one the entries in the lessor's books would be:

Dr Lease receivable	4,154	
Cr Interest revenue	4,154	

(To record the earning of interest revenue which will be transferred to the profit and loss)

Dr Bank	15,000	
Cr Lease receivable		15,000

(Being the receipt of the first payment under the lease)

Example where lessor manufactures the asset that is leased

The above example assumes the asset was purchased by the lessor for leasing on to the lessee. If the lessor has manufactured the asset then at the inception of the lease the lessor recognises a selling profit based on the fair value of the asset at the date of the lease or, if lower, the present value of the minimum lease payments.

Suppose, in the previous example, that the lessor had manufactured the leased asset at a total manufacturing cost of £48,000. The lessor would make the following accounting entries at the commencement of the finance lease:

	Debit £	Credit £	Comment
Revenue		60,000	Recording the 'sale' of the asset at the lower of its
Net investment in finance lease	60,000		fair value (£60,000) and the present value of the minimum lease payments (£62,000)
Inventory		48,000	Recording a cost of sale of £48,000 and therefore
Cost of sales	48,000		a gross profit of £12,000 (£60,000 − £48,000)
Cash		2,000	Recording the initial direct costs of establishing
Net investment in finance lease	2,000		the lease as part of the net investment in finance leases

The remainder of the accounting is as shown in the example above.

6.5.3 Operating leases in the books of the lessor

Where the lease is an operating lease the relevant asset is recorded as property, plant and equipment by the lessor. Lease rentals are recognised as income over the lease term, normally on a straight-line basis.

Example

A property company lets out two floors of an office block on a three-year operating lease. The lessee made an up-front payment of £120,000 followed by three annual payments of £70,000, payable in arrears.

The property would remain as property, plant and equipment of the lessor. The total lease rentals of £330,000 (£120,000 + 3 × £70,000) would be recognised as lease income over the three-year period at an amount of £110,000 each year. In year one, the lessor would make the following accounting entry:

Debit: Cash £190,000 (£120,000 + £70,000).

Credit: Profit or loss £110,000. (being rental income)

Credit: Deferred income £80,000.

In each of years two and three the lessor would make the following accounting entry:

Debit: Cash £70,000.

Debit: Deferred income £40,000 (£80,000 × $\frac{1}{2}$).

Credit: Profit or loss £110,000.

6.6 Sale and leaseback transactions

6.6.1 Introduction to sale and leaseback

Companies with valuable assets such as land and buildings have the possibility of raising finance by executing a mortgage over the land and buildings. However, it may be possible to raise more finance by selling the property to a finance company and the property is then leased to the original owner whereby the asset remains under the control of the original owner. Since the two transactions are really a single package which are negotiated together it is possible that the terms are such that profit recognition is managed across periods.

One possibility is that the sale price of the property is inflated but the financier recovers through higher interest/lease payments.

Another possibility is the price placed on the property is low with a lowered interest rate incorporated in the lease to compensate. To prevent any such manipulation rules have been placed around the accounting for sale and leasebacks.

Firstly, to record a sale the transaction must satisfy the conditions for recognising a sale under IFRS 15 *Revenue from Contracts with Customers*. The satisfaction of the relevant performance obligations under that standard would constitute an effective 'transfer' of asset to the lessor by the previous owner (now the lessee).

If it is a sale, the next step is to determine whether the whole of the asset has been sold or only a proportion. If effectively only a portion has been sold, the profit on sale in the lessee's books is only recorded in relation to the part that has been sold.

6.6.2 Transaction constituting a sale

If the transaction does constitute a 'sale' under IFRS 15 then the treatment is as follows:

- The seller-lessee shall measure the right-of-use asset arising from the leaseback. That is done to measure the part of the asset which effectively stays in the hands of the lessee and therefore is not treated as having been sold at that point in time. Accordingly, the seller-lessee shall recognise only the amount of any gain or loss that relates to the rights transferred to the buyer-lessor.

- The buyer-lessor shall account for the purchase of the asset applying applicable standards, and for the lease applying the lessor accounting requirements in IFRS 16.

If the fair value of the consideration for the sale of an asset does not equal the fair value of the asset, or if the payments for the lease are not at market rates, an entity shall make the following adjustments to measure the sale proceeds at fair value:

- Any below-market terms shall be accounted for as a prepayment of lease payments; and

- Any above-market terms shall be accounted for as additional financing provided by the buyer-lessor to the seller-lessee.

The entity shall measure any potential adjustment required by the above process on the basis of the more readily determinable of:

- The difference between the fair value of the consideration for the sale and the fair value of the asset; and

- The difference between the present value of the contractual payments for the lease and the present value of payments for the lease at market rates.

6.6.3 A numerical example (based on one of the IFRS 16 Illustrative examples)

Entity A sells a building to entity B for cash of £2,000,000 and leases it back for 18 years. The terms and conditions of the transaction are such that the transfer of the building by A satisfies the requirements for determining when a performance obligation is satisfied in IFRS 15 – *Revenue from Contracts with Customers,* i.e. it can be recognised as a sale.

Accordingly, A and B account for the transaction as a sale and leaseback with A entering into a contract with B for the right to use the building for 18 years, with annual payments of £120,000 payable at the end of each year.

Immediately before the transaction, the building is carried at a cost of £1,000,000 and its fair value at the date of sale and leaseback is £1,800,000. The interest rate incorporated in the lease is 4.5% per annum.

To account for these transactions we have to get to the substance of the transactions as opposed to the legal form. The first item of interest here is the agreement to 'sell' the asset above market value. A purchaser is not going to pay above market value unless they will recover that as part of the agreement. In this case it will be by increasing the lease payments. So the extra advance above the market value is an additional loan.

If an asset is sold and then leased for the whole of its economic life there would be no grounds for recognising a profit because, in essence, the control of the asset stays with the original owner and all that has happened is that finance has been raised using the asset as security.

However, if the asset is leased for only part of the life of the asset then part of the ownership rights have been transferred to the purchaser and hence to that extent a sale has been realised at the commencement of the lease when an amount for revenue, cost and profit will be reported.

The essence of the complicated arrangements in the example are as follows:

(a) A loan at 4.5% p.a. has been made by B to A through agreeing to a resale valuation of £2 million versus the £1.8 million market value. The difference of £200,000 being the amount of an additional loan.

(b) The 'lease payments of 120,000' discounted at 4.5% p.a. give a present value of £1,459,200. As £200,000 of this is really repayment of the additional loan then the true lease payments have a present value of £1,259,200. This figure relates to the 'value' of rights of use leased back.

Revenue

Therefore the part not covered by the lease and hence deemed transferred to B is the market value (1,800,000) minus the leased amount (1,259,200) equals 540,800. You can in this case treat as revenue from the sale of the asset £540,800.

Cost

The cost amount for that part that has been sold as part of the entering into the lease agreement is based on an apportionment of the total cost of the asset. The proportion sold is 540,800 at selling price as a fraction of the market value of the total asset namely 1,800,000. This fraction is then used to identify the part of the original cost of one million which has been sold. (540,800 ÷ 1,800,000) × 1,000,000 = 300,444.

Profit

The initial profit on sale is 540,800(proceeds) − 300,444(cost) = 240,356(profit).

(c) The 'real' lease payments would be arrived at by apportioning the agreement amount of 120,000 between the loan with a present value of 200,000 and the lease with a present value of 1,259,200. The loan calculation is:

$$\frac{120,000 \times 200,000}{(200,000 + 1,259,200)} = 16,447$$

The payments on the lease calculation:

As 16,447 represents payments on the additional loan, the remainder of the payment of 103,553 payments on the lease.

(d) The right of use asset is the original cost of the asset less the cost which relates to the sale or 1,000,0000 less 300,444 equals 699,556.

Accounting by A

Overall, on the sale and leaseback A would make the following accounting entry:

Debit: Cash £2,000,000

Debit: Right-of-use asset £699,556

Credit: Building £1,000,000

Credit: Financial liability (loan) £200,000

Credit: Lease liability £1,259,200

Credit: Gain on rights transferred £240,356

(Recognising the receipt of cash and the initial recording of the overall agreement)

Accounting by B

At the commencement date, B accounts for the transaction as follows.

Debit: Building £1,800,000 (recognising the acquired building at fair value)

Debit: Financial asset £200,000 (the 'financing' element of the transaction).

Credit: Cash £2,000,000

Going forward, B will account for the lease by treating £103,553 (see above for a derivation of this figure) of the annual payments of £120,000 as lease payments. The remaining £16,447 (£120,000 − £103,553) of annual payments received from A are accounted for as payments received to settle the financial asset of £200,000 and interest revenue. The split is illustrated below (the first five years only for illustrative purposes):

Year	Balance b/fwd £	Finance income (4.5%) £	Received £	Balance c/fwd £
1	200,000	9,000	(16,447)	192,553
2	192,553	8,665	(16,447)	184,771
3	184,771	8,315	(16,447)	176,639
4	176,639	7,949	(16,447)	168,141
5	168,141	7,566	(16,447)	159,260

The building will be depreciated in accordance with the company's policy for that class of assets.

6.6.4 Transaction not constituting a 'sale'

In the event that the agreement does not qualify as a sale under IFRS 15 then under those circumstances the seller does not 'transfer' the asset and continues to recognise it. The 'sales proceeds' are recognised as a financial liability and accounted for by applying IFRS 9 – *Financial Instruments*.

In the same circumstances, the 'buyer' recognises a financial asset equal to the 'sales proceeds'.

Summary

Leasing has been a difficult issue for accounting for a considerable time. The challenge was that, according to the predominant legal view, leases did not constitute a liability except for past use of assets which have not yet been paid. This resulted in an accounting treatment which was viewed by accountants as deficient in that it did not highlight the amount of leverage that heavy users of leases had and also made their operating performance in terms of return on assets higher. The solution of disclosure in notes to the accounts imposed costs on financial analysts and even then they were unsure whether their adjustments were accurate. The next step was to adopt substance over form and to require financial leases to be included in the balance sheet of lessees by recognise a right of use asset and the ongoing obligations under the lease as a liability. Operating leases however were effectively treated as an expense in the lessees' books as incurred. While that was an improvement it did not show the whole story and it encouraged writing of contracts to avoid having to treat them as financial leases. In its Effects Analysis the IFRS outlined the need for change stating that in 2005, the US Securities and Exchange Commission (SEC) estimated that US public companies may have approximately US$1.25 trillion of off-balance sheet leases. To overcome this situation the FASB and the IASB introduced new leasing standards which moved most of the off-balance sheet items on to the books in the accounts of the lessees. They adopted the same principles but differed in terms of adjustments to facilitate practical implementation.

Applying IFRS 16, a lessee company is required for all leases, except leases of low-value assets or short-term leases (at commencement has a twelve-month term or less), to:

(a) recognise lease assets and lease liabilities in the balance sheet, initially measuring the liability at the present value of expected cash flows associated with the lease;

(b) recognise depreciation of lease assets and interest on lease liabilities in the income statement over the lease term; and

(c) in the cash flow statement separate the total amount of cash paid into a principal portion (presented within financing activities) and interest which is treated in accordance with IAS 7 Statement of Cash Flows (normally operating or financing activities).

Applying IFRS 16 lessors recognise finance leases by recording a lease receivable rather than the cost of the physical asset. The lease payments received are effectively recognised as interest revenue and repayment of the lease receivable. Under operating leases, the lessor records the cost of the physical asset and amortises it in the normal way. Lease payments are matched to periods and recognised as revenue.

REVIEW QUESTIONS

1 'Can the legal position on leases be ignored now that substance over form is used for financial reporting?' Discuss.

2 State the factors that indicate that a lease is a finance lease under IFRS 16 and the extent to which this distinction is still relevant.

3 It could be argued that a lease is a long-term contract and that as soon as the lessee exercises control some consideration has passed and hence the contract is binding on both parties. Then accounting for leases is not substance over form but rather a recognition of the true legal position. Discuss.

4 The favourite off-balance sheet financing trick used to be leasing. Use any illustrative numerical examples you may wish to:

(a) Define the term 'off-balance sheet financing' and state why it is popular with companies.

(b) Suggest two other off-balance sheet financing techniques and discuss the effect that each technique has on statement of financial position assets and liabilities, and on the income statement.

5 The Tesco 2017 Annual Report included the following accounting policy:

'Leases

Leases are classified as finance whenever the terms of the lease transfer substantially all the risks and rewards of ownership to the lessee. All other leases are classified as operating leases.

The Group as a lessor
Amounts due from lessees under finance leases are recorded as receivables at the amount of the Group's net investment in the leases. Finance lease income is allocated to accounting periods so as to reflect a constant periodic rate of return on the Group's net investment in the lease. Rental income from operating leases is recognised on a straight-line basis over the term of the lease.

The Group as a lessee
Assets held under finance leases are recognised as assets of the Group at their fair value or, if lower, at the present value of the minimum lease payments, each determined at the inception of the lease. The corresponding liability is included in the Group balance sheet as a finance lease obligation. Lease payments are apportioned between finance charges and a reduction of the lease obligations so as to achieve a constant rate of interest on the remaining balance of the liability. Finance charges are charged to the Group income statement. Rentals payable under operating leases are charged to the Group income statement on a straight-line basis over the term of the lease.'

Provide answers to the following:

(a) Explain the meaning of 'minimum lease payments and fair value'.

(b) Explain why fair value might be higher than the discounted minimum lease payments.

(c) Explain why the aim is to arrive at a constant rate of interest.

(d) Explain why in 2017 the lessee accounts for the finance lease and the operating leases differently.

6 Given that the details of operating lease commitments were required to be disclosed in the notes to the accounts under IAS 17, discuss why it was necessary to issue a new standard which incorporates these into the statement of financial position when sophisticated investors already do such adjustments themselves?

7 Companies sometimes get special prices from suppliers if they undertake to purchase specified commodities from the supplier over a designated future period. These supply arrangements do not have to be recorded as assets and liabilities. However, in future leases will give rise to recording of assets and liabilities. Discuss why the transactions are to be treated differently.

8 Explain in your own words why in a finance lease the lessor shows in the statement of financial position a receivable rather than the unamortised amount of the initial investment in the physical asset being leased out.

9 Discuss why IFRS16 will have some impact on companies that are sensitive to gearing ratios, including those with banking covenants that are linked to balance sheet indebtedness.

10 Discuss the effect on the operating profit and EBITDA when the current operating lease expense is required to be replaced by depreciation of the lease asset and an interest expense on the lease liability.

11 Discuss the suggestion that enterprise value will rise as a result of the IFRS 16 accounting treatment of operating leases.

12 Explain why it has been suggested that the new rules in IFRS 16 could 'bring the biggest shake-up to retailers' financial statements for decades'.

13 State with your reasons:

(a) the three industries whose financial statements will be most affected by the implementation of IFRS 16, and

(b) the effect that will be seen on each of their primary financial standards.

EXERCISES

* Question 1

On 1 January 20X8, Grabbit plc entered into an agreement to lease a widgeting machine for general use in the business. The agreement, which may not be terminated by either party to it, runs for seven years and provides for Grabbit to make an annual rental payment of £92,500 on 31 December each year. The cost of the machine to the lessor was £450,329 and it has no residual value. There is no presumption that the lease will be extended. The machine has a useful economic life of eight years and Grabbit depreciates its property, plant and equipment using the straight-line method.

Required:
(a) Show how Grabbit plc will account for the above transaction in its statement of financial position at 31 December 20X8, and in its statement of comprehensive income for the year then ended, as required by IFRS 16. The rate of interest implicit in the lease is 10% if there are payments for seven years.
(b) Repeat the requirements in (a) above assuming the same lease will be extended for one year at the normal lease payment. (Note you will have to calculate the rate of interest implied by the new schedule of payments.)
(c) Explain why the standard setters considered accounting for leases to be an area in need of standardisation and discuss the rationale behind the approach adopted in the standard.
(d) The lessor has suggested that the lease could be drawn up with a minimum payment period of one year and an option to renew or purchase. The lessor alleges that this would mean the lease could be kept 'off balance sheet'. Discuss this suggestion.

* Question 2

(a) When accounting for leases, accountants prefer to overlook legal form in favour of commercial substance.

Required:

Discuss the above statement in the light of the requirements of IFRS 16 *Leases*.

(a) State briefly how you would distinguish between a finance lease and an operating lease and the extent to which it is relevant following the issue of IFRS 16.

(b) Smarty plc prepares financial statements to 31 March each year. On 1 October 20X7 it leased machinery from Hirer on the following terms:

   (i)   a lease rental of £50,000 is payable half-yearly in arrears for five years.

   (ii) the rate of interest implicit in the lease is reliably computed at 4% per half-year

   (iii) on completion of the primary period Smarty has an option to lease the asset for a further two years at a rental of £25,000, payable half-yearly in arrears. At the start of the lease it was considered unlikely that Smarty would exercise this option.

   (iv) the estimated useful economic life of the machinery at the inception of the lease was twelve years

Required:

1 Compute the carrying value of the 'right of use asset' in the statement of financial position of Smarty at 31 March 20X8 and 31 March 20X9.

2 Compute the finance cost of Smarty for the years ended 31 March 20X8 and 31 March 20X9.

3 Compute the lease liability that will be included in the statement of financial position of Smarty at 31 March 20X8 and 31 March 20X9. In both cases show the split into the current and non-current portions.

* Question 3

On 1 April 20Y1 Smarty (see question 2) reassessed its future strategy and concluded that it would take up the option to lease the machine for a further two years from 1 October 20Y2. This was regarded as a modification to the original lease and Smarty re-computed the rate of interest implicit in the lease at 3% per half year.

Required:

(a) Show how the modification would be reflected in the financial statements of Smarty for the year ended 31 March 20Y2, providing relevant extracts as in question 2.

(b) Hirer prepares financial statements to 30 September each year. Show how the lease would be accounted for by Hirer throughout its duration. You may assume that Hirer consistently retains the risks and rewards of ownership of the leased asset.

* Question 4

Bertie prepares financial statements to 31 December each year. On 1 January 20X1 Bertie purchased a machine for £200,000 and immediately leased the machine to Carter. The lease term was five years – equal to the expected useful life of the asset. Bertie estimated that the residual value of the asset at the end of the lease would be £2,000 and incurred initial direct costs of £1,500 in arranging the lease. Carter agreed to pay rentals of £50,000 per annum in arrears to lease the asset from Bertie

Required:

(a) Compute the rate of interest implicit in the lease by Bertie to Carter.

(b) Show how the arrangement will be reported in the financial statements of Bertie for the year ended 31 December 20X1. You should show the split of any relevant assets into their current and non-current portions.

* Question 5

Delta owned two assets which were sold on 1 April 20X1 – the first day of Delta's accounting period. Both assets were sold for their fair value. Details of the sales are as follows:

Asset 1

Asset 1 was sold for £500,000 and leased back on a five-year lease. The carrying amount of the asset at the date of sale was £360,000 and its estimated future economic life was ten years. The terms of the lease were that Delta would make five annual payments at the end of the financial year of £60,000 for the use of the asset. This transaction qualifies as a sale of the asset by Delta under the provisions of IFRS 15 – Revenue from Contracts with Customers.

Asset 2

Asset 2 was sold for £600,000 and leased back on a ten-year lease. The carrying amount of the asset at the date of sale was £540,000 and its estimated future economic life was ten years. The terms of the lease were that Delta would make ten annual payments of £77,703 at the end of the year for the use of the asset. This transaction does not qualify as a sale of the asset by Delta under the provisions of IFRS 15 – Revenue from Contracts with Customers.

Required:
Describe how both these assets and transactions would be reported under IFRS 16 in the financial statements of Delta for the year ended 31 March 20X2. The implicit rate of interest in both leases is 5% per annum.

* Question 6

Lightfooted purchases a machine for client Multiproductions and undertakes the installation and modifications at the premises of Multiproductions. The machine cost £63,000 and shipping and installation cost another £3,384 for a total cost of £66,384. The machine is expected to be scrapped at the end of the five-year lease and hence the residual value is expected to be zero. Lightfooted sets the interest rate at 6% per annum and receives payments at the end of the year for five years.

Required:
(a) Show all entries for the first two years in the books of Lightfooted. (Hint: first calculate the annual lease payment.)
(b) Multiproductions does not know the implicit interest rate in the lease but believes alternative sources of finance would cost 6.2% per annum. Show all the entries related to the lease in the books of Multiproductions in the first two years.

* Question 7

Under a contract between a customer named Charlie (C), and a freight carrier Solutions Ltd (S), S provides C with 10 rail cars for five years. The cars which are owned by S, are specified in the contract. C determines when, where and which goods are to be transported using the cars. When the cars are not in use, they are kept at C's premises. C can use the cars for another purpose (for example, storage) if it so chooses. If a particular car needs to be serviced or repaired, S is required to substitute a car of the same type. Otherwise, other than on default by C, S cannot retrieve the cars during the five-year period.

The contract also requires S to provide an engine and a driver when requested by C. S keeps the engines at its premises and provides instructions to the driver detailing C's requests to transport goods. S can choose to use any one of a number of engines to fulfil each of C's requests, and that one engine could be used to transport not only C's goods, but also the goods of other customers in other carriages (i.e. if other customers require the transportation of goods to same destinations or close to the destinations requested by C and within a similar timeframe), S can choose to attach up to 100 rail cars to the engine.

Required:
Advise Charlie if there is a lease in the contract under IFRS 16 in regard to the cars and the engines.

(Question based on one of the illustrative examples in IFRS 16)

CHAPTER 7

Preparation of financial statements of comprehensive income, changes in equity and financial position

7.1 Introduction

Annual Reports consist of primary financial statements, additional disclosures and narrative.

The primary financial statements should be presented using standardised formats as prescribed by International Financial Reporting Standards:

● a statement of income;

● a statement of other comprehensive income;

● a statement of changes in equity;

● a statement of financial position;

● a statement of cash flows;

● explanatory notes to the accounts.

Objectives

By the end of this chapter, you should be able to:

● understand the structure and content of published financial statements;
● prepare statements of comprehensive income, changes in equity and financial position;
● explain the nature of and reasons for notes to the accounts.

7.2 Preparing an internal statement of income from a trial balance

In this section we revise the steps taken to prepare an internal statement of income from a trial balance. These are to:

● identify year-end adjustments;

● calculate these adjustments;

● prepare an internal statement of income taking adjustments into account.

7.2.1 The trial balance of Wiggins SA

Accounts will be prepared for Wiggins SA from the trial balance set out in Figure 7.1.

7.2.2 Identify the year-end adjustments

During the year cash and credit transactions are recorded by posting to the individual ledger accounts as cash is paid or received and invoices received or issued. It is only

Figure 7.1 The trial balance for Wiggins SA as at 31 December 20X3

	€000	€000
Issued share capital (€1)		16,500
Share premium		750
Retained earnings		57,500
10% long-term loan (20X9)		63,250
Bank overdraft		6,325
Trade payables		30,650
Depreciation – buildings		2,300
– equipment		3,450
– vehicles		9,200
Freehold land	57,500	
Freehold buildings	57,500	
Equipment	14,950	
Motor vehicles	20,700	
Inventory at 1 January 20X3	43,125	
Trade receivables	28,750	
Cash in hand	4,600	
Purchases	258,750	
Bank interest	1,150	
Dividends	1,725	
Interest on loan	6,325	
Insurance	5,290	
Salaries and wages	20,355	
Motor expenses	9,200	
Taxation that was under provided	750	
Light, power, miscellaneous	4,255	
Sales		345,000
	534,925	534,925

when financial statements are being prepared that adjustments are made to ensure that the statement of income includes only income and expenses related to the current financial period.

The following information relating to accruals and prepayments has not yet been taken into account in the amounts shown in the trial balance:

- Inventory valued at cost at 31 December 20X3 was €25,875,000.
- Depreciation is to be provided as follows:
  - 2% on freehold buildings using the straight-line method;
  - 10% on equipment using the reducing balance method;
  - 25% on motor vehicles using the reducing balance method.
- €2,300,000 was prepaid for light, power and miscellaneous expenses and €5,175,000 has accrued for wages.
- Freehold land was revalued on 31 December 20X3 at €77,500,000, resulting in a gain of €20,000,000.
- Assume income tax at 20% of pre-tax profit.
- 1,500 €1 shares had been issued on 1 January 20X3 at a premium of 50c each.

7.2.3 Calculate the year-end adjustments

In this example they relate to accrued and prepaid expenses and depreciation.

W1 Salaries and wages:

€20,355,000 + accrued €5,175,000 = €25,530,000

W2 Depreciation:

Buildings	2% of €57,500,000	€1,150,000
Equipment	10% of (€14,950,000 − €3,450,000)	€1,150,000
Vehicles	25% of (€20,700,000 − €9,200,000)	€2,875,000
Total		€5,175,000

W3 Light, power and miscellaneous

€4,255,000 − prepaid €2,300,000 = €1,955,000

7.2.4 Prepare an internal statement of income after making the year-end adjustments

By way of revision, we have set out a statement of income prepared for internal purposes in Figure 7.2. We have arranged the expenses in descending monetary value. The method for doing this is not prescribed and companies are free to organise the expenses in other ways, for example in alphabetical order.

Figure 7.2 Statement of income of Wiggins SA for the year ended 31 December 20X3

		€000	€000
Sales			345,000
Less:			
Opening inventory		43,125	
Purchases		258,750	
		301,875	
Closing inventory		25,875	
Cost of sales			276,000
Gross profit			69,000
Less expenses:			
Salaries and wages	W1	25,530	
Motor expenses		9,200	
Loan interest		6,325	
Depreciation	W2	5,175	
Insurance		5,290	
Bank interest		1,150	
Light, power and miscellaneous	W3	1,955	
			54,625
Profit before tax			14,375
Income taxation (includes under-provision)			3,625
Profit after tax			10,750
Dividends (are disclosed in Statement of Changes in Equity in published format)			1,725
Retained earnings			9,025

7.3 Reorganising the income and expenses into one of the formats required for publication

Public companies are required to present their statement of income in a prescribed format to assist users making inter-company comparisons. IAS 1 allows a company two choices in the way in which it analyses the expenses, and the formats[1] are as follows:

- Format 1: Vertical with costs analysed according to function, e.g. cost of sales, distribution costs and administration expenses; or

- Format 2: Vertical with costs analysed according to nature, e.g. raw materials, employee benefits expenses, operating expenses and depreciation.

Many companies use Format 1 (unless there is an industry preference or possible national requirement to use Format 2) with the costs analysed according to function. If this format is used the information regarding the nature of expenditure (e.g. raw materials, wages and depreciation) must be disclosed in a note to the accounts. The analysis of expenses classified either by the nature of the expenses or by their function within the entity is decided by whichever provides information that is reliable and more relevant.

7.4 Format 1: classification of operating expenses and other income by function

In order to arrive at its operating profit (a measure of profit often recognised by many companies), a company needs to classify all of the operating expenses of the business into one of four categories:

- cost of sales;
- distribution and selling costs;
- administrative expenses;
- other operating income or expense.

We comment briefly on each to explain how a company might classify its trading transactions.

7.4.1 Cost of sales

Expenditure classified under cost of sales will typically include direct costs, overheads, depreciation and amortisation expense and adjustments. The items that might appear under each heading are as follows:

- Direct costs: direct materials purchased; direct labour; other external charges that comprise production costs from external sources, e.g. hire charges and subcontracting costs.
- Overheads: variable and fixed production overheads.
- Depreciation and amortisation: depreciation of non-current assets used in production and impairment expense.
- Adjustments: capitalisation of own work as a non-current asset. Any amount of the costs listed above that have been incurred in the construction of non-current assets for retention by the company will not appear as an expense in the statement of comprehensive income: it will be capitalised. Any amount capitalised in this way would be treated for accounting purposes as a non-current asset and depreciated.

7.4.2 Distribution costs

These are costs incurred after the production of the finished article and up to and including transfer of the goods to the customer. Expenditure classified under this heading will typically include the following:

- warehousing costs associated with the operation of the premises, e.g. rent, rates, insurance, utilities, depreciation, repairs and maintenance; wage costs, e.g. gross wages and pension contributions of warehouse staff;
- promotion costs, e.g. advertising, trade shows;
- selling costs, e.g. salaries, commissions and pension contributions of sales staff; costs associated with the premises, e.g. rent, rates; cash discounts on sales; travelling and entertainment;
- transport costs, e.g. gross wages and pension contributions of transport staff, vehicle costs, e.g. running costs, maintenance and depreciation.

7.4.3 Administrative expenses

These are the costs of running the business that have not been classified as either cost of sales or distribution costs. Expenditure classified under this heading will typically include:

- administration, e.g. salaries, commissions, and pension contributions of administration staff;
- costs associated with the premises, e.g. rent, rates;
- amounts written off the receivables that appear in the statement of financial position under current assets;
- professional fees.

7.4.4 Other operating income or expense

Under this heading a company discloses material income or expenses derived from ordinary activities of the business that have not been included elsewhere. If the amounts are not material, they would not be separately disclosed but included within the other captions. Items classified under these headings may typically include the following:

- income derived from intangible assets, e.g. royalties, commissions;
- income derived from third-party use of property, plant and equipment that is surplus to the current productive needs of the company;
- income received from employees, e.g. canteen, recreation fees;
- payments for rights to use intangible assets not directly related to operations, e.g. licences.

7.4.5 Finance costs

In order to arrive at the profit for the period, interest received or paid on loans and bank overdraft and investment income is disclosed under the Finance cost heading.

7.4.6 An analysis of expenses by function

An analysis of expenses would be carried out in practice in order to classify these under their appropriate function heading. These are allocated or apportioned as appropriate. The assumptions for this exercise are shown in Figure 7.3.

7.4.7 Accounting for current tax

The profit reported in the statement of income is subject to taxation at a percentage rate set by government. The resulting amount is treated as an expense in the statement of income and a current liability in the statement of financial position. However, this is an estimated figure and the amount agreed with the tax authorities in the following accounting period might be higher or lower than the estimate.

Underprovisions

If the agreed amount should be higher, it means the company has underprovided and will be required to pay an amount higher than the liability reported in the statement of financial

Figure 7.3 Assumptions made in analysing the costs

	Total €000	Cost of sales €000	Distribution costs €000	Administration expenses €000
Allocation of salaries and wages				
Factory staff	12,650	12,650		
Sales and warehouse	10,580		10,580	
Administration and accounts staff	2,300			2,300
Subtotal	25,530	12,650	10,580	2,300
An analysis of depreciation				
Freehold buildings	1,150	575	287.5	287.5
Equipment	1,150	575	287.5	287.5
Motor vehicles (allocated)	2,875		2,875	
Subtotal	5,175	1,150	3,450	575
Motor expenses (allocated)	9,200		9,200	
An apportionment of operating expenses				
on the basis of space occupied				
Insurance	5,290	2,645	1,322.5	1,322.5
Light, power and miscellaneous	1,955	977.5	488.75	488.75
Subtotal	16,445	3,622.5	11,011.25	1,811.25
TOTAL EXPENSES	47,150	17,422.5	25,041.25	4,686.25
Add material consumed	276,000	276,000		
TOTALS for statement of income	323,150	293,422.5	25,041.25	4,686.25

position – this results in a debit balance appearing in the trial balance prepared at the end of the following period. This underprovision will be added to the following year's estimated tax charged in the statement of income.

For example, if the company estimates €5,750,000 in Year 20X1 and pays €6,000,000 in 20X2 and estimates €5,220,000 in 20X2 on its 20X2 profits, then the charge in the statement of income for 20X2 will be €5,470,000 (€5,220,000 + €250,000).

Overprovisions

If overprovided the agreed tax payable will be lower, say €5,150,000, then the charge in 20X2 will be reduced by €600,000 (€5,750,000 − €5,150,000).

7.4.8 The statement of income using Format 1

Format 1 is favoured by capital markets and provides a multi-stage presentation reporting four profit measures for gross, operating, pre-tax and post-tax profit, as in Figure 7.4.

Figure 7.4 Statement of income of Wiggins SA for the year ended 31 December 20X3

	€000
Revenue	345,000.00
Cost of sales	293,422.50
Gross profit	51,577.50
Distribution costs	25,041.25
Administrative expenses	4,686.25
Operating profit	21,850.00
Finance costs	7,475.00
Profit on ordinary activities before tax	14,375.00
Income tax (2,875 + 750)	3,625.00
Profit for the year	10,750.00

7.5 Format 2: classification of operating expenses according to their nature

Note that if Format 2 is used the expenses are classified as change in inventory, raw materials, employee benefits expense, other expenses and depreciation as in Figure 7.5. The operating profit is unchanged from that appearing in Figure 7.4 using Format 1. If this format is used, the cost of sales has to be disclosed.

This method differs in that classification by nature does not require the allocation of expenses to functions. It is a format that is seen to be appropriate to particular industries such as the airline industry where it is adopted by Air China and EasyJet.

7.6 Other comprehensive income

When IAS 1 was revised in 2008 the profit and loss account or 'income statement' was replaced by the statement of comprehensive income, and a new section of 'Other comprehensive income' (OCI) was added to the previous statement of income.

Figure 7.5 Wiggins SA statement of income for the year ended 31 December 20X3

	€000	€000
Revenue		345,000
Decrease in inventory	(17,250)	
Raw materials	(258,750)	(276,000)
Employee benefit expense		
Salaries		(25,530)
Depreciation		(5,175)
Other operating expenses		
Motor expenses	(9,200)	
Insurance	(5,290)	
Light, power and miscellaneous	(1,955)	(16,445)
Operating profit		21,850

Other comprehensive income includes **unrealised** gains and losses resulting from changes in fair values of assets/liabilities such as changes in the fair value of intangible assets and property, plant and equipment; changes on the revaluation of equity investments; actuarial gains and losses on defined benefit plans and gains and losses from translating the financial statements of a foreign operation.

The statement was then retitled as 'Statement of Comprehensive Income'.

7.6.1 What is meant by comprehensive income?

Comprehensive income recognises the gains and losses, both realised **and unrealised,** that have increased or decreased the owners' equity in the business. Such gains and losses arise, for example, from the revaluation of non-current assets (Financial instruments) and 15 (Employee benefits). These are referred to as *Other comprehensive income.*

7.6.2 How to report other comprehensive income

IAS 1 allows a choice. It can be presented as a separate statement or as an extension of the statement of income. In our example we have presented it as an extension of the statement of income.

In this example, there is a revaluation gain on the freehold land which needs to be added to the profit on ordinary activities for the year in order to arrive at the comprehensive income. This is shown in Figure 7.6.

7.6.3 Analysing other comprehensive income

Analysts consider the implication for future profits and growth. For example, it prompts questions such as:

● If there is a gain on non-current asset revaluation: what will be the cash impact on plans for replacing or increasing operating capital? What do the notes to the accounts indicate about capital commitments?

Figure 7.6 Statement of comprehensive income of Wiggins SA for the year ended 31.12.20X3

	€000
Revenue	345,000.00
Cost of sales	293,422.50
Gross profit	51,577.50
Distribution costs	25,041.25
Administrative expenses	4,686.25
Operating profit	21,850.00
Finance costs	7,475.00
Profit on ordinary activities before tax	14,375.00
Income tax	3,625.00
Profit for the year	10,750.00
Other comprehensive income:	
Gains on property revaluation	20,000.00
Comprehensive income for the year	30,750.00

- If there is a gain or loss on foreign exchange: does it indicate a weakening or strengthening of the domestic currency? Will the translation of future overseas sales and profits result in higher or lower reported earnings per share?

7.7 How non-recurring or exceptional items can affect operating income

Operating income is one of the measures used by investors when attempting to predict future income. Management are, therefore, keen to highlight if the current year's operating income has been adversely affected by events that are unlikely to occur in future periods – these are referred to as 'exceptional items'. Such items are within the normal operating activities of the business but require to be separately disclosed because they are significant due to their non-recurring nature and materiality in both size and nature. A company's **quality of earnings** is important as seen in the following extract from the InterContinental Hotels Group 2015 Annual Report:

Exceptional items

The Group discloses certain financial information both including and excluding exceptional items. The presentation of information excluding exceptional items allows a better understanding of the underlying trading performance of the Group and provides consistency with the Group's internal management reporting.

There could be a number of exceptional reasons that result in a lower profit, for example costs incurred in restructuring the business or unusually high allowances for bad debts or material write-downs of inventories to net realisable value or non-current assets to recoverable amounts.

Exceptional items are not, however, always adverse – there might, for example, have been significant gains arising from the disposal of non-current assets. The following is an extract from the John Lewis 2016 Annual Report:

	2016	2015
Operating profit before exceptional item	399.4	439.8
Exceptional item	129.3	7.9
Operating profit	528.7	447.7

On 16 April 2015, the Group disposed of a property which was previously held for sale. The profit on disposal of £129.3m has been recorded as exceptional operating income in the period to 30 January 2016. A tax charge of £25.1m was recognised on the exceptional item.

They are a problem, however, when used to manipulate the figure for maintainable earnings, which led in 2013 to the UK's FRC issuing note PN 108 *FRC seeks consistency in the reporting of exceptional items,* which aims to discourage companies from smoothing profits by creating exceptional charges – which are then fed back in a later period as part of earnings.

7.7.1 Notes to the accounts

It is important to refer to information in the Notes because these items can have a material impact as seen in the Carrefour 2011 Annual Report where an operating profit is turned into an operating loss:

	2011	2010	% change
Total revenue	82,764	81,840	1.1%
Cost of sales	(64,912)	(63,969)	1.5%
Gross margin from recurring operations	17,852	17,871	(0.1)%
Sales, general and administrative expenses	(13,969)	(13,494)	3.5%
Depreciation, amortisation and provisions	(1,701)	(1,675)	1.6%
Recurring operating income	2,182	2,701	(19.2)%
Non-recurring income and expenses, net	(2,662)	(999)	–
Operating profit/(loss)	(481)	1,703	(128.2)%

Non-recurring income and expenses consist mainly of gains and losses on disposal of property and equipment or intangible assets, impairment losses on property and equipment or intangible assets (including goodwill), restructuring costs and provisions for claims and litigation that are material at Group level. They are presented separately in the income statement to 'help users of the financial statements to better understand the Group's underlying operating performance and provide them with useful information to assess the earnings outlook'.

The maintainable figure to concentrate on is the Recurring operating income – in 2012 and 2013 the company reports this as remaining relatively stable at €2,124m and €2,238m respectively.

7.7.2 Need for consistency in presentation

In the UK the Financial Reporting Council (FRC) issued a reminder in 2013 to Boards on the need to improve the reporting of additional and exceptional items by companies and ensure consistency in their presentation to comply with the Corporate Governance Code principle that the annual report and accounts as a whole should be fair, balanced and understandable. The Financial Reporting Review Panel (FRRP) made the point that it is important that investors should be able to identify the trend in underlying, i.e. maintainable profits.

This means, for example, that where the same category of material items recurs each year and in similar amounts (for example, restructuring costs), companies should consider whether such amounts should be included as part of underlying profit. Also where significant items of expense may be subsequently reversed, they should be treated as exceptional items in the subsequent period.

7.7.3 Columnar format

While the information could be disclosed as a note or a separate line item on the face of the statement of income, some companies emphasise the impact by preparing a three-column statement of income which is an alternative method for disclosing permitted by IAS 1.

7.8 How decision-useful is the statement of comprehensive income?

A key question we should ask whenever there is a proposal to present additional financial information is 'How will this be useful to users of the accounts?' There is no definitive answer, because some commentators[2] argue that there is no decision-usefulness in providing the comprehensive net income figure for investors, whereas others[3] take the opposite view. Intuitively, one might take a view that investors are interested in the total movement in equity regardless of the cause, which would lead to support for the comprehensive income figure. However, given that there is this difference of opinion and research findings, this would seem to be an area open to further empirical research to further test the decision-usefulness of each measure to analysts.

Interesting research[4] has since been carried out which supports the view that net income and comprehensive income are both decision-useful. The findings suggested that comprehensive income was more decision-relevant for assessing share returns and traditional net income more decision-relevant for setting executive bonus incentives.

7.9 Statement of changes in equity

This statement is designed to show the following:

- *Prior period adjustments.* The effect of any prior period adjustments is shown by adjusting the retained earnings figure brought forward (we will cover this in Chapter 8).
- *Capital transactions with the owners.* This includes dividends and a reconciliation between the opening and closing equity capital, reporting any change such as increases from bonus, rights or new cash issues and decreases from any buyback of shares.
- *Transfers from revaluation reserves.* When a revalued asset is disposed of, any revaluation surplus may be transferred directly to retained earnings, or it may be left in equity under the heading 'revaluation surplus'.
- *Comprehensive income.* The comprehensive income for the period is disclosed.

The statement for Wiggins SA is shown in Figure 7.7.

Note that the statement of changes in equity is a primary statement and is required to be presented with the same prominence as the other primary statements.

Figure 7.7 Statement of changes in equity for the year ended 31 December 20X3

	Share capital	Share premium	Retained earnings	Revaluation surplus	Total
Balance as at 1 January 20X3	15,000	—	57,500		74,750
Changes in equity for 20X3					
New shares issued	1,500	750			
Dividends			(1,725)		(1,725)
Total comprehensive income for the year			10,750	20,000	30,750
Balance as at 31 December 20X3	16,500	750	66,525	20,000	103,775

7.10 The statement of financial position

IAS 1 specifies which items are to be included on the face of the statement of financial position. These are referred to as alpha headings (a) to (r) – for example (a) Property, plant and equipment, (b) Investment property, . . . , (g) Inventories, . . . , (k) Trade and other payables.

It does not prescribe the order and presentation that are to be followed. It would be acceptable to present the statement as assets less liabilities equalling equity, or total assets equalling total equity and liabilities.

7.10.1 Current/non-current classification

● The standard does not absolutely prescribe that enterprises need to split assets and liabilities into current and non-current. However, it does state that this split would need to be done if the nature of the business indicates that it is appropriate.

● If it is more relevant, a presentation could be based on liquidity and, if so, all assets and liabilities would be presented broadly in order of liquidity. However, in almost all cases it would be appropriate to split items into current and non-current and the statement in Figure 7.8 follows the headings prescribed in IAS 1.

Figure 7.8 Wiggin SA statement of financial position as at 31.12.20X3

	€000	€000
Non-current assets:		
Property, plant and equipment (see Figure 3.10)		150,525
Current assets:		
Inventory	25,875	
Receivables	28,750	
Cash at bank and in hand	4,600	
Prepayments	2,300	
		61,525
Total assets		212,050
Equity:		
Share capital		16,500
Share premium		750
Revaluation reserve		20,000
Retained earnings		66,525
		103,775
Non-current liabilities:		
10% loan (20X9)		63,250
Current liabilities:		
Payables	30,650	
Provisions for income tax	2,875	
Accruals	5,175	
Bank overdraft	6,325	45,025
Total equity and liabilities		212,050

7.11 The explanatory notes that are part of the financial statements

Published accounts are supported by a number of explanatory notes. These have been expanded over time to satisfy various user needs. We will comment briefly on (a) notes setting out accounting policies, (b) notes giving greater detail of the make-up of items that appear in the statement of financial position, (c) notes providing additional information to assist predicting future cash flows, and (d) notes giving information of interest to other stakeholders.

(a) Accounting policies

Accounting policies are chosen by a company as being the most appropriate to the company's circumstances and **best able to produce a fair view.** They typically disclose the accounting policies followed for the basis of accounting, for example that the accounts have been prepared on a historical cost basis and how revenue, assets and liabilities have been reported. The policies relating to assets and liabilities will cover non-current and current items, for example the depreciation method used for non-current assets (as in Figure 7.9) and the valuation method used for inventory such as first-in-first-out (FIFO) or weighted average.

How do users know the effect of changes in accounting policy?

Accounting policies are required by IAS 1 to be applied consistently from one financial period to another. It is only permissible to change an accounting policy if required by a standard or

Figure 7.9 Extract from the 2017 financial statements of the Nestlé Group

Property, plant and equipment

Property, plant and equipment are shown on the balance sheet at their historical cost. Depreciation is provided on components that have homogeneous useful lives by using the straight-line method so as to depreciate the initial cost down to the residual value over the estimated useful lives. The residual values are 30% on head offices, 20% on distribution centres for products stored at ambient temperature and nil for all other asset types.

The useful lives are as follows:

Buildings	20–40 years
Machinery and equipment	10–25 years
Tools, furniture, information technology and sundry equipment	3–15 years
Vehicles	3–10 years

Land is not depreciated.

Useful lives, components and residual amounts are reviewed annually. Such a review takes into consideration the nature of the assets, their intended use including but not limited to the closure of facilities and the evolution of the technology and competitive pressures that may lead to technical obsolescence.

Depreciation of property, plant and equipment is allocated to the appropriate headings of expenses by function in the statement of comprehensive income.

if the directors consider that a change results in financial statements that are reliable and more relevant. When a change does occur IAS 8 requires:

- the comparative figures of the previous financial period to be amended if possible;
- the disclosure of the reason for the change;
- the effect of the adjustment in the statement of comprehensive income of the period and the effect on all other periods presented with the current period financial statements.

(b) Notes giving greater detail of the make-up of statement of financial position figures

Each of the alpha headings may have additional detail disclosed by way of a note to the accounts. For example, inventory of £25.875 million in the statement of financial position may have a note of its detailed make-up as follows:

	£m
Raw materials	11.225
Work in progress	1.500
Finished goods	13.150
	25.875

Property, plant and equipment normally have a schedule as shown in Figure 7.10. From this the net book value is read off the total column for inclusion in the statement of financial position.

Figure 7.10 Disclosure note: Property, plant and equipment movements

	Freehold land	Freehold buildings	Equipment	Motor vehicles	Total
	€000	€000	€000	€000	€000
Cost/valuation					
As at 1.1.20X3	57,500	57,500	14,950	20,700	150,650
Revaluation	20,000				20,000
Additions					
Disposals					
As at 31.12.20X3	77,500	57,500	14,950	20,700	170,650
Accumulated depreciation					
As at 1.1.20X3		2,300	3,450	9,200	14,950
Charge for the year		1,150	1,150	2,875	5,175
As at 31.12.20X3		3,450	4,600	12,075	20,125
Net book value					
As at 31.12.20X3	77,500	54,050	10,350	8,625	150,525
As at 31.12.20X2	57,500	55,200	11,500	11,500	135,700

(c) Notes giving additional information to assist prediction of future cash flows

These are notes intended to assist in predicting future cash flows. They give information on matters such as:

- capital commitments that have been contracted for but not provided in the accounts;
- capital commitments that have been authorised but not contracted for;
- future commitments, e.g. share options that have been granted; and
- contingent liabilities, e.g. guarantees given by the company in respect of overdraft facilities arranged by subsidiary companies or customers.

In deciding upon disclosures, management have an obligation to consider whether the omission of the information is material and could influence users who base their decisions on the financial statements. The management decision would be influenced by the size or nature of the item and the characteristics of the users. They are entitled to assume that the users have a reasonable knowledge of business and accounting and a willingness to study the information with reasonable diligence.

(d) Notes giving information that is of interest to other stakeholders

An example is information relating to staff. It is common for enterprises to provide a disclosure of the average number of employees in the period or the number of employees at the end of the period. IAS 1 does not require this information but it is likely that many businesses would provide and categorise the information, possibly following functions such as production, sales, and administration as in the following extract from the 2015 Annual Report of Wienerberger:

	Total (2015)	Total (2014)
Production	10,696	10,015
Administration	1,404	1,315
Sales	3,713	3,506
Total	15,813	14,836
Apprentices	94	96

This shows a significant increase in staff numbers with reasons given within the report. However, the annual report is not the only source of information – there might be separate employee reports and information obtained during labour negotiations such as the ratio of short-term and long-term assets to employee numbers, the capital–labour ratios and the average revenue and net profits per employee in the company with inter-period and inter-firm comparisons. For example, in 2017 John Lewis reported profit after tax of £353.5m with staff of 93,500 compared to Tesco which reported profit after tax of £645m with staff of 440,000 in 2016. Tesco also reports revenue per employee but there is no requirement to produce this figure and analysts would themselves need to calculate these – and questions should then perhaps be raised as to whether differing rates might mean that there is less customer satisfaction and the possibility of a fall with lower revenue or more employees.

7.12 Has prescribing the formats meant that identical transactions are reported identically?

That is the intention, but there are various reasons why there may still be differences. For example, let us consider some of the reasons for differences in calculating the cost of sales: (a) how inventory is valued, (b) the choice of depreciation policy, (c) management attitudes, and (d) the capability of the accounting system.

(a) Differences arising from the choice of the inventory valuation method

Different companies may assume different physical flows when calculating the cost of direct materials used in production. This will affect the inventory valuation. One company may assume a FIFO flow, where the cost of sales is charged for raw materials used in production as if the first items purchased were the first items used in production. Another company may use an average basis. This is illustrated in Figure 7.11 for a company that started trading on 1 January 20X1 without any opening inventory and sold 40,000 items on 31 March 20X1 for £4 per item.

Inventory valued on a FIFO basis is £60,000 with the 20,000 items in inventory valued at £3 per item, on the assumption that the purchases made on 1 January 20X1 and 1 February 20X1 were sold first. Inventory valued on an average basis is £40,000 with the 20,000 items in inventory valued at £2 per item on the assumption that sales made in March cannot be matched with a specific item.

The effect on the gross profit percentage would be as shown in Figure 7.12. This demonstrates that, even from a single difference in accounting treatment, the gross profit for the same transaction could be materially different in both absolute and percentage terms.

How can an investor determine the effect of different assumptions?

Although companies are required to disclose their inventory valuation policy, the level of detail provided varies and we are not able to quantify the effect of different inventory valuation policies.

For example, a clear description of an accounting policy is provided by AstraZeneca. Even so, it does not allow the user to know how net realisable value was determined. Was it, for example, primarily based upon forecasted short-term demand for the product?

Figure 7.11 Effect on sales of using FIFO and weighted average

Physical flow assumption			FIFO	Average
	Items	£	£	£
Raw materials purchased				
On 1 Jan 20X1 at £1 per item	20,000	20,000		
On 1 Feb 20X1 at £2 item	20,000	40,000		
On 1 Mar 20X1 at £3 per item	20,000	60,000		
On 1 Mar 20X1 in inventory	60,000	120,000	120,000	120,000
On 31 Mar 20X1 in inventory	20,000		60,000	40,000
Cost of sales	40,000		60,000	80,000

Figure 7.12 Effect of physical inventory flow assumptions on the percentage gross profit

	Items	FIFO £	Average £	% difference in gross profit
Sales	40,000	160,000	160,000	
Cost of sales	40,000	60,000	80,000	
		100,000	80,000	
Gross profit %		62.5%	50%	25%

AstraZeneca inventory policy (2017) Annual Report

Inventories

Inventories are stated at the lower of cost or net realisable value.

The first in, first out or an average method of valuation is used.

For finished goods and work in progress, cost includes directly attributable costs and certain overhead expenses (including depreciation).

Selling expenses and certain other overhead expenses (principally central administration costs) are excluded.

Net realisable value is determined as estimated selling price less all estimated costs of completion and costs to be incurred in selling and distribution.

Write-downs of inventory occur in the general course of business and are included in cost of sales in the income statement. However, if the write-off is regarded as material it would be reported as an exceptional item.

The following illustration is an extract from the 2017 Annual Report of R & R Ice Cream plc:

	Before exceptional items (€000)	Exceptional items (€000)	After exceptional items (€000)	Before exceptional items (€000)	Exceptional items (€000)	After exceptional items (€000)
Profit/(loss) before income tax	112,538	(69,796)	42,742	75,508	(103,122)	(27,614)

The group incurred substantial one-off and exceptional costs in 2013 and 2014, as part of a substantial reshaping of the group's activities and financing structure. Such exceptional costs reduced substantially in 2015, since the majority of the operational restructuring was conducted in earlier years. However, there has been a smaller amount of restructuring costs that extended into 2015, though the greater part of exceptional costs in 2015 relate to aborted refinancing costs (where the group explored refinancing opportunities) and the early stage costs in relation to the potential merger. A merger with Nestle's ice cream interest took place in 2016 and a new company Froneri Ltd was formed.

(b) Differences arising from the choice of depreciation method and estimates

Companies may make different choices:

- the accounting base to use, e.g. historical cost or revaluation; and
- the method that is used to calculate the charge, e.g. straight-line or reducing balance.

Companies make estimates that might differ:

- assumptions as to an asset's productive use, e.g. different estimates made as to the economic life of an asset; and
- assumptions as to the total cost to be expensed, e.g. different estimates of the residual value.

(c) Differences arising from management attitudes

Losses might be anticipated and measured at a different rate. For example, when assessing the likelihood of the net realisable value of inventory falling below the cost figure, the management decision will be influenced by the optimism with which it views the future of the economy, the industry and the company. There could also be other influences. For example, if bonuses are based on net income, there is an incentive to overestimate the net realisable value; whereas, if management is preparing a company for a management buy-out, there is an incentive to underestimate the net realisable value in order to minimise the net profit for the period.

(d) Differences arising from the capability of the accounting system to provide data

Accounting systems within companies differ and costs that are collected by one company may well not be collected by another company. For example, the apportionment of costs might be more detailed with different proportions being allocated or apportioned.

7.13 Fair presentation

IAS 1 *Presentation of Financial Statements* requires financial statements to give a **fair presentation** of the financial position, financial performance and cash flows of an enterprise. In paragraph 17 it states that:

> In virtually all circumstances, a fair presentation is achieved by compliance with applicable IFRSs. A fair presentation also requires an entity to:
>
> (a) select and apply accounting policies in accordance with IAS 8 *Accounting Policies, Changes in Accounting Estimates and Errors* [this is dealt with in Chapter 8];
>
> (b) present information, including accounting policies, in a manner that provides relevant, reliable, comparable and understandable information;
>
> (c) provide additional disclosures when compliance with the specific requirements in IFRSs is insufficient to enable users to understand the impact of particular transactions, other events and conditions on the entity's financial position and financial performance.

7.13.1 Legal opinions

In the UK we require financial statements to give a **true and fair view**. True and fair is a legal concept and can be authoritatively decided only by a court. However, the courts have never attempted to define 'true and fair'. In the UK the Accounting Standards Committee (ASC) obtained a legal opinion which included the following statement:

> Accounts will not be true and fair unless the information they contain is sufficient in quantity and quality to satisfy the reasonable expectations of the readers to whom they are addressed.

Accounting standards are an authoritative source of accounting practice.

However, an Opinion obtained by the FRC in May 2008 and again in 2013 advised that true and fair still has to be taken into consideration by preparers and auditors of financial statements whether prepared under UK company law or IFRSs. Directors have to consider whether the statements are appropriate and auditors have to exercise professional judgement when giving an audit opinion – it is not sufficient for either directors or auditors to reach a conclusion solely because the financial statements were prepared in accordance with applicable accounting standards.

7.13.2 Fair override

Standards are not intended to be a straitjacket and IAS 1 recognises that there may be occasions when application of an IAS/IFRS might be misleading and departure from the IAS/IFRS treatment is permitted. This is referred to as the **fair override** provision.

Although IAS 1 does not refer to true and fair or override, the FRC in a document issued in 2012 *True and Fair* concluded that preparers, those charged with governance and auditors should:

- always stand back and ensure that the accounts as a whole do give a true and fair view;
- provide additional disclosures when compliance with an accounting standard is insufficient to present a true and fair view;
- use the true and fair override where compliance with the standards does not result in the presentation of a true and fair view; and
- ensure that the consideration they give to these matters is evident in their deliberations and documentation.

Examples of the use of the IAS 1 override among European companies are very rare.

When do companies use the fair override?

Fair override can occur for a number[5] of reasons with the most frequent being the situation where the Accounting Standards may prescribe one method, which contradicts company law and thus requires an override, for example, providing no depreciation on investment properties. Next would be where Accounting Standards may offer a choice between accounting procedures, at least one of which contradicts company law. If that particular choice is adopted, the override should be invoked, for example grants not being shown as deferred income.

Fair override can be challenged

If a company in the UK relies on the fair override provision, it may be challenged by the Financial Reporting Review Panel and the company's decision overturned. For example, although Eurovestech had adopted an accounting policy in its 2005 and 2006 accounts not to consolidate two of its subsidiaries because its directors considered that to do so would not give a true and fair view, the FRRP decision was that this was unacceptable because the company was unable to demonstrate special circumstances warranting this treatment.

7.14 What does an investor need in addition to the primary financial statements to make decisions?

Investors attempt to estimate future cash flows when making an investment decision. As regards future cash flows, these are normally perceived to be influenced by past profits as reported in the statements of income and the asset base as shown by the statement of financial position.

In order to assist shareholders to predict future cash flows with an understanding of the risks involved, more information has been required by the IASB. For example:

- More quantitative information (discussed in Chapter 8):
  - financial statements are required to take account of events and information becoming available after the period-end;
  - segment reports are required;
  - disclosure is required of the impact of changes on the operation, e.g. a breakdown of turnover, costs and profits for both new and discontinued operations.
- More qualitative narrative information, including:
  - mandatory disclosures;
  - IFRS practice statement – management commentary.
- UK requirements:
  - Chairman's Statement;
  - Directors' Report;
    - Disclosure: Strategic Report
    - Viability Statement

We will comment briefly on the qualitative narrative disclosures.

7.14.1 IFRS mandatory disclosures

When making future predictions, investors need to be able to identify that part of the net income that is likely to be maintained in the future. IAS 1 provides assistance to users in this by requiring that certain items are separately disclosed. These are items within the ordinary activities of the enterprise which are of such size, nature or incidence that their separate disclosure is required in the financial statements in order for the financial statements to show a fair view.

These items are not extraordinary and must, therefore, be presented above the tax line. It is usual to disclose the nature and amount of these items in a note to the financial statements, with no separate mention on the face of the statement of comprehensive income; however, if sufficiently material, they can be disclosed on the face of the statement.

Examples of the type of item that may give rise to separate disclosures are:

- the write-down of assets to realisable value or recoverable amount;
- the restructuring of activities of the enterprise; discontinued operations; disposals of items of property, plant and equipment and long-term investments; litigation settlements.

7.14.2 Subjective nature of items classified as exceptional

The items reported as exceptional require the exercise of judgement and so need to be approached with a certain amount of scepticism.

Exercise of judgement

Judgement is required in determining the best manner in which information is presented. IAS 1 is not prescriptive and companies may choose to present exceptional items as a line item on the face of the accounts, as a disclosure note or in columnar format.

Judgement is also required when classifying items as operating or exceptional. IAS 1 states that it would be misleading and would impair comparability if items of an operating nature were excluded from the results of operating activities. This is aimed at preventing companies from classifying operating costs as exceptional in order to improve the headline figure that is frequently used to calculate key performance indicators such as return on equity and earnings per share.

Exercise of scepticism

Reporting an item as exceptional may cause operating profits to be boosted, as illustrated in a 2014 S&P study *'Why Inconsistent Reporting of Exceptional Items Can Cloud Underlying Profitability'* of non-financial FTSE 100 companies which reported that 89% adjusted profits and in 73% of cases this boosted operating profits.

A similar review[6] in 2013 by the Irish Auditing and Advisory Authority found that the costs presented as exceptional exceeded the income presented as exceptional by a factor of 5:1.

Investors need to exercise scepticism and carefully scrutinise underlying earnings and exceptional items before reaching their own view of a company's performance.

7.14.3 IFRS Management Commentary

In December 2010 the IASB issued an IFRS Practice Statement *Management Commentary*. Management commentary is defined in the statement as:

> A narrative report that relates to financial statements that have been prepared in accordance with IFRSs. Management commentary provides users with historical explanations of the amounts presented in the financial statements, specifically the entity's financial position, financial performance and cash flows. It also provides commentary on an entity's prospects and other information not presented in the financial statements. Management commentary also serves as a basis for understanding management's objectives and its strategies for achieving those objectives.

The commentary should give management's view not only about what has happened, including both positive and negative circumstances, but also why it has happened and what the implications are for the entity's future.

Following the Practice Statement is not mandatory and the financial statements and annual report of a business can still be compliant with IFRS even if the requirements are not followed. However, it is the first document to be issued by the IASB that solely covers information that is provided by companies outside the financial statements.

The guidance does not attempt to dictate exactly how management commentary should be prepared so as to avoid the tick-box approach to compliance. Instead it indicates the information that should be included within the commentary:

(a) the nature of the business;

(b) management's objectives and its strategies for meeting those objectives;

(c) the entity's most significant resources, risks and relationships;

(d) the results of operations and prospects; and

(e) the critical performance measures and indicators that management uses to evaluate the entity's performance against stated objectives.

It will be interesting to observe the effect that this has on future annual reports.

Who presents and approves a management commentary may depend on jurisdictional requirements.

7.14.4 Strategic Report

In the UK the 2006 Companies Act[7] provides that from 2013 quoted companies should issue a Strategic Report to help members to assess how the directors have performed their duty of promoting the success of the company.

The report must contain a description of the company's strategy, its business model, the principal risks and uncertainties facing the company and a balanced and comprehensive analysis of the development and performance of the company's business during the financial year and its position at the end of that year.

The review must also, where appropriate, include an analysis using financial and other key performance indicators including information relating to environmental, social, employee and human rights matters.

Potentially useful key performance indicators

The intention is that there should not be a list of all performance measures but only those key indicators considered by the board and used in management reporting.

They might include:

- Economic measures of ability to create value (with the terms defined):
  - Return on capital employed;
  - Economic profit-type measures, i.e. post-tax profits less cost of capital;
- Market position;
- Market share;
- Development, performance and position:
  - traditional financial measures such as asset turnover rates;
  - industry-specific measures such as sales per square metre;
- Customers, employees and suppliers: how they rate the company;
- Social, environmental and community issues.

Guidance on Strategic Report

Guidance[8] was issued by the FRC in 2014. Its objective is to ensure that relevant information that meets the needs of shareholders is presented in the Strategic Report and to encourage companies to experiment and be innovative in the drafting of their annual reports.

7.14.5 Chairman's Statement

This often tends to be a brief comment on the current year's performance and a view on the Outlook. For example, the following is a brief extract from Findel plc's 2016 Annual Report:

> We now have a well-financed Group focused solely on the growth of two core businesses – Express Gifts and Findel Education. We believe this represents a turning point in the development of Findel, as we can now focus on generating enhanced shareholder value from strong organic growth in our two core businesses as opposed to being focused on restructuring.

Notwithstanding this progress, the financial performance in the year was challenging. Overall profit before tax from continuing operations slipped from £27.7m in FY15 to £24.8m. Both of our core businesses contributed to this decline. This underlines the need for the prompt actions which we have taken and we are confident that these will improve our performance. A positive start to the current year supports our confidence.

7.14.6 Directors' Report

The paragraph headings from Findel's 2015 Annual Report illustrate the type of information that is published. The report covered matters such as:

- reference to the Corporate Governance Report as forming part of the Directors' Report;
- reference to the Strategic Report;
- comments on Going Concern;
- comments on changes sought to the capital structure;
- activities;
- review of the year and future prospects.

7.14.7 Developments in meeting narrative reporting needs for the future

Survey findings in 2010

In 2010 the ACCA issued the results of an international survey[9] of CFOs' views on narrative reporting, '*Hitting the notes, but what's the tune?*', based on a joint survey with Deloitte of some 230 chief financial officers and other preparers in listed companies in nine countries (Australia, China, Kenya, Malaysia, Singapore, Switzerland, the UAE, the UK and the US). The major findings were that:

- the principal audiences for narrative information were shareholders and regulators;
- the most important disclosures for shareholders were the explanation of financial results and financial position, identifying the most important risks and how they were managed, an outline of future plans and prospects, a description of the business model and a description of key performance indicators (KPIs);
- the interviewees supported a reporting environment with more discretion and less regulation.

FRC initiatives in 2014/2017

In 2014 the FRC started *The Clear & Concise Initiative* to bring together activities from across the FRC.

In 2015 as part of this initiative it produced *Guidance on the Strategic Report* and issued a report,[10] *Clear & Concise: Developments in Narrative Reporting,* that reviewed the impact of the Strategic Report with an analysis of recent research on the quality of the strategic reports, supplemented with a detailed review of a small sample of strategic reports.

In August 2017 it issued *Draft Amendments to Guidance on the Strategic Report - Non-financial Reporting.* This followed the publication by the government of Regulations to implement the EU Directive on disclosure of non-financial and diversity information ('non-financial reporting Directive'). The new Regulations amend the strategic report requirements arising from the government's agenda for corporate governance reform which places emphasis on the conduct of business. In particular, there have been calls, including from the FRC, for a greater focus on the directors' duty under section 172 'Duty to promote the success of the company'.

The need for a mature user response

The following is an extract from an ACCA paper 'Writing the narrative: the triumphs and tribulations'[11] by Afra Sajjad:

> We believe that the future of narrative reporting lies in reconciliation of competing information needs and expectations of primary users of annual reports, i.e. regulators and shareholders. This should be accompanied by nurturing of a culture of corporate reporting where integrity, probity and transparency are fundamental to reporting. Regulators also need to facilitate change in the culture of reporting by giving preparers the flexibility to use discretion and facilitate market led best practices.
> Shareholders . . . need also to be mature enough to encourage real transparency. If they respond with panic to disappointing news, it will inhibit the preparer's disclosure process.

7.14.8 Possible changes to financial performance statements' structure

Companies have been using many different subtotals (e.g. operating profit, EBIT, gross profit and profit before tax) that are not defined in IFRS and there is little consistency in the approach on how to measure such subtotals, which reduces understandability and comparability of the information provided to users. To address these issues, the IASB plans to explore requiring additional subtotals in the statement of financial performance.

This is a change in the structure of the statements. For example, some users might wish to identify the amount received by a company from its investments in addition to the return on its trading resources. One way to achieve this could be by disaggregating reported income and expenses into an additional category titled 'Investment income/expense'. Under this category it would report separately items such as:

- dividends received from equity investments;
- interest received from long-term loans and debentures;
- fair value changes on investment property;
- rental income from investment property;
- gains and losses on the disposal of investments.

A further category could be 'Finance income/expense' to include separate disclosure of items such as:

- interest payable on loans and debentures;
- lease payments;
- other financial income/expense which could include items such as the unwinding of interest on long-term provisions.

Definitions

Subtotals such as gross profit, operating profit or EBIT are often used by preparers, even though there is not a generally agreed definition for such terms and in many cases operating profit is similar or equal to EBIT. Providing guidance on any of these subtotals,[12] which could include disclosures on their definitions, would provide a comparable starting point for users' analysis as they often use an EBIT or EBITDA when developing estimates of future cash flows for their valuation purposes.

Options

At the present time there are two formats with expenses presented by function or by nature and in reporting other comprehensive income there could be a single statement or two statements.

Existing accounting options in IFRS Standards, including presentation options tend to reduce comparability across countries and industries. This raises the question as to whether the increased measures taken to improve comparability increase or reduce the relevance of the information.

Summary

In this chapter we have revised the preparation of internal financial statements making accrual adjustments to trial balance figures.

In order to assess stewardship and management performance, there have been mandatory requirements for standardised presentation, using the two formats prescribed by International Financial Reporting Standards. The required disclosures were explained for both formats.

The importance of referring to Notes to the accounts was illustrated with discussion of exceptional items and their impact on predicting operating income.

The disclosure of accounting policies which allow shareholders to make comparisons between years by requiring companies to be consistent in the application of accounting policies or requiring disclosure if there has been a change was discussed.

The need for explanatory notes was explained and described.

The need for financial statements to give a true and fair view of the income and net assets was explained with recognition that this requires the exercise of professional judgement. Having recorded the transactions and made the normal adjustments for accruals, do the resulting financial statements give a fair presentation?

The evolving practices for narrative reporting under IASB and UK were discussed in the IFRS Practice Statement *Management Commentary*, the UK *Strategic Report* and the FRC *Clear and Concise Initiative*.

REVIEW QUESTIONS

1 Explain the effect on income and financial position if (a) the amount of accrued expense were to be underestimated and (b) the inventory at the year-end omitted inventory held in a customs warehouse awaiting clearance.

2 Explain why two companies carrying out identical trading transactions could produce different gross profit figures.

3 Classify the following items into cost of sales, distribution costs, administrative expenses, other operating income or items to be disclosed after trading profit:

(a) Personnel department costs

(b) Computer department costs

(c) Cost accounting department costs

(d) Financial accounting department costs

(e) Bad debts

(f) Provisions for warranty claims

(g) Interest on funds borrowed to finance an increase in working capital

(h) Interest on funds borrowed to finance an increase in property, plant and equipment.

4 'We analyze a sample of UK public companies that invoked a True and Fair View (TFV) override during 1998–2000 to assess whether overrides are used opportunistically. We find overrides increase income and equity significantly, and firms with weaker performance and higher levels of debt employ overrides that are more costly . . . financial statements are not less informative than control sample.'[13]

Discuss the enquiries and action that you think an auditor should take to ensure that the financial statements give a more true and fair view than from applying standards.

5 When preparing accounts under Format 1, how would a bad debt that was materially larger than normal be disclosed?

6 'Annual accounts have been put into such a straitjacket of overemphasis on uniform disclosure that there will be a growing pressure by national bodies to introduce changes unilaterally which will again lead to diversity in the quality of disclosure. This is both healthy and necessary.' Discuss.

7 Explain the relevance to the user of accounts if expenses are classified as 'administrative expenses' rather than as 'cost of sales'.

8 IAS 1 *Presentation of Financial Statements* requires 'other comprehensive income' items to be included in the statement of comprehensive income and it also requires a statement of changes in equity. Explain the need for publishing this information, and identify the items you would include in them.

9 Discuss the major benefit to an investor from the UK Strategic Report.

10 The following are three KPIs for the retail sector:[14] capital expenditure, expected return on new stores and customer satisfaction. Discuss two further KPIs that might be significant.

11 Explain the difference between accounting policies, accounting estimates and prior period errors and how each affects the financial statements.

EXERCISES

* Question 1

The following trial balance was extracted from the books of Old NV on 31 December 20X1.

	€000	€000
Sales		12,050
Returns outwards		313
Provision for depreciation		
Plant		738
Vehicles		375
Rent receivable		100
Trade payables		738
Debentures		250
Issued share capital – ordinary €1 shares		3,125
Issued share capital – preference shares (treated as equity)		625
Share premium		350
Retained earnings		875
Inventory	825	
Purchases	6,263	
Returns inwards	350	
Carriage inwards	13	
Carriage outwards	125	
Salesmen's salaries	800	
Administrative wages and salaries	738	
Land	100	
Plant (includes €362,000 acquired in 20X1)	1,562	
Motor vehicles	1,125	
Goodwill	1,062	
Distribution costs	290	
Administrative expenses	286	
Directors' remuneration	375	
Trade receivables	3,875	
Cash at bank and in hand	1,750	
	19,539	19,539

Note of information not taken into the trial balance data:

(a) Provide for:
- (i) An audit fee of €38,000.
- (ii) Depreciation of plant at 20% straight-line.
- (iii) Depreciation of vehicles at 25% reducing balance.
- (iv) The goodwill suffered an impairment in the year of €177,000.
- (v) Income tax of €562,000.
- (vi) Debenture interest of €25,000.

(b) Closing inventory was valued at €1,125,000 at the lower of cost and net realisable value.

(c) Administrative expenses were prepaid by €12,000.

(d) Land was to be revalued by €50,000.

Required:
(a) Prepare a statement of income for internal use for the year ended 31 December 20X1.
(b) Prepare a statement of comprehensive income for the year ended 31 December 20X1 and
     a statement of financial position as at that date in Format 1 style of presentation.

* Question 2

Formatone plc produced the following trial balance as at 30 June 20X6:

	£000	£000
Land at cost	2,160.0	—
Buildings at cost	1,080.0	—
Plant and equipment at cost	1,728.0	—
Intangible assets	810.0	—
Accum. depreciation – 30.6.20X5		
Buildings	—	432.0
Plant and equipment	—	504.0
Interim dividend paid	108.0	
Receivables and payables	585.0	532.8
Cash and bank balance	41.4	—
Inventory as at 30.6.20X6	586.8	—
Taxation	—	14.4
Deferred tax	—	37.8
Distribution cost	529.2	—
Administrative expenses	946.8	—
Retained earnings b/f	—	891.0
Sales revenue	—	9,480.6
Cost of sales	5,909.4	—
Ordinary shares of 50p each	—	2,160.0
Share premium account	—	432.0
	14,484.6	14,484.6

The following information is available:

(i)   A revaluation of the Land and Buildings on 1 July 20X5 resulted in an increase of £3,240,000 in the
      Land and £972,000 in the Buildings. This has not yet been recorded in the books.

(ii) Depreciation:
      Plant and Equipment are depreciated at 10% using the reducing balance method.
      Intangible assets are to be written down by £540,000.
      Buildings have an estimated life of 30 years from date of the revaluation.

(iii) Taxation
      The current tax is estimated at £169,200.
      There had been an overprovision in the previous year.
      Deferred tax is to be increased by £27,000.

(iv) Capital
      150,000 shares were issued and recorded on 1 July 20X5 for 80p each.
      A further dividend of 5p per share has been declared on 30 June 20X6.

Required:
Prepare for the year ended 30 June 20X6 the statement of comprehensive income, statement of changes in equity and statement of financial position.

* Question 3

Basalt plc is a wholesaler. The following is its trial balance as at 31 December 20X0.

	Dr £000	Cr £000
Ordinary share capital: £1 shares		300
Share premium		20
General reserve		16
Retained earnings as at 1 January 20X0		55
Inventory as at 1 January 20X0	66	
Sales		962
Purchases	500	
Administrative costs	10	
Distribution costs	6	
Plant and machinery – cost	220	
Plant and machinery – provision for depreciation		49
Returns outwards		25
Returns inwards	27	
Carriage inwards	9	
Warehouse wages	101	
Salesmen's salaries	64	
Administrative wages and salaries	60	
Hire of motor vehicles	19	
Directors' remuneration	30	
Rent receivable		7
Trade receivables	326	
Cash at bank	62	
Trade payables		66
	1,500	1,500

The following additional information is supplied:

(i)   Depreciate plant and machinery 20% on straight-line basis.

(ii) Inventory at 31 December 20X0 is £90,000.

(iii) Accrue auditors' remuneration £2,000.

(iv) Income tax for the year will be £58,000 payable October 20X1.

(v) It is estimated that 7/11 of the plant and machinery is used in connection with distribution, with the remainder for administration. The motor vehicle costs should be allocated to distribution.

Required:
Prepare a statement of income and statement of financial position in a form that complies with IAS 1. No notes to the accounts are required.

* Question 4

HK Ltd has prepared its draft trial balance to 30 June 20X1, which is shown below.

Trial balance at 30 June 20X1		
$000	$000	
Freehold land	2,100	
Freehold buildings (cost $4,680,000)	4,126	
Plant and machinery (cost $3,096,000)	1,858	
Fixtures and fittings (cost $864,000)	691	
Goodwill	480	
Trade receivables	7,263	
Trade payables		2,591
Inventory	11,794	
Bank balance	11,561	
Development grant received		85
Profit on sale of freehold land		536
Sales		381,600
Cost of sales	318,979	
Administration expenses	9,000	
Distribution costs	35,100	
Directors' emoluments	562	
Bad debts	157	
Auditors' remuneration	112	
Hire of plant and machinery	2,400	
Loan interest	605	
Dividends paid during the year – preference	162	
Dividends paid during the year – ordinary	426	
9% loan		7,200
Share capital – preference shares (treated as equity)		3,600
Share capital – ordinary shares		5,400
Retained earnings		6,364
	407,376	407,376

The following information is available:

(a) The authorised share capital is 4,000,000 9% preference shares of $1 each and 18,000,000 ordinary shares of 50c each.

(b) Provide for depreciation at the following rates:

    (i)   Plant and machinery 20% on cost

    (ii) Fixtures and fittings 10% on cost

    (iii) Buildings 2% on cost

    Charge all depreciation to cost of sales.

(c) Provide $5,348,000 for income tax.

(d) The loan was raised during the year and there is no outstanding interest accrued at the year-end.

(e) Government grants of $85,000 have been received in respect of plant purchased during the year and are shown in the trial balance. One-fifth is to be taken into profit in the current year.

(f) During the year a fire took place at one of the company's depots, involving losses of $200,000. These losses have already been written off to cost of sales shown in the trial balance. Since the end of the financial year a settlement of $150,000 has been agreed with the company's insurers.

(g) $500,000 of the inventory is obsolete. This has a realisable value of $250,000.

(h) Acquisitions of property, plant and equipment during the year were:

Plant $173,000   Fixtures $144,000

(i) During the year freehold land which cost $720,000 was sold for $1,316,000.

(j) A final ordinary dividend of 3c per share is declared and was an obligation before the year-end, together with the balance of the preference dividend. Neither dividend was paid at the year-end.

(k) The goodwill has not been impaired.

(l) The land was revalued at the year-end at $2,500,000.

Required:
(a) **Prepare the company's statement of comprehensive income for the year to 30 June 20X1 and a statement of financial position as at that date, complying with the relevant accounting standards in so far as the information given permits.**
   (All calculations to nearest $000.)
(b) **Explain the usefulness of the schedule prepared in (a).**

* Question 5

Phoenix plc's trial balance at 30 June 20X7 was as follows:

	£000	£000
Freehold premises	2,400	
Plant and machinery	1,800	540
Furniture and fittings	620	360
Inventory at 30 June 20X7	1,468	
Sales		6,465
Administrative expenses	1,126	
Ordinary shares of £1 each		4,500
Trade investments	365	
Revaluation reserve		600
Development cost	415	
Share premium		500
Personal ledger balances	947	566
Cost of goods sold	4,165	
Distribution costs	669	
Overprovision for tax		26
Dividend received		80
Interim dividend paid	200	
Retained earnings		488
Disposal of warehouse		225
Cash and bank balances	175	
	14,350	14,350

The following information is available:

1 Freehold premises acquired for £1.8 million were revalued in 20X4, recognising a gain of £600,000. These include a warehouse, which cost £120,000, was revalued at £150,000 and was sold in June 20X7 for £225,000. Phoenix does not depreciate freehold premises.

2 Phoenix wishes to report plant and machinery at open market value which is estimated to be £1,960,000 on 1 July 20X6.

3 Company policy is to depreciate its assets on the straight-line method at annual rates as follows:

Plant and machinery 10%
Furniture and fittings 5%

4 Until this year the company's policy has been to capitalise development costs, to the extent permitted by relevant accounting standards. The company must now write off the development costs, including £124,000 incurred in the year, as the project no longer meets the capitalisation criteria.

5 During the year the company has issued one million shares of £1 at £1.20 each.

6 Included within administrative expenses are the following:

Staff salary (including £125,000 to directors) £468,000
Directors' fees £96,000
Audit fees and expenses £86,000

7 Income tax for the year is estimated at £122,000.

8 Directors propose a final dividend of 4p per share declared and an obligation, but not paid at the year-end.

Required:
In respect of the year ended 30 June 20X7:
(a) The statement of comprehensive income.
(b) The statement of financial position as at 30 June 20X7.
(c) The statement of movement of property, plant and equipment.

* Question 6

Olive A/S, incorporated with an authorised capital consisting of one million ordinary shares of €1 each, employs 64 persons, of whom 42 work at the factory and the rest at the head office. The trial balance extracted from its books as at 30 September 20X4 is as follows:

	€000	€000
Land and buildings (cost €600,000)	520	—
Plant and machinery (cost €840,000)	680	—
Proceeds on disposal of plant and machinery	—	180
Fixtures and equipment (cost €120,000)	94	—
Sales	—	3,460
Carriage inwards	162	—
Share premium account	—	150
Advertising	112	—
Inventory on 1 Oct 20X3	211	—
Heating and lighting	80	—
Prepayments	115	—
Salaries	820	—
Trade investments at cost	248	—
Dividend received (net) on 9 Sept 20X4	—	45
Directors' emoluments	180	—
Pension cost	100	—
Audit fees and expense	65	—
Retained earnings b/f	—	601
Sales commission	92	—
Stationery	28	—
Development cost	425	—
Formation expenses	120	—
Receivables and payables	584	296
Interim dividend paid on 4 Mar 20X4	60	—
12% debentures issued on 1 Apr 20X4	—	500
Debenture interest paid on 1 Jul 20X4	15	—
Purchases	925	—
Income tax on year to 30 Sept 20X3	—	128
Other administration expenses	128	—
Bad debts	158	—
Cash and bank balance	38	—
Ordinary shares of €1 fully called	—	600
	5,960	5,960

You are informed as follows:

(a) As at 1 October 20X3 land and buildings were revalued at €900,000. A third of the cost as well as all the valuation is regarded as attributable to the land. Directors have decided to report this asset at valuation.

(b) New fixtures were acquired on 1 January 20X4 for €40,000; a machine acquired on 1 October 20X1 for €240,000 was disposed of on 1 July 20X4 for €180,000, being replaced on the same date by another acquired for €320,000.

(c) Depreciation for the year is to be calculated on the straight-line basis as follows:
Buildings: 2% p.a.
Plant and machinery: 10% p.a.
Fixtures and equipment: 10% p.a.

(d) Inventory, including raw materials and work in progress on 30 September 20X4, has been valued at cost at €364,000.

(e) Prepayments are made up as follows:

	€000
Amount paid in advance for a machine	60
Amount paid in advance for purchasing raw materials	40
Prepaid rent	15
	€115

(f) In March 20X3 a customer had filed legal action claiming damages at €240,000. When accounts for the year ended 30 September 20X3 were finalised, a provision of €90,000 was made in respect of this claim. This claim was settled out of court in April 20X4 at €150,000 and the amount of the underprovision adjusted against the profit balance brought forward from previous years.

(g) The following allocations have been agreed upon:

	Factory	Administration
Depreciation of buildings	60%	40%
Salaries other than to directors	55%	45%
Heating and lighting	80%	20%

(h) Pension cost of the company is calculated at 10% of the emoluments and salaries.

(i) Income tax on 20X3 profit has been agreed at €140,000 and that for 20X4 estimated at €185,000.

(j) Directors wish to write off the formation expenses as far as possible without reducing the amount of profits available for distribution.

Required:
Prepare for publication:
(a) the statement of comprehensive income of the company for the year ended 30 September 20X4,
(b) the statement of financial position as at that date along with as many notes (other than the one on accounting policy) as can be provided on the basis of the information made available, and
(c) the statement of changes in equity.

* Question 7

The following is an extract from the trial balance of Imecet at 31 October 2005:

	$000	$000
Property valuation	8,000	
Factory at cost	2,700	
Administration building at cost	1,200	
Delivery vehicles at cost	500	
Sales		10,300
Inventory at 1 November 2004	1,100	
Purchases	6,350	
Factory wages	575	
Administration expenses	140	
Distribution costs	370	
Interest paid (6 months to 30 April 2005)	100	
Accumulated profit at 1 November 2004		3,701
10% loan stock		2,000
$1 ordinary shares (incl. issue on 1 May 2005)		4,000
Share premium (after issue on 1 May 2005)		1,500
Dividends (paid 1 June 2005)	400	
Revaluation reserve		2,500
Deferred tax		650

Other relevant information:

(i)   One million $1 ordinary shares were issued 1 May 2005 at the market price of $1.75 per ordinary share.

(ii)   The inventory at 31 October 2005 has been valued at $1,150,000.

(iii)   A current tax provision for $350,000 is required for the period ended 31 October 2005 and the deferred tax liability at that date has been calculated to be $725,000.

(iv)   The property has been further revalued at 31 October 2005 at the market price of $9,200,000.

(v)   No depreciation charges have yet been recognised for the year ended 31 October 2005.

(vi)   The depreciation rates are:

Factory – 5% straight-line.
Administration building – 3% straight-line.
Delivery vehicles – 25% reducing balance. The accumulated depreciation at 31 October 2004 was $10,000. No new vehicles were acquired in the year to 31 October 2005.

Required:
(a) **Prepare the income statement for Imecet for the year ended 31 October 2005.**
(b) **Prepare the statement of changes in equity for Imecet for the year ended 31 October 2005.**
(The Association of International Accountants)

* Question 8

Scott Ross, CFO of Ryan Industries PLC, is discussing the publication of the annual report with his managing director Nathan Davison. Graydon says: 'The law requires us to comply with accounting standards and at the same time to provide a true and fair view of the results and financial position. As half of the business consists of the crockery and brickmaking business which your great-great-grandmother Sasha started, and the other half is the insurance company which your father started, I am not sure that the consolidated accounts are very meaningful. It is hard to make sense of any of the ratios as you don't know what industry to compare them with. What say we also give them the comprehensive income statements and balance sheets of the two subsidiary companies as additional information, and then no one can complain that they didn't get a true and fair view?'

Nathan says: 'I don't think we should do that. The more information they have the more questions they will ask. Also they might realise we have been smoothing income by changing our level of pessimism in relation to the provisions for outstanding insurance claims. Anyway I don't want them to interfere with my business. Can't we just include a footnote, preferably a vague one, that stresses we are not comparable to insurance companies or brickmakers or crockery manufacturers because of the unique mix of our businesses? Don't raise the matter with the auditors because it will put ideas into their heads. But if it does come up we may have to charge head office costs to the two subsidiaries. You need to think up some reason why most of the charges should be passed on to the crockery operations. We don't want to show everyone how profitable that area is. I trust you will give that some thought so you will have a good answer ready.'

Required:
Discuss the professional, legal and ethical implications for Ross.

* Question 9

TYV is a manufacturing entity and produces a range of products in several factories.
TYV's trial balance at 30 September 2014 is shown below

	Notes	$000	$000
Accumulated depreciation at 30 September 2013:			
Buildings	(i)		1,700
Plant and equipment	(iv)		4,510
Administrative expenses		1,820	
Cash and cash equivalents		272	
Cost of sales		10,200	
Distribution costs		1,110	
Equity dividend paid		350	
Equity shares $1 each, fully paid at 30 September 2014			6,000
Finance charges for new factory building		113	
Income tax	(v)	80	
Inventory at 30 September 2014		575	
Land and buildings at cost at 30 September 2013	(ii) & (iii)	17,386	
Long-term borrowings	(vi)		5,000
Long-term borrowings loan interest	(vi)	233	
New factory building cost		1,014	
Plant and equipment at cost at 30 September 2013	(iv)	7,750	
Provision for deferred tax at 30 September 2013	(v)	625	
Receipt from disposal of plant and equipment	(iv)		7
Retained earnings at 30 September 2013			491
Sales revenue			19,460
Share premium at 30 September 2014			850
Short-term loan	(iii)		1,500
Suspense account	(ii)		1,130
Trade payables			1,880
Trade receivables		2,250	
		43,153	43,153

Notes:

(i) On 1 October 2013 two of TYV's factories, factory A and factory B, were deemed obsolete and no longer suitable for TYV's use. On 1 June 2014 both factories were closed and production moved to a new facility. TYV disposed of factory B with all legal formalities completed and cash received on 31 August 2014. Factory A was not sold by the financial year-end; however at 30 September 2014 negotiations for the sale of factory A were well advanced and TYV's management expected to conclude the sale by 31 December 2014. The cost and accumulated depreciation included in land and buildings along with the fair value of each factory is shown below:

Factory	Cost		Depreciation	Fair value less
	Land	Buildings	at 30 September 2013	cost of disposal at 30 Sept 2014
A	$1,375,000	$455,000	$364,000	$1,420,000
B	$1,120,000	$325,000	$286,000	$1,130,000

(ii) The suspense account is the cash received from the disposal of factory B. The only entries made in the ledgers for this item were in cash and cash equivalents and suspense account.

(iii) The cost of land included in land and buildings was $11,000,000 on 1 October 2013. TYV built the new factory on land it already owned, commencing on 1 October 2013 and completing it on 30 June 2014. To fund the project TYV raised a short-term loan on 1 October 2013, repayable on 30 September 2015.

(iv) Plant and equipment in factories A and B was relocated to the new factory, except for plant and equipment with a carrying value of $55,000 (cost $175,000) that was sold as scrap, realising $7,000. Buildings are depreciated at 2% per annum on the straight-line basis. Buildings depreciation is treated as an administrative expense. Plant and equipment is depreciated at 25% per annum using the reducing balance method and is charged to cost of sales. TYV's accounting policy for depreciation is to charge a full year in the year of acquisition and none in the year of disposal.

(v) The directors estimate the income tax charge on the year's profits at $940,000. The balance on the income tax account represents the under-provision for the previous year's tax charge. The deferred tax provision is to be reduced by $49,000.

(vi) The long-term borrowings consist of one loan issued in 2000 for 20 years at 7% interest per year. Interest is paid half yearly on 1 June and 1 December.

Required:
Prepare TYV's statement of profit or loss and a statement of changes in equity for the year ended 30 September 2014 and a statement of financial position at that date, in accordance with the requirements of International Financial Reporting Standards.
All workings should be to the nearest $000. Notes to the financial statements are not required but all workings must be clearly shown. Do not prepare a statement of accounting policies.

(CIMA Financial Operations November 2014)

Notes

1 IAS 1 *Presentation of Financial Statements*, IASB, December 2008.
2 D. Dhaliwal, K. Subramnayam and R. Trezevant, 'Is comprehensive income superior to net income as a measure of firm performance?', *Journal of Accounting and Economics*, vol. 26(1), 1999, pp. 43–67.
3 D. Hirst and P. Hopkins, 'Comprehensive income reporting and analysts' valuation judgments', *Journal of Accounting Research*, vol. 36 (Supplement), 1998, pp. 47–74.

4 G.C. Biddles and J.-H. Choi, 'Is comprehensive income irrelevant?', 12 June 2002. Available at SSRN: http://ssrn.com/abstract=316703

5 G. Livne and M. McNichols, *An Empirical Investigation of the True and Fair Override*, LBS Accounting Subject Area Working Paper No. 031 (www.bm.ust.hk/acct/acsymp2004/Papers/Livne.pdf).

6 www.iaasa.ie/publications/IAS1/ebook/IAS1_Commentary.pdf

7 Companies Act 2006 (Strategic Report and Directors Report) Regulations 2013.

8 Guidance for Strategic Report, FRC, August 2014.

9 www.accaglobal.com/gb/en/technical-activities/technical-resources-search/2010/september/hitting-the-notes.html

10 www.frc.org.uk/Our-Work/Publications/Accounting-and-Reporting-Policy/Clear-Concise-Developments-in-Narrative-Reporti.aspx

11 www.accaglobal.com/content/dam/acca/global/PDF-technical/narrative-reporting/writing_the_narrative.pdf

12 https://www.efrag.org/Assets/Download?assetUrl=%2Fsites%2Fwebpublishing%2FMeeting%20Documents%2F1607180830326300%2F10-02%20Issues%20Paper%20-%20Primary%20Financial%20Statements%20-%20Scope%20of%20the%20project%20-%20TEG%2017-01-25.pdf

13 G. Livne and M.F. McNichols, 'An empirical investigation of the true and fair override', *Journal of Business, Finance and Accounting*, pp. 1–30, January/March 2009.

14 www.pwc.com/gx/en/corporate-reporting/assets/pdfs/UK_KPI_guide.pdf

CHAPTER 8

Annual report: additional financial disclosures

8.1 Introduction

The main purpose of this chapter is to explain the additional content in an Annual Report that assists users to make informed assessments of stewardship and informed estimates of future financial performance. Investors need to be able to assess the effect on the published accounts of (a) transactions occurring after the year-end and (b) transactions occurring during the year that might not have been at arm's length. In looking at the future, investors need information on (a) the profitability of different product lines and markets and (b) the potential financial impact if any part of the business has been discontinued.

Objectives

By the end of this chapter, you should be able to:

- make appropriate entries in the financial statements and/or disclosure in the notes to the accounts in accordance with IAS 10 *Events after the Reporting Period*;
- make appropriate entries in the financial statements in accordance with IAS 8 *Accounting Policies, Changes in Accounting Estimates and Errors*;
- identify reportable segments in accordance with IFRS 8 *Operating Segments*;
- critically discuss the benefits and continuing concerns of segmental reporting;
- explain the meaning of the term and account for 'discontinued operations' in accordance with IFRS 5 *Non-current Assets Held for Sale and Discontinued Operations*;
- prepare financial statements applying IFRS 5;
- discuss the impact of such operations on the statement of comprehensive income;
- explain the criteria laid out in IFRS 5 that need to be satisfied before an asset (or disposal group) is classified as 'held for sale';
- explain how to identify key personnel for the purposes of IAS 24 *Related Party Disclosures* and why this is considered to be important.

8.2 IAS 10 *Events after the Reporting Period*[1]

We have seen that transactions listed in the trial balance need to be adjusted for accruals and prepayments. They may also need to be adjusted as a result of further information becoming available after the year-end. This is covered in IAS 10.

IAS 10 requires preparers of financial statements to review events that occur after the reporting date but before the financial statements have been authorised for issue by the directors to decide whether an **adjustment** is required to be made to the financial statements or explanatory information is required to be **disclosed** by way of a note.

8.2.1 Adjusting events

These are events after the reporting period that provide additional evidence of conditions that existed at the period-end. Examples of such events include, but are not limited to:

- *Inventory*: After-date sales of inventory that provide additional evidence that the net realisable value of the inventory at the reporting date was lower than cost.

- *Liabilities*: Evidence received after the year-end that provides additional evidence of the appropriate measurement of a liability that existed at the reporting date, such as the settlement of a contingent liability or the calculation of bonuses for which an obligation existed at the end of the reporting period.

- *Non-current assets*: The revaluation of an asset such as a property that indicates the likelihood of impairment at the reporting date.

- The discovery of fraud or errors that show that the financial statements are incorrect.

Under IAS 10 such information becoming available after the period-end means that the financial statements themselves have to be adjusted **provided** the information becomes available before the accounts have been approved. It is important to consider the date of the period-end, the date when the financial statements are approved and the date when transactions/events occurred.

For example, consider the following scenario. Financial statements are being prepared for the year ended 31 March 20X4 and are expected to be approved in the Annual General Meeting announced for 25 June 20X4. Reviewing the audit file on 15 May, it was noted that the audit staff had identified on 29 April that stores staff had misappropriated a material amount of stock before the year-end and concealed it by reporting it as damaged. The police have been informed and are investigating. Should the financial statements be adjusted?

Solution: As the fraud involves a material amount occurring during the reporting period but which is only discovered after the period-end, it is classified as an adjusting event and the financial statements would require amendment.

Consideration would then be required of the accounting implications. For example, what is the impact on the cost of sales and the gross profit if closing inventory has been over-stated? Is it necessary to disclose the loss as an exceptional item? What is the likelihood of recovering recompense from the staff themselves or the company's insurers? Is any recovery an asset or contingent asset?

8.2.2 Non-adjusting events

These are events occurring after the reporting period that concern conditions that did not exist at the statement of financial position date. Examples would include:

- Dividends proposed. These must be disclosed in the notes [IAS 1.137]: 'the amount of dividends proposed or declared before the financial statements were authorised for issue but not recognised as a distribution to owners during the period'. The concept of a 'dividend liability' for equity shares has effectively disappeared.

- Interim dividends are not non-adjusting events, because they will have been paid during the reporting period, whereas final dividends are at the discretion of the reporting entity until approved by shareholders at a general meeting.

- An issue or redemption of shares after the reporting date, as in the following extract from the 2015 Annual Report of the InterContinental Hotels Group:

Events after the reporting period
In February 2016, the Board proposed a $1.5 billion return of funds to shareholders via a special dividend with share consolidation.

- Potential restructuring implications, as in the following extract from the 2013 Annual Report of Mothercare plc:

As part of the Transformation and Growth plan an in-depth organisational review was conducted to streamline the group's structure and processes. As a result of the potential restructuring a number of employees in the head office in the UK and the overseas sourcing offices are in consultation. There are likely to be additional exceptional costs of approximately £5 million in respect of the implementation of this review and these will be charged in the next financial year.

- An announcement after the reporting date of a plan to acquire another company or discontinue an operation or entering into binding agreements to sell, all of which are non-adjusting but require to be disclosed, as in the following extract from the 2014 Metrogroup Annual Report.

As part of the decision taken during the reporting period to withdraw from the wholesale business in Denmark, METRO GROUP signed an agreement in October on the partial sale of METRO Cash & Carry Denmark to Euro Cater, a leading grocery wholesaler in Denmark and Sweden. Subject to the approval of Danish antitrust authorities, Euro Cater will take over the wholesale stores in Glostrup and Aarhus. In addition, METRO GROUP will close the remaining three wholesale stores in Denmark on 31 December 2014 and thus withdraw from the Danish market.

- The loss or other decline in value of assets due to events occurring after the reporting date.

- Entering into significant contracts, as in the following extract from the Deutz 2011 Annual Report:

On 12 January 2012, DEUTZ AG signed an agreement with the Chinese construction and agricultural equipment manufacturer Shandong Changlin Machinery Group to establish a company for the production of engines . . . . Over the medium term, the new plant will have a production capacity of around 65,000 engines . . . . At the moment, China represents the greatest area of potential growth for DEUTZ within the Asia region as a whole.

8.2.3 Going concern issues

Deterioration in the operating results or other major losses that occur after the period-end are basically non-adjusting events. However, if they are of such significance as to affect the going concern basis of preparation of the financial statements, then this impacts on the numbers in the financial statements, because the going concern assumption would no longer be appropriate. In this limited set of circumstances if the going concern assumption is no longer appropriate, IAS 10 requires the financial statements to be produced on a liquidation rather than going concern basis.

8.3 IAS 8 *Accounting Policies, Changes in Accounting Estimates and Errors*[2]

IAS 8 gives guidance when deciding whether to make a retrospective or prospective change to financial statements. A retrospective change means that the financial statements of the current and previous years will be affected. A prospective change means that accounting treatments in future years will be affected.

Let us now consider how to treat accounting policy changes, prior period adjustments and changes in accounting estimates in accordance with IAS 8.

8.3.1 Accounting policy changes

Accounting policies may be changed when required by a new IFRS or when management decide that it results in more relevant and reliable information being provided to users.

(a) When this occurs as a result of changes arising from the first application of a new IFRS

In this case there is normally a retrospective impact. For example, consider the effect on the financial statements if research costs had been capitalised by a company and a subsequent mandatory change then requires these costs to be expensed.

The research asset brought forward at the beginning of the year is treated as though it had already been expensed, which means it is eliminated and the retained earnings brought forward are reduced. The net result is that the opening assets and opening retained earnings are both reduced. Any research costs incurred in the current period will be charged to the current statement of income.

(b) When this occurs as a result of a change in circumstances

In this case, an entity might have applied one standard to an asset quite appropriately in one year and applied a different standard quite appropriately in the following year as its business circumstances change. For example, inventory reported under IAS 2 might be reported under IAS 16 if it is used in the construction of a capital asset. There would be no retrospective impact. The valuation would move from IAS 2 reporting at the lower of cost and net realisable value to reporting at cost/valuation less depreciation.

8.3.2 Prior period errors including both honest mistakes and fraud Materiality

Changes are only required if the errors are material. Omissions or misstatements of items are material if they could, individually or collectively, influence the economic decisions that users make on the basis of the financial statements. Materiality depends on the size and nature of the omission or misstatement judged in the surrounding circumstances.

A decision as to their materiality depends on the entity-specific circumstances and questions would need to be asked. For example, does it change a loss to a profit? Does it avoid failing to comply with a loan covenant? Does it have the effect of increasing management's bonuses?

Criteria

We need to be familiar with the criteria set out in the standard for prior period errors. These are as follows:

- Omissions from, and misstatements in, the entity's financial statements for one or more prior periods arising from a failure to use, or misuse of, reliable information that:
  - was available when financial statements for those periods were authorised for issue, and
  - could reasonably be expected to have been obtained and taken into account when preparing the financial statements.
- Possible scenarios:
  - Classification: current accounts payable have been classified as long-term liabilities. This might have occurred due to error or a deliberate attempt to improve the liquidity ratio – either way, the accounts payable and long-term debt must be restated;
  - Omission: trade payable invoices might have been concealed;
  - Valuation: inventory might have been overvalued by failing to record effect of obsolescence, or trade receivables overstated by failing to make adequate provision for bad debts. Expenses might have been incorrectly capitalised.

Retained earnings restated

In each case we have to consider the effect on the retained earnings brought forward. For example, a material expense that was incorrectly capitalised would require both retained earnings and the asset to be reduced. In such a case, we would need to also consider other consequential changes such as the reversal of depreciation if that had been charged against the capital item.

8.3.3 Accounting estimates

Changes in methods, such as a change from straight-line depreciation to reducing balance, and changes in assumptions, such as a change in the expected economic life of an asset, do not result in any adjustment of retained earnings. These are changes being made at the end of the financial period which have a *current* and *prospective* impact in future periods.

Management should disclose, in a note to the financial statements, details of the nature of the change, and the related amounts if the change in accounting estimate has a material effect on the current period.

If criteria for treatment as a prior period error cannot be satisfied, transactions are treated as changes in accounting estimates with a prospective impact. For example, the following is an extract from the 2012 Annual Report of Imtech NV:

> The prior period errors . . . stem from accounting irregularities. These accounting irregularities resulted in an overstatement of past results, net assets by overstating receivables, work-in-progress and revenue, and understating certain costs and payables. The reversal of the respective incorrect amounts results in a negative effect in the profit and loss account . . . and a correction . . . in the balance sheets.. . .
>
> Adjustments only qualified as prior period errors when an objective determination whether the adjustment was a prior period error could be made. When this was not the case, the adjustment was accounted for as a change in estimate in 2012.

8.4 What do segment reports provide?

Segment reports provide a more detailed breakdown of key numbers from the financial statements. Such a breakdown potentially allows a user to:

- be more aware of the balance between the different operations and thus able to assess the quality of the entity's reported earnings, the specific risks to which the company is subject, and the areas where long-term growth may be expected;
- appreciate more thoroughly the results and financial position by permitting a better understanding of past performance and thus a better assessment of future prospects;
- be aware of the impact that changes in significant components of a business may have on the business as a whole.

The IASB requirements are set out in IFRS 8 *Operating Segments.*

8.5 IFRS 8 *Operating Segments*[3]

IFRS 8 applies to both separate and consolidated financial statements of entities

- whose debt or equity instruments are traded in a public market; or
- that file financial statements with a securities commission or other regulatory organisation for the purpose of issuing any class of instruments in the public market.

We will comment briefly on the following four key areas:

- identification of segments;
- identification of reportable segments;
- measurement of segment information; and
- disclosures.

8.5.1 Identification of segments

IFRS 8 requires the identification of operating segments on the basis of internal reports that are regularly reviewed by the entity's chief operating decision maker (CODM) in order to allocate resources to the segment and assess its performance. A segment that sells exclusively or mainly to other operating segments of the group meets the definition of an operating segment if the business is managed in that way.

Criteria for identifying a segment

An operating segment is a component of an entity:

(a) that engages in business activities from which it may earn revenues and incur expenses;

(b) whose operating results are regularly reviewed by the entity's chief operating decision maker, to make decisions about resources to be allocated to the segment and to assess its performance; and

(c) for which discrete financial information is available.

Not every part of the entity will necessarily be an operating segment. For example, a corporate headquarters may not earn revenues.

Criteria for identifying the chief operating decision maker

The chief operating decision maker (CODM) may be an individual or a group of directors or others. The key identifying factors will be those of performance assessment and resource allocation. Some organisations may have overlapping sets of components for which managers are responsible, e.g. some managers may be responsible for specific geographic areas and others for products worldwide. If the CODM reviews the operating results of both sets of components, the entity determines which constitutes the operating segments using the core principles (a)–(c) above.

8.5.2 Identifying reportable segments

Once an operating segment has been identified, a decision has to be made as to whether it has to be reported. The segment information is required to be reported for any operating segment that meets any of the following criteria:

(a) its reported revenue, from internal and external customers, is 10% or more of the combined revenue (internal and external) of all operating segments; or

(b) the absolute measure of its reported profit or loss is 10% or more of the greater in absolute amount of (i) the combined profit of all operating segments that did not report a loss and (ii) the combined reported loss of all operating segments that reported a loss; or

(c) its assets are 10% or more of the combined assets of all operating segments.

Failure to meet any of the criteria does not, however, preclude a company from reporting a segment's results. Operating segments that do not meet any of the criteria may be disclosed voluntarily, if management think the information would be useful to users of the financial statements.

The 75% test

If the total external revenue of the reportable operating segments is less than 75% of the entity's revenue, additional operating segments need to be identified as reportable segments (even if they don't meet the criteria in (a)–(c) above) until 75% of the entity's revenue is included.

Combining segments

IFRS 8 includes detailed guidance on which operating segments may be combined to create a reportable segment, e.g. if they have mainly similar products, processes, customers, distribution methods and regulatory environments. Where there is an aggregation of operating segments an entity is required to disclose the judgements made by management in applying the aggregation criteria to operating segments.

Although IFRS 8 does not specify a maximum number of segments, it suggests that if the reportable segments exceed 10, the entity should consider whether a practical limit had been reached, as the disclosures may become too detailed.

EXAMPLE ● Varia plc is a large training and media entity with an important international component. It operates a state-of-the-art management information system which provides its directors with the information they require to plan and control the various businesses. The directors' reporting requirements are quite detailed and information is collected about the following divisions: Exam-based Training, E-Learning, Corporate Training, Print Media, Online Publishing and Cable Television. The following information is available for the year ended 31 December 20X9:

Division	Total revenue	Profit	Assets
	£m	£m	£m
Exam-based Training	360	21	176
E-Learning	60	3	13
Corporate Training	125	5	84
Print Media	232	27	102
Online Publishing	124	2	31
Cable TV	73	5	39
	974	63	445

Question

Which of Varia plc's divisions are reportable segments in accordance with IFRS 8 *Operating segments?*

Solution

- The revenues of Exam-based Training, Corporate Training, Print Media and Online Publishing are clearly more than 10% of total revenues and so these segments are reportable.

- All three numbers for E-Learning and Cable TV are under 10% of entity totals for revenue, profit and assets and so, unless these segments can validly be combined with others for reporting purposes, they are not reportable separately, although Varia could choose to provide separate information.

As a final check we need to establish that the combined revenues of reportable segments we have identified (£360million + £125million + £232million + £124million = £841million) is at least 75% of the total revenues of Varia of £974 million. £841 million is 86% of £974 million so this condition is satisfied. Therefore no other segments need to be added.

8.5.3 Measuring segment information

IFRS 8 specifies that the amount reported for each segment should be the measures reported to the chief operating decision maker for the purposes of allocating resources and assessing performance. It does not define segment revenue, segment expense, segment result, segment assets, and segment liabilities but rather requires an explanation of how segment profit or loss and segment assets and segment liabilities are measured for each reportable segment.

Allocations and adjustments to revenues and profit should only be included in segment disclosures if they are reviewed by the CODM.

8.5.4 Disclosure requirements for reportable segments

The principle in IFRS 8 is that an entity should disclose 'information to enable users to evaluate the nature and financial effect of the business activities in which it engages and the economic environment in which it operates'.

IFRS 8 requires disclosure of the following segment information:

(i) Factors used to identify the entity's operating segments such as whether management organises the entity around products and services, geographical areas, regulatory environments, or a combination of factors, and whether segments have been aggregated.

(ii) Types of products and services from which each reportable segment derives its revenues.

(iii) A measure of profit or loss for each reportable segment.

(iv) A measure of liabilities for each reportable segment if it is regularly provided to the chief operating decision maker.

(v)   The following items if they are disclosed in the performance statement reviewed by the chief operating decision maker:
- revenues from external customers and from transactions with other operating segments
- interest revenue and interest expense
- depreciation and amortisation
- 'exceptional' items
- income tax income or expense
- other material non-cash items.

(vi) Total assets; total amounts for additions to non-current assets if they are regularly provided to the chief operating decision maker.

(vii) Reconciliations of profit or loss to the group totals for the entity.

(viii) Reliance on major customers. If revenues from a single external customer are 10% or more of the entity's total revenue, it must disclose that fact and the segment reporting the revenue. It need not disclose the identity of the major customer or the amount of the revenue.

8.5.6 Sample disclosures under IFRS 8

We consider (1) the format for disclosure of segment profits or loss, assets and liabilities, (2) the reconciliations of reportable segment revenues and assets, and (3) information about major customers.

(1) Format for disclosure of segment profits or loss, assets and liabilities

	Hotels	Software	Finance	Other	Entity totals
	£m	£m	£m	£m	£m
Revenue from external customers	**800**	**2,150**	**500**	**100**[a]	**3,550**
Intersegment revenue	—	450	—	—	450
Interest revenue	125	250	—	—	375
Interest expense	95	180	—	—	275
Net interest revenue[b]	—	—	100	—	100
Depreciation and amortisation	30	155	110	—	295
Reportable segment profit	*27*	*320*	*50*	*10*	*407*
Other material non-cash items impairment of assets	20	—	—	—	20
Reportable segment assets	*700*	*1,500*	*5,700*	*200*	*8,100*
Expenditure for reportable segment non-current assets	100	130	60	—	290
Reportable segment liabilities	*405*	*980*	*3,000*	—	*4,385*

Reconciliations to group totals are in ***bold italics***.

Notes:

(a) Revenue from segments below the quantitative thresholds are attributed to four operating divisions. Those segments include a small electronics company, a warehouse leasing company, a retailer and an undertakers. None of these segments has ever met any of the quantitative thresholds for determining reportable segments.

(b) The finance segment derives most of its revenue from interest. Management primarily relies on net interest revenue, not the gross revenue and expense amounts, in managing that segment. Therefore, as permitted by paragraph 23, only net interest is disclosed.

(2) Reconciliations of reportable segment revenues and assets

Reconciliations are required for every material item disclosed. The following are just sample reconciliations.

Revenues	£m
Total revenues for reportable segments	3,900
Other revenues	100
Elimination of intersegment revenues	(450)
Entity's revenue	**3,550**

Profit or loss	£m
Total profit or loss for reportable segments	397
Other profit or loss	10
Entity profit	**407**

Assets	£m
Total assets for reportable segments	7,900
Other assets	200
Entity assets	**8,100**

(3) Information about major customers

A sample disclosure might be:

> Revenues from one customer of the software and hotels segments represent approximately £400 million of the entity's total revenue.

(Note that disclosure is not required of the customer's name or of the revenue for each operating segment.)

8.6 Benefits and continuing concerns following the issue of IFRS 8

8.6.1 The benefits of segment reporting

The majority of listed and other large entities derive their revenues and profits from a number of sources (or segments). This has implications for the investment strategy of the entity, as different segments require different amounts of investment to support their activities. Conventionally produced statements of financial position and statements of comprehensive income capture financial position and financial performance in a single column of figures.

The following is an extract from the Tesco 2011/12 Annual Report reporting on five segments within the group:

	Trading profit	Trading margin %	Growth %	Sales	Growth %
Group results	3,761m	5.8%	1.3%	72,035m	7.4%
UK	2,480m	5.8%	(1.0)%	47,355m	6.2%
Asia	737m	6.8%	21.5%	11,627m	10.4%
Europe	529m	5.3%	(0.4)%	11,371m	7.8%
US	(153m)	(24.2)%	17.7%	638m	31.5%
Tesco Bank	168m	16.1%	(36.4)%	1,044m	13.6%

We can see that the group is showing a trading profit growth of 1.3%. Within that, segments vary from negative growth of 36.4% to positive growth of 21.5%. Individual segments are also interesting, with sales in the US increasing by 31.5% whilst there is a trading loss.

To put the segment results into a group context we can see their relative importance to the group expressed as a percentage of the group totals as follows:

	Trading profit %	Sales %
UK	66	66
Asia	20	16
Europe	14	16
US	(4)	1
Tesco Bank	4	1

The losses are a red flag to investors and the problem is addressed in the Annual Report by the Chairman, who writes as follows:

> Elsewhere, we have continued the substantial reorientation of the US business to give it the best possible opportunity to secure its future with all the potential for longer-term growth that would bring. We have announced our intention to exit from Japan. We are willing to invest for the long term but where we cannot see a profitable, scalable business earning good returns within an acceptable timescale, we prefer to pursue better opportunities. And we have slowed down the development of Tesco Bank to increase its focus on quality, service and risk management.

8.6.2 Post-implementation Review: IFRS 8 *Operating Segments*[4]

IFRS 8 was the first standard to be subjected to a post-implementation review by the IASB. The review identified different opinions among the stakeholders.

Preparers

Standard setters, accounting firms and auditors generally supported the standard subject to suggestions for improvement.

Investors

Views were mixed. Some were concerned that operating segments are aggregated inappropriately. Also there were concerns that, as the segmentation process is based on the management perspective, there is a risk that commercially sensitive information might be concealed or segments reported to conceal loss-making activities within individual segments.

Others welcome the fact that the report is audited and discloses information about how management views the business. They see added value if the segments agree with the management commentary and analyst presentations.

Suggestions for improvement

Replace the term 'chief operating decision maker CODM' with a more common term such as key management personnel or governing body. Also, many entities present different definitions of 'operating result' or 'operating cash flow', making comparison difficult between entities. Investors would like defined line items so that they could calculate their own subtotals for operating result or cash flow.

8.6.4 Constraints on comparison between entities

Segment reporting is intrinsically subjective. This means that there are likely to be major differences in the way segments are determined and because costs, for instance, may be allocated differently by entities in the same industry, it is difficult to make inter-entity comparisons at the segment level and the user still has to take a great deal of responsibility for the interpretation of that information.

8.7 Discontinued operations – IFRS 5 *Non-current Assets Held for Sale and Discontinued Operations*[5]

IFRS 5 deals, as its name suggests, with two separate but related issues. We will first discuss the treatment of discontinued operations.

8.7.1 Criteria

We need to be familiar with the IFRS 5 definition of a discontinued operation. It is a component of an entity that, during the reporting period, either:

- has been disposed of (whether by sale or abandonment); or
- has been classified as held for sale, and *also*
  - represents a separate major line of business or geographical area of operations; or
  - is part of a single coordinated plan to dispose of a separate major line of business or geographical area of operations; or
  - is a subsidiary acquired exclusively with a view to resale (possibly as part of the acquisition of an existing group with a subsidiary that does not fit into the long-term plans of the acquirer).

Defining a component

The IFRS defines a component as a part of an entity which comprises operations and cash flows that can be clearly distinguished, operationally and for financial reporting purposes, from the rest of the entity. This definition is somewhat subjective and the IASB is considering amending this definition to align it with that of an operating segment in IFRS 8 and has issued an exposure draft to this effect.

8.7.2 Disclosure in the statement of income

The results of discontinued operations should be separately disclosed from those of other, continuing, operations in the income statement. As a minimum, on the face of the statement, entities should show, as a single amount, the total of:

- the post-tax profit or loss of discontinued operations; and
- the post-tax gain or loss recognised on the measurement to fair value less cost to sell or on the disposal of the assets or disposal group(s) constituting the discontinued operation.

Further analysis of this amount required, either on the face of the statement of comprehensive income or in the notes:

- the revenue, expenses and pre-tax profit or loss of discontinued operations;
- the related income tax expense as required by IAS 12;
- the gain or loss recognised on the measurement to fair value less costs to sell or on the disposal of the assets or disposal group(s) constituting the discontinued operation; and
- the related income tax expense as required by IAS 12.

The following is an extract from Premier Foods' 2011 consolidated income statement:

	2011 £m	2010 £m
Continuing operations		
(Loss)/profit before taxation from continuing operations	**(259.1)**	28.5
Taxation credit/(charge)	**29.1**	(24.4)
(Loss)/profit after taxation from continuing operations	**(230.0)**	4.1
Loss from discontinued operations	(109.0)	(103.4)
Loss for the year attributable to equity shareholders of the Parent Company	(339.0)	(99.3)

There is a supporting note which details the makeup of the £109m showing the revenue, operating expenses, tax and loss on disposal.

8.8 Held for sale – IFRS 5 *Non-current Assets Held for Sale and Discontinued Operations*

Let us now discuss the treatment of assets which have been classified as held for sale.

IFRS 5 deals with the appropriate reporting of an asset (or group of assets – referred to in IFRS 5 as a 'disposal group') that management has decided to dispose of. It states that an asset (or disposal group) is classified as 'held for sale' if its carrying amount will be recovered principally through a sale transaction rather than through continuing use.

It further provides that:

- the asset or disposal group must be **available for immediate sale** in its present condition; and
- its sale must be highly probable.

The criteria for the sale to be highly probable are:

- The appropriate level of management must be committed to a plan to sell the asset or disposal group.

- An active programme to locate a buyer and complete the plan must have been initiated.

- The asset or disposal group must be actively marketed for sale at a price that is reasonable in relation to its current fair value.

- The sale should be expected to qualify for recognition as a completed sale within one year from the date of classification.

- Actions required to complete the plan should indicate that it is unlikely that significant changes to the plan will be made or that the plan will be withdrawn.

There is a pragmatic recognition that there may be events outside the control of the enterprise which prevent completion within one year. In such a case the 'held for sale' classification is retained, provided there is sufficient evidence that the entity remains committed to its plan to sell the asset or disposal group and has taken all reasonable steps to resolve the delay.

It is important to note that IFRS 5 specifies that this classification is appropriate for assets (or disposal groups) that are to be **sold** or distributed. The classification does not apply to assets or disposal groups that are to be **abandoned**.

8.8.1 IFRS 5 – implications of classification as held for sale

Assets, or disposal groups, that are classified as held for sale should be removed from their previous position in the statement of financial position and shown under a single 'held for sale' caption – usually as part of **current** assets. Any liabilities directly associated with disposal groups that are classified as held for sale should be separately presented within liabilities.

As far as disposal groups are concerned, it is acceptable to present totals on the face of the statement of financial position, with a more detailed breakdown in the notes. The following is a disclosure note from the published financial statements of Unilever for the year ended 31 December 2015:

Assets and liabilities held for sale	2015	2014
	£m	£m
Groups held for sale		
Goodwill and intangibles	43	12
Property, plant and equipment	73	4
Inventories	35	1
Trade and other receivables	3	1
Other	5	5
	159	23
Non-current assets held for sale		
Property, plant and equipment	20	24
Liabilities associated with assets held for sale		1

Depreciable assets that are classified as 'held for sale' should not be depreciated from classification date, as the classification implies that the intention of management is primarily to recover value from such assets through sale, rather than through continued use.

When assets (or disposal groups) are classified as 'held for sale', their carrying value(s) at the date of classification should be compared with the 'fair value less costs to sell' of the asset (or disposal group). If the fair value less costs to sell exceeds the carrying value, the carrying value is the amount reported as the current asset. If the transfer occurs during an accounting period, the position is reassessed at the end of the period. For example, assume that a non-current asset acquired on 1 April 2014 at a cost of £100,000 and depreciated at 10% per annum on a straight-line basis is classified as held for sale on 1 October 2016 when fair value less cost to sell was £85,000 – reassessed on 31 March 2017 as £62,000.

The fair value of £85,000 exceeded the carrying value of £75,000 (£100,000 less 2.5 years' depreciation) which means that it is recorded as a current asset at its carrying value of £75,000. If the carrying value exceeds fair value less costs to sell then the excess should be treated as an impairment loss. As the fair value at 31 March 2017 was £62,000 there is an impairment of £13,000 recognised in profit or loss.

In the case of a disposal group, the impairment loss should be allocated to the specific assets in the order specified in IAS 36 *Impairment of Assets*. The treatment of impairment losses is discussed in detail in Chapter 3.

What if a non-current asset ceases to be classified as held for sale?

When a non-current asset ceases to be classified as held for sale paragraph 27 of IFRS 5 *Non-current Assets Held for Sale and Discontinued Operations* requires a new measurement basis. Paragraph 27 of IFRS 5 states:

> The entity shall measure a non-current asset that ceases to be classified as held for sale (or ceases to be included in a disposal group classified as held for sale) at the lower of:
>
> (a) its carrying amount before the asset (or disposal group) was classified as held for sale, adjusted for any depreciation, amortisation or revaluations that would have been recognised had the asset (or disposal group) not been classified as held for sale, and
>
> (b) its *recoverable amount* at the date of the subsequent decision not to sell.

8.9 IAS 24 *Related Party Disclosures*[6]

In the previous chapter we saw that after the financial statements have been drafted it is necessary to form a judgement as to whether or not they give a fair presentation of the entity's activities.

One of the considerations is whether there are any indications that transactions have not been carried out at arm's length. This can occur when one of the parties to the transaction is able to influence the management to enter into transactions which are not primarily in the best interest of the company. Where such a possibility exists, the person (or business) able to exert this influence is referred to in accounting terms as a 'related party'.

The users of financial statements would normally assume that the transactions of an entity have been carried out at arm's length and under terms which are in the best interests of the entity. The existence of related party relationships may mean that this assumption is not appropriate and IAS 24 therefore requires disclosure of such existence.

8.9.1 How to determine what is 'arm's length'

The Board of a company should consider a number of surrounding factors when determining whether a transaction has been at arm's length. These include considering:

● how the terms of the overall transaction compare with those of any comparable transactions between parties dealing on an arm's length basis in similar circumstances;

● the level of risk – how the transaction impacts on the company's financial position and performance, its ability to follow its business plan and the expected rate of return on the assets given the level of risk;

● other options – what other options were available to the company and whether any expert advice was obtained by the company.

8.9.2 IAS 24 disclosures required

The purpose of IAS 24 is to define the meaning of the term 'related party' and prescribe the disclosures that are appropriate for transactions with related parties (and in some cases for their mere existence). From the outset it is worth remembering that the term 'party' could refer to an individual (referred to as a person) or to another entity. IAS 24 breaks the definition down into two main sections relating to (a) persons and (b) entities. We will consider both below.

8.9.3 Definition of 'related party' when the party is a person

A person, or a close member of that person's family, whom we will refer to as P, is a related party to the reporting entity (RE) if:

- P has control or joint control over RE;
- P has significant influence over RE; or
- P is a member of the key management personnel of RE.

Close members of the family of P are those family members who may be expected to influence, or be influenced by, P in their dealings with RE and include:

- P's children and spouse or domestic partner; and
- children of the spouse or domestic partner; and
- dependants of P or P's spouse or domestic partner.

Key management personnel of RE are those persons having authority and responsibility for planning, directing and controlling the activities of RE, directly or indirectly, including any director (whether executive or otherwise) of RE.

Example: Individual as investor

Let us assume that Arthur has 60% of the shares in, and so controls, Garden Supplies Ltd and:

(a) he also has a 45% significant interest in Plant Growers Ltd. This means that in Garden Supplies Ltd's financial statements Plant Growers Ltd are a related party, and in Plant Growers Ltd's financial statements Garden Supplies Ltd are a related party; or

(b) a close member of his family (in this case his domestic partner) owns a 45% interest in Plant Growers Ltd. This means that a similar treatment would be required and the two companies are related; or

(c) Arthur still has the 60% interest in Garden Supplies Ltd but instead of having an investment in Plant Growers Ltd he is a member of Plant Growers Ltd's key management personnel. This means that a similar treatment would be required and the two companies are related.

8.9.4 Definition of 'related party' when the party is another entity

We have discussed the position where the related party relationship arises from an individual's relationship with two businesses. It also arises when companies are involved.

For example, let us now assume that Arthur, Garden Supplies and Plant Growers are all limited companies. We classify each company as follows:

- Arthur Ltd holds 60% of the shares and so is a parent of Garden Supplies Ltd.
- Plant Growers Ltd is an associate of Arthur Ltd because Arthur Ltd can exercise significant influence over Plant Growers Ltd.

This means that when any of the companies prepares its financial statements:

- Arthur Ltd is related to both Garden Supplies Ltd and Plant Growers Ltd.
- Garden Supplies Ltd is related to Plant Growers Ltd.
- Plant Growers Ltd is related to Garden Supplies Ltd.

8.9.5 Identifying related parties is not always clear

In the above examples we have clear knowledge of the relationship. However, there could be an intention to conceal the relationship, which requires ingenuity from any auditor. Steps might need to be taken such as discussions with lawyers and searching company records, referring to daily newspapers, trade magazines and phone books and, of course, using the Internet and social network sites.

The IASB has this area under review and, in its 2013 Annual Improvement Initiative, requires an entity that provides key management personnel services to be treated as a related party.

8.9.6 Parties deemed not to be related parties

IAS 24 emphasises that it is necessary to consider carefully the substance of each relationship to see whether or not a related party relationship exists. However, the standard highlights a number of relationships that would not normally lead to related party status:

- two entities simply because they have a director or other member of the key management personnel in common or because a member of the key management personnel of one entity has significant influence over the other entity;
- two venturers simply because they share control over a joint venture;
- providers of finance, trade unions, public utilities or government departments in the course of their normal dealings with the entity;
- a single customer, supplier, franchisor, distributor or general agent with whom an entity transacts a significant volume of business merely by virtue of the resulting economic dependence.

8.9.7 Disclosure of controlling relationships

IAS 24 requires that relationships between a parent and its subsidiaries be disclosed irrespective of whether there have been transactions between them. Where the entity is controlled, it should disclose:

- the name of its parent;
- the name of its ultimate controlling party (which could be an individual or another entity);
- if neither the parent nor the ultimate controlling party produces consolidated financial statements available for public use, the name of the next most senior parent that does produce such statements.

8.9.8 Exemption from disclosures re government-related entities

A reporting entity is exempt from the detailed disclosures referred to in Section 8.9.10 below in relation to related party transactions and outstanding balances with:

- a government that has control, joint control or significant influence over the reporting entity; and
- another entity that is a related party because the same government has control, joint control or significant influence over both parties.

If this exemption is applied, the reporting entity is nevertheless required to make the following disclosures about transactions with government-related entities:

● the name of the government and the nature of its relationship with the reporting entity;
● the following information in sufficient detail to enable users of the financial statements to understand the effect of related party transactions:
    ● the nature and amount of each individually significant transaction; and
    ● for other transactions that are collectively, but not individually, significant, a qualitative or quantitative indication of their extent.

The reason for the exemption is essentially pragmatic. In some jurisdictions where government control is pervasive it can be difficult to identify other government-related entities. In some circumstances the directors of the reporting entity may be genuinely unaware of the related party relationship. Therefore, the basis of conclusions to IAS 24 (BC 43) states that, in the context of the disclosures that are needed in these circumstances:

> The objective of IAS 24 is to provide disclosures necessary to draw attention to the possibility that the financial position and profit or loss may have been affected by the existence of related parties and by transactions and outstanding balances, including commitments, with such parties. To meet that objective, IAS 24 requires some disclosure when the exemption applies. Those disclosures are intended to put users on notice that related party transactions have occurred and to give an indication of their extent. The Board did not intend to require the reporting entity to identify **every** government-related entity, or to quantify in detail **every** transaction with such entities, because such a requirement would negate the exemption.

8.9.9 Disclosure of compensation of key management personnel

Compensation can be influenced by a person in this position. Consequently IAS 24 requires the disclosure of short-term employee benefits, post-employment benefits, other long-term benefits (e.g. accrued sabbatical leave), termination benefits and share-based payment.

8.9.10 Disclosure of related party transactions

A related party transaction is a transfer of resources or obligations between a reporting entity and a related party, regardless of whether a price is charged. Where such transactions have occurred, the entity should disclose the nature of the related party relationship as well as information about those transactions and outstanding balances to enable a user to understand the potential effect of the relationship on the financial statements. As a minimum, the disclosures should include:

● the amount of the transactions;
● the amount of the outstanding balances and:
    ● their terms and conditions, including whether they are secured, and the nature of the consideration to be provided in settlement; and
    ● details of any guarantees given or received;
● provisions for doubtful debts related to the amount of outstanding balances; and
● the expense recognised during the period in respect of bad or doubtful debts due from related parties.

The following extract from the Unilever 2017 Annual Report is an example of the required disclosures:

30 Related party transactions

A related party is a person or entity that is related to the Group. These include both people and entities that have, or are subject to the influence or control of the Group.

The following related party balances existed with associate or joint venture businesses at 31 December:

Related party balances

	2017 €million	2016 €million
Trading and other balances due from joint ventures	124	115

8.9.11 Possible impact of transactions with related parties

It is possible that there could be both beneficial and prejudicial impacts.

Beneficial transactions with related parties

It could be that the related party is actually offering support to the business. For example, the business might have received benefits in a variety of ways ranging from financial support on favourable terms such as guarantees or low or no interest loans to the provision of goods or services at less than market rates.

Prejudicial transactions with related parties

These can arise when the business enters into transactions on terms that would not be offered to an unrelated party. There are numerous ways that this could be arranged, such as:

- **Loans:**
  - borrowing at above market rates;
  - lending at below market rates;
  - lending with no agreement as to date for repayment;
  - lending with little prospect of being repaid;
  - lending with the intention of writing off;
  - guaranteeing debts where there is no commercial advantage to the business.
- **Assets:**
  - selling non-current assets at below market value;
  - selling goods at less than normal trade price;
  - providing services at less than normal rates;
  - transfer of know-how, or research and development transfers.
- **Trading:**
  - sales made where there is secret agreement to repurchase to inflate current period revenue;
  - sales to inflate revenue with funds advanced to the debtor to allow the debt to be paid;
  - paying for services which have not been provided.

Summary

The published accounts of a listed company are intended to provide a report to enable shareholders to assess current-year stewardship and management performance and to predict future cash flows. Financial statements prepared from a trial balance and adjusted for accruals might require further adjustments. These arise from:

(a) events after the reporting period that provide additional evidence of conditions that existed at the period-end which might require the financial statements to be adjusted; or

(b) prior period errors that may require retrospective changes to the opening balances in the statement of financial position that could affect assets, liabilities and retained earnings.

In addition to these adjustments, in order to assist shareholders to predict future cash flows with an understanding of the risks involved, more information has been required by the IASB. This has taken two forms:

(a) more quantitative information in the accounts, e.g. segmental analysis, and the impact of changes on the operation, e.g. a breakdown of turnover, costs and profits for both new and discontinued operations; and

(b) more qualitative information, e.g. related party disclosures and events occurring after the reporting period.

REVIEW QUESTIONS

1 Explain why non-adjusting items are not reported in the financial statements if they are of sufficient materiality to be disclosed.

2 Explain the criteria that have to be satisfied when identifying an operating segment.

3 Explain the criteria that have to be satisfied to identify a reportable segment.

4 Explain why it is necessary to identify a chief operating decision maker and describe the key identifying factors.

5 Discuss the review findings of the European Securities and Markets Authority (ESMA) in relation to the role of the chief operating decision maker.

6 A research report[7] found that users were worried about the lack of comparability among segmental disclosures of different companies following the issue of IFRS 8. Discuss:

    (a) why it should have resulted in a lack of comparability;

    (b) whether it is more relevant because its format and content are not closely defined;

    (c) whether any of the other financial statements would be more relevant to users if they were free to format as they wished;

    (d) whether inter-firm comparability is more important than inter-period comparability.

7 Explain the conditions set out in IFRS 5 for determining whether operations have been discontinued and the problems that might arise in applying them.

8 Explain the conditions that must be satisfied if a non-current asset is to be reported in the statement of financial position as held for sale.

9 Explain why it is important to an investor to be informed about assets held for sale.

10 Discuss how transactions with related parties can have

(a) a beneficial impact

(b) a prejudicial impact

on (i) the reported income and (ii) the financial position.

EXERCISES

Question 1

IAS 10 deals with events after the reporting period.

Required:
(a) Define the period covered by IAS 10.
(b) Explain when the financial statements should be adjusted.
(c) Why should non-adjusting events be disclosed?
(d) A customer made a claim for £50,000 for losses suffered by the late delivery of goods. The main part (£40,000) of the claim referred to goods due to be delivered before the year-end. Explain how this would be dealt with under IAS 10.
(e) After the year-end a substantial quantity of inventory was destroyed in a fire. The loss was not adequately covered by insurance. This event is likely to threaten the ability of the business to continue as a going concern. Discuss the matters you would consider in making a decision under IAS 10.
(f) The business entered into a favourable contract after the year-end that would see its profits increase by 15% over the next three years. Explain how this would be dealt with under IAS 10.

Question 2

Epsilon is a listed entity. You are the financial controller of the entity and its consolidated financial statements for the year ended 30 September 20X8 are being prepared. Your assistant, who has prepared the first draft of the statements, is unsure about the correct treatment of a transaction and has asked for your advice. Details of the transaction are given below.

On 31 August 20X8 the directors decided to close down a business segment which did not fit into its future strategy. The closure commenced on 5 October 2008 and was due to be completed on 31 December 20X8. On 6 September 2008 letters were sent to relevant employees offering voluntary redundancy or redeployment in other sectors of the business. On 13 September 20X8 negotiations commenced with relevant parties with a view to terminating existing contracts of the business segment and arranging sales of its assets. Latest estimates of the financial implications of the closure are as follows:

(i) Redundancy costs will total $30 million, excluding the payment referred to in (ii) below.

(ii) The cost of redeploying and retraining staff who do not accept redundancy will total $6 million.

(iii) Plant having a net book value of $11 million at 30 September 20X8 will be sold for $2 million.

(iv) The operating losses of the business segment for October, November and December 20X8 are estimated at $10 million.

Your assistant is unsure of the extent to which the above transactions create liabilities that should be recognised as a closure provision in the financial statements. He is also unsure as to whether or not the results of the business segment that is being closed need to be shown separately.

Required:
Explain how the decision to close down the business segment should be reported in the financial statements of Epsilon for the year ended 30 September 20X8.

* Question 3

Epsilon is a listed entity. You are the financial controller of the entity and its consolidated financial statements for the year ended 31 March 20X9 are being prepared. The board of directors is responsible for all key financial and operating decisions, including the allocation of resources.

Your assistant is preparing the first draft of the statements. He has a reasonable general accounting knowledge but is not familiar with the detailed requirements of all relevant financial reporting standards. He requires your advice and he has sent you a note as shown below:

We intend to apply IFRS 8 *Operating Segments* in this year's financial statements. I am aware that this standard has attracted a reasonable amount of critical comment since it was issued in November 2006.

The board of directors receives a monthly report on the activities of the five significant operational areas of our business. Relevant financial information relating to the five operations for the year to 31 March 20X9, and in respect of our head office, is as follows:

Operational area	Revenue for year to 31 March 20X9	Profit/(loss) for year to 31 March 20X9	Assets at 31 March 20X9
	$000	$000	$000
A	23,000	3,000	8,000
B	18,000	2,000	6,000
C	4,000	(3,000)	5,000
D	1,000	150	500
E	3,000	450	400
Sub-total	49,000	2,600	19,900
Head office	Nil	Nil	6,000
Entity total	49,000	2,600	25,900

I am unsure of the following matters regarding the reporting of operating segments:

● How do we decide what our operating segments should be?

● Should we report segment information relating to head office?

● Which of our operational areas should report separate information? Operational areas A, B and C exhibit very distinct economic characteristics but the economic characteristics of operational areas D and E are very similar.

● Why has IFRS 8 attracted such critical comment?

Required:
Draft a reply to the questions raised by your assistant.

* Question 4

Filios Products plc owns a chain of hotels through which it provides three basic services: restaurant facilities, accommodation, and leisure facilities. The latest financial statements contain the following information:

Statement of financial position of Filios Products

	£m
ASSETS	
Non-current assets at book value	1,663
Current assets	
Inventories and receivables	381
Bank balance	128
	509
Total Assets	2,172
EQUITY AND LIABILITIES	
Equity	
Share capital	800
Retained earnings	1,039
	1,839
Non-current liabilities:	
Long-term borrowings	140
Current liabilities	193
Total Equity and liabilities	2,172

Statement of comprehensive income of Filios Products

	£m	£m
Revenue		1,028
Less: Cost of sales	684	
Administration expenses	110	
Distribution costs	101	
Interest charged	14	(909)
Net profit		119

The following breakdown is provided of the company's results into three divisions and head office:

	Restaurants £m	Hotels £m	Leisure £m	Head office £m
Revenue	508	152	368	—
Cost of sales	316	81	287	—
Administration expenses	43	14	38	15
Distribution costs	64	12	25	—
Interest charged	10	—	—	4
Non-current assets at book value	890	332	364	77
Inventories and receivables	230	84	67	—
Bank balance	73	15	28	12
Payables	66	40	56	31
Long-term borrowings	100	—	—	40

Required:
(a) Outline the nature of segmental reports and explain the reason for presenting such information in the published accounts.
(b) Prepare a segmental statement for Filios Products plc complying, so far as the information permits, with the provisions of IFRS 8 *Operating Segments* so as to show for each segment and the business as a whole:
   (i) revenue;
   (ii) profit;
   (iii) net assets.
(c) Examine the relative performance of the operating divisions of Filios Products. The examination should be based on the following accounting ratios:
   (i) operating profit percentage;
   (ii) net asset turnover;
   (iii) return on net assets.

Question 5

The following is the draft trading and income statement of Parnell Ltd for the year ending 31 December 20X8:

	$m	$m
Revenue		563
Cost of sales		310
		253
Distribution costs	45	
Administrative expenses	78	
		123
Profit on ordinary activities before tax		130
Tax on profit on ordinary activities		45
Profit on ordinary activities after taxation – all retained		85
Profit brought forward at 1 January 20X8		101
Profit carried forward at 31 December 20X8		186

You are given the following additional information, which is reflected in the above statement of comprehensive income only to the extent stated:

1 Distribution costs include a bad debt of $15 million which arose on the insolvency of a major customer. There is no prospect of recovering any of this debt. Bad debts have never been material in the past.

2 The company has traditionally consisted of a manufacturing division and a distribution division. On 31 December 20X8, the entire distribution division was sold for $50 million; its book value at the time of sale was $40 million. The profit on disposal was credited to administrative expenses. (Ignore any related income tax.)

3 During 20X8, the distribution division made sales of $100 million and had a cost of sales of $30 million. There will be no reduction in stated distribution costs or administration expenses as a result of this disposal.

4 The company owns offices which it purchased on 1 January 20X6 for $500 million, comprising $200 million for land and $300 million for buildings. No depreciation was charged in 20X6 or 20X7, but

Financial Reporting and Advanced Financial Reporting

the company now considers that such a charge should be introduced. The buildings were expected to have a life of 50 years at the date of purchase, and the company uses the straight-line basis for calculating depreciation, assuming a zero residual value. No taxation consequences result from this change.

5 During 20X8 , part of the manufacturing division was restructured at a cost of $20 million to take advantage of modern production techniques. The restructuring was not fundamental and will not have a material effect on the nature and focus of the company's operations. This cost is included under administration expenses in the statement of comprehensive income.

Required:
(a) State how each of the items 1–5 above must be accounted for in order to comply with the requirements of international accounting standards.
(b) Redraft the income statement of Parnell Ltd for 20X8, taking into account the additional information so as to comply, as far as possible, with relevant standard accounting practice. Show clearly any adjustments you make. Notes to the accounts are not required. Where an IAS recommends information to be on the face of the income statement it could be recorded on the face of the statement.

* Question 6

Springtime Ltd is a UK trading company buying and selling as wholesalers fashionable summer clothes. The following balances have been extracted from the books as at 31 March 20X4:

	£000
Auditor's remuneration	30
Income tax based on the accounting profit:	
For the year to 31 March 20X4	3,200
Overprovision for the year to 31 March 20X3	200
Delivery expenses (including £300,000 overseas)	1,200
Dividends: final (proposed – to be paid 1 August 20X4)	200
interim (paid on 1 October 20X3)	100
Non-current assets at cost:	
Delivery vans	200
Office cars	40
Stores equipment	5,000
Dividend income (amount received from listed companies)	1,200
Office expenses	800
Overseas operations: closure costs of entire operations	350
Purchases	24,000
Sales (net of sales tax)	35,000
Inventory at cost:	
At 1 April 20X3	5,000
At 31 March 20X4	6,000
Storeroom costs	1,000
Wages and salaries:	
Delivery staff	700
Directors' emoluments	400
Office staff	100
Storeroom staff	400

Notes:

1 Depreciation is provided at the following annual rates on a straight-line basis: delivery vans 20%; office cars 25%; stores 1%.

2 The following taxation rates may be assumed: corporate income tax 35%; personal income tax 25%.

3 The dividend income arises from investments held in non-current investments.

4 It has been decided to transfer an amount of £150,000 to the deferred taxation account.

5 The overseas operations consisted of exports. In 20X3/X4 these amounted to £5,000,000 (sales) with purchases of £4,000,000. Related costs included £100,000 in storeroom staff and £15,000 for office staff.

6 Directors' emoluments include:

Chairperson	100,000	
Managing director	125,000	
Finance director	75,000	
Sales director	75,000	
Export director	25,000	(resigned 31 December 20X3)
	£400,000	

Required:
(a) **Produce a statement of comprehensive income suitable for publication and complying as far as possible with generally accepted accounting practice.**
(b) **Comment on how IFRS 5 has improved the quality of information available to users of accounts.**

Question 7

Omega prepares financial statements under International Financial Reporting Standards. In the year ended 31 March 20X7 the following transaction occurred:

Omega follows the revaluation model when measuring its property, plant and equipment. One of its properties was carried in the balance sheet at 31 March 20X6 at its market value at that date of $5 million. The depreciable amount of this property was estimated at $3.2 million at 31 March 20X6 and the estimated future economic life of the property at 31 March 20X6 was 20 years.

On 1 January 20X7 Omega decided to dispose of the property as it was surplus to requirements and began to actively seek a buyer. On 1 January 20X7 Omega estimated that the market value of the property was $5.1 million and that the costs of selling the property would be $80,000. These estimates remained appropriate at 31 March 20X7.

The property was sold on 10 June 20X7 for net proceeds of $5.15 million.

Required:
Explain, with relevant calculations, how the property would be treated in the financial statements of Omega for the year ended 31 March 20X7 and the year ending 31 March 20X8.

* Question 8

The following trial balance has been extracted from the books of Hoodurz as at 31 March 2006:

	$000	$000
Administration expenses	210	
Ordinary share capital, $1 per share		600
Trade receivables	470	
Bank overdraft		80
Provision for warranty claims		205
Distribution costs	420	
Non-current asset investments	560	
Investment income		75
Interest paid	10	
Property, at cost	200	
Plant and equipment, at cost	550	
Plant and equipment, accumulated depreciation (at 31.3.2006)		220
Accumulated profits (at 31.3.2005)		80
Loans (repayable 31.12.2010)		100
Purchases	960	
Inventories (at 31.3.2005)	150	
Trade payables		260
Sales		2,010
2004/2005 final dividend paid	65	
2005/2006 interim dividend paid	35	
	3,630	3,630

The following information is relevant:

(i)   The trial balance figures include the following amounts for a disposal group that has been classified as 'held for sale' under IFRS 5 *Non-current Assets Held for Sale and Discontinued Operations*:

	$000
Plant and equipment, at cost	150
Plant and equipment, accumulated depreciation	15
Trade receivables	70
Bank overdraft	10
Trade payables	60
Sales	370
Inventories (at 31.12.2005)	25
Purchases	200
Administration expenses	55
Distribution costs	60

The disposal group had no inventories at the date classified as 'held for sale'.

(ii)   Inventories (excluding the disposal group) at 31.3.2006 were valued at $160,000.

(iii) The depreciation charges for the year have already been accrued.

(iv) The income tax for the year ended 31.3.2006 is estimated to be $74,000. This includes $14,000 in relation to the disposal group.

(v) The provision for warranty claims is to be increased by $16,000. This is classified as administration expense.

(vi) Staff bonuses totalling $20,000 for administration and $20,000 for distribution are to be accrued.

(vii) The property was acquired during February 2006, therefore, depreciation for the year ended 31.3.2006 is immaterial. The directors have chosen to use the fair value model for such an asset. The fair value of the property at 31.3.2006 is $280,000.

Required:
Prepare for Hoodurz:
(a) an income statement for the year ended 31 March 2006; and
(b) a balance sheet as at 31 March 2006.
Both statements should comply as far as possible with relevant International Financial Reporting Standards. No notes to the financial statements are required nor is a statement of changes in equity, but all workings should be clearly shown.

(The Association of International Accountants)

Question 9

Omega prepares financial statements under International Financial Reporting Standards. In the year ended 31 March 20X7 the following transaction occurred. On 31 December 20X6 the directors decided to dispose of a property that was surplus to requirements. They instructed selling agents to procure a suitable purchaser and advertised the property at a commercially realistic price.

The property was being measured under the revaluation model and had been revalued at $15 million on 31 March 20X6. The depreciable element of the property was estimated as $8 million at 31 March 20X6 and the useful economic life of the depreciable element was estimated as 25 years from that date. Omega depreciates its non-current assets on a monthly basis.

On 31 December 20X6 the directors estimated that the market value of the property was $16 million, and that the costs incurred in selling the property would be $500,000. The property was sold on 30 April 20X7 for $15.55 million, being the agreed selling price of $16.1 million less selling costs of $550,000. The actual selling price and costs to sell were consistent with estimated amounts as at 31 March 20X7.

The financial statements for the year ended 31 March 20X7 were authorised for issue on 15 May 20X7.

Required:
Show the impact of the decision to sell the property on the income statement of Omega for the year ended 31 March 20X7, and on its balance sheet as at 31 March 20X7. You should state where in the income statement and the balance sheet relevant balances will be shown. You should make appropriate references to international financial reporting standards.

Question 10

(a) In 20X3 Arthur is a large loan creditor of X Ltd and receives interest at 20% p.a. on this loan. He also has a 24% shareholding in X Ltd. Until 20X1 he was a director of the company and left after a disagreement. The remaining 76% of the shares are held by the remaining directors.

(b) Brenda joined Y Ltd, an insurance broking company, on 1 January 20X0 on a low salary but high commission basis. She brought clients with her that generated 30% of the company's 20X0 revenue.

(c) Carrie is a director and major shareholder of Z Ltd. Her husband, Donald, is employed in the company on administrative duties for which he is paid a salary of £25,000 p.a. Her daughter, Emma, is a business consultant running her own business. In 20X0 Emma carried out various consultancy exercises for the company for which she was paid £85,000.

(d) Fred is a director of V Ltd. V Ltd is a major customer of W Ltd. In 20X0 Fred also became a director of W Ltd.

Required:
Discuss whether parties are related in the above situations.

* Question 11

Maxpool plc, a listed company, owned 60% of the shares in Ching Ltd. Bay plc, a listed company, owned the remaining 40% of the £1 ordinary shares in Ching Ltd. The holdings of shares were acquired on 1 January 20X0.

On 30 November 20X0 Ching Ltd sold a factory outlet site to Bay plc at a price determined by an independent surveyor.

On 1 March 20X1 Maxpool plc purchased a further 30% of the £1 ordinary shares of Ching Ltd from Bay plc and purchased 25% of the ordinary shares of Bay plc.
On 30 June 20X1 Ching Ltd sold the whole of its fleet of vehicles to Bay plc at a price determined by a vehicle auctioneer.

Required:
Explain the implications of the above transactions for the determination of related party relationships and disclosure of such transactions in the financial statements of (a) Maxpool Group plc, (b) Ching Ltd and (c) Bay plc for the years ending 31 December 20X0 and 31 December 20X1.

(ACCA)

Question 12

Gamma is a company that manufactures power tools. Gamma was established by Mr Lee, who owns all of Gamma's shares. Mrs Lee, Mr Lee's wife, owns a controlling interest in Delta, a distributor of power tools. Delta is one of Gamma's biggest customers, accounting for 70% of Gamma's sales. Delta buys exclusively from Gamma.

Gamma's official price list is based on the policy of selling goods at cost plus 50%; however, sales to Delta are priced at normal selling price less a discount of 30% to reflect the scale of the business transacted.

Gamma's terms of sale require payment within one month, but Delta is permitted three months to pay.

Mrs Lee has decided to sell her shares in Delta and has provided a potential buyer with financial information including the following:

Sales revenue for the year ended 30 September 2011	$12.0m
Cost of sales	$8.0m
Gross profit %	33%
Current assets (including bank $0.3m)	$4.0m
Trade payables	$3.0m
Other current liabilities	$0.8m
Current ratio	1.1:1 (in line with the ratios reported in each of the past three years)

The buyer conducted a due diligence investigation and discovered the relationship between Gamma and Delta. She has decided to restate the figures provided in the table above to reflect a 'worst case' scenario before arriving at a final decision concerning the purchase.

Required:

(a) Discuss the manner in which IAS 24 *Related Party Disclosures* should have alerted the potential buyer in this case.

(b) Recalculate the table of figures provided by Mrs Lee on the basis that Delta will not receive favourable terms from Gamma if Mrs Lee sells her shares, and discuss the resulting changes.

(The Association of International Accountants)

* Question 13

(a) IAS 8 Accounting Policies, Changes in Accounting Estimates and Errors lays down criteria for the selection of accounting policies and prescribes circumstances in which an entity may change an accounting policy. The standard also deals with accounting treatment of changes in accounting policies, changes in accounting estimates and correction of prior period errors.

Required:

(i) Define an accounting policy according to IAS 8. Explain briefly the difference between an accounting policy and an accounting estimate.

(ii) Outline the accounting treatment required to record (1) a change in accounting policy, (2) a change in accounting estimate and (3) the correction of an error.

(b) The following are summaries of the draft financial statements of Sigma plc for financial year ended 31 July 2015 together with the comparative figures for 2014. During August 2015, prior to the signing off of the financial statements, it was discovered that a fraud had been taking place in the company for the previous three years.

The chief financial officer had been misappropriating monies paid to the company by its customers, the amounts instead appearing as receivables. The effect of the fraud was that amounts shown in the financial statements as receivables need to be written off as they were in fact paid. There is no prospect of recovering the money as the employee lost it gambling and is now bankrupt. The amounts were as follows for each period ending on the following dates:

31 July 2013: €14,000
31 July 2014: €16,000
31 July 2015: €20,000.

Statements of Profit or Loss and Other Comprehensive Income for year ended 31 July:

	2015	2014
	€000	€000
Revenue	300	275
Cost of Sales	(225)	(212)
Gross Profit	75	63
Expenses	(30)	(26)
Profit for year	45	37

Statements of Changes in Equity (Retained Earnings only) for year ended 31 July:

	2015	2014
	€000	€000
Balance 1 August	258	236
Profit for the year	45	37
Dividends declared	(16)	(15)
Balance 31 July	287	258

Statements of Financial Position as at 31 July:

	2015	2014
	€000	€000
Non-current Assets	294	306
Net Current Assets	143	102
	437	408
Equity Share Capital	150	150
Retained Earnings	287	258
	437	408

Required:

Restate the above financial statements, including comparatives, incorporating the adjustments you deem necessary as a result of the fraud. Ignore the effect of taxation. Disclosure notes are not required.

(Institute of Certified Public Accountants (CPA), Professional Stage 1 Corporate Reporting Examination, August 2015)

Question 14

The Perry Company ('Perry') provides trust and investment services in an offshore location. Perry's main financial statements are prepared annually on an accruals basis with the last year end being the 31 December 2015.

During the preparation of the annual accounts, the following matters were identified by Perry's company secretary, who had been charged with making an initial review of the financial statements. No action has yet been taken on these matters.

Perry's turnover for the last year was £4,500,000, profit was £560,000.

Event 1

A client of Perry has taken a legal action against the company, stating that he received poor investment advice and suffered loss when the stock exchange in China lost significant value towards the end of 2015.

In a letter dated January 2016, the client is claiming £8,000 in lost capital from Perry. Perry's legal advice is that the client is very unlikely to succeed with the claim. The directors of Perry have made no adjustment to the financial statements following this advice.

Event 2

Up to 2015, Perry maintained a branch office on an island in the Caribbean. Towards the end of 2015, the directors of Perry decided to close this office with associated closure costs (staff relocation, ending of leases and so on) estimated at £45,000. The decision was recorded in the board minutes in December 2015 and announced to staff in January 2016 so as not to spoil their annual holiday at the end of December.

Full provision for closure costs has been included in Perry's financial statements to 31 December 2015.

Event 3

Towards the end of 2015, Perry upgraded its computerised accounting systems. In January 2016 it was discovered that information transfer from the old computer system was incomplete.

Specifically, billing information for special advice work carried out for 12 clients, along with invoices to a total of £6,500 in fees due, had been lost. Information from the old computer system was unavailable as the hard disks and backup copies had been destroyed and the computers sent for recycling. This meant that Perry had no record of services provided to these clients and was unable to prove that the debts were due to Perry.

The clients maintain that the advice requested was never received. Perry cannot prove that the work was done. No adjustment has been made to the financial statements.

Required

(a) Under the requirements of IAS 10 'Events After the Reporting Period', define:
    (i)   Events after the reporting period
    (ii) Adjusting events
    (iii) Non-adjusting events
(b) Explain whether the three events above are adjusting or non-adjusting events in accordance with IAS 10.
(c) Explain any actions that the directors of Perry can take to try and minimise the likelihood of similar events occurring in the future.

(ICSA Financial Reporting and Governance June 2016)

Notes

1 IAS 10 *Events after the Reporting Period*, IASB, revised 2003.
2 IAS 8 *Accounting Policies, Changes in Accounting Estimates and Errors.*
3 IFRS 8 *Operating Segments*, IASB, 2006.
4 Post-implementation Review, IFRS 8 *Operating Segments*, IFRS Foundation, July 2013.
5 IFRS 5 *Non-current Assets Held for Sale and Discontinued Operations*, IASB, revised 2009.
6 IAS 24 *Related Party Disclosures*, IASB, revised 2009.
7 L. Crawford, H. Extance and C. Helliar, *Operating Segments: The Usefulness of IFRS 8*, The Institute of Chartered Accountants of Scotland, 2012.

CHAPTER 9

Financial reporting – evolution of global standards

9.1 Introduction

The main purpose of this chapter is to describe the movement towards global standards for publicly and non-publicly accountable entities.

Objectives

By the end of the chapter, you should be able to:

- critically discuss the arguments for and against standards;
- describe standard setting and enforcement in the UK, the EU and the US;
- discuss the approach taken by the EU with the new Accounting Directive;
- describe and comment on the IASB approach to financial reporting by small and medium-sized entities (IFRS for SMEs);
- critically discuss the advantages and disadvantages of global standards;
- describe the reasons for differences in financial reporting.

9.2 Why do we need financial reporting standards?

Standards are needed because accounting numbers are important when defining contractual entitlements. Contracting parties frequently define the rights between themselves in terms of accounting numbers.[1] For example, the remuneration of directors and managers might be expressed in terms of a salary plus a bonus based on an agreed performance measure, e.g. Johnson Matthey's 2016 Annual Report states:

> Annual Bonus – which is paid as a percentage of basic salary . . . based on consolidated underlying profit before tax (PBT) compared with the annual budget. Provides a strong incentive aligned to strategy in the short term. The annual bonus are properly reflected in stretching but achievable annual budgets.

However, there is a risk of irresponsible behaviour by directors and managers if it appears that earnings will not meet performance targets. They might be tempted to adopt measures that increase the PBT but which are not in the best interest of the shareholders.

This risk is specifically addressed in the Johnson Matthey 2016 Annual Report as shown in the following extract:

> The Committee retains the discretion in awarding annual bonuses and . . . ensures that the incentive structure for senior management does not raise environmental, social and governance risks by inadvertently motivating irresponsible behaviour.

In its 2013 Annual Report the directors commented:

> At the start of the year, the board set ambitious targets, ahead of the prevailing industry analysts' consensus, but as the year unfolded, short term performance fell below that determined when setting the budget. As a result, no executive director bonuses will be paid this year, even though underlying earnings per share fell by just 2%.

This would not, however, preclude companies from taking typical steps such as **deferring discretionary expenditure**, e.g. research, advertising or training expenditure; **deferring amortisation**, e.g. making optimistic sales projections in order to classify research as development expenditure which can be capitalised; and **reclassifying** deteriorating current assets as non-current assets to avoid the need to recognise a loss under the lower of cost and net realisable value rule applicable to current assets.

The introduction of a mandatory standard that changes management's ability to adopt such measures **affects wealth distribution** within the firm. For example, if managers are able to delay the amortisation of development expenditure, then bonuses related to profit will be higher and there will effectively have been a transfer of wealth to managers from shareholders.

9.3 Why do we need standards to be mandatory?

Mandatory standards are needed, therefore, to define the way in which accounting numbers are presented in financial statements, so that their measurement and presentation are less subjective. It had been thought that the accountancy profession could obtain uniformity of disclosure by persuasion but, in reality, the profession found it difficult to resist management pressures.

During the 1960s the financial sector of the UK economy lost confidence in the accountancy profession when internationally known UK-based companies were seen to have published financial data that were materially incorrect. Shareholders are normally unaware that this occurs and it tends to become public knowledge only in restricted circumstances, e.g. when a third party has a **vested interest** in revealing adverse facts following a takeover, or when a company falls into the hands of an administrator, inspector or liquidator, **whose duty it is to enquire and report** on shortcomings in the management of a company.

Two scandals which disturbed the public at the time, GEC/AEI and Pergamon Press, were both made public in the restricted circumstances referred to above, when financial reports prepared from the same basic information disclosed a materially different picture.

9.3.1 GEC takeover of AEI in 1967

The first calamity for the profession involved GEC Ltd in its takeover bid for AEI Ltd when the pre-takeover accounts prepared by the old AEI directors differed materially from the post-takeover accounts prepared by the new AEI directors.

Under the control of the directors of GEC the accounts of AEI were produced for 1967 showing a **loss of £4.5 million**. Unfortunately, this was from basic information that was largely the same as that used by AEI when producing its profit forecast of £10 million.

There can be two reasons for the difference between the figures produced. Either the facts have changed or the judgements made by the directors have changed. In this case, it seems there was a change in the facts to the extent of a post-acquisition closure of an AEI factory; this explained £5 million of the £14.5 million difference between the forecast profit and the actual loss. The remaining £9.5 million arose because of differences in judgement. For example, the new directors took a different view of the value of stock and work in progress.

9.3.2 Pergamon Press

Audited accounts were produced by Pergamon Press Ltd for 1968 showing a profit of approximately £2 million.

An independent investigation by Price Waterhouse suggested that this profit should be reduced by 75% because of a number of unacceptable valuations, e.g. there had been a failure to reduce certain stock to the lower of cost and net realisable value, and there had been a change in policy on the capitalisation of printing costs of back issues of scientific journals – they were treated as a cost of closing stock in 1968, but not as a cost of opening stock in 1968.

9.3.3 Public view of the accounting profession following such cases

It had long been recognised that accountancy is not an exact science, but it had not been appreciated just how much latitude there was for companies to produce vastly different results based on the same transactions. Given that the auditors were perfectly happy to sign that those accounts showing either a £10 million profit or a £4.5 million loss were true and fair, the public felt the need for action if investors were to have any trust in the figures that were being published.

The difficulty was that each firm of accountants tended to rely on precedents within its own firm in deciding what was true and fair. In fairness, there could be consistency within an audit firm's approach but not across all firms in the profession. The auditors were also under pressure to agree to practices that the directors wanted because there were no professional mandatory standards.

This was the scenario that galvanised the City press and the investing public. An embarrassed, disturbed profession announced in 1969, via the ICAEW, that there was a majority view supporting the introduction of Statements of Standard Accounting Practice to supplement the legislation.

9.3.4 Does the need for standards and effective enforcement still exist in the twenty-first century?

The scandals involving GEC and Pergamon Press occurred more than 45 years ago. However, the need for the ongoing enforcement of standards for financial reporting and auditing continues unabated. We only need to look at the unfortunate events with Enron and Ahold to arrive at an answer.

Enron

Enron was formed in the mid-1980s and became by the end of the 1990s the seventh-largest company in revenue terms in the USA. However, this concealed the fact that it had off-balance-sheet debts and that it had overstated its profits by more than $500 million – falling into bankruptcy (the largest in US corporate history) in 2001.

Ahold

In 2003 Ahold, the world's third-largest grocer, reported that its earnings for the past two years were overstated by more than $500 million as a result of local managers recording promotional allowances provided by suppliers to promote their goods at a figure greater than the cash received. This may reflect on the pressure to inflate profits when there are option schemes for managers.

Tesco

In 2014 Tesco was investigated by the FRC and Serious Fraud Office following its overstatement of profits by £250m–£325m arising from the accelerated recognition of commercial income in the form of vendor allowances.

9.4 Arguments in support of standards

The setting of standards has both supporters and opponents. Those who support standards have a view that they are important in giving investors confidence and encouraging informed investment. In this section we discuss credibility, discipline and comparability.

Credibility

The accountancy profession would lose all credibility if it permitted companies experiencing similar events to produce financial reports that disclosed markedly different results simply because they could select different accounting policies. Uniformity was seen as essential if financial reports were to disclose a true and fair view. However, it has been a continuing view in the UK and IASB that standards should be based on principles and not be seen as rigid rules – they were not to replace the exercise of informed judgement in determining what constituted a true and fair view in each circumstance. The US approach has been different – its approach has been to prescribe detailed rules.

Discipline

Directors are under pressure to maintain and improve the market valuation of their company's securities. There is a temptation, therefore, to influence any financial statistic that has an impact on the market valuation, such as the trend in the earnings per share (EPS) figure, the net asset backing for the shares or the gearing ratios which show the level of borrowing relative to the amount of equity capital put in by the shareholders.

This is an ever-present risk and the Financial Reporting Council showed awareness of the need to impose discipline when it stated in its Annual Review as far back as 1991 that the high level of company failures in the then recession, some of which were associated with **obscure financial reporting,** damaged confidence in the high standard of reporting by the majority of companies.

Comparability

In addition to financial statements allowing investors to evaluate the management's performance, i.e. their stewardship, they should also allow investors to make predictions of future cash flows and make comparisons with other companies.

In order to be able to make valid inter-company comparisons of performance and trends, investors need relevant and reliable data that have been standardised. If companies were to continue to apply different accounting policies to identical commercial activities, innocently or with the deliberate intention of disguising bad news, then investors could be misled in making their investment decisions.

9.5 Arguments against standards

We have so far discussed the arguments in support of standard setting. However, there are also arguments that have been made against, such as consensus-seeking and information overload with IFRSs themselves exceeding 3,000 pages.

Consensus-seeking

Consensus-seeking can lead to the issuing of standards that are over-influenced by those who fear that a new standard will adversely affect their statements of financial position. For example, we see retail companies, who lease many of their stores, oppose the proposal to put operating leases onto the statement of financial position rather than reporting simply the future commitment as a note to the accounts.

Overload

Standard overload is not a new charge. It has been put forward by those who consider that:

- There are too many standard setters with differing requirements, e.g. the FRC in the UK with FRSs; the FASB in the US with the Accounting Standards Codification; the IASB with IFRSs and IFRICs; the EU with separate endorsement of IFRS giving us EU-IFRS; and the EU with its Directives and national Stock Exchange listing requirements.

- Standards are too detailed if rule-based and not sufficiently detailed if principle-based, leading to the need for yet further guidance from the standard setters. For example, further guidance has to be issued by the International Financial Reporting Interpretations Committee (IFRC) when existing IFRSs do not provide the answer.

- There are too many notes to the accounts to satisfy regulatory requirements, for example disclosing charitable donations.

- There are too many notes to the accounts put in by companies themselves. Various surveys by professional accounting firms including one by Baker Tilly in 2012[2] showed that the majority of financial directors were keen to cut 'clutter' from financial disclosures, believing that the financial statements are too long, and that key messages are being lost as a result. It was felt that existing standards lead to a checklist mentality and boiler-plate disclosures that are not material and can obscure relevant information.

- There has been no definition of a note by the standard setters. This is being addressed by EFRAG with the issue of a Discussion Paper in 2012, *Towards a Disclosure Framework for the Notes,* which proposes how notes should be defined. For example, it is proposed that relevance, for instance, should only apply to disclosures that fulfil some *specific* users' needs.

- International standards have, until 2009 with the issue of *IFRS for SMEs,* focused on the large multinational companies and failed to recognise the different users and information needs between large and smaller entities.

9.6 Standard setting and enforcement by the Financial Reporting Council (FRC) in the UK

The Financial Reporting Council (FRC) was set up in 1990 as an independent regulator. Under the FRC the Accounting Standards Board (ASB) issued standards and the Financial Reporting Review Panel (FRRP) reviewed compliance to encourage high-quality financial reporting.

Due to its success in doing this, the government decided, following corporate disasters such as that of Enron in the USA, to give it a more **proactive** role from 2004 onwards in the areas of corporate governance, compliance with statutes and accounting and auditing standards.

Countries experience alternating periods of favourable and unfavourable economic conditions – often described as 'boom and bust'. In the UK the FRC announced thematic reviews where there is a particular shareholder interest and scope for improvement and learning from good practice to include targeted aspects of smaller listed and AIM quoted company reports and accounts; the effect of the new International Financial Reporting Standards (IFRSs) on revenue and financial instruments on companies 2018 interim accounts; the expected effect of the new IFRS for lease accounting; and the effects of Brexit on companies' disclosure of principal risks and uncertainties.

The FRC has indicated that it will write to 40 smaller listed and AIM quoted companies prior to their year-end, informing them that it will review two specific aspects of their next published report and accounts. These specific aspects will be drawn from five areas of FRC focus that have featured in recent thematic reviews or Financial Reporting Lab reports.

In addition to the thematic reviews, the FRC will focus its routine corporate reporting review and audit monitoring activity on the reports and audits in the priority sectors of financial services, with particular emphasis on banks, other lenders and insurers; oil and gas; general retailers; and business support services. These routine reviews will focus on first- and last-year audits; the audit of fair value investments, including goodwill impairment; the nature and extent of the use of auditor's experts and specialists; and the approach to the audit of controls.

It also pays particular attention to the reports and accounts of companies whose shareholders have raised concerns about governance or where there have been specific complaints.

9.6.1 The FRC structure

The FRC structure has evolved to meet changing needs. It was restructured in 2012 to operate as a unified regulatory body with enhanced independence. The new structure is shown in Figure 9.1.

9.6.2 The FRC Board

The FRC Board is supported by three committees: the Codes and Standards Committee, the Conduct Committee and the Executive Committee.

Figure 9.1 FRC structure from 2012

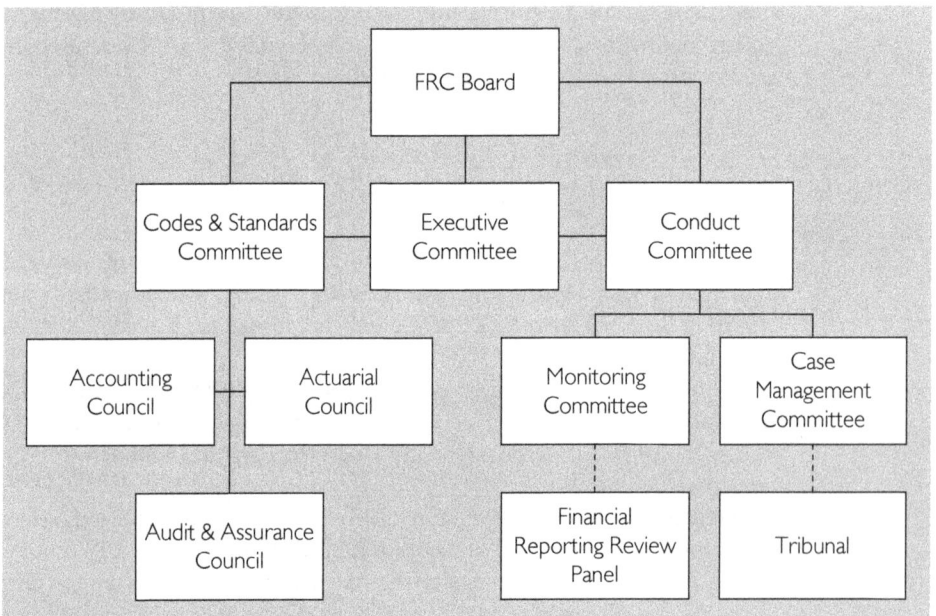

The Codes and Standards Committee

This will advise the FRC Board on matters relating to codes, standard setting and policy questions, through its Accounting, Actuarial and Audit & Assurance Councils. The *Accounting Council* replaces the Accounting Standards Board. It reports to the Codes and Standards Committee and is responsible for providing strategic input into the work-plan of the FRC as a whole and advising on draft national and international standards to ensure that high-quality, effective standards are produced.

The Conduct Committee

This will advise the FRC Board in matters relating to conduct to promote high-quality corporate reporting, including monitoring, oversight, investigative and disciplinary functions, through its Monitoring Committee and Case Management Committee. The *Monitoring Committee* will be concerned with the assessment and reviews of audit quality and decisions as to possible resulting sanctions and investigation leading to possible disciplinary action being taken.

The Executive Committee

This will support the Board by advising on strategic issues and providing day-to-day oversight of the work of the FRC.

9.6.3 The Financial Reporting Review Panel (FRRP)

Creative accounting

A research study[3] into companies that have been the subject of a public statement suggests that when a firm's performance comes under severe strain, even apparently well-governed firms can succumb to the pressure for creative accounting, and that good governance alone is not a sufficient condition for ensuring high-quality financial reporting. Enforcement is required.

Risk-based proactive approach to enforcement

The FRRP has a policing role with responsibility for overseeing some 2,500 companies. Its role is to review material departures from accounting standards and, where financial statements are defective, to require the company to take appropriate remedial action. It has the right to apply to the court to make companies comply, but it prefers to deal with defects by agreement and there has never been recourse to the court.

It selects companies and documents to be examined using a proactive risk-based approach or a mixed model where a risk-based approach is combined with a rotation and/or a sampling approach – a pure rotation approach or a pure reactive approach would not be acceptable.[4]

In 2015 it reported under Areas of Future Focus that there is a relatively mature corporate reporting environment, where UK Boards are:

> generally familiar with the requirements of IFRS and can apply them appropriately in most circumstances and an increasing proportion of time was spent evaluating the significant accounting judgements that Boards make and the quality of their conclusions, as areas are important to investors.

Cooperative approach to enforcement

There were, however, reservations expressed about the quality of reporting by some smaller listed and Alternative Investment Market (AIM) quoted companies that lacked the accounting expertise of their larger listed counterparts.

The FRC is looking at how to assist smaller listed and AIM quoted companies improve their financial reports and in June 2015 published a Discussion Paper on the FRC's findings and proposals, *Improving the Quality of Reporting by Smaller Listed and AIM Quoted Companies.*[5]

Feedback urged regulators not to impose any additional regulatory burdens on smaller quoted companies; agreed that all quoted companies should apply a common reporting framework and that IFRS represented the most appropriate framework; agreed that the FRC should encourage smaller quoted companies to participate in Financial Reporting lab projects; and welcomed the initiative to explore opportunities for providing more support for preparers of financial statements through training and CPD regimes.

This is in recognition that smaller listed and AIM quoted companies are important in generating future growth in the economy and need access to capital in order to invest and grow. The Organisation for Economic Co-operation and Development (OECD) reports that it considers small and medium-sized companies to be critical to ensuring that economic growth is sustainable and inclusive. In February 2015 the European Commission issued a Green Paper, *Building a Capital Markets Union*, which included the need for simpler reporting requirements.

9.7 The International Accounting Standards Board

The International Accounting Standards Board (IASB) has responsibility for all technical matters including the preparation and implementation of standards. The IASB website (www.iasb.org.uk) explains that:

> The IASB is committed to developing, in the public interest, a single set of high quality, understandable and enforceable global accounting standards that require transparent and comparable information in general purpose financial statements. In addition, the IASB co-operates with national accounting standard-setters to achieve convergence in accounting standards around the world.

The IASB adopted all current IASs and began issuing its own standards, International Financial Reporting Standards (IFRSs). The body of IASs and IFRSs is referred to collectively as 'IFRS'.

As a conceptual basis to assist when drafting Standards the IASC first issued a *Framework for the Preparation and Presentation of Financial Statements*[6] in 1989 (adopted by the IASB in 2001).

9.7.1 The Framework for the Preparation and Presentation of Financial Statements

The position was that different social, economic and legal circumstances had led to countries producing financial statements using different criteria for defining elements, recognising and measuring items appearing in the profit and loss account and balance sheet. The IASB approach was to attempt to harmonise national regulations and move towards the adoption by countries of International Standards (IFRSs). The *Framework* has been gradually revised and issued in 2018 as the *Conceptual Framework for Financial Reporting*. The objective of the Conceptual Framework is to improve financial reporting by providing the IASB with a complete and updated set of concepts to use when it develops or revises standards. It is discussed further in Chapter 10.

Adoption by countries of IFRS

IFRS has been adopted in the EU for consolidated accounts since 2005. It is interesting to see how the other G20 countries are gradually moving towards the use of IFRS. Of these, the position with the BRICS countries is that Brazil has required individual companies to use IFRS since 2008, Russia already uses it, India is converging with IFRS, China has substantially converged national standards and South Africa has required IFRS for listed companies since 2005. Japan required mandatory compliance by 2016.

What has been the impact of adopting IFRS

There have been numerous benefits claimed, for example:

● Multinationals see a reduction in the cost of capital and easier access to international equity markets.

● Investors see shares in companies adopting IFRS becoming more liquid and have greater confidence in earnings per share figures when making investment decisions.

● National standard setters see an advantage in the shared development of standards.

A detailed research report on the experience of converging IFRSs in China, *Does IFRS Convergence Affect Financial Reporting Quality in China?*, makes interesting reading.[7]

The report noted that there was a significant increase in the value relevance of reported earnings for the firms following mandatory adoption of IFRS-converged Chinese Accounting Standards (CAS). It also identified how access to external finance was an incentive to achieve improved quality of financial reporting, discussing the effect where companies are in the manufacturing sector, operating in less developed regions or operating under foreign ownership, in contrast to those under central government control or those that have financial problems and are tempted to manage earnings to avoid delisting.

Extant IASs and IFRSs are listed in Figure 9.2.

9.8 Standard setting and enforcement in the European Union (EU)[8]

A major aim of the EU has been to create a single financial market that requires access by investors to financial reports which have been prepared using common financial reporting standards. The initial steps were the issue of accounting directives – these were the Fourth Directive,[9] the Seventh Directive and the Eighth Directive which were required to be adopted by each EU country into their national laws – in the UK it is the Companies Act 2006. The existing Directives were subsumed in 2013 into a new Accounting Directive.

In the UK the requirements of the Accounting Directive were included into company law on the issue of The Companies, Partnerships and Groups (Accounts and Reports) Regulations 2015 effective from January 2016.

9.8.1 The new Accounting Directive[10]

There has been ongoing pressure to reduce the regulatory burden on small and medium-sized enterprises. The European Commission responded to this pressure by issuing a new Accounting Directive.

It is not a conceptual rewrite of the Directives. It aimed to address two of the major problems with the existing Directives, which were the lack of comparability arising from use of Member State Options (MSOs) and the unnecessary regulatory burden placed on SMEs.

The lack of comparability

The new Directive has achieved a small reduction in the number of options available to member states. It formalises fundamental accounting principles (although still with some

Figure 9.2 Extant international standards

IAS 1	Presentation of Financial Statements
IAS 2	Inventories
IAS 7	Statement of Cash Flows
IAS 8	Accounting Policies, Changes in Accounting Estimates and Errors
IAS 10	Events after the Reporting Period
IAS 11	Construction Contracts
IAS 12	Income Taxes
IAS 16	Property, Plant and Equipment
IAS 17	Leases
IAS 18	Revenue
IAS 19	Employee Benefits
IAS 20	Accounting for Government Grants and Disclosure of Government Assistance
IAS 21	The Effects of Changes in Foreign Exchange Rates
IAS 23	Borrowing Costs
IAS 24	Related Party Disclosures
IAS 26	Accounting and Reporting by Retirement Benefit Plans
IAS 27	Separate Financial Statements
IAS 28	Investments in Associates and Joint Ventures
IAS 29	Financial Reporting in Hyperinflationary Economies
IAS 32	Financial Instruments: Presentation
IAS 33	Earnings per Share
IAS 34	Interim Financial Reporting
IAS 36	Impairment of Assets
IAS 37	Provisions, Contingent Liabilities and Contingent Assets
IAS 38	Intangible Assets
IAS 39	Financial Instruments: Recognition and Measurement
IAS 40	Investment Properties
IAS 41	Agriculture
IFRS 1	First-time Adoption of International Financial Reporting Standards
IFRS 2	Share-based Payment
IFRS 3	(Revised) Business Combinations
IFRS 4	Insurance Contracts
IFRS 5	Non-current Assets Held for Sale and Discontinued Operations
IFRS 6	Exploration for and Evaluation of Mineral Resources
IFRS 7	Financial Instruments Disclosures
IFRS 8	Operating Segments
IFRS 9	Financial Instruments
IFRS 10	Consolidated Financial Statements
IFRS 11	Joint Arrangements
IFRS 12	Disclosure of Interests in Other Entities
IFRS 13	Fair Value Measurement
IFRS 14	Regulatory Deferral Accounts
IFRS 15	Revenue from Contracts with Customers
IFRS 16	Leases

Member State Options) for recognition and presentation in the financial statements. These are:

(i) There is a going concern presumption.

(ii) Accounts are to be prepared on an accrual basis.

(iii) Accounting policies and measurement bases are to be applied consistently between accounting periods.

(iv) Recognition and measurement are to be on a prudent basis, and in particular:

    (a) Items are to be measured at price or production cost.

        There is an option that allows for the revaluation of non-current assets and the use of fair values for financial and non-financial assets.

    (b) Only profits made at the balance sheet date are to be recognised.

    (c) Individual assets and liabilities are to be valued separately and set-off is not permitted.

    (d) All liabilities arising in the course of a financial year are to be recognised even if identified after the year.

    (e) All items are to be accounted for and presented in accordance with the substance of the transaction.

    (f) All negative value adjustments are to be recognised whether the result for the financial year is a profit or a loss.

(v) Materiality applies to recognition, measurement, presentation, disclosure and consolidation.

There have also been some arbitrary changes such as the requirement to write off goodwill over a period of between 5 and 10 years in exceptional cases, where the useful life of goodwill and development costs cannot be reliably estimated, and continuing options such as the option for the related costs of borrowing to be added to the cost of fixed and current assets.

Regulatory burden on SMEs

In order to further simplify the requirements for SMEs and micro-undertakings the European Commission adopted a 'bottom-up' approach that started with the requirements for small undertakings and then added additional accounting and reporting requirements as undertakings passed the thresholds for medium and large undertakings. It has set new size thresholds for determining the category as follows:

Undertakings	Turnover (£)	Balance sheet total (£)	Average number of employees
Micro	≤632,000	316,000	10
Small	≤10.2 m	≤5.1 m	50
Medium-sized	≤36.0 m	≤18 m	250

The undertaking must be within any two of the three thresholds for two successive accounting periods. The default thresholds for small undertakings' turnover and balance sheet total are €8 million and €4 million, respectively. However, member states have the option to increase either or both of these thresholds for small undertakings up to a maximum of €12 million and €6 million, respectively.

The need for small companies to be audited has been removed.

Progressive increase in requirements from the bottom up

The Directive starts by listing the reporting requirements applicable to a small company and then increases the disclosures required from a medium-sized and a large undertaking. A helpful summary of the requirements is provided by Accountancy Europe which was formerly called the Federation of European Accountants (FEE).[11]

9.8.2 Enforcement of standards in Europe

In 2014 ESMA issued[12] *Guidelines: Enforcement of Financial Information.* Together with European national enforcers it identifies common enforcement priorities, which for 2017 focused on new standards and will introduce significant change to financial statements. ESMA expects that issuers affected by these changes will provide entity-specific quantitative and qualitative disclosures about the application of the new standards and in particular financial institutions for IFRS 9 and corporates for IFRS 15.

It noted that investors increasingly value information on social and environmental impacts of issuers' activities. Consequently, ESMA highlights that both financial and non-financial reporting requirements are essential to support sustainable and long-term investment decision making in Europe.

9.8.3 The importance of enforcement

There is research evidence[13] that the cost of capital falls following the mandatory adoption of IFRS and that there is an increase in foreign equity investment. However, in addition to the standards, effective enforcement has to be in place.[14]

Even following the mandatory adoption of IFRS and enforcement of reporting standards, investors continue to consider national considerations such as the existence of good corporate governance, the degree of shareholder protection and the level of corruption.

9.8.4 What might the impact be on financial reporting following Brexit?

Here we are only considering the process of financial reporting rather than the likely impact of increased volatility on individual assets and liabilities.

At the time of writing (2018), the EU influence is exerted by the issue of the Accounting Directive 2013, which has to be adopted into national law and its requirement that IFRSs should be endorsed by the EU when applied to the consolidated accounts of listed companies. In practice EU endorsement has generally been quite accepting of the IASB produced IFRSs.

Details of all endorsements can be seen on the website of the European Financial Reporting Advisory Group (EFRAG) at www.efrag.org/Endorsement.

Position regarding IFRSs

Departure from the EU offers the UK three choices when preparing financial statements for listed companies, namely to

(i)   continue with EU-endorsed IFRS; or

(ii) move to full IFRS; or

(iii) revert to UK GAAP.

It is very unlikely that the UK would decide to revert to UK GAAP given the widespread internationally of the adoption of IFRSs. It might, however, consider UK-endorsed as opposed to EU-endorsed IFRSs. This would mean that the UK profession would have the ability to adapt IFRSs to its own needs.

9.9 Standard setting and enforcement in the US

Reporting standards are set by the Financial Accounting Standards Board (FASB) and enforced by the Securities Exchange Commission. Since 2002 it has also been necessary to satisfy the requirements of the Sarbanes–Oxley Act (normally referred to as SOX) which was passed following the Enron disaster.

9.9.1 Standard setting by the FASB and other bodies

The FASB is responsible for setting accounting standards in the USA. The FASB is financed by a compulsory levy on public companies, which should ensure its independence. (The previous system of voluntary contributions ran the risk of major donors trying to exert undue influence on the Board.) In 2009 the FASB launched the FASB *Accounting Standards Codi-fication* as the single source of authoritative non-governmental US Generally Accepted Accounting Principles (GAAP), combining and replacing the jumbled mix of accounting standards that have evolved over the last half-century.

9.9.2 Enforcement by the SEC

The Securities and Exchange Commission (SEC) is responsible for requiring the publication of financial information for the benefit of shareholders. It has the power to dictate the form and content of these reports. The largest companies whose shares are listed must register with the SEC and comply with its regulations. The SEC monitors financial reports filed in great detail and makes useful information available to the public via its website.[15] However, it is important to note that the majority of companies fall outside the SEC's jurisdiction.

9.9.3 SOX (the Sarbanes–Oxley Act 2002)

SOX came as a response to the failures in Enron. It is different from the UK's Code of Corporate Governance in that, rather than the comply-or-explain approach, compliance is mandatory with significant potential sanctions for individual directors where there is non-compliance.

Prevention of fraud

The SOX objectives are to reduce the risk of fraud. It provides that

> Whoever knowingly alters, destroys, mutilates, conceals, covers up, falsifies, or makes a false entry in any record, document, or tangible object with the intent to impede, obstruct, or influence the investigation or proper administration of any matter within the jurisdiction of any department or agency of the United States . . . shall be fined under this title, imprisoned not more than 20 years, or both. (Section 802(a))

Following the Enron and other scandals, a number of weaknesses were identified which allowed the frauds to go undetected. Weaknesses included (a) the accounting profession where there was inadequate oversight and conflicts of interest, (b) company management that had poor internal controls and had been subject to weak corporate governance procedures, and (c) investors under-protected with stock analysts giving biased investment advice, the FASB which was responsible for inadequate disclosure rules, and an under-funded enforcement agency in the Securities and Exchange Commission (SEC).

Management

CEOs of publicly traded companies are now directly responsible for ensuring that financial reports are accurate. To protect themselves CEOs rely on a sound system of internal control and management is accountable for the quality of those controls. Under SOX, management is required to certify the company's financial reports and both management and an independent accountant are required to certify the organisation's internal controls.

Investors

SOX aimed to reduce fraud and improve investor confidence in financial reports and the capital market by seeking improvements in corporate accounting controls. In doing so it has created mandatory requirements that might have disadvantaged US companies operating in a global market where there is a comply-or-explain approach to compliance as in the UK and OECD countries.

9.9.4 Progress towards adoption by the USA of international standards

There has been progress since 2002 following the Norwalk Agreement on making the US standards and IFRS fully compatible and to coordinate future work programmes.

The FASB and IASB have worked together on joint projects such as Revenue Recognition and Leasing. However, there is a view[16] that the future of further convergence remains uncertain as the Boards shift attention to their own independent agendas.

It has to be recognised that there appears to be little enthusiasm for the adoption of IFRS in place of US GAAP. This is understandable when realising that the question as to whether moving to IFRS is actually in the best interests of the US securities markets generally and US investors individually is unresolved. Their decision is also influenced by their view that (a) the IASB is underfunded and too reliant on the major accountancy firms and (b) their assessment that there is neither a consistent application nor enforcement of IFRSs globally.

9.10 Advantages and disadvantages of global standards for publicly accountable entities

Publicly accountable entities are those whose debt or equity is publicly traded. Many are multinational and listed on a stock exchange in more than one country.

9.10.1 Advantages

The main advantages arising from the development of international standards are that it reduces the cost of reporting under different standards, makes it easier to raise cross-border finance, leads to a decrease in firms' costs of capital with a corresponding increase in share prices, and enables investors to compare performance. For developing countries there is also the incentive to improve accountants' technical training and expertise.

9.10.2 Disadvantages

Complexity

However, one survey[17] carried out in the UK indicated that finance directors and auditors surveyed felt that IFRSs undermined UK reporting integrity. In particular, there was little support for the further use of fair values as a basis for financial reporting, which was regarded as making the accounts less reliable with comments such as 'I think the use of fair values increases the subjective nature of the accounts and confuses unqualified users'.

There was further reference to this problem of understanding with a further comment: 'IFRS/US GAAP have generally gone too far – now nobody other than the Big 4 technical departments and the SEC know what they mean. The analyst community doesn't even bother trying to understand them – so who exactly do the IASB think they are satisfying?'

Impact on net profit and equity

IFRS 1 *First-time Adoption of International Financial Reporting Standards* requires companies to produce a reconciliation of their IFRS equity and profit/loss to their equity and profit/ loss reported under national GAAP.

A research report[18] prepared for the Institute of Chartered Accountants in Scotland in 2008, *The Implementation of IFRS in the UK, Italy and Ireland,* analysed the impact on net profit and equity of selected standards which showed whether the standard had caused an increase or decrease in reported net profit due to the introduction of the standard.

Their analysis showed that adopting IFRS resulted in the net profit being increased in each of the countries with the net profit under national GAAP being 66% of the IFRS figure for UK companies, 89% for Italian and 89% for Irish companies. By contrast, the equity of the average company was less under IFRS, with the equity under national GAAP being 153% higher than that under IFRS.

These are average changes and the impact on an individual company might be very different. For example, there was a dramatic effect on the headline figures for Wassenan, a Dutch company, which reported an increase of over 400% in its net income figure when the Dutch GAAP accounts were restated under IFRS. In other cases, there may be some large adjustments to individual balances, but the net effect may be less obvious.

In the short term, these changes in reported figures can have important consequences for companies' contractual obligations (e.g. they may not be able to maintain the level of liquidity required by their loan agreements) and their ability to pay dividends. There may be motivational issues to consider where staff bonuses have traditionally been based on reported accounting profit. As a result, companies may find that they need to adjust their management accounting system to align it more closely with IFRS.

Volatility in the accounts

In most countries the use of IFRS will mean that earnings and statement of financial position values will be more volatile than in the past. This could be quite a culture shock for analysts and others used to examining trends that may have followed a fairly predictable straight line.

Lack of familiarity

While the change to IFRS was covered in the professional and the more general press, it was not clear whether users of financial statements fully appreciated the effect of the change in accounting regulations, although surveys by KPMG[19] and PricewaterhouseCoopers[20] indicated that most analysts and investors were confident that they understood the implications of the change. A survey following the issue of *IFRS for SMEs* in 2009 indicated that, as a new standard, there was naturally a fairly widespread lack of understanding of its provisions. This has been well addressed[21] by the IASB with supporting workshops and educational material.

9.11 How do reporting requirements differ for non-publicly accountable entities?

The EU, national governments and standard setters have realised that there are numerous small and medium-sized businesses that do not raise funds on the stock exchange and do not prepare general-purpose financial statements for external users. Countries adopting IFRS for publicly accountable entities have, therefore, been able to issue their own national standards for non-publicly accountable entities.

In the UK companies have a statutory obligation to submit accounts annually to the shareholders and file a copy with the Registrar of Companies. In recognition of the cost implications and need for different levels of privacy, there was provision for small and medium-sized companies to file abbreviated accounts and adopt *Financial Reporting Standard for Smaller Entities* (FRSSE).[22] This standard follows the top-down approach to standard setting by reducing some of the disclosures required by standards applicable to listed companies – such as disclosing an earnings per share figure. The FRSSE was withdrawn from 1 January 2016 and replaced by either FRS 105 *The Financial Reporting Standard for the Micro-entities Regime*, or Section 1A of FRS 102 *The Financial Reporting Standard*. Whereas the UK has FRS 105, the IASB has issued the *IFRS for SMEs*.

9.12 IFRS for SMEs

The IASB issued *IFRS for SMEs* in July 2009. The approach follows that adopted by the ASB with FRSSE:

- some topics omitted, e.g. IAS 33 Earnings per Share, IFRS 8 Operating Segments, IAS 34 Interim Financial Reporting, IFRS 5 Assets Held for Sale and IFRS 4 Insurance Contracts;
- some additional requirements as companies adopting the IFRS will have to comply with its mandatory requirement to produce a statement of cash flows and more information as to related party transactions;
- simpler options allowed, e.g. expensing rather than capitalising borrowing cost;
- simpler recognition, e.g. allowing an amortisation (with a maximum life of 10 years) rather than an annual impairment review for goodwill;
- simpler measurement, e.g. using the historical cost-depreciation model for property, plant and equipment;
- SMEs are not prevented from adopting other options available under full IFRS and may elect to do this if they so decide.

However, in defining an SME it has moved away from the size tests towards a definition based on qualitative factors such as public accountability whereby an SME would be a business that does not have public accountability. Public accountability is implied if outside stakeholders have a high degree of investment, commercial or social interest and if the majority of stakeholders have no alternative to the external financial report for financial information.

It is intended to have a three-yearly review of the implementation of the standard and it is reasonable to expect that the IFRS will evolve based on review findings such as permitting SMEs to revalue property, plant and equipment.

Longer-term future

This is in some doubt with the issue of the new Accounting Directive in 2013. This is designed to reduce unnecessary and disproportionate administrative costs on small companies by simplifying the preparation of financial statements and reducing the amount of information required by small companies in the notes to financial statements.

Under the Directive, small companies are only required to prepare a balance sheet, a profit and loss account and notes to meet regulatory requirements. When examining the various policy options available to replace the old Accounting Directives, the Commission examined and rejected the option to adopt the *IFRS for SMEs* at EU level as the Commission deemed that *IFRS for SMEs* did not meet the objective of reducing the administrative burden.

9.13 Why have there been differences in financial reporting?

Although there have been national standard-setting bodies, this has not resulted in uniform standards. A number of attempts have been made to identify reasons for differences in financial reporting.[23] The issue is far from clear but most writers agree that the following are among the main factors influencing the development of financial reporting:

- the character of the national legal system;
- the way in which industry is financed;
- the relationship of the tax and reporting systems;
- the influence and status of the accounting profession;
- the extent to which accounting theory is developed;
- accidents of history;
- language.

We will consider the effect of each of these.

9.13.1 The character of the national legal system

There are two major legal systems, that based on common law and that based on Roman law. It is important to recognise this because the legal systems influence the way in which behaviour in a country, including accounting and financial reporting, is regulated.

Countries with a legal system based on common law include the UK, Ireland, the USA, Australia, Canada and New Zealand. These countries rely on the application of equity to specific cases rather than a set of detailed rules to be applied in all cases. The effect in the UK, as far as financial reporting was concerned, was that there was limited legislation regulating the form and content of financial statements until the government was required to implement the EC Fourth Directive. The directive was implemented in the UK by the passing of the Companies Act 1981 and this can be seen as a watershed because it was the first time that the layout of company accounts had been prescribed by statute in the UK.

English common law heritage was accommodated within the legislation by the provision that the detailed regulations of the Act should not be applied if, in the judgement of the directors, strict adherence to the Act would result in financial statements that did not present a true and fair view.

Countries with a legal system based on Roman law include France, Germany and Japan. These countries rely on the codification of detailed rules, which are often included within their companies legislation. The result is that there is less flexibility in the preparation of financial reports in those countries. They are less inclined to look to fine distinctions to justify different reporting treatments, which is inherent in the common law approach. The existence of detailed rules or existing effective publication requirements also determines their approach to reporting standards as, for example, the reluctance in Germany to support the adoption of IFRS for SMEs.

However, it is not just that common law countries have fewer codified laws than Roman law countries. There is a fundamental difference in the way in which the reporting of commercial transactions is approached. In the common law countries there is an established practice of creative compliance. By this we mean that the spirit of the law is elusive[24] and management is more inclined to act with creative compliance in order to escape effective legal control. By creative compliance we mean that management complies with the form of the regulation but in a way that might be against its spirit, e.g. structuring leasing agreements in the most acceptable way for financial reporting purposes. This is addressed in an *ad hoc* manner with standards requiring the substance of a transaction to determine its treatment in the financial statements or revising individual standards to combat creative compliance.

9.13.2 The way in which industry is financed

Accountancy is the art of communicating relevant financial information about a business entity to users. One of the considerations to consider when deciding what is relevant is the way in which the business has been financed, e.g. the information needs of equity investors will be different from those of loan creditors. This is one factor responsible for international financial reporting differences because the predominant provider of capital is different in different countries. When making a comparison between domestic equity market capitalisation and gross domestic product (GDP) we can see that the higher the ratio, the greater the importance of the equity market compared with loan finance.

We see that in the USA companies have relied more heavily on individual investors to provide finance than in Europe or Japan. An active stock exchange has developed to allow shareholders to liquidate their investments. A system of financial reporting has evolved to satisfy a steward-ship need where prudence and conservatism predominate, and to meet the capital market need for fair information which allows interested parties to deal on an equal footing where the accruals concept and the doctrine of substance over form predominate. It is important to note that European statistics are *averages* that do not fully reflect the variation in sources of finance used between, say, the UK (where equity investment is very important) and Germany (where lending is more important). These could be important factors in the development of accounting.

We can see that the European countries have made continuing use of equity finance since 1998 rather than loan finance and this has led to a greater interest in the issue of International Financial Reporting Standards. Whereas lenders had access to management to obtain the information they sought, equity investors rely more on published information.

Since the 1990s there has been a growth globally of institutional investors, such as banks, insurance companies, retirement or pension funds, hedge funds and sovereign wealth funds. These form an ever-increasing proportion of shareholders. In theory, the information needs of these institutional investors should be the same as those of individual investors. However, in practice, they might be in a position to obtain information by direct access to management and the directors. One effect of this might be that they will become less interested in seeking disclosures in the financial statements – they will have already picked up the significant information at an informal level.

9.13.3 The relationship of the tax and reporting systems

In the UK separate rules have evolved for computing profit for tax and computing profit for financial reporting purposes in a number of areas. The legislation for tax purposes tends to be more prescriptive, e.g. there is a defined rate for capital allowances on fixed assets, which means that the reduction in value of fixed assets for tax purposes is decided by the government. The financial reporting environment is less prescriptive but this is compensated for by requiring greater disclosure. For example, there is no defined rate for depreciating non-current assets but there is a requirement for companies to state their depreciation accounting policy. Similar systems have evolved in the USA and the Netherlands.

However, certain countries give primacy to taxation rules and will only allow expenditure for tax purposes if it is given the same treatment in the financial accounts. In France and Germany, the tax rules effectively become the accounting rules for the accounts of individual companies, although the tax influence might be less apparent in consolidated financial statements.

This can lead to difficulties of interpretation, particularly when capital allowances, i.e. depreciation for tax purposes, are changed to secure public policy objectives such as encouraging investment in fixed assets by permitting accelerated write-off when assessing taxable profits. In fact, the depreciation charge against profit would be said by a UK accountant not to be fair, even though it could certainly be legal or correct.

Depreciation has been discussed to illustrate the possibility of misinterpretation because of the different status and effect of tax rules on annual accounts. Other items that require careful consideration include inventory valuations, bad debt provisions, development expenditure and revaluation of non-current assets. There might also be public policy arrangements that are unique to a single country, e.g. the existence of special reserves to reduce taxable profits was common in Scandinavia. It has recently been suggested that level of connection between tax and financial reporting follows a predictable pattern.[25]

9.13.4 The influence and status of the accounting profession

The development of a capital market for dealing in shares created a need for reliable, relevant and timely financial information. Legislation was introduced in many countries requiring companies to prepare annual accounts and have them audited. This resulted in the growth of an established and respected accounting profession able to produce relevant reports and attest to their reliability by performing an audit.

In turn, the existence of a strong profession had an impact on the development of accounting regulations. It is the profession that has been responsible for the promulgation of accounting standards and recommendations in a number of countries, such as the UK, the USA, Australia, Canada and the Netherlands.

In countries where there was not the same need to provide market-sensitive information, e.g. in Eastern Europe in the 1980s, accountants were seen purely as bookkeepers and were accorded a low status. However, the position has changed rapidly and there has been a growth in the training, professionalism and contribution for both financial and management accountants as these economies have become market economies.

9.13.5 The extent to which accounting theory is developed

Accounting theory can influence accounting practice. Theory can be developed at both an academic and a professional level, but for it to take root it must be accepted by the profession. For example, in the UK, theories such as current purchasing power and current cost accounting first surfaced in the academic world and there were many practising accountants who regarded them then, and still regard them now, as academic.

In the Netherlands, professional accountants receive academic accountancy training as well as the vocational accountancy training that is typical in the UK. Perhaps as a result of that, there is less reluctance on the part of the profession to view academics as isolated from the real world. This might go some way to explaining why it was in the Netherlands that we saw general acceptance by the profession of the idea that for information to be relevant it needed to be based on current value accounting. Largely as a result of pressure from the Netherlands, the Fourth Directive contained provisions that allowed member states to introduce inflation accounting systems.[26]

Attempts have been made to formulate a conceptual framework for financial reporting in countries such as the UK, the USA, Canada and Australia,[27] and the International Standards Committee has also contributed to this field. One of the results has been the closer collaboration between the regulatory bodies, which might assist in reducing differences in underlying principles in the longer term.

9.13.6 Accidents of history

The development of accounting systems is often allied to the political history of a country. Scandals surrounding company failures, notably in the USA in the 1920s and 1930s and in the UK in the 1960s and 1980s, had a marked impact on financial reporting in those countries.

In the USA the Securities and Exchange Commission was established to control listed companies, with responsibility to ensure adequate disclosure in annual accounts. Ever-increasing control over the form and content of financial statements through improvements in the accounting standard-setting process has evolved from the difficulties that arose in the UK.

International boundaries have also been crossed in the evolution of accounting. In some instances, it has been a question of pooling of resources to avoid repeating work already carried out elsewhere, e.g. the Norwegians studied the report of the Dearing Committee in the UK before setting up their new accounting standard-setting system in the 1980s.[28] Other changes in nations' accounting practices have been a result of external pressure, e.g. Spain's membership of the European Community led to radical changes in accounting.[29]

9.13.7 Language

Language has often played an important role in the development of different methods of accounting for similar items. Certain nationalities are renowned for speaking only their own language, which has prevented them from benefiting from the wisdom of other nations. There is also the difficulty of translating concepts as well as phrases, where one country has influenced another.

9.14 Move towards a conceptual framework

The process of formulating standards has encouraged a constructive appraisal of the policies being proposed for individual reporting problems and has stimulated the development of a conceptual framework. For example, the standard on leasing introduced the idea in UK standards of considering the commercial substance of a transaction rather than simply the legal position.

When the ASC was set up in the 1970s there was no clear statement of accounting principles other than that accounts should be prudent, be consistent, follow accrual accounting procedures and be based on the initial assumption that the business would remain a going concern.

The immediate task was to bring some order into accounting practice. The challenge of this task is illustrated by the ASC report *A Conceptual Framework for Financial Accounting and Reporting: The Possibilities for an Agreed Structure* by R. Macve, published in 1981, which considered that the possibility of an agreed body of accounting principles was remote at that time.

We will see in Chapter 10 the progress that has been made in developing a Conceptual Framework.

Summary

It is evident from cases such as AEI/GEC, Enron and Parmalat that management cannot be permitted to have total discretion in the way in which it presents financial information in its accounts and rules are needed to ensure uniformity in the reporting of similar commercial transactions. Decisions must then be made as to the nature of the rules and how they are to be enforced.

In the UK the standard-setting bodies have tended to lean towards rules being framed as general principles and accepting the culture of voluntary compliance with explanation for any non-compliance.

Although there is a preference on the part of the standard setters to concentrate on general principles, there is growing pressure from the preparers of the accounts for more detailed illustrations and explanations as to how the standards are to be applied.

Standard setters have recognised that small and medium-sized businesses are not publicly accountable to external users and are given the opportunity to prepare financial statements under standards specifically designed to be useful and cost-effective. The new Accounting Directive now adopts a bottom-up approach with additional requirements for medium-sized and large undertakings.

The expansion in the number of multinational enterprises and transnational investments has led to a demand for a greater understanding of financial statements prepared in a range of countries. This has led to pressure for a single set of high-quality international accounting standards. IFRSs are being used increasingly for reporting to capital markets. At the same time, national standards are evolving to come into line with IFRS.

REVIEW QUESTIONS

1 Why is it necessary for financial reporting to be subject to both (a) mandatory control and (b) statutory control?

2 Discuss how the Financial Reporting Review Panel plans its activities.

3 The increasing perception is that IFRS is overly complex and is complicating the search for appropriate forms of financial reporting for entities not covered by the EU Regulation.[30] Discuss:

   (a) whether the current criteria for defining small and medium-sized companies are appropriate; and

   (b) to what extent the provisions of the new Accounting Directive might alleviate the problem.

4 'The most favoured way to reduce information overload was to have the company filter the available information set based on users' specifications of their needs'.[31] Discuss how this can be achieved, given that users have differing needs.

5 Research[32] has indicated that narrative reporting in annual reports is not neutral, with good news being highlighted more than is supported by the statutory accounts and more than bad news. Discuss whether mandatory or statutory regulation could enforce objectivity in narrative disclosures and who should be responsible for such enforcement.

6 How is it possible to make shareholders aware of the significance of the exercise of judgement by directors which can turn profits of £6 million into losses of £2 million?

7 Discuss the effect on reporting standards of the way in which industry is financed.

8 'Foreign equity investment increases when countries have mandatory adoption of IFRS and effective enforcement'. Discuss why this may not be required by investors in bonds.

9 'The existence of a strong accounting profession is more important than uniform accounting standards in providing relevant information'. Discuss.

10 Discuss the extent to which creative compliance can have a positive influence on financial reporting standards.

11 Access the FRC Annual Review of Corporate Reports and discuss the main areas that it proposes to review over the following 2 years.

12 Using the following link, http://www.ifrs.org/about-us/how we set-standards/ Explain how IFRSs are set by the IFR Foundation's standard-setting body, the International Accounting Standards Boards.

EXERCISES

*Question 1

Review the Accounting policies of a company in the FTSE 100 and critically discuss the extent to which it satisfies the investor requirements identified in the FRC Lab project report *Accounting Policies and Integration of Related Financial Information July 2014* (www.frc.org.uk/Our-Work/Publications/Financial-Reporting-Lab/Accounting-policies-and-integration-of-related-fin.pdf).

*Question 2

FRS 105 *The Financial Reporting Standard applicable to the Micro-entities Regime* requires that a complete set of financial statements of a micro-entity should include the following: (a) a statement of financial position as at the reporting date with notes included at the foot of the statement; and (b) an income statement for the reporting period.

Required:
Critically discuss the adequacy of this requirement.

*Question 3

Consider the interest of the tax authorities in financial reporting regulations. Explain why national tax authorities might be concerned about the transition from domestic accounting standards to IFRS in companies' Annual Reports.

*Question 4

Select an Industry sector from the FTSE 100 companies.

(i)   Discuss risk factors you consider material.
(ii) Review the annual report of a company in that sector and critically comment on the coverage of risk factors.

*Question 5

(i)   Critically discuss the rationale for allowing businesses in the UK a choice as to which accounting standards to apply, such as IFRS for the Group accounts and FRS 102 for UK subsidiaries.
(ii) Critically evaluate the IASB decision to move from a size criterion to a qualitative criterion in issuing *IFRS for SMEs*.

*Question 6

The FRC in its 2010 publication *Cutting Clutter in Annual Reports* observed that much immaterial information is included in an Annual Report.

Required:
Review an Annual Report of a company that interests you and (a) as a potential investor critically comment on information you consider immaterial and (b) as the preparer justify its inclusion.

Notes

1 G. Whittred and I. Zimmer, *Financial Accounting Incentive Effects and Economic Consequences*, Holt, Rinehart & Winston, 1992, p. 8.
2 Baker Tilly, www.bakertilly.co.uk
3 K. Peasnell, P. Pope and S. Young, 'Breaking the rules', *Accountancy International*, February 2000, p. 76.
4 CESR, *Proposed Statement of Principles of Enforcement of Accounting Standards in Europe*, CESR02–188b Principle 13, October 2002.
5 https://www.frc.org.uk/getattachment/a072a946-15e2-486e-956b-24fd444f2407/;.aspx
6 IASC, *Framework for the Preparation and Presentation of Financial Statements*, 1989, adopted by IASB 2001.
7 E. Lee, M. Walker and C. Zeng, *Does IFRS Convergence Affect Financial Reporting Quality in China?*, ACCA Research Report 131. See www.accaglobal.com/content/dam/acca/global/PDF-technical/financial-reporting/rr-131-002.pdf
8 https://ec.europa.eu/info/business-economy-euro/company-reporting-and-auditing/company-reporting/financial-reporting_en
9 https://eur-lex.europa.eu/legal-content/EN/TXT/?uri=LEGISSUM%3Al26009
10 EU Directive 2013/34/EU.
11 https://www.accountancyeurope.eu/wp-content/uploads/Factsheet_Audit_Policy_SMEs_1404.pdf
12 www.a-tvp.si/Documents/guidelines_esma_1293en.pdf
13 S. Li, 'Does mandatory adoption of International Financial Reporting Standards in the European Union reduce the cost of equity capital?', *The Accounting Review*, vol. 85(2), 2009, pp. 607–636.
14 K.M. Shima and E.A. Gordon, 'ITFRS and the regulatory environment: the case of U.S. investor allocation choice', *Journal of Accounting and Public Policy*, vol. 30(5), 2011, pp. 481–500.
15 www.sec.gov
16 IFRS and US GAAP: similarities and differences, www.pwc.com/en_US/us/issues/ifrs-reporting/publications/assets/ifrs-and-us-gaap-similarities-and-differences-2013.pdf
17 V. Beattie, S. Fearnley and T. Hines, 'Does IFRS undermine UK reporting integrity?', *Accountancy*, December 2008, pp. 56–57.
18 T. Dunne, S. Fifield, G. Finningham, A. Fox, G. Hanna, C. Helliar, D. Power and M. Veneziani '*The implementation of IFRS in the UK, Italy and Ireland*', ICAS, 2008.
19 www.kpmg.co.uk/pubs/215748.pdf
20 http://download.pwc.com.ie/pubs/ifrs_survey.pdf
21 www.ifrs.org/IFRS-for-SMEs/Pages/SME-workshops.aspx
22 ASB, *Financial Reporting Standard for Smaller Entities*, 1997.
23 C. Nobes and R. Parker, *Comparative International Accounting* (7th edition), Pearson Education, 2002, pp. 17–33.
24 J. Freedman and M. Power, *Law and Accountancy: Conflict and Cooperation in the 1990s*, Paul Chapman Publishing, 1992, p. 105.

25 C. Nobes and H.R. Schwencke, 'Modelling the links between tax and financial reporting: a longitudinal examination of Norway over 30 years up to IFRS adoption', *European Accounting Review*, vol. 15(1), 2006, pp. 63–87.

26 Nobes and Parker, op. cit., pp. 73–75.

27 See S.P. Agrawal, P.H. Jensen, A.L. Meader and K. Sellers, 'An international comparison of conceptual frameworks of accounting', *International Journal of Accounting,* vol. 24, 1989, pp. 237–249.

28 *Accountancy,* June 1989, p. 10.

29 See, e.g. B. Chauveau, 'The Spanish *Plan General de Contabilidad:* Agent of development and innovation?', *European Accounting Review,* vol. 4(1), 1995, pp. 125–138.

30 S. Fearnley and T. Hines, 'How IFRS has destabilised financial reporting for UK non-listed entities', *Journal of Financial Regulation and Compliance,* vol. 15(4), 2007, pp. 394–408.

31 V. Beattie, *Business Reporting: The Inevitable Change?,* ICAS, 1999, p. 53.

32 V. Tauringana and C. Chong, 'Neutrality of narrative discussion in annual reports of UK listed companies', *Journal of Applied Accounting Research,* vol. 7(1), 2004, pp. 74–107.

CHAPTER 10

Concepts – evolution of an international conceptual framework

10.1 Introduction

The main purpose of this chapter is to discuss the rationale underlying financial reporting standards and concepts to apply when there are transactions for which there are no relevant standards.

> ### Objectives
>
> By the end of this chapter, you should be able to:
>
> - discuss how financial accounting theory has evolved;
> - discuss the accounting principles set out in the IASB *Conceptual Framework for Financial Reporting* 2018;
> - comment critically on rule-based and principles-based approaches;
> - outline the latest developments regarding disclosures and concepts of materiality.

10.2 Different countries meant different financial statements

In the previous chapter we discussed the evolution of national and international accounting standards. The need for standards arose initially as a means by which the accounting profession protected itself against litigation for negligence by relying on the fact that financial statements complied with the published professional standards. The standards were based on existing best practice and little thought was given to a theoretical basis.

Reactive process

Standards were developed by individual countries and it was a reactive process. For example, in the US the Securities and Exchange Commission (SEC) was set up in 1933 to restore investor confidence in financial reporting following the Great Depression. The SEC is an enforcement agency that enforces compliance with US GAAP, which comprises often rule-based standards issued by the FASB.

There has been a similar reactive response in other countries, often reacting to major financial crises and fraud, which has undermined investor confidence in financial statements. As a result, there has been a variety of national standards with national enforcement, e.g. in the UK principles-based standards are issued by the FRC Board.

National standards varied in their quality and in the level of enforcement. This is illustrated by the following comment by the International Forum on Accountancy Development (IFAD):

> **Lessons from the crisis**
>
> . . . the Asian crisis showed that under the forces of financial globalisation it is essential for countries to improve . . . the supervision, regulation and transparency of financial systems . . . Efficiency of markets requires reliable financial information from issuers. With hindsight, it was clear that local accounting standards used to prepare financial statements did not meet international standards. Investors, both domestic and foreign, did not fully understand the weak financial position of the companies in which they were investing.

Need for global standards

With the growth of the global economy there has been a corresponding growth in the need for global standards, so that investors around the world receive the same fair view of a company's results regardless of the legal jurisdiction in which the company is registered.

We will see in this chapter that, in addition to the realisation that global accounting standards were required, there was also growing interest in basing the standards on a conceptual framework rather than fire-fighting with pragmatic standards often dealing with an immediate problem. However, just as there have been different national standards, so there have been different conceptual frameworks.

Development of financial accounting theory

It is interesting to take a historical overview of the evolution of the financial accounting theory underpinning standards and guiding standard setters to see how it has moved through three phases from the empirical inductive to the deductive and then to a formalised conceptual framework.

10.3 Historical overview of the evolution of financial accounting theory

Financial accounting practices have not evolved in a vacuum. They are dynamic responses to changing macro- and micro-conditions which may involve political, fiscal, economic and commercial changes. These can give rise to various theories as to how they should be reflected in financial statements.

For example, in response to high rates of inflation different accounting theories for the accounting treatment of changing prices were proposed, such as proposals to:

- ignore and apply historical cost accounting; or
- adopt a modified historical cost system where tangible non-current assets are revalued, which has been the norm in the UK; or
- adopt current entry costs reflecting the operating capital maintenance concept; or
- adopt current exit costs; or
- adopt fair values.

Then, when inflation fell in many jurisdictions to levels that did not make historical cost accounting appear to misrepresent the transactions that had occurred, all alternative theories were abandoned.

It is clear from considering just the treatment of changing prices that there could be a variety of accounting treatments for similar transactions. It could be argued that, if annual financial reports are to be useful in making economic decisions, there is a need for **uniformity** or **harmonising** with all entities reporting similar transactions in similar ways and **consistency** in reporting over time within an entity.

We can see that over time there have been three approaches to achieving this: following an empirical inductive approach; or a deductive approach; and developing a conceptual framework. We will consider each of these briefly.

10.3.1 An empirical inductive approach

This was the approach followed by the accounting profession prior to 1970. It looked at the practices that existed and attempted to generalise from them.

This tended to be how the technical departments of accounting firms operated. By rationalising what they did, they ensured that the firm avoided clients adopting different financial reporting practices for similar transactions. The technical department's role was to advise partners and staff, i.e. it was a defensive role to avoid any potential charge from a user of the accounts that they had been misled.

Initially a technical circular was regarded as a private good and distribution was restricted to the firm's own staff. However, it then became recognised that it could benefit the firm if its practices were accepted as the industry benchmark, so that in the event of litigation it could rely on this fact.

When the technical advice ceased to be a private good, there was a perceived additional protection for the firm if their defence moved from a positive statement, i.e. this is how we always report inventories in the financial statements, to a normative statement, i.e. this is how we report and this is how all other financial reporters **ought** to report.

Consequently, there has been a growing trend since the 1980s for firms to publish rationalisations for their financial reporting practices. It has been commercially prudent for them to do so. It has also been extremely helpful to academic accountants and their students.

Typical illustrations of the result of such empirical induction are the wide acceptance of the historical cost model and various concepts such as matching and realisation. The early standards were produced under this regime, e.g. IAS 2, the standard on inventory valuation.

This approach has played an important role in the evolution of financial reporting practices and will continue to do so. After all, it is the preparers of the financial statements and their auditors who are first exposed to change, whether economic, political or commercial. They are the ones who have to think their way through each new problem that surfaces, for example how to measure and report financial instruments. This means that a financial reporting practice already exists by the time the problem comes to the attention of theoreticians.

This resulted in standards or reporting practices that were based on rationalising what happened in practice, i.e. it established best current practice as the norm. Under this approach there was a general disclosure standard, e.g. IAS 1 *Disclosure of Accounting Policies*, and standards for major specific items, e.g. IAS 2 *Inventories*.

It was thought that the limitations implicit in the empirical inductive approach could be overcome by the deductive approach.

10.3.2 A deductive approach

The deductive approach is not dependent on existing practice, which is often perceived as having been tainted because it has been determined by finance directors and auditors. However, the problem remains: from whose viewpoint is the deduction to be made?

Possible alternatives to the preparers and auditors of the accounts are economists and users. However, we saw in Chapter 6 that the economists' approach is appropriate for specific decisions such as capital investment decisions but impractical for financial reporting to stakeholders. As for users, the information they require for decisions has to be considered but their needs are so diverse that they can only be realistically satisfied in a single set of general-purpose accounts. This is why the IASB has been prompted by stakeholders to develop a conceptual framework to underpin IFRSs.

10.3.3 A conceptual framework approach

This was promoted in the late 1980s. It was recognised that standards needed to ensure that financial statements provided the information that users required both to check on management's stewardship and to be able to make informed economic investment decisions.

There were a number of constraints including the requirement that they should satisfy cost/benefit criteria and the acceptance at that time that their implementation could only be achieved by consensus. Consensus was required because a proposed accounting treatment could have different financial reporting consequences, such as when finance leases were required to be reported within the assets and liabilities, so affecting ratios. It could also have direct economic consequences on entities that changed the way in which they made investment decisions.

Consensus was only achieved by permitting entities a choice from alternative accounting treatments. Currently, the IASB is required to carry out an economic impact appraisal of any proposed reporting standard. The aim, then and now, was to base standards on a sound conceptual basis.

The outcome of the wish for a conceptual framework was the publication by the IASC (the predecessor body to the IASB) in 1989 of its *Framework for the Preparation and Presentation of Financial Statements*. This document was the first of a number of similarly titled documents. The documents were developed and published in response to changes in the global business environment.

10.4 Developing a Framework for the Preparation and Presentation of Financial Statements

A *Framework* is not a reporting standard. Its main purpose is to provide standard setters with concepts to inform them when developing standards. A secondary purpose is to provide guidance to management when deciding how to report on transactions for which there is no relevant international standard.

It is concerned with general-purpose financial statements that a business enterprise prepares and presents to meet the common information needs of a wide range of users to help them make economic decisions.

The user groups include current and potential investors, employees, lenders, suppliers and other trade creditors, customers, governments and their agencies and the general public. The approach taken by the *Framework* is that it accepts that not all of the information needs of each of the user groups can be met by a single set of financial statements. There has to be a primary user group.

The primary user group

It assumes, however, that as all users are making economic decisions, there is information in which all users have a common interest and that general-purpose financial statements should satisfy this. It further assumes that because investors are providers of risk capital to the enterprise, financial statements that meet their needs will also meet most of the general financial information needs of other users.

Typical economic decisions that are being made include:

- Assessing by stakeholders:
  - the stewardship or accountability of management;
  - when to buy, hold or sell an equity investment;
  - how much of the distributable profits to pay out as dividends;
  - the ability of the entity to pay and provide other benefits to its employees;
  - the security for amounts lent to the entity.
- Determining by regulatory authorities:
  - taxation policies;
  - how to regulate the activities of entities.

10.4.1 Revising the Framework for the Preparation and Presentation of Financial Statements

Just as with the convergence project, the IASB and FASB set up a joint project in 2004 to review the *Framework* in phases aiming to produce concepts relating to objectives and qualitative characteristics, elements and recognition, measurement and presentation and disclosure. There was also to be a phase aimed at reaching a converged IASB–FASB view on the secondary purpose of the framework.

The IASB and FASB worked jointly until 2010. After that date the FASB and the IASB suspended their work on the project to focus their resources on other projects. In 2012, following a public consultation that indicated that users regarded the revision of the Framework as a priority, the IASB revived the project as an *IASB-only comprehensive project.*

At that time the IASB resolved that:

- the conceptual framework project should focus on: elements of financial statements, measurement, reporting entity, presentation and disclosure;
- the aim should be to work towards a single discussion paper covering all these areas, rather than separate discussion papers for each area.

The idea was to add to the Framework which already existed. The Board published the following proposals over the course of the project:

- a Discussion Paper A Review of the Conceptual Framework for Financial Reporting in 2013 (2013 Discussion Paper); Exposure drafts in 2015 followed finally by the 2018 Conceptual Framework, which was issued in March 2018.

10.5 Conceptual Framework for Financial Reporting 2018

The 2018 version of the *Framework* has been produced in eight chapters as follows:

- Chapter 1 – The objective of general-purpose financial reporting
- Chapter 2 – Qualitative characteristics of useful financial information
- Chapter 3 – Financial statements and the reporting entity.
- Chapter 4 – The elements of financial statements

- Chapter 5 – Recognition and de-recognition
- Chapter 6 – Measurement
- Chapter 7 – Presentation and disclosure
- Chapter 8 – Concepts of capital and capital maintenance.

We outline the contents of each chapter.

10.5.1 Chapter 1 – The objective of general-purpose financial reporting

This chapter starts by stating that 'The objective of general-purpose financial reporting is to provide financial information about the reporting entity that is useful to existing and potential investors, lenders and other creditors in making decisions relating to providing resources to the entity'.

The chapter provides a number of (non-contentious) examples of the types of investment and lending decisions typical third parties might make on the basis of general-purpose financial information.

In order to make these decisions, Chapter 1 claims that users need information about both the economic resources the entity possesses and how efficiently and effectively its management have used those resources.

Chapter 1 stresses that general-purpose financial reports do **not** generally indicate the current value of an entity. This is because a number of 'assets' of an entity, most notably its internally generated goodwill (discussed further in Chapter 19), are not recognised in general-purpose financial reports.

The chapter goes on to state that individual primary users have different, and possibly conflicting, information needs and desires. The IASB, in developing Standards, will seek to provide the information set that will meet the needs of the maximum number of primary users. However, focusing on common information needs does not prevent the reporting entity from including additional information that is most useful to a particular subset of primary users. An example of this would be the requirement set out in IAS 33 (discussed further in Chapter 27) to disclose earnings per share.

General-purpose financial reports provide information about:

(a) The financial **position** of a reporting entity showing its economic resources (assets) and the claims against it (liabilities). It allows users to:

- identify the reporting entity's financial strengths and weaknesses;
- assess the reporting entity's liquidity and solvency;
- estimate its needs for additional financing and how successful it is likely to be in obtaining that financing; and
- assess management's stewardship of the entity's economic resources.

(b) The effects of transactions such as operating profits and losses that result in changes in the assets and liabilities. This provides users with the ability to calculate the return on the net assets which helps to:

- evaluate financial performance;
- assess management's stewardship;
- identify the historic trend; predict the variability of returns; and
- predict how efficiently and effectively management will use the entity's economic resources in future periods.

Such information would typically be presented in a statement of financial performance.

(c) The effect of non- financial performance events such as the issue and buyback of equity shares. Such information would typically be presented in a statement of changes in equity.

(d) The effect on cash flows of the trading transactions in (b) and the events in (c).

This helps the user to assess the short-term liquidity, the medium-term solvency and the longer-term viability of the business.

The chapter emphasises that both profit related (accruals accounting as discussed in Chapter 2) and cash flow related information (as discussed in Chapter 1) about changes in economic resources will be useful to general-purpose users for decision-making purposes.

Analysis of Chapter 1

The contents of Chapter 1 of the 2018 version of *The Framework* have been somewhat re-written compared with the previous version but they are relatively uncontroversial.

10.5.2 Chapter 2 – Qualitative characteristics of useful financial information

This chapter has largely been carried forward from the previous version of *The Framework* (although it was Chapter 3 in the previous version). There are two fundamental qualitative characteristics that information needs to portray in order to be decision-useful and not misleading. These are **relevance** and **faithful representation**. There are also characteristics which are referred to as **enhancing**. We will now discuss each of these.

(i) Relevance

Relevant financial information is capable of making a difference to the decisions made by users. Financial information is capable of making a difference to decisions if it has **predictive value, confirmatory value** or both.

Predictive value
Financial information has predictive value if it can be used as an input to processes employed by users to predict future outcomes. It is used by users in making their own predictions.

Confirmatory value
Financial information has confirmatory value if it provides feedback about (confirms or changes) previous evaluations.

Predictive and confirmatory values
Predictive and confirmatory values are interrelated. For example, revenue information for the current year, which can be used as the basis for predicting revenues in future years, can also be compared with revenue predictions for the current year that were made in past years.

Materiality in relation to relevance
Materiality is discussed in IAS 8 *Accounting Policies, Changes in Accounting Estimates and Errors*. IAS 8 says that items are material if they could, individually or collectively, influence the economic decisions of users by their omission or misstatement. Items can be material by their size or by their nature. An example of an item that is material by its nature is the existence of a related party relationship (as discussed in Chapter 4). IAS 24 – *Related Party*

Disclosures – requires the disclosure of related party relationships and transactions irrespective of their size. Having said this, the perception of materiality by size is clearly entity specific. Further developments in considerations of materiality will be discussed in Section 7.6 of this chapter.

(ii) Faithful representation

Financial reports represent the effect of economic activities in words and numbers. A faithful representation would need to be complete, neutral and free from error.

Neutral

This means that the information has not been slanted, weighted, emphasized or otherwise manipulated to increase the probability that financial information will be received favourably or unfavourably by users.

The *Framework* emphasizes that there is an inbuilt contradiction between a concept of neutrality and one of prudence (which was regarded as a fundamental concept in previous conceptual frameworks).

Prudence

The *Framework* states that 'The exercise of prudence does not imply a need for asymmetry, for example, a systematic need for more persuasive evidence to support the recognition of assets or income than the recognition of liabilities or expenses. Such asymmetry is not a qualitative characteristic of useful financial information. Nevertheless, particular Standards may contain asymmetric requirements if this is a consequence of decisions intended to select the most relevant information that faithfully represents what it purports to represent.' A particular example of such a standard is IAS 37 – *Provisions, Contingent Liabilities and Contingent Assets* (discussed further in Chapter 13) where the recognition criteria for possible liabilities are asymmetric with the recognition criteria for possible assets.

Free from error

Faithful representation does not mean the information is 100% accurate. 'Free from error' means there are no material errors or omissions in the description of the event or transaction and no errors in the process used to produce the reported information.

Taking the reporting of an estimate as an example, a representation of that estimate can be faithful if

(a) the amount is described clearly and accurately as being an estimate and

(b) the nature and limitations of the estimating process are explained and

(c) no errors have been made in selecting and applying an appropriate process for developing the estimate.

(iii) Enhancing qualities

There are other characteristics that may make the information more useful. These are:

- comparability – allowing for both inter-company and inter-period comparisons;
- verifiability – means that different knowledgeable and independent observers could broadly agree that the report provides a faithful representation of transactions;
- timeliness – information is available to decision-makers in time to be capable of influencing their decisions;
- understandability – assumes that users have a reasonable knowledge of business and economic activities.

Analysis of Chapter 2

As previously stated this chapter is derived very closely from Chapter 3 of the previous version of the *Framework*. Given that this chapter has 'stood the test of time' then much of its content will, as previously stated regarding Chapter 1, be relatively uncontroversial. The chapter makes a creditable attempt to reconcile the concept of 'neutrality' with the concept of 'prudence' that was previously regarded as sacrosanct by many accountants.

10.5.3 Chapter 3 – Financial Statements and the Reporting Entity

Financial statements

Chapters 1 and 2 of the *Framework* discuss information provided in general-purpose financial reports. The rest of the *Framework* discusses general-purpose financial *statements*, which are a particular form of general-purpose financial reports.

As far as financial *statements* are concerned-they are prepared from the perspective of the entity as a whole, rather than from the perspective of a particular user group and are for a specified period, typically a year. They provide information:

- in the statement of financial position, by recognising assets, liabilities and equity;
- in the statement of financial performance, by recognising income and expenses;
- in other statements and notes, by presenting and disclosing information about:

    (i)   assets and liabilities that have not been recognised such as internally created goodwill, including information about their nature and about the risks arising from them;

    (ii) contributions from holders of equity claims and distributions to them;

    (iii) the methods, assumptions and judgements used in estimating the amounts presented or disclosed, and changes in those methods, assumptions and judgements.

The statements are normally prepared on a going concern basis. However, if the going concern basis is not appropriate, then an alternative basis should be used and described in the financial statements. The most common alternative basis would be the break-up basis for insolvent entities (discussed further in Chapter 10).

The reporting entity

A reporting entity is defined as any entity that prepares financial statements, either by choice or under regulation. A reporting entity need not necessarily be a separate legal entity.

Consolidated financial statements are perhaps the most obvious example of the reporting entity (the group comprising the parent entity and its subsidiary entities) not being a single legal entity.

However, there could be other examples of where this is the case (e.g. financial statements dealing with one division of a single legal entity). In such other cases the accounting boundary can be more difficult to determine. The *Framework* states that in such circumstances the boundary is set so as to faithfully represent relevant information to the users of such financial statements.

Specifically, Chapter 3 states that:

(a) The boundary of the reporting entity should not contain an arbitrary or incomplete set of economic activities.

(b) Including that set of economic activities within the boundary of the reporting entity results in neutral information.

A description is provided of how the boundary of the reporting entity was determined and of what constitutes the reporting entity.

Analysis of Chapter 3

Chapter 3 contains, in the view of the writer, a sound overview of the nature and purpose of financial statements that are fundamental to the chapters that follow.

10.5.4 Chapter 4 – the Elements of Financial Statements

Summary of the definitions

The elements of financial statements defined in the *Conceptual Framework* are:

(a) assets, liabilities and equity, which relate to a reporting entity's financial position;

(b) income and expenses, which relate to a reporting entity's financial performance.

These five elements are linked to the concepts outlined in Chapter 1 of the *Framework* as follows:

Concept	Element	Definition or description
Economic resource	Asset	A present economic resource controlled by the entity as a result of past events. An economic resource is a right that has the potential to produce economic benefits.
Claim	Liability	A present obligation of the entity to transfer an economic resource as a result of past events.
	Equity	The residual interest in the assets of the entity after deducting all its liabilities.
Changes in economic resources and claims, reflecting financial performance	Income	Increases in assets, or decreases in liabilities, that result in increases in equity, other than those relating to contributions from holders of equity claims.
	Expenses	Decreases in assets, or increases in liabilities, that result in decreases in equity, other than those relating to distributions to holders of equity claims.
Other changes in economic resources and claims	–	Contributions from holders of equity claims, and distributions to them.
	–	Exchanges of assets or liabilities that do not result in increases or decreases in equity.

Definition of an asset – further detail

A right

A 'right' can take several forms. Examples include a right to receive cash, a right to receive goods or services, or a right to exchange economic resources with another entity on favourable terms (e.g. a derivative that is 'in the money'). Many rights are established via legal contracts but rights can arise in other ways (e.g. by creating knowhow that is not in the public domain) with the business making a decision to seek legal protection by registering or relying on trade secrets.

Economic resource

For a right to be an economic resource it has to have the potential to produce economic benefits, These economic benefits could manifest themselves in one or more of the following ways:

● receiving contractual cash flows or another economic resource;

● exchanging economic resources with another party on favourable terms;

- producing cash inflows or avoid cash outflows by, for example, using the economic resource either individually or in combination with other economic resources to produce goods or provide services;
- extinguishing liabilities by transferring the economic resource.

Control

For an economic resource to be an asset, the entity needs to control that resource. An entity controls an economic resource if it has the present ability to direct the use of the economic resource and obtain the economic benefits that may flow from it. Control includes the present ability to prevent other parties from directing the use of the economic resource and from obtaining the economic benefits that may flow from it. It follows that, if one party controls an economic resource, no other party controls that resource. Control of an economic resource usually arises from an ability to enforce legal rights.

However, control can also arise if an entity has other means of ensuring that it, and no other party, has the present ability to direct the use of the economic resource and obtain the benefits that may flow from it. For example, an entity could control a right to use know-how that is not in the public domain if the entity has access to the know-how and the present ability to keep the know-how secret, even if that know-how is not protected by a registered patent.

Definition of a liability – further detail

The first criterion for a liability is that the entity has an *obligation*. An obligation is a duty or responsibility that an entity has no practical ability to avoid. An obligation is always owed to another party (or parties). The other party (or parties) could be a person or another entity, a group of people or other entities, or society at large. It is not necessary to know the identity of the party (or parties) to whom the obligation is owed. Many obligations are established by contract, legislation or similar means and are legally enforceable by the party (or parties) to whom they are owed.

Obligations can also arise, however, from an entity's customary practices, published policies or specific statements if the entity has no practical ability to act in a manner inconsistent with those practices, policies or statements. The obligation that arises in such situations is sometimes referred to as a 'constructive obligation'. A typical example of a constructive obligation arises where an entity has a reputation for refunding retail customers who return unused goods (see IAS 37 – *Provisions, Contingent Liabilities and Contingent Assets*).

The second criterion for a liability is that the obligation is to transfer an economic resource. Obligations to transfer an economic resource include, for example:

(a) Obligations to pay cash.

(b) Obligations to deliver goods or provide services.

(c) Obligations to exchange economic resources with another party on unfavourable terms (e.g. a derivative that is 'out of the money').

(d) Obligations to transfer an economic resource if a specified uncertain future event occurs (e.g. the outcome of a pending legal case).

The third criterion for a liability is that the obligation is a present obligation that exists as a result of past events. A present obligation exists as a result of past events only if:

(a) The entity has already obtained economic benefits or taken an action.

(b) As a consequence, the entity will or may have to transfer an economic resource that it would not otherwise have had to transfer.

A present obligation can exist even if a transfer of economic resources cannot be enforced until some point in the future. For example, a contractual liability to pay cash may exist now even if the contract does not require a payment until a future date. Similarly, a contractual obligation for an entity to perform work at a future date may exist now even if the counterparty cannot require the entity to perform the work until that future date.

The unit of account (relevant to both assets and liabilities).

The 'unit of account' is the right or the group of rights, the obligation or the group of obligations, or the group of rights and obligations, to which recognition criteria and measurement concepts are applied. In some circumstances, it may be appropriate to select one unit of account for recognition and a different unit of account for measurement. For example, contracts may sometimes be recognised individually but measured as part of a portfolio of contracts, such as a portfolio of investments.

A unit of account is selected to provide useful information to the user. Decisions about the unit of account are linked to decisions about recognition and measurement that are made in developing Standards. Hence, the IASB concluded that decisions about selecting a unit of account will need to be made in developing Standards, not in the *Conceptual Framework*.

Possible units of account include:

(a) An individual right or individual obligation.

(b) All rights, all obligations, or all rights and all obligations, arising from a single source, for example the total amount payable in respect of a series of legal claims relating to the same issue.

(c) A subgroup of those rights and/or obligations – for example, a subgroup of rights over an item of property, plant and equipment for which the useful life and pattern of consumption differ from those of the other rights over that item. An example of this might be a component of a machine that requires periodic replacement and to which 'component deprecation' is applied.

(d) A group of rights and/or obligations arising from a portfolio of similar items.

(e) A group of rights and/or obligations arising from a portfolio of dissimilar items – for example, a portfolio of assets and liabilities to be disposed of in a single transaction. A practical example of this would be a disposal group as defined in IFRS 5 – *Non-current Assets Held for Sale and Discontinued Operations*.

(f) A risk exposure within a portfolio of items – if a portfolio of items is subject to a common risk, some aspects of the accounting for that portfolio could focus on the aggregate exposure to that risk within the portfolio. An example of this might be a derivative financial instrument that is held to hedge against a particular risk component of a portfolio of items (such as the currency risk associated with a portfolio of receivables or payables denominated in another currency).

Substance of contractual rights and contractual obligations

The terms of a contract create rights and obligations for an entity that is a party to that contract. To represent those rights and obligations faithfully, financial statements report their substance. In some cases, the substance of the rights and obligations is clear from the legal form of the contract. In other cases, the terms of the contract or a group or series of contracts require analysis to identify the substance of the rights and obligations.

Definition of equity – further detail

Equity is the residual interest in the assets of the entity after deducting all its liabilities. Equity claims are claims on the residual interest in the assets of the entity after deducting all its liabilities. In other words, they are claims against the entity that do not meet the definition of a liability.

Sometimes, legal, regulatory or other requirements affect particular components of equity, such as share capital or retained earnings. For example, some such requirements permit an entity to make distributions to holders of equity claims only if the entity has sufficient reserves that those requirements specify as being distributable.

Business activities are often undertaken by entities such as sole proprietorships, partnerships, trusts or various types of government business undertakings. The legal and regulatory frameworks for such entities are often different from frameworks that apply to corporate entities. For example, there may be few, if any, restrictions on the distribution to holders of equity claims against such entities. Nevertheless, the definition of equity already given applies to all reporting entities.

Definition of income and expenses – further detail

Income is increases in assets, or decreases in liabilities, that result in increases in equity, other than those relating to contributions from holders of equity claims.

Expenses are decreases in assets, or increases in liabilities, that result in decreases in equity, other than those relating to distributions to holders of equity claims. It follows from these definitions of income and expenses that contributions from holders of equity claims are not income, and distributions to holders of equity claims are not expenses.

Income and expenses provide users with information about financial performance, rather than financial position. The *Framework* regards information about financial performance as being of equal importance as information about financial position.

Analysis of Chapter 4

The basic definitions in Chapter 4 are unchanged from previous versions of the *Framework* but this version provides some helpful underpinning detail as well as useful guidance regarding the 'unit of account' to which basic recognition and measurement criteria are applied. There is, in some quarters, an on-going concern that the basic definitions all derive from the concept of assets and liabilities, rather than income and expenses. However, this does not represent a serious flaw in the chapter's logic given the clarity with which the definitions of income and expenses are articulated.

10.5.5 Chapter 5 – Recognition and de-recognition

Recognition

Recognition means including a monetary amount in the statement of financial position or the statement(s) of financial performance for an item that meets the definition of one of the elements of financial statements – an asset, a liability, equity, income or expenses. The amount at which an asset, a liability or equity is recognised in the statement of financial position is referred to as its 'carrying amount'.

Only items that meet the definition of an asset, a liability or equity are recognised in the statement of financial position. Similarly, only items that meet the definition of income or expenses are recognised in the statement(s) of financial performance. However, not all items that meet the definition of one of those elements are recognised. It has to be information that is useful, i.e. being

(a) relevant

(b) a faithful representation.

It is not possible, however, to always define precisely when recognition of an asset or liability will provide useful information to users of financial statements, at a cost that does not outweigh its benefits. What is useful to users depends on the item and the facts and circumstances. Consequently, judgement is required when deciding whether to recognise an item, and thus recognition requirements may need to vary between and within Standards. For example, on the whole the recognition requirements for intangible non-current assets are more onerous than those that apply to tangible non-current assets.

It is important when making decisions about recognition to then consider the information that would be given if an asset or liability were not recognised. For example, if the item is not recognised as an asset when expenditure is incurred, then it follows that an expense is recognised. Over time, recognising the expense may, in some cases, provide useful information, for example, information that enables users of financial statements to identify trends.

Even if an item meeting the definition of an asset or liability is not recognised, an entity may need to provide information about that item in the notes. It is important to consider how to make such information sufficiently visible to compensate for the fact that the item has not been reported in the statement of financial position and, if applicable, the statement(s) of financial performance.

Relevance

As we have already seen, relevance is one of the criteria that determines whether or not we recognise an element. Recognition of an element may not provide relevant information if:

(a) it is **uncertain** whether an asset or liability exists;

(b) an asset or liability exists, but the **probability** of an inflow or outflow of economic benefits is **low**.

If the probability of an inflow or outflow of economic benefits is low, the most relevant information about the asset or liability may be information about the magnitude of the possible inflows or outflows, their possible timing and the factors affecting the probability of their occurrence. The typical location for such information is in the notes. A practical example of this is the requirement of IAS 37 – *Provisions, Contingent Liabilities and Contingent Assets* – that contingent assets and liabilities are disclosed in the notes, rather than being recognised in the financial statements.

Faithful representation

Whether a faithful representation can be provided of a potentially recognisable element may be affected by the level of measurement uncertainty associated with the element. It might be unacceptably high if, for example:

(a) The range of possible outcomes is exceptionally wide and the probability of each outcome is exceptionally difficult to estimate.

(b) The measure is exceptionally sensitive to small changes in estimates of the probability of different outcomes – for example, if the probability of future cash inflows or outflows occurring is exceptionally low, but the magnitude of those cash inflows or outflows will be exceptionally high if they occur.

(c) Measuring the asset or liability requires exceptionally difficult or exceptionally subjective allocations of cash flows that do not relate solely to the asset or liability being measured.

Measurement issues are dealt with more comprehensively in Chapter 6 of the *Framework*.

De-recognition

De-recognition is the removal of all or part of a recognised asset or liability from an entity's statement of financial position. De-recognition normally occurs when that item no longer meets the definition of an asset or of a liability:

(a) For an asset, de-recognition normally occurs when the entity loses control of all or part of the recognised asset.

(b) For a liability, de-recognition normally occurs when the entity no longer has a present obligation for all or part of the recognised liability.

In some cases, an entity might appear to transfer an asset or liability, but that asset or liability might nevertheless remain an asset or liability of the entity. For example:

- If an entity has apparently transferred an asset but retains exposure to significant positive or negative variations in the amount of economic benefits that may be produced by the asset, this sometimes indicates that the entity might continue to control that asset.

- If an entity has transferred an asset to another party that holds the asset as an agent for the entity, the transferor still controls the asset.

De-recognition is not appropriate if an entity has transferred an asset and, at the same time, entered into another transaction that results in a present right or present obligation to reacquire the asset. Such present rights or present obligations may arise when, for example, an entity has transferred an asset and, at the same time, entered into another transaction that results in a present right or present obligation to reacquire the asset, for example, by sale and leaseback (discussed further in Chapter 18 Leases).

Such present rights or present obligations may arise from, for example, a forward contract, a written put option, or a purchased call option.

Suppose, for example, an entity (A) sells an equity share to another entity (B) but simultaneously gives entity B a call option to require entity A to re-purchase the share on a fixed future date. If the terms of the call option are such that it is highly probable the call option will be exercised then the transaction would not be depicted as a sale of shares by entity A to entity B and the simultaneous acquisition of an option derivative by entity B, but as a loan to entity A by entity B.

Analysis of Chapter 5
The recognition and de-recognition principles outlined in this chapter seem to be theoretically very sensible and logical but they are inevitably fairly vague. Much of the detail regarding recognition and de-recognition of individual items will need to be developed within individual *International Financial Reporting Standards (IFRSs)*.

10.5.6 Chapter 6 – Measurement

Introduction
The *Framework* basically states that assets and liabilities are measured either at their historical cost (adjusted in some cases to reflect the consumption of an asset – for example the depreciation of property, plant and equipment) or current value. Current value can either mean fair value, value in use, or current cost.

- Fair value is defined as 'the price that would be received to sell an asset, or paid to transfer a liability, in an orderly transaction between market participants'. This definition accords exactly with the definition given in IFRS 13 – *Fair Value Measurement*.

- Value in use is defined as 'the present value of the cash flows, or other economic benefits, that an entity expects to derive from the use of an asset and from its ultimate disposal'. This definition is basically the same as the definition given in IAS 36 - *Impairment of Assets*.

When applying the concept of 'value in use' to a liability the Framework describes 'fulfilment value'. This is regarded as 'the present value of the cash, or other economic resources, that an entity expects to be obliged to transfer as it fulfils a liability'.

- The current **cost** of an asset is the cost of an equivalent asset at the measurement date, comprising the consideration that would be paid at the measurement date plus the transaction costs that would be incurred at that date. The current cost of a liability is the consideration that would be received for an equivalent liability at the measurement date minus the transaction costs that would be incurred at that date.

The Framework notes that, like historical cost, current cost is an entry value measurement basis rather than an exit value measurement basis (both fair value and value in use are exit value measurement bases).

Selecting a measurement basis

The Framework notes that all four bases previously described can in theory provide useful information to users. In principle the measurement basis chosen should be the one that provides the most relevant information to users and that faithfully represents that information.

The most relevant measurement basis for an asset or liability depends on its characteristics. If the value of an asset or liability is sensitive to market factors or other risks, its historical cost might differ significantly from its current value. Consequently, historical cost may not provide relevant information if information about changes in value is important to users of financial statements. For example, amortised cost cannot provide relevant information about a financial asset or financial liability that is a derivative. However, changes in the fair value of an asset or liability reflect changes in expectations of market participants and changes in their risk preferences.

Depending on the characteristics of the asset or liability being measured and on the nature of the entity's business activities, information reflecting those changes may not always provide predictive value or confirmatory value to users of financial statements. This may be the case when the entity's business activities do not involve selling the asset or transferring the liability, for example, if the entity holds assets solely for use or solely for collecting contractual cash flows or if the entity is to fulfil liabilities itself. This principle is very much applied in IFRS 9 – *Financial Instruments* – when giving guidance on an appropriate measurement basis for financial assets.

Another factor in determining the most relevant measurement basis for an asset particularly is the way that asset generates future cash flows. If the asset generates cash flows directly then current value is often a more relevant measurement basis than historical cost. However, the reverse is stated to be true for an asset such as inventory, which typically cannot be sold to a customer, except by making extensive use of the entity's other economic resources. In such a case, historical cost often provides more relevant information to users.

The measurement basis that provides the more faithful representation of the asset or liability to users is largely dependent on the amount of uncertainty associated with the measurement (referred to in the *Framework* as 'measurement uncertainty'). A high level of measurement uncertainty does not necessarily prevent the use of a measurement basis that provides relevant information. However, in some cases the level of measurement uncertainty is so high that information provided by a measurement basis might not provide a sufficiently faithful representation. In such cases, it is appropriate to consider selecting a different measurement basis that would also result in relevant information.

In addition to relevance and faithful representation consideration should be given to the cost of using a particular measurement basis and also the comparability, understandability and verifiability of the selected measurement basis. A historical cost measurement basis is usually less costly, and easier to verify. However, when comparing assets and liabilities that we initially recognised at different times this basis could be said to be less useful. Conversely, while using a current value basis for all assets and liabilities might produce more comparable financial information, such measures are more costly to produce and harder to verify.

The *Framework* states that the measurement basis used will impact on the amount at which an asset or liability is initially recognised. If a transaction is established at 'arm's length' prices then whether the historical cost or the current cost method of valuation is used the amount initially recognised will be the amount paid for the asset, or the amount received for the liability. If the asset or liability is initially measured at fair value (or, in principle) value in use then the amount recognised will exclude transaction costs, which would normally be taken to profit or loss immediately (this happens in practice under IFRS 9 – *Financial Instruments* – where the 'fair value through profit or loss' classification is appropriate.

Where transactions are not established at 'arm's length' prices then even if the historical cost measurement basis is to be used the amount paid for the asset, or received to discharge the liability, may not faithfully represent the historical cost of the asset or liability. In such circumstances a 'deemed historical cost' is used for initial measurement, probably current value at the time of initial recognition.

Use of more than one measurement basis in the financial statements

Sometimes, preparers may conclude that more than one measurement basis is needed for an asset or liability and for related income and expenses in order to provide relevant information that faithfully represents both the entity's financial position and its financial performance. In most cases, the most understandable way to provide that information is to use a single measurement basis for the asset or liability in the statement of financial position and for related income and expenses in the statements of financial performance; and to provide in the notes additional information applying a different measurement basis. A practical example of this practice would be the use of the fair value model to measure property, plant and equipment with the provision of relevant historical cost information in the notes (see for example paragraph 77(e) of IAS 16 – *Property, Plant and Equipment*). In such circumstances, the *Framework* notes that when a fair value model is used in the statement of financial position, changes in the carrying amounts of relevant amounts are often presented in different parts of the statement of financial performance or, when there are two statements of financial performance, in different statements. Again, IAS 16 provides a practical example of this with the requirement to show depreciation of assets measured under the fair value model as part of the profit or loss for the period, while surpluses arising on the re-measurement of such assets to fair value are generally recognised in the statement of comprehensive income.

Other matters relevant to measurement

Equity is not measured directly. Equity is simply the difference between the total recognised assets and the total recognised liabilities of an entity. This is a direct corollary of the fact that financial statements do not purport to show the total value of an entity.

In some cases (particularly where the 'value in use' measurement basis is used) estimated future cash flows are used to compute measurements. Where such estimates potentially fall within a range of possible future outcomes the *Framework* states that estimates from the midpoint of the range are likely to be the most appropriate ones on which to base measurement. This is in line with the concept of neutrality that we discussed earlier in our summary of Chapter 2.

Analysis of Chapter 6

As similarly concluded regarding Chapter 5, the measurement principles outlined in this chapter will provide useful underpinning for the development of more specific requirements in individual IFRSs.

10.5.7 Chapter 7 – Presentation and disclosure

General principles

A reporting entity communicates information about its assets, liabilities, equity, income and expenses by presenting and disclosing information in its financial statements. It is only effective communication if the information is relevant and contributes to a faithful representation and also enhances the understandability and comparability of information in the financial statements.

When developing presentation and disclosure requirements in Standards a balance is needed between:

- giving entities the flexibility to provide relevant information that faithfully represents the entity's assets, liabilities, equity, income and expenses;
- requiring information that is comparable, both from period to period for a reporting entity and in a single reporting period across entities.

Classification

Classification is the sorting of assets, liabilities, equity, income or expenses on the basis of shared characteristics for presentation and disclosure purposes, for example, classifying by nature as in Vertical Format 2 (see Chapter 3) or function as in Vertical Format 1.

However, it may sometimes be appropriate to enhance usefulness by separating an asset or liability into components if the components have different characteristics and to classify those components separately.

A typical example of this practice would be a lease liability where the current portion of the liability would be shown within current liabilities and the non-current portion within non-current liabilities.

Presentation – offsetting

Offsetting occurs when an entity recognises and measures both an asset and liability as separate units of account, but groups them into a single net amount in the statement of financial position. Offsetting dissimilar items together is **generally** not appropriate. An exception to this general principle would be the requirement in IAS 12 – *Income Taxes* – to offset both current and deferred tax assets and liabilities in certain circumstances (see paragraphs 71 and 74 of IAS 12).

Presentation – equity

To provide useful information, it may be necessary to classify equity claims separately if those equity claims have different characteristics (for example ordinary shares are typically classified separately from preferred (or preference) shares).

Presentation – income and expenses

Income and expenses are included either in the statement of profit or loss or as 'other comprehensive income'. Because the statement of profit or loss is the primary source of information about an entity's financial performance for the period, all income and expenses are, in principle, included in that statement.

However, in developing Standards, the Board may decide in exceptional circumstances that income or expenses arising from a change in the current value of an asset or liability are to be included in other comprehensive income when doing so would:

(a) result in the statement of profit or loss providing more relevant information; or

(b) provide a more faithful representation of the entity's financial performance for that period.

A fairly common example of this is the requirement of IAS 16 – *Property, Plant and Equipment (PPE)* – to include most surpluses on the revaluation of PPE in other comprehensive income.

Reclassification

In principle, income and expenses included in other comprehensive income in one period are reclassified from other comprehensive income into the statement of profit or loss in a future period when doing so results in the statement of profit or loss providing more relevant information, or providing a more faithful representation of the entity's financial performance for that future period. An example of this practice would be the requirement in IFRS 9 – *Financial Instruments* – that gains or losses on the re-measurement of derivatives that are effective hedges of a cash-flow risk (and initially recognised in other comprehensive income) be reclassified into the statement of profit or loss when the cash-flow that the derivative is hedging is included in the statement of profit or loss.

However, if, for example, there is no clear basis for identifying the period in which reclassification would have that result, or the amount that should be reclassified, the Board may, in developing Standards, decide that income and expenses included in other comprehensive income are not to be subsequently reclassified. An example of this would be the requirement in IAS 16 – *Property, Plant and Equipment (PPE)* – that surpluses on the revaluation of PPE that were previously recognised in other comprehensive income are **not** reclassified into the statement of profit or loss when the relevant asset is disposed of.

Aggregation

Aggregation is the adding together of assets, liabilities, equity, income or expenses that have shared characteristics and are included in the same classification. Different levels of aggregation may be needed in different parts of the financial statements. For example, typically, the statement of financial position and the statement(s) of financial performance provide summarised information and more detailed information is provided in the notes.

Analysis of Chapter 7

Much of the theory included in this chapter is relatively uncontroversial. However, it could be argued that neglecting to provide a theoretical underpinning for when income and expenses are recognised in Other comprehensive income rather than profit or loss is a slightly unfortunate omission. The same argument could be applied to the lack of theoretical discussion regarding reclassification of items recognised in Other comprehensive income.

10.5.8 Chapter 8 – Concepts of capital and capital maintenance

The *Framework* discusses two concepts of capital and consequently two concepts of capital maintenance. These are the financial concept of capital and the physical concept of capital.

Under the financial concept of capital, a profit is earned only if the financial (or money) amount of the net assets at the end of the period exceeds the financial (or money) amount of net assets at the beginning of the period, after excluding any distributions to, and contributions from, owners during the period. Financial capital maintenance can be measured in either nominal monetary units or units of constant purchasing power. As levels of inflation in many areas of the world have reduced significantly over recent years the use of nominal monetary units is much more widespread than the use of 'constant purchasing power' units.

Under the physical concept of capital, a profit is earned only if the physical productive capacity (or operating capability) of the entity (or the resources or funds needed to achieve that capacity) at the end of the period exceeds the physical productive capacity at the beginning of the period, after excluding any distributions to, and contributions from, owners during the period.

Under the concept of financial capital maintenance, where capital is defined in terms of nominal monetary units, profit represents the increase in nominal money capital over the period. Thus, increases in the prices of assets held over the period, conventionally referred to as holding gains, are, conceptually, profits. They may not be recognised as such, however, until the assets are disposed of in an exchange transaction. An example of this would be the profit on disposal of inventory when that inventory is sold and the profit realised.

When the concept of financial capital maintenance is defined in terms of constant purchasing power units, profit represents the increase in invested purchasing power over the period. Thus, only that part of the increase in the prices of assets that exceeds the increase in the general level of prices is regarded as profit. The rest of the increase is treated as a capital maintenance adjustment.

Under the concept of physical capital maintenance when capital is defined in terms of the physical productive capacity, profit represents the increase in that capital over the period. All price changes affecting the assets and liabilities of the entity are viewed as changes in the measurement of the physical productive capacity of the entity; hence, they are treated as capital maintenance adjustments that are part of equity and not as profit.

The selection of the measurement bases and concept of capital maintenance will determine the accounting model used in the preparation of the financial statements. Different accounting models exhibit different degrees of relevance and reliability and, as in other areas, management must seek a balance between relevance and reliability. The *Conceptual Framework* is applicable to a range of accounting models and provides guidance on preparing and presenting the financial statements constructed under the chosen model. At the present time, it is not the intention of the Board to prescribe a particular model other than in exceptional circumstances, such as for those entities reporting in the currency of a hyperinflationary economy (and set out in IAS 29). This intention will, however, be reviewed in the light of world developments.

Analysis of Chapter 8

In many areas of the developed world, the issue of different concepts of capital maintenance is not such an urgent one. Overall levels of inflation have reduced markedly compared with the late 20th century and the financial concept of capital is widely used. However, in other areas of the world such as Venezuela the issue of price inflation is still very much a relevant one. Therefore it seems perfectly appropriate for the IASB to set out the differing capital maintenance concepts in the way that they have in Chapter 8.

10.5.9 Overall analysis of the new *Framework*

We now appear to have a comprehensive document that sets out theoretical principles in a logical order. There are inevitably specific issues that arguably could have been specified in further detail in the *Framework*. Examples could include specifying in more detail when fair value should be used as a measurement basis rather than historical cost (Chapter 18) and when gains and losses should be presented in Other comprehensive income rather than profit or loss (Chapter 10). Equally it could be argued that the lack of discussion of the meaning of 'true and fair' – a fundamental concept in financial reporting is an unfortunate omission. However, a fair assessment is that this final version of the *Framework* is a practical document that should assist the IASB in the further development of future accounting standards.

10.6 Current developments – concept of materiality

10.6.1 The issue

The concept of materiality is fundamental to financial reporting. Financial statements should provide useful financial information to the user. In order for financial information to be useful, it has to be reliable. Reliable financial information needs to present, in all *material* respects, a true and fair view of the financial performance of an entity for a reporting period and of its financial position at the end of the reporting period.

The IASB initiated a project on materiality in 2014. Its objective was to help preparers, auditors and regulators use judgement when applying the concept of materiality in order to make financial reports more meaningful.

A draft practice statement on materiality was issued in October 2015. However, it subsequently became clear that some of the proposed guidance needed to be authoritative to have the desired practical effect. Therefore the project was split into two parts. The first part would result in a new practice statement being published and the second part would result in minor amendments to IAS 1 *Presentation of Financial Statements* – and IAS 8 *Accounting Policies, Changes in Accounting Estimates and Errors*. Both IAS 1 and IAS 8 contain definitions of materiality that will potentially be updated to reflect the principles of the new *Framework* that we have already discussed. Both parts were published in draft form in September 2017

10.6.2 The latest IASB proposals

Revised practice statement

The Practice Statement discusses the general characteristics of materiality. In particular, it notes that:

- The need for materiality judgements is pervasive in the preparation of financial statements. A company makes materiality judgements when making decisions about presentation, disclosure, recognition and measurement.
- Requirements in IFRS Standards need only be applied if their effect is material.

The Practice Statement also provides some general guidance on identifying primary users and their information needs. In particular, it clarifies that:

- The primary users the company should consider when making materiality judgements are existing and potential investors, lenders and other creditors, as identified by the Conceptual Framework.
- Financial statements do not, and cannot, provide all the information that primary users need. Hence, in preparing its financial statements, the company should aim to meet the common information needs of its primary users.

The Practice Statement discusses the interaction between the materiality judgements a company is required to make and local laws and regulations. The Practice Statement clarifies that:

- The company's financial statements must comply with requirements in IFRS Standards, including requirements related to materiality, to state compliance with those Standards. Hence, a company that wishes to state compliance with IFRS Standards cannot provide less information than the information required by the Standards, even if local laws and regulations permit otherwise.

- Providing additional information to meet local legal or regulatory requirements is permitted by IFRS Standards even if, according to IFRS materiality requirements, that information is not material. However, such information must not obscure material information.

The Practice Statement is not an IFRS Standard and companies are not required to comply with a Practice Statement to state compliance with IFRS Standards. It sets out non-mandatory guidance developed by the IASB.

Proposed amendments to IAS 1 and IAS 8

The proposed revised definition of materiality is as follows:

'Information is material if omitting, misstating or obscuring it could reasonably be expected to influence decisions that the primary users of a specific reporting entity's general-purpose financial statements make on the basis of those financial statements'.

The exposure draft further states that:

'Materiality depends on the nature or magnitude of information, or both. An entity assesses whether information, either individually or in combination with other information, is material in the context of its financial statements. Material information might be obscured if it is not communicated clearly - for example, if it is obscured by immaterial information. A misstatement of information is material if it could reasonably be expected to influence decisions made by the primary users'.

The issue of materiality is partly 'user dependent'. The exposure draft finally states that 'Many existing and potential investors, lenders and other creditors cannot require reporting entities to provide information directly to them and must rely on general-purpose financial reports for much of the financial information they need. Consequently, they are the primary users to whom general-purpose financial statements are directed. Financial statements are prepared for users who have a reasonable knowledge of business and economic activities and who review and analyse the information diligently. At times, even well-informed and diligent users may need to seek the aid of an adviser to understand information about complex economic phenomena'.

Summary and evaluation of position to date

A revised version of the *Framework* has been issued. A detailed critique of this document has already been provided. Concepts of materiality have been refined to be consistent with the principles in the *Framework*. The IASB is to be applauded in its efforts to develop a comprehensive theoretical underpinning for financial statement preparation.

REVIEW QUESTIONS

1 'The replacement of accrual accounting with cash flow accounting would avoid the need for a conceptual framework.' Discuss.

2 The IASB has allowed the selective choice of a measurement base. Discuss why this may or may not be preferable to adopting a single measurement base for all elements.

3 Financial accounting theory has accumulated a vast literature. A cynic might be inclined to say that the vastness of the literature is in sharp contrast to its impact on practice.

(a) Describe the different approaches that have evolved in the development of accounting theory.

(b) Assess their varying impacts on standard setting.

4 'Rules-based accounting adds unnecessary complexity, encourages financial engineering and does not necessarily lead to a "true and fair view" or a "fair presentation".' Discuss.

5 'Tax avoidance would not occur if there was a principles rather than rules based approach.' Discuss.

6 Explain what you understand by a 'balance sheet approach' to income determination and how this is demonstrated in the definition of elements.

7 Explain how a company assesses materiality when attempting to report a true and fair view of its income.

8 'The key qualitative characteristics in the *Conceptual Framework* are relevance and faithful representation. Preparers of financial statements may face a dilemma in satisfying both criteria at once.' Discuss situations where there might be a conflict.

9 'An asset is to be defined in the *Framework* as 'a present economic resource controlled by the entity as a result of past events'. Discuss whether property, plant and equipment would automatically qualify as an asset.

10 'The *Conceptual Framework* regards neutrality as necessary for financial statements to provide a faithful representation of transactions. However, it could be argued that neutrality is impossible to achieve because if it is accepted that information must be relevant as a tool to influence decision making then it could not be neutral.' Discuss.

11 The concept of materiality is fundamental to financial statement preparation. Therefore the IASB's proposed *practice statement* on materiality should have the status of a financial reporting standard. Discuss this viewpoint.

12 Select three companies in any sector and review how the auditors have approached setting a materiality threshold in the new enhanced audit reports. Assess if there is a common approach to materiality in relation to profits and balance sheet items.

EXERCISES

*Question 1

The following extract is from the IASB *Conceptual Framework for Financial Reporting* published in March 2018: The *Conceptual Framework for Financial Reporting* (*Conceptual Framework*) describes the objective of, and the concepts for, general-purpose financial reporting. The purpose of the *Conceptual Framework* is to:

● Assist the International Accounting Standards Board (Board) to develop IFRS Standards (Standards) that are based on consistent concepts.

● Assist preparers to develop consistent accounting policies when no Standard applies to a particular transaction or other event, or when a Standard allows a choice of accounting policy.

● Assist all parties to understand and interpret the Standards.

Required:
(a) **Define a conceptual framework.**
(b) **Critically examine whether the purpose of the *Conceptual Framework* has been achieved given the detailed content.**

*Question 2

The following extract is from 'Comments of Leonard Spacek', in R.T. Sprouse and M. Moonitz, *A Tentative Set of Broad Accounting Principles for Business Enterprises*, Accounting Research Study No. 3, AICPA, New York, 1962, reproduced in A. Belkaoui, *Accounting Theory*, Harcourt Brace Jovanovich.

> A discussion of assets, liabilities, revenue and costs is premature and meaningless until the basic principles that will result in a fair presentation of the facts in the form of financial accounting and financial reporting are determined. This fairness of accounting and reporting must be for and to people, and these people represent the various segments of our society.

Required:
Discuss the extent to which the IASB conceptual framework satisfies the above definition of fairness.

*Question 3

A 2016 article by Alison Parker, CPA and Cheryl Hartfield, CPA, both executive editors of PPC products for the Tax & Accounting business of Thomson Reuters reflects on the arguments for and against US companies following International Financial Reporting Standards rather than US GAAP. Two of the arguments both for and against this development are as follows:

Arguments for
1 IFRS provides a single global accounting language.
2 The US is currently well-represented in the IFRS standard-setting process with three seats on the 14-member IASB.

Arguments against
1 Principles-based standards with a lack of industry-specific or transactional guidance may decrease the quality and consistency of reporting.
2 The IFRS standard-setting process is potentially subject to influence by political forces, which could lead to conflicts and inconsistent practices between jurisdictions.

Required:
Discuss whether the publication of the revised *Framework* by the IASB in March 2018 will be likely to persuade US standard setters that following IFRS would lead to financial reporting of sufficient quality and rigour.

*Question 4

The IASB has a number of projects underway to promote the effective communication of information in the financial statements. Key projects include Principles of Disclosure. The objective of this research project is to improve existing guidance in IFRS that helps entities determine the basic structure and content of a complete set of financial statements. The focus is on reviewing the general requirements in IAS 1 Presentation of Financial Statements, and considering how they may be revised. The aim is to develop a Disclosure Standard that improves and brings together the principles for determining the basic structure and content of the financial statements, in particular the notes. In March 2017, the IASB published a Discussion Paper *Disclosure Initiative – Principles of Disclosure*.

Required:
Critically discuss how a company could determine whether any disclosure is proportionate to the risks and whether this implies that there should be fewer mandatory disclosures which lead to ever more complexity.

The following are criticisms that could be made of the IASB's latest *Conceptual Framework* document.

(a) The framework does not consider the meaning of the term 'true and fair view' despite this being a fundamental characteristic discussed in International Financial Reporting Standards.

(b) The identification of prudence as a fundamental concept should focus on its asymmetric application because this is current practice in a number of specific areas.

(c) The discussion of measurement bases is incomplete as it does not address the issue of entry values versus exit values despite the use of such values by preparers under current practice.

(d) The *Framework* provides no guidance on the issue of reclassification of gains and losses despite this matter being dealt with inconsistently in a number of existing International Financial Reporting Standards.

Required:

Discuss the extent to which the above criticisms could be justified by reference to specific International Financial Reporting Standards.

CHAPTER 11

Corporate governance

11.1 Introduction

The main aim of this chapter is to create an awareness of what constitutes good corporate governance – how to achieve it, the threats to achieving it and the role of accountants and auditors.

Objectives

By the end of this chapter, you should be able to:

- understand the concept of corporate governance;
- have an awareness of how and why governance mechanisms may differ from jurisdiction to jurisdiction;
- have an appreciation of the role which accounting and auditing play in the governance process;
- have a greater sensitivity to areas of potential conflicts of interest.

11.2 A systems perspective

Corporations do not act in a vacuum. They are corporate citizens of society with rights and responsibilities. The way in which they exercise these rights and responsibilities is influenced by the history, institutions and cultural expectations of society. A systems perspective recognises that an entity is not independent but is interdependent with its environment. This has given rise to the need for corporate governance.

Corporate governance is defined by C. Oman[1] as:

> private and public institutions, including laws, regulations and accepted business practices, which together govern the relationship, in a market economy, between corporate managers and entrepreneurs ('corporate insiders') on the one hand, and those who invest resources in corporations on the other.

11.2.1 Good corporate governance – investor perspective

When we pause to contemplate the contribution of corporations to our standard of living, we are reminded how important their contribution is to most aspects of our existence. It is therefore vital that they operate as good citizens in their treatment of the investors who provide their funds and of other stakeholders. This includes actions by management when dealing with investors such as:

- complying with the laws and norms of society;
- striving to achieve the company objectives in a manner which does not involve taking risks which are greater than expected or acceptable to investors;
- balancing short- and long-term performance;
- establishing mechanisms to ensure that managers are acting in the interests of shareholders and are not directly or indirectly using their knowledge or positions to gain inappropriate benefits at the expense of shareholders;
- providing investors with relevant, reliable and timely information that allows them to assess the performance, solvency and financial stability of the business; and
- providing investors with an independent opinion that the financial statements are a fair representation.

This list does not cover all eventualities but is intended to indicate what could be expected from corporate governance – good being determined by the degree that the actions and information flows achieve fair outcomes.

11.2.2 Good corporate governance – other stakeholder perspective

A stakeholder perspective addresses all the other parties whose continued support is necessary to ensure the satisfactory performance of the business. The parties are normally seen as belonging to one of the following categories: loan creditors, employees, trade unions representing employees, customers, governments and suppliers.

Good corporate governance might include actions by management such as:

- fair treatment of employees, avoiding discrimination;
- establishing mechanisms for resolving conflicts of interests;
- establishing mechanisms for whistle-blowing so that if inappropriate behaviour is taking place it is highlighted as quickly as possible so as to minimise the cost to the organisation and society;
- paying suppliers, particularly small businesses, promptly within the agreed credit period; and
- providing suppliers with relevant, reliable and timely information that allows them to assess the solvency of the business.

11.2.3 Good corporate governance – stakeholder pressure on Boards of Directors

It is often difficult for stakeholders to exert effective influence in practice.

First, this is because shareholders are not a homogeneous group – some wish to invest for the long term others have a more speculative interest. This puts some capital-intensive companies in a quandary – if they invest in research for the long term, current profits available for paying dividends are hit which is less attractive to investors relying on dividends for their income.

Second, because as well as there being conflicting interests, there are also differences in the influence that a stakeholder can exert. Ideally, for example, dominant shareholders, institutional investors and major customers should have a greater ability to hold management to account and achieve good corporate governance outcomes. However, when we look at the makeup of shareholdings in the UK stock market we see that the fragmentation calls into question just how much influence any single group has – for example, over 50% is held by the rest of the world and only 6% held by insurance companies and 3% by pension funds.

Even accepting the existence of an ability to influence does not necessarily mean that it is put into effect, since the individual stakeholder's private interest might not be advanced by taking action – it might, for example, divert their management's attention away from their own business.

11.2.4 Good corporate governance – all sectors

The objective is to influence behaviour so that all parties act within the spirit of good governance. The actions and information flows above have been oriented towards business entities but we should expect all organisations to behave in the same way. For example, in the case of a not-for-profit enterprise such as a charity it is important that the methods by which money are raised are ethical and the manner in which the money used is consistent with the uses envisaged by the donors, and that an appropriate balance be achieved between administrative costs and the money devoted to assisting the beneficiaries of the charity.

Good governance requires constant vigilance, and in the UK fundraising has been the subject of a government report, House of Commons Public Administration and Constitutional Affairs Committee *The 2015 Charity Fundraising Controversy: Lessons for Trustees, the Charity Commission, and Regulators,* Third Report of Session 2015–16.[2]

A charity's reputation is not just dependent on the funds it raises and distributes, it also depends on the behaviour of its staff and volunteers in the field. There is a Charity Governance Code[3] giving advice to Trustees but how they discharge their obligations has been seriously challenged with complaints about unethical behaviour.[4]

The approach to enforcement of good corporate governance by charities varies internationally.

11.3 Different jurisdictions have different governance priorities

The predominant conflicts of interest will vary from country to country depending on each country's history, economic and legal developments, norms and religion.

In the UK and the United States, with their similar considerable reliance on stock exchanges for the financing of public companies, there is a need for an active, efficient capital market. This leads to their focus being on potential conflicts between management and shareholders.

In Germany, where companies have a board of directors made up of investors as well as an advisory board representing both management and employees, there is a recognition that there is a need to reconcile both management and employee long-term interests and to ensure that both groups are motivated to achieve the organisation's long-term goals.

In south-east Asia, with many of the large corporations having substantial shareholdings owned by members of a single family, the emphasis has been on avoiding conflicts between family and minority shareholders.

In Muslim countries companies should not be involved in activities related to alcohol and gambling; they cannot pay or charge interest and they have religious obligations to make a minimum level of donations. This means there is a need for corporate governance mechanisms to ensure that there is no conflict between commercial activity and religious obligations.

From the above we can see how the governance priorities differ from country to country. They result from the role of the political institutions, the stage of economic development, the diversity of stakeholder perspectives and a country's heritage in so far as it shapes the law, the religion and the social norms.

The large number of multinational companies means that these companies have to be sensitive to the approaches taken in all countries in which they have subsidiary companies and joint ventures. They also have to be aware of the provisions of the US Foreign Corrupt Practices Act 1977 which is far reaching and has teeth – for example in 2011 the SEC found that London-based Diageo plc[5] paid more than $2.7 million through its subsidiaries to obtain lucrative sales and tax benefits relating to its Johnnie Walker and Windsor Scotch whiskeys, among other brands. Diageo agreed to pay more than $16 million to settle the SEC's charges. The company also agreed to cease and desist from further violations of the FCPA's books and records and internal controls provisions. In the UK, the Bribery Act 2010, creates a corporate offence and personal liability for failing to prevent bribery by persons associated with a corporation securing its first successful prosecution in 2016 of the Sweet Group.[6]

Companies identifying bribery and corruption risk management in their Annual Reports

The following is an extract from the Centrica 2016 Annual Report:

> Financial health, risk and anti-bribery and corruption due diligence and monitoring is implemented in supplier selection and contract renewal processes.

Just as governance priorities differ, so do the institutions and methods for controlling corporate governance. The institutions include statutory bodies enforcing detailed prescriptive requirements and statutory bodies that encourage voluntary adoption of good practices with disclosure, through voluntary organisations such as Transparency International UK to professional accounting bodies that have built the awareness of good corporate governance into their examination syllabi.

11.3.1 Corporate governance culture

In China, Russia and the former communist countries in Eastern Europe, the economies are being changed from state-controlled businesses to privately owned companies. The 'model' of these companies is similar to those in the US and UK. So, the trend is towards the US and UK model of companies' shares being listed on their national stock exchange. This trend to wider share ownership will encourage the development of corporate governance criteria similar to those in the US and the UK. For some countries this is a real cultural shift and it will take time for the concept of good corporate governance to be applied. The following is an extract from an OECD Note of a meeting on Corporate Governance Development in State-owned Enterprises in Russia:[7]

> Finally, as stressed by investors, the OECD, and government officials at this expert's meeting, the emergence of a true corporate governance culture is vital. Such a culture-based approach should involve the understanding of the principles and values behind corporate governance, and replace the 'box-ticking' mechanistic approach in which superficial institutions fulfill certain criteria but do not bring real benefits in terms of effective achievement of corporate goals. This would complement the creation of specific incentives intended to guide the behaviour of economic actors.

11.4 Pressures on good governance behaviour vary over time

History shows that business behaviour is influenced by where we are in the economic cycle, whether it's a time of boom or bust.

11.4.1 Behaviour in boom times

During the booms there has always been a tendency to be over-optimistic and to expect the good times to continue indefinitely. In such periods there is a tendency for everyone to focus on making profits. The safeguards that are in the system to prevent conflicts of interest and to limit undesirable behaviour are seen as slowing down the business and causing genuine opportunities to be missed. Over-optimism leads to a business taking risks that the shareholders had not sanctioned and is, to that extent, excessive.

This is accompanied by a tendency to water down the controls or to simply ignore them. When that happens there will always be some unethical individuals who will exploit some of the opportunities for themselves rather than for the business.

11.4.2 Behaviour in bust times

We see a repetitive reaction from bust to bust. When it occurs some of the malpractices will come to light, there will be a public outcry and governance procedures will be tightened up. Although controls are weakly enforced during boom times, it is a fact of life that vigilance is required at all times. Fraud, misrepresentation, misappropriation and anti-social behaviour will be constantly with us and robust corporate governance systems need to be in place and monitored.

The ideal would be that the controls in place develop a culture that makes individuals constrain their own behaviour to that which is ethical, having previously sensitised themselves to recognise the potential conflicts of interest. It is interesting to see the approach taken by the professional accounting bodies which are concentrating on sensitising students and members to ethical issues.

11.5 Types of past unethical behaviour

Some of the unethical behaviour that has been identified in earlier periods and which our governance systems should attempt to prevent are listed below:

- Inflating profits by overstating revenues and understating expenses. For example, in 2016 the US Securities and Exchange Commission (SEC)[8] announced financial fraud cases against two companies, Logiteck and Ener1, and their executives. The SEC alleged deficiencies in Ener1's failure to properly impair assets on its balance sheet and Logitech's failure to write down the value of its inventory to avoid the financial consequences of disappointing sales.

In the Ener1 case, the SEC also found that Robert D. Hesselgesser, the engagement partner for PricewaterhouseCoopers LLP's audit of Ener1's 2010 financial statements, violated professional auditing standards when he failed to perform sufficient procedures to support his audit conclusions that Ener1 management had appropriately accounted for its assets and revenues. He was suspended from participating in the financial reporting or audits of public companies for two years.

'Auditors play a critical role regarding the accuracy of financial statements relied upon by investors, and they must be held accountable when they fail to do everything required under professional auditing standards,' said Michael Maloney, Chief Accountant of the SEC's Division of Enforcement.

- Insider trading, particularly around major events such as a forthcoming company buyout, takeover or development of a new product. In the UK, the Financial Conduct Authority (FCA) has been cracking down on behaviour over the past decade and in 2017 had opened 84 insider-dealing probes.[9]

- Excessive remuneration so that the rewards flow disproportionately to management compared to other stakeholders and often with the major risks being borne by the other stakeholders.

- Excessive risk taking which is hidden from shareholders and stakeholders until after the catastrophe has struck.

- Unsuccessful managers being given 'golden handshakes' to leave and thus being rewarded for poor performance. For example, in Denmark it was reported that 'Banks are facing criticism for giving their CEOs million-kroner "golden handshakes", despite poor performances'.[10]

- Auditors, bankers, lawyers, credit rating agencies, and stock analysts, who might put their fees before the interests of the public for honest reporting.

- Directors who do not stand up to authoritarian managing directors or seriously question their ill-advised plans. For example, it was reported in 2010 that 'A dominant CEO and a weak board of directors was a recipe for disaster at Orion Bank of Naples [Florida]. Orion failed last November because Chief Executive Jerry Williams and his inexperienced board could not handle the bank's overly aggressive growth strategy, according to a new report by the Federal Reserve's Office of Inspector General'.[11]

- Management setting incentives for employees which encourage action that is not in the firm's interests.

- Procurement fraud schemes including kickbacks (usually 5–20% on large contracts), corrupt payments or influence and excluding qualified bidders.[12]

11.6 The effect on capital markets of good corporate governance

Good governance is important to facilitate large-scale commerce. The mechanism of legal structures such as limited liability of companies exists because it allows the capital of many investors to be combined in the pursuit of economic activities which need large quantities of capital to be economically viable. There are also statutory provisions relating to directors' duties and shareholders' rights. This is a good backcloth which is necessary but not sufficient to ensure the effective working of the capital market.

In addition, there has to be a high level of trust by shareholders in their relationship with management. Firstly, they need to believe the company will deal with them in an honest and prudent manner and act diligently. This means that shareholders need to be confident that:

- their money will be invested in ventures of an appropriate degree of risk;
- efforts will be made to achieve a competitive return on equity;
- management will not take personal advantage of their greater knowledge of events in the business; and
- the company will provide a flow of information that will contribute to the market fairly valuing shares at the times of purchase and sale.

Failure to achieve appropriate levels of trust will lead to the risk of the loss of potential investors or the provision of lesser amounts of funds at higher costs. Similarly, if other stakeholders, such as the bank, do not trust the management, there will be fewer participants and the terms will be less favourable. Another way of addressing this is to say that people have a strong sense of what is or is not fair. While economic necessity may lead to participation, the level of commitment is influenced by the perceived fairness of the transaction.

Also, from a macro perspective, the more efficient and effective the individual firms, the better allocation of resources and the higher the average standard of living. If management as a group is not diligent in its activities and fair in its treatment of stakeholders, there will be lower standards of living both economically and socially.

In addition, the current focus on corporate social responsibility could be seen as a response to governance failures by some companies. For example, some managers ignored externalities such as the costs to society of rectifying pollution because management was only judged on the financial results of the firm, and not the net benefit to society.

11.7 Risk management

We have seen with the issue by the IASB of its *Practice Statement Management Commentary* and the UK with its *Strategic Report* that there is a growing pressure internationally for a company to disclose its risk management policy. In any company there is a range of risks that have to be managed. It is not a matter of just avoiding risks but rather of systematically analysing the risks and then deciding how to decide what risks should be borne, which to avoid, and how to minimise the possible adverse consequences of those which it is not economic to shift. A good governance system will ensure that (a) comprehensive risk management occurs as a normal course of events (b) action taken is proportional and (c) there is transparent disclosure to shareholders and regulators of the nature, extent and management of these risks.

There is a variety of approaches which could be adopted to the process of identifying the types of risks associated with a company. In this chapter we will discuss briefly strategic, operational and legal/regulatory risks.

11.7.1 Strategic risks

Strategic risk is associated with maintaining the attractiveness and economic viability of the product and service offerings. In other words, current product decisions have to be made with a strong sense of their probable future consequences. To do that the business has to be constantly monitoring trends in the current markets, potential merging of markets,[13] shifting demographics and consumer tastes, technological developments, political developments and regulations so as to capitalise on opportunities and to counter threats. It must be remembered that to do nothing may involve as much or more risk as entering into new ventures. When entering into new projects there needs to be a thorough risk analysis to ensure that there are no false assumptions in the projections, there has been pilot testing, and the question of the exit strategy if the project fails has been seriously considered and costed.

11.7.2 Operational risks

Operational risks include (a) insurable risks, (b) transferable risks and (c) potential hazards.

Insurable risks

These include such risks as physical damage from fire, flood or accident and reputational damage from quality and public liability issues. The question then is 'If this event should happen could we comfortably bear the cost?' If the answer is no, then we should insure at least for the amount we couldn't afford to bear.

Transferable risks

These include such risks as difficulty recruiting skilled staff to meet orders or dependence on a key supplier.

On staffing, the question may be 'Could work be outsourced?' However, that in itself creates risks such as dependence, quality control, reliability of delivery, lack of involvement in technological developments, and financial risks associated with the subcontractor.

On supply policy, the question may be 'Should the company opt for multiple suppliers?' This would protect against normal hazards such as strikes at the supplier, adverse weather conditions blocking supply, or threats to supply caused by political factors but at a probable increase in cost.

Hazards

In relation to risks like occupational health and safety, the steps involve identification of potential hazards, identifying the best physical process for handling them, and developing standard ways of operating, then training personnel in those standard operating procedures, and regularly checking to ensure those procedures are being followed.

11.7.3 Legal and regulatory risks

This refers to the possibility that the firm will breach its legal or regulatory requirements and thus expose the company to fines and injury to its reputation. This involves being aware of the requirements of each country in which it operates or in which its products and services are used. Further, the staff of the company need to know of the relevant requirements which apply to their activities. They should also have access to advice in order to avoid problems or to address issues that do arise. Once again, standard operating procedures and standard documentation can help reduce the risks. Many businesses now have a Compliance Officer responsible for making sure outside regulatory requirements are being followed. Many of these now have a degree in accountancy, business or finance. In some companies the protection of intellectual property should be of considerable relevance.

11.7.4 IASB Practice Statement Management Commentary

Adequate disclosure of risk is now being addressed in the UK by the *Strategic Report* and by the IASB *Practice Statement Management Commentary*, which states:

> Management should disclose an entity's principal risk exposures and changes in those risks, together with its plans and strategies for bearing or mitigating those risks, as well as disclosure of the effectiveness of its risk management strategies.

11.8 The role of internal control, internal audit and audit committees in corporate governance

Good governance is supported by (a) adequate internal controls, (b) effective internal audit and (c) effective audit committees.

11.8.1 Adequate internal control

In some jurisdictions the company and the external auditors have to explicitly state that the company has adequate internal controls and the accounts present a fair view. In other jurisdictions it is implied that if the company receives a clean audit report then the internal controls are adequate.

In the US when the explicit requirement was introduced many companies spent considerable sums after the introduction of the Sarbanes–Oxley Act 2002 in upgrading their systems, particularly as the CEO and CFO were made personally liable for the effectiveness of the internal controls.

There is, however, an opportunity cost in CEOs focusing on compliance issues rather than on strategic issues and an actual cost in upgrading systems. This led to some arguing that the costs were unjustified.

While the need to consider cost–benefit considerations in relation to all corporate governance measures is a valid concern, it is also important to remember the costs of bad corporate governance. Good governance will not stop all fraud and excessive risk taking but it will stop them from being so widespread. The internal control systems should limit the ability of management to misdirect resources to their personal use or to publish financial statements with material misrepresentation.

11.8.2 Effective internal audit

Sound internal controls combined with an effective internal audit unit should make it more difficult for senior managers to misappropriate resources or misrepresent the financial position. Naturally we know that the more senior the managers the more likely it is that they can override the internal controls or pressure others to do so. It can be argued that such a situation justifies the requirement that the internal audit unit (if one exists) should report direct to the Audit Committee.

11.8.3 Effective audit committees

Financial Reporting Council

In June 2016 the Financial reporting Council (FRC) published a revised version of the Guidance on Audit Committees. The Guidance provides recommendations on the audit committee's establishment and effectiveness, role and responsibilities and communications with shareholders.

Establishment and effectiveness of the audit committee

There should be at least two independent non-executive directors if below the FTSE 350 index or at least three members if above. At least one member should have recent and relevant financial experience. The 2016 UK Corporate Governance Code states that audit committee as a whole should have competence relevant to the sector in which the company operates.

Role and responsibilities

The audit committee should review the annual report to determine whether taken as a whole, it is fair, balanced and understandable and provides the information necessary for shareholders to assess the company's position and performance, business model and strategy.

Communications with shareholders

The chairman of the audit committee should be present at the AGM to answer questions on the separate section of the annual report describing the audit committee's activities and matters within the scope of the audit committee's responsibilities.

The Institute of Internal Auditors Model Audit Committee Charter

The Charter[14] states that the Audit Committee should:

Approve the risk-based internal audit annual plan.

Review with management and the chief audit executive the activities, staffing, and organisational structure of the internal audit function and, at least once per year, the performance of the chief audit executive, the effectiveness of the internal audit function, and significant accounting and reporting issues.

Ensure there are no unjustified restrictions or limitations, and review and concur in the appointment, replacement, or dismissal of the chief audit executive.

11.9 External audits in corporate governance

External audits are intended to increase participation in financial investing and to lower the cost of funds. They may be *ad hoc* reports or audit reports giving an opinion on the fair view of annual financial statements.

Ad hoc reports

In the case of lending to companies it is not uncommon for lenders to impose restrictions to protect the interests of the lenders. Such restrictions or covenants include compliance with certain ratios such as liquidity and leverage or gearing ratios. Auditors then report to lenders or trustees for groups of lenders on the level of compliance. In this way auditors facilitate the flows of funds at good rates.

Statutory audit reports

Similarly for shareholders the audit report is intended to create confidence that the financial statements are presenting a fair view of financial performance and position. If that confidence is undermined by examples of auditors failing to detect misrepresentation or material misstatement, the public becomes wary of holding shares, share prices in the market tend to fall and the availability of new funds shrinks.

Enhanced audit reports

The IAASB responded to the need to improve investor confidence and communications between investors and the auditor by requiring[15] the auditor to discuss in the audit report matters such as audit risks, materiality used in the conduct of the audit and scope of audit work undertaken, including responses to audit risks.

In January 2016 the FRC issued *Extended auditor's reports A further review of experience*[16] based on 278 reports which was nearly 80% of the UK's largest companies from the main UK listed market. The key findings included that Investors greatly valued the enhanced information it provided and the reports which earned the greatest praise from investors was for clear, concise and transparent disclosures about risk, scope and materiality, as well as the critical areas where professional judgement and assumptions have been addressed.

Investor confidence

Confidence depends on shareholders accepting that:

(a) the auditors:
- are independent; approach the audit with a degree of scepticism; are professionally competent; have industry knowledge; carry out a quality audit; report the results of the audit in a clear manner; and

(b) the profession enforces audit standards.

11.9.1 Auditor independence

The external auditors should keep in mind that their main responsibility is to shareholders. However, there is a potential governance conflict in that for all practical purposes they are appointed by the board, their remuneration is agreed with the board and their day-to-day dealings are with the management. Appointments and remuneration have to be approved by the shareholders but this is normally a rubber-stamping exercise.

It is not uncommon for auditors to talk of the management as the customer, which is of course the wrong mindset. To reduce the identification with management and loss of independence arising from a personal interest in the financial performance of the client, a number of controls are often put in place, for example:

- Financial threats to independence:
  - Auditors and close relatives should not have shares or options in the company
  - Auditors must not accept contingency fees or gifts, nor should relatives or close associates receive benefits.
  - Undertaking non-audit work the loss of which, if a significant amount, might be perceived as affecting the auditor's independence. This is a contentious issue with some advocating that auditors should not undertake non-audit work, whereas the client might consider it to be cost-effective. All the indications are that current practice will continue with disclosure of the amounts involved.
- Familiarity threats:

  - Appointments, terminations and the remuneration of auditors should be handled by the audit committee.
  - Auditors should not have worked for the company or its associates.
  - Audit partners should be rotated periodically so the audit is looked at with fresh eyes.
  - Audit tests should vary so that employees cannot anticipate what will be audited.
  - It is not desirable that audit staff be transferred to senior positions in a client company. This happens but it does mean that they will continue to have close relations with the auditors and knowledge of their audit procedures. Clients might regard this as a benefit.

However, this is not a rule-based approach. Good governance depends on the auditors behaving independently, with professional competence, and identifying with shareholders and other stakeholders whose interests they are supposed to be protecting. Failing to do this leads to what is described as the expectation gap.

11.9.2 Lack of independence – Enron

The following is an extract from the United Nations Conference on Trade and Development G-24 Discussion Paper Series illustrating the dangers when there is a lack of independence:[17]

> Regarding auditing good corporate governance requires high-quality standards for preparation and disclosure, and independence for the external auditor. Enron's external auditor was Arthur Andersen, which also provided the firm with extensive internal auditing and consulting services . . . lack of independence linked to its multiple consultancy roles was a crucial factor in Andersen's failure to fulfill its obligations as Enron's external auditor.

11.9.3 Professional scepticism and competence

Professional scepticism is defined[18] as 'an attitude that includes a questioning mind, being alert to conditions which may indicate possible misstatement due to error or fraud, and a critical assessment of audit evidence'. The auditor is explicitly required to plan and perform an audit with professional scepticism recognising that circumstances may exist that cause the financial statements to be materially misstated.

In the UK Audit Quality Inspections are carried out and consider all aspects of an audit. For example, it produced a report[19] on BDO LLP in 2015, where one of the findings was:

> On six audits we identified concerns regarding the level of professional scepticism applied in key audit areas. Whilst the firm has developed a number of initiatives intended to embed professional scepticism in the culture of the firm, including improved training, our file review findings continue to suggest that more needs to be done to achieve changes on individual audits.

Professional competence

As the Competent Authority for audit in the UK, the FRC sets auditing and ethical standards and monitors and enforces audit quality. In this role it has imposed fines on various of the audit firms. For example:

- *Quindell.* The FRC fined KPMG £3.2m in 2018 and said the big four accountant and its partner's errors 'included failure to obtain reasonable assurance that the financial statements as a whole were free from material misstatement, failure to obtain sufficient appropriate audit evidence and failure to exercise sufficient professional scepticism.'
- *Connaught.* The FRC fined PWC £5m in 2018 for failure to obtain sufficient audit evidence for the audit of the 2009 accounts and failure to exercise sufficient professional scepticism. PWC accepted this finding but said its auditors had been intentionally misled by the company's management.

KPMG and PWC are not alone and these examples are to illustrate that the FRC is responding actively to complaints that it had not been sufficiently vigorous in pursuing audit firms that failed to conduct an audit with professional competence or appropriate degree of professional scepticism.

Warning flags

The individual circumstances will vary but there are indicators such as the following that should be considered:

- Internal conditions:
  - Lack of personnel with appropriate accounting and financial reporting skills.
  - Changes in key personnel including departure of key executives.
  - Deficiencies in internal control, especially those not addressed by management.
  - Changes in the IT environment.
- Trading conditions:
  - Operations in regions that are economically unstable, for example countries with significant currency devaluation or highly inflationary economies.
  - Changes in the industry in which the entity operates.
  - Developing or offering new products or services, or moving into new lines of business.
  - Changes in the supply chain.

- Scale of operations:
  - Expanding into new locations.
  - Changes in the entity such as large acquisitions or reorganisations or other unusual events.
  - Entities or business segments likely to be sold.
  - The existence of complex alliances and joint ventures.
- Financial conditions:
  - Going concern and liquidity issues including loss of significant customers.
  - Constraints on the availability of capital and credit.
  - Use of off-balance-sheet finance, special-purpose entities, and other complex financing arrangements.
  - Significant transactions with related parties.
  - Excessive reliance on management representations.

11.9.4 Example of where there was excessive reliance on management representations

In the normal course of an audit it is usual to obtain a letter of representation from management, for example providing information regarding a subsequent event occurring after year-end and the existence of off-balance-sheet contingencies. It is confirmation to the auditor that management has made full disclosure of all material activities and transactions in its financial records and statements.

However, the representations do not absolve the auditor from obtaining sufficient and appropriate audit evidence. The following is an extract[20] from an SEC finding relating to two Certified Public Accountants who were auditing a company (Structural Dynamics Research Corporation) which had improperly recorded sales and then written them off in the following accounting period:

> Despite the fact that the language in purchase orders clearly stated the orders were conditional and subject to cancellation, the auditors accepted the controller's explanation and did not take exception to the recognition of revenue on these orders. This undue reliance on management's representations constitutes insufficient professional skepticism by Present [the engagement partner].
>
> Moreover, Present failed to corroborate management's representations regarding conditional purchase orders with sufficient additional evidence that these sales were properly recorded . . . Overall, Present failed to exercise due professional care in the performance of the audit.

11.9.5 Developing and enforcing audit standards

The IAASB

There are international audit standards set by the International Auditing and Assurance Standards Board (IAASB). The IAASB in developing standards has to have regard to developments in financial reporting which has grown more complex with a greater variety of disclosures than those traditionally disclosed and the need for greater transparency in the audit work that has been carried out. As with the development of IFRSs, the IAASB follows a process of Discussion Papers, Exposure Drafts and IASs.

In 2014 it published a *Framework for Audit Quality: Key Elements that Create an Environment for Audit Quality* and in 2015 published revised IASs.

The International Forum of Independent Audit Regulators (IFIAR)

The IFIAR is composed of 51 independent audit regulators from jurisdictions in Africa, the Americas, Asia, Europe, the Middle East and Oceania. It was formed in 2006 to provide a forum for regulators to share knowledge of the audit market environment and the practical experience gained from their independent audit regulatory activity.

IFIAR publishes the results of its surveys to inform investors, regulators, the financial community, auditors and the public about the current state of inspections of audits of public companies.

IFIAR's 2017 *Survey of Inspection Findings*[21] found that the two areas with the highest rate and greatest number of findings were Accounting Estimates and Internal Control Testing. For Accounting Estimates, most findings related to failure to assess the reasonableness of assumptions, including consideration of contrary or inconsistent evidence. For Internal Control Testing, the most common type of finding was the failure to obtain sufficient persuasive evidence to support reliance on manual internal controls. The next most common type of finding was the failure to sufficiently test controls over, or the accuracy and completeness of, data or reports produced by management.

While the standards are international, the enforcement of the standards is carried out nationally. National practice varies. In the UK, the Financial Reporting Council (FRC) is the independent regulator for corporate reporting and corporate governance. Through its Codes and Standards Committee the FRC has primary responsibility for setting, monitoring and enforcement of auditing standards in the UK.

11.9.6 Governance within audit firms

Within the audit practices there is also the need to apply systems to ensure that there are adequate reviews of the performance of individual auditors and that the individual partners do not take advantage of their positions of trust.

The greatest control mechanism within an audit firm is the culture of the firm. Arthur Wyatt made the following observation:[22]

> The leadership of the various firms needs to understand that the internal culture of firms needs a substantial amount of attention if the reputation of the firms is to be restored. No piece of legislation is likely to solve the behavioural changes that have evolved within the past thirty years.

Impact of consultancy on audit attitudes

Wyatt, drawing on his experience in Arthur Andersen and his observation of competitors, indicated that in earlier times there was a culture of placing the maintenance of standards ahead of retention of clients; the smaller size of firms meant there was more informal monitoring of compliance with firm rules and ethical standards. Promotion was more likely to flow to those with the greatest technical expertise and compliance with ethical standards, rather than an ability to bring in more fees. The values of conservative accountants predominated over the risk-taking orientation of consultants.

Wyatt's view was that the growth and risk orientations of consulting are incompatible with the values needed to perform auditing in a manner which is independent in attitude.

11.9.7 The expectation gap

Another area of corporate governance and auditing relates to the expectation gap. The gap is between the stakeholders' expectation of the outcomes that can be expected from the auditors' performance and the outcomes that could reasonably be expected given the audit work that should have been performed.

The stakeholders' expectation is that the auditor guarantees that the financial statements are accurate, that every transaction has been 100% checked and any fraud would have been detected. The auditors' expectation is that the audit work carried out should identify material errors and misstatements based on a judgemental or statistical sampling approach.

Loss of confidence following corporate scandals

There have been a number of high-profile corporate failures and irregularities; for example, in the US, Enron failed, having inflated its earnings and hidden liabilities in SPEs (special-purpose entities). In 2008 the same problem of hiding liabilities appears to have occurred with Lehman Brothers where according to the Examiner's report[23] Lehman used what amounted to financial engineering to temporarily shuffle $50 billion of troubled assets off its books in the months before its collapse in September 2008 to conceal its dependence on borrowed money, and senior Lehman executives as well as the bank's accountants at Ernst & Young were aware of the moves. In Italy, Parmalat created a false paper trail and created assets where none existed; and in the US, the senior management of Tyco looted the company.

This raises questions such as (a) Were the auditors independent? (b) Did they carry out the work with due professional competence? and (c) Did they rely unduly on management representations?

11.9.8 Action by auditors to limit liability

In each of the above there is good reason for the expectation gap in that the audit had not been conducted in accordance with generally accepted audit standards and there was a lack of due professional care. If the auditors have been negligent then they are liable to be sued in a civil action. In the UK the profession has sought to obtain a statutory limit on their liability and, failing that, some have registered as limited liability partnerships – the path taken by Ernst & Young in 1996 and KPMG in 2002. In Australia some accountants operate under a statutory limit on their liability and in return ensure they have a minimum level of professional indemnity insurance.

11.9.9 Detection of fraud

An audit is designed to obtain evidence that the financial statements present a fair view and do not contain material misstatements. It is not a forensic investigation commissioned to detect fraud. Such an investigation would be expensive and in the majority of cases not be cost-effective. It has been argued that auditors should be required to carry out a fraud and detection role to avoid public concerns that arise when hearing about the high-profile corporate failures. However, it would appear that it is not so much a question of making every audit a forensic investigation to detect fraud but rather enforcing the exercise of due professional care in the conduct of all audits. The audit standards reinforce this when they emphasise the importance of scepticism.

11.9.10 Educating users

Many surveys have shown that there has been a considerable difference between auditors and audit report users regarding auditors' responsibilities for discovering fraud and predicting failure. Users of published financial statements need to be made aware that auditors rely on systems reviews and *sample testing* to evaluate the company's annual report. Based on those evaluations they form an opinion on the *likelihood* that the accounts provide a true and fair view or fairly present the accounts. However, they cannot guarantee the accounts are 100% accurate.

A number of major companies have collapsed without warning signs and the public have criticised the auditors. It is difficult when there are such high-profile corporate failures to persuade the public that lack of due professional care is not endemic. In response to these pressures auditors have modified their audit standards to place more emphasis on scepticism.

11.10 Executive remuneration in the UK

It is worth reinforcing the fact that the objective of corporate governance is to focus management on achieving the objectives of the company whilst keeping risks to appropriate levels and positioning the firm for a prosperous future. At the same time, sufficient safeguards must be in place to reduce the risks of resources being inappropriately diverted to any group at the expense of other groups involved.

11.10.1 The problem

The following is an extract[24] from a speech by Vince Cable, UK Secretary of State for business and industry, in 2012:

> The issue is **partly** about 'rewards for failure'. But it is not just that.
> There is also a ratchet in executive pay with everyone believing that they should be paid well above average and that they should be benchmarked against US peers when they live and work in the UK. It is of course a logical absurdity for everyone to be paid above the average, let alone in the top quartile. Imagine if this happened with workers' pay awards. There would be galloping wage inflation and loud business objections about our loss of competitiveness.
> While it is true that rising executive pay is a global phenomenon, trends in inequality at the very top are very divergent between countries, despite them all operating in the same global economy. There are world class companies in the Nordic countries, Japan, Holland and Germany who take a very different approach to the UK and US.
> But let me be clear. There is a legitimate role for high pay for exceptional talent and performance – quite apart from high returns to successful entrepreneurs – and I will defend that.

Since management is the group with the most discretion and power, it is important to ensure they do not obtain excessive remuneration or perks, or be allowed to shirk, or to gamble with company resources by taking excessive risks.

11.10.2 UK government response

In 2014 the UK introduced new requirements[25] for directors' remuneration reports. The report is split into three parts – a statement from the Chairman of the Remuneration Committee, a Policy Report and an Annual Report on remuneration. The Policy Report contains details of the performance measures (not the actual targets which are commercially sensitive) and is subject to a shareholder binding vote. The Annual Report includes a single figure for each director and the link between pay and performance. This follows the approach that disclosure should gradually result in change. This is supported when looking, for example, at the Kingfisher Remuneration Report[26] 2016, which comments positively on shareholder involvement:

> We were pleased by the level and quality of engagement and with the support received for our principles and proposed design. We welcomed the constructive feedback provided through the consultation process and this has been taken on board in our final proposals. To align incentives with the creation of long-term value, our proposed remuneration arrangements are a departure from the traditional UK executive pay model in some respects.
>
> Shareholders appreciated:
>
> • the reduced focus on annual bonus; the increased five year performance period for the long-term incentive (Transformation Incentive); and the balance between the short-term strategic objectives on the annual bonus, and the long-term business and financial measures on the equity elements of pay.

11.10.3 What is fair?

In the UK the statistics show[27] that in recent years the remuneration of executives relative to the average employee has been considerably higher than it was 20 years ago, and the remuneration of the top executive compared to the average of the next four executives is also higher than in the past.

From 1 January 2017 the Securities and Exchange Commission in the US requires public companies to disclose the ratio of the compensation of the chief executive officer (CEO) to the median compensation of its employees. The intention is that the disclosure of this information can be used to evaluate a CEO's compensation.

Just how this will play out is far from certain – the optimists hope that it will act as a restraint to ever increasing pay ratios, others might be inclined to see this as yet another ratio that CEOs will use to ratchet up their remuneration.

In 2017, the UK government proposed secondary legislation to require:

• quoted companies to report annually on the ratio of CEO pay to the average pay of their UK workforce with an explanation of changes to that ratio from year to year and a clearer explanation of potential outcomes from complex, share-based incentive schemes.

In the UK it had previously been is left to private organisations like the High Pay Centre[28] to calculate pay ratios. It reported in 2014 that average FTSE 100 CEO pay in 2016 was 138 times the earnings of the average full-time UK worker, down from 156 times in 2015 and 160 times in 2010.

Such high ratios seem intuitively unfair – but what is fair? Perhaps the question should be whether this higher relative remuneration reflects a greater contribution to performance, whether it reflects that as businesses increase in size the remuneration of the chief executive tends to increase to reflect the higher responsibilities, or whether it has been achieved simply because directors have been effectively able to set their own remuneration.

11.10.4 How to set criteria – in principle

There are a number of issues that will require a judgement to be made:

• What is the right balance between short-term performance and long-term performance? It is interesting to note that one of the measures[29] proposed in the European parliament is that:

The remuneration policy for company directors should also contribute to the long-term growth of the company so that it corresponds to a more effective practice of corporate governance and is not linked entirely or largely to short-term investment objectives.

- What if there are revenues and costs that are beyond the control or influence of management? Should these be excluded from the measure?
- Also, to the extent that performance may be influenced by general economic conditions, should managers be assessed on absolute performance or relative performance?

Relative performance means that if the performance fell from 10% to minus 3% during an economic downturn, and competitors' performance fell to minus 5%, managers would qualify for a bonus recognising that their performance had been relatively better. This may be resented by shareholders who have seen the share price fall.

Often companies resort to outside consultants, but the observation has been made that one doesn't hear of outside consultants recommending a pay cut and they are in part responsible for ratcheting up the levels of remuneration.

11.10.5 Where do accountants feature in setting directors' remuneration?

The equity of the remuneration is not normally seen as an accounting matter, but accountants should ensure transparent disclosure of the performance criteria and of the payments. In some jurisdictions there is legislation setting out in some detail what has to be disclosed.

For example, in the UK The Large and Medium-sized Companies and Groups (Accounts and Reports) (Amendment) Regulations 2013 requires the annual report to contain a single total figure table comprising six columns, reporting for each director (with certain conditions):

- the total amount of salary and fees;
- all taxable benefits;
- money or other assets received or receivable for the relevant financial year as a result of the achievement of performance measures and targets relating to a period ending in that financial year;
- money or other assets received or receivable for periods of more than one financial year where final vesting is determined as a result of the achievement of performance measures or targets relating to a period ending in the relevant financial year;
- all pension-related benefits including payments (whether in cash or otherwise) in lieu of retirement benefits and all benefits in year from participating in pension schemes; and
- the total amount of the sums set out in the previous five columns.

It is interesting to see companies carrying out sensitivity tests to show the maximum that is achievable if all targets are met. For example, the following is an extract from the IMI Annual Report and Accounts 2017:[30]

> To illustrate the opportunity available to our executive directors, and the **sensitivity** of pay to performance, the adjacent graphs set out pay outcomes for three performance scenarios:
>
> - minimum, where pay is limited to fixed, non-performance components (based on 2018 salaries, the corresponding pension allowance and other benefits);
> - 'on-target', where annual bonus and long-term incentives vest at on-target levels; and;
> - maximum, where all variable pay components vest in full

11.10.6 Performance criteria

Directors are expected to produce increases in the share price and dividends. Traditional measures have been largely based on growth in earnings per share (EPS), which has encouraged companies to seek to increase short-term earnings at the expense of long-term earnings, e.g. by cutting back capital programmes. Even worse, concentrating on growth in earnings per share can result in a reduction in shareholder value, e.g. by companies borrowing and investing in projects that produce a return in excess of the interest charge, but less than the return expected by equity investors.

11.10.7 Institutional investor guidelines

One of the problems is the innovative nature of the remuneration packages that companies might adopt and the fact that there is no uniquely correct scheme. The following are examples of the various criteria which have evolved and which have been adopted:

Absolute Measures or Targets
Normalised earnings per share measured by reference to a percentage margin, for example 2% per annum growth, in excess of inflation over a 3 year period. It is important that the figures for earnings be smoothed where appropriate to avoid distortions arising from one-off extraordinary or exceptional items included within the FRS 3 definition of earnings per share.

Comparative Measures
Outperformance of an index or of the median or weighted average of a pre-defined peer group in the case of basic options: or the achievement of top quartile performance in the case of super-options:

(i) *Normalised earnings per share*
Outperformance of the median or weighted average rate of increase in normalised earnings of a peer group.

(ii) *Net Asset Value per Share*
Net asset value per share measured, for example against a predefined peer group or index.

(iii) *Total Shareholder Return (i.e. share price performance plus gross dividend per share)*
Where total shareholder return is used this should be based on exceeding the relevant benchmark within a predefined peer group but, as this formula relies substantially on share price, attainment of the criterion should also be supported by a defined secondary criterion validating sustained and significant improvement in the underlying financial performance.

(iv) *Comparative Share Price*
Comparative share price relative to a peer group would be an acceptable alternative to total shareholder return, conditional in the same way on a secondary performance criterion validating sustained and significant improvement in underlying financial performance over the same period.

11.10.8 Institutional investors' statements of principles

In the UK, in response to The Large and Medium-sized Companies and Groups (Accounts and Reports) (Amendment) Regulations 2013, the Association of British Insurers (ABI)[31] and the National Association of Pension Funds (NAPF)[32] have issued statements of principles that they expect companies to consider when setting remuneration policies.

These include proactive proposals that schemes should ensure that executive rewards reflect long-term returns to shareholders by expecting executive management to make a material long-term investment in shares of the businesses they manage. There are also proposals to address the criticisms that have been made that poor performance has still been rewarded by proposing that there should be provisions that allow a company to forfeit all or part of a bonus or long-term incentive award before it has vested and been paid and claw back moneys already paid.

11.11 Corporate governance, legislation and codes

Investors looking to the safety and adequacy of the return on their investment are influenced by their level of confidence in the ability of the directors to achieve this. Good governance has not been fully defined and various reports have attempted to set out principles and practices which they perceive to be helpful in making directors accountable. These principles and practices are set out in a variety of Acts, e.g. Sarbanes–Oxley in the US and the Companies Act and regulations in the UK, and codes such as the Singapore Code of Corporate Governance 2012 and the UK Corporate Governance Code (formerly the Combined Code).

The various laws and codes that have been published set out principles and recommended best practice relating to the board of directors, directors' remuneration, relations with shareholders, accountability and audit.

The European Corporate Governance Institute[33]

This is an excellent resource that covers pretty well all the corporate governance codes in the world. It is interesting to refer to the Institute's website to observe the number of new and amended codes since 2010 which reflects the growing importance attached to corporate governance in terms of investor confidence.

11.11.1 Codes as a partial solution

As the nature of business and expectations of society change, the governance requirements evolve to reflect the new laws and regulations. By anticipating changing requirements, companies can prepare for the future. At the same time, they should identify the special areas of potential conflict in their own operations and develop policies to manage those relationships.

Good governance is a question of having the right attitudes. All the corporate governance codes will not achieve much if they focus on form rather than substance. Codes work because people want to achieve good governance. People can always find ways around rules.

The FRC took the view in 2014 that more effective application of, and reporting on, existing code principles may often have a greater impact on actual standards of governance and stewardship than managing further change.

Furthermore, rules cannot cover all cases, so good governance needs a commitment to the fundamental idea of fairness.

The research on whether good governance leads to lower cost of capital is very mixed, reflecting both the difficulty of identifying the impact of good governance and the fact that some engage with the spirit of the concept and some do not. There are those who question the impact of good corporate governance, and supporting the case of those who doubt that there is a positive impact on performance is an Australian research project[34] looking at companies in the S&P/ASX 200 index which found that companies which the researcher classified as having poor corporate governance outperformed companies classified as having good corporate governance over a range of measures including EBITDA growth and return on assets. There is an ongoing need for further research, particularly as to the effect on smaller listed companies, and it will be interesting to await the outcome.

11.12 Corporate governance – the UK experience

In the UK there have been a number of initiatives in attempting to achieve good corporate governance through (a) legislation, (b) the UK Corporate Governance Code, (c) non-executive directors (NEDs), (d) shareholder activism and (e) audit. We discuss each of these briefly below.

11.12.1 Legislation

Legislation is in place that attempts to ensure that investors receive sufficient information to make informed judgements. For example, there are requirements for the audit of financial statements, majority voting on directors' remuneration policy and disclosure of directors' remuneration. There could be a case for increased statutory involvement in the affairs of a company by, for example, putting a limit on benefits and specifying how share options should be structured. However, the government has gone down the road of disclosure and transparency to encourage and empower shareholder activism.

11.12.2 The UK Corporate Governance Code 2016[35]

The Code sets standards of good practice in relation to board leadership and effectiveness, remuneration, accountability and relations with shareholders. It is routinely reviewed every two years since first published in 2010.
Since 2012 revisions include:

The Board
- Boards will be expected to confirm that the report and accounts, taken as a whole, is fair, balanced and understandable and provides the information needed for shareholders to assess the company's performance, business model and strategy.
- A description of the board's policy on diversity, including gender, any measurable objectives that it has set for implementing the policy, and progress on achieving the objectives.
- Evaluation of the board should consider the balance of skills, experience, independence and knowledge of the company on the board, its diversity, including gender, how the board works together as a unit, and other factors relevant to its effectiveness.

Going concern, risk management and internal control
- Companies should state whether they consider it appropriate to adopt the going concern basis of accounting and identify any material uncertainties to their ability to continue to do so.
- Companies should robustly assess their principal risks and explain how they are being managed or mitigated.

- Companies should state whether they believe they will be able to continue in operation and meet their liabilities taking account of their current position and principal risks, and specify the period covered by this statement and why they consider it appropriate. It is expected that the period assessed will be significantly longer than 12 months.
- Companies should monitor their risk management and internal control systems and, at least annually, carry out a review of their effectiveness, and report on that review in the annual report.

Remuneration

- Greater emphasis be placed on ensuring that remuneration policies are designed with the long-term success of the company in mind, and that the lead responsibility for doing so rests with the remuneration committee.
- Companies should put in place arrangements that will enable them to recover or withhold variable pay when appropriate to do so, and should consider appropriate vesting and holding periods for deferred remuneration.

11.12.3 Non-executive directors (NEDs)

The main function of non-executive directors is to ensure that the executive directors are pursuing policies consistent with shareholders' interests.[29]

Review of their contribution

Considering the qualities that are required, the Cadbury Report recommended that the board should include non-executive directors of sufficient calibre and number for their views to carry significant weight in the board's decisions. Research[37] indicated that they are concerned to maintain their reputation in the external market in order to maintain their marketability.

NEDs on many boards bring added or essential commercial and financial expertise, for example on a routine basis as members of the audit committee, or on an *ad hoc* basis providing experience when a company is preparing to float or having specific industry knowledge. They are also valued as having a role in questioning investment decisions and entering into unduly risky projects.

Limitations

However, NEDs are not and never can be a universal panacea. It has to be recognised that there may be constraints such as:

- They might have divided loyalties, having been nominated by the chairman, the CEO or another board member.
- This has been addressed by the Code which states 'An explanation should be given if neither an external search consultancy nor open advertising has been used in the appointment of a nonexecutive director. Where an external search consultancy has been used, it should be identified in the report and a statement should be made as to whether it has any other connection with the company.'
- They might have other NED appointments and/or executive appointments which limit the time they can give to the company's affairs.
- This is addressed by some companies such as BUPA[38] which requires non-executive directors to disclose their other significant commitments to the board before appointment, with a broad indication of the time involved; and inform the board of any subsequent changes.

- They might not be able to restrain an overbearing CEO, particularly if the CEO is also the chairman.
- A 2009 survey[39] indicated that a third of non-executive directors feel they are unable to control their chairmen and chief executives, and almost 40% feel they would be unable to sack underperforming board colleagues.

With so many caveats, it would be reasonable to assume that NEDs could not easily divert a dominant CEO or executive directors from a planned course of action. In such cases, their influence on good corporate governance is reduced unless the interest of directors and shareholders already happen to coincide. However, if the issue is serious enough for one or more independent director to resign it is likely that the market will certainly take note.

Independent NEDs and risk – a negative view

Research[40] commented that the view that outside directors brought experience and strategic expertise, together with vigilance in monitoring management decisions, to prevent strategic mistakes and/or opportunistic behaviour by management was not supported by much evidence that governance reduces risks. The researchers found little evidence that governance was effective in reducing the volatility of share prices or the chance of large adverse share price movements. As with the financial sector in the credit crunch, independent directors seem not to be a protection against companies adopting risky strategies.

Independent NEDs and risk – a positive view

However, on a more positive note, the presence of NEDs is perceived to be indicative of good corporate governance, and a research report[41] indicated that good governance has a positive impact on investor confidence. The research examined 654 UK FTSE All-Share companies from 2003 to 2007 using unique governance data from the ABI's Institutional Voting and Information Service (IVIS). An extract from the ABI research is as follows:

> New research from the ABI (Association of British Insurers) shows that companies with the best corporate governance records have produced returns 18% higher than those with poor governance. It was also revealed that a breach of governance best practice (known as a red top in the ABI's guidance) reduces a company's industry-adjusted return on assets (ROA) by an average of 1 percentage point a year. For even the best performing companies (those within the top quartile of ROA performance), that equates to an actual fall of 8.6% in returns per year.
>
> The research also shows that shareholders investing in a poorly governed company suffer from low returns. £100 invested in a company with no corporate governance problems leads to an average return of £120 but if invested in the worst governed companies the return would have been just £102.

There are many highly talented, well-experienced NEDs but their ability to influence good governance should not be overestimated. Their effectiveness might be reduced if they have limited time, limited access to documents, limited respect from full-time executive directors and limited expertise within the remuneration and/or audit committees. When a company is prospering their influence could be extremely beneficial; when there are problems they may not have the authority to ensure good governance.

11.12.4 Shareholder activism

In the UK the need for good corporate governance is affected by how widely shares are held.

In the US and the UK, a large number of financial institutions and individuals hold shares in listed companies, so there is a greater need for corporate governance requirements. In Japan and most European countries (except the UK) shares in listed companies tend to be held by a small number of banks, financial institutions and individuals. Where there are few shareholders in a company, they can question the directors directly, so there is less need for corporate governance requirements.

The UK Office for National Statistics[42] reported that at the end of 2016, shares in quoted UK domiciled companies (that is, their country of incorporation is the UK) were worth a total of £2.04 trillion. An analysis of holdings showed:

The rest of the world sector	53.9%
UK individuals	12.3%
UK Unit trusts	9.3%
Other financial institutions based in the UK	8.1%
Insurance companies	4.9%

Individual shareholder influence on corporate governance

With the rest of the world holding 53.9% and individual shareholders holding only 12.3% it is difficult for the latter group to exercise any significant group influence on management behaviour. In passing legislation, there is an implicit view that individual shareholders have a responsibility to achieve good corporate governance. Statutes can provide for disclosure and be fine-tuned in response to changing needs but they are not intended to replace shareholder activism. When the economy is booming there is a temptation to sit back, collect the dividends and capital gains, bin the annual report and post in proxy forms.

Shareholder influence has to rely on that exercised by the institutional investors.

Large-block investors' influence on corporate governance

There is mixed evidence about the influence of large-block shareholders. The following is an extract from a Department of Trade and Industry report:[43]

> The report observed from a review of economics, corporate finance and 'law and economics' research literature that there was no unambiguous evidence that presence of large-block and institutional investors among the firm's shareholders performed monitoring and resource functions of 'good' corporate governance. However, management and business strategy research suggests that it does have a significant effect on *critical* organisational decisions, such as executive turnover, value-enhancing business strategy, and limitations on anti-takeover defences.

Feedback from the experts' evaluation of the governance roles of various types of shareholders provided the following pattern:[43]

	Mean	Standard deviation
Pension funds, mutual funds, foundations	4.58	1.50
Private equity funds	4.52	1.76
Individual (non-family) blockholders	4.36	1.70
Family blockholders	4.20	1.63
Corporate pension funds	3.85	1.55
Insurance companies	3.69	1.69
Banks	3.31	1.49
Dispersed individual shareholders	2.18	1.41

The highest scores were assigned to the governance roles of pension funds, mutual funds, foundations and private equity investors:

> Some respondents also suggested that various associations of institutional investors such as NAPF, ABI, etc., play strong governance roles, as do individual blockholders and family owners. At the other end of the spectrum are dispersed individual shareholders whose governance roles received the lowest score. However, it must be kept in mind that none of the individual scores is above 5 indicating that, on average, our experts were rather sceptical about the effectiveness of large blockholders from the 'good' governance perspective.[43]

A further related factor is that US and UK companies have tended to have a low gearing with most of the finance provided by shareholders. However, in other countries the gearing of companies is much higher, which indicates that most finance for companies comes from banks. If the majority of the finance is provided by shareholders, then there is a greater need for corporate governance requirements than if finance is in the form of loans where the lenders are able to stipulate conditions and loan covenants, e.g. the maximum level of gearing and action available to them if interest payments or capital repayments are missed.

However, institutional investors do not represent a majority in any company. Their role is to achieve the best return on the funds under their management consistent with their attitude to environmental and social issues. Their expertise has been largely directed towards the strategic management and performance of the company with, perhaps, an excessive concern with short-term gains. Issues such as directors' remuneration might well be of far less significance than the return on their investment.

The Stewardship Code[44]

Whereas the UK Corporate Governance Code related to conduct of the Board, the **Stewardship Code** is a set of principles or guidelines issued by the FRC in 2010. Its principal aim is to make institutional investors take an active role to protect the interests of the people who have placed their money with them to invest.

The code consists of seven principles which, if followed, should benefit corporate governance. The principles are that

Institutional investors should:

1 **publicly disclose their policy on how they will discharge their stewardship responsibilities.** Such a policy should include how investee companies will be monitored with an active dialogue on the board and its policy on voting and the use made of proxy voting.

2 **have a robust policy on managing conflicts of interest in relation to stewardship and this policy should be publicly disclosed.** Such a policy should include how to manage conflicts of interest when, for example, voting on matters affecting a parent company or client.

3 **monitor when it is necessary to enter into an active dialogue with their boards.** The objective is to identify problems at an early stage to minimise any loss of shareholder value. They do this by satisfying themselves that the board and sub-committee structures are effective, and that independent directors provide adequate oversight and maintain a clear audit trail of the institution's decisions.

4 **establish clear guidelines on when and how they will escalate their activities as a method of protecting and enhancing shareholder value.** They may want to intervene when they have concerns about the company's strategy and performance, its governance or its approach to the risks arising from social and environmental matters. This would

normally be by meetings with management although it could lead on to requisitioning an EGM, possibly to change the board.

5 **be willing to act collectively with other investors where appropriate.** Such action is proposed in extreme cases when the risks posed threaten the ability of the company to continue.

6 **have a clear policy on voting and disclosure of voting activity.** This means seeking to vote all shares held, not automatically supporting the board and, if they have been unable to reach a satisfactory outcome through active dialogue, registering an abstention or voting against the resolution.

7 **report periodically on their stewardship and voting activities.** Regularly explaining how they have discharged their responsibilities whilst remaining aware of the need for confidentiality in specific situations.

The FRC proposes to extend these principles to all listed companies and review the Code again in 2018

The Kay Review[45]

The Kay Review of UK Equity Markets and Long-term Decision Making was published in 2012. It recommended that the Stewardship Code should be developed to incorporate a more expansive form of stewardship, focusing on strategic issues as well as questions of corporate governance. This is in keeping with the increasing pressure for companies to report risks and how they are addressing them. It also recommended that an investors' forum should be established to facilitate collective engagement by investors in UK companies. This recommendation has been acted on[46] and the 'Investors Forum' has been launched by the Collective Engagement Working Group.

- There has been recognition that a cultural change is needed with investors and companies developing a shared sense of partnership to promote long-term strategies that can generate sustainable wealth creation for all stakeholders. One way forward is for all major listed companies to hold an annual strategy meeting for institutional investors, outside the results cycle, where investors and company executives can link governance to the company's long-term strategy without the focus on short-term results. Where there are shared concerns about a particular company it is proposed that an Engagement Action Group should operate.

- An investors' forum should be established to facilitate collective engagement by investors in UK companies.

- Companies should consult their major long-term investors over major board appointments.

- High-quality, succinct narrative reporting should be strongly encouraged.

- Companies should structure directors' remuneration to relate incentives to sustainable long-term business performance. Long-term performance incentives should be provided only in the form of company shares to be held at least until after the executive has retired from the business.

- Asset management firms should similarly structure managers' remuneration so as to align the interests of asset managers with the interests and timescales of their clients. Pay should therefore not be related to short-term performance of the investment fund or asset management firm. Rather a long-term performance incentive should be provided in the form of an interest in the fund (either directly or via the firm) to be held at least until the manager is no longer responsible for that fund.

Legal safeguards

Corporate governance has to react to changing circumstances and threats. It evolves and will continue to need to be revised and updated. The law provides minimum safeguards but in the ever-changing complexities of global trade and finance, good governance is dependent on the behaviour of directors and their commitment to principles and values. The UK system is heavily dependent on codes which set out principles and the requirement for directors to explain if they fail to comply. The UK Corporate Governance Code and Stewardship Code will rely for their effectiveness on investor engagement. This recognises that investors cannot delegate all responsibility to their agents, the directors, accept their dividends and be dormant principals.

UK experience and international initiatives

It is interesting to note that what constitutes good corporate governance is evolving with new initiatives being taken globally. For example, the OECD is responding to weaknesses in corporate governance that became apparent in the financial crisis by developing recommendations for improvements in board practices, the remuneration process and how shareholders should actively exercise their rights. It is also reviewing governance in relation to risk management which featured as such a threat in the way financial institutions conducted their business. However, there is some concern that measures that might be essential for the control of the financial sector should not be imposed arbitrarily on non-financial sector organisations.

11.12.5 Employee involvement

The UK Government proposed in 2017 measures aimed at strengthening corporate governance through mostly non-legislative means relating to: executive pay; strengthening the employee voice, customer, and supplier voice; governance in large privately held businesses.

The employee voice

It was proposed[47] that this should take the form of:

- Director from the workforce
- Designated non-executive director
- Formal employee advisory council

Director from the workforce

This places a single worker on the Board who will be subject to all the statutory and fiduciary duties of a director. It is questionable whether a single director could adequately represent all the varied labour issues and pressure would grow to increase the number. There is also the risk that other directors might make decisions outside the formal Board meetings to avoid the employee scrutiny or comment.

Designated non-executive director

Such a director could be an independent professional, such as an academic or judge who then becomes are a full board member whose primary duty is to have the company's interests at heart. Of course, there could be cases when company and employee interests may conflict as when the Board is making decisions on pay, site closures or dealing with large-scale employment disputes.

Formal employee advisory council

This form of consultation occurs in Europe, as in Germany. It has the advantage that an advisory council member is not subject to statutory director's obligations, is able to represent the views of the workforce without having to balance the wider competing interests of the company and does not need to be privy to the full range of business confidential or strategic information being considered by the Board.

11.12.6 Audit

There has been audit reform in the EU[48] with a Directive setting out new rules which addresses independence, the expectation gap and competition.

Independence

These include the mandatory rotation of auditors every 10 years (or 20 years subject to tendering), the prohibition on the provision of certain non-audit services to audit and the introduction of a cap on fees that can be earned from the provision of permitted non-audit services.

The *expectation* gap

This is to be improved by ensuring increased audit quality and more detailed and informative audit reports with meaningful data for investors and better accountability with a provision for 5% of the shareholders in a company to initiate actions to dismiss the auditors.

Competition

Medium-sized audit practices have been precluded from obtaining audit work with some major companies that have had a 'Big Four only' policy. This restrictive practice is now prohibited. In addition there will be the impact of the prohibition of certain non-audit services to audit clients.

Auditors are subject to professional oversight to ensure that they are independent, up-to-date and competent. However, where there is a determined effort to mislead the auditors, for example by creating false paper trails and misstatement at the highest level, then there is the risk that fraud will be missed.

There have been allegations of audit negligence in some high-profile corporate failures, in some of which auditors have been found liable or agreed to pay a settlement.

The following two examples in 2018 relate to the audit by PwC of the Colonial Bank and the audit by Deloitte of a mortgage lending firm Taylor, Bean & Whitaker (TBW).

- PricewaterhouseCoopers LLP was negligent in connection with one of the biggest bank failures of the financial crisis, a federal judge has ruled,[49] opening up the Big Four accounting firm to the potential of hundreds of millions of dollars in damages. PwC violated auditing rules and didn't take steps that could have detected a $2 billion fraud scheme that contributed to the 2009 failure of Alabama's Colonial Bank, the judge ruled. The ruling Thursday came in a lawsuit brought against PwC by the Federal Deposit Insurance Corpn. This decision, if it stands, will have a significant extension of an auditor's liability for detecting fraud.

- The US Department of Justice alleged[50] that: "Deloitte's audits knowingly deviated from applicable auditing standards and therefore failed to detect TBW's fraudulent conduct and materially false and misleading financial statements."

Furthermore, the Justice Department claimed that Deloitte's failure to detect misconduct enabled TBW's improper behaviour to continue and thus contributed to its collapse. Deloitte came to a settlement with the department, agreeing to pay $149.5m, which makes no determination of liability.

In general, while the audit appears to be a reliable mechanism for ensuring that the financial statements give a true and fair view, there is a need for audit staff to acquire a detailed understanding of the industry being audited and the risks attaching.

Summary

Good governance is achieved when all parties feel that they have been fairly treated. It is achieved when behaviour is prompted by the idea of fairness to all parties. Independent behaviour is expected of the NEDs and auditors and they are expected to have the strength of character to act professionally with proper regard for the interest of the shareholders. The shareholders in turn should be exercising their rights and not be inert. They have a role to play and it is not fair of them to sit on their hands and complain.

Good corporate governance cannot be achieved by rules alone. The principle-based approach such as that of the FRC with the UK Corporate Governance Code recognises that it is behaviour that is the key – it sets out broad principles and a recommended set of provisions/rules which are indicative of good practice, and disclosure is required if there is a reason why they are not appropriate in a specific situation.

Good corporate governance depends on directors behaving in the best interest of shareholders. Corporate governance mechanisms to achieve this include legislation, corporate governance codes, appointment of NEDs, shareholder activism and audit. Such mechanisms are necessary when companies are financed largely by equity capital. It is noticeable that they are being developed in many countries in response to wider share ownership.

Corporate governance best practice is being regularly reviewed and improved internationally.

REVIEW QUESTIONS

1 Explain in your own words what you understand corporate governance to mean.

2 Explain why governance procedures may vary from country to country.

3 What are the implications of governance for the Big 6 and their audit practices?

4 Auditors should take a more combative position and start with presumptive doubt and a more sceptical frame of mind, even though past experience of the FD and client staff has never revealed any cause for suspicion. Discuss the extent to which the requirement to adopt a different approach will increase the auditor's responsibility for detecting fraud.

5 The Big 6 audit firms have had their professional competence found to be lacking on various audits. Discuss the measures that might be taken to avoid a re-occurrence.

See https://www.ft.com/content/ad09f204-3c90-11e8-b9f9-de94fa33a81e as a starting point.

6 The Association of British Insurers held the view that options should be exercised only if the company's earnings per share growth exceeded that of the Retail Price Index. The National Association of Pension Funds preferred the criterion to be a company's outperformance of the FTA All-Share Index.

(a) Discuss the reasons for the differences in approach.

(b) Discuss the implication of each approach to the financial reporting regulators and the auditors.

7 Research[51] suggests that companies whose managers own a significant proportion of the voting share capital tend to violate the UK Corporate Governance Code recommendations on board composition far more frequently than other companies. Discuss the advantages and disadvantages of enforcing greater compliance.

8 'Good corporate governance is a myth – just look at these frauds and irregularities:

- Enron www.sec.gov/litigation/litreleases/lr18582.htm
- WorldCom www.sec.gov/litigation/litreleases/lr17588.htm
- Xerox Corporation www.sec.gov/litigation/complaints/complr17465.htm
- Dell www.sec.gov/news/press/2010/2010-131.htm
- Lehman http://lehmanreport.jenner.com/VOLUME%201.pdf'

How realistic is it to expect good governance to combat similar future behaviour?

9 'Stronger corporate governance legislation is emerging globally but true success will only come from self-regulation, increased internal controls and the strong ethical corporate culture that organisations create.' Discuss.

10 In the modern commercial world, auditors provide numerous other services to complement their audit work. These services include the following:

(a) Accountancy and book-keeping assistance, e.g. in the maintenance of ledgers and in the preparation of monthly and annual accounts.

(b) Consultancy services, e.g. advice on the design of information systems and organisational structures, advice on the choice of computer equipment and software packages, and advice on the recruitment of new executives.

(c) Investigation work, e.g. appraisals of companies that might be taken over.

(d) Taxation work, e.g. tax planning advice and preparation of tax returns to HM Revenue and Customs for both the company and the company's senior management.

Discuss:

(i) Whether any of these activities is unacceptable as a separate activity because it might weaken an auditor's independence.

(ii) The advantages and disadvantages to the shareholders of the audit firm providing this range of service.

11 The following is an extract from the *Sunday Times* of 8 March 2009:

Marc Jobling, the ABI's assistant director of investment affairs, said: 'Pay consultants are a big contributor to the problems around executive pay. We have heard of some who admit that they work for both management and independent directors – which is a clear conflict of interest and not acceptable. We believe that remuneration consultants, whose livelihood appears to depend on pushing an ever-upward spiral in executive pay, should be obliged to develop a code of ethics.'

Discuss the types of issues which should be included in such a code of ethics and how effective they would be in achieving good corporate governance.

12 There has been much criticism of the effectiveness of non-executive directors following failures such as Enron. Some consider that their interests are too close to those of the executive directors and they have neither the time nor the professional support to allow them to be effective monitors of the executive directors. Draft a job specification and personal criteria that you think would allay these criticisms.

13 In 2000, the chairman of the US Securities and Exchange Commission (SEC), Arthur Levitt, proposed that other services provided by audit firms to their audit clients should be severely restricted, probably solely to audit and tax work.[52] Discuss why this has still not happened.

14 Discuss how remuneration policies may adversely affect good corporate governance and how these effects may be reduced or prevented.

15 Discuss the major risks which will need to be managed by a pharmaceutical company and the extent to which these should be disclosed.

16 Egypt is a country in which many of the public companies have substantial shareholders in the form of founding families or government shareholders. How do you think that would affect corporate governance?

17 'Management will become accountable only when shareholders receive information on corporate strategy, future-based plans and budgets, and actual results with explanations of variances.' Discuss whether this is necessary, feasible and in the company's interest.

18 The Chartered Institute of Management Accountants (CIMA) has warned that linking directors' pay to EPS or return on assets is open to abuse, since these are not the objective measures they might appear.

   (a) Identify four ways in which the directors might manipulate the EPS and return on assets without breaching existing standards.

   (b) Suggest two alternative bases for setting criteria for bonuses.

19 Review reporting requirements in relation to disclosure of related party transactions and discuss their adequacy in relation to the avoidance of conflicts of interest.

20 Discuss in what situations audit independence could be compromised.

21 It has been suggested that an Investors Forum will make management more accountable to the shareholders. Discuss how this might be achieved when shareholdings are so widely held.

22 It has been suggested that there would be less of an expectation gap if there were to be a note to the accounts giving in relation to those assets and liabilities which involved estimates, the range of values and confidence level in the reported figure – for example, land, inventory, trade receivables.

   Discuss the pros and cons of this suggestion from the viewpoint of the shareholder and the auditor.

23 Access the FRC Guidance on the Strategic Report issued in June 2014 and refer to section 7 'The strategic report: content elements'. Then select a set of published accounts and review the extent to which the company has satisfied the guidance. (www.frc.org.uk/Our-Work/Publications/Accounting-and-Reporting-Policy/Guidance-on-the-Strategic-Report.pdf)

24 The IASB should issue a Practice Statement giving detailed guidance on the calculation of an alternative EPS figure if used to set targets for executive bonus.

   Discuss.

25 Access the Kingman Report (https://www.gov.uk/government/publications/financial-reporting-council-review-2018).

Discuss: (a) Why proposal for a new regulator- Audit. Reporting and Governance Authority (b) Proposals relating to internal control, viability statements, discussion documents, corporate governance reporting Stewardship Code and the audit expectation gap.

26 Discuss the factors that you consider might limit the ability to use non-financial information when making investment decisions as an analyst.[53]

27 There is a concern that the audit of FTSE 100 companies is dominated by the Big Four audit firms. One proposal is that there should be joint audits which include mid-tier firms.

Discuss the objection that has been raised that these firms lack the technical expertise to act as joint auditors with the Big Four and how this could be resolved.

28 PwC were severely reprimanded and fined £5m for misconduct in relation to the 2009 audit of Connaught plc, a FTSE 250 company which went into administration in 2010. What is the FRC's role in relation to enforcement matters?

Findings of misconduct were found in relation to which areas of the audit?

Access http://www.frc.org.uk/may-2017/connaught-tribunal-case-report-published

29 Carillion, the UK's second-largest construction company, collapsed under a debt pile of £1.5bn on 15 January 2018.

What are the wider implications of the Carillion collapse for the accounting profession?

Access http://www.bbc.co.uk/news/business-43275605

30 In discussing in Parliament the directors' remuneration in Carillion: Rt Hon Frank Field MP, Chair of the Committee, said: 'It's greed on stilts, pure and simple.'

Discuss the actions of the Remuneration Committee, how shareholder activism might be able to limit excesses and the likelihood of this being effective.

Access https://www.parliament.uk/business/committees/committees-a-z/commons-select/work-and-pensions-committee/news-parliament-2017/carillion-board-greed-17-19/

EXERCISES

Question 1

Manufacturing Co. has been negotiating with Fred Paris regarding the sale of some property that represented an old manufacturing site which is now surplus to requirements. Because part of the site was used for manufacturing, it has to be decontaminated before it can be subdivided as a new housing development. This has complicated negotiations. Fred is a property developer and has a private company (Paris Property Development Pty Ltd) and is also a major (15%) shareholder of FP Development of which he is chairman. The negotiators for Manufacturing Co. note that the documents keep switching between Paris Property Development and FP Development and they use that as feedback as to how well they are negotiating.

Required:
Is there a corporate governance failure? Discuss.

Question 2

Harvey Storm is chief executive of West Wing Savings and Loans. Harvey authorises a loan to Middleman Properties secured on the land it is about to purchase. Middleman Properties has little money of its own. Middleman Properties subdivides the land and builds houses on them. It offers buyers a house and finance package under which West Wing provides the house loans up to 97% of the house price even to couples with poor credit ratings. This allows Middleman Properties to ask for higher prices for the houses.

Middleman Properties appoints Frontman Homes as the selling agent who kindly provides buyers with the free services of a solicitor to handle all the legal aspects including the conveyancing. Most of the profits from the developments are paid to Frontman Homes as commissions. Harvey Storm's wife has a 20% interest in Frontman Homes.

Required:
Are these corporate governance failures? Discuss.

Question 3

Conglomerate plc was a family company which was so successful that the founding Alexander family could not fully finance its expansion. So the company was floated on the Stock Exchange with the Alexander family holding 'A' class shares and the public holding 'B' class shares. 'A' class shares held the right to appoint six of the eleven directors. 'B' class shares could appoint five directors and had the same dividend rights as the 'A' class shares. The company could not be wound up unless a resolution was passed by 75% or more of 'A' class shareholders.

Required:
Is there any risk of a governance failure? Discuss.

Question 4

The board of White plc is discussing the filling of a vacant position arising from the death of Lord White. A list of possible candidates is as follows:

(a) Lord Sperring, who is a well-known company director and who was the managing director of Sperring Manufacturers before he switched to being a professional director.

(b) John Spate, B.Eng., PhD, who is managing director of a successful, innovative high-technology company and will be taking retirement in four months' time.

(c) Gerald Stewart, B. Com, who is the retired managing director of Spry and Montgomery advertising agency which operates in six countries, being the UK and five other Commonwealth countries.

The managing director leads the discussion and focuses on the likelihood of the three candidates being able to work in harmony with other members of the board. He suggests that John Spate is too radical to be a member of the board of White plc. The other members of the board agree that he has a history of looking at things differently and would tend to distract the board.

The chairman of the board suggests that Lord Sperring is very well connected in the business community and would be able to open many doors for the managing director. It was unanimously agreed that the chairman should approach Lord Sperring to see if he would be willing to join the board.

Required:
Critically discuss the appointment process.

Question 5

(a) Describe the value to the audit client of the audit firm providing consultancy services.

(b) Why is it undesirable for audit firms to provide consultancy services to audit clients?

(c) Why do audit firms want to continue to provide consultancy services to audit clients?

Question 6

How is the relationship between the audit firm and the audit client different for:

(a) the provision of statutory audit when the auditor reports to the shareholders;

(b) the provision of consultancy services by audit firms?

Question 7

Why is there a prohibition of auditors owning shares in client companies? Is this prohibition reasonable? Discuss.

Notes

1 C. Oman (ed.), *Corporate Governance in Development: The Experiences of Brazil, Chile, India and South Africa*, OECD Development Centre and Center for International Private Enterprise, Paris and Washington, DC, 2003, cited in N. Meisel, *Governance Culture and Development*, Development Centre, OECD, Paris, 2004, p. 16.

2 http://www.publications.parliament.uk/pa/cm201516/cmselect/cmpubadm/980/980.pdf

3 https://charitycommission.blog.gov.uk/2017/07/13/the-new-charity-governance-code-essential-reading-for-all-trustees/

4 https://www.thirdsector.co.uk/regulator-tells-oxfam-conduct-review-sexual-abuse-claims/management/article/1452535

5 https://www.sec.gov/news/press/2011/2011-158.htm

6 https://www.walkermorris.co.uk/publications/brief-walker-morris-legal-update-may-2016/first-ever-corporate-conviction-uk-bribery-act/

7 www.oecd.org/dataoecd/28/62/38699164.pdf

8 www.sec.gov/news/pressrelease/2016-74.html4

9 https://www.bloomberg.com/news/articles/2017-12-21/u-k-insider-trading-investigations-set-record-as-fca-cleans-up

10 http://cphpost.dk/business/ruin-bank-and-earn-ten-million-kroner

11 www.heraldtribune.com/article/20100719/COLUMNIST/7191018

12 http://iacrc.org/procurement-fraud/the-most-common-procurement-fraud-schemes-and-their-primary-red-flags/

13 An example of this is the convergence of computing, telephone, television and entertainment markets as new devices impinge on all fields compared to ten years ago when they were quite distinct fields.

14 https://na.theiia.org/standards-guidance/Public%20Documents/MODEL_AUDIT_COMMITTEE_CHARTER.pdf

15 *The New Auditor's Report: Enhancing Auditor Communications*, January 2015, Greater Transparency into the Financial Statement Audit. IAASB, www.ifac.org/system/files/uploads/IAASB/Auditor-Reporting-Fact-Sheet.pdf

16 https://www.frc.org.uk/getattachment/76641d68-c739-45ac-a251-cabbfd2397e0/Report-on-the-Second-Year-Experience-of-Extended-Auditors-Reports-Jan-2016.pdf

17 A. Cornford, 'Enron and internationally agreed principles for corporate governance and the financial sector', G-24 Discussion Paper Series, United Nations.

18 ISA 200, *Overall Objectives of the Independent Auditor and the Conduct of an Audit in Accordance with International Standards on Auditing,* paragraph 13(l).

19 www.frc.org.uk/Our-Work/Publications/Audit-Quality-Review/Audit-Quality-Inspection-Report-May-2016-BDO-LLP.pdf

20 www.sec.gov/litigation/admin/3438494.txt

21 https://www.ifiar.org

22 A.R. Wyatt (2003), 'Accounting professionalism – they just don't get it!', http://aaahq.orgAM2003/WyattSpeech.pdf

23 http://lehmanreport.jenner.com/

24 www.bis.gov.uk/news/speeches/vince-cable-executive-pay-remuneration-2012

25 The Large and Medium-sized Companies and Groups (Accounts and Reports) (Amendment) Regulations 2013 www.legislation.gov.uk/uksi/2013/1981/schedule/made

26 www.kingfisher.com/files/pdf/directors_remuneration_report_2016.pdf

27 L. Bebchuk, M. Cremers and U. Peyer, 'Higher CEO salaries don't always pay off', *The Australian Financial Review,* 12 February 2010, p. 59.

28 http://highpaycentre.org/files/7571_CEO_pay_in_the_FTSE100_report_%28FINAL%29.pdf

29 www.europarl.europa.eu/sides/getDoc.do?pubRef=|minus|//EP//TEXT+TA+P8-TA-2015-0257+0+DOC+XML+V0//EN

30 http://www.imiplc.com/~/media/Files/I/IMI/annual-reports/imi-ara-2017.pdf

31 www.ivis.co.uk/guidelines

32 www.napf.co.uk/PolicyandResearch/DocumentLibrary/~/media/Policy/Documents/0351_3_remuneration_principles_for_building_and_reinforcing%20_longterm_business_success_nov2013.pdf

33 www.ecgi.org

34 M. Gold, 'Corporate governance reform in Australia: the intersection of investment fiduciaries and issuers', in P. Ali and G. Gregoriou (eds), *International Corporate Governance after Sarbanes–Oxley,* John Wiley and Sons, New York, 2006.

35 https://www.frc.org.uk/directors/corporate-governance-and-stewardship/uk-corporate-governance-code

36 E. Fama, 'Agency problems and the theory of the firms', *Journal of Political Economy,* vol. 88, 1980, pp. 288–307.

37 E. Fama and M. Jensen, 'Separation of ownership and control', *Journal of Law and Economics,* vol. 26, 1983, pp. 301–325.

38 www.bupa.com/investor-relations/our-status-and-governance/our-corporate-governance/role-of-the-sid

39 www.guardian.co.uk/business/2009/feb/01/ftse-royal-bank-scotland-group

40 A. Abdullah and M. Page, *Corporate Governance and Corporate Performance: UK FTSE 350 Companies,* The Institute of Chartered Accountants of Scotland, Edinburgh, 2009.

41 ABI Research, *Corporate Governance 'Pays' for Shareholders and Company Performance,* ABI, 27 February 2008, Ref: 12/08.

42 https://www.ons.gov.uk/economy/investmentspensionsandtrusts/bulletins/ownershipofukquotedshares/2016

43 G. Igor Filatochev, H.G. Jackson and D. Allcock, *Key Drivers to Good Corporate Governance and Appropriateness of UK Policy Responses,* DTI, 2007, www.berr.gov.uk/files/file36671.pdf

44 www/frc.org.uk/Our-Work/Codes-Standards/Corporate-governance/UK-Corporate-Governance-Code.aspx

45 www.bis.gov.uk/assets/biscore/business-law/docs/k/12-917-kay-review-of-equity-markets-final-report.pdf

46 file:///C:/Users/Barry/Downloads/20131203-cewginvestorforum%20(1).pdf

47 https://www.financialdirector.co.uk/2017/09/21/will-new-employee-corporate-governance-reforms-affect/

48 http://europa.eu/rapid/press-release_STATEMENT-14-104_en.htm

49 https://www.wsj.com/articles/judge-says-pricewaterhousecoopers-was-negligent-in-colonial-bank-failure-1514762610

50 https://www.justice.gov/. . . /deloitte-touche-agrees-pay-1495-million-settle-claims-arisin. . .

51 K. Peasnell, P. Pope and S. Young, 'A new model board', *Accountancy*, July 1998, p. 115.

52 'PwC and E&Y in favour of rules to restrict services', *Accountancy*, October 2000, p. 7.

53 https://www.cfainstitute.org/learning/future/Documents/ESG_Survey_Report_July_2017.pdf

CHAPTER 12

Accounting for price-level changes

12.1 Introduction

The main purpose of this chapter is to explain the impact of inflation on profit and capital measurement and the concepts that have been proposed to incorporate the effect into financial reports by adjusting the historical cost data. The chapter gives further detail to support the concepts introduced in Chapter 10 dealing with Conceptual Framework 2018 (Concepts of Capital and Capital Maintenance). These concepts are periodically discussed but there is no general support for any specific concept among practitioners in the field.

Objectives

By the end of the chapter, you should be able to:

- describe the problems of historical cost accounting (HCA);
- explain the approach taken in each of the price-level changing models;
- prepare financial statements applying each model (HCA, CPP, CCA, NRVA);
- critically comment on each model (HCA, CPP, CCA, NRVA);
- describe the approach being taken by standard setters and future developments.

12.2 Review of the problems of historical cost accounting (HCA)

The transaction-based historical cost concept was unchallenged in the UK until price levels started to hedge upwards at an ever-increasing pace during the 1950s and reached an annual rate of increase of 20% in the mid-1970s. The historical cost base for financial reporting witnessed growing criticism. The inherent faults of the system were discussed in Chapter 9, but inflation exacerbates the problem in the following ways:

- Profit is overstated when inflationary changes in the value of assets are ignored.
- Comparability of business entities, which is so necessary in the assessment of performance and growth, becomes distorted when assets are acquired at different times.
- The decision-making process, the formulation of plans and the setting of targets may be suboptimal if financial base data are out of date.
- Financial reports become confusing at best, misleading at worst, because revenue is mismatched with differing historical cost levels as the monetary unit becomes unstable.
- Unrealised profits arising in individual accounting periods are increased as a result of inflation.

In order to combat these serious defects, current value accounting became the subject of research and controversy as to the most appropriate method to use for financial reporting.

12.3 Inflation accounting

A number of versions of current value accounting (CVA) were eventually identified, but the current value postulate was said to suffer from the following disadvantages:

- It destroys the factual nature of HCA, which is transaction-based: the factual characteristic is to all intents and purposes lost as transaction-based historic values are replaced by judgemental values.
- It is not as objective as HCA because it is less verifiable from auditable documentation.
- It entails recognition of unrealised profit, a practice that is anathema to the traditionalist.
- The claimed improvement in comparability between commercial entities is a myth because of the degree of subjectivity in measuring current value by each.
- The lack of a single accepted method of computing current values compounds the subjectivity aspect. One fault-laden system is being usurped by another that is also faulty.

In spite of these criticisms, the search for a system of financial reporting devoid of the defects of HCA and capable of coping with inflation has produced a number of CVA models.

12.4 The concepts in principle

Several current income and value models have been proposed to replace or operate in tandem with the historical cost convention. However, in terms of basic characteristics, they may be reduced to the following three models:

- current purchasing power (CPP) or general purchasing power (GPP);
- current entry cost or replacement cost (RC);
- current exit cost or net realisable value (NRV).

We discuss each of these models below.

12.4.1 Current purchasing power accounting (CPPA)

The CPP model measures income and value by adopting a price index system. Movements in price levels are gauged by reference to price changes in a group of goods and services in **general** use within the economy. The aggregate price value of this **basket** of commodities-cum-services is determined at a base point in time and indexed as 100. Subsequent changes in price are compared on a regular basis with this base period price and the change recorded. For example, the price level of our chosen range of goods and services may amount to £76 on 31 March 20X1, and show changes as follows:

£76	at 31 March 20X1
£79	at 30 April 20X1
£81	at 31 May 20X1
£84	at 30 June 20X1

and so on.

The change in price may be indexed with 31 March as the base:

20X1	Calculation	Index
31 March	i.e. £76	100
30 April	i.e. $\dfrac{79}{76} \times 100$	103.9
31 May	i.e. $\dfrac{80}{76} \times 100$	106.6
30 June	i.e. $\dfrac{84}{76} \times 100$	110.5

In the UK, index systems similar in construction to this are known as the Retail or Consumer Price Index (RPI). The index is a barometer of fluctuating price levels covering a miscellany of goods and services as used by the average household. Thus it is a **general** price index. It is amended from time to time to take account of new commodities entering the consumer's range of choice and needs. As a model, it is unique owing to the introduction of the concept of gains and losses in **purchasing power.**

12.4.2 Current entry or replacement cost accounting (RCA)

The replacement cost (RC) model assesses income and value by reference to entry costs or current replacement costs of materials and other assets utilised within the business entity. The valuation attempts to replace like with like and thus takes account of the quality and condition of the existing assets. A motor vehicle, for instance, may have been purchased brand new for £25,000 with an expected life of five years, an anticipated residual value of nil and a straight-line depreciation policy. Its HCA carrying value in the statement of financial position at the end of its first year would be £25,000 less £5,000 = £20,000. However, if a similar new replacement vehicle cost £30,000 at the end of year 1, then its gross RC would be £30,000; depreciation for one year based on this sum would be £6,000 and the net RC would be £24,000. The increase of £4,000 is a holding gain and the vehicle with an HCA carrying value of £20,000 would be revalued at £24,000.

12.4.3 Current exit cost or net realisable value accounting (NRVA)

The net realisable value (NRV) model is based on the economist's concept of opportunity cost. It is a model that has had strong academic support, most notably in Australia from Professor Ray Chambers who referred to this approach as Continuous Contemporary Accounting (CoCoA). If an asset cost £25,000 at the beginning of year 1 and at the end of that year it had an NRV of £21,000 after meeting selling expenses, it would be carried in the NRV statement of financial position at £21,000. This amount represents the cash forgone by holding the asset, i.e. the opportunity of possessing cash of £21,000 has been sacrificed in favour of the asset. There is effectively a holding loss for the year of £25,000 less £21,000 = £4,000.

12.5 The four models illustrated for a company with cash purchases and sales

We will illustrate the effect on the profit and net assets of Entrepreneur Ltd.

Entrepreneur Ltd commenced business on 1 January 20X1 with a capital of £3,000 to buy and sell second-hand computers. The company purchased six computers on 1 January 20X1 for £500 each and sold three of the computers on 15 January for £900 each.

The following data are available for January 20X1:

	Retail Price Index	Replacement cost per computer £	Net realisable value £
1 January	100		
15 January	112	610	
31 January	130	700	900

The statements of income and financial position are set out in Figure 12.1 with the detailed workings in Figure 12.2.

12.5.1 Financial capital maintenance concept

HCA and CPP are both transaction-based models that apply the financial capital maintenance concept. This means that profit is the difference between the opening and closing net assets (expressed in HC £) or the opening and closing net assets (expressed in HC £ indexed for RPI changes) adjusted for any capital introduced or withdrawn during the month.

Figure 12.1 Trading account for the month ended 31 January 20X1

Statements of income for the month ended 31 January 20X1	HCA		CPP		RCA		NRVA	
	£		CPP£		£		£	
Sales	2,700	W1	3,134	W5	2,700	W1	2,700	W1
Opening inventory	—		—		—		—	
Purchases	3,000	W2	3,900	W6	3,000	W2	3,000	W2
Closing inventory	(1,500)	W3	(1,950)	W7	(1,500)	W3	(1,500)	W3
COSA	na		na		330	W10	na	
Cost of sales	1,500		1,950		1,830		1,500	
Holding gain	na		na		na		1,200	W15
Profit	1,200		1,184		870		2,400	

Statement of financial position as at 31 January 20X1	£		PCP£		£		£	
Current assets								
Inventory	1,500	W3	1,950	W7	2,100	W11	2,700	W14
Cash	2,700	W4	2,700		2,700		2,700	
Capital employed	4,200		4,650		4,800		5,400	
Capital	3,000		3,900	W8	3,000		3,000	
Holding gains								
On inventory consumed	na		na		330	W12		
On inventory in hand	na		na		600	W13		
Profit	1,200		1,184		870		2,400	
Loss on monetary items	na		(434)	W9	na		na	
	4,200		4,650		4,800		5,400	

na = not applicable

Figure 12.2 Workings (W)

HCA

W1 Sales	$3 \times £900 = £2,700$	
W2 Purchases	$6 \times £500 = £3,000$	
W3 Closing inventory	$3 \times £500 = £1,500$	
W4 Cash	1 January 20X1 Capital	3,000
	1 January 20X1 Purchases	(3,000)
	1 January 20X1 Balance	nil
	15 January 20X1 Sales	
	$3 \times £900 =$	£2,700
	31 January 20X1 Balance	£2,700

CPP

		CPP£
W5 Sales	$£2,700 \times 130/112 =$	3,134
W6 Purchases	$£3,000 \times 130/100 =$	3,900
W7 Closing inventory	$£1,500 \times 130/100 =$	1,950
W8 Capital	$£3,000 \times 130/100 =$	3,900

W9   Balance of cash was nil until 15 January when sales generated £2,700. This sum was held until 31 January during which period cash, a monetary item, lost purchasing power. The loss of purchasing power is measured by applying the general index to the cash held: $£2,700 \times 130/112 - £2,700 = $ CPP £434

RCA

W8   Additional replacement cost of inventory consumed as at the date of sale is measured as a cost of sales adjustment (COSA). COSA is calculated as follows:

	$3 \times £610 =$	1,830
Less:	$3 \times £500 =$	1,500
COSA		£330

W11   Closing inventory: $3 \times £700 = £2,100$

W12   Holding gains on inventory consumed: as for W10 $= £330$

W13	Inventory at replacement cost	$= 3 \times £700 = 2,100$
	Less: inventory at cost	$= 3 \times £500 = 1,500$
	Holding gains on closing inventory	£600

NRVA

W14   Closing inventory at net realisable value $= 900 \times 3 = £2,700$

W15	$3 \times £900 =$	2,700
	$3 \times £500 =$	1,500
	Holding gain	£1,200

CPP adjustments

- All historical cost values are adjusted to a common index level for the month. In theory this can be the index applicable to any day of the financial period concerned. However, in practice it has been deemed preferable to use the last day of the period; thus the financial statements show the latest price level appertaining to the period.

- The application of a general price index as an adjusting factor results in the creation of an **alien** currency of **purchasing power,** which is used in place of sterling. Note, particularly, the impact on the entity's sales and capital compared with the other models. **Actual** sales shown on **invoices** will still read £2,700.

- Note the application of the concept of gain or loss on holding monetary items. In this example there is a monetary loss of CPP £434 as shown in Working 9 in Figure 12.2.

12.5.2 Operating capital maintenance concept

Under this concept capital is only maintained if sufficient income is retained to maintain the business entity's physical operating capacity, i.e. its ability to produce the existing level of goods or services. Profit is, therefore, the residual after increasing the cost of sales to the cost applicable at the date of sale.

- Basically, only two adjustments are involved: the additional replacement cost of inventory consumed and holding gains on closing inventories. However, in a comprehensive exercise an adjustment will be necessary regarding non-current assets and you will also encounter a gearing adjustment.

- Notice the concept of holding gains. This model introduces, in effect, unrealised profits in respect of closing inventories. The holding gain concerning inventory consumed at the time of sale has been realised and deducted from what would have been a profit of £1,200. The statement discloses profits of £870.

12.5.3 Capacity to adapt concept under the NRVA model

The HCA, CPP and RCA models have assumed that the business will continue as a going concern and only distribute realised profits after retaining sufficient profits to maintain either the financial or operating capital.

The NRVA concept is that a business has the capacity to realise its net assets at the end of each financial period and reinvest the proceeds and that the NRV accounts provide management with this information.

- This produces the same initial profit as HCA, namely £1,200, but a peculiarity of this system is that this realised profit is supplemented by **unrealised** profit generated by holding stocks. Under RCA accounting, such gains are shown in a separate account and are not treated as part of real income.

- This simple exercise has ignored the possibility of investment in non-current assets, thus depreciation is not involved. A reduction in the NRV of non-current assets at the end of a period compared with the beginning would be treated in a similar fashion to depreciation by being charged to the revenue account, and consequently profits would be reduced. An increase in the NRV of such assets would be included as part of the profit.

12.5.4 The four models compared

Dividend distribution

We can see from Figure 12.1 that if the business were to distribute the profit reported under HCA, CPP or NRVA the physical operating capacity of the business would be reduced and it would be paying dividends out of capital:

	HCA	*CPP*	*RCA*	*NRVA*
Realised profit	1,200	1,184	870	1,200
Unrealised profit	—	—	—	1,200
Profit for month	1,200	1,184	870	2,400

Shareholder orientation

The CPP model is shareholder-oriented in that it shows whether shareholders' funds are keeping pace with inflation by maintaining their purchasing power. Only CPP changes the value of the share capital.

Management orientation

The RCA model is management-oriented in that it identifies holding gains which represent the amounts required to be retained in order to simply maintain the operating capital.

RCA measures the impact of inflation on the individual firm, in terms of the change in price levels of its **raw materials and assets,** i.e. inflation peculiar to the company, whereas CPP measures general inflation in the economy as a whole. CPP may be meaningless in the case of an individual company. Consider a firm that carries a constant volume of stock valued at £100 in HCA terms. Now suppose that price levels double when measured by a general price index (GPI), so that its inventory is restated to £200 in a CPP system. If, however, the cost of that **particular** inventory has risen by 500%, then under the RCA model the value of the stock should be £500.

In the mid-1970s, when the accountancy profession was debating the problem of changing price-level measurement, the general price level had climbed by some 23% over a period during which petroleum-based products had risen by 500%.

12.6 Critique of each model

A critique of the various models may be formulated in terms of their characteristics and peculiarities as virtues and defects in application.

12.6.1 HCA

This model's virtues and defects have been discussed in Chapter 9 and earlier in this chapter.

12.6.2 CPP

Virtues

- It is an **objective measure** since it is still transaction-based, as with HCA, and the possibility of subjectivity is constrained if a GPI is used that has been constructed by a central agency such as a government department. This applies in the UK, where the Retail Price Index is currently published by the Office for National Statistics.

- It is a **measure of shareholders' capital** and that capital's maintenance in terms of purchasing power units. Profit is the residual value after maintaining the money value of capital funds, taking account of changing price levels. Thus it is a measure readily understood by the shareholder/user of the accounts. It can prevent payment of a dividend out of real capital as measured by GPPA.

- It **introduces the concept of monetary items** as distinct from non-monetary items and the attendant concepts of gains and losses in holding net monetary liabilities compared with holding net monetary assets. Such gains and losses are experienced on a disturbing scale in times of inflation. They are **real** gains and losses. The **basic RCA** and NRV models do not recognise such 'surpluses' and 'deficits'.

Defects

- It is **HCA-based but adjusted** to reflect general price movements. Thus it possesses the characteristics of HCA, good and bad, but with its values updated in the light of an arithmetic measure of general price changes. The major defect of becoming out of date is mitigated to a degree, but the impact of inflation on the entity's income and capital may be at variance with the rate of inflation affecting the economy in general.

- It may be **wrongly assumed that the CPP statement of financial position is a current value statement.** It is not a current value document because of the defects discussed above; in particular, asset values may be subject to a different rate of inflation than that reflected by the GPI.

- It **creates an alien unit of measurement** still labelled by the £ sign. Thus we have the HCA £ and the CPP £. They are different pounds: one is the *bona fide* pound, the other is a synthetic unit. This may not be fully appreciated or understood by the user when faced with the financial accounts for the recent accounting period.

- Its **concept of profit is dangerous.** It pretends to cater for changing prices, but at the same time it fails to provide for the additional costs of replacing stocks sold or additional depreciation due to the escalating replacement cost of assets. The inflation encountered by the business entity will not be the same as that encountered by the whole economy. Thus the maintenance of the CPP of shareholders' capital via this concept of profit is not the maintenance of the entity's operating capital in physical terms, i.e. its capacity to produce the same volume of goods and services. The use of CPP profit as a basis for decision making without regard to RCA profit can have disastrous consequences.

12.6.3 RCA

Virtues

- Its **unit of measurement** is the monetary unit and consequently it is understood and accepted by the user of accountancy reports. In contrast, the CPP system employs an artificial unit based on arithmetic relationships, which is different and thus unfamiliar.

- It **identifies and isolates holding gains** from operating income. Thus it can prevent the inadvertent distribution of dividends in excess of operating profit. It satisfies the prudence criterion of the traditional accountant and **maintains the physical operating capacity** of the entity.

- It introduces **realistic current values** of assets in the statement of financial position, thus making the statement of financial position a 'value' statement and consequently more meaningful to the user. This contrasts sharply with the statement of financial position as a list of unallocated carrying costs in the HCA system.

Defects

- It is a **subjective measure,** in that replacement costs are often necessarily based on estimates or assessments. It does not possess the factual characteristics of HCA. It is open to manipulation within constraints. Often it is based on index numbers which themselves may be based on a compound of prices of a mixture of similar commodities used as raw material or operating assets. This subjectivity is exacerbated in circumstances where rapid technological advance and innovation are involved in the potential new replacement asset, e.g. computers and printers.

- It **assumes replacement of assets** by being based on their replacement cost. Difficulties arise if such assets are not to be replaced by similar assets. Presumably, it will then be assumed that a replacement of equivalent value to the original will be deployed, however differently, as capital within the firm.

12.6.4 NRVA

Virtues

- It is a concept readily understood by the user. The value of any item invariably has two measures – a buying price and a selling price – and the twain do not usually meet. However, when considering the value of an **existing** possession, the owner instinctively considers its 'value' to be that in potential sale, i.e. NRV.

- It **avoids the need to estimate depreciation** and, in consequence, the attendant problems of assessing lifespan and residual values. Depreciation is treated as the arithmetic difference between the NRV at the end of a financial period and the NRV at its beginning.

- It is **based on opportunity cost** and so can be said to be more meaningful. It is the **sacrificial** cost of possessing an asset, which, it can be argued, is more authentic in terms of being a true or real cost. If the asset were not possessed, its cash equivalent would exist instead and that cash would be deployed in other opportunities. Therefore, NRV = cash = opportunity = cost.

Defects

- It is a **subjective measure** and in this respect it possesses the same major fault as RCA. It can be said to be less prudent than RCA because NRV will tend to be higher in some cases than RCA. For example, when valuing finished inventories, a profit content will be involved.

- **It is not a realistic measure** as most assets, except finished goods, are possessed in order to be utilised, not sold. Therefore, NRV is irrelevant.

- **It is not always determinable.** The assets concerned may be highly specialist and there may be no ready market by which a value can be easily assessed. Consequently, any particular value may be fictitious or erroneous, containing too high a holding gain or, indeed, too low a holding loss.

- **It violates the concept of the going concern,** which demands that the accounts are drafted on the basis that there is no intention to liquidate the entity. Admittedly, this concept was formulated with HCA in view, but the acceptance of NRV implies the possibility of a cessation of trading.

- It is less reliable and verifiable than HC.

- The statement of comprehensive income will report a more volatile profit if changes in NRV are taken to the statement of comprehensive income each year.

- The profit arising from the changes in NRV may not have been realised.

12.7 Operating capital maintenance – a comprehensive example

In Figure 12.1 we considered the effect of inflation on a cash business without fixed assets, credit customers or credit suppliers. In the following example, Economica plc, we now consider the effect where there are non-current assets and credit transactions.

The HCA statements of financial position as at 31 December 20X4 and 20X5 are set out in Figure 12.3 and index numbers required to restate the non-current assets, inventory and monetary items in Figure 12.4.

12.7.1 Restating the opening statement of financial position to current cost

The non-current assets and inventory are restated to their current cost as at the date of the opening statement as shown in W1 and W2 below. The increase from HC to CC represents an unrealised holding gain which is debited to the asset account and credited to a reserve account called a current cost reserve, as in W3 below.

Figure 12.3 Economica plc HCA statement of financial position

		20X5		20X4
Statements of financial position as at 31 December on the basis of HCA				
	£000	£000	£000	£000
Non-current assets				
Cost	85,000		85,000	
Depreciation	34,000		25,500	
		51,000		59,500
Current assets				
Inventory	25,500		17,000	
Trade receivables	34,000		23,375	
Cash and bank	17,000		11,875	
	76,500		42,250	
Current liabilities:				
Trade payables	25,500		17,500	
Income tax	8,500		4,250	
Dividend declared	5,000		4,000	
	39,000		25,250	
Net current assets	37,500		17,000	
Less: 8% debentures	11,000		11,000	
		26,500		6,000
		77,500		65,500
Share capital and reserves:				
Authorised and issued £1 ordinary shares		50,000		50,000
Share premium		1,500		1,500
Retained earnings		26,000		14,000
		77,500		65,500

Figure 12.4 Index data relating to Economica plc

1	Index numbers as prepared by the Office for National Statistics for non-current assets

1 January 20X2	100
1 January 20X5	165
1 January 20X6	185
Average for 20X4	147
Average for 20X5	167

2   All non-current assets were acquired on 1 January 20X2. There were no further acquisitions or disposals during the four years ended 31 December 20X5

3   Indices as prepared by the Office for National Statistics for inventories and monetary working capital adjusments were:

1 October 20X4	115
31 December 20X4	125
15 November 20X4	120
1 October 20X5	140
31 December 20X5	150
15 November 20X5	145
Average for 20X5	137.5

4   Three months' inventory is carried.

5   Depreciation: historical cost based on 10% p.a. straight-line with a residual value of nil:

	£ HCA
20X4	8,500,000
20X5	8,500,000

The calculations are as follows. First we shall convert the HCA statement of financial position in Figure 12.3, as at 31 December 20X4, to the CCA basis, using the index data in Figure 12.4.

The **non-monetary items,** comprising the non-current assets and inventory, are converted and the converted amounts are taken to the CC statement and the increases taken to the current cost reserve, as follows.

(W1) Property, plant and equipment

	HCA £000		Index		CCA £000	Increase £000
Cost	85,000	×	$\dfrac{165}{100}$	=	140,250	55,250
Depreciation	25,500	×	$\dfrac{165}{100}$	=	42,075	16,575
	59,500				98,175	38,675

The CCA valuation at 31 December 20X4 shows a net increase in terms of numbers of pounds sterling of £38,675,000. The £59,500,000 in the HCA statement of financial position will be replaced in the CCA statement by £98,175,000.

(W2) Inventories

HCA £000		Index		CCA £000		Increase £000
17,000	×	$\dfrac{125}{120}$	=	17,708	=	708

Note that Figure 12.4 specifies that three months' inventories are held. Thus on average they will have been purchased on 15 November 20X4, on the assumption that they have been acquired and consumed evenly throughout the calendar period. Hence, the index at the time of purchase would have been 120. The £17,000,000 in the HCA statement of financial position will be replaced in the CCA statement of financial position by £17,708,000.

(W3) Current cost reserve

The total increase in CCA carrying values for non-monetary items is £39,383,000, which will be credited to CC reserves in the CC statement. It comprises £38,675,000 on the non-current assets and £708,000 on the inventory.

Note that monetary items do not change by virtue of inflation. Purchasing power will be lost or gained, but the carrying values in the CCA statement will be identical to those in its HCA counterpart. We can now compile the CCA statement as at 31 December 20X4 – this will show net assets of £104,883,000.

12.7.2 Adjustments that affect the profit for the year

The statement of comprehensive income for the year ended 31 December 20X5 set out in Figure 12.5 discloses a profit before interest and tax of £26,350,000. We need to deduct realised holding gains from this profit to avoid the distribution of dividends that would reduce the operating capital. These deductions are a cost of sales adjustment (COSA), a depreciation adjustment (DA) and a monetary working capital adjustment (MWCA). The accounting treatment is to debit the statement of comprehensive income and credit the current cost reserve.

The adjustments are calculated as follows.

(W4) Cost of sales adjustment (COSA) using the average method

We will compute the cost of sales adjustment by using the average method. The average purchase price index for 20X5 is 137.5. If price increases have moved at an even pace throughout the period, this implies that consumption occurred, on average, at 30 June, the mid-point of the financial year.

	HCA £000		Adjustment		CCA £000		Difference £000
Opening inventory	17,000	×	$\dfrac{137.5}{120}$	=	19,479	=	2,479
Purchases	—		—		—		—
	17,000				19,479		
Closing inventory	(25,500)	×	$\dfrac{137.5}{145}$	=	24,181	=	1,319
	(8,500)				(4,702)		3,798

Figure 12.5 Economica plc HCA statement of comprehensive income

Statement of income for the year ended 31 December 20X5, on the basis of HCA

	20X5 £000		20X4 £000
Turnover	42,500		38,250
Less: Cost of sales	(12,070)		(23,025)
Gross profit	30,430		15,225
Less: Distribution costs	2,460	2,210	
Less: Administrative expenses	1,620	1,540	
	(4,080)		(3,750)
Profit before interest and tax	26,350		11,475
Interest	(880)		(880)
Profit before tax	25,470		10,595
Income tax expense	(8,470)		(4,250)
Profit after tax	17,000		6,345
Dividend	(5,000)		(4,000)
Retentions	12,000		2,345
Balance b/f	14,000		11,655
Balance b/f	26,000		14,000
EPS	34p		13p

The impact of price changes on the cost of sales would be an increase of £3,798,000, causing a profit decrease of like amount and a current cost reserve increase of like amount.

(W5) Depreciation adjustment: average method

As assets are consumed throughout the year, the CCA depreciation charge should be based on average current costs.

	HCA £000	Adjustment		CCA £000		Difference £000
Depreciation	8,500	$\times$	$\dfrac{167}{100}$ =	14,195	=	5,695

(W6) Monetary working capital adjustment (MWCA)

The objective is to transfer from the statement of comprehensive income to CC reserve the amount by which the need for monetary working capital (MWC) has increased due to rising price levels. The change in MWC from one statement of financial position to the next will be the consequence of a combination of changes in volume and escalating price movements. Volume change may be segregated from the price change by using an average index.

	20X5	20X4		Change
	£000	*£000*		*£000*
Trade receivables	34,000	23,375		
Trade payables	25,500	17,000		
MWC	8,500	6,375	Overall change =	2,125

The MWC is now adjusted by the average index for the year. This adjustment will reveal the change in volume.

$$\left(8,500 \times \frac{137.5}{150}\right) - \left(6,375 \times \frac{137.5}{125}\right)$$

= 7,792 − 7,012		= Volume change	780
So price change =			1,345

The profit before interest and tax will be reduced as follows:

	£000	*£000*
Profit before interest and tax		26,350
Less:		
COSA (from W4)	(3,798)	
DA (from W5)	(5,695)	
MWCA (from W6)	(1,345)	
Current cost operating adjustments		(10,838)
Current cost operating profit		15,512

The adjustments will be credited to the current cost reserve.

12.7.3 Unrealised holding gains on non-monetary assets as at 31 December 20X5

The holding gains as at 31 December 20X4 were calculated in Section 12.7.1 above for non-current assets and inventory. A similar calculation is required to restate these at 20X5 current costs for the closing statement of financial position. The calculations are as in Working 7 below.

(W7) Non-monetary assets

(i)   Holding gain on non-current assets

	£000
Revaluation at year-end	
Non-current assets at 1 January 20X5 (as W1) at CCA revaluation	140,250
CCA value at 31 December 20X5 = $140,250 \times \dfrac{185}{165}$ =	157,250
Revaluation holding gain for 20X5 to CC reserve in W8	17,000

This holding gain of £17,000,000 is transferred to CC reserves.

(ii) Backlog depreciation on non-current assets

	£,000
CCA aggregate depreciation at 31 December 20X5 for CC statement of financial position	
$= \text{HCA } £34,000,000 \times \dfrac{185}{100}$ in CC **Statement of financial position**	**62,900**
Less: CCA aggregate depreciation at 1 January 20X5 (as per W1 and statement of financial position at 1 January 20X5)	42,075
Being CCA depreciation as revealed between opening and closing statements of financial position	20,825
But CCA depreciation charged in revenue accounts (i.e. £8,500,000 in £HCA plus additional depreciation of £5,695,000 per W5) =	14,195
So total backlog depreciation to CC reserve in W8	6,630

	£000
The CCA value of non-current assets at 31 December 20X5:	
Gross CCA value (above)	157,250
Depreciation (above)	62,900
Net CCA carrying value in the CC statement of financial position in W8	94,350

This £6,630,000 is backlog depreciation for 20X5. Total backlog depreciation is not expensed (i.e. charged to revenue account) as an adjustment of HCA profit, but is charged against CCA reserves. The net effect is that the CC reserve will increase by £10,370,000, i.e. £17,000,000 − £6,630,000.

(iii) Inventory valuation at year-end

CCA valuation at 31 December 20X5		CCA £,000
HCA £,000	*CCA £,000*	
= 25,500 × 150/145 = 26,379 = increase of		879
CCA valuation at 1 January 20X5 (per W2)		
= 17,000 × 125/120 = 17,708 = increase of		708
Inventory holding gain occurring during 20X5 to W8		171

12.7.4 Current cost statement of financial position as at 31 December 20X5

The current cost statement as at 31 December 20X5 now discloses non-current assets and inventory adjusted by index to their current cost and the retained profits reduced by the current cost operating adjustments. It appears as in Working 8 below.

(W8) Economica plc: CCA statement of financial position as at 31 December 20X5

		20X5			20X4
Non-current assets	£000	£000		£000	£000
Cost	157,250 (W7(i))			140,250 (W1)	
Depreciation	62,900 (W7(ii))			42,075 (W1)	
		94,350 (W7(ii))			98,175
Current assets					
Inventory	26,379 (W7(iii))			17,708 (W2)	
Trade receivables	34,000			23,375	
Cash	17,000			1,875	
	77,379			42,958	
Current liabilities					
Trade payables	25,500			17,000	
Income tax	8,500			4,250	
Dividend declared	5,000			4,000	
	39,000			25,250	
Net current assets	38,379			17,708	
Less: 8% debentures	11,000			11,000	
		27,379			6,708
		121,729			104,883
Financed by					
Share capital: authorised and issued £1 shares		50,000			50,000
Share premium		1,500			1,500
CC reserve (Note 1)		55,067			39,383
Retained profit (Note 2)		15,162			14,000
Shareholders' funds		121,729			104,883

Note 1: CC reserve	£000	£000	
Opening balance		39,383 (W3)	
Holding gains			
Non-current assets	17,000 (W7(i))		
Inventory	171 (W7(iii))		
		17,171	
COSA	3,798 (W4)		
MWCA	1,345 (W6)		
Less: backlog depreciation	(6,630) (W7(ii))	(1,487)	
		55,067	

Note 2: Retained profit			
Opening balance		14,000 (Figure 12.5)	
HCA profit for 20X5	12,000		
COSA	(3,798) (W4)		
Extra depreciation	(5,695) (W5)		
MWCA	(1,345) (W6)		
		1,162	
CCA profit for 20X5		15,162	

12.7.5 How to take the level of borrowings into account

We have assumed that the company will need to retain £10,838,000 from the current year's earnings in order to maintain the physical operating capacity of the company. However, if the business is part financed by borrowings then part of the amount required may be assumed to come from the lenders. One of the methods advocated is to make a gearing adjustment. The gearing adjustment that we illustrate here has the effect of reducing the impact of the adjustments on the profit after interest, i.e. it is based on the realised holding gains only.

The gearing adjustment will change the carrying figures of CC reserves and retained profit, but not the shareholders' funds, as the adjustment is compensating. The gearing adjustment cannot be computed before the determination of the shareholders' interest because that figure is necessary in order to complete the gearing calculation.

(W9) Gearing adjustment

The CC operating profit of the business is quantified after making such retentions from the historical profit as are required in order to maintain the physical operating capacity of the entity. However, from a shareholder standpoint, there is no need to maintain in real terms the portion of the entity financed by loans that are fixed in monetary values. Thus, in calculating profit attributable to shareholders, that part of the CC adjustments relating to the proportion of the business financed by loans can be deducted:

$$\text{Gearing adjustment} = \frac{\text{Average net borrowing for year}}{\text{Average net borrowing for year} + \text{Average shareholders' funds for year}} \times \text{Aggregate adjustments}$$

This formula is usually expressed as $\frac{L}{(L + S)} \times A$ where L = loans (i.e. net borrowings); S = shareholders' interest or funds; and A = adjustments (i.e. extra depreciation + COSA + MWCA). Note that L/(L + S) is often expressed as a percentage of A (see example below where it is 6.31%).

Net borrowings

This is the sum of all liabilities less current assets, excluding items included in MWC or utilised in computing COSA. In this instance it is as follows.

Note: in some circumstances (e.g. new issue of debentures occurring during the year) a weighted average will be used.

	Closing balance £000	Opening balance £000
Debentures	11,000	11,000
Income tax	8,500	4,250
Cash	(17,000)	(1,875)
Total net borrowings, the average of which equals L	2,500	13,375

$$\text{Average net borrowings} = \frac{2,500,00 + 13,375,000}{2} = £7,937,500$$

Net borrowings plus shareholders' funds

Shareholders' funds in CC £ (inclusive of proposed dividends)	126,729	108,883
Add: net borrowings	2,500	13,375
	129,229	122,258

Or, alternatively:

	£000	£000
Non-current assets	94,350	98,175
Inventory	26,379	17,708
MWC	8,500	6,375
	129,229	122,258

$$\text{Average } L + S = \frac{129,229,000 + 122,258,000}{2} = 125,743,500$$

$$\text{So gearing} = \frac{L}{L+S} \times A = \frac{7,937,500}{125,743,500} \times \frac{(\text{COSA} + \text{MWCA} + \text{extra depreciat}}{(3,798,000 + 1,345,000 + 5,695,000)}$$

$$= 6.31\% \text{ of } £10,838,000 = £683,877, \text{ say } £684,000$$

Thus the CC adjustment of £10,838,000 charged against historical profit may be reduced by £684,000 due to a gain being derived from net borrowings during a period of inflation as shown in Figure 12.6. The £684,000 is shown as a deduction from interest payable.

Figure 12.6 Economica plc CCA statement of income

Economica plc CCA statement of comprehensive income for year ended 31 December 20X5
(i.e. under the operating capital maintenance concept)

		£000
Turnover		42,500
Cost of sales		(12,070
Gross profit		**30,430**
Distribution costs		(2,460)
Administrative expenses		(1,620)
Historical cost operating profit		26.350
Current cost operating adjustments (from Section 7.7.2 above)		**(10.838)**
Current cost operating profit		15,512
Interest payable	(880)	
Gearing adjustment	**684**	(196)
Current profit on ordinary activities before taxation		15,316
Tax on profit on ordinary activities		(8,470)
Current cost profit for the financial year		6,846
Dividends declared		(5,000)
Current cost profit retained		1,846
EPS		13.7p

12.7.6 The closing current cost statement of financial position

The closing statement with the non-current assets and inventory restated at current cost and the retained profit adjusted for current cost operating adjustments as reduced by the gearing adjustment is set out in Figure 12.7.

Figure 12.7 Economica plc CCA statement of financial position

		Economica plc CCA statement of financial position as at 31 December 20X5		
20X4			*20X5*	
£000	*£000*	Non-current assets	*£000*	*£000*
140,250		Property, plant and equipment	157,250	
42,075		Depreciation	62,900	
	98,175			94,350
		Current assets		
17,708		Inventory	26,379	
23,375		Trade receivables	34,000	
1,875		Cash	17,000	
42,958			77,379	
		Current liabilities		
17,000		Trade payables	25,500	
		Other payables		
4,250		— income tax	8,500	
4,000		— dividend declared	5,000	
25,250			39,000	
	17,708	*Net current assets*		38,379
	(11,000)	*Non-current liabilities*		(11,000)
	6,708			27,379
	104,883			121,729
	£000	*Capital and reserves*		*£000*
	50,000	Called-up share capital		50,000
	1,500	Share premium account		1,500
	53,383	Total of other reserves		70,229
	104,883			121,729
		Analysis of 'Total of other reserves'		
	£000			*£000*
	14,000	Statement of income		15,846
	39,383	Current cost reserve		54,383
	53,383			70,229

continued

Figure 12.7 continued

Movements on reserves

(a) Statement of income: £000

    Balance at 1 January 20X5   14,000 (from Figure 7.5)

    Current cost retained profit   1,846 (from Figure 7.6)

    Balance at 31 December 20X5   15,846

(b) Current cost reserve:

	Total	Non-current assets	Inventory	MWCA	Gearing
	£000	£000	£000	£000	£000
Balance as at 1 January 20X5	39,383	38,675	708		
Movements during the year:					
Unrealised holding gains in year	10,541	10,370	171		
Gearing adjustment	(684)				(684)
MWCA	1,345			1,345	
COSA	3,798		3,798		
Balance as at 31 December 20X5	54,383	49,045	4,677	1,345	(684)

12.7.7 Real terms system

The real terms system combines both CPP and current cost concepts. This requires a calculation of total unrealised holding gains and an inflation adjustment as calculated in Workings 10 and 11 below.

(W10) Total unrealised holding gains to be used in Figure 12.8

[Closing statement of financial position at CC − Closing statement of financial position at HC] − [Opening statement of financial position at CC − Opening statement of financial position at HC]

  = (£121,729,000 − £77,500,000) − (£104,883,000 − £65,500,000) = £4,846,000

    (Working 8)   (Figure 10.3)   (Working 8)   (Figure 10.3)

(W11) General price index numbers to be used to calculate the inflation adjustment in Figure 12.8

General price index at 1 January 20X5 = 317.2

General price index at 31 December 20X5 = 333.2

Opening shareholders' funds at CC × percentage change in GPI during the year =

$$104,883,000 \times \frac{333.2 - 317.2}{317.2} = £5,290,435, \text{ say } £5,290,000$$

The GPP (or CPP) real terms financial capital

The real terms financial capital maintenance concept may be incorporated within the CCA system as in Figure 12.8 by calculating an inflation adjustment.

Figure 12.8 Economica plc real terms statement of comprehensive income

Economica plc CCA statement of income under the real terms system for the year ended 31 December 20X5	£000	£000
Historical cost profit after tax for the financial year		17,000
Add: Total unrealised holding gains arising during the year (see W10)	4,846	
Less: Realised holding gains previously recognised as unrealised	none	
	4,846	
Less: Inflation adjustment to CCA shareholders' funds (W11)	(5,290)	
Real holding gains		(444)
Total real gains		16,556
Deduct: dividends declared		5,000
Amount retained		11,556

Real terms system: analysis of reserves

20X4 £000		20X5 £000
53,383	Statement of income	64,939
—	Financial capital maintenance reserve	5,290
53,383		70,229

Movements on reserves

	Income statement £000	Financial capital maintenance reserve £000
Balances at 1 January 20X5	53,383	—
Amount retained	11,556	—
Inflation adjustment for year		5,290
Balances as at 31 December 20X5	64,939	5,290

12.8 Critique of CCA statements

Considerable effort and expense are involved in compiling and publishing CCA statements. Does their usefulness justify the cost? CCA statements have the following uses:

1 The operating capital maintenance statement reveals CCA profit. Such profit has removed inflationary price increases in raw materials and other inventories, and thus is more realistic than the alternative HCA profit.

2 Significant increases in a company's buying and selling prices will give the HCA profit a holding gains content. That is, the reported HCA profit will include gains consequent upon holding inventories during a period when the cost of buying such inventories increases. Conversely, if specific inventory prices fall, HCA profit will be reduced as it takes account of losses sustained by holding inventory while its price drops. Holding gains

and losses are quite different from operating gains and losses. HCA profit does not distinguish between the two, whereas CCA profit does.

3 HCA profit might be adjusted to reflect the moving price-level syndrome:

   (a) by use of the operating capital maintenance approach, which regards only the CCA **operating** profit as the authentic result for the period and which treats any holding gain or loss as a movement on reserves;

   (b) by adoption of the real terms **financial** capital maintenance approach, which applies a general inflation measure via the RPI, combined with CCA information regarding holding gains.

   Thus the statement can reveal information to satisfy the demands of the management of the entity itself – as distinct from the shareholder/proprietor, whose awareness of inflation may centre on the **RPI**. In this way the concern of operating management can be accommodated with the different interest of the shareholder. The HCA profit would fail on both these counts.

4 CC profit is important because:

   (a) it quantifies cost of sales and depreciation after allowing for changing price levels; hence trading results, free of inflationary elements, grant a clear picture of entity activities and management performance;

   (b) resources are maintained, as a result of having eliminated the possibility of paying dividend out of real capital;

   (c) yardsticks for management performance are more comparable as a time series within the one entity and between entities, the distortion caused by moving prices having been alleviated.

12.9 Measurement bases

We saw in Chapter 10 that the Conceptual Framework exposure draft described different measurement bases (historical cost and current value (fair value and value in use – for assets – or fulfilment value – for liabilities)), the information that they provide and their advantages and disadvantages. The factors to be considered when selecting a measurement basis (relevance, faithful representation, enhancing qualitative characteristics, and factors specific to initial measurement) mean that it is likely to result in the selection of different measurement bases for different assets, liabilities and items of income and expense.

12.10 The IASB position where there is hyperinflation

12.10.1 What do we mean by hyperinflation?

IAS 29 *Financial Reporting in Hyperinflationary Economies* states that hyperinflation occurs when money loses purchasing power at such a rate that comparison of amounts from transactions that have occurred at different times, even within the same accounting period, is misleading.

12.10.2 What rate indicates that hyperinflation exists?

IAS 29 does not specify an absolute rate – this is a matter of qualitative judgement – but it sets out certain pointers, such as people preferring to keep their wealth in non-monetary assets, people preferring prices to be stated in terms of an alternative stable currency rather than the domestic currency, wages and prices being linked to a price index, or the cumulative inflation rate over three years approaching 100%.

Countries where hyperinflation has been a risk include Iran, Sudan and Venezuela.

12.10.3 How are financial statements adjusted?

The current year financial statements, whether HCA or CCA, must be restated using the domestic measuring unit current at the statement of financial position date. The domestic statements may be adjusted using an index as in the following extract from the Diageo 2013 Annual Report:

> Since December 2009 Venezuela has been classified as a hyperinflationary economy. Hyperinflationary accounting requires the restatement of the subsidiary undertaking's income statement to current purchasing power. The index used to calculate the hyperinflationary adjustment was the Indice Nacional de Precios al Consumidor which changed from 285.5 to 398.6 in the year ended 30 June 2013.

12.11 Future developments

A mixed picture emerges when we try to foresee the future of changing price levels and financial reporting. The accounting profession has been reluctant to abandon the HC concept in favour of a 'valuation accounting' approach. In the UK and Australia many companies have stopped revaluing their non-current assets, with a large proportion opting instead to revert to the historical cost basis, with the two main factors influencing management's decision being cost-effectiveness and future reporting flexibility.[1]

The pragmatic approach is prevailing with each class of asset and liability being considered on an individual basis. For example, non-current assets may be reported at depreciated replacement cost if this is lower than the value in use we discussed in Chapter 9; financial assets are reported at market value (exit value in the NRV model); and current assets reported at the lower of HC and NRV. In each case the resulting changes, both realised and unrealised, in value now find their way into the financial performance statement(s).

12.11.1 Increasing use of fair values

A number of IFRSs now require or allow the use of fair values, e.g. IFRS 3 *Business Combinations* in which fair value is defined as 'the amount for which an asset could be exchanged or a liability settled between knowledgeable, willing parties in an arm's length transaction'. This is equivalent to the NRVA model discussed above. It is defined as an exit value rather than a cost value but like NRVA it does not imply a forced sale, i.e. it is the best value that could be obtained.

It is very possible that the number of international standards requiring or allowing fair values will increase over time and reflect the adoption on a piecemeal basis. In the meantime, efforts[2] are in hand for the FASB and IASB to arrive at a common definition of fair value which can be applied to value assets and liabilities where there is no market value available. Agreeing a definition, however, is only a part of the exercise. If analysts are to be able to compare corporate performance across borders, then it is essential that both the FASB and the IASB agree that all companies should adopt fair value accounting – this has been proving difficult.

12.11.2 The move to defining how to measure fair value

The IASB addressed this by issuing IFRS 13 *Fair Value Measurement* in 2011. This standard[3] does not state when fair values are to be used but applies when the decision has been made to measure at fair value so that there is uniformity in the measurement process.

IFRS 13 *Fair Value Measurement*

The standard (a) defines fair value, (b) sets out a framework for measuring it and (c) sets out the disclosures that are required.

Fair value definition

IFRS 13 defines fair value as the price that would be received to sell an asset or paid to transfer a liability in an orderly transaction between market participants at the measurement date. This means that it is a market-based measurement we would refer to as an exit price – it is not an entity-specific measurement so that the entity's intention to hold an asset or to settle a liability is not relevant when measuring fair value.

Fair value measurement

An entity has to identify the particular asset or liability being measured, the market in which an orderly transaction would take place and the appropriate valuation technique.

Fair value hierarchy

It is not always possible to obtain a directly comparable market value. The IFRS establishes, therefore, a fair value hierarchy that categorises the inputs to a valuation into three levels. It provides a framework to increase comparability but it does not remove the judgement that is required in arriving at a fair value.

Level 1 typically applies to financial investments when there are inputs such as quoted prices in an active market for identical assets or liabilities at the date the fair value is being measured.

Level 2 applies when there are not quoted prices as in Level 1 but there is observable data such as the price per square metre that had been achieved locally in an orderly market when valuing retail space.

Level 3 applies when there are no comparable observable inputs and reliance has to be on judgement using data such as discounted cash flows.

Judgement is required in arriving at a fair value

Judgement is required in selecting the level input appropriate to a particular asset. For example, consider Retail Properties plc:

> Retail Properties plc has a portfolio of investments linked to the retail property market which it had acquired 5 years earlier when property prices were buoyant. At the end of the current financial period it had received an offer from a private equity vulture fund of £2m to acquire the portfolio. The company has been advised that this fund had acquired similar portfolios from companies that had gone into administration – however, Retail Properties plc was solvent and under no liquidity pressure to accept this offer.

The company obtained advice from Commercial Property Valuers that from their current experience with sales in this sector the portfolio could be sold for £3m in the current market and, with the expected upturn in the retail sector, could probably realise up to £5m in 2 to 3 years' time. There are three valuations and in determining the fair value the company has to (a) bear in mind that the fair value has to be that obtainable at the current date and (b) measured applying the IFRS 13 three hierarchy levels approach. So, taking each in turn:

Level 1 does not apply because it requires an active market such as the availability of quoted prices on a stock exchange.

Level 2 would seem to apply as there is *observable* evidence provided by commercial property valuers of the results on the sale of *similar* assets at the *current* time.

Level 3 is based on an estimated improvement of market conditions in the *future*. It is *not observable* and it is *not current* – it is not appropriate on those grounds.

The best estimate of fair value based on this analysis is the figure of £3m arrived at applying the Level 2 input which is observable and based on an orderly market – unlike the forced sale conditions that applied to the vulture fund offer.

Note: If there were no observable direct or indirect comparators and the Level 3 valuation used discounted cash flows, improvements in cash flows arising from action taken by the company would be acceptable provided those actions would also have been taken by any party taking over the asset. The cash flows used should reflect only the cash flows that market participants would take into account when assessing fair value. This includes both the type of cash flows (e.g. future capital expenditure) and the estimated amount of cash flows.

How will financial statements be affected if fair values are adopted?

The financial statements will have the same virtues and defects as the NRVA model (Section 12.6.4 above). Some concerns have been raised that reported annual income will become more volatile and the profit that is reported may contain a mix of realised and unrealised profits. Supporters of the use of fair values see the statements of comprehensive income and financial position as more relevant for decision making while accepting that the figures might be less reliable and not as effective as a means of assessing the stewardship by the directors.

This means that in the future historical cost and realisation will be regarded as less relevant[4] and investors, analysts and management will need to come to terms with increased volatility in reported annual performance.

This is one of the reasons that narrative reports such as the Strategic Report and Management Commentary are increasingly important when investors make their predictions about future performance and position.

Summary

The traditional HCA system reveals disturbing inadequacies in times of changing price levels, calling into question the value of financial reports using this system. Considerable resources and energy have been expended in searching for a substitute model able to counter the distortion and confusion caused by an unstable monetary unit.

Three basic models have been developed: RCA, NRVA and CPP. Each has its merits and defects; each produces a different income value and a different capital value.

In the search for more relevant decision-useful financial statements we will see the gradual replacement of historical cost figures.

The contemporary financial reporting scene continues to be dynamic.

We see value in use used as a criterion in measuring the impairment of non-current tangible and intangible assets (discussed further in Chapter 3); we see financial assets valued at fair values; we see current assets valued at lower of cost and NRV; we see the addition of a statement of comprehensive income required as a primary financial statement to report fair value adjustments.

REVIEW QUESTIONS

1 Explain why financial reports prepared under the historical cost convention are subject to the following major limitations:

- periodic comparisons are invalidated; the depreciation charge may be understated;
- gains and losses on net monetary assets are undisclosed.

2 Explain how each of the limitations in Question 1 could be overcome.

3 Compare the operating and financial capital maintenance concepts and discuss if they are mutually exclusive.

4 Explain how the CPP model differs from the CCA model as a basis for making dividend decisions.

5 '[T]he IASB's failure to decide on a capital maintenance concept is regrettable as users have no idea as to whether total gains represent income or capital and are therefore unable to identify a meaningful "bottom line".'[5] Discuss.

6 'To be relevant to investors, the profit for the year should include both realised and unrealised gains/losses.' Discuss.

7 Discuss why there are objections to financial statements being prepared using the NRVA model.

8 Explain the criteria for determining whether hyperinflation exists.

9 'Investors benefit when unrealised changes in assets arising from fair value measurement are incorporated in the financial report even if this means that there is greater volatility in income and balance sheet ratios.' Discuss.

10 Retail plc had a portfolio linked to retail properties. Discuss the information that would be required if Level 1 and Level 2 inputs were unavailable. Explain the judgements that would be required.

EXERCISES

*Question 1

Raiders plc prepares accounts annually to 31 March. The following figures, prepared on a conventional historical cost basis, are included in the company's accounts to 31 March 20X5.

1 In the income statement:

	£000	£000
(i) Cost of goods sold:		
Inventory at 1 April 20X4	9,600	
Purchases	39,200	
	48,800	
Inventory at 31 March 20X5	11,300	37,500
(ii) Depreciation of equipment		8,640

2 In the statement of financial position:

	£000	£000
(iii) Equipment at cost	57,600	
Less: Accumulated depreciation	16,440	41,160
(iv) Inventory		11,300

The inventory held on 31 March 20X4 and 31 March 20X5 was in each case purchased evenly during the last six months of the company's accounting year.

Equipment is depreciated at a rate of 15% per annum, using the straight-line method. Equipment owned on 31 March 20X5 was purchased as follows: on 1 April 20X2 at a cost of £16 million; on 1 April 20X3 at a cost of £20 million; and on 1 April 20X4 at a cost of £21.6 million.

	Current cost of inventory	Current cost of equipment	Retail Price Index
1 April 20X2	109	145	313
1 April 20X3	120	162	328
30 September 20X3	128	170	339
31 December 20X3	133	175	343
31 March/1 April 20X4	138	180	345
30 September 20X4	150	191	355
31 December 20X4	156	196	360
31 March 20X5	162	200	364

Required:
(a) Calculate the following current cost accounting figures:
    (i)   The cost of goods sold of Raiders plc for the year ended 31 March 20X5.
    (ii) The statement of financial position value of inventory at 31 March 20X5.
    (iii) The equipment depreciation charge for the year ended 31 March 20X5.
    (iv) The net statement of financial position value of equipment at 31 March 20X5.
(b) Discuss the extent to which the figures you have calculated in (a) above (together with figures calculated on a similar basis for earlier years) provide information over and above that provided by the conventional historical cost statement of comprehensive income and statement of financial position figures.
(c) Outline the main reasons why the standard setters have experienced so much difficulty in their attempts to develop an accounting standard on accounting for changing prices.

*Question 2

The finance director of Toy plc has been asked by a shareholder to explain items that appear in the current cost statement of comprehensive income for the year ended 31.8.20X9 and the statement of financial position as at that date:

		£	£
Historical cost profit			143,000
Cost of sales adjustment	(1)	10,000	
Additional depreciation	(2)	6,000	
Monetary working capital adjustment	(3)	2,500	18,500
Current cost operating profit before tax			124,500
Gearing adjustment	(4)		2,600
CCA operating profit			127,100

		£	£
Non-current assets at gross replacement cost		428,250	
Accumulated current cost depreciation	(5)	(95,650)	332,600
Net current assets			121,400
12% debentures			(58,000)
			396,000
Issued share capital			250,000
Current cost reserve	(6)		75,000
Retained earnings			71,000
			396,000

Required:

(a) Explain what each of the items numbered 1–6 represents and the purpose of each.

(b) What do you consider to be the benefits to users of providing current cost information?

*Question 3

The statements of financial position of Parkway plc for 20X7 and 20X8 are given below, together with the income statement for the year ended 30 June 20X8.

Statement of financial position

	20X8			20X7		
	£000	£000	£000	£000	£000	£000
Non-current assets	Cost	Depn	NBV	Cost	Depn	NBV
Freehold land	60,000	—	60,000	60,000	—	60,000
Buildings	40,000	8,000	32,000	40,000	7,200	32,800
Plant and machinery	30,000	16,000	14,000	30,000	10,000	20,000
Vehicles	40,000	20,000	20,000	40,000	12,000	28,000
	170,000	44,000	126,000	170,000	29,200	140,800
Current assets						
Inventory		80,000			70,000	
Trade receivables		60,000			40,000	
Short-term investments		50,000			—	
Cash at bank and in hand		5,000			5,000	
		195,000			115,000	
Current liabilities						
Trade payables		90,000			60,000	
Bank overdraft		50,000			45,000	
Taxation		28,000			15,000	
Dividends declared		15,000			10,000	
		183,000			130,000	
Net current assets			12,000			(15,000)
			138,000			125,800
Financed by						
ordinary share capital			80,000			80,000
Share premium			10,000			10,000
Retained profits			28,000			15,800
			118,000			105,800
Long-term loans			20,000			20,000
			138,000			125,800

Statement of income of Parkway plc for the year
ended 30 June 20X8

	£000
Sales	738,000
Cost of sales	620,000
Gross profit	118,000

Notes

1   The freehold land and buildings were purchased on 1 July 20X0. The company policy is to depreciate buildings over 50 years and to provide no depreciation on land.
2   Depreciation on plant and machinery and motor vehicles is provided at the rate of 20% per annum on a straight-line basis.
3   Depreciation on buildings and plant and equipment has been included in administration expenses, while that on motor vehicles is included in distribution expenses.
4   The directors of Parkway plc have provided you with the following information relating to price rises:

	RPI	Inventory	Land	Buildings	Plant	Vehicles
1 July 20X0	100	60	70	50	90	120
1 July 20X7	170	140	290	145	135	180
30 June 20X8	190	180	310	175	165	175
Average for year ending 30 June 20X8	180	160	300	163	145	177

Required:
(a) **Making and stating any assumptions that are necessary, and giving reasons for those assumptions, calculate the monetary working capital adjustment for Parkway plc.**
(b) **Critically evaluate the usefulness of the monetary working capital adjustment.**

*Question 4

The historical cost accounts of Smith plc are as follows:

Smith plc Statement of income for the year ended 31 December 20X8

	£000	£000
Sales		2,000
Cost of sales:		
Opening inventory 1 January 20X8	320	
Purchases	1,680	
	2,000	
Closing inventory at 31 December 20X8	280	
		1,720
Gross profit		280
Depreciation	20	
Administration expenses	100	
		120
Net profit		160

Statement of financial position of Smith plc as at 31 December 20X8

	20X7		20X8	
Non-current assets	£000		£000	
Land and buildings at cost	1,360		1,360	
Less aggregate depreciation	(160)		(180)	
	1,200		1,180	
Current assets				
Inventory	320		280	
Trade receivables	80		160	
Cash at bank	40		120	
	440		560	
Trade payables	200		140	
		240		420
		1,440		1,600
Ordinary share capital		800		800
Retained profit		640		800
		1,440		1,600

Notes

1 Land and buildings were acquired in 20X0 with the buildings component costing £800,000 and depreciated over 40 years.
2 Share capital was issued in 20X0.
3 Closing inventories were acquired in the last quarter of the year.
4 RPI numbers were:

Average for 20X0	120
20X7 last quarter	216
At 31 December 20X7	220
20X8 last quarter	232
Average for 20X8	228
At 31 December 20X8	236

Required:
(i) Explain the basic concept of the CPP accounting system.
(II) Prepare CPP accounts for Smith plc for the year ended 20X8.
  The following steps will assist in preparing the CPP accounts:
  (a) Restate the statement of comprehensive income for the current year in terms of £CPP at the year-end.
  (b) Restate the closing statement of financial position in £CPP at the year-end, but excluding monetary items, i.e. trade receivables, trade payables, cash at bank.
  (c) Restate the opening statement of financial position in £CPP at the year-end, but including monetary items, i.e. trade receivables, trade payables and cash at bank, and showing equity as the balancing figure.
  (d) Compare the opening and closing equity figures derived in (b) and (c) above to arrive at the total profit/loss for the year in CPP terms. Compare this figure with the CPP profit calculated in (a) above to determine the monetary gain or monetary loss.
  (e) Reconcile monetary gains/loss in (d) with the increase/decrease in net monetary items during the year expressed in £CPP compared with the increase/decrease expressed in £HC.

*Question 5

Shower Ltd was incorporated towards the end of 20X2, but it did not start trading until 20X3. Its historical cost statement of financial position at 1 January 20X3 was as follows:

	£
Share capital, £1 shares	2,000
Loan (interest free)	8,000
	£10,000
Non-current assets, at cost	6,000
Inventory, at cost (4,000 units)	4,000
	£10,000

A summary of Shower Limited's bank account for 20X3 is given below:

		£	£
1 Jan 20X3	Opening balance		nil
30 Jun 20X3	Sales (8,000 units)		20,000
Less			
29 Jun 20X3	Purchase (6,000 units)	9,000	
	Sundry expenses	5,000	14,000
31 Dec 20X3	Closing balance		£6,000

All the company's transactions are on a cash basis.

The non-current assets are expected to last for five years and the company intends to depreciate its non-current assets on a straight-line basis. The non-current assets had a resale value of £2,000 at 31 December 20X3.

Notes
1 The closing inventory is 2,000 units and the inventory is sold on a first-in-first-out basis.
2 All prices remained constant from the date of incorporation to 1 January 20X3, but thereafter, various relevant price indices moved as follows:

		Specific indices	
	General price level	Inventory	Non-current assets
1 January 20X3	100	100	100
30 June 20X3	120	150	140
31 December 20X3	240	255	200

Required:
Produce statements of financial position as at December 20X3 and statements of comprehensive income for the year ended on that date on the basis of:
(i)   historical cost;
(ii) current purchasing power (general price level);
(iii) replacement cost;
(iv) continuous contemporary accounting (NRVA).

*Question 6

Aspirations Ltd commenced trading as wholesale suppliers of office equipment on 1 January 20X1, issuing ordinary shares of £1 each at par in exchange for cash. The shares were fully paid on issue, the number issued being 1,500,000.

The following financial statements, based on the historical cost concept, were compiled for 20X1.

Aspirations Ltd

Statement of income for the year ended 31 December 20X1

	£	£
Sales		868,425
Purchases	520,125	
Less: Inventory 31 December 20X1	24,250	
Cost of sales		495,875
Gross profit		372,550
Expenses	95,750	
Depreciation	25,250	
		121,000
Net profit		251,550

Statement of financial position as at 31 December 20X1

	Cost	Depreciation	
Non-current assets	£	£	£
Freehold property	650,000	6,500	643,500
Office equipment	375,000	18,750	356,250
	1,025,000	25,250	999,750
Current assets			
Inventories		24,250	
Trade receivables		253,500	
Cash		1,090,300	
		1,368,050	
Current liabilities		116,250	
		1,251,800	
Non-current liabilities		500,000	751,800
			1,751,550
Issued share capital			
1,500,000 £1 ordinary shares			1,500,000
Retained earnings			251,550
			1,751,550

The year 20X1 witnessed a surge of inflation and in consequence the directors became concerned about the validity of the revenue account and statement of financial position as income and capital statements.

Specific index numbers reflecting replacement costs

	1 January 20X1	31 December 20X1	Average for 20X1
Inventory	115	150	130
Freehold property	110	165	127
Office equipment	125	155	145
General price index numbers	135	170	155

Regarding current exit costs

Inventory is anticipated to sell at a profit of 75% of cost.

Value of assets at 31 December 20X1

	£
Freehold property	640,000
Office equipment	350,000

Index numbers reflecting price changes were:

Initial purchases of inventory were effected on 1 January 20X1 amounting to £34,375; the balance of purchases was evenly spread over the 12-month period. The non-current assets were acquired on 1 January 20X1 and, together with the initial inventory, were paid for in cash on that day.

Required:
Prepare the accounts adjusted for current values using each of the three proposed models of current value accounting: namely, the accounting methods known as replacement cost, general (or current) purchasing power and net realisable value.

Notes

1 Ernst & Young, 'Revaluation of non-current assets', Accounting Standard, Ernst & Young, January 2002, www.ey.com/Global/gcr.nsf/Australia.
2 *SFAS 157 Fair Value Measurement*, FASB, 2006.
3 IFRS 13 *Fair Value Measurement*, IASSB, 2011.
4 A. Wilson, 'IAS: the challenge for measurement', *Accountancy*, December 2001, p. 90.
5 N. Fry and D. Bence, 'Capital or income?', *Accountancy*, April 2007, p. 81.

Bibliography

W.T. Baxter, *Depreciation*, Sweet and Maxwell, 1971.
W.T. Baxter, *Inflation Accounting*, Philip Alan, 1984.
W.T. Baxter, *The Case for Deprival Accounting*, ICAS, 2003.
E.O. Edwards and P.W. Bell, *The Theory and Measurement of Business Income*, University of California Press, 1961.
J.R. Hicks, *Value and Capital* (2nd edition), Oxford University Press, 1975.
T.A. Lee, *Income and Value Measurement: Theory and Practice* (3rd edition), Van Nostrand Reinhold (UK), 1985, Chapter 5.
D.R. Myddleton, *On a Cloth Untrue – Inflation Accounting: The Way Forward*, Woodhead-Faulkner, 1984.
R.H. Parker and G.C. Harcourt (eds), *Readings in the Concept and Measurement of Income*, Cambridge University Press, 1969.
D. Tweedie and G. Whittington, *Capital Maintenance Concepts*, ASC, 1985.
D. Tweedie and G. Whittington, *The Debate on Inflation in Accounting*, Cambridge University Press, 1985.

CHAPTER 13

Accounting for groups at the date of acquisition

13.1 Introduction

The main purpose of this chapter is to explain how to prepare consolidated financial statements at the date of acquisition and the IFRS 10 and 13 requirements.

Objectives

By the end of this chapter, you should be able to:

- prepare consolidated accounts at the date of acquisition:
  - for a wholly owned subsidiary;
  - for a partly owned subsidiary with non-controlling interests, calculating goodwill under the two options available in IFRS 3;
  - where the fair value of a subsidiary's net assets are more or less than their book values;
- explain IFRS 10, IFRS 3 and IFRS 13 provisions;
- discuss the usefulness of group accounts to stakeholders.

13.2 Preparing consolidated accounts for a wholly owned subsidiary

When a company acquires the shares of another company it records the cost as an Investment. If the shares acquired give it control over the acquired company, then the acquirer is referred to as a parent or holding company and the acquired company as a subsidiary.

The shareholders of the parent company want to know how well the directors of their company have managed all of the net assets which they control. This information is provided by the preparation of consolidated accounts which aggregates the assets and liabilities of both companies. In doing this it replaces the Investment in subsidiary in the parent's accounts with the fair value of the assets and liabilities of the subsidiary.

The parent may well have had to pay a premium over and above the fair value of the net assets in order to obtain control – this is referred to as Goodwill.

13.3 IFRS 10 *Consolidated Financial Statements*

IFRS 10 *Consolidated Financial Statements* which defines a group and how to determine control and also requires the use of fair values for a subsidiary.

13.3.1 IFRS 10 definition of a group

One of IASB's main objectives had been to develop a consistent basis for determining when a company consolidates the financial statements of another company to prepare group accounts. For this, it has stated that control should be the determining factor.

Under IFRS 10 *Consolidated Financial Statements,* a group exists where one enterprise (the parent) controls, either directly or indirectly, another enterprise (the subsidiary). A group consists of a parent and its subsidiaries.

13.3.2 IFRS 10 definition of control

Under IFRS 10 an investor is a parent[1] when it is exposed, or has rights, to variable returns from its involvement with the investee and has the ability to affect those returns through its power over the investee.

An investor controls[2] an investee if and only if the investor satisfies all of the following requirements:

- exposure, or rights, to variable returns whether positive or negative from its involvement with the investee;
- power over the investee whereby the investor has existing rights that give it the ability to direct those activities that significantly affect the investee's returns;
- the ability to use its power over the investee to affect the amount of the investor's returns.

The following is an extract from the 2017 Linde AG annual report:

Scope of consolidation

The Group financial statements comprise Linde AG and all the companies over which Linde AG is able to exercise control as defined by IFRS 10.

What if the shares acquired are less than 50%?

Even in this situation, it may still be possible to identify an acquirer when one of the combining enterprises, as a result of the business combination, acquires:

(a) power over more than one-half of the voting rights of the other enterprise by virtue of an agreement with other investors;

(b) power to govern the financial and operating policies of the other enterprise under a statute or an agreement;

(c) power to appoint or remove the majority of the members of the board of directors; or

(d) power to cast the majority of votes at a meeting of the board of directors.

What if the parent holds options or potential voting rights?

IFRS 10 provides that if those options give the entity control then this could result in an entity being consolidated. For example, if the investee's management always followed the wishes of the option holder, this may be viewed as having control. The following is an extract from the BMW 2015 Annual Report:

Subsidiaries are those enterprises which, either directly or indirectly, are under the uniform control of the management of BMWAG or in which BMWAG, either directly or indirectly – holds the majority of the voting rights – has the right to appoint or remove the majority of the members of the Board of Management or equivalent governing body, and in which

BMWAG is at the same time (directly or indirectly) a shareholder – has control (directly or indirectly) over another enterprise on the basis of a control agreement or a provision in the statutes of that enterprise.

What if a company has significant voting rights in comparison to other shareholders?

If an investor is so powerful through their voting rights compared to others, for example one investor has 40% while the other 60% is widely dispersed between unconnected investors, this can also give control and result in the investee being consolidated. Both of these areas will require directors to exercise judgement in determining whether control exists.

13.3.3 Requirement to use fair values

When one company acquires a controlling interest in another and the combination is treated as an acquisition, the assets and liabilities of the subsidiary are recorded in the acquirer's consolidated statement of financial position at their fair value.

On consolidation, if the acquirer has acquired less than 100% of the ordinary shares, any differences (positive or negative) between the fair values of the net assets and their book value are recognised in full and the parent and non-controlling interests are credited or debited with their respective percentage interests.

13.4 Fair values

The **fair value** of the consideration paid to acquire an investment in a subsidiary is set against the **fair value** of the identifiable net assets in the subsidiary at the date of acquisition.

Fair value of the consideration

Consideration may be in the form of shares in the acquiring company. If these are quoted then the fair value is the market price of the shares. If the shares are not quoted on an exchange, then they would need to be valued – for the purposes of this chapter the value is given (how to value unquoted shares is discussed in Chapter 19).

Consideration may also be in cash or a combination of shares and cash. If the cash element is deferred for more than a year the consideration is discounted to its present value. The difference is reported as an accrued finance charge.

Under IFRS3, acquisition costs (such as legal, accounting and valuation fees) must be expensed and cannot be capitalised.

If there is contingent consideration it will be accounted for as a provision under IAS37 and, if it falls to be paid more than one year later, it will be necessary to review the amount and treat any changes as an error in accordance with IAS 8 *Accounting Policies, Accounting Estimates and Errors.*

Fair value of the net assets

The starting point is the book values in the subsidiary's statement of financial position. These are required to be re-stated at fair values when incorporating into the consolidated accounts. First, each asset and liability is reviewed. For example, land may be revalued to market value, raw materials to replacement price, finished goods to selling price less estimated profit, loans may be revalued if there has been a change in interest rates that impacts on their value. In addition to the assets and liabilities in the accounts, it is also necessary to estimate a fair value for any contingent liabilities – if unable to value then they are disclosed.

If the investment is greater than the share of net assets then the difference is regarded as the purchase of goodwill – see the Rose Group example below

13.5 Illustration where there is a wholly owned subsidiary

The **fair value** of the parent company's investment in a subsidiary is set against the **fair value** of the identifiable net assets in the subsidiary at the date of acquisition. If the investment is greater than the share of net assets then the difference is regarded as the purchase of goodwill – see the Rose Group example below.

EXAMPLE • The Rose group on 1 January 20X0 Rose plc acquired 100% of the 10,000 £1 ordinary voting shares in Tulip plc for £1.50 per share in cash and so gained control. We are assuming for this example that the fair value of Tulip's net assets at that date was the same as their book value. The individual and group statements of financial position immediately after the acquisition were as in the following schedule:

	Rose plc £	Tulip plc £	Adjustments Dr	Cr	Group £	
Non-current assets	20,000	11,000			31,000	Step 2
Investment in Tulip	15,000	—		10,000 (a)	—	
				4,000 (b)	1,000	Step 1
Net current assets	8,000	3,000			11,000	
Net assets	43,000	14,000			43,000	
Share capital	16,000	10,000	10,000 (a)		16,000	Step 3
Retained earnings	27,000	4,000	4,000 (b)		27,000	Step 3
	43,000	14,000	14,000	14,000	43,000	

(a) and (b) identify the entries in the calculations below.

Step 1: First we calculate the goodwill

Goodwill arises if Rose has to pay the Tulip shareholders more than the book value of the net assets in order to acquire control over those net assets.

		£	£
The parent company's investment			15,000
Less: The parent's share of			
(a) the subsidiary's share capital	(100% × 10,000)	10,000	
(b) the subsidiary's retained earnings	(100% × 4,000)	4,000	14,000
Goodwill reported in statement of financial position			1,000

Step 2: Aggregate the assets and liabilities

Having cancelled the investment in Tulip against the share capital and reserves acquired, we then add together the assets and liabilities of the two companies including any goodwill:

		£
Non-current assets other than goodwill	(20,000 + 11,000)	31,000
Goodwill (as calculated in Step 1)		1,000
Net current assets	(8,000 + 3,000)	11,000
		43,000

Note that the total of the net assets in the consolidated account is the same as the net assets in the individual statement of financial position except that Rose's investment in Tulip has been replaced by Tulip's net assets of £14,000 **plus** the previously unrecorded £1,000 goodwill.

Step 3: Calculate the consolidated share capital and reserves

This is the final step.

	£
Share capital (parent company only)	16,000
Retained earnings (parent company only)	**27,000**
	43,000

Note that in a consolidated statement of financial position we only **ever** include the parent's share capital because, as we have seen above, the subsidiary's share capital has been cancelled as in Step 1 above.

13.6 Preparing consolidated accounts when there is a partly owned subsidiary

A parent company does not need to purchase all the shares of another company to gain control. The holders of any shares not acquired by the parent are collectively referred to as a **non-controlling interest.** They are part-owners of the subsidiary. However, although the parent does not **own** all the net assets of the acquired company, it does **control** them and the parent company directors are accountable for their use.

Indeed, one of the main purposes of preparing group accounts is to show how effectively the directors have used this power to control. Therefore, all of the net assets of the subsidiary will be included in the group statement of financial position and the non-controlling interest will be shown as partly financing those net assets.

How is a non-controlling interest measured?

IFRS 3[3] allows for two different methods of measuring the non-controlling interest in the statement of financial position:

- **Method 1** requires the non-controlling interest to be measured as the *proportionate share of the net assets* of the subsidiary at the date of acquisition. At each subsequent reporting date the non-controlling interest is measured as its percentage share of the subsidiary's net assets.

- **Method 2** requires the non-controlling interest to be measured at *fair value* at the date of acquisition. Using fair value rather than a percentage of book value means that there could be a difference for goodwill. At each subsequent reporting date the non-controlling interest is measured as the share of the net assets of the subsidiary, plus any goodwill.

13.6.1 Illustration where there is a partly owned subsidiary using Method 1

We will continue with our Rose Group example on the basis that it acquired less than 100% of Tulip's shares.

On 1 January 20X0 Rose plc acquired 80% of the 10,000 £1 ordinary shares in Tulip plc for £1.50 per share in cash and so gained control. The fair value of Tulip's net assets at that date was the same as their book value.

The consolidation schedule is as follows:

	Rose £	Tulip £	Adjustment Dr £	Cr £	Group £	
Non-current assets	20,000	11,000			31,000	Step 3
Investment in Tulip	12,000	—		8,000 (a)	—	
				3,200 (b)		
Goodwill	—	—			800	Step 1
Net current assets	**11,000**	**3,000**			**14,000**	Step 3
Net assets	43,000	14,000			45,800	
Share capital	16,000	10,000	8,000 (a)			Step 4
			2,000 (c)	16,000		
Retained earnings	**27,000**	**4,000**	3,200 (b)			Step 4
			800 (d)	27,000		
	43,000	14,000			43,000	
Non-controlling interest		—		**2,000 (c)**		Step 2
				800 (d)	**2,800**	
	43,000	14,000	14,000	14,000	45,800	

(a), (b), (c) and (d) identify the entries in the calculations below.

Step 1: Calculate goodwill

	£	£
The parent company's investment in Tulip		12,000
Less: (a) parent's share of Tulip's share capital (80% × 10,000)	8,000	
(b) parent's share of the retained earnings (80% × 4,000)	**3,200**	
Goodwill		**11,200**
		800

Step 2: Calculate the non-controlling interest in Tulip

(c) Non-controlling interest in the share capital	(20% × 10,000)	2,000
(d) Non-controlling interest in the retained earnings	(20% × 4,000)	800
Representing the non-controlling interest in Tulip's net assets		2,800

In the published consolidated accounts the non-controlling interest will be shown as a separate item in the equity of the group as follows:

Share capital	16,000
Retained earnings	**27,000**
Rose shareholders' share of equity	43,000
Non-controlling interest	**2,800**
Total equity	45,800

This recognises that the non-controlling shareholders are part of the ownership of the group rather than a liability.

Step 3: Aggregate the assets and liabilities of the parent and subsidiary

		£
Non-current assets other than goodwill	(20,000 + 11,000)	31,000
Goodwill (as calculated in Step 1)		800
Net current assets	(11,000 + 3,000)	**14,000**
		45,800

Step 4: Calculate the consolidated share capital and reserves

	£
Share capital (*parent company only*)	16,000
Retained earnings (*parent company only*)	**27,000**
	43,000

Note it is only the parent's share capital that is **ever** reported in the group accounts. As for the retained earnings, it is only the earnings that arise **after** the date when the parent obtains control that are reported as part of the group retained earnings – this is dealt with further in the next chapter.

13.6.2 Illustration where there is a partly owned subsidiary using Method 2

Let us now consider the impact on the previous example of using Method 2 to measure the non-controlling interest. In order to use this method, we need to know the fair value of the non-controlling interest in the subsidiary at the date of acquisition. Let us assume in this case that the fair value of a share in Tulip is £1.45, giving a value for the 2,000 shares of £2,900.

Two figures are different in the consolidated accounts if this method is used. The use of Method 2 affects two figures – goodwill and the non-controlling interest. Whereas under Method 1 the goodwill represented the cost of Rose obtaining control, under Method 2 we also credit the non-controlling interest with its own goodwill. It is computed as follows:

		£
Fair value of non-controlling interest at date of acquisition		2,900
20% of the net assets at the date of acquisition	(£14,000)	**(2,800)**
Attributable goodwill		100

The consolidated statement of financial position would now be as follows:

		£
Non-current assets other than goodwill		31,000
Goodwill	(£800 + £100)	900
Net current assets		**14,000**
		45,900
Share capital		16,000
Retained earnings		27,000
Non-controlling interest	(£2,800 + £100)	**2,900**
		45,900

How to determine the value of a share not acquired by the parent

Note that we assumed that the fair value of the non-controlling interest at the date of acquisition was £2,900. If Tulip's shares are quoted then the fair value estimate would be based on the share price prior to a bid. This price could be different from that paid by Rose on the assumption that in seeking to obtain control it would probably have paid more than the current share price. In exercises or exam questions the total figure might be given (as in this example) or a price per share might be given.

In the Rose example the goodwill relating to the parent (Rose's) shareholding of 80% is £800, i.e. 10p per share. The goodwill relating to the non-controlling interest in 2,000 shares, however, based on a £2,900 valuation is £100, i.e. 5p per share.

13.7 The treatment of differences between a subsidiary's fair value and book value

In our examples so far we have assumed that the book value of the net assets in the subsidiary is equal to their fair value. In practice, book value rarely equals fair value and it is necessary to revalue the group's share of the assets and liabilities of the subsidiary prior to consolidation.

The following is an extract from the BMW 2015 Annual Report:

Consolidation principles

The equity of subsidiaries is consolidated in accordance with IFRS 3 (Business Combinations). IFRS 3 requires that all business combinations are accounted for using the acquisition method, whereby identifiable assets and liabilities acquired are measured at their fair value at acquisition date. An excess of acquisition cost over the Group's share of the net fair value of identifiable assets, liabilities and contingent liabilities is recognised as goodwill in a separate balance sheet line item and allocated to the relevant cash-generating unit (CGU).

The following is an extract from the EnBW 2015 Annual Report:

Basis of consolidation

Non-controlling interests are measured at the proportionate share of fair value of assets identified and liabilities assumed.

Note that, when consolidating, the **parent** company's assets and liabilities remain **unchanged** at book value – it is only the subsidiary's that are adjusted for the purpose of the consolidated accounts.

For example, let us assume that the fair value of Tulip's non-current assets was £600 above their book value at £11,600. If Rose owned 100% of Tulip, then the Rose hareholders would have the benefit of the £600 and the goodwill would be reduced from £800 to £200. However, as Tulip is part-financed by non-controlling shareholders, they are entitled to their 20% share of the £600 as seen in the following schedule:

	Rose £	Tulip £	Group £	Dr	Cr	Group fair value £	
Non-current assets	20,000	11,000	31,000	600		31,600	Step 3
Goodwill	—	—	800		480	320	Step 1
Investment in Tulip	12,000	—	—			—	
Net current assets	11,000	3,000	14,000			14,000	
Net assets	43,000	14,000	45,800			45,920	
Share capital	16,000	10,000	16,000			16,000	
Retained earnings	27,000	4,000	27,000			27,000	
	43,000	14,000	43,000			43,000	
Non-controlling interest	—	—	2,800		120	2,920	Step 2
	43,000	14,000	45,800			45,920	

Step 1: Goodwill is adjusted when fair value exceeds book value

As goodwill is the difference between the consideration and the net assets acquired, any increase in the net assets will mean that the difference is lower.

		£
The parent company's investment in Tulip		12,000
Less: The parent's share of the subsidiary's share (80% × 10,000) capital	8,000	
The parent's share of retained earnings (80% × 4,000)	3,200	
The parent's share of the revaluation (80% × 600)	480	11,680
Goodwill		320

* This is equivalent to the share of net assets, 80% × (11,000 + 3,000 + 600).

Step 2: Non-controlling interest adjusted for fair value in excess of book value

Non-controlling interest in share capital of Tulip	(20% × 10,000)	2,000
Non-controlling interest in retained earnings of Tulip	(20% × 4,000)	800
Revaluation to fair value of the subsidiary's assets	(20% × 600)	120
		2,920

Step 3: Aggregate the parent's non-current assets which remain at book value and the subsidiary's which have been restated to fair value

The non-current assets would be reported as £31,600 (20,000 + 11,000 + 600). Remember that the revaluation of the subsidiary's assets is only necessary for the consolidated accounts. No entries need be made in the individual accounts of the subsidiary or its books of account. The preparation of consolidated accounts is *a separate exercise* that in no way affects the records of the individual companies.

13.8 The parent issues shares to acquire shares in a subsidiary

Shares in another company can be purchased with cash or through an exchange of shares. In the former case, the cash will be reduced and exchanged for another asset called 'investment in the subsidiary company'. If there is an exchange of shares, there will be an increase in the parents' share capital and often in the share premium.

Let us assume that Rose issued its own shares to 80% of the Tulip shareholders who wanted £1.50 for each share, totalling £12,000. Rose would in this case have to set a value of its own shares that was acceptable to the Tulip shareholders.

For illustration purposes, let us assume that the Rose shares were valued at £2.50 each and 4,800 were issued (£12,000/£2.50). The consolidation schedule would show that Rose's cash had not been reduced but the share capital and share premium had increased as follows:

		Rose £	Tulip £	Group £
Non-current assets		20,000	11,600	31,600
Investment in Tulip		12,000	—	—
Goodwill		—	—	320
Net current assets	11,000 + 12,000*	**23,000**	**3,000**	**26,000**
Net assets		55,000	14,000	57,920
Share capital	16,000 + 4,800 at par	20,800	10,000	20,800
Share premium	4,800 × £1.50	7,200		7,200
Retained earnings		27,000	4,000	27,000
Parent company's equity		55,000	14,000	55,000
Non-controlling interest		—	—	**2,920**
		55,000	14,000	57,920

* This is showing cash at £23,000 which was the position before we assumed that the shares in Tulip had been acquired for cash.

Note that there is no effect on the accounts of the acquired company as the payment of cash or exchange of shares is with the subsidiary company's individual shareholders, not the company itself.

13.9 IFRS 3 *Business Combinations* treatment of goodwill at the date of acquisition

Any differences between the fair values of the net assets and the consideration paid to acquire them is treated as positive goodwill or a bargain purchase (also referred to as badwill or negative goodwill) and dealt with in accordance with IFRS 3 *Business Combinations*.

The treatment of positive goodwill

Positive purchased goodwill, where the investment exceeds the total of the net assets acquired, should be recognised as an asset with no amortisation. In subsequent years goodwill must be subject to impairment tests in accordance with IAS 36 *Impairment of Assets*. These tests will be annual, or more frequently if circumstances indicate that the goodwill might be impaired.[4] Once recognised, an impairment loss for goodwill may not be reversed in a subsequent period, which helps in preventing the manipulation of period profits.

The treatment of a bargain purchase

The acquiring company does not always pay more than the fair value of the identifiable net assets. Paying less (sometimes referred to as negative goodwill) can arise[5] when:

(a) there have been errors measuring the fair value of either the cost of the combination or the acquiree's identifiable assets, liabilities or contingent liabilities; or

(b) future costs such as losses have been taken into account; or

(c) there has been a bargain purchase.

Where a parent pays less than the fair value of the net assets, IFRS 3 requires it to review the fair value exercise to ensure that no asset has been overstated or liability understated. Assuming this review reveals no errors, then the resulting difference is recognised immediately in the statement of income.

13.10 When may a parent company not be required to prepare consolidated accounts?

It may not be necessary for a parent company to prepare consolidated accounts if the parent is itself a wholly owned subsidiary and the ultimate parent produces consolidated financial statements available for public use that comply with International Financial Reporting Standards (IFRSs).[6]

If the parent company is a partially owned subsidiary of another entity, then, if its other owners have been informed and do not object, the parent company need not present consolidated financial statements; nor if its debt or equity instruments are not traded in a public foreign or domestic market.

13.11 When may a parent company exclude or not exclude a subsidiary from a consolidation?

13.11.1 Exclusion permitted

Subsidiaries may be excluded if they are immaterial or there are substantial rights exercisable by non-controlling interests.

Materiality

Exclusion is permissible on grounds of non-materiality[6] as the International Accounting Standards are not intended to apply to immaterial items.

For example, Linde AG states in its 2017 Annual Report:

Non-consolidated subsidiaries and other investments, when taken together, are immaterial from the Groups point of view in terms of total assets, revenue and profit or loss for the year and do not have a significant impact on the net assets, financial position and results of operations of the Group.

Substantial rights exercisable by the non-controlling interest

Exclusion might also be appropriate where there are substantial rights exercisable by a non-controlling interest as seen in the following extract from the Mitsubishi Logistics Corporation 2013 Annual Report:

The company holds 51% of the voting rights in MICLTL Logistics Company Ltd, however, the other shareholder's agreement is necessary to decide important policies of finance and trade. Therefore, the Company does not treat MICLTL as a subsidiary.

13.11.2 Exclusion not permitted

Exclusion on the grounds that a subsidiary's activities are dissimilar from those of the others within a group is not permitted.[7] This is because information is required under IFRS 8 *Operating Segments* on the different activities of subsidiaries, and users of accounts can, therefore, make appropriate adjustments for their own purposes if required.

13.12 IFRS 13 *Fair Value Measurement*

IFRS 13 *Fair Value Measurement*[8] defines fair value as the price that would be received to sell an asset or paid to transfer a liability in an orderly transaction between market participants at the measurement date. The detailed guidance for determining fair value is also set out in IFRS 3.

The main provisions are that as from the date of acquisition, an acquirer should:

(a) incorporate into the statement of income the results of operations of the acquiree; and

(b) recognise in the statement of financial position the identifiable assets, liabilities and contingent liabilities of the acquiree and any goodwill or negative goodwill arising on the acquisition.

The identifiable assets, liabilities and contingent liabilities acquired that are recognised should be those of the acquiree that existed at the date of acquisition.

Treatment of future liabilities

Liabilities should not be recognised at the date of acquisition if they result from the acquirer's intentions or actions. Therefore liabilities for terminating or reducing the activities of the acquiree should **only** be recognised where the acquiree has, at the acquisition date, an existing liability for restructuring recognised in accordance with IAS 37 *Provisions, Contingent Liabilities and Contingent Assets.*

Treatment of future losses

Liabilities should also not be recognised for future losses[9] or other costs expected to be incurred as a result of the acquisition, whether they relate to the acquirer or the acquiree.

Treatment of contingent liabilities

Under IFRS 3 only those contingent liabilities assumed in a business combination that are a **present** obligation and can be measured reliably are recognised. If not recognised then they are disclosed in the same way as other contingent liabilities.

Treatment of intangible assets

There is a requirement to identify both tangible and intangible assets that are acquired. For example, fair values would be attached to intangibles such as brands and customer lists if these can be measured reliably. If it is not possible to measure them reliably, then the goodwill would be reported at a higher figure, as in the following extract from the AstraZeneca 2015 Annual Report:

Business Combinations and Goodwill
On the acquisition of a business, fair values are attributed to the identifiable assets and liabilities and contingent liabilities unless the fair value cannot be measured reliably in which case the value is subsumed into goodwill.

Why revalue net assets?
The reason why all the net assets, including the intangible assets that did not appear in the subsidiary's statement of financial position must be identified and fair-valued at the date of acquisition is to prevent distortion of EPS in periods following the acquisition. For example, we have seen in Chapter 4 that intangible assets are required to be amortised with an annual charge against profits, whereas goodwill is not subject to an annual amortisation charge but is reviewed for impairment. Subsuming intangible assets into the goodwill figure means that a regular amortisation charge is avoided. This reason for valuing the intangible assets would not apply if goodwill were to be amortised as it had been in the UK prior to 2008.

13.13 What advantages are there for stakeholders from requiring groups to prepare consolidated accounts?

Advantages include investor protection, help in predicting future earnings per share and means to assess management performance.

(a) **Investor protection:** Consolidation prevents the publication of misleading accounts by such means as inflating the sales through selling to another member of a group.

(b) **Prediction:** Consolidation provides a more meaningful EPS figure. Consolidated accounts show the full earnings on a parent company's investment while the parent's individual accounts only show the dividend received from the subsidiaries.

(c) **Accountability:** Consolidation provides a better measurement of the performance of a parent company's directors as the total earnings of a group can be compared with its total assets in arriving at a group's return on capital employed (ROCE).

It is important to remember that the ROCE prepared from the consolidated financial statements is regarded by management as a ratio that is an important measure of performance and one to be maximised. For example, Northgate plc reported in its 2013 Annual Report:

Return on capital employed (ROCE) – In a capital intensive business, ROCE is a more important measure of performance than profitability alone, as low margin business returns low value to shareholders . . . ROCE is maximised through a combination of managing utilisation, hire rates, vehicle holding costs and improvements in operational efficiency.

Summary

When one company acquires a controlling interest in another and the combination is treated as an acquisition, the investment in the subsidiary is recorded in the acquirer's statement of financial position at the fair value of the investment.

On consolidation, if the consideration exceeds the fair value of the net assets it is referred to as goodwill and appears as an asset in the statement of financial position. If the consideration is less than the fair value of the net assets it is regarded as a bargain purchase and it will be taken to profit in accordance with IFRS 3.

On consolidation, if the acquirer has acquired less than 100% of the equity shares, any differences between the fair values of the assets or liabilities and their face value are recognised in full and the parent and non-controlling interests credited or debited with their respective percentage interests.

REVIEW QUESTIONS

1 Explain how negative goodwill (bargain purchase) may arise and its accounting treatment.

2 Explain how the fair value is calculated for:
   - tangible non-current assets
   - inventories
   - monetary assets.

3 Explain why only the net assets of the subsidiary and not those of the parent are adjusted to fair value at the date of acquisition for the purpose of consolidated accounts.

4 The 2013 Annual Report of Bayer AG states:

   Subsidiaries that do not have a material impact on the Group's net worth, financial position or earnings, either individually or in aggregate, are accounted for at cost of acquisition less any impairment losses.

   Discuss what criteria might have applied in determining that a subsidiary does not have a material impact.

5 Parent plc acquired Son plc at the beginning of the year. At the end of the year there were intangible assets reported in the consolidated accounts for the value of a domain name and customer lists. These assets did not appear in either Parent or Son's statements of financial position.

   Discuss why these assets only appeared in the consolidated accounts.

6 In each of the following cases you are required to give your opinion, with reasons, on whether or not there is a parent/subsidiary under IFRS 3. Suggest other information, if any, that might be helpful in making a decision.

   (a) Tin acquired 15% of the equity voting shares and 90% of the non-voting preferred shares of Copper. Copper has no other category of shares. The directors of Tin are also the directors of Copper, there is a common head office with shared administration departments and the functions of Copper are mainly the provision of marketing and transport facilities for Tin. Another company, Iron, holds 55% of the equity voting shares of Copper but has never used its voting power to interfere with the decisions of the directors.

(b) Hat plc owns 60% of the voting equity shares in Glove plc and 25% of the voting equity shares in Shoe plc. Glove owns 30% of the voting equity shares in Shoe plc and has the right to appoint a majority of the directors.

(c) Morton plc has 30% of the voting equity shares of Berry plc and also has a verbal agreement with other shareholders, who own 40% of the shares, that those shareholders will vote according to the wishes of Morton.

(d) Bean plc acquired 30% of the shares of Pea plc several years ago with the intention of acquiring influence over the operating and financial policies of that company. Pea sells 80% of its output to Bean. While Bean has a veto over the operating and financial decisions of Pea's board of directors it has only used this veto on one occasion, four years ago, to prevent that company from supplying one of Bean's competitors.

EXERCISES

* Questions 1–5

Required in each case:

Prepare the statements of financial position of Parent Ltd and the consolidated statement of financial position as at 1 January 20X7 after each transaction, using for each question the statements of financial position of Parent Ltd and Daughter Ltd as at 1 January 20X7 which were as follows:

	Parent Ltd £	Daughter Ltd £
Ordinary shares of £1 each	40,500	9,000
Retained earnings	4,500	1,800
	45,000	10,800
Cash	20,000	2,000
Other net assets	25,000	8,800
	45,000	10,800

* Question 1

(a) Assume that on 1 January 20X7 Parent Ltd acquired all the ordinary shares in Daughter Ltd for £10,800 cash. The fair value of the net assets in Daughter Ltd was their book value.

(b) The purchase consideration was satisfied by the issue of 5,400 new ordinary shares in Parent Ltd. The fair value of a £1 ordinary share in Parent Ltd was £2. The fair value of the net assets in Daughter Ltd was their book value.

Required: see above.

* Question 2

(a) On 1 January 20X7 Parent Ltd acquired all the ordinary shares in Daughter Ltd for £16,200 cash. The fair value of the net assets in Daughter Ltd was their book value.

(b) The purchase consideration was satisfied by the issue of 5,400 new ordinary shares in Parent Ltd. The fair value of a £1 ordinary share in Parent Ltd was £3. The fair value of the net assets in Daughter Ltd was their book value.

Required: see above.

* **Question 3**

(a) On 1 January 20X7 Parent Ltd acquired all the ordinary shares in Daughter Ltd for £16,200 cash. The fair value of the net assets in Daughter Ltd was £12,000.

(b) The purchase consideration was satisfied by the issue of 5,400 new ordinary shares in Parent Ltd. The fair value of a £1 ordinary share in Parent Ltd was £3. The fair value of the net assets in Daughter Ltd was £12,000.

Required: see above.

* **Question 4**

On 1 January 20X7 Parent Ltd acquired all the ordinary shares in Daughter Ltd for £6,000 cash. The fair value of the net assets in Daughter Ltd was their book value.

Required: see above.

* **Question 5**

On 1 January 20X7 Parent Ltd acquired 75% of the ordinary shares in Daughter Ltd for £9,000 cash. The fair value of the net assets in Daughter Ltd was their book value. Assume in each case that the non-controlling interest is measured using Method 1.

Required: see above.

* **Question 6**

Rouge plc acquired 100% of the common shares of Noir plc on 1 January 20X0 and gained control. At that date the statements of financial position of the two companies were as follows:

	Rouge € million	Noir € million
ASSETS		
Non-current assets		
Property, plant and equipment	100	60
Investment in Noir	132	
Current assets	80	70
Total assets	312	130
EQUITY AND LIABILITIES		
Ordinary €1 shares	200	60
Retained earnings	52	40
	252	100
Current liabilities	60	30
Total equity and liabilities	312	130

Note: The fair values are the same as the book values.

Required:
Prepare a consolidated statement of financial position for Rouge plc as at 1 January 20X0.

* **Question 7**

Ham plc acquired 100% of the common shares of Burg plc on 1 January 20X0 and gained control. At that date the statements of financial position of the two companies were as follows:

	Ham €000	Burg €000
ASSETS		
Non-current assets		
Property, plant and equipment	250	100
Investment in Burg	90	
Current assets	100	70
Total assets	440	170
EQUITY AND LIABILITIES		
Capital and reserves		
€1 shares	200	100
Retained earnings	160	10
	360	110
Current liabilities	80	60
Total equity and liabilities	440	170

Notes:

1 The fair value is the same as the book value.

2 €15,000 of the negative goodwill (badwill) arises because the net assets have been acquired at below their fair value and the remainder covers expected losses of €3,000 in the year ended 31/12/20X0 and €2,000 in the following year.

Required:
(a) **Prepare a consolidated statement of financial position for Ham plc as at 1 January 20X0.**
(b) **Explain how the negative goodwill (badwill) will be treated.**

* Question 8

Set out below is the summarised statement of financial position of Berlin plc at 1 January 20X0.

	£000
ASSETS	
Non-current assets	
Property, plant and equipment	250
Current assets	150
Total assets	400
EQUITY AND LIABILITIES	
Capital and reserves	
Share capital (£5 shares)	200
Retained earnings	80
	280
Current liabilities	120
Total equity and liabilities	400

On 1/1/20X0 Berlin acquired 100% of the shares of Hanover for £100,000 and gained control.

Required:
Prepare the statement of financial position of Berlin immediately after the acquisition if:
(a) **Berlin acquired the shares for cash.**
(b) **Berlin issued 10,000 shares of £5 (market value £10).**

* Question 9

Bleu plc acquired 80% of the shares of Verte plc on 1 January 20X0 and gained control. At that date the statements of financial position of the two companies were as follows:

	Bleu £m	Verte £m
ASSETS		
Non-current assets		
Property, plant and equipment	150	120
Investment in Verte	210	
Current assets	108	105
Total assets	468	225
EQUITY AND LIABILITIES		
Capital and reserves		
Share capital (£1 shares)	300	120
Retained earnings	78	60
	378	180
Current liabilities	90	45
Total equity and liabilities	468	225

Note: The fair values are the same as the book values.

Required:
Prepare a consolidated statement of financial position for Bleu plc as at 1 January 20X0. Non-controlling interests are measured using Method 1.

* Question 10

Base plc acquired 60% of the common shares of Ball plc on 1 January 20X0 and gained control. At that date the statements of financial position of the two companies were as follows:

	Base £000	Ball £000
ASSETS		
Non-current assets		
Property, plant and equipment	250	100
Investment in Ball	90	
Current assets	100	70
Total assets	440	170
EQUITY AND LIABILITIES		
Capital and reserves		
Share capital	200	80
Share premium		20
Retained earnings	160	10
	360	110
Current liabilities	80	60
Total equity and liabilities	440	170

Note: The fair value of the property, plant and equipment in Ball at 1/1/20X0 was £120,000. The fair value of the non-controlling interest in Ball at 1/1/20X0 was £55,000. The 'fair value method' should be used to measure the non-controlling interest.

Required:
Prepare a consolidated statement of financial position for Base as at 1 January 20X0.

...l in IFRS 10 *Consolidated Financial Statements,* as described in Section ...equired to consider whether certain investments of Austin plc are

...umber of companies, and the company's accountant has asked your ...se companies should be treated as subsidiaries under IFRS 10 *Consoli-*

...voting shares of Bond Ltd.

...oting shares of Bradford Ltd and Bradford Ltd owns 30% of the voting ...tly, Austin plc purchased 70% of the voting shares of Coventry Ltd. ...e voting shares of Derby Ltd. The accountant believes Derby Ltd is not a subsidiary of Austin, as Austin effectively owns only 39% of the shares of Derby – 60% × 30% = 18% through Bradford and 70% × 30% = 21% through Coventry.

(c) Recently, Austin plc purchased 60% of the ordinary shares of Norwich plc.

Prior to the purchase, Norwich plc had in issue 6,000,000 'A' shares of £1 each. Each 'A' share carries a single vote. These shares were owned equally by each of the directors of Norwich plc. For the purchase, the directors of Norwich plc sold 2,000,000 'A' shares to Austin plc, and Norwich plc issued 4,000,000 'B' shares of £1 each to Austin plc. 'B' shares do not carry a vote.

Required:
Consider and, where appropriate, discuss whether the following companies are subsidiaries of Austin plc:
(a) Bond Ltd
(b) Derby Ltd
(c) Norwich plc.

* Question 12

(a) On 1 October 2012, Paradigm acquired 75% of Strata's equity shares by means of a share exchange of two new shares in Paradigm for every five acquired shares in Strata. In addition, Paradigm issued to the shareholders of Strata a $100 10% loan note for every 1,000 shares it acquired in Strata. Paradigm has not recorded any of the purchase consideration, although it does have other 10% loan notes already in issue.

The market value of Paradigm's shares at 1 October 2012 was $2 each.

The summarised statements of financial position of the two companies as at 31 March 2013 are:

	Paradigm	*Strata*
Assets	$000	$000
Non-current assets Property, plant and equipment	47,400	25,500
Financial asset: equity investments (notes (i) and (iv))	7,500	3,200
	54,900	28,700
Current assets		
Inventory (note (ii))	20,400	8,400
Trade receivables (note (iii))	14,800	9,000
Bank	2,100	nil
Total assets	92,200	46,100

	Paradigm	Strata
Equity and liabilities		
Equity		
Equity shares of $1 each	40,000	20,000
Retained earnings/(losses) – at 1 April 2012	19,200	(4,000)
– for year ended 31 March 2013	7,400	8,000
	66,600	24,000
Non-current liabilities		
10% loan notes	8,000	nil
Current liabilities		
Trade payables (note (iii))	17,600	13,000
Bank overdraft nil 9,100		
Total equity and liabilities	92,200	46,100

The following information is relevant:

(i)   At the date of acquisition, Strata produced a draft statement of profit or loss which showed it had made a net loss after tax of $2 million at that date. Paradigm accepted this figure as the basis for calculating the pre- and post-acquisition split of Strata's profit for the year ended 31 March 2013.

Also at the date of acquisition, Paradigm conducted a fair value exercise on Strata's net assets which were equal to their carrying amounts (including Strata's financial asset equity investments) with the exception of an item of plant which had a fair value of $3 million below its carrying amount. The plant had a remaining economic life of three years at 1 October 2012.

Paradigm's policy is to value the non-controlling interest at fair value at the date of acquisition. For this purpose, a share price for Strata of $1.20 each is representative of the fair value of the shares held by the non-controlling interest.

(ii) Each month since acquisition, Paradigm's sales to Strata were consistently $4.6 million. Paradigm had marked these up by 15% on cost. Strata had one month's supply ($4.6 million) of these goods in inventory at 31 March 2013. Paradigm's normal mark-up (to third party customers) is 40%.

(iii) Strata's current account balance with Paradigm at 31 March 2013 was $2.8 million, which did not agree with Paradigm's equivalent receivable due to a payment of $900,000 made by Strata on 28 March 2013, which was not received by Paradigm until 3 April 2013.

(iv) The financial asset equity investments of Paradigm and Strata are carried at their fair values as at 1 April 2012. As at 31 March 2013, these had fair values of $7.1 million and $3.9 million respectively.

(v) There were no impairment losses within the group during the year ended 31 March 2013.

Required:
Prepare the consolidated statement of financial position for Paradigm as at 31 March 2013.

(b) Paradigm has a strategy of buying struggling businesses, reversing their decline and then selling them on at a profit within a short period of time. Paradigm is hoping to do this with Strata.

Required:
As an adviser to a prospective purchaser of Strata, explain any concerns you would raise about basing an investment decision on the information available in Paradigm's consolidated financial statements and Strata's entity financial statements.

(ACCA Financial Reporting June 2013)

Notes

1 IFRS 10 *Consolidated Financial Statements*, IASB, 2011, B 92-93.
2 Ibid., para. 7.
3 IFRS 3 *Business Combinations*, 2008, B 44.
4 IAS 36 *Impairment of Assets*, IASB, revised 2004, para. 34.
5 IFRS 3 *Business Combinations*, 2008, B 34.
6 IFRS 10 *Consolidated Financial Statements*, IASB, 2011.
7 Ibid., paras 5, 6 and 8.
8 IFRS 13 *Fair Value Measurement*, IASB, 2011, Appendix A.
9 IFRS 10 *Consolidated Financial Settlements*, IASB, 2011, B 92-93.

CHAPTER 14

Preparation of consolidated statements of financial position after the date of acquisition

14.1 Introduction

The main purpose of this chapter is to prepare consolidated financial statements after a period of trading.

Objectives

By the end of this chapter, you should be able to:

- explain uniform accounting policies;
- account for the pre- and post-acquisition profits of a subsidiary;
- eliminate inter-company balances and deal with reconciling items;
- account for unrealised profits on inter-company transactions;
- calculate group retained earnings;
- prepare consolidated statements of financial position.

14.2 Uniform accounting policies and reporting dates

Consolidated financial statements are required to adopt uniform accounting policies on a consistent basis in accordance with IFRS 10 *Consolidated Financial Statements*. The following is an extract from the 2015 Annual Report of Munksjo AB:

Accounting policies for subsidiaries are changed where necessary to ensure consistent application of the Group's policies.

If this is not practicable then disclosure must be made of that together with details of the items involved.[1]

The financial statements of the parent and subsidiaries used in the consolidated accounts are usually drawn up to the same date but IFRS 10 continues to allow up to three months' difference providing that appropriate adjustments are made for significant transactions outside the common period.[2]

14.3 Pre- and post-acquisition profits/losses

Pre-acquisition profits

Any profits or losses of a subsidiary made **before** the date of acquisition are referred to as **pre-acquisition profits/losses** in the consolidated financial statements. These are represented by the retained earnings that existed in the subsidiary as at the date of acquisition and, as we have seen in Chapter 13, they are taken into account when calculating the goodwill.

It is important to remember that the calculation of the initial goodwill as at the date of acquisition is unchanged in subsequent accounting periods. The goodwill only changes in subsequent accounting periods if there should be an impairment charge or amortisation charge if that should be the regulatory requirement in the local jurisdiction.

Post-acquisition profits

Any profits or losses made **after** the date of acquisition are referred to as **post-acquisition profits/losses**. Because these will have arisen while the subsidiary was under the control of the parent company, they will be included in the group consolidated statement of income and so will be included in the retained earnings figure in the statement of financial position. The following example for the Bend Group illustrates the approach for dealing with pre- and post-acquisition profits.

14.4 The Bend Group – assuming there have been no inter-group transactions

On 1 January 20X1 Bend plc acquired 80% of the 10,000 £1 ordinary shares in Stretch plc for £1.50 per share in cash which gave it control.

- Investment in the subsidiary cost £12,000.
- The retained earnings of Stretch plc were £4,000.
- The fair value of the non-current assets in Stretch plc was £600 above book value.
- The fair value of the non-controlling interest at the date of acquisition was £2,950 and Method 2 has been adopted.

Remember that in the subsidiary's own accounts the assets may be either left at book values or restated at their fair values. If restated at fair values, they will then become subject to the requirements of IAS 16 *Property, Plant and Equipment*[3] which states that revaluations should be made with sufficient regularity that the statement of financial position figure is not materially different from the fair value at that date. This is one reason why the fair value adjustment is usually treated simply as a consolidation adjustment each year.

At 31 December 20X1 the closing statements of financial position of Bend plc and Stretch plc together with the group accounts were as follows:

	Bend £	Stretch £	Group £	
ASSETS				
Non-current assets	26,000	12,000	38,600	Step 3
Goodwill	—	—	350	Step 1
Investment in Stretch	12,000	—	—	
Net current assets	13,000	4,000	17,000	Step 3
Net assets	51,000	16,000	55,950	
EQUITY				
Share capital	16,000	10,000	16,000	Step 4
Retained earnings	35,000	6,000	36,600	Step 4
	51,000	16,000	52,600	
Non-controlling interest	—	—	3,350	Step 2
	51,000	16,000	55,950	

Step 1: Goodwill calculated as at 1 January 20X1

	£	£
Goodwill on Bend's 80% shareholding in Stretch		
The cost of the parent company's investment in Stretch		12,000
Less:		
(a) Bend's share of Stretch share capital:		
80% × share capital of Stretch (80% × 10,000)	8,000	
(b) Pre-acquisition profit		
Bend's share of Stretch's retained earnings:		
80% × retained earnings as at 1 January 20X1 (80% × 4,000)	3,200	
(c) Fair value adjustment		
Bend's share of any change in the book values:		
80% × revaluation of fixed assets at 1 January 20X1 (80% × 600)	480	
		11,680
Goodwill attributable to the parent company shareholders		320
Goodwill on non-controlling interest's 20% shareholding in Stretch		
Fair value of non-controlling interest at date of acquisition		2,950
20% of net assets at date of acquisition (10,000 + 4,000 + 600)		(2,920)
Goodwill attributable to the non-controlling interest		30
Total goodwill of parent and non-controlling interest (£320 + £30)		£350

Step 2: Non-controlling interest in the net assets of subsidiary calculated as at 31.12.20X1

	£
(a) Subsidiary share capital	
Non-controlling interest in the share capital of Stretch (20% × 10,000)	2,000
(b) Total retained earnings as at 31.12.20X1	
Non-controlling interest in retained earnings of Stretch (20% × 6,000)	1,200
(c) Fair value adjustment of subsidiary's non-current assets	
Non-controlling interest in fair value increase (20% × 600)	120
Non-controlling interest in the net assets of Stretch as at 31.12.20X1	3,320
Non-controlling interest in goodwill	30
Reported in the statement of financial position as at 31 December 20X1	3,350

Step 3: Add together the assets and liabilities of the parent and subsidiary for the group

	Parent	*Subsidiary*	*Group*
	£	£	£
Non-current tangible assets	26,000	+ (12,000 + revaluation 600)	38,600
Goodwill as calculated in Step 1			350
Net current assets	13,000	+ 4,000	17,000
Total			55,950

Step 4: Calculate the consolidated share capital and reserves for the group accounts

			£	£
Share capital	Parent only			16,000
Retained earnings	Parent		35,000	
	Bend's share of			
	post-acquisition			
	retained earnings	(80% of (6,000 − 4,000))	1,600	36,600
Total				52,600

Notes:

1 The separation of the retained earnings into pre- and post-acquisition is only of relevance to the parent with the pre-acquisition (£4,000) used when calculating the goodwill and the post-acquisition (£2,000) reported as part of the group earnings.

2 The non-controlling shareholders are entitled to their percentage share of the closing net assets. The pre-acquisition and post-acquisition division is irrelevant to the non-controlling interests – they are entitled to their percentage share of the **total** retained earnings at the date the consolidated statement of financial position is prepared.

14.5 Inter-company transactions

In the Bend example we assumed that there had been no inter-company transactions. In most groups, however, there are inter-company transactions that take place. On consolidation IFRS 10 requires[4] all inter-company transactions to be eliminated. So, if goods have been sold by Many plc, the parent, for £1,500 to Few plc, a subsidiary, the sales that had been reported in Many's statement of income and the cost of sales reported in Few's statement of income would both be eliminated. This is accomplished by a consolidation journal entry:

	Dr	Cr
Sales	1,500	
Cost of sales		1,500
Eliminating intra-group sales		

Note that no entries are made in the individual company's accounts and the elimination is simply to ensure that the consolidated sales and cost of sales only include transactions with non-group parties.

14.5.1 Adjustment when inter-company sales include a profit loading

Where sales have been made between two companies within the group, it is only necessary to provide for an unrealised profit from intra-group sales to the extent that the goods are still in the inventories of the group at the date of the statement of financial position.

We will illustrate the accounting treatment where there is unrealised profit with the Many Group example.

Let us assume that Many plc has bought £1,000 worth of goods for resale and sold them to Few plc for £1,500, making a profit of £500 in Many's own accounts.

We have already seen that one of the consolidated journal entries would be to debit sales £1,500 and credit cost of sales £1,500, whether or not the goods had been sold on to a third party.

If at the year-end Few plc still has these goods in inventory, the group has not yet made a sale to a third party and the £500 profit is therefore 'unrealised'. It must be removed from the consolidated statement of financial position by:

● reducing the retained earnings of Many by £500; and

● reducing the inventories of Few by £500.

The £500 is called a 'provision for unrealised profit'.

If the sale is made by a subsidiary to the parent and there are non-controlling interests, these will be debited with their 'proportion of the unrealised profit'.

14.5.2 Eliminating inter-company current account balances

If the sale were made for cash, then the cash in the seller would have increased and the cash in the buyer would have decreased. On consolidation no adjustment is, therefore, required. However, if the invoice has not been settled, there would be an account receivable in the seller's and an account payable in the buyer's statement of financial position. These must be eliminated by cancelling each.

In our Many Group example, the £1,500 would be cancelled.

Reconciling inter-company balances

In practice, temporary differences may arise for such items as cash or inventory in transit that are recorded in one company's books but of which the other company is not yet aware. If so, this is reconciled on consolidation for cash in transit, debit Cash and credit Accounts receivable and for inventory in transit, debit Inventory and credit Accounts payable.

If Few had sent cash of £400 to Many in part settlement of the £1,500 owing but it had not been recorded in the books of Many at the period-end date, the Many accounts would show £1,500 owing, whereas the Few accounts would show £1,100 owing and the cash balance reduced by the £500. On consolidation the Accounts receivable would be reduced to £1,100 and the cash increased by £400. The Account receivable and payable balances are both £1,100 and would be cancelled.

14.5.3 Inter-company dividends payable/receivable

If the subsidiary company has declared a dividend before the year-end, it will appear in the current liabilities of the subsidiary company and in the current assets of the parent company. It needs to be cancelled by set-off.

If the subsidiary is wholly owned by the parent the whole amount will be cancelled. If, however, there is a non-controlling interest in the subsidiary, the non-cancelled amount of the dividend payable in the subsidiary's statement of financial position will be the amount payable to the non-controlling interest and will be reported as part of the non-controlling interest in the consolidated statement of financial position.

Where a final dividend has not been declared by the year-end date there is no liability under IAS 10 *Events after the Reporting Period Date* and no liability will be reported.

Companies include a reference to these adjustments in their accounting policies, as seen in the following extract from the 2017 Annual Report of Munksjo AB:

> **Transaction eliminated on consolidation**
>
> Transactions between Group companies, including intra–group receivables and liabilities, income or expenses and unrealized gains or losses are eliminated in full.

The Prose Group example that follows incorporates the main points dealt with so far on the preparation of a consolidated statement of financial position.

14.6 The Prose Group – assuming there have been inter-group transactions

On 1 January 20X1 Prose plc acquired 80% of the equity shares in Verse plc for £21,100 to gain control and 10% of the 5% loans for £900. The retained earnings as at 1 January 20X1 were £4,000. The fair value of the land in Verse was £1,000 above book value.

During the year Prose sold some of its inventory to Verse for £3,000, which represented cost plus a markup of 25%. Half of these goods are still in the inventory of Verse at 31/12/20X1.

The consolidated statement of financial position as at 31 December 20X1 is shown below with supporting notes. Note that depreciation is not charged on land and Method 1 is used to compute the non-controlling interest.

	Prose £	Verse £	Adjustments Dr	Group Cr	£	
ASSETS						
Non-current assets	25,920	33,400	1,000		60,320	
Investment in Verse/goodwill	22,000	—		21,500	500	Step 1
Current assets						
Inventories	9,600	4,000		300	13,300	Step 3
Verse current account	8,000			8,000	—	Step 2
Loan interest receivable	35			35	—	Step 2
Other current assets	3,965	13,350			17,315	
Total assets	69,520	50,750			91,435	
EQUITY and LIABILITIES						
Equity share capital	24,000	21,000	21,000		24,000	
Retained earnings	30,000	8,500	5,200		33,300	Step 5
Non-controlling interest	—	—		6,100	6,100	Step 4
Non-current liabilities						
5% loan 2017/18	5,000	7,000	700		11,300	Step 2
Current liabilities						
Prose current account		8,000	8,000		—	
Loan interest payable		350	35		315	
Other current liabilities	10,520	5,900			16,420	
	69,520	50,750	35,935	35,935	91,435	

Step 1: Calculation of goodwill

(Note that this calculation will be the same as when calculated at the date of acquisition)

	£	£
Cost of investment in shares and loan		22,000
Less:		
1 80% × equity shares of Verse (80% × 21,000)	16,800	
2 80% × retained earnings balance at 1.1.20X1 (80% × 4,000)	3,200	
3 80% × fair value increase at 1.1.20X1 (80% × 1,000)	800	
4 10% × loans of Verse (10% × 7,000)	700	21,500
5 Goodwill in statement of financial position		500

Step 2: Inter-company elimination by set-off of inter-company balances

1 The current accounts of £8,000 between the two companies are cancelled. Note that the accounts are equal, which indicates that there are no items such as goods in transit or cash in transit which would have required a reconciliation.

2 The loan interest receivable by Prose is cancelled with £35 (10% of £350) of the loan interest payable by Verse, leaving £315 (90% of £350) payable to outsiders. This is not part of the non-controlling interest as loan holders have no ownership rights in the company.

3 The loan of £700 in Prose's accounts is set off against the £7,000 in Verse's accounts, leaving 6,300 owing to non-group members.

Step 3: Unrealised profit in inventory

Markup on the inter-company sales (£3,000 × 20%)	£600
Half the goods are still in inventories at the year-end.	
Unrealised profit	£300

Step 4: Calculation of non-controlling interest as at 31/12/20X1

Note that the non-controlling interest is calculated as at the year-end while goodwill is calculated at the date of acquisition.

		£
Non-controlling interest in the equity shares of Verse	(20% × 21,000)	4,200
Non-controlling interest in the retained earnings of Verse	(20% × 8,500)	1,700
Non-controlling interest in the fair value increase	(20% × 1,000)	200
Statement of financial position figure		6,100

Step 5: Calculation of consolidated share capital and reserves for the group accounts

	£	£
Share capital:		
Equity share capital (parent company's only)		24,000
Retained earnings (parent company's)	30,000	
Less: Provision for unrealised profit	(300)	29,700
Parent's share of the post-acquisition profit of the subsidiary		
(80% × 8,500)	6,800	
Less: 80% of pre-acquisition profits (80% × 4,000)	(3,200)	3,600
Retained earnings in the consolidated statement of financial position		33,300

Summary

When consolidated accounts are prepared after the subsidiary has traded with other members of the group, the goodwill calculation remains as at the date of the acquisition but all inter-company transactions and unrealised profits arising from inter-company transactions must be eliminated.

REVIEW QUESTIONS

1 An accounting policy states that all inter-company transactions, receivables, liabilities and unrealised profits, as well as intra-group profit distributions, are eliminated.

  (a) Discuss three examples of inter-company (also referred to as intra-group) transactions.

  (b) Explain what is meant by 'are eliminated'.

  (c) Explain what effect there could be on the reported group profit if inter-company transactions were not eliminated.

2 Explain why the non-controlling interest is not affected by the pre- and post-acquisition division.

3 Explain why pre-acquisition profits of a subsidiary are treated differently from post-acquisition profits when consolidating.

4 Explain the effect of a provision for unrealised profit on a non-controlling interest:

  (a) where the sale was made by the parent to the subsidiary; and

  (b) where the sale was made by the subsidiary to the parent.

5 A consolidated journal adjustment set off the dividend receivable reported in the parent's statement of financial position against the dividend declared by the subsidiary. Explain why this may not fully eliminate the dividend that is reported in the group statement of financial position.

6 Explain reasons why the current accounts in the parent and subsidiary may not agree. If not, how could the two accounts be set off?

EXERCISES

* Question 1

Sweden acquired 100% of the equity shares of Oslo on 1 March 20X1 and gained control. At that date the balances on the reserves of Oslo were as follows:

Revaluation reserve	Kr10 million
Retained earnings	Kr70 million

The statements of financial position of the two companies at 31/12/20X1 were as follows:

	Sweden Krm	Oslo Krm
ASSETS		
Non-current assets		
Property, plant and equipment	264	120
Investment in Oslo	200	
Current assets	160	140
Total assets	624	260

	Sweden Krm	Oslo Krm
EQUITY AND LIABILITIES		
Kr10 shares	400	110
Retained earnings	104	80
Revaluation reserve	20	10
	524	200
Current liabilities	100	60
Total equity and liabilities	624	260

Notes:

1. The fair values were the same as the book values on 1/3/20X1.
2. There have been no movements on share capital since 1/3/20X1.
3. 20% of the goodwill is to be written off as an impairment loss.
4. Method 1 is to be used to compute the non-controlling interest.

Required:
Prepare a consolidated statement of financial position for Sweden as at 31 December 20X1.

* Question 2

Summer plc acquired 60% of the equity shares of Winter Ltd on 30 September 20X1 and gained control. At the date of acquisition, the balance of retained earnings of Winter was €35,000.

At 31 December 20X1 the statements of financial position of the two companies were as follows:

	Summer €000	Winter €000
ASSETS		
Non-current assets		
Property, plant and equipment	200	200
Investment in Winter	141	
Current assets	100	140
Total assets	441	340
EQUITY AND LIABILITIES		
Equity shares	200	180
Retained earnings	161	40
	361	220
Current liabilities	80	120
Total equity and liabilities	441	340

Notes:

1. The fair value of the non-controlling interest at the date of acquisition was £92,000. The non-controlling interest is to be measured using Method 2. The fair values of the identifiable net assets of Winter at the date of acquisition were the same as their book values.

2. There have been no movements on share capital since 30/9/20X1.

Required:
Prepare a consolidated statement of financial position for Summer plc as at 31 December 20X1.

* Question 3

On 30 September 20X0 Gold plc acquired 75% of the equity shares, 30% of the preferred shares and 20% of the bonds in Silver plc and gained control. The balance of retained earnings on 30 September 20X0 was £16,000. The fair value of the land owned by Silver was £3,000 above book value. No adjustment has so far been made for this revaluation.

The statements of financial position of Gold and Silver at 31 December 20X1 were as follows:

	Gold £	Silver £
ASSETS		
Property, plant and equipment (including land)	82,300	108,550
Investment in Silver	46,000	—
Current assets		
Inventory	23,200	10,000
Silver current account	20,000	
Bond interest receivable	175	
Other current assets	5,000	7,500
Total assets	176,675	126,050
EQUITY AND LIABILITIES		
Equity share capital	60,000	27,600
Preferred shares	10,000	20,000
Retained earnings	75,000	21,200
	145,000	68,800
Non-current liabilities – bonds	12,500	17,500
Current liabilities		
Gold current account		20,000
Bond interest payable	625	875
Other current liabilities	18,550	18,875
Total equity and liabilities	176,675	126,050

Notes:

1 The recoverable amount for purposes of calculating the impairment of goodwill is £50,040.

2 During the year Gold sold some of its inventory to Silver for £3,000, which represented cost plus a markup of 25%. Half of these goods are still in the inventory of Silver at 31.12.20X1.

3 There is no depreciation of land.

4 There has been no movement on share capital since the acquisition.

5 Method 1 is to be used to compute the non-controlling interest.

Required:
Prepare a consolidated statement of financial position as at 31 December 20X1.

* Question 4

Prop and Flap have produced the following statements of financial position as at 31 October 2008:

	Prop		Flap	
	$m	$m	$m	$m
ASSETS				
Non-current assets				
Plant and equipment		2,100		480
Investments		800		
Current assets				
Inventories	880		280	
Receivables	580		420	
Cash and cash equivalents	400		8	
		1,860		708
Total assets		4,760		1,188
EQUITY and LIABILITIES				
Equity share capital		2,400		680
Retained earnings		860		200
		3,260		880
Non-current liabilities				
Long-term borrowing		400		
Current liabilities				
Payables	1,100		228	
Bank overdraft	—		80	
		1,100		308
Total equity and liabilities		4,760		1,188

The following information is relevant to the preparation of the financial statements of the Prop Group:

1 Prop acquired 80% of the issued ordinary share capital of Flap many years ago when the retained earnings of Flap were $72 million. Consideration transferred was $800 million. Flap has performed well since acquisition and so far there has been no impairment to goodwill.

2 At the date of acquisition the plant and equipment of Flap was revalued upwards by $40 million, although this revaluation was not recorded in the accounts of Flap. Depreciation would have been $32 million greater had it been based on the revalued figure.

3 Flap buys goods from Prop upon which Prop earns a margin of 20%. At 31 October 2008 Flap's inventories include $180 million goods purchased from Prop.

4 At 31 October 2008 Prop has receivables of $140 million owed by Flap and payables of $60 million owed to Flap.

5 The market price of the non-controlling interest shares just before Flap's acquisition by Prop was $1.30. It is the group's policy to value the non-controlling interest at fair value.

Required:
Prepare the Prop Group consolidated statement of financial position as at 31 October 2008.

(Association of International Accountants)

* Question 5

On 1 January 20X0 Hill plc purchased 70% of the ordinary shares of Valley plc for £1.3 million. The fair value of the non-controlling interest at that date was £0.5 million. At the date of acquisition, Valley's retained earnings were £0.4 million.

The statements of financial position of Hill and Valley at 31 December 20X0 were:

	Hill	Valley
Capital and reserves	£000	£000
Share capital	5,000	1,000
Retained earnings	3,500	200
	8,500	1,200
Net assets	8,500	1,200

Because of Valley's loss in 20X0, the directors of Hill decided to write down the value of goodwill by £0.3 million. The directors of Hill propose to use Method 2 to calculate goodwill in the consolidated statement of financial position. The goodwill is to be written down in proportion to the respective holdings of Valley's shares by Hill and the non-controlling interest.

Required:
(a) Calculate the goodwill of Valley relating to Hill plc and the non-controlling interest.
(b) Show how the goodwill will be written down at 31 December 20X0, for both Hill plc and the non-controlling interest.
(c) Comment on your answer to part (b).

* Question 6

The following accounts are the consolidated statement of financial position and parent company statement of financial position for Alpha Ltd as at 30 June 20X2:

	Consolidated statement of financial position		Parent company statement of financial position	
	£	£	£	£
Ordinary shares		140,000		140,000
Capital reserve		92,400		92,400
Retained earnings		79,884		35,280
Non-controlling interest		12,329		—
		324,613		267,680
Non-current assets				
Property		127,400		84,000
Plant and equipment		62,720		50,400
Goodwill		85,680		
Investment in subsidiary (50,400 shares)				151,200
Current assets				
Inventory	121,604		71,120	
Trade receivables	70,429		51,800	
Cash at bank	24,360		—	
	216,393		122,920	

	Consolidated statement of financial position		Parent company statement of financial position	
	£	£	£	£
Current liabilities				
Trade payables	140,420		80,920	
Income tax	27,160		20,720	
Bank overdraft	—		39,200	
	167,580		140,840	
Working capital		48,813		(17,920)
		324,613		267,680

Notes:

1 There was only one subsidiary, called Beta Ltd.

2 There were no capital reserves in the subsidiary.

3 Alpha produced inventory for sale to the subsidiary at a cost of £3,360 in May 20X2. The inventory was invoiced to the subsidiary at £4,200 and was still on hand at the subsidiary's warehouse on 30 June 20X2. The invoice had not been settled at 30 June 20X2.

4 The retained earnings of the subsidiary had a credit balance of £16,800 at the date of acquisition. No fair value adjustments were necessary.

5 There was a right of set-off between overdrafts and bank balances.

6 The parent owns 90% of the subsidiary.

Required:
Prepare the statement of financial position as at 30 June 20X2 of the subsidiary company from the information given above. The non-controlling interest is measured using Method 1.

Notes

1 IFRS 10 *Consolidated Financial Statements*, IASB, 2011, para. 19.
2 Ibid., B 92–93.
3 IAS 16 *Property, Plant and Equipment*, IASB, revised 2003, para. 31.
4 IFRS 10 *Consolidated Financial Statements*, IASB, 2011, B 86.

CHAPTER 15

Preparation of consolidated statements of income, changes in equity and cash flows

15.1 Introduction

The main purpose of this chapter is to explain how to prepare a consolidated statement of income.

Objectives

By the end of this chapter, you should be able to:

- eliminate inter-company transactions;
- prepare a consolidated statement of income;
- attribute income to the non-controlling shareholders;
- prepare a consolidated statement of changes in equity;
- prepare a consolidated statement of income when a subsidiary is acquired partway through a year;
- prepare a consolidated statement of cash flows.

15.2 Eliminate inter-company transactions

Many business combinations occur because the acquirer seeks closer links with the acquired company. There are many examples of this, such as a clothing manufacturer in Europe acquiring a denim supplier in Hong Kong with inter-company purchases and sales following the acquisition.

Inter-company sales

When the consolidated statement of income is prepared the inter-company sales are eliminated. This avoids the possibility that the group could inflate its revenue merely by group companies selling to each other. The sales and purchases both need to be reduced by the invoiced amount of the inter-company sales. This is achieved in the consolidation process by reducing the aggregate sales and aggregate cost of sales figures.

Unrealised profit

In the previous chapter we treated any unrealised profit by reducing the inventory figure and reducing the retained earnings figure. The retained earnings figure would have incorporated the retained earnings balance from the statement of income, i.e. the adjustment for the unrealised profit would have already been reported in the statement of income.

In the consolidation process the unrealised profit is added to the cost of sales to achieve the reduction in group gross profit.

Dividends and interest

Having set off the sales and cost of sales and adjusted for any unrealised profit, further adjustments may be required[1] to establish the profit before tax earned by the group as a whole. This requires us to eliminate any dividends (and interest if any) that have been credited in the parent's statement of income for amounts paid or payable to the parent by the subsidiaries.

If this were not done, there would be double-counting because we would be including in the consolidated statement of income the subsidiary's profit from operations and again as dividends and interest received/receivable by the parent.

Group profits before tax

We can see, therefore, that group profit before tax is arrived at after setting-off inter-company sales against the cost of sales, adding the unrealised profit to the cost of sales figure, and eliminating any dividends or interest received or receivable from a subsidiary.

We will illustrate this in the following Ante Group example.

15.3 Preparation of a consolidated statement of income – the Ante Group

The following information is available:

At the date of acquisition on 1 January 20X3:
Ante plc acquired 75% of the ordinary shares in Post plc. (*This shows that Ante had control.*) At that date the retained earnings of Post were £30,000. (*These are pre-acquisition profits and should not be included in the group profit for the year.*)

At the end of 20X3:
The retained earnings of Ante were £69,336 and the retained earnings of Post were £54,000.

During the year ended 31 December 20X4:
Ante had sold Post goods at their cost price of £9,000 plus a markup of one-third. These were the only inter-company sales. (*This indicates that the group sales and cost of sales require reducing.*)

At the end of the financial year on 31 December 20X4:
Half of these goods were still in the inventory at the end of the year. (*There is unrealised profit to be removed from the group gross profit by adding the unrealised amount to the cost of sales figure.*)

Dividends paid in 20X4 by group companies were as follows:

	Ante	*Post*
On ordinary shares	£40,000	£5,000

Set out below are the individual statements of income of Ante and Post together with the consolidated statement of income for the year ended 31 December 20X4 with explanatory notes.

Statements of comprehensive income for the year ended 31 December 20X4

	Ante £	Post £	Consolidated £	
Sales	200,000	120,000	308,000	Note 1
Cost of sales	60,000	60,000	109,500	Notes 1 and 2
Gross profit	140,000	60,000	198,500	
Expenses	59,082	40,000	99,082	Note 3
Profit from operations	80,918	20,000	99,418	
Dividends received – ordinary shares	3,750	—	—	
Profit before tax	84,668	20,000	99,418	Note 4
Income tax expense	14,004	6,000	20,004	Note 5
Profit for the period	70,664	14,000	79,414	
Attributable to:				
Ordinary shareholders of Ante (balance)			75,914	
Non-controlling shareholders in Post			3,500	Note 6
			79,414	

Notes:

1 Eliminate inter-company sales on consolidation
   Cancel the inter-company sales of £12,000 (£9,000 × 1⅓) by

   (i)   reducing the sales of Ante from £200,000 to £188,000; and

   (ii) reducing the cost of sales of Post by the same amount from £60,000 to £48,000.
         (Remember that the same amount is deducted from both sales and cost of sales – a sale to one party is the amount of the purchase by the other party.)

   (iii) Group sales are £188,000 + £120,000 = £308,000.

   (iv) Group cost of sales (before any adjustment for unrealised profit) is £60,000 + £48,000 = £108,000.

2 Eliminate unrealised profit on inter-company goods still in closing inventory

   (i)   Ante had sold the goods to Post at a markup of £3,000.

   (ii) Half of the goods remain in the inventory of Post at the year-end.

   (iii) From the group's view there is an unrealised profit of half of the markup, i.e. £1,500. Therefore:

         ● deduct £1,500 from the gross profit of Ante by adding this amount to the cost of sales;

         ● reduce the inventories in the consolidated statement of financial position by the amount of the provision (as explained in the previous chapter).

   (iv) Cost of sales has been increased from £108,000 to £109,500.

3 Aggregate expenses

   In this example we do not have any inter-company transactions such as Head Office management fees that need to be set off. No adjustment is, therefore, required to the parent or subsidiary total figures.

4 **Profit before tax, accounting for the inter-company dividends**

The ordinary dividend of £3,750 received by Ante is an inter-company item that does not appear in the group profit before tax.

5 **Aggregate the taxation figures**

No adjustment is required to the parent or subsidiary total figures.

6 **Allocation of profit to equity holders and non-controlling interest**

Adjustment is required[2] to establish how much of the profit after tax is attributable to equity holders of the parent. The amount is that remaining after deducting the non-controlling interest's percentage of the subsidiary's after-tax figure, i.e. 25% of £14,000 = £3,500.

15.4 The statement of changes in equity (SOCE)[3]

In practice the opening figures for the SOCE would be available from the 20X3 group accounts. It is not uncommon in an examination context to require you to calculate the opening figure for the group SOCE. The calculation is as follows:

Opening balance for the Ante group

	£
Ante's retained earnings at the start of the year	69,336
Group share of Post's post-acquisition earnings (75% × (54,000 − 30,000))	18,000
	87,336

Opening balance for the non-controlling interest

Total retained earnings as at 31.12.20X3	25% of 54,000	13,500

We can then complete the group SOCE as follows:

	Ante	Non-controlling interest	Total
	£	£	£
Opening balance	87,336	13,500	100,836
Income for the period	75,914	3,500	79,414
Dividends paid	(40,000)	(1,250)	(41,250)
Closing balance	123,250	15,750	139,000

Dividends paid

In the Ante column the dividends paid are those of the parent only. The parent company's share of Post's dividend cancels out with the parent company's investment income. The non-controlling share is £5,000 minus the £3,750 paid to the parent. This is the amount dealt with in their column.

15.5 Other consolidation adjustments

In the above example we dealt with adjustments for intra-group sale of goods, unrealised profit on inventories and dividends received from a subsidiary. There are other adjustments that often appear in examinations relating to depreciation and dividends paid by a subsidiary out of pre-acquisition profits.

15.5.1 Depreciation adjustment when fair value is higher than book value

If the fair value of depreciable non-current assets is different from their book value, it is necessary to adjust the depreciation that has been charged in the subsidiary's books.

For example, assume that the parent acquired a non-current asset from a subsidiary which had a book value of £100,000 that was being depreciated by the subsidiary on a straight-line basis over five years and the scrap value was nil. The annual charge in the subsidiary's statement of income would be £20,000.

If the fair value on acquisition was £150,000, the charge in the consolidated statement of income should be based on the £150,000, i.e. £30,000 (£150,000/5) with the depreciation increased by £10,000. If there is no information as to the type of non-current asset, the £10,000 would be added to the cost of sales figure. If the type of asset is identified, for example as delivery vehicles, then the adjustment would be made to the appropriate expense, e.g. distribution costs.

15.5.2 Depreciation adjustment when transfer has been at cost plus a profit loading

Let us consider Digdeep plc, a civil engineering company that has a subsidiary, Heavylift plc, that manufactures digging equipment. Assume that at the beginning of the financial year Heavylift sold equipment costing £80,000 to Digdeep for £100,000. It is Digdeep's depreciation policy to depreciate at 5% using the straight-line method with nil scrap value.

On consolidation, the following adjustments are required:

(i) Revenue is reduced by £20,000 and the asset is reduced by £20,000 to bring the asset back to its cost of £80,000.

Dr: Revenue	£20,000	
Cr: Asset		£20,000

(ii) Revenue is then reduced by £80,000 and cost of sales reduced by £80,000 to eliminate the inter-company sale.

Dr: Revenue	£80,000	
Cr: Cost of sales		£80,000

(iii) Depreciation needs to be based on the cost of £80,000. The depreciation charge was £5,000 (5% of £100,000); it should be £4,000 (5% of £80,000) so the adjustment is:

Dr: Accumulated depreciation	£1,000	
Cr: Depreciation in the statement of income		£1,000

15.5.3 Dividends or interest paid by the subsidiary out of pre-acquisition profits

When a parent acquires the net assets of a subsidiary it is paying for all of the assets including the cash. If the subsidiary then pays part of this to the parent as a dividend it is in effect transferring an asset that the parent had already paid for. The dividend received by the parent is not, therefore, income but a return of part of the purchase price. It is credited by the parent to the investment in subsidiary account. This is illustrated in the Bow plc example below.

Illustration of a dividend paid out of pre-acquisition profits

Bow plc acquired 75% of the shares in Tie plc on 1 January 20X4 for £80,000 when the balance of the retained earnings of Tie was £40,000. On 10 January 20X4 Bow received a dividend of £3,000 from Tie out of the profits for the year ended 31/12/20X3. The draft summarised statements of income for the year ended 31/12/20X4 were as follows:

	Bow £	Tie £	Consolidated £
Gross profit	130,000	70,000	200,000
Expenses	50,000	40,000	90,000
Profit from operations	80,000	30,000	110,000
Dividends received from Tie (see note)	3,000	—	—
Profit before tax	83,000	30,000	110,000
Income tax expense	24,000	6,000	30,000
Profit for the period	59,000	24,000	80,000

Note:
The treatment is incorrect. The £3,000 dividend received from Tie is not income and must not therefore appear in Bow's statement of income. The correct treatment is to deduct it from the investment in Tie, which will then become £77,000 (80,000 − 3,000) with a debit to dividends received and a credit to the Investment in Tie.

15.5.4 Goodwill

We know that there is no amortisation charge for goodwill. However, if there has been any impairment then this would appear as an expense in the group column of the consolidated statement of income.

For example, if in our Ante example above you were informed that the goodwill on acquisition was £10,000 and that it had been impaired by £2,000, the consolidated statement of income would have an entry in the group column and appear as follows:

	Ante £	Post £	Consolidated £	
Sales	200,000	120,000	308,000	Note 1
Cost of sales	60,000	60,000	109,500	Notes 1/2
Gross profit	140,000	60,000	198,500	
Expenses	59,082	40,000	99,082	Note 3
Goodwill impairment			2,000	
Profit from operations	80,918	20,000	97,418	

15.6 A subsidiary acquired part-way through the year

It would be attractive for a company whose results had not been as good as expected to acquire a profitable subsidiary at the end of the year and take its current year's profit into the group accounts. However, this is window dressing and it is not permitted. The group can only bring in a subsidiary's profits from the date of the acquisition when it assumed control. The Tight plc example below illustrates the approach.

15.6.1 Illustration of a subsidiary acquired part-way through the year – Tight plc

The following information is available:

At the date of acquisition on 30 September 20X1
Tight acquired 75% of the shares and 20% of the 5% long-term loans in Loose. The book value and fair value were the same amount.

During the year
There have been no inter-company sales. If there had been then normal set-off would apply. All income and expenses are deemed to accrue evenly through the year and the dividend received may be apportioned to pre- and post-acquisition on a time basis.

At the end of the financial year
The Tight Group prepares its accounts as at 31 December each year.

Set out below are the individual statements of income of Tight and Loose together with the consolidated statement of income for the year ended 31 December 20X1.

	Tight	Loose	Time-apportion		Consolidated
	£	£		£	£
Revenue	200,000	120,000	3/12	30,000	230,000
Cost of sales	60,000	60,000	3/12	15,000	75,000
Gross profit	140,000	60,000	3/12	15,000	155,000
Expenses	59,082	30,000	3/12	7,500	66,582
Interest paid on 5% loans		10,000		2,500	2,000
Interest received on Loose loans	2,000		Set off		NIL
	82,918	20,000			86,418
Dividends received	3,600	NIL	Set off		NIL
Profit before tax	86,518	20,000			86,418
Income tax expense	14,004	6,000	3/12	1,500	15,504
Profit for the period after tax	72,514	14,000		3,500	70,914
Attributable to:					
Ordinary shareholders of Tight (balance)		70,039			
Non-controlling shareholders in Loose		875			
					70,914

Notes:

1   Time-apportion and aggregate the revenue, cost of sales, expenses and income tax Group items include a full year for the parent company and three months for the subsidiary (1 October to 31 December).

2   Account for inter-company interest.

Inter-company expense items need to be eliminated or cancelled by set-off against the interest paid by Loose. Interest is an expense which is normally deemed to accrue evenly over the year and is to be apportioned on a time basis.

(i)   It has been assumed that interest is paid annually in arrears. This means that the interest received by Tight has to be apportioned on a time basis: $^9/_{12} \times £2,000 = £1,500$

is treated as being pre-acquisition. It is therefore deducted from the cost of the investment in Loose.

(ii) The remainder (£500) is cancelled with £500 of the post-acquisition element of the interest paid by Loose. The interest paid figure in the consolidated financial statements will be the post-acquisition interest less the inter-company elimination, which represents the amount payable to the holders of 80% of the loan capital.

(iii) The interest of £10,000 paid by Loose to its loan creditors is time-apportioned with £7,500 being pre-acquisition. The post-acquisition amount of £2,500 includes £500 that was included in the £2,000 reported by Tight in its statement of income. This is cancelled, leaving £2,000 which was paid to the 80% non-group loan creditors.

3 Account for inter-company dividends

Amount received by Tight =	£3,600
The dividend received by Tight is apportioned on a time basis, and the pre-acquisition element is credited to the cost of investment in Tight, i.e. $^{9}/_{12} \times £3,600 =$	(£2,700)
The post-acquisition element is cancelled	(£900)
Amount credited to consolidated statement of income	NIL

4 Calculate the share of post-acquisition consolidated profits belonging to the non-controlling interest

As only the post-acquisition proportion of the subsidiary's profit after tax has been included in the consolidated statement of income, the amount deducted as the non-controlling interest in the profit after tax is also time-apportioned, i.e. 25% of £3,500 = £875.

15.7 Published format statement of income

The statement of comprehensive income follows the classification of expenses by function as illustrated in IAS 1:

	£
Revenue	230,000
Cost of sales	75,000
Gross profit	155,000
Distribution costs	42,562
Administrative expense	24,020
	66,582
	88,418
Finance cost	2,000
	86,418
Income tax expense	15,504
Profit for the period	70,914
Attributable to:	
Equity holders of the parent	70,039
Non-controlling interest	875
	70,914

15.8 Consolidated statements of cash flows

Statements of cash flows are explained in Chapter 2 for a single company. A consolidated statement of cash flows differs from that for a single company in two respects:

(a) there are additional items such as dividends paid to non-controlling interests; and

(b) adjustments may be required to the actual amounts to reflect the assets and liabilities brought in by the subsidiary which did not arise from cash movements.

15.8.1 Adjustments to changes between opening and closing statements of financial position

Adjustments are required if the closing statement of financial position items have been increased or reduced as a result of non-cash movements. Such movements occur if there has been a purchase of a subsidiary to reflect the fact that the assets and liabilities from the new subsidiary have not necessarily resulted from cash flows. The following illustrates such adjustments in relation to a subsidiary acquired at the end of the financial year where the net assets of the subsidiary were as follows:

Net assets acquired	£000	Effect in consolidated statement of cash flows
Working capital:		
Inventory	10	Reduce inventory increase
Trade payables	(12)	Reduce trade payables increase
Non-current assets:		
Vehicles	20	Reduce capital expenditure
Cash/bank:		
Cash	5	Reduce amount paid to acquire subsidiary in investing section
Net assets acquired	23	

Let us assume that the consideration for the acquisition was as follows:

Shares	10	Reduce share cash inflow
Share premium	10	Reduce share cash inflow
Cash	3	Payment to acquire subsidiary in investing section
	23	

The consolidated statement of cash flows can then be prepared using the indirect method.

Statement of cash flows using the indirect method

		£000	£000
Cash flows from operating activities			
Net profit before tax		500	
Adjustments for:			
Depreciation		102	
Operating profit before working capital changes		602	
Increase in inventories	(400)		
Less: **Inventory brought in on acquisition**	10	(390)	
Decrease in trade payables	(40)		
Add: **Trade payables brought in on acquisition**	(12)	(52)	
Cash generated from operations		160	
Income taxes paid (200 + 190 − 170)		(220)	
Net cash from operating activities			(60)
Cash flows from investing activities			
Purchase of property, plant and equipment	(563)		
Less: **Vehicles brought in on acquisition**	20	(543)	
Payment to acquire subsidiary		(3)	
Cash acquired with subsidiary		5	
Net cash used in investing activities			(541)
Cash flows from financing activities			
Proceeds from issuance of share capital	300		
Less: **Shares issued on acquisition not for cash**	(20)	280	
Dividends paid (from statement of income)		(120)	
Net cash from financing activities			160
Net decrease in cash and cash equivalents			(441)
Cash and cash equivalents at the beginning of the period			72
Cash and cash equivalents at the end of the period			(369)

Supplemental disclosure of acquisition

	£
Total purchase consideration	23,000
Portion of purchase consideration discharged by means of cash or cash equivalents	3,000
Amount of cash and cash equivalents in the subsidiary acquired	5,000

Summary

The retained earnings of the subsidiary brought forward are divided into pre-acquisition profits and post-acquisition profits – the group share of the former are used in the goodwill calculation, and the share of the latter are brought into the consolidated shareholders' equity.

Revenue and cost of sales are adjusted in order to eliminate intra-group sales and unrealised profits.

Finance expenses and income are adjusted to eliminate inter-company payments of interest and dividends.

The non-controlling interest in the profit after tax of the subsidiary is deducted to arrive at the profit for the year attributable to the equity holders of the parent.

If a subsidiary is acquired during a financial year, the items in its statement of income require apportioning. In the illustration in the text we assumed that trading was evenly spread throughout the year – in practice you would need to consider any seasonal patterns that would make this assumption unrealistic, remembering that the important consideration is that the group accounts should only be credited with profits arising whilst the subsidiary was under the parent's control.

REVIEW QUESTIONS

1 Explain why the dividends deducted from the group in the statement of changes in equity are only those of the parent company.

2 Explain two ways in which unrealised profits might arise from transactions between companies in a group and why it is important to remove them.

3 Explain why it is necessary to apportion a subsidiary's profit or loss if acquired part-way through a financial year.

4 Explain why dividends paid by a subsidiary to a parent company are eliminated on consolidation.

5 Give four examples of inter-company income and expense transactions that will need to be eliminated on consolidation and explain why each is necessary.

6 A shareholder was concerned that following an acquisition the profit from operations of the parent and subsidiary were less than the aggregate of the individual profit from operations figures. She was concerned that the acquisition, which the directors had supported as improving earnings per share, appeared to have reduced the combined profits. She wanted to know where the profits had gone. Give an explanation to the shareholder.

7 Explain how a management charge made by a parent company would be dealt with on consolidation.

8 Explain how the impairment of goodwill is dealt with on consolidation.

9 Explain why unrealised profits on inventory purchased from another member of the group is added to the cost of sales when it is not a cost.

10 Explain why differences between the opening and closing statements of financial position are adjusted when preparing a consolidated statement of cash flows when a subsidiary is acquired.

EXERCISES

* Question 1

Hyson plc acquired 75% of the shares in Green plc on 1 January 20X0 for £6 million when Green plc's accumulated profits were £4.5 million. At acquisition, the fair value of Green's non-current assets were £1.2 million in excess of their carrying value. The remaining life of these non-current assets is six years.

The summarised statements of comprehensive income for the year ended 31.12.20X0 were as follows:

	Hyson	Green
	£000	£000
Revenue	23,500	6,400
Cost of sales	16,400	4,700
Gross profit	7,100	1,700
Expenses	4,650	1,240
Profit before tax	2,450	460
Income tax expense	740	140
Profit for the period	1,710	320

There were no inter-company transactions. Depreciation of non-current assets is charged to cost of sales.

Required:
Prepare a consolidated statement of comprehensive income for the year ended 31 December 20X0.

* Question 2

Forest plc acquired 80% of the ordinary shares of Bulwell plc some years ago. At acquisition, the fair values of the assets of Bulwell plc were the same as their carrying value. Bulwell plc manufacture plant and equipment.

On 1 January 20X3, Bulwell sold an item of plant and equipment to Forest plc for $2 million. Forest plc depreciate plant and equipment at 10% per annum on cost, and charge this expense to cost of sales. Bulwell plc made a gross profit of 30% on the sale of the plant and equipment to Forest plc.

The income statements of Forest and Bulwell for the year ended 31 December 20X3 are:

	Forest	Bulwell
	$000	$000
Revenue	21,300	8,600
Cost of sales	14,900	6,020
Gross profit	6,400	2,580
Other operating expenses	3,700	1,750
Profit before tax	2,700	830
Taxation	820	250
Profit after tax	1,880	580

Required:
Prepare an income statement for the Forest plc group for the year ended 31 December 20X3.

* Question 3

Bill plc acquired 80% of the common shares and 10% of the preferred shares in Ben plc on 31 December three years ago when Ben's retained profits were €45,000. During the year Bill sold Ben goods for €8,000 plus a markup of 50%. Half of these goods were still in stock at the end of the year. There was goodwill impairment loss of €3,000. Non-controlling interests are measured using Method 1.

The statements of comprehensive income of the two companies for the year ended 31 December 20X1 were as follows:

	Bill	Ben
	€	€
Revenue	300,000	180,000
Cost of sales	90,000	90,000
Gross profit	210,000	90,000
Expenses	88,623	60,000
	121,377	30,000
Dividends received – common shares	6,000	—
Dividends received – preferred shares	450	—
Profit before tax	127,827	30,000
Income tax expense	21,006	9,000
Profit for the period	106,821	21,000

Required:
Prepare a consolidated statement of comprehensive income for the year ended 31 December 20X1.

* Question 4

Morn Ltd acquired 90% of the shares in Eve Ltd on 1 January 20X1 for £90,000 when Eve Ltd's accumulated profits were £50,000. On 10 January 20X1 Morn Ltd received a dividend of £10,800 from Eve Ltd out of the profits for the year ended 31/12/20X0. On 31/12/20X1 Morn increased its non-current assets by £30,000 on revaluation. The summarised statements of comprehensive income for the year ended 31/12/20X1 were as follows:

	Morn	Eve
	£	£
Gross profit	360,000	180,000
Expenses	120,000	110,000
	240,000	70,000
Dividends received from Eve Ltd	10,800	—
Profit before tax	250,800	70,000
Income tax expense	69,000	18,000
Profit for the period	181,800	52,000

There were no inter-company transactions, other than the dividend. There was no goodwill.

Required:
Prepare a consolidated statement of comprehensive income for the year ended 31 December 20X1.

* Question 5

River plc acquired 90% of the common shares and 10% of the 5% bonds in Pool Ltd on 31 March 20X1. All income and expenses are deemed to accrue evenly through the year. On 31 January 20X1 River sold Pool goods for £6,000 plus a markup of one-third. 75% of these goods were still in stock at the end of the year. There was a goodwill impairment loss of £4,000. On 31/12/20X1 River increased its non-current assets by £15,000 on revaluation. Non-controlling interests are measured using Method 1. Set out below are the individual statements of comprehensive income of River and Pool:

Statements of comprehensive income for the year ended 31 December 20X1

	River	Pool
	£	£
Net turnover	100,000	60,000
Cost of sales	30,000	30,000
Gross profit	70,000	30,000
Expenses	20,541	15,000
Interest payable on 5% bonds		5,000
Interest receivable on Pool Ltd bonds	500	—
	49,959	10,000
Dividends received	2,160	NIL
Profit before tax	52,119	10,000
Income tax expense	7,002	3,000
Profit for the period	45,117	7,000

Required:
Prepare a consolidated statement of comprehens[...]   for the year ended 31 December 20X1.

* Question 6

The statements of financial position of Mars plc and Jupiter plc at 31 December 20X2 are as follows:

	Mars £	Jupiter £
ASSETS		
Non-current assets at cost	550,000	225,000
Depreciation	220,000	67,500
	330,000	157,500
Investment in Jupiter	187,500	
Current assets		
Inventories	225,000	67,500
Trade receivables	180,000	90,000
Current account – Jupiter	22,500	
Bank	36,000	18,000
	463,500	175,500
Total assets	981,000	333,000
EQUITY AND LIABILITIES		
Capital and reserves		
£1 common shares	196,000	90,000
General reserve	245,000	31,500
Retained earnings	225,000	135,000
	666,000	256,500
Current liabilities		
Trade payables	283,500	40,500
Taxation	31,500	13,500
Current account – Mars		22,500
	315,000	76,500
Total equity and liabilities	981,000	333,000

Statements of comprehensive income for the year ended 31 December 20X2

	£	£
Sales	1,440,000	270,000
Cost of sales	1,045,000	135,000
Gross profit	395,000	135,000
Expenses	123,500	90,000
Dividends received from Jupiter	9,000	NIL
Profit before tax	280,500	45,000
Income tax expense	31,500	13,500
Profit for the period	249,000	31,500
Dividends paid	180,000	11,250
	69,000	20,250
Retained earnings brought forward from previous years	156,000	114,750
	225,000	135,000

Mars acquired 80% of the shares in Jupiter on 1 January 20X0 when Jupiter's retained earnings were £80,000 and the balance on Jupiter's general reserve was £18,000. Non-controlling interests are measured using Method 1. During the year Mars sold Jupiter goods for £18,000 which represented cost plus 50%. Half of these goods were still in stock at the end of the year.

During the year Mars and Jupiter paid dividends of £180,000 and £11,250 respectively. The opening balances of retained earnings for the two companies were £156,000 and £114,750 respectively.

Required:
Prepare a consolidated statement of income for the year ended 31/12/20X2, a statement of financial position as at that date, and a consolidated statement of changes in equity. Also prepare the retained earnings columns of the consolidated statement of changes in equity for the year.

* Question 7

The statements of financial position of Red Ltd and Pink Ltd at 31 December 20X2 are as follows:

	Red $	Pink $
ASSETS		
Non-current assets	225,000	100,000
Depreciation	80,000	30,000
	145,000	70,000
Investment in Pink Ltd	110,000	
Current assets		
Inventories	100,000	30,000
Trade receivables	80,000	40,000
Current account – Pink Ltd	10,000	
Bank	16,000	8,000
	206,000	78,000
Total assets	461,000	148,000
EQUITY AND LIABILITIES		
Capital and reserves		
$1 common shares	176,000	40,000
General reserve	20,000	14,000
Revaluation reserve	25,000	
Retained earnings	100,000	60,000
	321,000	114,000
Current liabilities		
Trade payables	125,996	18,000
Taxation payable	14,004	6,000
Current account – Red Ltd		10,000
	140,000	34,000
Total equity and liabilities	461,000	148,000

Statements of comprehensive income for the year ended 31 December 20X2

	$	$
Sales	200,000	120,000
Cost of sales	60,000	60,000
Gross profit	140,000	60,000
Expenses	59,082	40,000
Dividends received	3,750	NIL
Profit before tax	84,668	20,000
Income tax expense	14,004	6,000
	70,664	14,000
Surplus on revaluation	25,000	
Total comprehensive income	95,664	14,000

Red Ltd acquired 75% of the shares in Pink Ltd on 1 January 20X0 when Pink Ltd's retained earnings were $30,000 and the balance on Pink's general reserve was $8,000. The fair value of the non-controlling interest at the date was £32,000. Non-controlling interests are to be measured using Method 2.

On 31 December 20X2 Red revalued its non-current assets. The revaluation surplus of £25,000 was credited to the revaluation reserve.

During the year Pink sold Red goods for $9,000 plus a markup of one-third. Half of these goods were still in inventory at the end of the year. Goodwill suffered an impairment loss of 20%.

Required:
Prepare a consolidated statement of comprehensive income for the year ended 31/12/20X2 and a statement of financial position as at that date.

* **Question 8**

H Ltd has one subsidiary, S Ltd. The company has held a controlling interest for several years. The latest financial statements for the two companies and the consolidated financial statements for the H Group are as shown below:

Statements of comprehensive income for the year ended 30 September 20X4

	H Ltd	S Ltd	H Group
	€000	€000	€000
Turnover	4,000	2,200	5,700
Cost of sales	(1,100)	(960)	(1,605)
	2,900	1,240	4,095
Administration	(420)	(130)	(550)
Distribution	(170)	(95)	(265)
Dividends received	180		
Profit before tax	2,490	1,015	3,280
Income tax	(620)	(335)	(955)
Profit after tax	1,870	680	2,325
Attributable to:			
Equity shareholders of H Ltd			2,155
Non-controlling shareholders in S Ltd			170
			2,325

Statements of financial position at 30 September 20X4

	H Ltd €000	€000	S Ltd €000	€000	H Group €000	€000
Non-current assets:						
Tangible	7,053		2,196		9,249	
Investment in S Ltd	1,700	8,753	—	2,196	—	9,249
Current assets:						
Inventory	410		420		785	
Receivables	535		220		595	
Bank	27	972	19	659	46	1,426
Current liabilities:						
Payables	(300)		(260)		(355)	
Dividend to non-controlling interest	—		—		(45)	
Taxation	(605)	(905)	(375)	(635)	(980)	(1,380)
		8,820		2,220		9,295

	H Ltd £000	S Ltd £000	H Group £000
Share capital	4,500	760	4,500
Retained earnings	4,320	1,460	4,240
	8,820	2,220	8,740
Non-controlling interest	—	—	555
	8,820	2,220	9,295

Goodwill of €410,000 was written off at the date of acquisition following an impairment review.

Required:

(a) Calculate the percentage of S Ltd which is owned by H Ltd.

(b) Calculate the value of sales made between the two companies during the year.

(c) Calculate the amount of unrealised profit which had been included in the inventory figure as a result of inter-company trading and which had to be cancelled on consolidation.

(d) Calculate the value of inter-company receivables and payables cancelled on consolidation.

(e) Calculate the balance on S Ltd's retained earnings when H Ltd acquired its stake in the company. Non-controlling interests are measured using Method 1.

(CIMA)

Rumpus plc is a public listed manufacturing company. Its summarised consolidated financial statements for the year ended 31 March 2014 (and 2013 comparatives where relevant) are as follows:

Rumpus plc: Consolidated Statement of Profit or Loss and Other Comprehensive Income for the year ended 31 March 2014:

	€ million
Revenue	310
Cost of sales	(270)
Gross profit	40
Distribution costs	(10)
Administrative expenses	(29)
Share of profit for year from associate	14
Finance costs	(6)
Profit (loss) before taxation	9
Income tax expense	(3)
Profit for the year	**6**
Other comprehensive income (net of tax)	
Items that will not be reclassified to profit or loss:	
Revaluation gains on group property	13
Share of revaluations gains from associate's property	4
	17
Total comprehensive income for the year	23
Profit for the year attributable to:	
Owners of the parent	5
Non-controlling interest	1
	6
Total comprehensive income for the year attributable to:	
Owners of the parent	22
Non-controlling interest	1
	23

Rumpus plc: Consolidated Statements of Financial Position as at 31 March:

	2014 € million	2013 € million
Non-current assets:		
Property, plant and equipment	290	245
Goodwill	6	—
Investments in associates	64	40
	360	285
Current assets:		
Inventory and work-in-progress	22	19
Trade receivables	42	28
Cash & cash equivalents	18	1
	82	48
Total assets	**442**	**333**
Equity:		
Equity shares of €1 each	160	106

	2014	2013
	€ million	*€ million*
Share premium	39	----
Revaluation reserve	62	45
Retained earnings	68	65
	329	216
Non-controlling interests	23	14
	352	230
Non-current liabilities:		
12% debentures 2016	50	50
Long-term provisions	12	7
	62	57
Current liabilities:		
Trade payables	23	33
Current tax payable	5	13
	28	46
Total equity and liabilities	442	333

The following additional information is available:

(i)   The group acquired an 80% interest in Sacker plc during the year on the following terms:

 ● Cost of purchase of 80% of the equity shares of Sacker plc was €45 million.

 ● The agreed payment for the purchase was settled by issuing 25 million equity shares valued at €35 million plus cash of €10 million.

 ● The non-controlling interest was fair-valued at €11 million on the acquisition date.

 ● The net assets of Sacker plc at the acquisition date consisted entirely of the following:

  ● property plant & equipment €33 million;

  ● inventory €8 million;

  ● cash €6 million.

   Sacker plc was correctly accounted for and fully consolidated in the above financial statements.

(ii)   No disposals of non-current assets took place during the year.

(iii)   Depreciation charged to cost of sales during the year amounted to €41 million.

(iv)   The group purchased an interest in an associate company for cash of €13 million during the year.

(v)   Equity dividends were paid during the year out of retained earnings.

(vi)   Goodwill was tested for impairment at the reporting date. An impairment loss was recognised and charged to expenses.

Required:
(a) **Prepare a consolidated statement of cash flows for year ended 31 March 2014 in accordance with IAS 7.**
(b) **Evaluate the liquidity position of Rumpus plc as portrayed by the above financial statements and the statement of cash flows you have prepared.**

(Institute of Certified Public Accountants (ICPA), Professional I Stage I Corporate Reporting Examination, August 2014)

The following are the financial statements of two trading companies, Arch and Roads, for the financial year ended 31 August 20x1.

Statements of income for the year ended 31 August 20x1

	Arch $m	Roads $m
Turnover	250	190
Cost of sales	(138)	(86)
Gross profit	112	104
Expenses	(44)	(46)
Investment income	42	10
Interest receivable	8	6
Finance charges	(10)	(6)
Net profit before taxation	108	68
Taxation	(30)	(20)
Profit for the year after tax	78	48

Statements of Financial Position as at 31 August 20x1

	Arch	Roads
ASSETS		
Non-current assets	$m	$m
Tangible assets at net book value	580	580
Investments at cost	530	26
	1,110	606
Current assets	266	94
Total assets	1,376	700
EQUITY and LIABILITIES		
Equity		
Ordinary shares of £1	600	360
Retained earnings	464	160
	1,064	520
Non-current liabilities	200	132
Current liabilities	112	48
Total equity and liabilities	1,376	700

The following information is available:

(i) Arch acquired 90% of the ordinary shares in Roads for $480m on 1 September 20x0 when the reserves of Roads were $152m. Each ordinary share in Roads carries one vote and there are no voting rights other than those attaching to the ordinary shares. Roads has not issued any additional shares since its acquisition by Arch.

(ii) Arch made a long-term loan of $46m to Roads during the year ended 31 August 20x1. Roads has made interest payments on this loan of $6m. There was no interest outstanding as at 31 August 20x1.

(iii) During the year ended 31 August 20x1 Arch made sales to Roads totalling $80m. The goods sold to Roads had cost Arch $48m and by 31 August 20x1 75% had been resold by Roads.

As at 31 August 20x1 Roads owed Arch $20m due on unpaid invoices.

(iv) During the year ended 31 August 20x1 dividends paid by Arch totalled $60m and those paid by Roads totalled $40m.

Required:

Prepare:

(a) The consolidated statement of comprehensive income of Arch for the year ended 31 August 20x1, and

(b) The consolidated statement of financial position of Arch as at 31 August 20x1.

Note: round all figures correct to the nearest $m.

Notes

1 IFRS 10 *Consolidated Financial Statements*, IASB, 2011, B 86.
2 *Ibid.*, B 94, B 89.
3 IAS 1 *Presentation of Financial Statements*, IASB, revised 2007, Implementation Guidance.

CHAPTER 16

Accounting for associates and joint arrangements

16.1 Introduction

The previous three chapters have focused on the need for consolidated financial statements where an investor has control over an entity. In those circumstances line-by-line consolidation is appropriate. Where the size of an investment is not sufficient to give sole control, but where the investment gives the investor significant influence or joint control, then a modified form of accounting is appropriate. We will consider this issue further in this chapter.

Objectives

By the end of this chapter, you should be able to:

- define an associate;
- incorporate a profit-making associate into the consolidated financial statements using the equity method;
- incorporate a loss-making associate into the consolidated financial statements using the equity method;
- define and describe a joint operation and a joint venture and prepare financial statements incorporating interests in joint ventures;
- explain disclosure requirements.

16.2 Definitions of associates and of significant influence

An associate is an entity over which the investor has significant influence and which is neither a subsidiary nor a joint venture of the investor.[1] **Significant influence** is the power to participate in the financial and operating policy decisions of the investee but is not control over these policies.[2]

Significant influence will be assumed in situations where one company has 20% or more of the voting power in another company, unless it can be shown that there is no such influence. Unless it can be shown to the contrary, a holding of less than 20% will be assumed insufficient for associate status. The circumstances of each case must be considered.[2]

IAS 28 *Investments in Associates and Joint Ventures* suggests that one or more of the following might be evidence of an associate:

(a) representation on the board of directors or equivalent governing body of the investee;

(b) participation in policy-making processes;

(c) material transactions between the investor and the investee;

(d) interchange of managerial personnel; or

(e) provision of essential technical information.[3]

16.3 The treatment of associated companies in consolidated accounts

Associated companies will be shown in consolidated accounts under the equity method, unless the investment meets the criteria of a disposal group held for sale under IFRS 5 *Non-current Assets Held for Sale and Discontinued Operations*. If this is the case it will be accounted for under IFRS 5 at the lower of carrying value and fair value less costs to sell.

The equity method is a method of accounting whereby:

● The investment is reported in the consolidated statement of financial position in the non-current asset section.[4] It is reported initially at cost adjusted, at the end of each financial year, for the post-acquisition change in the investor's share of the net assets of the investee.[5]

● In the consolidated statement of comprehensive income, income from associates is reported after profit from operations together with finance costs and finance expenses.[6] The income reflects the investor's share of the post-tax results of operations of the investee.[5]

16.4 The Brill Group – group accounts with a profit-making associate

Brill plc was the parent of the Brill Group which consisted of Brill and a single subsidiary, Bream plc. On 1 January 20X0 Brill acquired 20% of the ordinary shares in Cod Ltd for £20,000. At that date the retained earnings of Cod were £22,500 and the general reserve was £6,000.

Set out below are the consolidated accounts of Brill and its subsidiary Bream and the individual accounts of the associated company, Cod, together with the consolidated group accounts.

16.4.1 Consolidated statement of financial position

Statements of financial position of the Brill Group (parent plus subsidiary already consolidated) and Cod (an associate company) as at 31 December 20X2 are as follows:

	Brill and subsidiary	Cod	Group	
	£	£	£	
Non-current assets				
Property, plant and equipment	172,500	59,250	172,500	
Goodwill on consolidation	13,400		13,400	
Investment in Cod	20,000		23,600	Note 1
Current assets				
Inventories	132,440	27,000	132,440	
Trade receivables	151,050	27,000	151,050	
Current account – Cod	2,250		2,250	Note 2
Bank	36,200	4,500	36,200	
Total assets	527,840	117,750	531,440	
Current liabilities				
Trade payables	110,250	25,500	110,250	
Taxation	27,750	6,000	27,750	
Current account – Brill		2,250		
	138,000	33,750	138,000	
Total net assets	389,840	84,000	393,440	
EQUITY				
£1 ordinary shares	187,500	37,500	187,500	
General reserve	24,900	9,000	25,500	Note 3
Retained earnings	145,940	37,500	148,940	Note 4
	358,340	84,000	361,940	
Non-controlling interest	31,500	—	31,500	Note 5
	389,840	84,000	393,440	

Notes:

1 **Investment in associate** £ £

Initial cost of the 20% holding ... 20,000

Share of post-acquisition reserves of Cod:

Retained earnings 20% × (37,500 − 22,500) 3,000

General reserve 20% × (9,000 − 6,000) 600 3,600

23,600

Note that (a) unlike subsidiaries the assets and liabilities are not joined line-by-line with those of the companies in the group; (b) where necessary the investment in the associate is tested for impairment under IAS 28;[7] and (c) goodwill is not reported separately and is only calculated initially to establish a figure when considering possible impairment.

2 **The Cod current account** is received from outside the group and must therefore continue to be shown as receivable by the group. *It is not cancelled.*

3 **General reserve consists of:**

	£
Parent's general reserve	24,900
General reserve of Cod:	
The group share of the post-acquisition general reserve,	
i.e. 20% × (9,000 − 6,000)	600
Consolidated general reserve	**25,500**

4 **Retained earnings consist of:**

	£
Brill group's retained earnings	145,940
Retained earnings of Cod:	
The group share of the post-acquisition retained profits,	
i.e. 20% × (37,500 − 22,500)	3,000
Consolidated retained earnings	**148,940**

5 **Non-controlling interest**

Note that there is no non-controlling interest in Cod. Only the group share of Cod's net assets has been brought into the total net assets above (see Note 1). This is unlike the consolidation of a subsidiary when all of the subsidiary's assets and liabilities are aggregated into the consolidation.

16.4.2 Consolidated statement of income

Statements of income for the year ended 31 December 20X2 are as follows:

	Brill and subsidiary £	Cod £	Group £	
Sales	329,000	75,000	329,000	
Cost of sales	114,060	30,000	114,060	
Gross profit	214,940	45,000	214,940	
Expenses	107,700	22,500	107,700	
Profit from operations	107,240	22,500	107,240	
Dividends received	1,200	—	NIL	Note 1
Share of associate's **post-tax** profit	—	—	3,300	Note 2
Profit before tax	108,440	22,500	110,540	
Income tax expense	27,750	6,000	27,750	
Profit for the period	80,690	16,500	82,790	

Notes:

1 **Dividend received from Cod** is not shown because the share of Cod's profits (before dividend) has been included in the group account (see Note 2). To include the dividend as well would be double-counting.

2 **Share of Cod's profit after tax** = 20% × £16,500 = £3,300

As in the statement of financial position, there is no need to account for a non-controlling interest in Cod. This is because the consolidated statement of income only included the group share of Cod's profits.

There are no additional complications in the statement of changes in equity. The group retained earnings column will include the group share of Cod's post-acquisition retained earnings. There will be no additional column for a non-controlling interest in Cod.

16.4.3 The treatment of unrealised profits

It is never appropriate in the case of associated companies to remove 100% of any unrealised profit on inter-company transactions because only the group's share of the associate's profit and net assets are shown in the group accounts. For example, let us assume that Brill had purchased goods from Cod during the year at an agreed markup of £10,000, and a quarter of the goods were held by Brill in inventory at the year-end.

The Brill Group will provide for 20% of £2,500 (i.e. £500) by reducing the group share of the associate's profit in the statement of income and reducing the investment in the associate reported in the statement of financial position.

If the sale had been made by Brill, the cost of sales would be increased by £500 and the investment in the associate would be reduced by £500.

16.5 The Brill Group – group accounts with a loss-making associate

The treatment of losses in and impairment of an associate are described below.

Losses

Losses in an associate are normally treated the same way as profits. The group statement of income will show a loss after tax of the associate, and the statement of financial position will continue to show the associate at cost plus its share of post-acquisition profits or less its share of post-acquisition losses.

If the losses were such that they exceeded the carrying amount of the investment in the associate, the investment would be reduced to zero. After that point, additional losses are recognised by a provision (liability) only to the extent that the investor has incurred legal or constructive obligations or made payments on behalf of the associate.

If the associate subsequently reports profits, the investor resumes recognising its share of those profits only after its share of the profits equals the share of losses not recognised.[8]

Impairment

IAS 36 *Impairment of Assets* says (paragraph 9): 'An entity shall assess at the end of each reporting period whether there is any indication that an asset may be impaired. If any such indication exists [*such as making losses or small profits*], the entity shall estimate the recoverable amount of the asset.'

Brill and its subsidiary have a loss-making associate, Herring, which is 20% owned by Brill. On 1 January 20X0 Brill acquired 20% of the ordinary shares in Herring for £20,000. At that date the retained earnings of Herring were £22,500 and the general reserve was £6,000. For the year ended 31 December 20X2, Herring's loss after tax was £18,500.

Because of the losses incurred by Herring, Brill has carried out an impairment test on the value of the investment in the associate. The recoverable amount of a 20% shareholding in Herring at 31 December 20X2 is £10,000.

Statements of financial position of the Brill Group and Herring as at 31 December 20X2

	Brill group £	Herring £	Group £	
Non-current assets				
Property, plant and equipment	172,500	59,250	172,500	
Goodwill on consolidation	13,400		13,400	
Investment in Herring	20,000		10,000	Note 1
Current assets				
Inventories	132,440	10,500	132,440	
Trade receivables	151,050	12,000	151,050	
Current account – Herring	2,250		2,250	Note 2
Bank	36,200	500	36,200	
	527,840	82,250	517,840	
Current liabilities				
Trade payables	110,250	25,500	110,250	
Taxation	27,750	—	27,750	
Current account – Herring		2,250		
	138,000	27,750	138,000	
Total net assets	389,840	54,500	379,840	
EQUITY				
£1 ordinary shares	187,500	37,500	187,500	
General reserve	24,900	7,000	25,100	Note 3
Retained earnings	145,940	10,000	135,740	Note 4
	358,340	54,500	348,340	
Non-controlling interest	31,500	—	31,500	
	389,840	54,500	379,840	

Notes:

1 **Investment in associate**

	£	£
Initial cost of 20% holding		20,000
Share of post-acquisition reserves of Herring		
20% × (10,000 − 22,500) (retained earnings)	(2,500)	
20% × (7,000 − 6,000) (general reserves)	200	(2,300)
Carrying value (before impairment)		17,700
Impairment (write down to recoverable amount)		(7,700)
Value in statement of financial position		10,000

The post-acquisition loss of £12,500 gives a loss of £2,500 in the group financial statements. As the carrying value (before impairment) is higher than the recoverable amount of £10,000, the value of the associate in Brill's statement of financial position is reduced to £10,000.

2 **The Herring current account remains at £2,250.**

3 **General reserve consists of:**

	£
Parent's general reserve	24,900
General reserve of Herring:	
The group share of the post-acquisition general reserve,	
i.e. 20% × (7,000 − 6,000)	200
Consolidated general reserve	25,100

4 **Retained earnings consist of:**

	£
Parent's retained earnings	145,940
Retained earnings of Herring:	
The group share of the post-acquisition retained earnings,	
i.e. 20% × (10,000 − 22,500)	(2,500)
Impairment of investment in associate (see Note 1)	(7,700)
Consolidated general reserve	135,740

Statements of income for the year ended 31 December 20X2

	Brill group £	Herring £	Group £	
Sales	329,000	75,000	329,000	
Cost of sales	114,060	66,000	114,060	
Gross profit	214,940	9,000	214,940	
Expenses	107,700	27,500	107,700	
Profit/(loss) from operations	107,240	(18,500)	107,240	
Share of associate's after-tax loss			(3,700)	Note 1
Impairment of investment in associate			(7,700)	Note 2
Profit before tax	107,240	(18,500)	95,840	
Income tax expense	27,750	—	27,750	
Profit/(loss) for the period	79,490	(18,500)	68,090	

Notes:

1 Share of associate's loss after tax = 20% × (18,500) = (3,700).

2 Impairment of investment in associate: this figure comes from the investment in associate in the statement of financial position. It reduces the carrying value of £17,700 to its recoverable amount of £10,000.

16.6 The acquisition of an associate part-way through the year

In order to match the cost (the investment) with the benefit (share of the associate's net assets), the associate's profit will only be taken into account from the date of acquiring the holding in the associate. The associate's profit at the date of acquisition represents part of the net assets that are being acquired at that date. The Puff example below is an illustration of the accounting treatment. The adjustment for unrealised profit is made against the group's share of the associate's profit and investment in the associate.

16.6.1 The Puff Group

At date of acquisition on 31 March 20X4 of shares in the associate:

● Puff plc acquired 30% of the shares in Blow plc.
● At that date the retained earnings of Blow were £61,500.

During the year:

● On 1/10/20X4 Blow sold Puff goods for £15,000, which was cost plus 25%.
● All income and expenditure for the year in Blow's statement of comprehensive income accrued evenly throughout the year.

At end of financial year on 31 December 20X4:

- 75% of the goods sold to Puff by Blow were still in inventory.

Set out below are the consolidated statement of income of Puff and its subsidiaries and the individual statement of income of an associated company, Blow, together with the consolidated group statement of income.

	Puff and subsidiaries	Blow	Group accounts	
	£	£	£	
Revenue	225,000	112,500	225,000	Note 1
Cost of sales	75,000	56,250	75,000	Note 2
Gross profit	150,000	56,250	150,000	
Expenses	89,850	30,000	89,850	
	60,150	26,250	60,150	
Dividends received from associate	1,350	NIL	NIL	Note 3
Share of associate's profit	—	—	3,713	Note 4
Profit before taxation	61,500	26,250	63,863	
Income tax for the period	15,000	6,750	15,000	
Profit for the period	46,500	19,500	48,863	

Notes:

1 The revenue, cost of sales and all other income and expenses of the associated company are not added on a line-by-line basis with those of the parent company and its subsidiaries. The group's share of the profit after taxation of the associate is shown as one figure (see Note 4) and added to the remainder of the group's profit before taxation.

2 The group accounts 'cost of sales' figure has not been adjusted for unrealised profit, as this has been deducted from the share of the associate's profit.

3 The dividend received of £1,350 is eliminated, being replaced by the group share of its underlying profits.

4 Share of profits after tax of the associate:

	£
Profit after tax	19,500
Apportion for 9 months ($^9/_{12} \times 19,500$)	14,625
Less: Unrealised profit ($^{25}/_{125} \times 15,000$) $\times$ 75%	2,250
	12,375
Group share (30% $\times$ 12,375)	3,713

5 There is no share of the associated company's retained earnings brought forward because the shares in the associate were purchased during the year.

16.7 Joint arrangements

IFRS 11 *Joint Arrangements* was issued by the IASB in 2011. Under this standard, joint arrangements are classified as either *joint operations* or *joint ventures* depending upon the parties' rights and obligations.

Joint control[9]

Notice that both joint operations and joint ventures require that there should be joint control.

Joint control exists where there is a contractually agreed sharing of control of an arrangement under which decisions require the *unanimous* consent of the parties sharing control.

This may be by implicit agreement such as when two parties establish an arrangement in which each has 50% of the voting rights and the contractual arrangement between them specifies that at least 51% of the voting rights are required to make decisions, which results in joint control.

This does not mean the unanimous consent of *all* parties but of those who *collectively control* an arrangement, as illustrated in the following example.[10]

EXAMPLE ● Assume that three parties establish an arrangement: A has 50% of the voting rights in the arrangement, B has 30% and C has 20%. The contractual arrangement between A, B and C specifies that at least 75% of the voting rights are required to make decisions. Even though A can block any decision, it does not control the arrangement because it needs the agreement of B. The terms of their contractual arrangement requiring at least 75% of the voting rights to make decisions about the relevant activities imply that A and B have joint control of the arrangement, because decisions about the relevant activities of the arrangement cannot be made without both A and B agreeing.

Joint operations[11]

This is where the parties, called joint operators, have joint control of the arrangement which gives rights to the assets and obligations for the liabilities. It is the existence of rights and obligations that is critical to determining whether a joint operation exists as opposed to the legal structure of the joint venture. In the predecessor standard, IAS 31, a joint operation could only exist where no new entity was formed.

There may be situations where the ownership rights have been varied by contract. For example, the contractual arrangement might provide for the allocation of revenues and expenses on the basis of the relative performance of each party to the joint arrangement, such as when companies control and finance an oil pipeline equally but pay according to the amount of their throughput. In other instances, the parties might have agreed to share the profit or loss on the basis of a specified proportion such as the parties' ownership interest in the arrangement. These contractual arrangements would not prevent the arrangement from being a joint operation so long as the parties have rights to the assets and obligations for the liabilities.

Joint ventures[12]

This is where the parties, called joint venturers, have joint control of the arrangement which gives rights to the *net* assets of the arrangement. Typically in a joint venture the venturers take a share of the overall profit or loss earned by the joint venture as opposed to taking a share of the output of the venture.

16.7.1 Consolidated financial statements

Joint operations

IFRS 11 says:[13]

A joint operator shall recognise in relation to its interest in a joint operation:

(a) its assets, including its share of any assets held jointly;

(b) its liabilities, including its share of any liabilities incurred jointly;

(c) its revenue from the sale of its share of the output arising from the joint operation;

(d) its share of the revenue from the sale of the output by the joint operation; and

(e) its expenses, including its share of any expenses incurred jointly.

As there are no numerical examples in the standard, it is not clear how the assets, liabilities, revenue and expenses of the joint operation will be shown in the financial statements of each contributor to the joint venture.

The following example suggests how the joint operation would be shown in the financial statements of Sherwood plc.

EXAMPLE ● The joint operators are Sherwood plc and Arnold plc. Sherwood provides the land and buildings for the joint operation, and Sherwood and Arnold have provided equal cash sums to set up the joint venture. The profit is allocated equally between Sherwood and Arnold, after a payment to Sherwood of 5% of the carrying value of the land and buildings. On liquidation of the joint operation, the land and buildings will be returned to Sherwood, and the remaining assets and liabilities split equally between Sherwood and Arnold.

Sherwood's statement of financial position will include all the value of the land and buildings, and half the value of all the other assets and liabilities. It appears that these figures will be combined with the other assets and liabilities of Sherwood and not shown separately.

On the income statement, the joint operation's revenue will be included with other revenue. It would be helpful to the users of the financial statements if the revenue of the joint operation was shown separately.

On expenses, the standard is not clear whether they will be shown separately (in total) or combined with the other individual expense items of Sherwood. It may be shown as a separate figure (in total) as this would be helpful to the users of the financial statements. The rent on the land and buildings (of 5% of their carrying value) is likely to be shown separately in the income statement.

Joint operations can be very complex and require detailed analysis to identify the specific rights and obligations. Already audit firms are considering the practical implication of applying the standard and the possible restatement of prior years' financial statements if accounting policy and treatment changes.

Joint ventures

A joint venturer recognises[14] its interest in a joint venture as an investment which is accounted for using the equity method in accordance with IAS 28 *Investments in Associates and Joint Ventures*.

What if a party participates but does not have joint control?

If it is a joint operation the party would include its interest in the assets and liabilities. If a joint venture, the treatment then depends on the extent of influence that can be exerted. If it is significant then it is accounted for as an associate in accordance with IAS 28. If it is not significant then it is accounted for accordance with IFRS 9 *Financial Instruments*.

16.7.2 Determining whether we are dealing with a joint operation or a joint venture

The following is a helpful extract from www.kpmg.com:

> An entity determines the type of joint arrangement by considering the structure, the legal form, the contractual arrangement and other facts and circumstances.

Structure	Is the arrangement structured through a vehicle that is separate from the parties?	No →

↓ Yes

Legal form	Does the legal form of the separate vehicle give the parties rights to the assets and obligations for the liabilities of the arrangement?	Yes →

↓ No

Contractual arrangement	Do the contractual arrangements give the parties rights to the assets and obligations for the liabilities of the arrangement?	Yes →

↓ No

Other facts and circumstances	Do the parties have rights to substantially all of the economic benefits of the assets relating to the arrangement; and does the arrangement depend on the parties on a continuous basis for settling its liabilities?	Yes →

↓ No

Joint venture

Joint operation

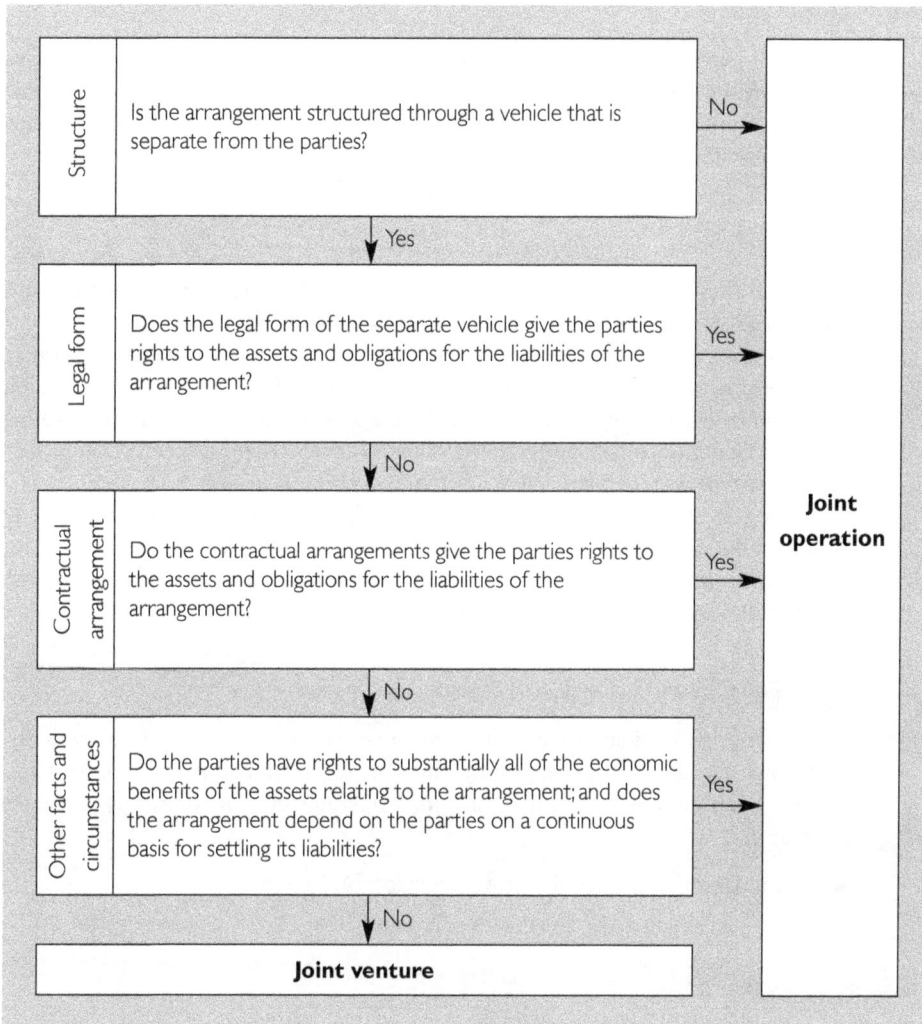

16.7.3 The accounting treatment required where the investment is a subsidiary, associate or joint operation

To illustrate the accounting treatments, we will take a parent company, Pete, which has an investment in another company, Sid.

Subsidiary – IFRS 10 *Consolidated Financial Statements applies*

If Pete owns more than 50% of the shares of Sid then Pete is presumed to have control of Sid. Sid is, therefore, classified as a subsidiary and the Pete group accounts will include all Sid's assets and liabilities as Pete has *control* over *all* of Sid's assets and liabilities.

Associate – IAS 28 *Investments in Associates and Joint Ventures applies*

If Pete owns between 20% and 50% of Sid's shares, then it is presumed that Pete is able to exercise significant influence and Sid will be classified as an associated company. In the Pete group accounts the investment in Sid is shown as a single figure in non-current assets. It will be reported at Pete's share of Sid's net assets at the date of acquisition plus goodwill plus post-acquisition profits.

Joint venture

If Sid is a joint venture, then Sid is treated like an associated company of Pete. Even if Pete owns more than 50% of the shares in Sid, it would be treated like an associated company (using equity accounting) rather than a subsidiary. The reason for this is that one of the requirements of a joint venture is that decisions must be with the agreement of all the parties to the joint venture so that Pete does not have control of Sid. Thus Sid cannot be a subsidiary.

Joint operation – IFRS 11 *Joint Arrangements* applies

The definition of a joint operation in IFRS 11 (para. 15) says that the parties that have joint control have rights to the assets and obligations for the liabilities.

So, in the example above, Pete will include in its statement of financial position the assets and liabilities of Sid over which it has the rights. So, if Pete purchased Sid's building, then the building will be included in Pete's statement of financial position. After allocating all Sid's assets and liabilities attributable to Pete in Pete's statement of financial position, any residual amount will be included in current assets and current liabilities.

In the statement of income Pete will include its share of the revenue and expenses of Sid over which it has rights. So, if £1 million of Sid's revenue is wholly attributable to Pete and £2 million of Sid's revenue over which Pete has a 40% share, the revenue of Sid which Pete will include in its financial statements would be £1.8 million (£1 million + 40% of £2 million).

16.7.4 Separate financial statements

The accounting for joint arrangements in an entity's separate financial statements depends on the involvement of the entity in that joint arrangement and the type of the joint arrangement.[15] For example, if the entity is a joint operator or joint venturer, it accounts for its interest in

- a joint operation in accordance with Section 16.7.1 above;
- a joint venture in accordance with paragraph 10 of IAS 27 *Separate Financial Statements*.

16.8 Disclosure in the financial statements

IFRS 12 *Disclosure of Interests in Other Entities* was issued by the IASB in 2011 to bring 'off-balance-sheet finance' onto the financial statements and to enable[16] users of financial statements to evaluate:

(a) the nature of, and risks associated with, its interests in other entities; and

(b) the effects of those interests on its financial position, financial performance and cash flows.

In terms of this chapter, there is a general requirement to disclose information about significant judgements and assumptions made when determining control, joint control, significant influence and classification of joint arrangements. In relation to interest in subsidiaries and joint arrangements, there are specific disclosure requirements.

Interests in subsidiaries disclosures

An entity shall disclose information that enables[17] users of its consolidated financial statements to:

(a) understand the composition of the group and the interest that non-controlling interests have in the group's activities and cash flows; and

(b) evaluate the nature and extent of significant restrictions on its ability to access or use assets, and settle liabilities, of the group; the nature of, and changes in, the risks associated with its interests in consolidated structured entities; the consequences of changes in its ownership interest in a subsidiary that do not result in a loss of control; and the consequences of losing control of a subsidiary during the reporting period.

Interests in joint arrangements and associates disclosures

An entity shall disclose information that enables[18] users of its financial statements to evaluate:

(a) the nature, extent and financial effects of its interests in joint arrangements and associates; and

(b) the nature of, and changes in, the risks associated with its interests in joint ventures and associates.

16.9 Parent company use of the equity method in its separate financial statements

In 2014 the IASB issued Equity Method in Separate Financial Statements to amend IAS 27 *Separate Financial Statements* so that an entity can use the equity method to account for investments in subsidiaries, joint ventures and associates in its separate financial statements.

IAS 27 (2011) required entities to account for investments in subsidiaries, joint ventures and associates either:

(a) at cost, or

(b) in accordance with IFRS 9 *Financial Instruments.*

This proposed amendment would allow the entity to use equity accounting to account for such investments.

Essentially, both IAS 28 *Investments in Associates* and, for joint ventures, IFRS 11 *Joint Arrangements* require equity accounting to be used for these arrangements.

Allowing subsidiaries to use equity accounting is a new alternative. Using equity accounting will reduce disclosure of the subsidiary:

(a) in the statement of financial position, a single figure in non-current assets of the cost plus share of profit since acquisition less any impairment (or share of net assets plus goodwill less impairment) (note: the two methods produce the same figure);

(b) in the statement of income, the share of the profit of the subsidiary after tax.

This means that there is far less disclosure in the parent company's financial statements. This reduces the work of the preparer of the financial statements but provides less information to the user.

Where the parent company elects not to prepare consolidated financial statements and instead prepares separate financial statements, it must disclose:

(a) the fact the financial statements are separate financial statements and that the exemption from consolidation has been used;

(b) a list of significant investments in subsidiaries, joint ventures and associates, including:

    (i) the name of those investees;

    (ii) the principal place of business of those investees;

    (iii) the proportion of ownership interest held in those investees;

(c) a description of the method used to account for the investments.

The option to use equity accounting (rather than cost or treating it as an investment) provides more useful information to shareholders as it gives the share of profit for the year and a measure of the value of the subsidiary/associated company/joint venture.

16.9.1 Critique of Equity Method in Separate Financial Statements

For associates and joint ventures

The permission to use equity accounting will produce the same figures and disclosure as are required by IAS 28 *Investments in Associates* and, for joint ventures, IFRS 11 *Joint Arrangements*. This is certainly much better than valuing them at cost, and, where these investments are to be held for the long term, it is more relevant information (and less subject to fluctuation) than using IFRS 7 *Financial Instruments*.

For subsidiaries

It is much easier for the preparer of the financial statements to include the subsidiary using the equity method, as all that is required is:

(i) for the income statement, the share of the profit after tax;

(ii) for the statement of financial position, the cost plus the share of profit since acquisition.

However, for the user/investor significantly less information is provided than a full consolidation. This would be acceptable if the subsidiary is small compared with the parent company (or the parent company and other subsidiaries). Compared with full consolidation, the reduced information will give the same profit (after tax) in the income statement and the same value of equity in the statement of financial position.

    This is ignoring, however, the definition of a subsidiary which is that the parent company has **control** – so the subsidiary's results should be combined with those of the parent company. This is not what happens when the proposed amendment to IAS 27 is applied (essentially, only the parent company's detailed results are included in the separate financial statements).

    Thus, applying the equity method to the parent's financial statements could well produce misleading financial statements, particularly when the subsidiary is a significant part of the group's activities (separate financial statements would suggest the group is much smaller than it is, and it would hide any risks associated with the subsidiary).

    In conclusion, unless the subsidiary is immaterial, it is apparent that the user's needs are not satisfied by the reduced disclosure of IAS 27, and these reduced financial statements could be misleading. The separate financial statements may reduce the work of the preparer of the financial statements, but there is a greater loss to the user of the financial statement. Thus, the parent company should continue to consolidate the subsidiary, and not be permitted to reduce the subsidiary's disclosure solely to that required by equity accounting.

Summary

Associates and joint ventures are accounted for under IAS 28 (revised 2011) using the equity method whereby there is a single-line entry in the statement of financial position carried initially at cost and the balance adjusted annually for the investor's share of the associate's current year's profit or loss. For joint venture entities, IAS 31 (now superseded by IFRS 11) permitted alternative treatments with investors able to adopt the equity accounting method or proportionate consolidation. Proportionate consolidation is no longer permitted. Joint operations are accounted for in accordance with IFRS 11.

REVIEW QUESTIONS

1 Why are associated companies accounted for under the equity method rather than consolidated?

2 IAS 28, paragraph 17, states:

> The recognition of income on the basis of distributions received may not be an adequate measure of the income earned by an investor on an investment in an associate.

Explain why this may be so.

3 How does the treatment of inter-company unrealised profit differ between subsidiaries and associated companies?

4 The result of including goodwill by valuing the non-controlling shares at their market price using Method 2 is to value the non-controlling shares on a different basis to valuing an equity investment in an associate.

Discuss whether there should be a uniform approach to both.

5 Where an associate has made losses, IAS 28, paragraph 30, states:

> After the investor's interest is reduced to zero, additional losses are provided for, and a liability is recognised, only to the extent that the investor has incurred legal or constructive obligations or made payments on behalf of the associate. If the associate subsequently reports profits, the investor resumes recognising its share of those profits only after its share of the profits equals the share of losses not recognised.

Explain why profits are recognised only after its share of the profits equals the share of losses not recognised.

6 The following is an extract from the notes to the 2013 consolidated financial statements of the Chugoku Electric Power Company, Incorporated:

> For the year ended March 31, 2013, 10 affiliated companies were stated at cost without applying the equity method.

Discuss:

(a) why these affiliated companies are being reported at cost;

(b) the effect on the consolidated retained earnings if they had been reported using the equity method.

7 Explain the difference between a joint operation and a joint venture.

8 Explain the approach to determining whether an arrangement is a joint operation or a joint venture.

EXERCISES

* Question 1

The statements of income for Continent plc, Island Ltd and River Ltd for the year ended 31 December 20X9 were as follows:

	Continent plc	Island Ltd	River Ltd
	€	€	€
Revenue	825,000	220,000	82,500
Cost of sales	(616,000)	(55,000)	(8,250)
Gross profit	209,000	165,000	74,250
Administration costs	(33,495)	(18,700)	(3,850)
Distribution costs	(11,000)	(14,300)	(2,750)
Dividends receivable from Island and River	4,620		
Profit before tax	169,125	(132,000)	67,650
Income tax	(55,000)	(33,000)	(11,000)
Profit after tax	114,125	99,000	56,650

Continent plc acquired 80% of Island Ltd for €27,500 on 1 January 20X3, when Island Ltd's retained earnings were €22,000 and share capital was €5,500. During the year, Island Ltd sold goods costing €2,750 to Continent plc for €3,850. At the year-end, 10% of these goods were still in Continent plc's inventory.

Continent plc acquired 40% of River Ltd for €100,000 on 1 January 20X5, when River Ltd's share capital and reserves totalled €41,250 (share capital consisted of 11,000 50c shares). During the year River Ltd sold goods costing €1,650 to Continent plc for €2,200. At the year-end, 50% of these goods were still in Continent plc's inventory.

Goodwill in Island Ltd had suffered impairment charges in previous years totalling €2,200 and goodwill in River Ltd impairment charges totalling €7,700. Impairment has continued during 2009, reducing the goodwill in Island by €550 and the goodwill in River by €3,850.

Continent plc includes in its revenue management fees of €5,500 charged to Island Ltd and €2,750 charged to River Ltd. Both companies treat the charge as an administration cost.

Non-controlling interests are measured using Method 1.

Required:
Prepare Continent plc's consolidated statement of income for the year ended 31 December 20X9.

Question 2

The statements of comprehensive income for Highway plc, Road Ltd and Lane Ltd for the year ended 31 December 20X9 were as follows:

	Highway plc $	Road Ltd $	Lane Ltd $
Revenue	184,000	152,000	80,000
Cost of sales	(48,000)	(24,000)	(16,000)
Gross profit	136,000	128,000	64,000
Administration costs	(13,680)	(11,200)	(20,800)
Distribution costs	(11,200)	(17,600)	(8,000)
Dividends receivable from Road	2,480		
Profit before tax	113,600	99,200	35,200
Income tax	(32,000)	(8,000)	(4,800)
Profit for the period	81,600	91,200	30,400

Highway plc acquired 80% of Road Ltd for $160,000 on 1.1.20X6 when Road Ltd's share capital was $64,000 and reserves were $16,000.

Highway plc acquired 30% of Lane Ltd for $40,000 on 1.1.20X7 when Lane Ltd's share capital was $8,000 and reserves were $8,000.

Goodwill of Road Ltd had suffered impairment charges of $14,400 in previous years and $4,800 was to be charged in the current year. Goodwill of Lane Ltd had suffered impairment charges of $3,520 in previous years and $1,760 was to be charged in the current year.

During the year Road Ltd sold goods to Highway plc for $8,000. These goods had cost Road Ltd $1,600. 50% were still in Highway's inventory at the year-end.

During the year Lane Ltd sold goods to Highway plc for $6,400. These goods had cost Lane Ltd $3,200. 50% were still in Highway's inventory at the year-end.

Highway's revenue included management fees of 5% of Road and Lane's turnover. Both of those companies have treated the charge as an administration cost.

Non-controlling interests are measured using Method 1.

Required:
Prepare Highway's consolidated statement of comprehensive income for the year ended 31.12.20X9.

The following are the financial statements of the parent company Alpha plc, a subsidiary company Beta and an associate company Gamma.

Statements of financial position as at 31 December 20X9

	Alpha	Beta	Gamma
ASSETS	£	£	£
Non-current assets			
Land at cost	540,000	256,500	202,500
Investment in Beta	216,000		
Investment in Gamma	156,600		
Current assets			
Inventories	162,000	54,000	135,000
Trade receivables	108,000	72,900	91,800
Dividend receivable from Beta	10,800		
Dividend receivable from Gamma	1,620		
Current account – Beta	10,800		
Current account – Gamma	13,500		
Cash	237,600	62,100	67,500
Total current assets	544,320	189,000	294,300
Total assets	1,456,920	445,500	496,800
EQUITY AND LIABILITIES			
£1 shares	540,000	67,500	27,000
Retained earnings	769,500	329,400	391,500
	1,309,500	396,900	418,500
Current liabilities			
Trade payables	93,420	24,300	59,400
Dividends payable	54,000	13,500	5,400
Current account – Alpha	—	10,800	13,500
Total equity and liabilities	1,456,920	445,500	496,800

On 1 January 20X5 Alpha plc acquired 80% of Beta plc for £216,000 when Beta plc's share capital and reserves were £81,000, and 30% of Gamma Ltd for £156,600 when Gamma Ltd's share capital and reserves were £40,500. The fair value of the land at the date of acquisition was £337,500 in Beta plc and £270,000 in Gamma Ltd. Both companies have kept land at cost in their statement of financial position. All other assets are recorded at fair value. There have been no further share issues or purchases of land since the date of acquisition.

At the year-end, Alpha plc has inventory acquired from Beta plc and Gamma Ltd. Beta plc had invoiced the inventory to Alpha plc for £54,000 – the cost to Beta plc had been £40,500. Gamma Ltd had invoiced Alpha plc for £13,500 – the cost to Gamma Ltd had been £8,100. Goodwill has been impaired by £52,650. The whole of the impairment relates to Beta.

Non-controlling interests are measured using Method 1.

Required:
Prepare Alpha plc's consolidated statement of financial position as at 31.12.20X9.

Question 4

The following are the statements of financial position of Garden plc, its subsidiary Rose Ltd and its associate Petal Ltd:

Statements of financial position as at 31 December 20X9

	Garden £	Rose £	Petal £
ASSETS			
Non-current assets			
Land at cost	240,000		84,000
Land at valuation		180,000	
Investment in Rose	300,000		
Investment in Petal	72,000		
Investments	18,000		
Current assets			
Inventories	15,000	99,000	5,400
Trade receivables	33,000	98,400	1,200
Current account – Rose	18,000		
Current account – Petal	2,400		
Cash	6,600	67,200	300
Total current assets	75,000	264,600	6,900
Total assets	705,000	444,600	90,900
EQUITY AND LIABILITIES			
£1 shares	300,000	120,000	30,000
Revaluation reserve		90,000	
Retained earnings	270,000	216,000	57,600
	570,000	426,000	87,600
Current liabilities			
Trade payables	135,000	3,600	900
Current account – Garden	—	15,000	2,400
Total equity and liabilities	705,000	444,600	90,900

On 1 January 20X3 Garden plc acquired 75% of Rose Ltd for £300,000 when Rose's share capital and reserves were £252,000. Prior to the acquisition, the net book value of Rose's non-current assets was £90,000. Rose revalued its non-current assets immediately prior to the acquisition to fair value and included the revaluation in its statement of financial position.

On 1 January 20X5 Garden acquired 20% of Petal Ltd for £72,000 when the fair value of Petal's net assets were £42,000.

Goodwill has been impaired in Rose by £77,700 and in Petal by £31,800.

At the year-end, Garden plc has inventory acquired from Rose and Petal. Rose had invoiced the inventory to Garden for £6,000 – the cost to Rose had been £1,200. Petal had invoiced Garden for £3,000 – the cost to Petal had been £1,800.

Non-controlling interests are measured using Method 1.

Required:
Prepare Garden plc's consolidated statement of financial position as at 31.12.20X9.

Question 5

On 1 January 2017 Picus acquired 8 million $1 equity shares in Sol for $20 million cash. The consideration paid was considerably lower than the market price because the vendor required a quick sale due to cash flow problems.

The financial statements of Picus and Sol for the year ended 30 September 2017 are shown below:

Statements of profit or loss:

	Picus	Sol
	$000	$000
Revenue	85,000	25,000
Cost of sales	(40,000)	(15,000)
Gross profit	45,000	10,000
Other income	2,000	—
Operating expenses	(17,000)	(4,000)
Finance costs	(1,000)	(200)
Profit before taxation	29,000	5,800
Income tax expense	(6,000)	(1,200)
Profit for the period	23,000	4,600

Statements of financial position:

	Picus	Sol
Assets	$000	$000
Non-current assets		
Property, plant and equipment	72,000	30,000
Investments	33,000	—
	105,000	30,000
Current assets	37,000	25,000
Total assets	142,000	55,000
EQUITY AND LIABILITIES		
Equity Share capital – $1 equity shares	20,000	10,000
Retained earnings	70,000	23,000
	90,000	33,000
Non-current liabilities	30,000	10,000
Current liabilities	22,000	12,000
Total equity and liabilities	142,000	55,000

The following information is relevant:

1   On 1 January 2017, the fair value of Sol's net assets acquired were equal to the book value, except for plant and equipment whose fair value was $1.2 million lower than the book value. It is estimated that the plant and equipment has a remaining life of four years from 1 January 2017.

2   On 1 April 2017 Sol sold plant and equipment with a carrying value of $3 million to Picus for $4 million. The plant and equipment had a remaining life of two years at 1 April 2017.

3   On 1 July 2017 Picus acquired a 30% interest in Acquilo for $10 million when its retained earnings were $5 million. Picus exerts a significant influence over the financial and operating policies of Acquilo. Acquilo's reported profit for the year ended 30 September 2017 was $3 million.

4   On 1 September 2017 Sol paid a dividend out of post-acquisition profits of $2 million. Picus recorded its share of the dividend in other income.

5 It is group policy to value the non-controlling interest at the proportionate share of the fair value of the subsidiary's net assets at the date of acquisition.

6 Assume profits accrue evenly throughout the year.

Required
(a) **Prepare the consolidated statement of profit or loss for the year ended 30 September 2017.**
(b) **Prepare the consolidated statement of financial position for the year ended**

(The Association of International Accountants)

Question 6

Set out below are the financial statements of Ant Co., its subsidiary Bug Co. and an associated company Nit Co. for the accounting year-end 31 December 20X9.

Statements of financial position as at 31 December 20X9

	Ant $	Bug $	Nit $
ASSETS			
Non-current assets			
Property, plant and equipment at cost	240,000	135,000	75,000
Depreciation	150,000	52,500	15,750
	90,000	82,500	59,250
Investment in Bug	90,000		
Investment in Nit	30,000		
Current assets			
Inventories	105,000	45,000	27,000
Trade receivables	98,250	52,500	27,000
Current account – Bug	11,250		
Current account – Nit	2,250		
Bank	17,250	5,250	4,500
Total current assets	234,000	102,750	58,500
Total assets	444,000	185,250	117,750
EQUITY AND LIABILITIES			
$1 ordinary shares	187,500	45,000	37,500
General reserve	22,500	15,000	9,000
Retained earnings	112,500	90,000	37,500
	322,500	150,000	84,000
Current liabilities			
Trade payables	99,000	18,750	25,500
Taxation payable	22,500	5,25 0	6,000
Current account – Ant		11,250	2,250
Total equity and liabilities	444,000	185,250	117,750

Statements of comprehensive income for the year ended 31 December 20X9

	Ant	Bug	Nit
	$	$	$
Sales	225,000	120,000	75,000
Cost of sales	67,500	60,000	30,000
Gross profit	157,500	60,000	45,000
Expenses	70,500	37,500	30,000
Dividends received	7,500	NIL	7,500
Profit before tax	94,500	22,500	22,500
Taxation	22,500	5,250	6,000
Profit for the year	72,000	17,250	16,500
Dividends paid in year	30, 000	7,500	6,000

Ant Co. acquired 80% of the shares in Bug Co. on 1 January 20X7 when the balance on the retained earnings of Bug Co. was $45,000 and the balance on the general reserve of Bug Co. was $12,000. The fair value of the non-controlling interest in Bug on 1 January 20X7 was $21,000. Group policy is to measure non-controlling interests using Method 2. Ant Co. also acquired 25% of the shares in Nit Co. on 1 January 20X8 when the balance on Nit's retained earnings was $22,500 and the general reserve $6,000.

During the year Ant Co. sold Bug Co. goods for $12,000, which included a markup of one-third. 90% of these goods were still in inventory at the end of the year.

Required:

(a) Prepare a consolidated statement of income for the year ending 31/12/20X9, including the associated company Nit's results.

(b) Prepare a consolidated statement of financial position at 31/12/20X9, including the associated company.

* Question 7

Epsilon acquired 40% of Zeta when Zeta's retained earnings were $50,000, 25% of Kappa when Kappa's retained earnings were $40,000, and 25% of Lambda when Lambda's retained earnings were $50,000.

The four companies' statements of financial position as at 31 October 2011 were as follows:

	Epsilon $000	Zeta $000	Kappa $000	Lambda $000
ASSETS				
Non-current assets	1,900	170	140	160
Investment in Zeta	100			
Investment in Kappa	55			
Investment in Lambda	60			
	2,115	170	140	160
Current assets:				
Inventory	8	6	12	11
Trade receivables	12	5	4	7
Bank	5	4	3	2
	25	15	19	20
Total assets	2,140	185	159	180
LIABILITIES				
Equity:				
Share capital	500	50	60	70
Reserves	1,563	124	91	98
	2,063	174	151	168
Non-current liabilities	50			
Current liabilities:				
Trade payables	27	11	8	12
	2,140	185	159	180

Epsilon is entitled to appoint three members of Zeta's board. Zeta's articles state that the board of directors is restricted to five members and that board decisions are binding whenever a simple majority of the directors agree.

Epsilon used its voting rights to secure a place on Kappa's board for one of its own directors. This director has access to internal management reports and can exert some influence on decision making within the company.

Epsilon does not have a representative on the board of Lambda. The directors of Epsilon attempted to secure a place on the board, but were rebuffed by Ms Strong, who owns 75% of the shares. Ms Strong takes a very direct role in the management of Lambda.

Required:
(a) Discuss how each of Epsilon shareholdings should be accounted for in the Epsilon group's consolidated financial statements.
(b) Prepare a consolidated statement of financial position for the Epsilon Group as at 31 October 2011.

(The Association of International Accountants)

Question 8

This question concerns an associated company making a loss and possible impairment of goodwill.

Hyson plc acquired a 30% interest in the ordinary shares of Green plc on 1 January 20X3 when Green's general reserve was £25,000 and its retained earnings were £40,000.

In the year ended 31 December 20X8 Green made a loss after tax of £65,000 because of a recession in its principal sales market.

The statements of financial position of Hyson plc and Green plc at 31 December 20X8 are as follows:

	Hyson £	Green £
ASSETS		
Non-current assets:		
Property, plant and equipment	650,000	230,000
Depreciation	(310,000)	(105,000)
	340,000	125,000
Investment in Green	90,000	
Current assets:		
Inventories	145,000	64,000
Trade receivables	180,000	85,000
Current account – Green	5,000	
Bank	25,000	3,000
Total current assets	355,000	152,000
Total assets	785,000	277,000
EQUITY AND LIABILITIES		
£1 ordinary shares	300,000	200,000
General reserve	60,000	30,000
Retained earnings	225,000	(57,000)
	585,000	173,000
Current liabilities:		
Trade payables	163,000	99,000
Taxation payable	37,000	—
Current account – Hyson	—	5,000
Total equity and liabilities	785,000	277,000

The statements of income of Hyson and Green for the year ended 31 December 20X8 are:

	£	£
Sales	1,045,000	350,000
Cost of sales	683,000	320,000
Gross profit	362,000	30,000
Distribution expenses	42,000	20,000
Administration expenses	152,000	75,000
Profit/(loss) before tax	168,000	(65,000)
Income tax expense	33,000	—
Profit for the period	135,000	(65,000)
Dividend paid (shown in equity)	40,000	—

Because of the losses of Green in 20X8, the recoverable amount of a 30% interest in Green is £40,000 at 31 December 20X8.

Required:
(a) Prepare a consolidated statement of financial position of Hyson plc as at 31 December 20X8.
(b) Prepare a consolidated statement of income of Hyson plc, including the associated company Green, for the year ended 31 December 20X8.
(c) State the changes to your answers in (a) and (b) above if the recoverable amount of a 30% interest in Green was £65,000.

Question 9

Arnold plc and Bunny plc agreed to establish a Joint Operation, Carlton, which started trading on 1 January 20X1. Carlton is an unincorporated business, which is financed and managed by Arnold and Bunny.

Arnold agreed to provide land at an agreed price of £1,000,000 and plant at £600,000. In addition, Arnold and Bunny provided £200,000 in cash for working capital.

It was agreed that, on consolidation, the land and plant would remain in the statement of financial position of Arnold. All other assets and liabilities (except cash at the bank) of the joint operation would be divided equally between the partners. Cash at the bank would be divided so the capital of each partner was equal to their respective assets less liabilities.

The trial balance of the Joint Operation at 31 December 20X1 is given below:

	£000	£000
Sales		1,500
Purchases	700	
Direct wages	500	
Land	1,000	
Plant	600	
Trade receivables	400	
Trade payables		300
Office expenses	80	
Heat, light & telephone	70	
Motor & travelling expenses	60	
Advertising & marketing	46	
Finance costs	30	
Capital – Arnold		1,800
Capital – Bunny		200
Bank balance	314	
	3,800	3,800

The value of inventory at 31 December 20X1 was £200,000. No depreciation is to be charged on the land. Plant is to be depreciated at 5% per annum on cost.

Profit for the year is to be distributed to the partners:

(i) 5% per annum on capital; then

(ii) the remaining profit is to be divided equally between Arnold and Bunny.

Required:
For the year ended 31 December 20X1, prepare an income statement and statement of financial position of the Joint Operation at the year-end.

Notes

1 IAS 28 *Investments in Associates and Joint Ventures*, IASB, revised 2011, para. 3.
2 Ibid., para. 5.
3 Ibid., para. 8.
4 Ibid., para. 15.
5 Ibid., para. 10.
6 IAS 1 *Presentation of Financial Statements*, IASB, revised 2003, Implementation Guidance.
7 IAS 28 *Investments in Associates and Joint Ventures*, IASB, revised 2011, para. 40.
8 Ibid., para. 30.
9 Ibid., para. 7.
10 IFRS 11 *Joint Arrangements*, IASB, 2011, B8.
11 Ibid., para. 15.
12 Ibid., para. 16.
13 Ibid., para. 20.
14 Ibid., paras 24–25.
15 Ibid., para. 26.
16 IFRS 12 *Disclosure of Interest in Other Entities*, IASB, 2011, para. 1.
17 Ibid., para. 10.
18 Ibid., para. 20.

CHAPTER 17

Introduction to accounting for exchange differences

17.1 Introduction

The increasing globalisation of business means that it is becoming more and more common for companies to enter into transactions that have to be paid for in a foreign currency.

When currency fluctuations occur, the exchange rate will have changed between the date the goods or services have been invoiced and the date that payment is made. The difference impacts on cash flows and will be reported as a realised exchange gain or loss in the statement of income.

In this chapter we also consider how to prepare consolidated accounts when there is a foreign subsidiary that maintains its own accounts in the local currency which is different from that of its parent. IAS 21 refers to the local currency as the **functional** currency and the parent's currency as the **presentation** currency. The restatement of the functional currency into the presentation is referred to as translation. Any difference on exchange arising on translation has not been realised and is reported as other comprehensive income.

Objectives

By the end of this chapter, you should be able to:

- account for foreign transactions where differences arise on actual cash inflows and outflows resulting in realised gains or losses;
- translate the financial statements of foreign subsidiaries into the parent company's currency and report any exchange differences under other comprehensive income;
- explain the criteria when determining 'functional' and 'presentation' currency;
- prepare consolidated financial statements to include subsidiaries whose financial statements prepared using the local functional currency have to be translated into a different presentation currency on consolidation;
- explain the characteristics of a hyperinflationary economy and restatement of the functional currency financial statements.

17.2 How to record foreign currency transactions in a company's own books

We will comment briefly on the IAS 21 provisions relating to (i) how a foreign currency transaction is defined, (ii) the amount entered into the company's accounting records on entering into a transaction, (iii) the accounting treatment of exchange differences when the transaction is settled within the current accounting period, (iv) the accounting treatment when settlement occurs in the next accounting period, (v) the accounting treatment when settlement occurs in an accounting period beyond the next, and (vi) hedging the amount payable.

17.2.1 Defining foreign transactions

IAS 21 *The Effects of Changes in Foreign Exchange Rates* defines foreign transactions as follows:[1]

A foreign transaction is a transaction which is denominated in or requires settlement in a foreign currency, including transactions arising when an entity:

(a) buys or sells goods or services whose price is denominated in a foreign currency;

(b) borrows or lends funds when the amounts payable or receivable are denominated in a foreign currency;

(c) otherwise acquires or disposes of assets, or incurs or settles liabilities, denominated in a foreign currency.

17.2.2 The amount recorded on entering into a transaction

On initial recognition,[2] transactions are entered in the books at the spot currency exchange rate at the transaction date.

For example, let us assume that Brie SA buys vintage cheese from a UK company, Cheddar Ltd, on 1 October 20X1 for £100,000 when the exchange rate was £1 = €1.20. This will be recorded by Brie as Purchases €120,000 and Trade payable (Cheddar) at €120,000.

Where it is more practical an average rate may be used for a period to translate the month's purchases (it will be inappropriate where exchange rates fluctuate significantly).

17.2.3 The accounting treatment of exchange differences when the transaction is settled within the current accounting period

Amounts paid or received in settlement of foreign currency monetary items during an accounting period are translated at the date of settlement, and any exchange difference is taken to the statement of income as a realised gain or loss.

For example, if the rate at the date of payment on 31 October 20X1 was £1 = €1.22, then Brie would pay €122,000 to obtain the sterling amount of £100,000. The exchange difference of €2,000 (€122,000 − €120,000) is debited to the statement of income as an operating expense. If the rate had changed to £1 = €1.18 then there would have been an operating income of €2,000.

The following is an extract from the accounting policies in Nemetschek's 2011 report:

Currency translation
Exchange rate differences arising on the settlement of monetary items at rates different from those at which they were initially recorded during the period, are recognized as other operating income or other operating expenses in the period in which they arise.

17.2.4 The accounting treatment of exchange differences at the year-end when settlement is to occur in the next accounting period

The treatment depends on the ledger balances outstanding. For instance:

- Monetary balances are retranslated at the closing rate as at the date of the statement of financial position.
- Non-monetary items such as property, plant, equipment and inventory reported at historical cost remain translated at their original transaction rate.
- Non-monetary items at fair value are translated at the rate on the date the fair value was determined.[3]

Continuing with our Brie example on accounting for inventory, there are the following possibilities.

Inventory has been sold but the account payable is still outstanding

Assuming that all of the cheese had been sold but Cheddar had still not been paid, then there is no inventory to consider, only the amount payable to Cheddar. This balance is required to be translated at the closing rate. If the closing rate is £1 = €1.24 then the liability to Cheddar would be restated at €124,000 and there would be a resulting exchange loss of €4,000 which is reported in the statement of income.

Inventory has still not been sold and the account payable is still outstanding

If the cheese had not been sold and was still held as inventory, it is required to be reported at the rate as at the date of the initial transaction and not the closing rate, i.e. reported in the statement of financial position as €120,000 – the cost as at 1 October 20X1, the date of purchase. The account payable would still be reported at €124,000.

Inventory has still not been sold but net realisable value is lower than cost

If enquiry established that the cheese had deteriorated and the net realisable value was 50% of cost, then this would be translated at the closing rate as €62,000 (£50,000 × 1.24) and a loss reported of €58,000.

17.2.5 The accounting treatment of exchange differences when settlement occurs in a yet later accounting period

If a monetary item remains unpaid beyond the next accounting period then it will need to be retranslated at the closing rate as at the end of that period.

Let us assume the following:

- Brie has translated the €120,000 due to Cheddar as €124,000 and recognised an operating loss of €4,000 in the year ended 31 December 20X1.
- Brie has reached an agreement with Cheddar that the cheese needs a further period to mature and settlement in full is to be on 1 January 20X3.
- The exchange rate is £1 = €1.23 on 31 December 20X2.

At 31 December 20X2 Brie would report that there was €123,000 owing and there would be an operating gain reported in the 20X2 statement of income of €1,000 (€124,000 − €123,000). If the exchange rate had weakened to a rate higher than £1 = €1.24 there would have been a further operating loss reported in 20X2.

17.2.6 Hedging a foreign currency transaction to crystallise the amount of any exchange difference

A company might enter into a hedging transaction under IAS 39 or IFRS 9 *Financial Instruments*. The intention is to neutralise the exchange risk so that the company knows exactly how much a transaction will cost when settlement is required at a later date. This can be achieved in a number of ways such as entering into a forward contract or an options contract.

For example, let us continue with our Brie example and assume that the euro is weakening and Brie's finance director wants to fix the exact amount it is required to pay in euros on 31 October 20X1 to settle the debt currently recorded as €120,000. His worry is that the end-of-month rate might be £1 = €1.30 which would result in an operating loss of €10,000. In order to take away the uncertainty, Brie enters into a forward contract to buy £100,000 at the end of the month at a rate of say €1.25. This means that there is a known loss of €5,000 as opposed to the risk of a potential loss of up to €10,000.

17.3 Boil plc – a more detailed illustration

Let us assume the following transactions were entered into by Boil plc, a UK company that buys and sells catering equipment in New Zealand, during the year ended 31 December 20X4:

1/11	Buys goods for $30,000 on credit from Napier Ltd
15/11	Sells goods for $40,000 on credit to Wellington Ltd
15/11	Pays Napier Ltd $20,000 on account for the goods purchased
10/12	Receives $25,000 on account from Wellington Ltd in payment for the goods sold
10/12	Buys machinery for $80,000 from Auckland Ltd on credit
22/12	Pays Auckland Ltd $80,000 for the machinery

Boil's functional currency is sterling and the New Zealand companies' functional currency is NZ$.

The exchange rates at the relevant dates were:

1/11	£1 = $2.00	15/11	£1 = $2.20	10/12	£1 = $2.40
22/12	£1 = $2.50	31/12	£1 = $2.60		

(Assume that Boil plc buys foreign currency to pay for goods and non-current assets on the day of settlement and immediately converts into sterling any currency received from sales.)

Translating monetary accounts

We need to calculate any exchange differences on monetary accounts that are to be reported in the statement of income which arise on changes between the date of the initial transaction and the rate on the date of its settlement or the statement of financial position date, whichever is the earlier. Profits or losses on exchange differences will arise on the following monetary accounts:

Napier Ltd	Trade payables
Wellington Ltd	Trade receivable
Auckland Ltd	Payable for machinery

The profit or loss on foreign exchange in these cases will be as follows:

	Napier *Payable*				Wellington *Receivable*				Auckland *Payable*		
NZ$	*Rate*	*£*		*NZ$*	*Rate*	*£*		*NZ$*	*Rate*	*£*	

(i)   Record using the exchange rate on the date of transaction:
      30,000 @ 2.00 = 15,000   40,000 @ 2.20 = (18,182)   80,000 @ 2.40 = 33,333

(ii) Record using the exchange rate at the settlement date:
      20,000 @ 2.20 = (9,091)   25,000 @ 2.40 = 10,417   80,000 @ 2.50 = (32,000)

(iii) Retranslate and record using the closing exchange rate as at the year-end:
      10,000 @ 2.60 = (3,846)   15,000 @ 2.60 = 5,769

(iv) Calculate any gain (loss) on exchange:

2,063	(1,996)	1,333

The exchange gains of £2,063 and £1,333 and exchange loss of £1,996 have been realised and are reported in the statement of income as operating income and operating expense.

Accounting treatment of other balances

All other balances, i.e. purchases and sales in the statement of income and machinery (non-monetary), will be translated on the day of the initial transaction and no profit or loss on foreign exchange will arise. These balances will therefore appear in the financial statements as follows:

Purchases	$30,000/2.00 = £15,000
Sales	$40,000/2.20 = £18,182
Machinery	$80,000/2.40 = £33,333

17.4 IAS 21 *Concept of Functional and Presentation Currencies*

All companies have a functional and a presentation currency. In a group with foreign subsidiaries these currencies often differ.

Many groups consist of a parent with a number of foreign subsidiaries that prepare their accounts in the local currency, their functional currency. At the year-end each set of foreign subsidiary accounts is translated into the currency of the parent, the presentation currency or presentational currency.

17.4.1 The functional currency

The functional currency is the currency of the primary economic environment in which the entity operates. For example, the following extract is from the Rio Tinto 2015 financial statements:

> The functional currency for each entity in the Group . . . is the currency of the primary economic environment in which that entity operates. For many entities, this is the currency of the country in which they are located.

Factors to consider when determining the functional currency for an individual company

IAS 21 sets out the factors which a reporting entity (a company preparing financial statements) will consider in determining its functional currency.[1] These are:

● the currency that mainly influences sales prices for goods and services;

● the currency that mainly influences labour, materials and other costs of providing goods and services; and

- the currency in which funds from financing activities are generated and the currency in which the receipts from operating activities are usually retained, which also provide evidence of an entity's functional currency.[4]

If the functional currency is not obvious from the above, then managers have to make a judgement as to which currency most represents the economic effects of its transactions.

Factors a parent considers when deciding with a subsidiary on the subsidiary's functional currency

In making its decision the following factors will be considered:[5]

(a) Whether the activities of the foreign operation are carried out as an extension of the reporting entity (the parent), rather than being carried out with a significant degree of autonomy. An example of the former is when the foreign operation only sells goods imported from the parent and remits the proceeds to it. An example of the latter is when the operation accumulates cash and other monetary items, incurs expenses, generates income and arranges borrowings, all substantially in its local currency.

(b) Whether transactions with the parent are a high or low proportion of the foreign operation's activities.

(c) Whether cash flows from the activities of the foreign operation directly affect the cash flows of the parent and are readily available for remittance to it.

(d) Whether cash flows from the activities of the foreign operation are sufficient to service existing and normally expected debt obligations without funds being made available by the parent.

If the functional currency of the foreign operation is the same as that of the parent, there will of course be no need for translation and the consolidation will be just as for any other subsidiary.

17.4.2 The presentation currency[6]

The **presentation currency** is the currency a parent chooses for its financial statements. The parent is entitled to present its group accounts in any currency, so that in some cases the parent's presentation currency may differ from its own functional currency. There are various reasons for this, such as the principal or potential investors tending to function in a country with a different currency. For example, a parent whose functional currency is the euro might decide to raise finance in the US and so translates its euro financial statements into US$.

The following is an extract from a Press Announcement in 2010 by Tullow Oil plc:

Change in presentation currency
Tullow Oil plc ('the Company', together with its subsidiaries, 'the Group') will present its results in US dollars with effect from 1 January 2010. The Group has decided it is appropriate to change the presentational currency from Sterling as the majority of the Group's activities are in Africa where oil revenues and costs are dollar denominated.

17.5 Translating the functional currency into the presentation currency

Whenever the presentational currency is different from the functional currency, it is necessary to translate the financial statements into the presentational currency. In this situation there is no impact on cash flows and so there is no realised exchange gain or loss to be reported in the statement of income.

Any gain or loss will, therefore, be reported as other comprehensive income. The translation rules used in this situation are set out in paragraph 39 of IAS 21 as follows:

(a) assets and liabilities . . . shall be translated at the closing rate at the date of the statement of financial position;

(b) income and expenses . . . shall be translated at exchange rates at the dates of the transactions [or average rate if this is a reasonable approximation]; and

(c) all resulting exchange differences shall be recognised as a separate component of equity.

The following is an extract from Nemetschek AG's 2017 annual report:

Currency translation
The group's consolidated financial statements are prepared in Euros, which is the group's presentation currency.

Functional currency policy
Each entity in the group determines its own functional currency which is the currency of the primary economic environment in which the company operates. Items included in the financial statements of each entity are measured using the functional currency. Transactions in foreign currencies are initially recorded at in the functional currency at the spot rate ruling on of the date of the transaction.

Monetary assets and liabilities denominated in foreign currencies are retranslated at the functional currency exchange spot rate as at the balance sheet date. Foreign exchange differences are recognised in profit or loss . . .

Non-monetary items that are measured in terms of historical cost in a foreign currency are translated using the exchange rate as of the date of the initial transaction. Non-monetary items measured at fair value in a foreign currency are translated using the exchange rates at the date when the fair value is determined.

Group policy re subsidiaries
Assets and liabilities of foreign companies are translated to the Euro at the closing rate (incl. goodwill). Income and expenses are translated at the average exchange rate. Any resulting exchange differences are recognised separately in equity.

17.6 Preparation of consolidated accounts

The consolidated accounts are prepared for the Pau Group from the following data.

On 1 January 20X1 Pau Inc. acquired 80% of the ordinary shares of a Brazilian company Briona for $18m when Briona's retained earnings were R$2m and the share premium was R$7m. Briona's financial statements have been audited in their functional currency of

Brazilian reals and comply with IAS 21. The summarised statements of income and financial position as at 31 December 20X1 were as follows:

Statements of income for the year ended 31 December 20X1

		Pau		*Briona*
	US$000	*US$000*	*R$000*	*R$000*
Sales		200,000		80,000
Opening inventories	20,000		10,000	
Purchases	130,000		60,000	
Closing inventories	(40,000)		(30,000)	
Cost of sales		110,000		40,000
Gross profit		90,000		40,000
Other expenses		(15,000)		(14,000)
Interest paid				(1,000)
Total expenses		(15,000)		(15,000)
Profit before taxation		75,000		25,000
Taxation		(15,000)		(5,000)
Profit after taxation		60,000		20,000

Statement of financial position as at 31 December 20X1

	US$000	*R$000*
Non-current assets	70,000	30,000
Investment in Briona	18,000	
Current assets		
Inventories	40,000	30,000
Trade receivables	27,000	25,000
Cash	2,000	1,000
Total current assets	69,000	56,000
Current liabilities		
Trade payables	35,000	12,000
Taxation	15,000	5,000
Total current liabilities	50,000	17,000
Debentures		6,000
Total assets less liabilities	107,000	63,000
Share capital	20,000	34,000
Share premium		7,000
Retained earnings	87,000	22,000
	107,000	63,000

The following information is also available:

(i) The opening inventory was acquired when the exchange rate was US$1 = R$2.0 and the closing inventory when the rate was US$1 = R$2.4.

(ii) Exchange rates were as follows:

At 1 January 20X1	US$1 = R$2.0
Average for the year ending 31 December 20X4	US$1 = R$2.25
At 31 December 20X1	US$1 = R$2.5

Required:

(a) Prepare a consolidated statement of income.

(b) Prepare a consolidated statement of financial position:

    (i) Show the goodwill calculation.

    (ii) Show the non-controlling interest calculation.

    (iii) Complete with retained earnings as a balancing figure.

(c) Reconcile the retained earnings figure showing exchange gains and losses.

17.6.1 Pau Group draft consolidated accounts

(a) Statement of income

	Pau US$000	Briona R$000	Rate	Briona US$000	Pau Group US$000
Sales	200,000	80,000	2.25	35,555.6	235,555.6
Opening inventories	20,000	10,000	2.0	5,000.0	25,000.0
Purchases	130,000	60,000	2.25	26,666.7	156,666.7
Closing inventories	−40,000	−30,000	2.4	−12,500.0	−52,500.0
Cost of sales	110,000	40,000		19,166.7	129,166.7
Gross profit	90,000	40,000		16,388.9	106,388.9
Other expenses	−15,000	−14,000	2.25	−6,222.2	−21,222.2
Interest paid		−1,000	2.25	−444.4	−444.4
Total expenses	15,000	15,000		6,666.7	21,666.7
Profit before tax	75,000	25,000		9,722.2	84,722.2
Income tax	−15,000	−5,000	2.5	−2,000.0	−17,000.0
Profit after tax	60,000	20,000		7,722.2	67,722.2

(b) Statement of financial position

	Pau US$000	Briona R$000	Rate	Briona US$000		Pau Group US$000
Non-current assets	70,000	30,000	2.5	12,000		82,000
Investment in Briona	18,000				Goodwill (b1)	640
Current assets						
Inventories	40,000	30,000	2.5	12,000		52,000
Trade receivables	27,000	25,000	2.5	10,000		37,000
Cash	2,000	1,000	2.5	400		2,400
	69,000	56,000		22,400		91,400
Current liabilities						
Trade payables	35,000	12,000	2.5	4,800		39,800
Taxation	15,000	5,000	2.5	2,000		17,000
Total current liabilities	50,000	17,000		6,800		56,800
Debentures		6,000	2.5	2,400		2,400
Total assets less liabilities	107,000	63,000		25,200		114,840
Share capital	20,000	34,000	2.5	13,600		20,000
Share premium		7,000	2.5	2,800		
Retained earnings	87,000	22,000	2.5	8,800	(b3)	89,800
	107,000	63,000		25,200		109,800
Non-controlling interest					(b2)	5,040
	107,000	63,000		25,200		114,840

(b1) Goodwill

	R$000	R$000	Rate at 1.1.20X1	US$000
Cost		36,000		
Share capital	34,000			
Share premium	7,000			
Retained earnings	2,000			
	43,000 × 80%	34,400		
Goodwill		1,600	2.0	800
Required to restate at year-end:				
Goodwill		1,600	2.5	640

(b2) Non-controlling interest (NCI) at 31.12.20X1

	R$000	Rate	US$000	US$000
Share capital	34,000	2.5	13,600	
Share premium	7,000	2.5	2,800	
Retained earnings	22,000	2.5	8,800	
			25,200 × 20%	5,040

(b3) The consolidated statement of financial position could be completed by inserting a balancing figure of US$89,800 for the retained earnings made up of Pau's retained earnings of £87,000 and Briona's post-acquisition profit of £2,800. This can be proved as follows:

(c) Subsidiary post-acquisition profit included in the $89,800 group retained earnings

	R$000	Rate	US$000	US$000 Parent	US$000 NCI
Retained profit per Income Statement			7,722.2	6,177.8	1,544.4
At closing rate	20,000	2.5	8,000		
Gain on exchange			277.8	222.2	55.6
Loss on opening shareholders' funds					
Share capital	34,000				
Share premium	7,000				
Retained earnings	2,000				
	43,000	Opening rate 2.0	21,500		
		Closing rate 2.5	17,200		
Loss			−4,300	(3,440)	(860)
Loss on goodwill		Opening rate			
Goodwill	1,600	2.0	800		
		Closing rate 2.5	640		
Loss			−160	(160)	
Post-acquisition profit of Briona attributable to Pau				2,800	
Post-acquisition profit attributable to NCI					740
Opening NCI (43,000 × 20%/2.0)					4,300
Closing NCI (63,000 × 20%/2.5)					5,040
Group retained profit at 31.12.20X1		US$000			
Pau		87,000			
Briona post-acquisition (above)		2,800			
Group retained profit		89,800			

Note that there is no post-acquisition share premium, as the subsidiary's balance at acquisition and at 31.12.20X1 is the same at R$7m.

17.7 How to reduce the risk of translation differences

We have seen that when a parent invests in a foreign subsidiary it is required at each year-end to translate the assets and liabilities from the subsidiary's functional currency into that of the parent.

For example, let us assume that a UK parent has spent $10m on acquiring a US trading subsidiary and at the year-end the net assets of the US subsidiary are also $10m.

On consolidation by the UK parent, the $10m net assets of the US subsidiary are translated into sterling for inclusion in the consolidated statement of financial position. At each year-end the sterling value of any foreign exchange differences are taken to reserves. This means that the group's consolidated shareholders' funds will fluctuate up and down as exchange rates move.

The parent is able to reduce the extent of such fluctuations by hedging the translation risk. It normally does so by acquiring a matching foreign exchange liability. One way is to take on a debt such as a $10m loan.

Assuming that the opening exchange rate is £1 = $2 and the closing rate is £1 = $2.5, without hedging there would be an exchange loss on holding the net assets of £1,000. If the same amount is borrowed there would be an exchange gain on holding the debt of £1,000 ($10m at 2.0 less $10m at 2.5).

In practice, it may be difficult for the parent to borrow as much as $10m unless it gave a guarantee to the lender. By borrowing all its investment in its subsidiary in dollars, the parent would minimise its exchange gains and losses in its subsidiary. In this example, the dollar depreciates against the pound and there is a loss (without hedging). If the dollar appreciated against the pound, there would be a gain (without hedging).

17.8 Critique of the use of presentational currency

Multinational companies may have subsidiaries in many different countries, each of which may report by choice or legal requirement internally in their local currency. With globalisation, reporting the group in a presentation currency assists the efficiency of international capital markets, particularly where a group raises funds in more than one market. Although each subsidiary might be controlled through financial statements prepared in the local currency, realism requires the use of a single presentation currency.

17.9 IAS 29 *Financial Reporting in Hyperinflationary Economies*[7]

IAS 29 applies where an entity's functional currency is that of a hyperinflationary economy. Its objective is to give guidance on (a) determining when an economy is hyperinflationary, and (b) restating financial statements to make them meaningful.

17.9.1 Determining when an economy is hyperinflationary

There is no precise criterion, although there is a view that there is hyperinflation when the cumulative inflation rate over three years exceeds 100%. The IAS 29 approach is to leave it as a matter of judgement, based on indicators (IAS 29.3) such as:

- the general population preferring to keep its wealth in non-monetary assets or in a relatively stable foreign currency, with amounts of local currency held being immediately invested to maintain purchasing power;
- the general population regarding monetary amounts not in terms of the local currency but in terms of a relatively stable foreign currency in which prices may be quoted;
- sales and purchases on credit taking place at prices that compensate for the expected loss of purchasing power during the credit period, even if the period is short;
- interest rates, wages and prices being linked to a price index; and
- the cumulative inflation rate over three years approaching, or exceeding, 100%.

17.9.2 How to restate financial statements

Having decided that hyperinflation has occurred, the standard requires the financial statements (and corresponding figures for previous periods) of an entity with a functional currency that is hyperinflationary to be restated for the changes in the general pricing power of the functional currency using the measuring unit current at the year-end date.

17.9.3 Restatement treatment of statements of income and financial position

The statement of comprehensive income

All items in the statement of comprehensive income are expressed in terms of the measuring unit current at the end of the reporting period. All amounts need to be restated by applying the change in the general price index from the dates when the items of income and expenses were initially recorded in the financial statements.

The statement of financial position

Amounts not already expressed in terms of the measuring unit current at the end of the reporting period are restated by applying a general price index.

Monetary items

● Monetary items are not restated because they are already expressed in terms of the monetary unit.

● Inventory also as it has been written down to net realisable value under IAS 2.

Non-monetary items

Non-monetary items are restated from the date of acquisition if they are historical cost financial statements or from date of valuation if any asset has been reported at valuation.

If they are current cost financial statements then there is no restatement because they are already expressed in the unit of measurement current at the end of the reporting period.

17.9.4 Disclosures

The following disclosures are required:

(a) the fact that the financial statements and the corresponding figures for previous periods have been restated in terms of the measuring unit current at the end of the reporting period;

(b) whether the financial statements are based on a historical cost approach or a current cost approach; and

(c) the price index that has been used and the level of the price index at the end of the reporting period and the movement in the index during the current and the previous reporting periods.

Summary

When accounts are prepared in the functional currency, exchange differences arising on the settlement of monetary items or on translating monetary items at rates that are different from those which applied on initial recognition (i.e. settled in a later accounting period) are recognised in profit or loss in the period in which they arise.

When functional currency financial statements are translated into a different presentation currency, assets and liabilities are translated at closing rate, income and expenses are translated at the rate as at the date of the transactions (an average may be practical if appropriate), and resulting exchange gains are recognised in other comprehensive income.

REVIEW QUESTIONS

1   Discuss the desirability or otherwise of isolating profits or losses caused by exchange differences from other profit or losses in financial statements.

2   Explain the term functional currency and describe the factors an entity should take into account when determining which is the functional currency.

3   Explain why exchange differences are treated differently in financial statements prepared in a functional currency and those prepared in a presentation currency.

4   Discuss why a company that is not part of a group might decide to translate its financial statements into a presentation currency.

5   Explain why exchange differences might appear in other comprehensive income.

6   How does the treatment of changes in foreign exchange rates relate to the prudence and accruals concepts?

7   It was reported[8] that 'Belarus' cumulative inflation index will exceed 100%, which means that IAS 29 is likely to be applicable to Belarus up to 2014 . . . does not expect any significant microeconomic consequences of Belarus' qualifying as a country with hyperinflationary economy, except for the significant deterioration in financial performance indicators of banks and enterprises applying IFRS.'

Discuss what financial performance indicators might be adversely affected by applying IAS 29.

EXERCISES

* Question I

Fry Ltd has the following foreign currency transactions in the year to 31/12/20X0:

15/11	Buys goods for $40,000 on credit from Texas Inc.
15/11	Sells goods for $60,000 on credit to Alamos Inc.
20/11	Pays Texas Inc. $40,000 for the goods purchased
20/11	Receives $30,000 on account from Alamos Inc. in payment for the goods sold
20/11	Buys machinery for $100,000 from Chicago Inc. on credit
20/11	Borrows $90,000 from an American bank
21/12	Pays Chicago Inc. $80,000 for the machinery

The exchange rates at the relevant dates were:

15/11	£1 = $2.60
20/11	£1 = $2.40
21/12	£1 = $2.30
31/12	£1 = $2.10

Required:
Calculate the profit or loss to be reported in the financial statements of Fry Ltd at 31/12/20X0.

* Question 2

On 1 January 20X1 Fibre plc acquired 80% of the ordinary shares of a Singaporean company, Fastlink Ltd, for £6m when Fastlink's retained earnings were $15.5m and the share premium was $0.8m. Fastlink's financial statements have been prepared in their functional currency of Singapore dollars and comply with IAS 21. The summarised statements of income and financial position as at 31 December 20X1 were as follows:

Statements of income for the year ended 31 December 20X1

	Fibre	Fastlink
	£000	$000
Sales	200,000	50,000
Opening inventories	20,000	8,000
Purchases	130,000	30,000
Closing inventories	(40,000)	(6,000)
Cost of sales	110,000	32,000
Gross profit	90,000	18,000
Expenses	(15,000)	(6,500)
Profit before taxation	75,000	11,500
Taxation	(15,000)	(3,000)
Profit after taxation	60,000	8,500

Statement of financial position as at 31 December 20X1

	£000	$000
Non-current assets	90,000	25,000
Investment in Fastlink	6,000	
Current assets:		
Inventories	40,000	6,000
Trade receivables	27,000	5,000
Cash	2,000	4,000
Total current assets	69,000	15,000
Current liabilities:		
Trade payables	35,000	11,000
Taxation	15,000	3,000
Total current liabilities	50,000	14,000
Total assets less liabilities	115,000	26,000
Share capital	20,000	1,200
Share premium		800
Retained earnings	95,000	24,000
	115,000	26,000

The following information is also available:

(i) The opening inventory was acquired when the exchange rate was £1 = $2.6 and the closing inventory when the rate was £1 = $2.2.

(ii) Exchange rates were as follows:

At 1 January 20X1	£1 = $2.5
Average for the year ending 31 December 20X4	£1 = $2.25
At 31 December 20X1	£1 = $2.0

Required:
(a) Prepare a consolidated statement of income.
(b) Prepare a consolidated statement of financial position:
  (i) Show the goodwill calculation.
  (ii) Show the non-controlling interest calculation.
  (iii) Complete with retained earnings as a balancing figure.
(c) Reconcile the retained earnings figure showing exchange gains and losses.

* Question 3

On 1 January 20X0 Walpole Ltd acquired 90% of the ordinary shares of a French subsidiary Paris SA. At that date the balance on the retained earnings of Paris SA was €10,000. The non-controlling interest in Paris was measured as a percentage of identifiable net assets. No shares have been issued by Paris since acquisition. Paris SA's dividend was paid on 31 December 20X2. The summarised statements of comprehensive income and statements of financial position of Walpole Ltd and Paris SA at 31 December 20X2 were as follows:

Statements of comprehensive income for the year ended 31 December 20X2

	Walpole Ltd	Paris SA
	£000	£000
Sales	317,200	200,000
Opening inventories	50,000	22,000
Purchases	180,000	90,000
Closing inventories	60,000	12,000
Cost of sales	170,000	100,000
Gross profit	147,200	100,000
Dividend received from Paris SA	1,800	NIL
Depreciation	30,000	30,000
Other expenses	15,000	7,000
Interest paid	6,000	3,000
Total expenses	51,000	40,000
Profit before taxation	98,000	60,000
Taxation	21,000	15,000
Profit after taxation	77,000	45,000
Dividend paid	20,000	10,000

Statement of financial position as at 31 December 20X2

	Walpole Ltd	Paris SA
	£000	£000
Non-current assets	94,950	150,000
Investment in Paris SA	41,050	
Current assets:		
Inventories	60,000	12,000
Trade receivables	59,600	40,000
Paris SA	2,400	
Cash	11,000	11,000
Total current assets	133,000	63,000
Current liabilities:		
Trade payables	45,000	18,000
Walpole Ltd		12,000
Taxation	21,000	15,000
Total current liabilities	66,000	45,000
Debentures	40,000	10,000
Total assets less liabilities	163,000	158,000
Share capital	80,000	60,000
Share premium	6,000	20,000
Revaluation reserve	10,000	12,000
Retained earnings	67,000	66,000
	163,000	158,000

The following information is also available:

(i)   The revaluation reserve in Paris SA arose from the revaluation of non-current assets on 1/1/20X2.

(ii) No impairment of goodwill has occurred since acquisition.

(iii) Exchange rates were as follows:

At 1 January 20X0	£1 = €2
Average for the year ending 31 December 20X2	£1 = €4
At 31 December 20X1/1 January 20X2	£1 = €3
At 31 December 20X2	£1 = €5

Required:
Assuming that the functional currency of Paris SA is the euro, prepare the consolidated accounts for the Walpole group at 31 December 20X2.

* Question 4

(a) According to IAS 21 *The Effects of Changes in Foreign Exchange Rates*, how should a company decide what its functional currency is?

(b) Until recently Eufonion, a UK limited liability company, reported using the euro (€) as its functional currency. However, on 1 November 2007 the company decided that its functional currency should now be the dollar ($).

The summarised balance sheet of Eufonion as at 31 October 2008 in € million was as follows:

ASSETS		€m
Non-current assets		420
Current assets		
Inventories	26	
Trade and other receivables	42	
Cash and cash equivalents	8	
		76
Total assets		496
EQUITY AND LIABILITIES		
Equity		
Share capital		200
Retained earnings		107
		307
Non-current liabilities	85	
Current liabilities		
Trade and other payables	63	
Current taxation	41	
	104	
Total liabilities		189
Total equity and liabilities		496

Non-current liabilities includes a loan of $70 million which was raised in dollars ($) and translated at the closing rate of $1 = €0.72425.

Trade receivables include an amount of $20 million invoiced in dollars ($) to an American customer which has been translated at the closing rate of $1 = €0.72425.

All items of property, plant and equipment were purchased in euros (€) except for plant which was purchased in British pounds (£) in 2007 and which cost £150 million. This was translated at the exchange rate of £1 = €1.46015 as at the date of purchase. The carrying value of the equipment was £90 million as at 31 October 2008.

Required:
Translate the balance sheet of Eufonion as at 31 October 2008 into dollars ($m), the company's new functional currency.

(c) The directors of Eufonion (as in (b) above) are now considering using the British pound (£) as the company's presentation currency for the financial statements for the year ended 31 October 2009.

Required:
Advise the directors how they should translate the company's income statement for the year ended 31 October 2009 and its balance sheet as at 31 October 2009 into the new presentation currency.

(d) Discuss whether or not a reporting entity should be allowed to present its financial statements in a currency which is different from its functional currency.

(The Association of International Accountants)

* **Question 5**

Helvatia GmbH is a Swiss company which is a wholly owned subsidiary of Corolli, a UK company. Helvatia GmbH was formed on 1 November 2005 to purchase and manage a property in Zürich in Switzerland. The reporting and functional currency of Helvatia GmbH is the Swiss franc (CHF).

As a financial accountant in Corolli you are converting the financial statements of Helvatia GmbH into £ sterling in order to be consolidated with the results of Corolli which reports in £s.

The following are the summarised income statements and balance sheet (in thousands of Swiss francs) of Helvatia GmbH:

Helvatia GmbH income statement and retained earnings for the year ended 31 October 2007

	CHF (000)
Revenue	8,800
Depreciation	(1,370)
Other operating expenses	(1,900)
Net income	5,530
Retained earnings at 1 November 2006	3,760
	9,290
Dividends paid	(1,000)
Retained earnings at 31 October 2007	8,290

Helvatia GmbH balance sheet as at 31 October

	2007 CHF (000)		2006 CHF (000)	
ASSETS				
Non-current assets				
Land		6,300		3,300
Buildings		12,330		13,700
		18,630		17,000
Current assets				
Receivables	550		1,550	
Cash	5,610		610	
		6,160		2,160
		24,790		19,160
LIABILITIES AND EQUITY				
Non-current liabilities				
Mortgage loan		10,800		10,000
Current liabilities				
Payables		700		400
Equity				
Issued share capital	5,000		5,000	
Retained earnings	8,290	13,290	3,760	8,760
		24,790		19,160

The following exchange rates are available:

	1 Swiss franc = £
At 1 November 2005	0.40
At 1 November 2006	0.55
At 30 November 2006	0.53
At 31 January 2007	0.53
At 31 October 2007	0.45
Weighted average for the year ended 31 October 2007	0.50

The non-current assets and mortgage loan of Helvatia GmbH as at 31 October 2006 all date from 1 November 2005. Helvatia GmbH purchased additional land and increased the mortgage loan on 31 January 2007. There were no other purchases of non-current assets. Land is not depreciated but the building is depreciated at 10% a year using the reducing balance method. Helvatia GmbH's dividends were paid on 31 January 2007.

The sterling equivalent of Helvatia GmbH's retained earnings as at 31 October 2006 was £1,222,000.

Required:
Prepare the following statements for Helvatia GmbH in £000 sterling:
(a) A summarised income statement for the year ended 31 October 2007.
(b) A summarised balance sheet as at 31 October 2007.
(c) A statement of cash flows for the year ended 31 October 2007 using the indirect method. Additional notes are not required.

(The Association of International Accountants)

* Question 6

The following Statements of Profit or Loss and other Comprehensive Income relate to Allen plc (Allen) and its investee companies, Corrib plc (Corrib) and Neagh plc (Neagh). Neagh is based in Northern Ireland. It produces, sells, and is managed autonomously in Northern Ireland. Accordingly, its financial statements are presented in GB£ Sterling as the functional currency.

Statements of Profit or Loss and Other Comprehensive Income for year ended 31 July 2017

	Allen plc €million	Corrib plc € million	Neagh plc GB£ million
Revenue	225	240	60
Cost of sales	(130)	(123)	(18)
Gross profit	95	117	42
Operating expenses	(27)	(75)	(18)
Finance costs	(12)	(21)	(2.4)
Other income	8		
Investment income	14	—	—
Profit before taxation	78	21	21.6
Taxation	(10)	(3)	(4)
Profit for the year	68	18	17.6
Other comprehensive income (items that will not be reclassified to profit or loss):			
Gains on revaluation of property	24	6	—
Total comprehensive income for the year	92	24	17.6

The following additional information is provided:

1 Allen purchased a 70% holding in the equity of Corrib on 1 December 2016. The purchase price was 200 million paid in cash. Goodwill arising on acquisition was calculated at €30 million, using the fair value method. On 3 July 2017, impairment losses amounting to €10 million had been incurred. No accounting entry was made ttto reflect the impairment.

2 Allen purchased a 60% holding in Neagh on 1 August 2016, for an immediate cash payment of £80 million. On that date, the fair values of the identifiable net assets of Neagh totalled £100 million, which was the same as their carrying values in the books of Neagh. The 40% non-controlling interest had a fair value of £50 million on 1 August 2016. No impairment of goodwill had occurred by 31 July 2017. The directors of Allen wish to use the fair value method for all acquisitions.

3 On 1 December 2016, the fair value of certain plant & equipment held by Corrib was €3 million more than its carrying value. This plant & equipment had a useful economic life of 5 years from the date of acquisition. The revised values have not been incorporated into the books of Corrib and depreciation was accounted for based on the original carrying values.

4 During the post-acquisition period Corrib sold goods to Allen for €4 million. These goods were sold at a gross margin of 25% of transfer price. 30% of the goods remained in the inventory of Allen at 31 July 2017.

5 Corrib declared a dividend of €6 million during the year from post-acquisition profits. Allen has recognised its share of this dividend within 'investment income'.

6 All workings may be taken to the nearest €0.1 million. The £ / € exchange rate was as follows during the relevant period:

Date	£ per €1
1 August 2016	0.89
31 July 2017	0.81
Average for period	0.85

Requirement:

(a) Calculate the following:
   (i) the goodwill arising on the acquisition of Neagh at the date of acquisition; and
   (ii) the goodwill figure in respect of Neagh to be reported in the group accounts for the Allen Group at 31 July 2017.
   Explain clearly the accounting treatment of any difference between the two figures.

(b) Prepare a consolidated Statement of Profit or Loss and Other Comprehensive Income for the Allen Group for year ended 31 July 2017 in accordance with IFRS. Your answer should show clearly the amount of any exchange gains or losses recognised during the period.

(c) Discuss what is meant by the concept of an entity's functional currency and how it may be determined in accordance with IAS 21 *The Effects of Changes in Foreign Exchange Rates*.

(Institute of Certified Public Accountants (CPA), Professional Stage 1 Corporate Reporting Examination, August 2017)

Notes

1 IAS 21 *The Effects of Changes in Foreign Exchange Rates*, IASB, revised 2003, para. 20.
2 Ibid., para. 21.
3 Ibid., para. 23.
4 Ibid., para. 10.
5 Ibid., para. 11.
6 Ibid., para. 38.
7 IAS 29 *Financial Reporting in Hyperinflationary Economies*, IASB, 1989.
8 www.prime-tass.by/english/News/show.asp?id=96939

Earnings per share

18.1 Introduction

The main purpose of this chapter is to understand the importance of earnings per share (EPS) and the PE ratio as a measure of the financial performance of a company (or 'an enterprise'). This chapter will enable you to calculate the EPS according to IAS 33 for both the current year and prior years, when there is an issue of shares in the year. Also, it will enable you to understand and calculate the diluted earnings per share, for future changes in share capital arising from exercising of share options and conversion of other financial instruments into shares.

Objectives

By the end of this chapter, you should be able to:

- define earnings per share and the PE ratio;
- comment critically on alternative EPS figures;
- calculate the basic earnings per share;
- calculate the diluted earnings per share.

18.2 Why is the earnings per share figure important?

One of the most widely publicised ratios for a public company is the price/earnings or PE ratio. The PE ratio is significant because, by combining it with a forecast of company earnings, analysts can decide whether the shares are currently over- or undervalued.[1]

The ratio is published daily in the financial press and is widely employed by those making investment decisions. The following is a typical extract:

Breweries, Pubs and Restaurants

Company	Price 31/10/12	PE ratio
Company A	283	8.9
Company B	471	11.0
Company C	705	17.0

The PE ratio is calculated by dividing the market price of a share by the earnings that the company generated for that share. Alternatively, the PE figure may be seen as a multiple of the earnings per share, where the multiple represents the number of years' earnings required to recoup the price paid for the share. For example, it would take a shareholder in Company B 11 years to recoup her outlay if all earnings were to be distributed, whereas it would take a shareholder in Company A almost nine years to recoup his outlay, and one in Company C 17 years.

18.2.1 What factors affect the PE ratio?

The PE ratio for a company will reflect investors' confidence and hopes about the international scene, the national economy and the industry sector, as well as about the current year's performance of the company as disclosed in its financial report. It is difficult to interpret a PE ratio in isolation without a certain amount of information about the company, its competitors and the industry within which it operates.

For example, a **high PE ratio** might reflect investor confidence in the existing management team: people are willing to pay a high multiple for expected earnings because of the underlying strength of the company. Conversely, it might also reflect lack of investor confidence in the existing management, but an anticipation of a takeover bid which will result in transfer of the company assets to another company with better prospects of achieving growth in earnings than has the existing team.

A **low PE ratio** might indicate a lack of confidence in the current management or a feeling that even a new management might find problems that are not easily surmounted. For example, there might be extremely high gearing, with little prospect of organic growth in earnings or new capital inputs from rights issues to reduce it.

These reasons for a difference in the PE ratios of companies, even though they are in the same industry, are market-based and not simply a function of earnings. However, both the current earnings per share figure and the individual shareholder's expectation of future growth relative to that of other companies also have an impact on the share price.

18.3 How is the EPS figure calculated?

Because of the importance attached to the PE ratio, it is essential that there be a consistent approach to the calculation of the EPS figure. IAS 33 *Earnings per Share*[2] was issued in 1998 for this purpose. A revised version of the standard was issued in 2003.

The EPS figure is of major interest to shareholders not only because of its use in the PE ratio calculation, but also because it is used in the earnings yield percentage calculation. It is a more acceptable basis for comparing performance than figures such as dividend yield percentage because it is not affected by the distribution policy of the directors. The formula is:

$$\text{EPS} = \frac{\text{Earnings}}{\text{Weighted number of ordinary shares}}$$

The standard defines two EPS figures for disclosure, namely,

- basic EPS based on ordinary shares currently in issue; and
- diluted EPS based on ordinary shares currently in issue plus potential ordinary shares.

18.3.1 Basic EPS

Basic EPS (BEPS) is defined in IAS 33 as follows:[3]

- Basic earnings per share is calculated by dividing the net profit or loss for the period attributable to ordinary shareholders by the weighted average number of ordinary shares outstanding during the period.

For the purpose of the BEPS definition:

- **Net profit** is the profit for the period attributable to the parent entity after deduction of preference dividends (assuming preference shares are equity instruments).[4]

- The **weighted average number of ordinary shares** should be adjusted for events, other than the conversion of potential ordinary shares, that have changed the number of ordinary shares outstanding, without a corresponding change in resources.[5]

- An **ordinary share** is an equity instrument that is subordinate to all other classes of equity instruments.[6]

Earnings per share is calculated on the overall profit attributable to ordinary shareholders but also on the profit from continuing operations if this is different from the overall profit for the period.

18.3.2 Diluted EPS

Diluted EPS is defined as follows:

- For the purpose of calculating diluted earnings per share, the net profit attributable to ordinary shareholders and the weighted average number of shares outstanding should be *adjusted for the effects of all dilutive potential ordinary* shares.[7]

This means that *both* the earnings *and* the number of shares used *may* need to be adjusted from the amounts that appear in the profit and loss account and statement of financial position.

- **Dilutive** means that earnings in the future may be spread over a larger number of ordinary shares.

- **Potential ordinary shares** are financial instruments that may entitle the holders to ordinary shares.

18.4 The use to shareholders of the EPS

Shareholders use the reported EPS to estimate future growth which will affect the future share price. It is an important measure of growth over time. There are, however, limitations in its use as a performance measure and for inter-company comparison.

18.4.1 How does a shareholder estimate future growth in the EPS?

The current EPS figure allows a shareholder to assess the wealth-creating abilities of a company. It recognises that the effect of earnings is to add to the individual wealth of shareholders in two ways: first, by the payment of a dividend which transfers cash from the company's control to the shareholder; and, secondly, by retaining earnings in the company for reinvestment, so that there may be increased earnings in the future.

The important thing when attempting to arrive at an estimate is to review the statement of comprehensive income of the current period and identify the earnings that can reasonably be expected to continue. In accounting terminology, you should identify the **maintainable post-tax earnings** that arise in the **ordinary course of business**.

Companies are required to make this easy for the shareholder by disclosing separately, by way of note, any unusual items and by analysing the profit and loss on trading between discontinuing and continuing activities.

Shareholders can use this information to estimate for themselves the maintainable post-tax earnings, assuming that there is no change in the company's trading activities. Clearly, in a dynamic business environment it is extremely unlikely that there will be no change in the current business activities. The shareholder needs to refer to any information on capital commitments which appear as a note to the accounts and also to the chairman's statement and any coverage in the financial press. This additional information is used to adjust the existing maintainable earnings figure.

18.4.2 Limitations of EPS as a performance measure

EPS is thought to have a significant impact on the market share price. However, there are limitations to its use as a performance measure.

The limitations affecting the use of EPS as an inter-period performance measure include the following:

- It is based on historical earnings. Management might have made decisions in the past to encourage current earnings growth at the expense of future growth, e.g. by reducing the amount spent on capital investment and research and development. Growth in the EPS cannot be relied on as a predictor of the rate of growth in the future.
- EPS does not take inflation into account. Real growth might be materially different from the apparent growth.

The limitations affecting inter-company comparisons include the following:

- The earnings are affected by management's choice of accounting policies, e.g. whether non-current assets have been revalued or interest has been capitalised.
- EPS is affected by the capital structure, e.g. changes in number of shares by making bonus issues.

However, the **rate of growth** of EPS is important and this may be compared between different companies and over time within the same company.

18.5 Illustration of the basic EPS calculation

Assume that Watts plc had post-tax profits for 20X1 of £1,250,000 and an issued share capital of £1,500,000 comprising 1,000,000 ordinary shares of 50p each and 1,000,000 £1 10% preference shares that are classified as equity. The basic EPS (BEPS) for 20X1 is calculated at £1.15 as follows:

	£000
Profit on ordinary activities after tax	1,250
Less preference dividend	(100)
Profit for the period attributable to ordinary shareholders	1,150

BEPS = £1,150,000/1,000,000 shares = £1.15

Note that it is the *number* of issued shares that is used in the calculation and *not the nominal value* of the shares. The market value of a share is not required for the BEPS calculation.

18.6 Adjusting the number of shares used in the basic EPS calculation

The earnings per share is frequently used by shareholders and directors to demonstrate the growth in a company's performance over time. Care is required to ensure that the number of shares is stated consistently to avoid distortions arising from changes in the capital structure that have changed the number of shares outstanding without a corresponding change in resources during the whole or part of a year. Such changes occur with (a) bonus issues and share splits; (b) new issues and buybacks at full market price during the year; and (c) the bonus element of a rights issue.

We will consider the appropriate treatment for each of these capital structure changes in order to ensure that EPS is comparable between accounting periods.

18.6.1 Bonus issues

A bonus issue, or capitalisation issue as it is also called, arises when a company capitalises reserves to give existing shareholders more shares. In effect, a simple transfer is made from reserves to issued share capital. In real terms, neither the shareholder nor the company is giving or receiving any immediate financial benefit. The process indicates that the reserves will not be available for distribution, but will remain invested in the physical assets of the company. There are, however, more shares.

Treatment in current year

In the Watts plc example, assume that the company increased its shares in issue in 20X1 by the issue of another 1 million shares and achieved identical earnings in 20X1 as in 20X0. The EPS reported for 20X1 would be immediately halved from £1.15 to £0.575. Clearly, this does not provide a useful comparison of performance between the two years.

Restatement of previous year's BEPS

The solution is to restate the EPS for 20X0 that appears in the 20X1 accounts, using the number of shares in issue at 31.12.20X1, i.e. £1,150,000/2,000,000 shares = BEPS of £0.575.

18.6.2 Share splits

When the market value of a share becomes high some companies decide to increase the number of shares held by each shareholder by changing the nominal value of each share. The effect is to reduce the market price per share but for each shareholder to hold the same total value. A share split would be treated in the same way as a bonus issue.

For example, if Watts plc split the 1,000,000 shares of 50p each into 2,000,000 shares of 25p each, the 20X1 BEPS would be calculated using 2,000,000 shares. It would seem that the BEPS had halved in 20X1. This is misleading and the 20X0 BEPS is therefore restated using 2,000,000 shares. The total market capitalisation of Watts plc would remain unchanged. For example, if, prior to the split, each share had a market value of £4 and the company had a total market capitalisation of £4,000,000, after the split each share would have a market price of £2 and the company market capitalisation would remain unchanged at £4,000,000.

A split is frequently taken as a sign that the board is confident of improved future performance, plus the fact that the fall in the share price makes the shares become more attractive to smaller investors means that the share price might rise above £4 due to the increased demand.

The following is an extract relating to Starbucks:

18 March 2015 Shareholders of record as of March 30, 2015 will receive one additional share for each share held on the record date. The new shares will be payable on April 8, 2015. Starbucks common stock will begin trading on a split-adjusted basis on April 9, 2015. This is the sixth two-for-one split of the company's common stock since its initial public offering in 1992 . . .

This split is a direct reflection of the past seven years of increasing shareholder value, enhancing the liquidity of our shares, and building an attractive share price. It also takes place at a time when Starbucks shareholders are experiencing an all-time high in value as we continue to deliver world-class customer service and, in turn, record profits and revenue.

Effect on ratios of a share split

Those ratios that are expressed as 'per share' are restated in proportion to the split as with the earnings, dividends and asset per share ratios. For example, if the earnings per share are 50c before a two-for-one split, this will be restated as 25c per share.

Reverse share split

The board might decide to recommend a reverse if the share price is considered too low. There are different reasons for a company making this decision. For example:

● it might be to avoid the shares appearing to be low-quality following poor results, or
● it might be to satisfy listing requirements for a minimum share price in order to avoid being delisted, or
● it might be to make the shares more attractive to institutional investors who might avoid low price shares.

Just as with a share split, the market capitalisation is unchanged. The ratio tends to be significantly higher than for a share split with 1 for 10 or higher being the norm. For example, if there were 5 million shares with a market value of 80c and there was a reverse split of one share for twenty currently held, the share price would increase to €16; however, the market capitalisation would remain at €4m.

18.6.3 New issue at full market value

Selling more shares to raise additional capital should generate additional earnings. In this situation we have a real change in the company's capital and there is no need to adjust any comparative figures. However, a problem arises in the year in which the issue took place. Unless the issue occurred on the first day of the financial year, the new funds would have been *available to generate profits* for only a part of the year. It would therefore be misleading to calculate the EPS figure by dividing the earnings generated during the year by the number of shares in issue at the end of the year. The method adopted to counter this is to use a time-weighted average for the number of shares.

For example, let us assume in the Watts example that the following information is available:

	No. of shares
Shares (nominal value 50p) in issue at 1 January 20X1	1,000,000
Shares issued for cash at market price on 30 September 20X1	500,000

The time-weighted number of shares for EPS calculation at 31 December 20X1 will be:

	No. of shares
Shares in issue for 9 months to date of issue (1,000,000 × 9/12)	750,000
Shares in issue for 3 months from date of issue (1,500,000 × 3/12)	375,000
Time-weighted shares for use in BEPS calculation EPS for 20X1	1,125,000

will be £1,150,000/1,125,000 shares = £1.02

18.6.4 Buybacks at market value

Companies are prompted to buy back their own shares when there is a fall in the stock market. The main arguments that companies advance for purchasing their own shares are:

- to reduce the cost of capital when equity costs more than debt;
- the shares are undervalued;
- to return surplus cash to shareholders; and
- to increase the apparent rate of growth in BEPS.

The following is an extract from the 2012 Vodafone Group plc Annual Report:

> Our business is highly cash generative and in the last four years we have returned over 30% of our market capitalisation to shareholders in the form of dividends and share buybacks, while still investing around £6 billion a year in our networks and infrastructure.

> **Earnings per share**
> Adjusted earnings per share was 14.91 pence, a decline of 11.0% year-on-year, reflecting the loss of our 44% interest in SFR and Polkomtel's profits, the loss of interest income from investment disposals and mark-to-market items charged through finance costs, *partially offset by a reduction in shares arising from the Group's share buyback programme.*

Shares bought back by the company are included in the basic EPS calculation time-apportioned from the beginning of the year to the date of buyback.

For example, let us assume in the Watts example that the following information is available:

	No. of shares
Shares (50p nominal value) in issue at 1 January 20X1	1,000,000
Shares bought back on 31 May 20X1	240,000
Profit attributable to ordinary shares	£1,150,000

The time-weighted number of shares for EPS calculation at 31 December 20X1 will be:

1.1.20X1	Shares in issue for 5 months to date of buyback	(1,000,000 × 5/12)	416,667
31.5.20X1	Number of shares bought back by company	(240,000)	
31.12.20X1	Opening capital less shares bought back	(760,000 × 7/12)	443,333
	Time-weighted shares for use in BEPS calculation		860,000

BEPS for 20X1 will be £1,150,000/860,000 shares = £1.34

Note that the effect of this buyback has been to increase the BEPS for 20X1 from £1.15 as calculated in Section 18.5 above. This is a mechanism for management to lift the BEPS and achieve EPS growth.

18.7 Rights issues

A rights issue involves giving existing shareholders 'the right' to buy a set number of additional shares at a price below the fair value which is normally the current market price. A rights issue has two characteristics, being both an issue for cash and, because the price is below fair value, a bonus issue. Consequently the rules for *both* a cash issue *and* a bonus issue need to be applied in calculating the weighted average number of shares for the basic EPS calculation.

This is an area where students frequently find difficulty with Step 1 and we will illustrate the rationale without accounting terminology.

The following four steps are required:

Step 1:   Calculate the average price of shares before and after a rights issue to identify the amount of the bonus the company has granted.

Step 2:   Calculate the weighted average number of shares for the current year.

Step 3:   Calculate the BEPS for the current year.

Step 4:   Adjust the previous year's BEPS for the bonus element of the rights issue.

Step 1: Calculate the average price of shares before and after a rights issue to identify the amount of the bonus the company has granted

Assume that Mr Radmand purchased two 50p shares at a market price of £4 each in Watts plc on 1 January 20X1 and that on 2 January 20X1 the company offered a 1:2 rights issue (i.e. one new share for every two shares held) at £3.25 per share.

If Mr Radmand had bought at the market price, the position would simply have been:

		£
Two shares at market price of £4 each on 1 January 20X1	=	8.00
One share at market price of £4 on 2 January 20X1	=	4.00
Total cost of three shares as at 2 January 20X1		12.00
Average cost per share unchanged at		4.00

However, this did not happen. Mr Radmand paid only £3.25 for the new share. This meant that the total cost of three shares to him was:

		£
Two shares at market price of £4 each on 1 January 20X1	=	8.00
One share at discounted price of £3.25 on 2 January 20X1	=	3.25
Total cost of three shares	=	11.25
Average cost per share (£11.25/3 shares)	=	3.75

The rights issue has had the effect of reducing the cost per share of each of the three shares held by Mr Radmand on 2 January 20X1 by £0.25 per share.

The accounting terms applied are:

- The average cost per share after the rights issue (£3.75) is *the theoretical ex-rights value*.

- The amount by which the average cost of each share is reduced (£0.25) is *the bonus element*.

In accounting terminology, Step 1 is described as follows:

Step 1:   *Theoretical ex-rights calculation.* The bonus element is ascertained by calculating the theoretical ex-rights value, i.e. the £0.25 is ascertained by calculating the £3.75 and deducting it from £4 pre-rights market price.

In accounting terminology, this means that existing shareholders get an element of bonus per share (£0.25) at the same time as the company receives additional capital (£3.25 per new share). The bonus element may be quantified by the calculation of a **theoretical ex-rights price** (£3.75), which is compared with the last market price (£4.00) prior to the issue; the difference is a bonus. The theoretical ex-rights price is calculated as follows:

	£
Two shares at fair value of £4 each prior to rights issue	= 8.00
One share at discounted rights issue price of £3.25 each	= 3.25
Three shares at fair value after issue (i.e. ex-rights)	= 11.25
Theoretical ex-rights price (£11.25/3 shares)	= 3.75
Bonus element (fair value £4 less £3.75)	= 0.25

Note that for the calculation of the number of shares and the time-weighted number of shares for a bonus issue, share split and issue at full market price per share, the market price per share is not relevant. The position for a rights issue is different and the market price becomes a relevant factor in calculating the number of bonus shares.

Step 2: Calculate the weighted average number of shares for the current year

Assume that Watts plc made a rights issue of one share for every two shares held on 1 January 20X1. There would be no need to calculate a weighted average number of shares. The total used in the BEPS calculation would be as follows:

		No. of shares
Shares to date of rights issue:		
1,000,000 shares held for a full year	=	1,000,000
Shares from date of rights issue:		
500,000 shares held for a full year	=	500,000
Total shares for BEPS calculation		1,500,000

However, if a rights issue is made part-way through the year, a time-apportionment is required. For example, if we assume that a rights issue is made on 30 September 20X1, the time-weighted number of shares is calculated as follows:

		No. of shares
Shares to date of rights issue:		
1,000,000 shares held for a full year	=	1,000,000
Shares from date of rights issue:		
500,000 shares held for 3 months (500,000 × 3/12)	=	125,000
Weighted average number of shares		1,125,000

Note, however, that the 1,125,000 has not taken account of the fact that the new shares had been issued at less than market price and that the company had effectively granted the existing shareholders a bonus. We saw above that when there has been a bonus issue the number of shares used in the BEPS is increased. We need, therefore, to calculate the number of bonus shares that would have been issued to achieve the reduction in market price from £4.00 to £3.75 per share. This is calculated as follows:

Total market capitalisation 1,000,000 shares @ £4.00 per share	= £4,000,000
Number of shares that would reduce the market price to £3.75	= £4,000,000/£3.75
	= 1,066,667 shares
Number of shares prior to issue	= 1,000,000
Bonus shares deemed to be issued to existing shareholders	= 66,667
Bonus shares for period of 9 months to date of issue (66,667 × 9/12)	= 50,000

The bonus shares for the nine months are added to the existing shares and the time-apportioned new shares as follows:

Figure 18.1 Formula approach to calculating weighted average number of shares

					No. of shares
Shares to date of rights issue:					
No. of shares	×	Increase by bonus fraction	×	Time adjustment	
1,000,000			×	9/12 =	750,000
Bonus:		((1,000,000 × 4/3.75) − 1,000,000)	×	9/12 =	50,000
Shares from date of issue:					
1,500,000	×		×	3/12 =	375,000
Weighted average number of shares					1,175,000

		No. of shares
Shares to date of rights issue:		
1,000,000 shares held for a full year	=	1,000,000
Shares from date of rights issue:		
500,000 shares held for 3 months (500,000 × 3/12)	=	125,000
Weighted average number of shares		1,125,000
Bonus shares:		
66,667 shares held for 9 months (66,667 × 9/12)	=	50,000
		1,175,000

The same figure of 1,175,000 can be derived from the following approach using the relationship between the market price of £4.00 and the theoretical ex-rights price of £3.75 to calculate the number of bonus shares.

The relationship between the actual cum-rights price and theoretical ex-rights price is shown by the bonus fraction:

$$\frac{\text{Actual cum-rights share price}}{\text{Theoretical ex-rights share price}}$$

This fraction is applied to the number of shares before the rights issue to adjust them for the impact of the bonus element of the rights issue. This is shown in Figure 18.1.

Step 3: Calculate the BEPS for the current year

The BEPS for 20X1 is then calculated as £1,150,000/1,175,000 shares = £0.979.

Step 4: Adjust the previous year's BEPS for the bonus element of the rights issue

The 20X0 BEPS of £1.15 needs to be restated, i.e. reduced to ensure comparability with 20X1.

In Step 2 above we calculated that the company had made a bonus issue of 66,667 shares to existing shareholders. In recalculating the BEPS for 20X0 the shares should be increased by 66,667 to 1,066,667. The restated BEPS for 20X0 is as follows:

Earnings/restated number of shares
£1,150,000/1,066,667 = £1.078125

Assuming that the earnings for 20X0 and 20X1 were £1,150,000 in each year, the 20X0 BEPS figures will be reported as follows:

As reported in the 20X0 accounts as at 31.12.20X0 = £1,150,000/1,000,000 = £1.15
As restated in the 20X1 accounts as at 31.12.20X1 = £1,150,000/1,066,667 = £1.08

The same result is obtained using the bonus element approach by reducing the 20X0 BEPS as follows by multiplying it by the reciprocal of the bonus fraction:

$$\frac{\text{Theoretical ex-rights fair value per share}}{\text{Fair value per share immediately before the exercise of rights}} = \frac{£3.75}{£4.00}$$

As restated in the 20X1 accounts as at 31.12.20X1 $= £1.15 \times (3.75/4.00) = £1.08.$

18.7.1 Would the BEPS for the current and previous years be the same if the company had made a separate full market price issue and a separate bonus issue?

This section is included to demonstrate that the BEPS is the same, i.e. £1.08, if we approach the calculation on the assumption that there was a full price issue followed by a bonus issue. This will demonstrate that the BEPS is the same as that calculated using theoretical ex-rights. There are five steps, as follows.

Step 1: Calculate the number of full value and bonus shares in the company's share capital

	No. of shares
Shares in issue *before* bonus	1,000,000
Rights issue at full market price	
(500,000 shares × £3.25 issue price/£4 full market price)	406,250
	1,406,250
Total number of bonus shares	93,750
Total shares	1,500,000

Step 2: Allocate the total bonus shares to the 1,000,000 original shares

(Note that the previous year will be restated using the proportion of original shares: original shares + bonus shares allocated to these original 1,000,000 shares.)

	No. of shares
Shares in issue before bonus	1,000,000
Bonus issue applicable to pre-rights:	
93,750 bonus shares × (1,000,000/1,406,250) = 66,667 × 9/12 = 50,000	
Bonus issue applicable to post-rights:	
93,750 bonus shares × (1,000,000/1,406,250) = 66,667 × 3/12 = 16,667	
Total bonus shares allocated to existing 1,000,000 shares	66,667
Total original holding plus bonus shares allocated to that holding	1,066,667

Step 3: Time-weight the rights issue and allocate bonus shares to rights shares

Rights issue at full market price:

500,000 shares × (£3.25 issue price/£4 full market price) × 406,250 × 3/12	=	101,563

Bonus issue applicable to rights issue:

93,750 bonus shares × (406,250/1,406,250) × 27,083 × 3/12	=	6,770
Weighted average ordinary shares (includes shares from Steps 2 and 3)		1,175,000

Step 4: BEPS calculation for 20X1

Calculate the BEPS using the post-tax profit and weighted average ordinary shares, as follows:

$$20\text{X1 BEPS} = \frac{£1,150,000}{1,175,000} = £0.979$$

Step 5: BEPS restated for 20X0

There were 93,750 bonus shares issued in 20X1. The 20X0 BEPS needs to be reduced, therefore, by the same proportion as applied to the 1,000,000 ordinary shares in 20X1, i.e. 1,000,000:1,066,667:

$$20\text{X0 BEPS} \times \text{bonus adjustment} = \text{restated 20X0 BPES}$$

$$= £1.15 \times (1,000,000/1,066,667) = £1.08.$$

This approach illustrates the rationale for the time-weighted average and the restatement of the previous year's BEPS. The adjustment using the theoretical ex-rights approach produces the same result and is simpler to apply but the rationale is not obvious.

18.8 Adjusting the earnings and number of shares used in the diluted EPS calculation

We will consider briefly what dilution means and the circumstances which require the weighted average number of shares and the net profit attributable to ordinary shareholders used to calculate BEPS to be adjusted.

18.8.1 What is dilution?

In a modern corporate structure, a number of classes of person such as the holders of convertible bonds, the holders of convertible preference shares, members of share option schemes and share warrant holders may be entitled as at the date of the statement of financial position to become equity shareholders at a future date.

If these people exercise their entitlements at a future date, the EPS would be reduced. In accounting terminology, the EPS will have been *diluted*. The effect on future share price could be significant. Assuming that the share price is a multiple of the EPS figure, any reduction in the figure could have serious implications for the existing shareholders; they need to be aware of the potential effect on the EPS figure of any changes in the way the capital of the company is or will be constituted. This is shown by calculating and disclosing both the basic and 'diluted EPS' figures.

IAS 33 therefore requires a diluted EPS figure to be reported using as the denominator potential ordinary shares that are dilutive, i.e. would decrease net profit per share or increase net loss from continuing operations.[8]

18.8.2 Circumstances in which the number of shares used for BEPS is increased

The holders of convertible bonds, the holders of convertible preference shares, members of share option schemes and the holders of share warrants will each be entitled to receive ordinary shares from the company at some future date. Such additional shares, referred to as potential ordinary shares, *may* need to be added to the basic weighted average number *if they are dilutive*. It is important to note that if a company has potential ordinary shares they are not automatically included in the fully diluted EPS calculation. There is a test to apply to see if such shares actually are dilutive – this is discussed further in Section 18.9 below.

18.8.3 Circumstances in which the earnings used for BEPS are increased

The earnings are increased to take account of the post-tax effects of amounts recognised in the period relating to dilutive potential ordinary shares that will no longer be incurred on their conversion to ordinary shares, e.g. the loan interest payable on convertible loans will no longer be a charge after conversion and earnings will be increased by the post-tax amount of such interest.

18.8.4 Procedure where there are share warrants and options

Where options, warrants or other arrangements exist which involve the issue of shares below their fair value (i.e. at a price lower than the average for the period) then the impact is calculated by notionally splitting the potential issue into shares issued at fair value and shares issued at no value for no consideration.[9] Since shares issued at fair value are not dilutive, that number is ignored, but the number of shares at no value is employed to calculate the dilution. The calculation is illustrated here for Watts plc.

Assume that Watts plc had at 31 December 20X1:

- an issued capital of 1,000,000 ordinary shares of 50p each nominal value;
- profit attributable to shareholders of £1,150,000;
- an average market price per share of £4; and
- share options in existence 500,000 shares issuable in 20X2 at £3.25 per share.

The computation of basic and diluted EPS is as follows:

	Per share	*Earnings*	*Shares*
Profit attributable to shareholders		£1,150,000	
Weighted average shares during 20X1			1,000,000
Basic EPS (£1,150,000/1,000,000)	1.15		
Number of shares under option			500,000
Number that would have been issued at fair value (500,000 × £3.25/£4)			(406,250)
Adjusted earnings and number of shares		£1,150,000	1,093,750
Diluted EPS (£1,150,000/1,093,750)	1.05		

18.8.5 Procedure where there are convertible bonds or convertible preference shares

The post-tax profit should be adjusted[10] for:

- any dividends on dilutive potential ordinary shares that have been deducted in arriving at the net profit attributable to ordinary shareholders;
- interest recognised in the period for the dilutive potential ordinary shares; and
- any other changes in income or expense that would result from the conversion of the dilutive potential ordinary shares, e.g. the reduction of interest expense related to convertible bonds results in a higher post-tax profit but this could lead to a consequential increase in expense if there were a non-discretionary employee profit-sharing plan.

18.8.6 Convertible preference shares calculation

Assume that Watts plc had at 31 December 20X1:

- an issued capital of 1,000,000 ordinary shares of 50p each nominal value;
- profit attributable to ordinary shareholders of £1,150,000;
- convertible 8% preference shares of £1 each totalling £1,000,000, convertible at one ordinary share for every five convertible preference shares.

The computation of basic and diluted EPS for convertible bonds is as follows:

	Per share	Earnings	Shares
Post-tax net profit for 20X1 (after interest)		£1,150,000	
Weighted average shares during 20X1			1,000,000
Basic EPS (£1,150,000/1,000,000)	£1.15		
Number of shares resulting from conversion			200,000
Add back the preference dividend paid in 20X1		80,000	
Adjusted earnings and number of shares		1,230,000	1,200,000
Diluted EPS (£1,230,000/1,200,000)	£1.025		

18.8.7 Convertible bonds calculation

Assume that Watts plc had at 31 December 20X1:

- an issued capital of 1,000,000 ordinary shares of 50p each nominal value;
- profit attributable to ordinary shareholders of £1,150,000;
- convertible 10% loan of £1,000,000;
- an average market price per share of £4;

and the convertible loan is convertible into 250,000 ordinary shares of 50p each.
The computation of basic and diluted EPS for convertible bonds is as follows:

	Per share	Earnings	Shares
Post-tax net profit for 20X1 (after interest)		£1,150,000	
Weighted average shares during 20X1			1,000,000
Basic EPS (£1,150,000/1,000,000)	£1.15		
Number of shares resulting from conversion			250,000
Interest expense on convertible loan		100,000	
Tax liability relating to interest expense, assuming the firm's marginal tax rate is 40%		(20,000)	
Adjusted earnings and number of shares		1,230,000	1,250,000
Diluted EPS (£1,230,000/1,250,000)	£0.98		

18.9 Procedure where there are several potential dilutions

Where there are several potential dilutions the calculation must be done in progressive stages starting with the most dilutive and ending with the least.[11] Any potential 'antidilutive' issues (i.e. potential issues that would increase earnings per share) are ignored.

Assume that Watts plc had at 31 December 20X1:

- an issued capital of 1,000,000 ordinary shares of 50p each nominal value;
- profit attributable to ordinary shareholders of £1,150,000;

- an average market price per share of £4;
- share options in existence of 500,000 shares exercisable in year 20X2 at £3.25 per share;
- a convertible 10% loan of £1,000,000 convertible in year 20X2 into 250,000 ordinary shares of 50p each; and
- convertible 8% preference shares of £1 each totalling £1,000,000 convertible in year 20X4 at one ordinary share for every 40 preference shares.

There are two steps in arriving at the diluted EPS, namely:

Step 1: Determine the increase in earnings attributable to ordinary shareholders on conversion of potential ordinary shares.

Step 2: Determine the potential ordinary shares to include in the computation of diluted earnings per share.

Step 1: Determine the increase in earnings attributable to ordinary shareholders on conversion of potential ordinary shares

	Increase in earnings	Increase in number of ordinary shares	Earnings per incremental share
Options			
Increase in earnings			
Incremental shares issued for no consideration			
500,000 × (£4 − 3.25)/£4	NIL	93,750	NIL
Convertible preference shares			
Increase in net profit 8% of £1,000,000	80,000		
Incremental shares 1,000,000/40		25,000	3.20
10% convertible bond			
Increase in net profit £1,000,000 × 0.10 × (60%) (assuming a marginal tax rate of 40%)	60,000		
Incremental shares 1,000,000/4		250,000	0.24

Step 2: Determine the potential ordinary shares to include in the computation of diluted earnings per share

	Net profit attributable to continuing operations	Ordinary shares	Per share
As reported for BEPS	1,150,000	1,000,000	1.15
Options	—	93,750	
	1,150,000	1,093,750	1.05 dilutive
10% convertible bonds	60,000	250,000	
	1,210,000	1,343,750	0.90 dilutive
Convertible preference shares	80,000	25,000	
	1,290,000	1,368,750	0.94 antidilutive

Since the diluted earnings per share is increased when taking the convertible preference shares into account (from 90p to 94p), the convertible preference shares are antidilutive and are ignored in the calculation of diluted earnings per share. The lowest figure is selected and the diluted EPS will, therefore, be disclosed as 90p.

18.10 Exercise of conversion rights during the financial year

Shares actually issued will be in accordance with the terms of conversion and will be included in the BEPS calculation on a time-apportioned basis from the date of conversion to the end of the financial year.

18.10.1 Calculation of BEPS assuming that convertible loan has been converted and options exercised during the financial year

This is illustrated for the calculation for the year 20X2 accounts of Watts plc as follows. Assume that Watts plc had at 31 December 20X2:

- an issued capital of 1,000,000 ordinary shares of 50p each as at 1 January 20X2;
- a convertible 10% loan of £1,000,000 **converted** on 1 January 20X2 into 250,000 ordinary shares of 50p each; and
- share options for 500,000 ordinary shares of 50p each **exercised** on 1 January 20X2.

The weighted average number of shares for BEPS is calculated as follows:

	Net profit attributable to continuing operations	Ordinary shares	Per share
As reported for BEPS	1,150,000	1,000,000	1.15
Options	—	93,750	
	1,150,000	1,093,750	1.05
10% convertible bonds	60,000	250,000	
	1,210,000	1,343,750	0.90
Convertible preference shares	80,000	25,000	
	1,290,000	1,368,750	0.94

18.11 Disclosure requirements of IAS 33

The standard[12] requires the following disclosures. For the current year:

- Companies should disclose the basic and diluted EPS figures for profit or loss from continuing operations and for profit or loss with equal prominence, whether positive or negative, on the face of the statement of comprehensive income for each class of ordinary share that has a different right to share in the profit for the period.
- The amounts used as the numerators in calculating basic and diluted earnings per share, and a reconciliation of those amounts to the net profit or loss for the period.
- The weighted average number of shares used as the denominator in calculating the basic and diluted earnings per share and a reconciliation of these denominators to each other.

For the previous year (if there has been a bonus issue, rights issue or share split):

- BEPS and diluted EPS should be adjusted retrospectively.

18.11.1 Alternative EPS figures

Alternative EPS figures are permitted to be reported in the Annual Report by IAS 33. It is not, however, to be given greater prominence than the basic and diluted EPS figures and can only be disclosed in the notes and not on the face of the statement of comprehensive income. The adjusted earnings figure must be reconciled to the earnings reported in the statement of comprehensive income and the same weighted average number of shares must be used.

The intention is that investors are presented with an EPS figure based on sustainable or permanent earnings unaffected by exceptional and non-recurring items. The IASB does not provide a definition of permitted adjustments and it an opportunity for management to high-light or customise the earnings. The adjustments should lead to less volatility in the earnings used for the EPS figure and improve the market value of the shares.

The following is an extract from the Cello Group 2015 Annual Report:

11 EARNINGS PER SHARE

	Year ended 31 December 2014 £000	Year ended 31 December 2015 £000
Profit attributable to owners of the parent	3,042	2,283
Adjustments to earnings:		
Restructuring costs	694	534
Charge for VAT payable and related costs	1,301	2,109
Start-up losses	1,037	446
Acquisition costs	–	106
Amortisation of intangible assets	445	965
Acquisition-related employee remuneration expenses	1,591	1,200
Share-based payments charge	204	212
Tax thereon	(907)	(976)
Headline earnings for the year	7,407	6,879
Basic earnings per share	3.54p	2.70p
Diluted earnings per share	3.44p	2.63p

In addition to basic and diluted earnings per share, headline earnings per share, which is a non- GAAP measure, has also been presented.

Headline earnings per share

Headline basic earnings per share	8.61p	8.14p
Headline diluted earnings per share	8.39p	7.93p

Headline earnings per share is calculated using headline post-tax earnings for the year, which excludes the effect of restructuring costs, start-up losses, amortisation of intangibles, impairment charges, acquisition accounting adjustments, share option charges, fair value gains and losses on derivative financial instruments and other exceptional costs.

Earnings defined

While disclosure and calculation of headline earnings is not an IFRS requirement, the South African Institute of Chartered Accountants issued a Circular[13] to its members at the request of the Johannesburg Stock Exchange (JSE), providing detailed guidance on whether an adjustment is permitted. The JSE Listings Requirements require the calculation of headline earnings and disclosure of a detailed reconciliation of headline earnings to the earnings used in the calculation of the IAS 33 basic earnings per share. The aim is to achieve uniform treatment across all listed companies.

Research into reasons why companies publish an alternative EPS

The initial approach was to exclude non-recurring items and provide investors with a more informative alternative figure.

An interesting 2013 research paper[14] suggested that the choice to disclose an alternative EPS figure is positively related to firms where the vesting of executive share options (ESOs) is contingent on the achievement of growth in EPS.

18.11.2 IAS 33 disclosure requirements

If an enterprise discloses an additional EPS figure using a reported component of net profit other than net profit for the period attributable to ordinary shareholders, IAS 33 requires that:

- it must still use the weighted average number of shares determined in accordance with IAS 33;
- if the net profit figure used is not a line item in the statement of comprehensive income, then a reconciliation should be provided between the figure and a line item which is reported in the statement of comprehensive income; and
- the additional EPS figures cannot be disclosed on the face of the statement of comprehensive income.

18.12 Enhanced disclosures

The FRC published[15] *Lab implementation study: Disclosure of dividends – policy and practice* in October 2017.

This contained extracts from annual reports which illustrated improvements in disclosures:

- detailing the policy and providing insight into factors relevant to the setting of the dividend (ITV);
- providing information about factors relevant to setting dividend and level of reserves (Moneysupermarket);
- highlighting level of reserves (Hammerson); and
- highlighting the link between risk and distributable reserves (Rathbone).

It commented on the continuing improvements made by companies identified in the study where they were responding to investor calls to add clarity to disclosures around distributable profit/reserves. It observed that best practice continued to develop and encouraged companies to continue to enhance disclosures.

Summary

The increased globalisation of stock market transactions places an increasing level of importance on international comparisons. The EPS figure is regarded as a key figure with a widely held belief that management performance could be assessed by the comparative growth rate in this figure. This has meant that the earnings available for distribution, which was the base for calculating EPS, became significant. Management action has been directed towards increasing this figure: sometimes by healthy organic growth; sometimes by buying in earnings by acquisition; sometimes by cosmetic manipulation, e.g. structuring transactions so that all or part of the cost bypassed the statement of comprehensive income; and at other times by the selective exercise of judgement, e.g. underestimating provisions. Regulation by the IASB has been necessary.

IAS 33 permits the inclusion of an EPS figure calculated in a different way, provided that there is a reconciliation of the two figures. Analysts have expressed the view that EPS should be calculated to show the future maintainable earnings and in the UK have arrived at a formula designed to exclude the effects of unusual events and of activities discontinued during the period.

REVIEW QUESTIONS

1 Explain: (i) basic earnings per share; (ii) diluted earnings per share; (iii) potential ordinary shares; and (iv) limitation of EPS as a performance measure.

2 In connection with IAS 33 *Earnings per Share*:

(a) Define the profit used to calculate basic and diluted EPS.

(b) Explain the relationship between EPS and the price/earnings (PE) ratio. Why may the PE ratio be considered important as a stock market indicator?

3 Would the following items justify the calculation of a separate EPS figure under IAS 33?

(a) A charge of £1,500 million that appeared in the accounts, described as additional provisions relating to exposure to countries experiencing payment difficulties.

(b) Costs of £14 million that appeared in the accounts, described as redundancy and other non-recurring costs.

(c) Costs of £62.1 million that appeared in the accounts, described as cost of rationalisation and withdrawal from business activities.

(d) The following items that appeared in the accounts:

(i) Profit on sale of property £80m

(ii) Reorganisation costs £35m

(iii) Disposal and discontinuance of hotels £659m.

4 Explain the adjustments made to earnings when reporting an underlying or headline EPS figure and discuss why this is more relevant than an EPS calculated in accordance with IAS 33.

5 The following note appeared in the 2013 Annual Report of Mercer International Inc.:

Net income (loss) per share attributable to common shareholders:

	2013	2012	2011
Basic	$(0.47)	$(0.28)	$1.39
Diluted	$(0.47)	$(0.28)	$1.24

The calculation of diluted net income (loss) per share attributable to common shareholders does not assume the exercise of any instruments that would have an anti-dilutive effect on net income (loss) per share.

Explain what is meant by antidilutive.

6 Why are issues at full market value treated differently from rights issues?

7 Explain why companies buy back shares and the effect that this has on the earnings per share figure.

8 Explain reverse share splits and the effect that this has on a company's market capitalisation.

9 Discuss the limitations of an IAS 33 calculated EPS figure for performance reporting.

10 Discuss the limitations of EPS as a criterion for setting executive remuneration targets.

EXERCISES

Question 1

Alpha plc had an issued share capital of 2,000,000 ordinary shares at 1 January 20X1. The nominal value was 25p and the market value £1 per share. On 30 September 20X1 the company made a rights issue of 1 for 4 at a price of 80p per share. The post-tax earnings were £4.5m and £5m for 20X0 and 20X1 respectively.

Required:
(a) Calculate the basic earnings per share.
(b) Restate the basic earnings per share for 20X0.

* Question 2

Beta Ltd had the following changes during 20X1:

1 January	1,000,000 shares of 50c each
31 March	500,000 shares of 50c each issued at full market price of $5 per share
30 April	Bonus issue made of 1 for 2
31 August	1,000,000 shares of 50c each issued at full market price of $5.50 per share
31 October	Rights issue of 1 for 3. Rights price was $2.40 and market value was $5.60 per share.

Required:
Calculate the time-weighted average number of shares for the basic earnings per share denominator. Note that adjustments will be required for time, the bonus issue and the bonus element of the rights issue.

* **Question 3**

The computation and publication of earnings per share (EPS) figures by listed companies are governed by IAS 33 *Earnings per Share*.

Nottingham Industries plc
Statement of comprehensive income for the year ended 31 March 20X6
(extract from draft unaudited accounts)

		£000
Profit on ordinary activities before taxation	(Note 2)	1,000
Tax on profit on ordinary activities	(Note 3)	(420)
Profit on ordinary activities after taxation		580

Notes:

1 Called-up share capital of Nottingham Industries plc:
   In issue at 1 April 20X5:
   16,000,000 ordinary shares of 25p each
   1,000,000 10% cumulative preference shares of £1 each classified as equity
   1 July 20X5: Bonus issue of ordinary shares, 1 for 5.
   1 October 20X5: Market purchase of 500,000 of own ordinary shares at a price of £1.00 per share.

2 In the draft accounts for the year ended 31 March 20X6, 'profit on ordinary activities before taxation' is arrived at after charging or crediting the following items:

   (i) accelerated depreciation on fixed assets, £80,000;

   (ii) book gain on disposal of a major operation, £120,000.

3 Profit after tax included a write-back of deferred taxation (accounted for by the liability method) in consequence of a reduction in the rate of corporation tax from 45% in the financial year 20X4 to 40% in the financial year 20X5.

4 The following were charged:

   (i) Provision for bad debts arising on the failure of a major customer, £150,000. Other bad debts have been written off or provided for in the ordinary way.

   (ii) Provision for loss through expropriation of the business of an overseas subsidiary by a foreign government, £400,000.

5 In the published accounts for the year ended 31 March 20X5, basic EPS was shown as 2.2p; fully diluted EPS was the same figure.

6 Dividends paid totalled £479,000.

Required:

(a) On the basis of the facts given, compute the basic EPS figures for 20X6 and restate the basic EPS figure for 20X5, stating your reasons for your treatment of items that may affect the amount of EPS in the current year.

(b) Compute the diluted earnings per share for 20X6 assuming that on 1 January 20X6 executives of Nottingham plc were granted options to take up a total of 200,000 unissued ordinary shares at a price of £1.00 per share: no options had been exercised at 31 March 20X6. The average fair value of the shares during the year was £1.10.

(c) Give your opinion as to the usefulness (to the user of financial statements) of the EPS figures that you have computed.

* Question 4

The following information relates to Simrin plc for the year ended 31 December 20X0:

	£
Turnover	700,000
Operating costs	476,000
Trading profit	224,000
Net interest payable	2,000
	222,000
Exceptional charges	77,000
	145,000
Tax on ordinary activities	66,000
Profit after tax	79,000

Simrin plc had 100,000 ordinary shares of £1 each in issue throughout the year. Simrin plc has in issue warrants entitling the holders to subscribe for a total of 50,000 shares in the company. The warrants may be exercised after 31 December 20X5 at a price of £1.10 per share. The average fair value of shares was £1.28. The company had paid an ordinary dividend of £15,000 and a preference dividend of £9,000 on preference shares classified as equity.

Required:
(a) Calculate the basic EPS for Simrin plc for the year ended 31 December 20X0, in accordance with best accounting practice.
(b) Calculate the diluted EPS figure, to be disclosed in the statutory accounts of Simrin plc in respect of the year ended 31 December 20X0.
(c) Briefly comment on the need to disclose a diluted EPS figure and on the relevance of this figure to the shareholders.
(d) In the past, the single most important indicator of financial performance has been earnings per share. In what way has the profession attempted to destroy any reliance on a single figure to measure and predict a company's earnings, and how successful has this attempt been?

* Question 5

Gamma plc had an issued share capital at 1 April 20X0 of:

● £200,000 made up of 20p shares; and
● 50,000 £1 convertible preference shares classified as equity receiving a dividend of £2.50 per share. These shares were convertible in 20X6 on the basis of one ordinary share for one preference share.

There was also loan capital of:

● £250,000 10% convertible loans. The loan was convertible in 20X9 on the basis of 500 shares for each £1,000 of loan, and the tax rate was 40%.

Earnings for the year ended 31 March 20X1 were £5,000,000 after tax.

Required:
(a) Calculate the diluted EPS for 20X1.
(b) Calculate the diluted EPS assuming that the convertible preference shares were receiving a dividend of £6 per share instead of £2.50.

Question 6

Delta NV has share capital of €1m in shares of €0.25 each. At 31 May 20X9 shares had a market value of €1.1 each. On 1 June 20X9 the company makes a rights issue of one share for every four held at €0.6 per share. Its profits were €500,000 in 20X9 and €440,000 in 20X8. The year-end is 30 November.

Required:
Calculate
(a) the theoretical ex-rights price;
(b) the bonus issue factor;
(c) the basic earnings per share for 20X8;
(d) the basic earnings per share for 20X9.

Question 7

The following information is available for X Ltd for the year ended 31 May 20X1:

Net profit after tax and minority interest	£18,160,000
Ordinary shares of £1 (fully paid)	£40,000,000
Average fair value for year of ordinary shares	£1.50

Notes:

1 Share options have been granted to directors giving them the right to subscribe for ordinary shares between 20X1 and 20X3 at £1.20 per share. The options outstanding at 31 May 20X1 were 2,000,000 in number.

2 The company has £20 million of 6% convertible loan stock in issue. The terms of conversion of the loan stock per £200 nominal value of loan stock at the date of issue were:

Conversion date	No. of shares
31 May 20X0	24
31 May 20X1	23
31 May 20X2	22

No loan stock has as yet been converted. The loan stock had been issued at a discount of 1%.

3 There are 1,600,000 convertible preference shares in issue classified as equity. The cumulative dividend is 10p per share and each preference share can convert into two ordinary shares. The preference shares can be converted in 20X2.

4 Assume a corporation tax rate of 33% when calculating the effect on income of converting the convertible loan stock.

Required:
(a) Calculate the diluted EPS according to IAS 33.
(b) Discuss why there is a need to disclose diluted earnings per share.

Question 8

(a) The issued share capital of Manfred, a quoted company, on 1 November 2004 consisted of 36,000,000 ordinary shares of 75 cents each. On 1 May 2005 the company made a rights issue of 1 for 6 at $1.46 per share. The market value of Manfred's ordinary shares was $1.66 before announcing the rights issue. Tax is charged at 30% of profits.

Manfred reported a profit after taxation of $4.2 million for the year ended 31 October 2005 and $3.6 million for the year ended 31 October 2004. The published figure for earnings per share for the year ended 31 October 2004 was 10 cents per share.

Required:
Calculate Manfred's earnings per share for the year ended 31 October 2005 and the comparative figure for the year ended 31 October 2004.

(b) Brachly, a publicly quoted company, has 15,000,000 ordinary shares of 40 cents each in issue throughout its financial year ended 31 October 2005. There are also:

- 1,000,000 8.5% convertible preference shares of $1 each in issue classified as equity. Each preference share is convertible into 1.5 ordinary shares.

- $2,000,000 12.5% convertible loan notes. Each $1 loan note is convertible into two ordinary shares.

- Options granted to the company's senior management giving them the right to subscribe for 600,000 ordinary shares at a cost of 75 cents each.

The statement of comprehensive income of Brachly for the year ended 31 October 2005 reports a net profit after tax of $9,285,000 and preference dividends paid of $85,000. Tax on profits is 30%. The average market price of Brachly's ordinary shares was 84 cents for the year ended 31 October 2005.

Required:
Calculate Brachly's basic and diluted earnings per share figures for the year ended 31 October 2005.

(The Association of International Accountants)

Question 9

The following trial balance relates to Amethyst as at 31 March 2015:

	$000	$000
Revenue		818,000
Cost of sales	583,000	
Distribution costs	89,000	
Administrative expenses	91,000	
Investment Income		1,000
Loan stock interest paid	600	
Overdraft interest	100	
Equity shares of $1 each at 31 March 2015		110,000
Share premium at 31 March 2015		5,000
Retained earnings at 1 April 2014		40,950
Freehold land buildings at cost 1 April 2014 (Land cost $50m)	200,000	
Plant and equipment at 1 April 2014	120,000	

	$000	$000
Accumulated depreciation at 1 April 2014		
Buildings		75,000
Plant and equipment		40,000
Inventory at 31 March 2015	44,000	
Trade receivables	17,000	
Bank		7,500
Trade payables		25,000
Current tax	2,750	
Deferred tax		5,000
6% $1 Loan stock (2020)		20,000
	1,147,450	1,147,450

The following information is relevant:

1 After the year end stock take it was discovered that goods worth $4 million, which were stored in a temporary holding facility, had been accidently omitted from the stock count.

2 Amethyst previously held its land and buildings under the cost model basis. On 1 April 2014 the directors decided to adopt the policy of revaluation and obtained an external valuation of $160 million (of which $60 million related to land). The property had a total estimated useful life of 50 years at the date of acquisition and a remaining life of 25 years at the date of the revaluation. The directors decided to make the transfer from the revaluation reserve to retained earnings each year in respect of the excess depreciation.

3 Deferred tax on the revaluation is to be provided for at a tax rate of 20%.

4 Depreciation for the year is to be provided for. Depreciation on plant and equipment is charged to cost of sales on a 15% reducing balance basis. Depreciation on buildings is charged to administrative expenses.

5 On 1 January 2015 the company made a 1:10 rights issue at $1.50 per share and this was correctly accounted for and included in the trial balance above. Share issue costs of $1 million were incurred and posted to administrative expenses.

6 The share price immediately before the rights issue was $1.80 per share. Earnings per share in the year ended 31 March 2014 was $2.53.

7 Loan stock interest paid represents the interim interest paid on 30 September 2014.

8 A provision for income tax of $10 million is required at the year end. The balance on the current tax account represents the under/overprovision of tax for the year ended 31 March 2014. The deferred tax liability in the trial balance relates to the taxable temporary differences on plant and equipment. As at 31 March 2015 the deferred tax liability arising on these items has increased to $10 million (excluding the effect of the revaluation in note 2).

Required:
(a) **Prepare the statement of profit or loss and other comprehensive income for the year ended 31 March 2015.**
(b) **Prepare the statement of changes in equity for the year ended 31 March 2015.**
(c) **Prepare the statement of financial position for the year ended 31 March 2015.**
(d) **Calculate the earnings per share for the year ended 31 March 2015 and the restated figure for the year ended 31 March 2014.**

(The Association of International Accountants)

Notes

1 J. Day, 'The use of annual reports by UK investment analysts', *Accounting Business Research*, Autumn 1986, pp. 295–307.
2 IAS 33 *Earnings per Share*, IASB, 2003.
3 Ibid., para. 10.
4 Ibid., para. 12.
5 Ibid., para. 26.
6 Ibid., para. 5.
7 Ibid., para. 31.
8 Ibid., para. 31.
9 Ibid., para. 45.
10 Ibid., para. 33.
11 Ibid., para. 44.
12 Ibid., paras 66 and 70.
13 www.jse.co.za/content/jsecircularitems/circular_2_2013_headline_earnings.pdf
14 C. Grey, K. Stathopoulos and M. Walker, 'The impact of executive pay on the disclosure of alternative earnings per share figures', *International Review of Financial Analysis*, vol. 29, September 2013, pp. 227–236.
15 https://www.frc.org.uk/getattachment/3a7972af-35ae-4354-8136-0b395f5bbbba/Dividends-implementation-study-Lab.pdf

CHAPTER 19

Analysis of Published Financial Statements

19.1 Introduction

In Chapter 1 we considered the way in which we could 'make the numbers talk' from a set of published financial statements. We explained the importance of taking a 'helicopter perspective' initially and identifying key issues before focusing on specific areas of detail. We showed how powerful ratio analysis could be used as an analytical tool provided the ratios were interpreted appropriately. A particularly important issue was the need to differentiate between changes to ratios that were caused by operational and business factors and changes caused by accounting policies and accounting estimates.

When we are interpreting the financial statements of an entity a key issue is the amount of financial information actually available. If we are performing an analysis on behalf of management, or a controlling shareholder, then the amount of financial information available to us is likely to be sufficient to perform any analysis we consider appropriate. On the other hand, where we are performing an analysis from a purely external perspective there will be a limit to the amount of information available to us, because published financial statements generally contain only the information that is required by the appropriate regulatory framework.

Objectives

By the end of this chapter, you should be able to:

- discuss steps taken to improve information for shareholders;
- critically discuss the limitations of published financial data as a source of useful information for interpretation purposes;
- consider the disclosure of business risk in financial statements;
- discuss additional entity-wide cash-based performance measures;
- explain the use of ratios in determining whether a company is Shariah-compliant;
- explain the use of ratios in debt covenants;
- critically discuss various scoring systems for predicting corporate failure;
- critically discuss remuneration performance criteria;
- critically discuss the role of credit rating agencies;
- calculate the value of unquoted investments.

19.2 Improvement of information for shareholders

There have been a number of discussion papers, reports and voluntary code provisions from professional firms and regulators making recommendations on how to provide additional information to allow investors to form a view as to the business's future prospects by (a) making financial information more understandable and easier to analyse and (b) improving the reliability of the historical financial data. This would help ensure the equal treatment of all investors and improve accountability for stewardship.

19.2.1 Making financial information more understandable

There has been a view that users should bring a reasonable level of understanding when reading an annual report. This view could be supported when transactions were relatively simple. It no longer applies when even professional accountants comment that the only people who understand some of the disclosures are the technical staff of the regulator and the professional accounting firms.

Statutory measures

Users need the financial information to be made more accessible. This is being achieved in part by initiatives such as the Strategic Report in the UK with the requirement to publish information on the past year, including a fair review of the company's business, a description of the principal risks and uncertainties facing the company, and a balanced and comprehensive analysis of the performance of the company's business during the financial year.

As regards the future, a description of the company's strategy, a description of the company's business model and the main trends and factors likely to affect the future development, performance and position of the company's business are also required.

Need to understand volatility

There is a need on the part of investors to understand the volatility that can arise as a result of a company's strategy, such as recognising the short- and medium-term impact on earnings of R&D investment. There has been a view that investors are unhappy with an uneven profit trend and that companies have responded by smoothing earnings from year to year to maintain investor confidence.

An ICAEW report[1] produced in 1999 *No Surprises: The Case for Better Risk Reporting* recognised the need for management to disclose their strategies and how they managed risk whilst stating that the intention was not to encourage profit-smoothing but rather a better management of risk and a better understanding by investors of volatility.

19.2.2 Disclosure of business risk

Listed companies in the UK are now required to describe 'business risks' in their annual financial statements.

To illustrate how this is disclosed, the business risks have been taken from the Civil Aero Engine division of Rolls-Royce Holdings plc. Rolls-Royce is best known for producing motor cars. However, this activity is now undertaken by a subsidiary of the German motor manufacturer, BMW, where Rolls-Royce cars are produced under licence at Goodwood, near Chichester in the South of England.

The principal activity of Rolls-Royce Holdings plc is the manufacture and servicing of Civil aero engines. Other activities include military aero engines, nuclear, marine and 'power systems'.

Civil aero engines are 'jet engines' (gas turbine engines) for aircraft. This division's turn-over is just over 50% of the total turnover of the Group. The two main activities are production of new aero engines (47% of turnover) and servicing & repair of the engines in service (53%).

The annual financial statements for 2015 state the business risks as:

1 If we experience a major product failure in service, then this could result in a loss of life and critical damage to our reputation

2 If an external event or severe economic downturn significantly reduces air travel, then our financial performance may be impacted

3 If our airframe customers significantly delay their production rates, then our financial performance may be impacted

4 If we fail to achieve cost reductions at the necessary pace, then our ability to invest in future programmes and technology may be reduced

5 If we suffer a major disruption in our supply chain, then our delivery schedules may be delayed, damaging our financial performance and reputation

6 If there are significant changes to the regulatory environment for the airline industry, then our market position may be impacted

The problem with this disclosure is that it doesn't quantify the risk (it is likely/unlikely to happen), and the financial consequences. Any attempt to assess the level of risk requires a reader to have detailed industry knowledge.

For instance, in item 1, a 'major product failure' could be overcome by different handling of the engine. For instance, an aircraft with a Rolls-Royce engine crashed just short of the runway at London Airport, because of loss of power on both engines. This was due to icing of the fuel at the front of an oil cooler, which blocked the flow of fuel to the engines. Short-term, this was overcome by periodically accelerating the engines during descent to avoid build-up of the ice. Longer term, a change was made to the oil cooler.

However, a major failure could result in the withdrawal of all aircraft with that engine from service. It could take time to identify the fault and produce revised components. There also could be damages claims from aircraft manufacturers, airlines and passengers.

On items 2 and 6, this will equally affect manufacturers of similar aero engines. The 'servicing' of aero engines is likely to be more stable than demand for new manufactured ones.

Item 3 is 'possible', such as when Boeing started to manufacture aircraft from 'composites' (e.g. carbon fibre) rather than aluminium. 'New technology' is likely to increase the risk of delays compared with using existing technology.

Item 4, 'cost reductions', will range from little success in cost reductions to having substantial reductions in costs.

Item 5, 'major disruption in supply chain' looks unlikely.

The list of 'risks' gives the impression that aero engines is a mature business. However, there may be significant technical developments by competitors which Rolls-Royce may either not be able to match or it would take them a long time to make them successful and reliable.

Including 'business risks' can be helpful. In the case of Rolls-Royce (and probably many other companies), it tends to state obvious risks, but does not quantify them (how likely are they and how significant is the potential financial risk). It also fails to mention other risks that could be significant.

19.2.3 Improving the reliability of financial information

Investors rely on the fact that annual reports are audited and so present a fair view of a company's financial performance and position. However, accounting scandals, such as in Enron, Satyam and the SEC probe in 2012 into the auditing of Chinese companies, have led to a feeling that auditors are not protecting their interests. The profession is aware of this view and of the existence of an expectation gap between what investors expect from an audit and what can reasonably be delivered. This is discussed further in Chapter 11.

Reliability of narrative information in the Annual Report

The following is an indication of the work carried out by an auditor.

- Other information contained in the Annual Report is read and considered as to whether it is consistent with the audited financial statements.

- The other information comprises only the Directors' Report, the unaudited part of the Directors' Remuneration Report, the Chairman's Statement, the Viability Report, the Strategic Report and the Corporate Governance Statement.

- The implications for the audit report are considered if there is an awareness of any apparent misstatements or material inconsistencies with the financial statements.

- The responsibilities of the auditor do not extend to any other information.

19.3 Published financial statements – their limitations for interpretation purposes

Assuming that the financial statements have been audited and present a fair view, there remain limitations such as lack of detail and the impact of unaudited information when attempting to analyse the statements.

19.3.1 Limitation 1 – Lack of detail

This limitation is due to the amount that corporate entities are required to disclose by the appropriate regulatory framework. Only that information that is required to be disclosed would be subject to objective external scrutiny through audit and that information is strictly limited. For example:

- When analysing the profitability of a corporate entity, whether gross or net profit, the extent to which expenses can be broken down into categories is strictly limited. Most current frameworks require the disclosure of cost of sales and other operating expenses but do not require further analysis. Therefore, when, say, the gross margin shows a variation (either from one period to another for single-entity comparison or between entities) we cannot further investigate the components of gross margin because the published financial statements do not provide the required detail.

- Most frameworks require analysis of expenses into a number of headings but do not prescribe exactly where certain expenses (e.g. advertising) would fit. This means that when we compare the gross margin of one corporate entity with that of another we may not be comparing like with like, because one may have treated advertising as part of cost of sales and another may have treated equivalent costs as other operating expenses and the amount could be significant.

● Lack of detailed information prevents the computation of certain useful ratios in their 'purest' from. For example, one of the ratios we discussed in Chapter 1 was 'payables days' – trade payables as a number of days' credit purchases. If we tried to compute this ratio from the published financial statements we would have a problem – credit purchases are not required to be disclosed in the published financial statements of corporate entities in most regulatory frameworks. It is possible to use cost of sales as a proxy for credit purchases. However, this 'contrived' ratio is not as useful as the ratio would be were credit purchases to be available.

Limitation 2 – The impact of unaudited information

There is a varying amount of information relating to areas such as strategy, risk and KPIs and an ongoing move for improvement. For example, an interesting report issued by the FRC in 1999, *Rising to the Challenge: A Review of Narrative Reporting by UK Listed Companies*,[2] found the following:

● For KPIs, the best companies linked KPIs to strategy and provided an explanation of each measure along with some targets, reconciliations, graphical illustrations of year-on-year comparatives and tables to link KPIs to strategy and targets or future intentions. However, many reports still featured an isolated KPI table with no accompanying discussion or link to the remainder of the document.

● For principal risks, best-practice reports provided some context for the risk, indicating whether it was increasing or decreasing, and provided some idea of the impact of a risk crystallising, supported by numbers. However, users would find it difficult to assess risk where there was too little detail or too many risks identified that obscured those which were important.

19.4 Published financial statements – additional entity-wide cash-based performance measures

When making inter-firm comparisons there is the problem that accrual accounting requires a number of subjective judgements to be made such as the non-cash adjustments for depreciation, amortisation and impairment. Inter-firm comparison schemes overcome this by requiring member companies to restate their results using uniform policies such as restating non-current assets at current values and applying uniform depreciation policies.

External analysts are unable to achieve this and have, therefore, developed additional performance measures which are becoming more frequently met in published financial statements. However, there are concerns that they are not mandatory or uniformly defined. This is being addressed by a number of bodies including the International Federation of Accountants (IFAC) with its exposure draft for an International Good Practice Guidance on *Developing and Reporting Supplementary Financial Measures – Definition, Principles, and Disclosures*, the European Securities and Markets Authority (ESMA) with its draft *Guidelines on Alternative Performance Measures* and the IASB which has indicated an intention to research the presentation and disclosure of non-IFRS financial information as part of its *Disclosure Initiative project*.

The position then at present is that management defines the additional performance measures that they report which they consider best assist users to understand how these are used by management in making business decisions.

We discuss some of these measures below.

19.4.1 EBITDA

EBITDA is fairly widely used by external analysts. It stands for 'earnings before interest, tax, depreciation and amortisation'.

EBITDA more closely reflects the cash effect of earnings by adding back depreciation and amortisation charges to the operating profit. The figure can be derived by adding back the depreciation and amortisation that is disclosed in the statement of cash flows.

By taking earnings before depreciation and amortisation we eliminate differences due to different ages of plant and equipment when making inter-period comparisons of performance and also differences arising from the use of different depreciation methods when making inter-firm comparisons. By taking earnings before interest it shows how much is available to pay interest.

Note that there is no standard definition – for example some companies define it as earnings before interest, depreciation, tax, amortisation, *impairment* and *exceptional items.*

EBITDA shows an approximation to the cash impact of earnings. It differs from the cash flow from operations reported in the statement of cash flows in that it is before adjustment for working capital changes.

Comparing segment performance

EBITDA information is useful where an entity has a number of segments. It allows performance to be compared by calculating the EBITDA for each segment which provides a figure that is independent of the age structure of the non-current assets.

For example, the following is an extract from the Vodafone 2017 Annual Report:

	Adjusted EBITDA £m	EBITDA margin %
31 March 2017		
Germany	3,617	34.1
Italy	2,229	36.5
Spain	1,360	27.3
UK	1,212	17.5
Other Europe	1,865	30.4
Europe	**10,283**	**29.8**

Interestingly, the company states that it uses EBITDA as an operating performance measure which is reviewed by the Chief Executive to assess internal performance in conjunction with EBITDA margin, which is an alternative sales margin figure.

19.4.2 Other 'EBITDA-based' ratios commonly produced

The use of EBITDA in annual reports of listed companies is becoming more frequent. However, fewer companies are using 'other EBITDA-based ratios'. These other EBITA-based ratios include the following.

EV (Enterprise value)/EBITDA

EV is the market capitalisation of equity plus debt, non-controlling interest and preference shares less total cash equivalents.

Net debt/EBITDA

This ratio shows the number of years that it would take to 'pay off' the debt.

Debt service coverage ratio

This is defined as EBITDA/annual debt repayments and interest

EBITDA/Interest

This shows the number of times interest is covered. Most companies use the more familiar ratio, Profit before interest/Interest

EBITDAR

This is a variant of EBITDA. It stands for 'earnings before interest, tax, depreciation, amortisation and **rental expense**'.

Adding this rental expense back allegedly makes performance comparisons between entities with different proportions of assets leased under operating leases more valid. It also removes the subjectivity introduced by lease classification as operating or finance.

The following is an extract from the J Sainsbury plc 2015 Annual Report:

Key financial ratios	2015	2014
Adjusted net debt to EBITDAR[1]	**4.1 times**	3.9 times
Interest cover[2]	**7.4 times**	8.2 times
Fixed charge cover[3]	**2.9 times**	3.1 times
Gearing[4]	42.3%	39.7%
Gearing excluding pension deficit[5]	37.9%	35.7%

1. Net debt of £2,343 million plus capitalised lease obligations of £5,417 million (5.5 per cent discount rate), divided by Group underlying EBITDAR of £1,890 million.
2. Underlying profit before interest and tax divided by underlying net finance costs.
3. Group underlying EBITDAR divided by net rent and underlying net finance costs.
4. Net debt divided by net assets.
5. Net debt divided by net assets, excluding pension deficit.

EBITDAR in supermarket companies such as Sainsbury and Tesco refers to *rent*. It may also be defined differently, for example, as *restructuring*. In the aviation industry it is the key earnings-oriented operational performance indicator, referring to the profit before interest, taxes, depreciation, amortization, impairment and leasing costs for aircraft. EBITDAR is generally recognised and used by the aviation industry and investors and analysts as the ratio used for measuring operational success.

EBITDARM

EBITDARM stands for 'earnings before interest, tax, depreciation, amortisation, rental expense and management fees'. The rationale behind this measure is that management fees are extracted from different entities in different proportions.

Management charges may not always be totally representative of the services provided. Therefore management fees might sometimes be a form of profit extraction rather than a genuine expense and adding them back once again facilitates inter-entity comparison.

19.4.3 Evaluating the use of EBITDA

EBITDA is often used when valuing a company. It helps when comparing the performance of companies which may have differently geared capital structures, depreciation policies and tax rates.

However, it is not a substitute for cash flow in that it does not take into account changes in working capital that may be significant in a fast-growing company, material finance charges that may exist in a highly leveraged company and potential cash required by a capital-intensive company.

It needs to be used in conjunction with other ratios. For example, in reviewing a highly leveraged company the debt service coverage ratio and EBITDA/Interest would be considered. In reviewing a capital-intensive company reference would be made to Free cash flow discussed in Chapter 13. In assessing dividend potential the Free cash flow to Equity would be considered by calculating the cash after interest, taxes and reinvestment have been paid.

19.5 Ratio thresholds to satisfy Shariah compliance

In addition to considering the range of cash-based earnings ratios, investors might also require a company to satisfy certain threshold ratios *before* making an investment. An example is seen with the ratios relevant for shariah compliance.

Shariah law is a regulatory system that is derived from the Islamic religion. Islam commands followers to avoid consumption of alcohol and pork and so adherents avoid investments in those industries. There is screening to check that (a) business activities are not prohibited and (b) certain of the financial ratios do not exceed specified limits.

This use of ratios is included because of the growing importance of investment in shariah-compliant companies. Islamic banking is gaining popularity all over the world. Global Islamic finance assets had reached $2.07 trillion by the end of 2017, which is 1% of world total finance. Some are predicting that this might increase to over $3 trillion by 2020, subject of course to the performance of the overall global economy.

Investors interested in establishing whether an entity is shariah-compliant are assisted by the service provided by various Islamic indices such as where the constituent companies have been screened to confirm that they are shariah-compliant with reference to the nature of the business and debt ratios.

The indices are compiled after:

- screening companies to confirm that their business activities are not prohibited (or fall within the 5% permitted threshold);
- calculating three financial ratios based on total assets; and
- calculating a dividend adjustment factor which results in more relevant benchmarks, as they reflect the total return to an Islamic portfolio net of dividend purification.

Details are provided below.

19.5.1 Screening

Shariah investment principles do not allow investment in entities which are directly active in, or derive more than 5% of their revenue (cumulatively) from, the following activities ('prohibited activities'):

- Alcohol: distillers, vintners and producers of alcoholic beverages, including producers of beer and malt liquors, owners and operators of bars and pubs.
- Tobacco: cigarettes and other tobacco products manufacturers and retailers.
- Pork-related products: companies involved in the manufacture and retail of pork products.
- Conventional financial services: an extensive range including commercial banks, investment banks, insurance companies, consumer finance such as credit cards, and leasing.
- Defence/weapons: manufacturers of military aerospace and defence equipment, parts or products, including defence electronics and space equipment.
- Gambling/casinos: owners and operators of casinos and gaming facilities, including companies providing lottery and betting services.
- Music: producers and distributors of music, owners and operators of radio broadcasting systems.
- Hotels: owners and operators of hotels.

Key ratios

Shariah investment principles do not allow investment in companies deriving significant income from interest or companies that have excessive leverage. MSCI Barra uses the following three financial ratios to screen for these companies:

- total debt over total assets;
- sum of an entity's cash and interest-bearing securities over total assets;
- sum of an entity's accounts receivables and cash over total assets.

None of the financial ratios may exceed 33.33%.

Dividend adjustment (or 'purification')

If an entity does derive part of its total income from interest income and/or from prohibited activities, shariah investment principles state that this proportion must be deducted from the dividend paid out to shareholders and given to charity.

Dividend purification may be calculated by dividing prohibited income (including interest income) by total income and multiplying by the dividend received. An alternative is to divide total prohibited income (including interest income) by the number of shares issued at the end of the period and multiply by the number of shares held. MSCI Barra applies a 'dividend adjustment factor' to all reinvested dividends.

The 'dividend adjustment factor' is defined as:

$$\frac{\text{Total earnings} - (\text{Income from prohibited activities} + \text{Interest income})}{\text{Total earnings}}$$

In this formula, total earnings are defined as gross income, and interest income is defined as operating and non-operating interest.

19.6 Use of ratios in restrictive loan covenants

Whereas the shariah compliance criteria apply *before* making a financial commitment, frequently lenders set specific threshold ratios that a company must comply with when making a loan in order to limit the lender's risk – these are described as affirmative or negative debt covenants.

When a corporate entity borrows, the borrowing agreement often includes a provision which requires that specified accounting ratios such as gearing (relationship between debt and equity) of the entity be kept below a certain level. The loan agreement would of course have to specify exactly how any ratio is computed for this purpose.

The existence of a debt covenant or covenants has a number of potential implications for an entity and for analysts:

- An entity with a debt covenant that is close to its limit will be unable to raise funds by borrowing, so it will need to raise any required funds by an equity issue. Given the attitude of investors to risk, the return required by equity shareholders in a highly geared entity will be higher than that of an entity in which the gearing is lower. This will affect the overall amount of funding an entity can raise.

- Where a ratio of an entity subject to a debt covenant approaches the limit set out in the covenant, there is an inevitable temptation for the preparers to ensure the ratio is kept within the limit, leading to a potential temptation to misstate the financial statements.

The potential existence of a debt covenant is a factor that should be borne in mind by external analysts. The problem is that the existence of such debt covenants is not normally a required disclosure by relevant regulatory frameworks. Therefore a concerned analyst would need to attempt to obtain this information from the management of the entity. The success or otherwise of this attempt will depend on the bargaining power of the analyst.

19.6.1 Affirmative and negative covenants

Lenders may require borrowers to do certain things by affirmative covenants or refrain from doing certain things by negative covenants.

Affirmative covenants may, for example, include requiring the borrower to:

- provide quarterly and annual financial statements;
- remain within certain ratios whilst ensuring that each agreed ratio is not so restrictive that it impairs normal operations:
    - maintain a current ratio of not less than an agreed ratio – say 1.6 to 1;
    - maintain a ratio of total liabilities to tangible net worth at an agreed rate – say no greater than 2.5 to 1;
    - maintain tangible net worth in excess of an agreed amount – say £1 million;
- maintain adequate insurance.

    Negative covenants may, for example, include requiring the borrower *not* to:

- grant any other charges over the company's assets;
- repay loans from related parties without prior approval;
- change the group structure by acquisitions, mergers or divestment without prior agreement.

19.6.2 What happens if a company is in breach of its debt covenants?

Borrowers will normally have prepared forecasts to assure themselves and the lenders that compliance is reasonably feasible. Such forecasts will also normally include the worst-case scenario, e.g. taking account of seasonal fluctuations that may trigger temporary violations with higher borrowing required to cover higher levels of inventory and trade receivables.

If any violation has occurred, the lender has a range of options, such as:

- amending the covenant, e.g. accepting a lower current ratio; or
- granting a waiver period when the terms of the covenant are not applied; or
- renegotiating the credit facility and restructuring the finance.

In addition, companies may increase their equity capital, possibly by a rights issue as the current shareholders have a greater incentive to provide additional capital than new investors.

For example, it was reported in 2012 that Lonmin planned a $800m rights issue to avoid possibly breaching its covenants.

In times of recession a typical reaction is for companies to take steps to reduce their operating costs, align production with reduced demand, tightly control their working capital and reduce discretionary capital expenditure.

19.6.3 Risk of aggressive earnings management

In 2001, before the collapse of Enron, there was a consensus amongst respondents to the UK Auditing Practices Board Consultation Paper *Aggressive Earnings Management* that aggressive earnings management was a significant threat and actions should be taken to diminish it.

Reasons for earnings management

It was considered that aggressive earnings management could occur to increase earnings in order to avoid losses, to meet profit forecasts, to ensure compliance with loan covenants and when directors' and managements' remuneration were linked to earnings. It could also occur to reduce earnings to reduce tax liabilities or to allow profits to be smoothed.

In 2004, as a part of the *Information for Better Markets* initiative, the Audit and Assurance Faculty commissioned a survey.[3] This showed that the vulnerability of corporate reporting to manipulation is perceived as being always with us but at a lower level following the greater awareness and scrutiny by non-executive directors and audit committees.

Sector variations

The analysts interviewed in the survey believed the potential for aggressive earnings management varied from sector to sector, e.g. in the older, more established sectors followed by the same analysts for a number of years, they believed that company management would find it hard to disguise anything aggressive even if they wanted to. However, this was not true of newer sectors (e.g. IT) where the business models may be loss-making initially and imperfectly understood.

Levels of confidence

While analysts and journalists tend to have low confidence in the reported earnings where there are pressures to manipulate, there is a research report[4] which paints a rather more optimistic picture. This report aimed to assess the level of confidence investors had in different sources of company information, including audited financial information, when making investment decisions. As far as audited financial information was concerned, the levels of confidence in UK audited financial information among UK and US investors remained very high, with 87% of UK respondents having either a 'great deal' or a 'fair amount' of confidence in UK audited financial information.

Need for scepticism

The auditing profession continues to respond to the need to contain aggressive earnings management. This is not easy because it requires a detailed understanding not only of the business but also of the process management follows when making its estimates. ISA 540 Revised, *Auditing Accounting Estimates, including Fair Value Accounting Estimates, and Related Disclosures,* requires auditors to exercise greater rigour and scepticism and to be particularly aware of the cumulative effect of estimates which in themselves fall within a normal range but which, taken together, are misleading.

19.6.4 Audit implications when there is a breach of a debt covenant

Auditors are required to bring a healthy scepticism to their work. This applies particularly at times such as when there is a potential debt covenant breach. There may then well be a temptation to manipulate to avoid reporting a breach. This will depend on the specific covenant. For example, if the current ratio is likely to fall below the agreed figure, management might be more optimistic when setting inventory obsolescence and accounts receivable provisions and assessing the probability of contingent liabilities crystallising.

19.6.5 Impact on share price

If there is a risk of bank covenants being breached, there can be a significant adverse effect on the share price. For example, in 2018 Mothercare's share price fell when it revealed that it expected to breach banking covenants while seeking to raise additional funds.

However, both the company and the lender might prefer to keep potential breaches private unless there is a risk that enforced disclosure is imminent.

19.7 Investor-specific ratios

The analysis we carried out in Chapter 1 (and the additional performance measures we discussed in Section 19.4 above) was done from the perspective of the performance and position of the entity. In this section we will focus on additional ratios and measures that have as their focus the position of the shareholders of the entity. Some of these measures are 'financial statement measures' and others are 'market-based measures'.

19.7.1 Return on equity

We discussed ROE in Chapter 1 so this section is included as a brief reminder. In Chapter 1 we stated that a primary entity profitability measure is 'Return on equity', i.e. 'Profit'/Capital employed. Where the focus is on the equity shareholders the applicable ratio is ROE where the numerator is the post-tax profit.

If capital employed is funded by sources other than equity, then there is a financial leverage impact on the ROCE when calculating the ROE to reflect the potential benefit to equity shareholders of the company borrowing and investing at a higher rate.

As far as the equity shareholders are concerned, it might appear that the higher the financial leverage the better. However:

● If borrowings are high, it might be difficult to obtain additional loans to take advantage of new opportunities. For example, HSBC raised £12.5 billion in 2009 by a rights issue on the basis that this would give the bank a competitive advantage over its rivals by restoring its position as having the strongest statement of financial position, i.e. high borrowings limit a company's flexibility.

● Interest has to be paid even in bad years with the risk that loan creditors could put the company into administration if interest is not paid.

The relationship is illustrated using data from the financial statements of Vertigo plc for the year ended 31 December 20X9 presented in Section 28.3.1:

	£000
Total assets	4,587
Equity	3,353
Pre-tax profit	116
Tax	25
Sales	3,461

The effect of leverage on ROE is:

$$\text{Pre} - \text{tax margin } (3.35\%) \times \text{Asset turnover } (0.755) = \text{Return on assets } (2.53\%)$$
$$(116/3,461) \quad (3,461/4,587)$$

$$\text{Return on assets } (2.53\%) \times \text{Leverage } (1.37) \times (1 - \text{tax rate}) \ (0.785) = \text{ROE } (2.72)$$
$$(4,587/3,353) \quad (1 - 0.215)$$

The effect of leverage on EPS (assuming 3 million shares in issue) is:

$$\text{ROE } (2.72) \times \text{Book value } (1.12) = \text{EPS } (3.05)$$
$$(3,353/3,000)$$

19.7.2 Price/earnings (PE) ratio

The PE ratio is computed as:

$$\frac{\text{Market value of a share}}{\text{Earnings per share}}$$

The PE ratio is a market-based measure and a high ratio indicates that investors are relatively confident in the maintainability and quality of the earnings of the entity. Entities in certain sectors (e.g. the retail sector) tend to have higher PE ratios than those in other sectors (e.g. the construction sector). Higher PE ratios imply a greater level of market confidence, which usually means that (given the attitude an average investor takes to risk) the entity with a higher PE ratio operates in a sector which is less cyclical.

We will see in Section 19.11 that competitor or industry PE ratios (or their reciprocal, the earnings yield) are used as a base for valuing shares in unquoted companies – comparators being obtained from trade association schemes or sites such as https://csimarket.com/Industry/Industry_Valuation.php.

Earnings yield

This is the reciprocal of the PE ratio. For example, a PE ratio of 10 becomes an earnings yield of 10% ($1/10 \times 100$).

19.7.3 Earnings per share (EPS)

EPS is computed as:

$$\frac{\text{Profit attributable to the ordinary (equity) shareholders}}{\text{Weighted average number of ordinary shares in issue during the periods}}$$

The detailed calculation of basic and diluted EPS was dealt with in Chapter 18.

EPS could be said to be a more reliable indicator of the true trend in profitability than the actual profit numbers because the denominator of the fraction factors in any change in the issued capital during the period. The fact that the weighted average number is used removes the potential inconsistency that arises when dividing a 'period' number like profit by a 'point of time' number like the number of shares.

How EPS might be manipulated

The appropriateness of EPS as a performance measure can be influenced by the subjectivity of the directors when preparing the financial statements. For example, their remuneration may be based on the growth in EPS. Looking at calculation of the EPS of 3.05 (rounded) we can see that it is affected by:

- the number of shares in issue which can be changed by issuing bonus shares, share splits and reverse share splits;
- the profit which can be manipulated by adjusting accrued liabilities, depreciation, amortisation and impairment charges.

Simply buying back one-sixth of the shares can lift the EPS by more than 10%.

19.7.4 Dividend cover

Dividend cover is computed as:

$$\frac{\text{Profit for the period}}{\text{Dividends paid}} \text{ or } \frac{\text{EPS}}{\text{Dividend per share}}$$

Dividend cover is a measure of the vulnerability of the dividend to a fall in profits. The legality of a dividend payment is normally based on cumulative profits rather than the profits for a single period, but in practice an entity would wish the dividend declared for a particular period to be 'covered' by profits made in that period. Therefore this ratio is seen as a measure of the 'security' of the dividend.

An issue with this ratio is whether a high dividend cover is good or bad. In one sense, a shareholder might be content with a high dividend cover, because this would mean that profits could potentially fall quite significantly without the dividend necessarily falling, and retained earnings are being employed profitably within the company. Alternatively, a shareholder might feel disgruntled that the dividend itself is not higher. Therefore conclusions about whether a change in dividend cover is 'good' or 'bad' need to be made with caution – the trend and inter-firm comparators from the same industry need to be looked at. For example, some companies may target the rate of dividend cover as a key performance indicator as shown in the following extract from the Morrisons 2017 Annual Report:

> Our aim is that dividend cover will be the same as the average for the European food retail sector. Our dividend cover is 2.4 times, in line with the European food retail sector average. This has resulted in dividend growth of 17%.

19.7.5 Dividend yield

Dividend yield is computed as:

$$\frac{\text{Dividend per share}}{\text{Market value of a share}} \text{ (expressed as a percentage)}$$

This ratio measures the 'effective' current investment by the shareholder in the entity, because by deciding to keep the share rather than dispose of it the shareholder is forgoing an amount that would be available were the shareholder to make a disposal decision.

This ratio is a 'market-based' ratio, because it is influenced by the share price of the entity. We need to interpret any 'market-based' ratio with caution. In this case a high dividend yield could mean that the shareholder is receiving a very healthy dividend (which would be very positive) or that the share price was very low (which would clearly not be a desirable position either for the entity or for the shareholder).

Indeed, in times of disappointing prices on securities markets, dividend yields often tend to be very high because entities are reluctant to cut their dividends for fear the share price will fall even further. A combination of a static dividend and falling share prices leads inevitably to a rise in dividend yields. This would become more apparent if dividend growth were considered in addition to dividend yield.

19.7.6 Total shareholder return approach

Shareholder value (SV)

It has been a long-standing practice for analysts to arrive at shareholder value of a share by calculating the internal rate of return (IRR %) on an investment from the dividend stream and realisable value of the investment at date of disposal, i.e. taking account of dividends received and capital gains. However, it is not a generic measure in that the calculation is specific to each shareholder. The reason for this is that the dividends received will depend on the length of period the shares are held and the capital gain achieved will depend on the share price at the date of disposal – and, as we know, the share price can move significantly even over a week.

For example, consider the SV for each of the three shareholders, Miss Rapid, Mr Medium and Miss Undecided, who each invested £10,000 on 1 January 20X6 in Spacemobile Ltd which pays a dividend of £500 on these shares on 31 December each year. Miss Rapid sold her shares on 31 December 20X7. Mr Medium sold his on 31 December 20X9, whereas Miss Undecided could not decide what to do with her shares. The SV for each shareholder is as follows:

Shareholder	Date acquired	Investment at cost	Dividends amount (total)	Date of disposal	Sale proceeds	IRR %
Miss Rapid	1.1.20X6	10,000	1,000	31.12.20X7	11,000	10%*
Mr Medium	1.1.20X6	10,000	2,000	31.12.20X9	15,000	15%
Miss Undecided	1.1.20X6	10,000	2,000	Undecided		

$*(500 \times 0.9091) + (11,500 \times 0.8265) - 10,000 = 0$

We can see that Miss Rapid achieved a shareholder value of 10% on her shares and Mr Medium, by holding until 31.12.20X9, achieved an increased capital gain raising the SV to

15%. We do not have the information as to how Miss Rapid invested from 1.1.20X8 and so we cannot evaluate her decision – it depends on the subsequent investment and the economic value added by that new company.

19.7.7 Total shareholder return

Miss Undecided has a notional SV at 31.12.20X9 of 15% as calculated for Mr Medium. However, this has not been realised and, if the share price changed the following day, the SV would be different. The notional 15% calculated for Miss Undecided is referred to as the total shareholder return (TSR) – it takes into account market expectation on the assumption that share prices reflect all available information but it is dependent on the assumption made about the length of the period the shares are held.

19.7.8 Performance-based remuneration using TSR

Performance monitoring
TSR has been used by companies to monitor their performance by comparing their own TSR with that of comparator companies. It is also used to set strategic targets. For example, Unilever set itself a TSR target in the top third of a reference group of 21 international consumer goods companies. Unilever calculates the TSR over a three-year rolling period which it considers 'sensitive enough to reflect changes but long enough to smooth out short-term volatility'.

Statutory requirement
The Directors' Report Regulations 2002 now require a line graph to be prepared showing such a comparison. Marks & Spencer Group's 2012 Annual Report contained the following:

Total shareholder return performance graph

The graph illustrates the performance of the Company against the FTSE 100 over the past five years. The FTSE 100 has been chosen as it is a recognised broad equity market index of which the Company has been a member throughout the period.

Management and investors assess a company's performance based on the use of ratios described in Chapter 1 and earlier in the present chapter. This follows the pyramid approach of starting with the ROE and drilling down to identify possible causes of change.

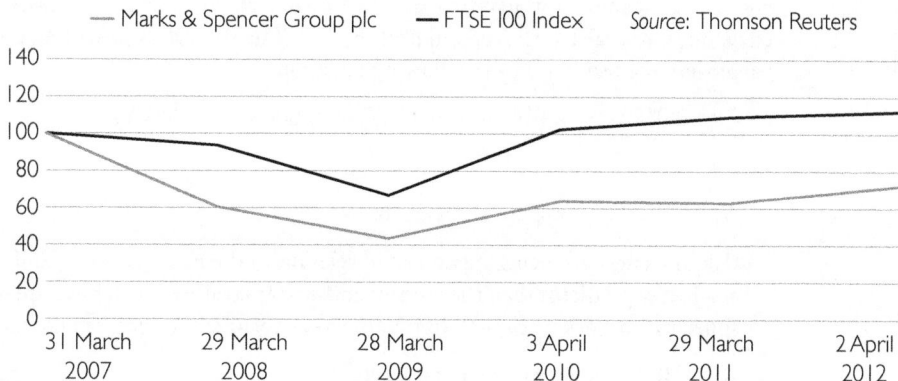

Marks & Spencer Group plc — FTSE 100 Index   *Source:* Thomson Reuters

19.8 Predicting corporate failure

The models that attempt to predict corporate failure combine selected ratios to produce a single-figure score. There are a number of such models and we will discuss a selection.

In the preceding chapter we extolled the virtues of ratio analysis for the interpretation of financial statements. However, ratio analysis is an excellent indicator only when applied properly. Unfortunately, a number of limitations impede its proper application. How do we know which ratios to select for the analysis of company accounts? Which ratios can be combined to produce an informative end-result? How should individual ratios be ranked to give the user an overall picture of company performance? How reliable are all the ratios – can users place more reliance on some ratios than others? We will consider which ratios have been selected to produce Z-scores and H-scores.

Z-score analysis can be employed to overcome some of the limitations of traditional ratio analysis. It evaluates corporate stability and, more importantly, predicts potential instances of corporate failure. All the forecasts and predictions are based on publicly available financial statements.[5] The aim is to identify potential failures so that 'the appropriate action to reverse the process [of failure] can be taken before it is too late'.[6]

19.8.1 What are Z-scores?

Inman[7] describes what Z-scores are designed for:

> Z-scores attempt to replace various independent and often unreliable and misleading historical ratios and subjective rule-of-thumb tests with scientifically analysed ratios which can reliably predict future events by identifying benchmarks above which 'all's well' and below which there is imminent danger.

Z-scores provide a single-value score to describe the combination of a number of key characteristics of a company. Some of the most important predictive ratios are weighted according to perceived importance and then summed to give the single Z-score. This is then evaluated against the identified benchmark.

The two best-known Z-scores are Altman's Z-score and Taffler's Z-score.

Altman's Z-score

The original Z-score equation was devised by Professor E. Altman in 1968 and developed further in 1977.[8]

Altman selected 66 manufacturing companies with an equal number of failed and going concern companies. Twenty-two ratios were calculated from five categories – leverage, solvency, liquidity, sales turnover and profitability. The five ratios providing the best predictive value were then set out in the following equation:

$$Z = 0.012X_1 + 0.014X_2 + 0.033X_3 + 0.006X_4 + 0.999X_5$$

where:

X_1 = Working capital/Total assets

(Liquid assets are being measured in relation to the business's size and this may be seen as a better predictor than the current and acid test ratios which measure the interrelationships within working capital. For X_1 the more relative Working capital, the more liquidity.)

X_2 = Retained earnings/Total assets

(In early years the proportion of retained earnings used to finance the total asset base may be quite low and the length of time the business has been in existence has been seen as a factor in insolvency. In later years the more earnings that are retained the more funds that could be available to pay creditors. X_2 also acts as an indication of a company's dividend policy – a high dividend payout reduces the retained earnings with impact on solvency and creditors' position.)

X_3 = Earnings before interest and tax (EBIT)/Total assets

(Adequate operating profit is fundamental to the survival of a business.)

X_4 = Market capitalisation/Book value of debt

(This is an attempt to include market expectations which may be an early warning as to possible future problems. Solvency is less likely to be threatened if shareholders' interest is relatively high in relation to the total debt.)

X_5 = Sales/Total assets

(This indicates how assets are being used. If efficient, then profits available to meet interest payments are more likely. It is a measure that might have been more appropriate when Altman was researching companies within the manufacturing sector. It is a relationship that varies widely between manufacturing sectors and even more so within knowledge-based companies.)

It can be seen from the weighting (0.999) that X_5 is the most important ratio.

Altman identified two benchmarks. Companies scoring over 3.0 are unlikely to fail and should be considered safe, while companies scoring under 1.8 are very likely to fail. The value of 3.0 has since been revised down to 2.7.[9] Z-scores between 2.7 and 1.8 fall into the grey area. The 1968 work is claimed to be able to distinguish between successes and failures up to two or three years before the event. The 1977 work claims an improved prediction period of up to five years before the event.

The Zeta model

This was a model developed by Altman and Zeta Services, Inc. in 1977. It is the same as the Z-score for identifying corporate failure one year ahead but it is more accurate in identifying potential failure in the period two to five years ahead. The model is based on the following variables:

X_1 return on assets:	earnings before interest and tax/total assets;
X_2 stability of earnings:	normalised return on assets around a five- to ten-year trend;
X_3 interest cover:	earnings before interest and tax/total interest;
X_4 cumulative profitability:	retained earnings/total assets;
X_5 liquidity:	the current ratio;
X_6 capitalisation:	equity/total market value;
X_7 size:	total tangible assets.

Zeta is available as a subscription service and the coefficients have not been published.

Taffler's Z-score

The exact definition of Taffler's Z-score[10] is unpublished, but the following components form the equation:

$$Z = c_0 + c_1X_1 + c_2X_2 + c_3X_3 + c_4X_4$$

where:

X_1 = Profit before tax/Current assets (53%)

X_2 = Current assets/Current liabilities (13%)

X_3 = Current liabilities/Total assets (18%)

X_4 = No credit interval = Length of time which the company can continue to finance its operations using its own assets with no revenue inflow (16%)

In the equation, c_0 to c_4 are the coefficients, and the percentages in brackets represent the ratios' contributions to the power of the model.

The benchmark used to detect success or failure is 0.2. Companies scoring above 0.2 are unlikely to fail, while companies scoring less than 0.2 demonstrate the same symptoms as companies that have failed in the past.

PAS-score: performance analysis score

Taffler adapted the Z-score technique to develop the PAS-score. The PAS-score evaluates company performance relative to other companies in the industry and incorporates changes in the economy.

The PAS-score ranks all company Z-scores in percentile terms, measuring relative performance on a scale of 0 to 100. A PAS-score of X means that $100 - X\%$ of the companies have scored higher Z-scores. So, a PAS-score of 80 means that only 20% of the companies in the comparison have achieved higher Z-scores.

The PAS-score details the relative performance trend of a company over time. Any downward trends should be investigated immediately and the management should take appropriate action.

SMEs and failure prediction

The effectiveness of applying a failure prediction model is not restricted to large companies. This is illustrated by research[11] conducted in New Zealand where such a model was applied to 185 SMEs and found to be useful. As with all models, it is also helpful to refer to other supplementary information that may be available, e.g. other credit reports, credit managers' assessments and trade magazines.

19.8.2 H-scores

An H-score is produced by Company Watch to determine overall financial health. The H-score is an enhancement of the Z-score technique in giving more emphasis to the strength of the statement of financial position. The Company Watch system calculates a score ranging from 0 to 100 with below 25 being in the danger zone. It considers profit management, asset management and funding management using seven factors: profit from the statement of income; three factors from the asset side of the statement of financial position, namely current asset cover, inventory and trade receivables management and liquidity; and three factors from the liability side of the statement of financial position, namely equity base, debt dependence and current funding.

The factors are taken from published financial statements, which makes the approach taken by the IASB to bring off-balance-sheet transactions onto the statement of financial position particularly important.

The ability to chart each factor against the sector average and to 25 level criteria over a five-year period means that it is valuable for a range of user needs, from trade creditors considering extending or continuing to allow credit to potential lenders and equity investors and the big four accounting firms in reviewing audit risk. The model also has the ability to process 'what-ifs'.

It appears to be a robust, useful and exciting tool for all user groups. It is not simply a tool for measuring risk. It can also be used by investors to identify companies whose share price might have fallen but which might be financially strong with the possibility of the share price recovering – it can indicate 'buy' situations. It is also used by leading firms of accountants for the purpose of targeting companies in need of turnaround. Further information appears on the company's website at www.companywatch.net which includes additional examples.

19.8.3 The A-score model

This is a qualitative model which concentrates on non-financial signs of failure.[12] This method sets out to quantify different judgemental factors.

Management defects and strategic mistakes

The whole basis of the analysis is that financial difficulties are the direct result of management defects and strategic mistakes which can be evidenced by symptoms. A weighting is then attached to individual defects and mistakes.

For example, in looking at management defects a weighting system might be applied such as:

Defects in operational management:	*Weight*
The chief executive is an autocrat	8
The chief executive is also the chairman	4
The board is unbalanced, e.g. too few with finance experience	2
Defects in financial management:	
There are no budgets for budgetary control	3
Weak finance director	3
There is a poor response to change, e.g. out-of-date plant, old-fashioned products, poor marketing	15

To calculate a company A-score, different scores are allocated to each defect, mistake and symptom according to their importance. Then this score is compared with the benchmark values. If companies achieve an overall score of over 25, or a defect score of over 10, or a mistakes score of over 15, then the company is demonstrating typical signs leading up to failure. Generally, companies not at risk will score below 18, and companies which are at risk will score well over 25.

Symptoms

With an adverse A-score, symptoms of failure will start to arise. These are directly attributable to preceding management mistakes. Typical symptoms are financial signs (e.g. poor ratios, poor Z-scores); creative accounting (management might attempt to 'disguise' signs of failure in the accounts); non-financial signs (e.g. investment decisions delayed; market share drops); and terminal signs (when the financial collapse of the company is imminent).

It is interesting to see the weighting given to the chief executive being an autocrat, which is supported by the experience in failures such as Worldcom in 2002 where Ebbers was the CEO with the following extract:[13]

'Autocratic style'
Ebbers was *autocratic* in his dealings with the board, and the board permitted it. The members of the board were reluctant to challenge Ebbers even when they disagreed with him.

However, there are also limitations to participative management which could lead to slow reaction to change in a fast-moving environment.[14]

19.8.4 Failure prediction combining cash flow and accrual data

There is a continuing interest in identifying variables which have the ability to predict the likelihood of corporate failure – particularly if this only requires a small number of variables. One study[15] indicated that a parsimonious model that included only three financial variables, namely a cash flow, a profitability and a financial leverage variable, was accurate in 83% of the cases in predicting corporate failure one year ahead.

19.9 Professional risk assessors

Credit agencies such as Standard & Poor and Moody's Investor Services assist investors, lenders and trade creditors by providing a credit rating service. Companies are given a rating that can range from AAA for companies with a strong capacity to meet their financial commitments down to D for companies that have been unable to make contractual payments or have filed for bankruptcy, with more than 10 ratings in between, e.g. BBB for companies that have adequate capacity but which are vulnerable to internal or external economic changes.

19.9.1 How are ratings set?

The credit agencies take a broad range of internal company and external factors into account. Internal company factors may include:

- an appraisal of the financial reports to determine:
  - trading performance, e.g. return on equity (ROE) and return on assets (ROA); earnings volatility; how well a company has coped with business cycles and severe competition;
  - cash flow adequacy, e.g. EBITDA interest cover; EBIT interest cover; free operating cash flow;
  - capital structure, e.g. gearing ratio; any off-balance-sheet financing;
- a consideration of the notes to the accounts to determine possible adverse implications, e.g. contingent liabilities, whether the company is fixed-capital- or working-capital-intensive or has heavy capital investment commitments;
- meetings and discussions with management;
- monitoring expectation, e.g. against quarterly reports, company press releases, profit warnings;

- monitoring changes in company strategy, e.g. changes to funding structure with company buyback of shares, new divestment or acquisition plans and implications for any debt covenants.

However, experience with companies such as Enron makes it clear that off-balance-sheet transactions can make appraisal difficult even for professional agencies if companies continue to avoid transparency in their reporting.

External factors may include:

- growth prospects, e.g. trends in industry sector; technology possible changes; peer comparison;

- competitors, e.g. the major domestic and foreign competitors; product differentiation; barriers to entry;

- keeping a watching brief on macroeconomic factors, e.g. environmental statutory levies, tax changes, political changes such as restrictions on the supply of oil, foreign currency risks.

19.9.2 Regulation of credit rating agencies

Since the credit crisis there has been severe criticism that credit rating agencies had not been independent when rating financial products. The agencies have been self-regulated but this has been totally inadequate in curtailing conflicts of interest. The conflicts have arisen because they were actively involved in the design of products (collateralised debt obligations) to which they then gave an 'objective' credit rating which did not clearly reflect the true risks associated with investing in them. This conflict of interest was compounded by the fact that (a) agency staff were free to join a company after rating its products, and (b) the companies issuing the products paid their fees.

This led to a call for both Europe and the US to regulate the agencies.

In 2014 the Commission adopted a report on the feasibility of a network of smaller credit rating agencies to facilitate their growth to become more competitive market players.

19.10 Valuing shares of an unquoted company – quantitative process

The valuation of shares brings together a number of different financial accounting procedures that we have covered in previous chapters. The assumptions may be highly subjective, but there is a standard approach. This involves the following:

- Estimate the maintainable income flow based on earnings defined in accordance with the IIMR guidelines, as described in Chapter 18. Normally the profits of the past five years are used, adjusted for any known or expected future changes.

- Estimate an appropriate dividend yield, as described in Section 19.7.5, if valuing a non-controlling holding.

- Estimate an appropriate PE or earnings yield if valuing a majority holding. In the UK there is now a Valuation Index[15] focused on SMEs which is the result of UK200's Corporate Finance members providing key data on actual transactions involving the purchase or sale of real businesses (in the form of asset or share deals) over the past five years. The average PE ratio at November 2017 stood at 5.4. Average deal size in the last two years was £3.4m.

- Make a decision on any adjustment to the required yields. For example, the shares in the unquoted company might not be as marketable as those in the comparative quoted companies and the required yield would therefore be increased to reflect this lack of marketability; or the statement of financial position might not be as strong with lower current/acid test ratios or higher gearing, which would also lead to an increase in the required yield.

- Calculate the economic capital value, as described in Chapter 18, by applying the required yield to the income flow.
- Compare the resulting value with the net realisable value (NRV), as described in Chapter 3, when deciding what action to take based on the economic value.

Example The Doughnut Ltd is an unlisted company engaged in the baking of doughnuts. The statement of financial position of the Doughnut Ltd as at 31 December 20X9 showed:

	£000	£000
Freehold land		100
Non-current assets at cost	240	
Accumulated depreciation	40	
		200
Current assets	80	
Current liabilities	(60)	
		20
		320
Share capital in £1 shares		300
Retained earnings		20
		320
Estimated net realisable values:		
Freehold land		180
Plant and equipment		120
Current assets		70

The company achieved the following profit after tax (adjusted to reflect maintainable earnings) for the past five years ended 31 December:

	20X5	20X6	20X7	20X8	20X9
Maintainable earnings (£000)	36	40	44	38	42
Dividend payout history: Dividends	10%	10%	12%	12%	12%

Current yields for comparative quoted companies as at 31 December 20X9:

	Earnings yield %	Dividend yield %
Ace Bakers plc	14	8
Busi-Bake plc	10	8
Hard-to-beat plc	13	8

Acquiring a majority holding

You are required to value a holding of 250,000 shares for a shareholder, Mr Quick, who makes a practice of buying shares for sale within three years.

Now, the 250,000 shares represent an 83% holding. This is a majority holding and the steps to value it are as follows:

1 Calculate average maintainable earnings (in £000):

$$\frac{36{,}000 + 40{,}000 + 44{,}000 + 38{,}000 + 42{,}000}{5} = £40{,}000$$

2 Estimate an appropriate earnings yield:

$$\frac{14\% + 10\% + 13\%}{3} = 12.3\%$$

3 Adjust the rate for lack of marketability by, say, 3% and for the lower current ratio (of 1.3:1) by, say, 2%. Both these adjustments are subjective and would be a matter of negotiation between the parties.

Required yield	= 12.3
Lack of marketability weighting	= 3.0
Statement of financial position weakness	= 2.0
Required earnings yield	= 17.3

The adjustments depend on the actual circumstances. For instance, there might be negotiation over the use of the average of £40,000 with differing views on growth and, if Mr Quick were intending to hold the shares as a long-term investment, there might be less need to increase the required return for lack of marketability.

4 Calculate share value:

$$(£40{,}000 \times 100/17.3)/300{,}000 = 77p$$

5 Compare with the net realisable values on the basis that the company was to be liquidated:

	£
Net realisable values = 70,000 + 120,000 + 180,000	= 370,000
Less: Current liabilities	60,000
	310,000
Net asset value per share = £310,000/300,000	= £1.03

The comparison indicates that, on the information we have been given, Mr Quick is paying less than the net realisable value, but the difference may not be enough to justify acquiring the shares in order to asset strip and liquidate the company to make an immediate capital gain.

Acquiring a minority holding

Let us extend our illustration by assuming that, if Mr Quick acquires control, it is intended to replace the non-current assets at a cost of £20,000 per year out of retained earnings. One of the remaining minority shareholders, Ms Croissant, wishes to dispose of shares and is in discussion with Mr Small who has £10,000 to invest. You are required to calculate for Mr Small how many shares he should aim to acquire from Ms Croissant.

There are two significant changes: the cash available for distribution as dividends will be reduced by £20,000 per year, which is used to replace non-current assets; and Mr Small is acquiring only a minority holding, which means that the appropriate valuation method is the **dividend yield** rather than the **earnings yield.**

The share value will be calculated as follows:

1 Estimate income flow:

	£
Maintainable earnings	40,000
Less: CAPEX	20,000
Cash available for distribution	20,000

Note that we are here calculating not distributable profits, but the available cash flow.

2 Required dividend yield:

	%
Average dividend yield	8.0
Lack of negotiability, say	2.0
Financial risk, say	1.5
	11.5

3 Share value:

$$\frac{£20,000}{300,000} \times \frac{100}{11.5} = 58p$$

At this price it would be possible for Mr Small to acquire $(£10,000/58p) = 17,241$ shares.

19.11 Valuing shares of an unquoted company – qualitative process

In the section above we illustrated how to value shares using the capitalisation of earnings and capitalisation of dividends methods. However, share valuation is an extremely subjective exercise.

A company's future cash flows may be affected by a number of factors. These may occur as a result of a change of control, action within the company (e.g. management change, revenue investment) or external events (e.g. change in the rate of inflation, change in competitive pressures).

- **Change of control:**
  - Aer Lingus said the offer in 2012 of €1.30 (£1.02) per share by Ryanair was 31% below the €1.87 cash per share based on the company's cash balance of €1bn.
  - Ryanair in its offer document said it would grow jobs at Aer Lingus and raise the flag carrier's passenger numbers from 9.5 million a year to 14 million, by cutting Aer Lingus ticket prices and improving the productivity of Aer Lingus staff in order to hold down costs and maintain profit margins.
- **Management change** often heralds a significant change in a company's share price. For example, car and bike parts retailer Halfords' share price jumped after the company appointed a new Chief Executive Officer in October 2012 following the abrupt departure of David Wild in the summer, as it revealed that full-year profits would be at the top end of guidance after a strong second quarter.

- **Revenue investment** refers to discretionary revenue expenditure, such as charges to the income statement for research and development, training and advertising. It also relates to expenditure on costs such as amount of office space provided and travel expense allowed. Where in the recession there had been a reduction in face-to-face meetings and an increase in video- and web-conferencing, there is ongoing pressure to maintain this process into the future.

- **Changes in the rate of inflation** can affect the required yield. If, for example, it is expected that inflation will fall, this might mean that past percentage yields will be higher than the percentage yield that is likely to be available in the future.

- **Change in competitive pressures** can affect future sales. For example, increased foreign competition could mean that past maintainable earnings are not achievable in the future and the historic average level might need to be reduced.

These are a few of the internal and external factors that can affect the valuation of a share. The factors that are relevant to a particular company may be industry-wide (e.g. change in rate of inflation), sector-wide (e.g. change in competitive pressure) or company-specific (e.g. loss of key managers or employees).

If the company supports the acquisition of the shares, the valuer will be able to gain access to relevant internal information. For example, details of research and development expenditure may be available analysed by type of technology involved, by product line, by project and by location, and distinguishing internal from externally acquired R&D.

If the acquisition is being considered without the company's knowledge or support, the valuer will rely more heavily on information gained from public sources, e.g. statutory and voluntary disclosures in the annual accounts and industry information such as trade journals. Information on areas such as R&D may be provided in the OFR (Operating and Financial Review or Strategic Report), but probably in an aggregated form, constrained by management concerns about use by potential competitors.[16]

There is an increasing wealth of financial and narrative disclosures to assist investors in making their investment decisions. There are external data such as the various multivariate Z-scores and H-scores and professional credit agency ratings; and there is greater internal disclosure of financial data such as TSR and EVA data indicating how well companies have managed value in comparison with a peer group and of narrative information such as the IFRS Practice Statement *Management Commentary*. It is also easier to access companies' financial data through the Web.

Literature search of qualitative factors which can lead to improved or reduced valuations

There is an interesting research report[17] investigating the nature of SME intangible assets in which the researchers have reported the following:

- **Factors identified in the literature as enhancing achieved price:** transportable business with a transferable customer base; non-cancellable service agreements and beneficial contractual arrangements; unexploited property situations; synergistic and cost-saving benefits; under-exploited brands and products; customer base providing cross-selling opportunities; competitor elimination, increased market share; complementary product or service range; market entry – a quick way of overcoming entry barriers; buy into new technology; access to distribution channels; and non-competition agreements.

- **Factors identified in the literature as diminishing achieved price:** confused accounts; poor housekeeping, doubtful debts, under-utilised equipment, outstanding litigation, etc.; over-dependence upon owner and key individuals; over-dependence on a small number of customers; unrelated side activities; poor or out-of-date company image; long-term contracts about to finish; poor liquidity; poor performance; minority and 'messy' ownership structures; inability to substantiate ownership of assets; and uncertainties surrounding liabilities.

Not all of these satisfy the criteria for recognition in annual financial statements.

19.12 Possible effect of 'Brexit' on financial statements

We have seen in Chapters 1 and 19 that ratio analysis is used to assess past performance and the strength of the statement of financial position with a view to (a) satisfying that there is appropriate stewardship over the assets under the management's control and (b) making predictions about the future performance and financial health of a company.

'Brexit' (the word coined in the UK media to describe the UK's 2016 referendum vote to leave the EU and consequences thereof) does not mean that we have to change our use of the pyramid of ratios when analysing financial statements. Our approach and interpretation are, however, coloured by the increased uncertainty that Brexit has created.

Effect of uncertainty

One of the major effects of Brexit from the viewpoint of all stakeholders has been that it has created a higher level of uncertainty that affects both the income statement and the statement of position. Investors and analysts will, therefore, need to be aware of any potential industry-wide effects and the risks that arise from these.

(a) Income statement

(i) Revenue – the effect depends on the industry, with varying opportunities and threats. In the tourist industry, for example, foreign holidays might be adversely affected by any fall in the rates of exchange, which could in turn lead to possible pressure on the cash flow and even the collapse of a tour company. On the other hand, the UK hospitality sector might well benefit from the opportunity for increased local demand and increased overseas visitors enjoying the benefit of any fall in sterling.

(ii) Costs – again the effect depends on the industry – airlines and transport might be adversely affected by possible increases in any costs denominated in US dollars.

Audit implications

Auditors will be considering how risks, such as a lower profit, might impact on company behaviour where, say, remuneration and bonuses are based on earnings growth or there is the risk of breaching loan covenants.

Particular attention will need to be paid to all discretionary expenses and the possible future impact if these are reduced – what effect is likely, for instance, from any reduction in advertising, marketing or supplier inducements? Costs that are based on management's subjective estimation will also need to be viewed carefully – has the percentage wastage rate in a retail organisation, for instance, suddenly been forecast to be at a lower rate?

Of course, it is not all negative, and it may well be that new trade deals lead to lower costs with alternative sources of supply becoming available.

(a) Statement of financial position

(i) Assets – intangible, tangible non-current and current assets will all need to be reviewed carefully to identify any specific adverse changes that might arise from Brexit.

Longer-term economic changes that might arise following the referendum vote to leave the EU could trigger a company's need to test its finite-lived intangibles such as goodwill, customer relationships and royalty agreements for impairment.

How, for example, is goodwill affected if it has arisen on the acquisition of a financial services company if EU passporting (where, by using a UK licence as a European passport, foreign financial firms can offer their financial services throughout the EEA) should be no longer available?

(ii) Liabilities – if financial difficulties arise due to Brexit there might be a need to restructure debt at a different interest rate to strengthen the balance sheet or avoid breaching loan covenants.

Narrative

Given the uncertainty it is increasingly important to read the narrative in the Annual Report – the Strategic Report, the Chairman's Statement, the enhanced auditor's report and explanations if there has been changes in, say, accounting policies or levels of exceptional items.

Auditors have always had to approach an audit with a degree of scepticism – following Brexit, this has become even more so.

Summary

This chapter has introduced a number of additional analytical techniques to complement the pyramid approach to ratio analysis discussed in the previous chapter.

The increasing use of 'non-GAAP' cash-based ratios was discussed to reduce the effect of subjective judgements. The use of ratio thresholds was discussed in determining shariah compliance and in setting debt covenants.

The calculation of TSR was explained, statuary disclosures in the UK were illustrated and their use in the context of performance-related remuneration was discussed. In addition, this chapter has described the use of ratios in the valuation of unquoted shares.

All users of financial statements (both internal and external users) should be prepared to utilise any or all of the interpretive techniques suggested in this chapter and the preceding one. These techniques help to evaluate the financial health and performance of a company. Users should approach these financial indicators with real curiosity – any unexplained or unanswered questions arising from this analysis should form the basis of a more detailed examination of the company accounts.

REVIEW QUESTIONS

I It has been suggested that the growth in profits can be achieved by accounting sleight of hand rather than genuine economic growth. Consider how 'accounting sleight of hand' can be used to report increased profits and discuss what measures can be taken to mitigate against the possibility of this happening.

2 Explain how the use of debt can improve returns to equity shareholders in good years and increase their losses in poor years.

3 Telecomsabroad plc has a dividend payout ratio of 95%. Discuss why using the ratio of free cash flow to dividend might influence your assessment of dividend growth.

4 Discuss the difficulties when attempting to identify comparator companies for benchmarking as, for example, when selecting a TSR peer group.

5 The Unilever annual review stated:

Total Shareholder Return (TSR) is a concept used to compare the performance of different companies' stocks and shares over time. It combines share price appreciation and dividends paid to show the total return to the shareholder. The absolute size of the TSR will vary with stock markets, but the relative position is a reflection of the market perception of overall performance relative to a reference group. The Company calculates the TSR over a three-year rolling period . . . Unilever has set itself a TSR target in the top third of a reference group of 21 . . . companies.

Discuss (a) why a three-year rolling period has been chosen, and (b) the criteria you consider appropriate for selecting the reference group of companies.

6 Discuss Z-score analysis with particular reference to Altman's Z-score and Taffler's Z-score. In particular:

(i) What are the benefits of Z-score analysis?

(ii) What criticisms can be levelled at Z-score analysis?

7 Identify the two most significant variables in the Altman's and Taffler's Z-scores and discuss why each variable might have been selected.

8 Discuss three situations when management might be under pressure to adopt an aggressive earnings management approach.

9 Compare the risks experienced by a lender in Islamic and non-Islamic finance.

Access: www.futurelearn.com and see Video presentation by Professor Lawrence Harris 'Risk Management in the Global Economy'

I0 Discuss the advantages and disadvantages of all companies adopting the ratio criteria required to be shariah-compliant.

II Describe the measures taken to reduce the risk that credit rating agencies can mislead investors.

I2 Discuss how the following might be used by a shareholder and by the management:

(i) The ratio of dividends plus share price movement to the opening share price.

(ii) Accounting profit less an additional charge for the use of equity capital.

13 The finance director was investigating a potential acquisition. As part of the exercise she gave your colleague the current value of total assets, the post-tax operating income, the economic life of the assets and the scrap value of the assets with a request to calculate the cash flow return on investment (CFROI) for the company. Your colleague has asked you to explain to him (a) how this is done or where he could find further information about this on the Web, and (b) how the CFROI will be used.

14 There is evidence (Black, Christensen, Joo and Schmardebeck) suggesting that managers prefer to meet expectations based on neutral reporting of solid operational performance.

They also found that, conditional on missing analysts' expectations after employing both accruals and real earnings management, firms are more likely to report non-GAAP earnings.

Access: https://www.researchgate.net/publication/310512924_The_Relation_Between_Earnings_Management_and_Non-GAAP_Reporting

Discuss whether this is a reason for not permitting the reporting of APMs in Annual Reports.

15 There are differences of opinion as to whether alternative performance measures (APMs) should be regulated by standard setters such as the IASB or whether they should remain entity-specific as defined by management. Discuss arguments for and against regulation.

16 Investors want a better understanding of how boards identify and manage risk to protect the sustainability of companies. By reference to the FRC's Financial Reporting Lab, identify one good corporate example of each of (i) risk reporting and (ii) viability statement reporting.

Access https://www.frc.org.uk/getattachment/76e21dee-2be2-415f-b326-932e8a3fc1e6/Risk-and-Viability-Reporting.pdf

17 Discuss the HMRC approach to valuing unquoted shares in (i) an Established trading company and (ii) a Start up company with no external investment.

Access https://www.gov.uk/government/publications/hmrc-shares-and-assets-valuations-sav/hmrc-shares-and-assets-valuations-sav#unquoted-shares

EXERCISES

* Question 1

Belt plc and Braces plc were in the same industry. The following information appeared in their 20X9 accounts:

	Belt	Braces
	€m	€m
Revenue	200	300
Total operating expenses	180	275
Average total assets during 20X9	150	125

Required:

(a) Calculate the following ratios for each company and show the numerical relationship between them:

      (i)   Their rate of return on the average total assets.

      (ii) The net profit percentages.

      (iii) The ratio of revenue to average total assets.

(b) Comment on the relative performance of the two companies.

(c) State any additional information you would require as:

      (i)   A potential shareholder.

      (ii) A potential loan creditor.

* Question 2

Quickserve plc is a food wholesale company. Its financial statements for the years ended 31 December 20X8 and 20X9 are as follows:

Statements of income

	20X9	20X8
	£000	£000
Sales revenue	12,000	15,000
Gross profit	3,000	3,900
Distribution costs	500	600
Administrative expenses	1,500	1,000
Operating profit	1,000	2,300
Interest receivable	80	100
Interest payable	(400)	(350)
Profit before taxation	680	2,050
Income taxation	240	720
Profit after taxation	440	1,330
Dividends in SOCE	800	600

Statements of financial position

	20X9	20X8
	£000	£000
Non-current assets:		
Intangible assets	200	—
Tangible assets	4,000	7,000
Investments	600	800
	4,800	7,800
Current assets:		
Inventory	250	300
Trade receivables	1,750	2,500
Cash & bank	1,500	200
	3,500	3,000
Total assets	8,300	10,800
Equity and reserves:		
Ordinary shares of 10p each	1,000	1,000
Share premium account	1,000	1,000
Revaluation reserve	1,110	1,750
Retained earnings	3,190	3,550

	20X9	20X8
	£000	£000
	6,300	7,300
Debentures	1,000	2,000
Current liabilities	1,000	1,500
	8,300	10,800

Required:

(a) Describe the concerns of the following users and how reading an annual report might help satisfy these concerns:
  (i) employees;
  (ii) bankers;
  (iii) shareholders.

(b) Calculate relevant ratios for Quickserve and suggest how each of the above user groups might react to these.

* Question 3

The following are the accounts of Bouncy plc, a company that manufactures playground equipment, for the year ended 30 November 20X6.

Statements of comprehensive income for years ended 30 November

	20X6	20X5
	£000	£000
Profit before interest and tax	2,200	1,570
Interest expense	170	150
Profit before tax	2,030	1,420
Taxation	730	520
Profit after tax	1,300	900
Dividends paid in SOCE	250	250

Statements of financial position as at 30 November 20X6

	20X6	20X5
	£000	£000
Non-current assets (written-down value)	6,350	5,600
Current assets		
Inventories	2,100	2,070
Receivables	1,710	1,540
Total assets	10,160	9,210
Creditors: amounts due within one year		
Trade payables	1,040	1,130
Taxation	550	450
Bank overdraft	370	480
Total assets less current liabilities	8,200	7,150
Creditors: amounts due after more than one year		
10% debentures 20X7/20X8	1,500	1,500
	6,700	5,650
Capital and reserves		

	20X6	20X5
	£000	£000
Share capital: ordinary shares of 50p fully paid up	3,000	3,000
Share premium	750	750
Retained earnings	2,950	1,900
	6,700	5,650

The directors are considering two schemes to raise £6,000,000 in order to repay the debentures and finance expansion estimated to increase profit before interest and tax by £900,000. It is proposed to make a dividend of 6p per share whether funds are raised by equity or loan. The two schemes are:

1. an issue of 13% debentures redeemable in 30 years;

2. a rights issue at £1.50 per share. The current market price is £1.80 per share (20X5: £1.50; 20X4: £1.20).

Assume a corporation tax rate of 40%.

Required:
(a) Calculate the return on equity and any three investment ratios of interest to a potential investor.
(b) Calculate three ratios of interest to a potential long-term lender.
(c) Report briefly on the performance and state of the business from the viewpoint of a potential shareholder and lender using the ratios calculated above and explain any weaknesses in these ratios.
(d) Advise management which scheme they should adopt on the basis of your analysis above and explain what other information may need to be considered when making the decision.

Question 4

Sally Gorden seeks your assistance to decide whether she should invest in Ruby plc or Sapphire plc. Both companies are quoted on the London Stock Exchange. Their shares were listed on 20 June 20X4 as Ruby 110p and Sapphire 120p.

The performance of these two companies during the year ended 30 June 20X4 is summarised as follows:

	Ruby plc	Sapphire plc
	£000	£000
Operating profit	588	445
Interest and similar charges	(144)	(60)
	444	385
Taxation	(164)	(145)
Profit after taxation	280	240
Interim dividend paid	(30)	—
Preference dividend paid	(90)	—
Ordinary dividend paid	(60)	(160)

The companies have been financed on 30 June 20X4 as follows:

	Ruby plc	Sapphire plc
	£000	£000
Ordinary shares of 50p each	1,000	1,500
15% preference shares of £1 each	600	—

	Ruby plc	Sapphire plc
	£000	£000
Share premium account	60	—
Retained earnings	250	450
17% debentures	800	—
12% debentures	—	500
	2,710	2,450

On 1 October 20X3 Ruby plc issued 500,000 ordinary shares of 50p each at a premium of 20%. On 1 April 20X4 Sapphire plc made a 1 for 2 bonus issue. Apart from these, there has been no change in the issued capital of either company during the year.

Required:
(a) Calculate the earnings per share (EPS) of each company.
(b) Determine the price/earnings ratio (PE) of each company.
(c) Based on the PE ratio alone, which company's shares would you recommend to Sally?
(d) On the basis of appropriate accounting ratios (which should be calculated), identify three other matters Sally should take account of before she makes her choice.
(e) Describe the advantages and disadvantages of gearing.

* Question 5

Growth plc made a cash offer for all of the ordinary shares of Beta Ltd on 30 September 20X9 at £2.75 per share. Beta's accounts for the year ended 31 March 20X9 showed:

	£000
Profit for the year after tax	750
Dividends paid	250

Statement of financial position as at 31 March 20X9

		£000
Buildings		1,600
Other tangible non-current assets		1,400
		3,000
Current assets	2,000	
Current liabilities	1,400	
		600
		3,600
£1 ordinary shares		2,500
Retained earnings		1,100
		3,600

Additional information:

(i) The half yearly profits to 30 September 20X9 show an increase of 25% over those of the corresponding period in 20X8. The directors are confident that this pattern will continue, or increase even further.

(ii) The Beta directors hold 90% of the ordinary shares.

(iii) The following valuations are available:

Realisable values

	£000
Buildings	2,500
Other non-current assets	700
Current assets	2,500
Net replacement values	
Buildings	2,600
Other non-current assets	1,800
Current assets	2,200

(iv) Shares in quoted companies in the same sector have a PE ratio of 10. Beta Ltd is an unquoted company.

(v) One of the shareholders is a bank manager who advises the directors to press for a better price.

(vi) The extra risk for unquoted companies is 25% in this sector.

Required:
(a) Calculate valuations for the Beta ordinary shares using four different bases of valuation.
(b) Draft a report highlighting the limitations of each basis and advise the directors whether the offer is reasonable.

Question 6

R. Johnson inherited 810,000 £1 ordinary shares in Johnson Products Ltd on the death of his uncle in 20X5. His uncle had been the founder of the company and managing director until his death. The remainder of the issued shares were held in small lots by employees and friends, with no one holding more than 4%.

R. Johnson is planning to emigrate and is considering disposing of his shareholding. He has had approaches from three parties, who are:

1 A competitor – Sonar Products Ltd. Sonar Products Ltd considers that Johnson Products Ltd would complement its own business and is interested in acquiring all of the 810,000 shares. Sonar Products Ltd currently achieves a post-tax return of 12.5% on capital employed.

2 Senior employees. Twenty employees are interested in making a management buyout with each acquiring 40,500 shares from R. Johnson. They have obtained financial backing, in principle, from the company's bankers.

3 A financial conglomerate – Divest plc. Divest plc is a company that has extensive experience of acquiring control of a company and breaking it up to show a profit on the transaction. It is its policy to seek a pre-tax return of 20% from such an exercise.

The company has prepared draft accounts for the year ended 30 April 20X9. The following information is available.

(a) Past earnings and distributions:

Year ended 30 April	Profit/(Loss) after tax	Gross dividends declared
	£	%
20X5	79,400	6
20X6	(27,600)	—
20X7	56,500	4
20X8	88,300	5
20X9	97,200	6

(b) Statement of financial position of Johnson Products Ltd as at 30 April 20X9:

	£000	£000
Non-current assets		
Land at cost		376
Premises at cost	724	
Aggregate depreciation	216	
		508
Equipment at cost	649	
Aggregate depreciation	353	
		296
Current assets		
Inventories	141	
Receivables	278	
Cash at bank	70	
	489	
Payables due within one year	(335)	
Net current assets		154
Non-current liabilities		(158)
		1,176
Represented by:		
£1 ordinary shares		1,080
Retained earnings		96
		1,176

(c) Information on the nearest comparable listed companies in the same industry:

Company	Profit after tax for 20X9 £000	Retention %	Gross dividend yield %
Eastron plc	280	25	15
Westron plc	168	16	10.5
Northron plc	243	20	13.4

Profit after tax in each of the companies has been growing by approximately 8% per annum for the past five years.

(d) The following is an estimate of the net realisable values of Johnson Products Ltd's assets as at 30 April 20X9:

	£000
Land	480
Premises	630
Equipment	150
Receivables	168
Inventories	98

Required:

(a) As accountant for R. Johnson, advise him of the amount that could be offered for his shareholding with a reasonable chance of being acceptable to the seller, based on the information given in the question, by each of the following:

   (i) Sonar Products Ltd;

(ii) the 20 employees;

(iii) Divest plc.

(b) As accountant for Sonar Products Ltd, estimate the maximum amount that could be offered by Sonar Products Ltd for the shares held by R. Johnson.

(c) As accountant for Sonar Products Ltd, state the principal matters you would consider in determining the future maintainable earnings of Johnson Products Ltd and explain their relevance.

(ACCA)

Question 7

Harry is about to start negotiations to purchase a controlling interest in NX, an unquoted limited liability company. The following is the statement of financial position of NX as at 30 June 2006, the end of the company's most recent financial year.

NX
Statement of financial position as at 30 June 2006

	$
ASSETS	
Non-current assets	3,369,520
Current assets	
Inventories, at cost	476,000
Trade and other receivables	642,970
Cash and cash equivalents	132,800
	1,251,770
Total assets	4,621,290
LIABILITIES AND EQUITY	
Non-current liabilities	
8% loan note	260,000
	260,000
Current liabilities	
Trade and other payables	467,700
Current tax payable	414,700
	882,400
Equity	
Ordinary shares, 40 cent shares	2,000,000
5% preferred shares of $1	200,000
Retained profits	1,278,890
	3,478,890
Total liabilities	1,142,400
Total liabilities and equity	4,621,290

The non-current assets of NX comprise:

	Cost	Depreciation	Net
	$	$	$
Property	2,137,500	262,500	1,875,000
Equipment	1,611,855	515,355	1,096,500
Motor vehicles	696,535	298,515	398,020
	4,445,890	1,076,370	3,369,520

NX has grown rapidly since its formation in 2000 by Albert Bell and Candy Dale who are currently directors of the company and who each own half of the company's issued share capital. The company was formed to exploit knowledge developed by Albert Bell. This knowledge is protected by a number of patents and trademarks owned by the company. Candy Dale's expertise was in marketing and she was largely responsible for developing the company's customer base. Figures for turnover and profit after tax taken from the statements of comprehensive income of the company for the past three years are:

	Turnover	Profit after tax
	$	$
Profit for 2004	8,218,500	1,031,000
Profit for 2005	10,273,100	1,288,720
Profit for 2006	11,414,600	991,320

NX's property has recently been valued at $3,000,000 and it is estimated that the equipment and motor vehicles could be sold for a total of $1,568,426. The net realisable values of inventory and receivables are estimated at $400,000 and $580,000 respectively. It is estimated that the costs of selling off the company's assets would be $101,000.

The 8% loan note is repayable at a premium of 30% on 31 December 2006 and is secured on the company's property. It is anticipated that it will be possible to repay the loan note by issuing a new loan note bearing interest at 11% repayable in 2012.

As directors of the company, Albert Bell and Candy Dale receive annual remuneration of $99,000 and £74,000 respectively. Both would cease their relationship with NX because they wish to set up another company together. Harry would appoint a general manager at an annual salary of $120,000 to replace Albert Bell and Candy Dale.

Investors in quoted companies similar to NX are currently earning a dividend yield of 6% and the average PE ratio for the sector is currently 11. NX has been paying a dividend of 7% on its common stock for the past two years.

Ownership of the issued common stock and preferred shares is shared equally between Albert Bell and Candy Dale.

Harry wishes to purchase a controlling interest in NX.

Required:

(a) On the basis of the information given, prepare calculations of the values of a preferred share and an ordinary share in NX on each of the following bases:

(i)   net realisable values;

(ii) future maintainable earnings.

(b) Advise Harry on other factors which he should be considering in calculating the total amount he may have to pay to acquire a controlling interest in NX.

(The Association of International Accountants)

Question 8

Briefly state:

(i)   the case for segmental reporting;

(ii) the case against segmental reporting.

Question 9

Discuss the following issues with regard to financial reporting for risk:

(a) How can a company identify and prioritise its key risks?

(b) What actions can a company take to manage the risks identified in (a)?

(c) How can a company measure risk?

* Question 10

Amalgamated Engineering plc makes specialised machinery for several industries. In recent years, the company has faced severe competition from overseas businesses, and its sales volume has hardly changed. The company has recently applied for an increase in its bank overdraft limit from £750,000 to £1,500,000. The bank manager has asked you, as the bank's credit analyst, to look at the company's application.

You have the following information:

(i)   *Statements of financial position as at 31 December 20X5 and 20X6*

	20X5		20X6	
	£000	£000	£000	£000
Tangible non-current assets:				
Freehold land and buildings, at cost		1,800		1,800
Plant and equipment, at net book value		3,150		3,300
		4,950		5,100
Current assets:				
Inventory	1,125		1,500	
Trade receivables	825		1,125	

	20X5		20X6	
	£000	£000	£000	£000
Short-term investments	300		—	
	2,250		2,625	
Current liabilities:				
Bank overdraft	225		675	
Trade payables	300		375	
Taxation payable	375		300	
Dividends payable	225		225	
	1,125		1,575	
Net current assets		1,125		1,050
		6,075		6,150
Long-term liability				
8% debentures, 20X9		1,500		1,500
		4,575		4,650
Capital and reserves:				
Ordinary shares of £1 each		2,250		2,250
Share premium account		750		750
Retained earnings		1,575		1,650
		4,575		4,650

(ii)   *Statements of comprehensive income for the years ended 31 December 20X5 and 20X6*

	20X5		20X6	
	£000	£000	£000	£000
Revenue		6,300		6,600
Cost of sales: materials	1,500		1,575	
: labour	2,160		2,280	
: production: overheads	750		825	
		4,410		4,680
		1,890		1,920
Administrative expenses		1,020		1,125
Operating profit		870		795
Investment income		15		—
		885		795
Interest payable: debentures	120		120	
: bank overdraft	15		75	
		135		195
Profit before taxation		750		600
Taxation		375		300
Profit attributable to shareholders		375		300
Dividends		225		225
Retained earnings for year		150		75

(iii)   The general price level rose on average by 10% between 20X5 and 20X6. Average wages also rose by 10% during this period.

(iv)   The debenture stock is secured by a fixed charge over the freehold land and buildings, which have recently been valued at £3,000,000. The bank overdraft is unsecured.

(v) Additions to plant and equipment in 20X6 amounted to £450,000: depreciation provided in that year was £300,000.

Required:

(a) Prepare a statement of cash flows for the year ended 31 December 20X6.

(b) Calculate appropriate ratios to use as a basis for a report to the bank manager.

(c) Draft the outline of a report for the bank manager, highlighting key areas you feel should be the subject of further investigation. Mention any additional information you need, and where appropriate refer to the limitations of conventional historical cost accounts.

(d) On receiving the draft report the bank manager advised that he also required the following three cash-based ratios:

(i)   Debt service coverage ratio defined as EBITDA/annual debt repayments and interest.

(ii) Cash flow from operations to current liabilities.

(iii) Cash recovery rate defined as ((cash flow from operations proceeds from sale of non-current assets)/average gross assets) × 100.

The director has asked you to explain why the bank manager has requested this additional information given that he has already been supplied with profit-based ratios.

Question 11

Plymbridge Ltd is a company which manufactures and sells modular pre-cast buildings to retail customers. The directors have adopted a policy of steady expansion following the Brexit decision in 2016 into the manufacture and sale of modular warehouse facilities to commercial customers.

It has revalued its property with a view of raising further loan in the future and benefited from an increase in the market value of its Available for sale investments

The company has prepared the following draft statements of performance and financial position.

The Statement of financial performance for the year ended 31 March:

	2019	2018
	$000	$000
Revenue	30,780	26,010
Cost of sales	21,600	18,225
Gross profit	9,180	7,785
Distribution costs	1,500	960
Administration expenses	3,108	2,010
Operating profit	4,572	4,815
Finance costs	468	405
Profit before tax	4,104	4,410
Tax	1,170	1,260
Profit after tax	2,934	3,150

	2019	2018
	$000	$000
Non-current assets		
Property, plant and equipment	23,337	16,092

Available for sale investments	5,580	4,860
Total non-current assets	28,917	20,952
Current assets		
Inventories	4.050	3,240
Trade receivables	3,870	4,680
Cash and cash equivalents	-	108
	7,920	8,028
Total assets	36,837	28,980
Equity and liabilities		
Share capital	9,000	9,000
Revaluation reserve	3,780	990
Other reserves – investment	1,620	900
Retained earnings	6,714	3,780
Total equity	21,114	14,670
Non-current liabilities		
Loan repayable 2020	4,860	4,680
Other loans	5,400	5,400
Total non-current liabilities	10,260	10,080
Current liabilities		
Trade payables	4,200	2,970
Bank overdraft	93	-
Tax payable	1,170	1,260
Total current liabilities	5,463	4,230
Total liabilities	15,723	14,310
Total equity and liabilities	36,837	28,980

Required:

The finance director is submitting a report to the Board at their April meeting and has instructed his assistant to prepare a draft memo to explain:

(a) the company's financial performance and position with supporting ratios; and
(b) the matters to be taken into account when considering the feasibility of a further planned rapid expansion.

Notes

1 *No Surprises:* The Case for Better Risk Reporting, ICAEW, 1999.
2 www.frc.org.uk/Our-Work/Publications/ASB/Rising-to-the-Challenge/Full-results-of-a-Review-of-Narrative-Reporting-by.aspx
3 J. Collier, *Aggressive Earnings Management: Is It Still a Significant Threat?*, ICAEW, October 2004.
4 Alpa A. Virdi, *Investors' Confidence in Audited Financial Information*, Research Report, ICAEW, December 2004.
5 C. Pratten, *Company Failure*, Financial Reporting and Auditing Group, ICAEW, 1991, pp. 43–5.

6 R.J. Taffler, 'Forecasting company failure in the UK using discriminant analysis and financial ratio data', *Journal of the Royal Statistical Society*, Series A, vol. 145, part 3, 1982, pp. 342–358.

7 M.L. Inman, 'Altman's Z-formula prediction', *Management Accounting*, November 1982, pp. 37–39.

8 E.I. Altman, 'Financial ratios, discriminant analysis and the prediction of corporate bankruptcy', *Journal of Finance*, vol. 23(4), 1968, pp. 589–609.

9 M.L. Inman, 'Z-scores and the going concern review', *ACCA Students' Newsletter*, August 1991, pp. 8–13.

10 R.J. Taffler, 'Z-scores: an approach to the recession', *Accountancy*, July 1991, pp. 95–97.

11 K. Van Peursem and M. Pratt, 'Failure prediction in New Zealand SMEs: measuring signs of trouble', *International Journal of Business Performance Management (IJBPM)*, vol. 8 (2/3), 2006.

12 J. Argenti, 'Predicting corporate failure', Accountants Digest, no. 138, Summer 1983, pp. 18–21.

13 P. Gottschalk, *CEOs and White-Collar Crime: A Convenience Perspective*. Palgrave Macmillan, London, 2016, p. 70

14 www.managementstudyguide.com/limitations-of-participitative-management.htm

15 www.uk200group.co.uk/Members/SpecialistGroups/SpecialistPanels/CorporateFinance/Sp_Valuations/Sp_Valuations_Home.aspx

16 W.A. Nixon and C.J. McNair, 'A measure of R&D', *Accountancy*, October 1994, p. 138.

17 C. Martin and J. Hartley, *SME Intangible Assets*, Certified Accountants Research Report 93, London, 2006.

CHAPTER 20

Integrated reporting: sustainability, environmental and social

20.1 Introduction

Previous chapters have introduced the techniques involved in financial accounting and financial statement analysis and discussed Corporate Governance. However, annual reporting to shareholders and other interested parties also involves management explaining past performance and indicating future opportunities, challenges and risks. To truly understand the performance of a company one needs to understand the strategies adopted by management, the business environment in which they operate and what they have done to prepare the company to meet the challenges of the future. Part of that involves choices about the level of risk the company wants to take.

Integrated reporting is an attempt to provide a systematic way of addressing the reporting of the performance of the company which incorporates awareness of the broad strategic approach of the company and links that strategy to performances in economic, environmental and social spheres.

In other words, a company should spell out how the company is going to achieve in a competitive environment and what that approach necessitates in terms of both its economic operations and its environmental and social activities.

The chapter objectives will be achieved by illustrating the way in which a company manages and integrates environmental and social information in its annual report. This requires greater attention by management to social and environmental issues as well as to traditional economic operations – it stresses the linkages between economic, environmental and social activities and measures performance in all those areas.

However, the extent to which environmental and social performance are considered key aspects of performance is likely to vary across companies and countries, being influenced by management views as to:

- how critical they are perceived to be in terms of achieving the economic strategy of the organisation;
- the appropriate roles and responsibility of business for environmental and social issues;
- how appropriate it is felt for environmental and social dimensions to be embedded in day-to-day management decisions and actions;
- how much the evaluation of an individual manager's performance is influenced by environmental and social performance.

Integrated reporting is important not only because it allows a better evaluation of the company's performance but also because it allows for a better evaluation of potential serious economic consequences if such issues are mismanaged.

Objectives

By the end of this chapter, you should be able to:

- understand the objectives and frameworks of integrated reporting;
- be sensitised to the broad range of factors that companies need to address to reduce the future strategic risks;
- understand the historical context of the development of integrated reporting;
- be familiar with the major organisations who have contributed to the development of integrated reporting and the resources that they provide to report preparers;
- be able to explain the accountant's and auditor's roles in integrated reporting;
- be able to formulate well-thought-out views on the possible implications and future developments of the above.

20.2 Environmental and social disasters, the adverse consequences that can follow and the lessons to be learnt

The objective of this section is to bring home the magnitude of the economic consequences, and the level of social disruption, which can flow from inadequate management of such risks particularly in the areas of environmental risks, health and safety, resource protection, intellectual knowledge and protection, and supply chain management. Two examples will be briefly discussed to stress the significance of these to both economic success and the type of world in which we would like to live.

20.2.1 Environmental disasters

BP plc and its group

In April 2010 an oil rig in the Gulf of Mexico experienced a high-pressure methane gas surge from its well. It ignited and the explosion engulfed the drilling platform and oil flowed into the ocean for 87 days before the well was closed off. This had major adverse consequences:

- **Social** – 11 workers were never found and their families were affected.
- **Environmental** – the beaches which were spoilt by the oil or other chemicals took a substantial period to rectify, substantial numbers of wildlife were killed and many of the wildlife survivors had their habitats rendered unliveable.
- **Economic** – the oil spill caused major disruption to companies operating in fishing and tourism in the area and of course there was a knock-on effect for all their suppliers.

For BP and the two other companies involved this was the start of major stress in trying to contain the oil flows, reducing the impact of the oil flows that couldn't be stopped, responding to government departments, trying to directly or indirectly help those suffering as a consequence of the disaster, defending court cases and trying to minimise the damage to the reputation of the company. Also some employees were subjected to criminal legal cases, which irrespective of the outcome would be very stressful.

According to the BP Group 2016 Strategic Report:

Following the 2015 settlements with the United States and the Gulf states further significant progress was made in 2016 towards resolving outstanding claims arising from the 2010 Deepwater Horizon accident and oil spill. . . . As a result of this progress, we have clarified the remaining material uncertainties arising from the incident. The cumulative pre-tax income statement charge since the incident, in April 2010, amounted to $62.6 billion.

Our objective is not to focus on BP. It is rather to stress that environmental and safety issues are major management problems and require continued vigilance by management. Furthermore, if precautions fail to prevent such events then considerable time, energy and money will be consumed in handling the physical problems, business interruption, social and reputational aspects of such disasters. For investors the costs of managing environmental aspects (both prevention and rectification) are significant costs which they would like to think management has given the attention it deserves.

VW

Another example in this section is VW, whose employees were under pressure to reduce the pollution levels of diesel cars so that the company could get a larger market share, particularly in the USA. Being unable to satisfy US requirements, and also apparently unwilling to tell top management of their failure, they resorted to using software in the cars which reduced pollution levels (from the car's exhaust) when tested in the laboratory but did not reduce the pollution under normal driving conditions.

The result was that in normal operation the pollution level was in excess of US mandatory limits and sometimes considerably in excess. When the situation was uncovered VW was exposed to costs to fix 600,000 cars so they have lower pollution levels, compensation to car owners, and fines. By 2018 it had set aside a provision of $18.2bn with the further prospect of a class action in the UK.[2] VW was 'removed from the Dow Jones Sustainability Indices'[3] which meant it was no longer deemed a leader of its Industry Group in terms of environmental, social and governance factors and unattractive to ethical investors. A Volkswagen AG compliance executive who pleaded guilty in the U.S. for his role in the company's $30 billion emissions cheating scandal has since been sentenced to 7 years in prison.[4]

This case viewed from the outside would seem to suggest that the culture in the organisation (i.e. do employees feel they can share bad news with their superiors) was a major factor. It also highlights that the cost of failure can be high, particularly where companies use environmental credentials as a marketing tool.

20.2.2 Social disasters

Rana Plaza

It would be wrong to think that other industries do not face their own challenges in terms of the possibility of disasters which could reflect badly on their businesses and affect customer attitudes to their products. We have become used to cheap clothing, but often that is supplied by countries with working conditions that would be condemned in developed countries. It takes a disaster or action by activists to bring these conditions to the attention of customers in developed countries.

One example of such a disaster occurred in 2013 at Rana Plaza in Bangladesh, where 1,129 people died because 'shoddy construction turned a building in Dhaka into a death trap when a garment manufacturing complex collapsed'.[5] To be fair, the UK retailers were more likely to have been assessing the factories for fire risks than for structural problems. Primark acted quickly to provide food parcels and financial support to the families affected, but they were only one of many well-known brands linked to the factory.[6]

The disaster led to campaigners for garment workers' rights brokering a significant break-through, with 31 brands signing the Bangladesh Safety Accord. The Accord will sound dry to many fashion lovers. It is a contract between brands, retailers and trade unions in Bangladesh, and is a legally binding, five-year pact that makes independent safety inspections of 1,000 factories and public reporting on them mandatory. It is also the first-ever multi-buyer collective agreement. This was a historic moment for the campaign to clean up fashion.

Once again this demonstrates the need for and the difficulty of anticipating and eliminating potential problems. When such events do occur, management has to decide what it is going to do both in terms of ethical responsibilities and in terms of protecting their brand image.

20.2.3 The lessons

The objective of this section is to use a few examples to demonstrate that managing corporate social responsibility is a major task of management. It is not easy but it can have a major impact on the company's brand and reputation, not to mention the financial impacts in the short and medium term. These in turn can affect access to resources such as loans, share capital, mineral reserves, rights to operate in a location, recruitment of quality employees and customer loyalty.

All industries face these corporate social responsibility problems which are not restricted just to the industries discussed above. For example, another industry which has been criticised for inappropriate cultures is the finance industry, where it has been argued that reward systems have encouraged some employees to ignore their moral and legal obligations to customers when giving financial advice or manipulating interest rates as seen in the Libor scandal.[7] Obviously the form they take will vary from industry to industry but the underlying issues will be similar. Further it is no longer a separate activity over and above profit making. It is main stream, as it has to be integrated into day-to-day activities. Thus, when a product is being designed, trade-offs might have to be made between costs and safety (e.g. toy designs), efficiency and health and safety (e.g. building construction or paramedic well-being), and pressure for financial results versus risk mitigation.

20.3 Management accountability for environmental and social responsibility

This section will address the issue of the normative views on the role(s) of business. As pointed out earlier, the subjective views held by managers as to *the appropriate roles and responsibility of business will influence their day-to-day actions.* As these views become more widely held they will also influence the *legislation* of a country.

We set out below a discussion of competing views as to those responsibilities. While we spell out a few possibilities, the reality is that a wide range of views are held and the discussion is designed to highlight some of those views. Subsequently there will be a discussion of the legal responsibility of directors of companies in the United Kingdom for the management and reporting on economic, environmental and social issues.

20.3.1 Shareholder primacy

Maximising profits

Sometimes the question is raised whether management's role should actually include environmental and social responsibility. Such discussions normally start with a quotation from

Milton Friedman, a famous American economist, who said that management is responsible for providing maximum returns to shareholders (shareholder primacy theory), and social and environmental applications of funds by companies are normally inappropriate. According to that approach the shareholders themselves should be the ones who decide whether to donate to environmental or social activities out of their dividends or capital gains.

Difficulties with this approach

Friedman himself did not rule out expenditures on environmental and social activities if it increased shareholder returns. It is interesting to note, for example, that many companies which have undertaken initiatives to reduce energy costs purely based on environmental concerns have found that the cost savings have generated very attractive returns on investments.

Shareholder primacy is difficult, however, to apply in a complex world. How to decide, for example, over what period are profits to be maximised; how to determine whether the use of management resources for environmental and social purposes contributes to maximising earnings and share prices? Certainly as demonstrated above, if insufficient weight is given to the social and environmental activities then the costs of not doing so may be substantially greater than would have been incurred to avoid the environmental and social malpractices in the first place.

Economic and societal pressures that operate against profit maximising

Direct investment

Companies that give insufficient attention to environmental and social issues may find that direct investment into the company incurs an increase in the cost of capital, i.e. the cost of borrowing and the rate of return that is required by shareholders to justify the increased risks that they bear. Conversely, there is some empirical evidence that companies taking positive action on environmental impacts have a lower cost of capital.[8]

Shareholder activity

An increasing number of investment funds are avoiding companies which are deemed to be involved in anti-social activities such as being contributors to pollution (e.g. coal companies) or financing anti-social organisations (e.g. banks supporting companies which are contributing to anti-social activities) or producing unhealthy products (e.g. cigarettes).

Others may need to decide whether to disinvest. For example, in 2018 the world's largest fund manager which oversees more than $6 trillion, decided not to disinvest and outlined steps to ensure the three publicly traded arms manufacturers in which it owns stock make 'a positive contribution to society.' It won't solve America's gun-violence epidemic, but by engaging with gunmakers and distributors rather than divesting, BlackRock provides a blueprint for how shareholders can bring about social change and safeguard their investments.[9]

These decisions not to invest/disinvest in certain companies may be based on social attitudes to the companies' activities or on assessments of higher risks – such as possible future liabilities for rectification, class actions for injury caused by products or threats to future rights to operate.

Cost and risk trade-offs

It must be stressed that in a large corporation many executives will make decisions which make cost and risk trade-offs as part of normal operations. The way in which they are rewarded and achievements recognised will influence their priorities and the trade-offs they make. Individuals at lower levels may experience different pressures from those impinging on senior management and as a result they may make choices which are inappropriate from the perspective of senior management. This means that senior management, even under shareholder primacy, has to ensure that at all levels of the organisation decisions are made which give sufficient weight to environmental and social issues in line with top management priorities, and must avoid giving unintended messages that increasing sales or short-term profitability takes total priority. This was not ensured, apparently, in the case of VW.

Move to the opposite profit-maximising shareholder primacy

Companies in the past have been able to disregard of the impact of externalities. Externalities are the costs borne by society, and not the company, as a result of the actions or the inactions of the company. Thus if a company discharges inadequately treated effluent from its manufacturing activities into the adjacent river the costs they impose on others are the externalities.

Mandatory regulations have gradually been imposed to make companies responsible for externalities, and voluntary initiatives have been encouraged to allow management more discretion in focusing on social and environmental issues. For example, in some US states it is possible to establish Benefit Corporations, which are a new type of company that uses the power of business to solve social and environmental problems, and where being good corporate citizens is one of the legal objectives of the company.

However, the widespread US view is that normal businesses should exercise shareholder primacy, but one legal authority[10] suggests that shareholders are just another party with a contract with the corporation, much the same as a supplier of raw materials. As such, the corporation as a separate legal entity manages its shareholder relations (the suppliers of finance) in the same way as it manages other supplier relations.

Given the dominant culture in the USA, and the heavy reliance on stock market financing, it is likely that in the main environmental and social action and reporting is likely to be less extensive than in continental Europe. (Obviously this is a generalisation and many US companies are very environmentally oriented, but in the main one would expect more environmental and social accounting in more 'socialistic cultures' such as Europe.)

In summary, the shareholder primacy view is that company management has a responsibility to maximise shareholder returns, which implies that environmental and social costs are incurred if, and only if, they contribute to the level of shareholder returns or are required under the law.

20.3.2 Stakeholder theory

Another normative view of the corporation is what is called stakeholder theory. Under such an approach, incorporation with limited liability is a privilege granted by the state because it is of benefit to the whole community. Thus the company should respect the need to contribute back to the state/community in generating employment, taxes and a good community environment if it is to retain its privileges.

Under stakeholder theory, management has a range of contributors to the operation whose continued contribution is of benefit or essential if the corporation is to achieve its aims. Thus the company is dependent on satisfying customers and suppliers of finance (shareholders and lenders); developing skills and knowledge (employees, professional firms, and suppliers); securing reliable sources of raw materials; and enjoying a productive environment.

A productive environment can be said to exist where the state supplies a transparent legal environment in which to operate and there are efficient transport links, sound exchange rate management, educated employees and protection of property and property-rights such as patents, etc. Under this view it is management's task to keep all stakeholders committed to the well-being of the company. It has to set strategic directions for the company so as to ensure the continued success of the business, and this includes the attraction and retention of satisfied stakeholders.[11]

Thus, under stakeholder theory, management has to keep stakeholders committed to supporting the operation of the company. One way of doing this is to use the Annual Report to communicate to the major stakeholders how the company will continue to satisfy their needs into the future.

20.3.3 Management obligations

Irrespective of which framework is adopted (shareholder primacy or stakeholder theory or just a sense of moral responsibilities or some other view of the world) management has considerable discretion and with that comes responsibility to communicate clearly the results of their actions and priorities.

It is the challenge of the current time to identify what and how the reporting should be extended to show how the management have positioned the company to deal with the risks inherent in an uncertain future. Part of the issue is how to focus on the important issues and provide greater insights without over-burdening the business and the readers of the Report.

There are certain statutory requirements relating to the environmental and social issues that need to be addressed in a Report, but it has to be recognised that management has considerable discretion in deciding what issues are important to the major community strategies, which may well vary from country to country. In South Africa, for example, the community is very concerned with the development of the skills of the black community and the improvement of health including reducing and treating Aids.

UK statutory position

In the United Kingdom the law states that the company is primarily accountable to shareholders. However, the Companies Act 2006 qualifies this to some extent when it says that the duty of a director is to act:[12]

in the way [s]he considers, in good faith, would be most likely to promote the success of the company for the benefit of its members as a whole, and in doing so have regard (amongst other matters) to:

(a) the likely consequences of any decision in the long term;

(b) the interests of the company's employees;

(c) the need to foster the company's business relationships with suppliers, customers and others;

(d) the impact of the company's operations on the community and the environment;

(e) the desirability of the company maintaining a reputation for high standards of business conduct; and

(f) the need to act fairly as between members of the company.

Thus it takes a shareholder primacy approach but also requires selective stakeholder activities.

From October 2014 new regulations became operational which require companies to produce a Strategic Report, and the Financial Reporting Council produced a report, *Guidance on the Strategic Report,*[13] giving non-binding guidance on the content of the report. A quoted company must provide a description of its strategy and its business model. The FRC expanded on this when it recommended that the Strategic Report stress linkages between the items discussed in the strategic report and the annual report (paragraphs 6.15 to 7.26) and in paragraph 7.29 it says:

> To the extent necessary for an understanding of the development, performance or position of the entity's business, the Strategic Report should include information about:
>
> (a) environmental matters (including the impact of the business of the entity on the environment);
>
> (b) the entity's employees; and
>
> (c) social, community and human rights issues.

The information should include a description of any relevant policies in respect of those matters and the effectiveness of those policies.

Thus the Financial Reporting Council has adopted a set of policies which are reflected in the principles of integrated reporting covering economic, environmental, social and human rights issues, and governance. In this context, governance refers to developing appropriate corporate policies and decisions supported by a system which provides reasonable assurance that those are being implemented as intended.

Monitoring performance

Stakeholders need to know whether the firm has governance systems to ensure management strategies and policies are implemented correctly and ethically, and that reporting systems capture accurate information and report fairly on those activities.

Given the emphasis on clear reporting and the focus on key issues there is still room for considerable discretion, which has both advantages and disadvantages. The major advantages include a better understanding of management's strategies and the risks they may be exposing the business to; the disadvantages include a lack of comparability, and possible selective reporting in not showing unsatisfactory areas of performance.

Decisions taken by companies shape the future

Therefore business needs to be conscious that its actions and those of other businesses will shape the future environment in which they have to operate, which includes future laws and the economic conditions that they will be faced with. Businesses in general, especially large businesses, have such a major impact on the future of the world, and those in it, that they must take responsibility for their major impacts. Thus the Stern Review[14] suggests that inadequate attention to the environmental impacts of human and business activities means that business is potentially facing large reductions in gross domestic product (i.e. reduced business revenue).

There is much discussion of climate change, and the Report says there is evidence that climate change is already creating more extreme weather conditions with the resulting destruction of property and thus additional costs to business. On the other hand, the challenge of reducing environmental impacts potentially provides new business opportunities. Unilever in their 2015 Strategic Report[15] reports that since 2008 it has saved €600m by adopting eco-production.

The above discussions have highlighted the fact that different countries are likely to view the appropriate level of regulation differently, reflecting cultural norms.

20.4 Integrated reporting concepts

The International Integrated Reporting Council (IIRC) has been established to foster and guide the development of integrated reporting. Its activities include establishing principles to guide those wishing to adopt integrated reporting.[16] It has a wide range of businesses using their principles and providing feedback on their experiences. Presently integrated reporting is most widely reported by listed companies, particularly those in South Africa where it is a legal requirement, and to a lesser extent in Europe.

The expectation is that management should convey how they expect the business or organisation to achieve its goals and to keep its major stakeholders satisfied with the achievability of forecast profits and with the solvency and viability of the company over the short term, medium term and long term. How the various components of that strategy support each other needs to be explained.

Reporting to the suppliers of financial capital is seen as the primary role

As stated earlier, to understand the organisation and its potential for future success one needs to understand all of the resources it has at its disposal and how it intends to combine those resources to achieve its aims. The approach adopted is to get businesses to also report on progress in terms of improving key non-financial resources. The International $<$ IR $>$ Framework suggests six resources (called capitals), which most (but not all) organisations will be dependent on, as a starting framework to guide management in selecting the items to report upon. These capitals are financial, manufactured, intellectual, human, social and relationships, and natural.

- **Financial capital.** Reporting on financial performance has traditionally focused on the maintenance of financial capital concept. In other words, *progress has not been made until the financial base has been increased.* Profit (or loss) represents the increase (decrease) in the financial capital invested in the business. However, an organisation is more than simply a financial investment. It involves the coordinated use of people, knowledge, legal privileges, reputations and customer relationships, supply chains, production facilities and natural resources to achieve acceptable returns and continuing viability.

- **Manufactured capital** is the manufactured physical objects used in the production of goods and services.[17] Being manufactured items they exclude natural resources. Note that production is used in a very broad sense. It includes plant and machinery, goods manufactured for sale, roads and port facilities used in say a stevedoring firm or a mining operation, office equipment, etc. Thus a call centre would have office equipment as part of its production facilities. In summary it would include all tangible non-current assets and finished goods inventory. But the perspective is not the financial amount but the ability to service a given level of business activity at the required quality of performance.

- **Intellectual capital** includes both the knowledge base of the organisation which supports its operations and the legal rights which protect specific items of knowledge (e.g. patents, copyright), or provide access to use of specific knowledge (e.g. licences). Once again it is very broad in application. It would cover the intangible assets reported in the statement of financial position and would also include internally generated intangibles and systems knowledge which enable the company to provide high-quality services.

  Note also that some firms do not patent new inventions either because patenting is expensive to enforce or because it discloses confidential information to competitors, for example, A study on patenting activity in Australia indicates that 44% of the firms used patents, while 74% used trade secrets as a way of protecting their ideas.[18]

  Thus if intellectual knowledge evolves rapidly it may not be worth patenting but rather the competitive advantage is dependent on continuous improvement and rapid incorporation of new ideas into the products. The degree to which the company is at the forefront of intellectual knowledge may be important to the competitive advantage which the company wants to exploit. If it is at the centre of the company's strategy then it is important to know whether it is likely that the company has maintained its intellectual advantage.

- **Human capital** includes the skill levels of employees, their level of commitment to their jobs, and their ability to contribute to improvements in operations in all areas. The level of staff commitment may, of course, depend on things such as the opportunity for enhancing their skills and knowledge, opportunities for promotion without unfair discrimination and the provision of a safe working environment.

It also includes their identification and conformity with the governance strategies and corporate strategy, particularly in relation to the level of risk that management consider acceptable. An illustration of the latter is in a financial organisation where traders are given specific limits, and it is their willingness to comply not only with those limits but also the spirit of those limits that is key to management being able to control the firm. Thus what is required is an organisational culture that supports fair and ethical values and compliance with company governance processes.

Insights into whether a company has improved human capital could be captured by independent surveys of staff morale,[19] staff injury and death statistics, health issues including those resulting from work situations (e.g. exposure to chemicals) and the external environments (in some countries aids and malaria are major issues), and staff turnover rates.

- **Social and relationship capital** relates to maintaining good relationships with all major stakeholders. For example, the perceptions of customers that the company will treat them appropriately in providing safe products, honouring commitments (delivery performance, replacing damaged goods), providing products sourced ethically, etc. Similarly relations with employees, suppliers, industry associations, and the communities in which they are located are all important in ensuring the ongoing level of support which the firm is dependent upon for current and future operations

- **Natural capital,** as the name implies, are the environmental resources that the organisation needs and uses in its operations. These environmental resources include those that can be renewed, such as forests which can be replaced by systematic replanting and husbandry.

Resources that cannot be renewed include oil, gas and minerals. If it is in the oil industry the firm needs to find new oil deposits or to develop new technology to make it economically viable to extract at least the same quantity of oil at the end of the period as at the beginning. Resource companies are already required to report on the level of their reserves as it is vital to making an assessment of the future prospects of such companies. Below are two extracts. The first is an extract from the accounts of Shell to illustrate the type of information provided:[20]

	2015	2014	2013
Oil and gas production available for sale (thousand boe/d)	2,954	3,080	3,199
Equity sales of LNG (million tonnes)	22.6	24.0	19.6
Proved oil and gas reserves at December 31 (million boe)	11,747	13,081	13,944

Note: boe/d = barrels of oil equivalent per day

The second is Marks and Spencer's 'Our Sustainable Value Creation Model' diagram:

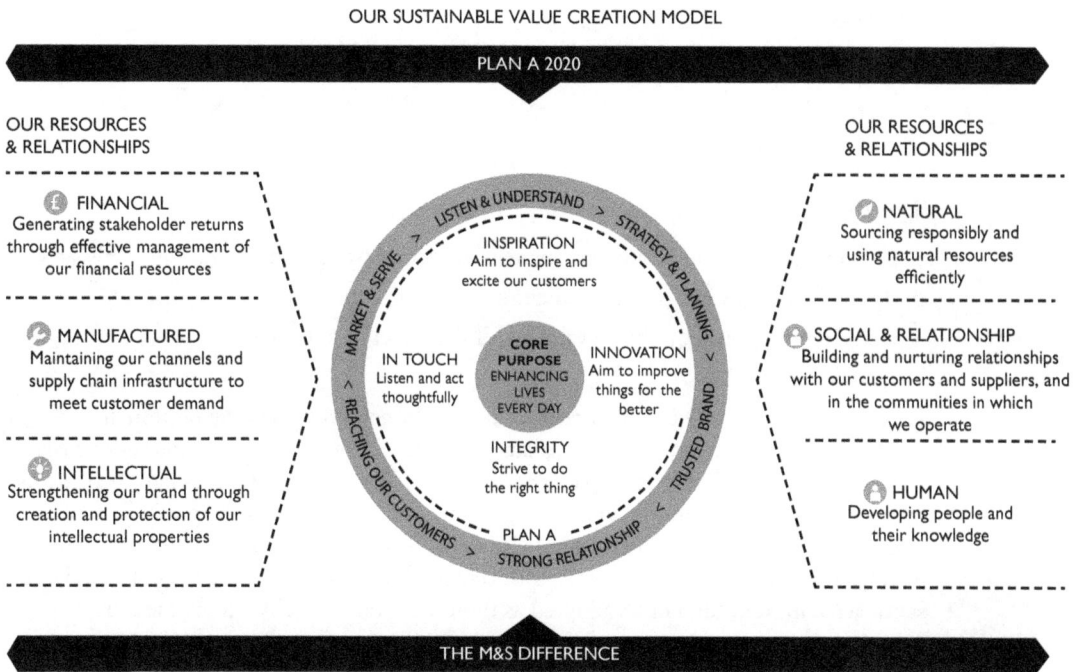

OUR SUSTAINABLE VALUE CREATION MODEL

PLAN A 2020

OUR RESOURCES & RELATIONSHIPS

FINANCIAL
Generating stakeholder returns through effective management of our financial resources

MANUFACTURED
Maintaining our channels and supply chain infrastructure to meet customer demand

INTELLECTUAL
Strengthening our brand through creation and protection of our intellectual properties

LISTEN & UNDERSTAND
STRATEGY & PLANNING
MARKET & SERVE

INSPIRATION
Aim to inspire and excite our customers

IN TOUCH
Listen and act thoughtfully

CORE PURPOSE
ENHANCING LIVES EVERY DAY

INNOVATION
Aim to improve things for the better

INTEGRITY
Strive to do the right thing

REACHING OUR CUSTOMERS
TRUSTED BRAND
PLAN A
STRONG RELATIONSHIP

OUR RESOURCES & RELATIONSHIPS

NATURAL
Sourcing responsibly and using natural resources efficiently

SOCIAL & RELATIONSHIP
Building and nurturing relationships with our customers and suppliers, and in the communities in which we operate

HUMAN
Developing people and their knowledge

THE M&S DIFFERENCE

20.4.1 The benefits of integrated reporting

Integrated reporting:

- should help us judge the quality of earnings and the level of associated risks;
- will force management to more clearly articulate their strategies and pay attention to performance of all capitals and to ensure the work in the various areas is coordinated; and
- is an attempt to get management to focus on the sustainability of their business.[21]

What integrated accounting is not

The International < IR > Framework does not provide standard reporting formats. Reporting according to a generic format would make it more difficult to fully appreciate the thinking and motivation of management. However, where the companies have chosen to report on specific elements of social and environmental accounting then common definitions would be an advantage for comparative purposes.

It also does not say that every capital should be reported upon. After all we don't want a company to spend valuable resources collecting information that may be important for other firms but is relatively unimportant for it, nor to overwhelm the reader with unimportant information.

Integrated reporting is not new

It is important to know that some companies have been reporting on the triple bottom line (financial, environmental and social issues[22]), and multiple bottom line, for some time and professional organisations with that expertise already exist. Some of those bodies will be discussed in this chapter. However, the important point is that since the reporting is tied into the strategy of the firm the coverage and emphasis must reflect the nature and approach of each specific firm.

20.5 The historical context of the evolution of integrated reporting[23] including the drivers of this movement

The evolution of integrated accounting can be seen as:

- attempts to tackle limitations in financial reporting by academics and the profession;
- driven by socially aware management in business; and
- a reaction to growing public awareness of the effect of pollution.

Attempts to tackle limitations in financial reporting by academics and the profession

In 1976 a new academic journal was started called *Accounting, Organization and Society*, reflecting the interest in these broader issues. Since that time these issues have become more mainstream in the accounting and management literature. In 1975 the profession published 'The Corporate Report', which essentially took a stakeholder approach and advocated producing a value added statement and an employment report. It took the view at that date that social accounting could not be adopted as there were no generally agreed measures.[24]

The value added statement

The value added statement flourished for a period of time and is still reported by some companies. The business is seen as buying in inputs (say materials and services like electricity) and processing them to sell at a higher price. The increase in value (the value added) is then shared among four groups:

- investors in the form of dividends and interest;
- the company as reinvestment in the business;
- payments to employees; and
- taxes to various levels of government.

The statement focuses on the split of the 'value added' between the various parties. Management used the statement to demonstrate that shareholders were not getting an excessive share of the value created. However, it did not address the split between different classifications of employees. It was not possible to assess whether management was receiving a fair share compared to other employees and shareholders and there was little incentive to provide this breakdown. The content of the report will be explained in a separate section below.

20.5.1 Failure to report human assets

It has been noted that in annual reports there are often statements like: 'We would like to thank our employees for their efforts during the year. Our employees are our greatest asset.' But the accounts do not directly reflect this. Human resources were reflected in some accounts during the period of the slave trade but since then they have generally not been treated as assets because they are not bound to the firm and can leave at any time.

Attempts have been made to develop methods of accounting for human resources such as:

- reflecting their replacement costs, recruitment costs, relocation costs paid to new employees, sign on bonuses, costs of lower productivity until they become familiar with company operations; or
- capitalising and amortising training costs; or
- valuing the assets based on future earning potential multiplied by the probabilities that they would continue with the firm for each year of the projections.

Such suggestions have not gained acceptance, however, partly due to cost considerations and ethical concerns about treating humans as assets, but mainly due to the failure to satisfy the IASB's conceptual definition of an asset.

This discussion is intended to highlight the fact that there has been serious concern about the completeness of accounting reports that do not include information about resources that are important if the business is to operate successfully in the future.

Another argument in favour of accounting for human resources in the statement of financial position is that management might be less willing to downsize during hard economic times if they had to recognise the cost of earlier financial investment in staff that they are discarding.

20.5.2 Drive by more socially aware management

In business initially the drive for reporting on environmental issues came altruistically from a small group of environmentally and socially aware individuals who did not want current generations to jeopardise the ability of future generations to have an equally rewarding existence. This was remarked on in the Brundtland Report.[25]

This was followed by other organisations acting from self-interest when becoming aware that they could face a possible community backlash from damaging environmental impacts they caused. Their interest was to manage public relations by reporting on the action they were taking to rectify environmental damage and to improve their production processes.

The difference between these two groups is that the former were interested in giving a comprehensive insight into the environmental impacts of their businesses and were seriously working to improve processes wherever possible. The second group were more interested in public relations and were selective in their disclosures, for example, deciding whether to include fines in their reported expenditures on environmental matters.

20.5.3 Reaction to the growing public awareness of the effect of pollution

Pollution of the environment has always been with us but until it reaches a level that impacts on most of us it tends to be ignored. Thus while it occurs out of sight or out of mind, then little is done. Further there needs to be potential for reducing it in terms of having the resources and knowledge to do so. Thus at the time of the industrial revolution there were chronic living and working conditions for the poor but they had little power to influence decision making.

Since those times, however, rising living standards, greater political power for the working classes, expanding cities making it more difficult to hide pollution and increases in knowledge have made it more important and feasible to tackle pollution.

Example of China's recent experience

China provides a good example. In the last 30 years China has focused on providing higher standards of living by acting as a cheap supplier to developed countries. However, there was a cost in that cheap forms of production often created high levels of pollution. As an economic solution it was extremely effective. The pollution impacted on the quality of life and the health of inhabitants so political pressure built for improved air quality and safer agricultural products. Government is now seeking to reduce the level of pollution by closing down old polluting factories, limiting expansion of motor cycle and car fleets, and installing more pollution controls in new factories. Similar changes in practices have also been seen in many countries, China only being different in that the cycle was condensed into a much shorter period.

Over time the proportion of the population placing importance on economic, environmental and social conditions has increased and they have placed pressure on companies to reflect these changing values.

20.5.4 Other limitations of traditional financial reporting

The growing awareness of the limitations of traditional accounting formed another driver for more comprehensive reporting. We discussed accounting for human resources above and the varying suggested treatment for goodwill in Chapter 4.

We saw that how to account for goodwill has been debated over a long period of time without a satisfactory resolution. Approaches that have been used include:

- an immediate write off (either to retained earnings or the profit statement);
- capitalisation of the amount paid which is retained until there is evidence of significant impairment; and
- initial treatment of the cost as an asset but with annual amortisation.

The assessment of whether the asset has decreased in value is very subjective in the absence of a sale.

The accounting for trademarks, patents, software, research and development, and other intangibles have similar problems. In particular, the increased importance of information technology highlights the problems of accounting for intangibles, especially as such items are notoriously associated with rapid and unexpected obsolescence.

Rapid changes in technology are disrupting industries and causing industries to converge leading to major changes to competition, manufacturing processes, and distribution systems and hence knowledge of these potential impacts and the company's preparedness are important in valuing the organisation.

Finally, technology is making knowledge of what is happening in the supply chain more quickly and more widely known with the possibility of boycotts being more easily coordinated. Thus greater management of supply chains is necessary to maintain earning capacity.

The fact that *financial accounting has inherent limitations* has given added impetus to integrated accounting. As mentioned previously this has evolved from environmental accounting to triple bottom line accounting (financial, environmental and social accounting).

The first country to incorporate integrated reporting into its regulatory requirements was South Africa in 2011. The requirement was that listed companies had to provide an integrated report or explain why not. The motivation is thought to have been *to increase trust in South African companies* following the removal of apartheid. It was hoped that with increased trust the South African companies would find it easier to attract foreign investments in companies and in joint ventures.[26]

20.5.5 The South African experience in more detail

This country will be examined because it highlights the interaction of social and historical forces in shaping the move to integrated reporting and the emphasis placed upon it. Obviously countries such as the USA with different history and culture are likely to approach sustainability and social dimensions slightly differently.

Under the apartheid regime in South Africa there was a concentration of wealth, managerial positions, educational opportunities and pleasant life styles in the hands of parts of the white minority. This was viewed by international groups as unfair, and boycotts occurred in athletics from the 1960s onwards followed by a wide range of boycotts of other sports including football, rugby, golf and cricket. By 1980 the pressure was widespread.

What may be less well known is that businesses were under pressure to stop dealing with South Africa and those multinationals with investments in South Africa felt they had to withdraw. When Nelson Mandela became the first black president in 1994 he was faced with improving the lot of black and coloured South Africans. Part of this was to improve living conditions, access to education and training, and employment opportunities. To increase employment he needed to attract more investment to South Africa.

Investment activities require confidence in the governance of companies in the country. To improve investment inflows there was a need for confidence that business would be conducted:

● appropriately according to fair laws;

● that conflicts of interest would be dealt with appropriately and ethically; and

● that companies would have good systems to ensure operations follow strategies in an orderly fashion.

In other words, there needed be confidence in good corporate governance. To create the necessary environment that would attract more investment, the Institute of Directors of Southern Africa in 1993 appointed a committee under the chairmanship of Mervyn King, a retired Supreme Court judge, to look at governance and that committee reported in 1994.

By 2002 it was time to update the code and this occurred in an environment in which environmental issues were attracting attention worldwide. So the second version of the corporate code, called King 2, recommended the use of triple bottom line reporting (reporting on financial, environmental and social performance). In particular, there is specific mention of policies and strategies in relation to HIV (Aids), procurement and black empowerment, and policies on disclosure of non-financial matters.[27] Aids was at that time a major issue in South Africa and obviously impinged both on the well-being of employees and on the performance of the business. Similarly by focusing on black sources of inputs firms could contribute to their living standards.

In 2009 the South African code was updated again, to King 3, and emphasises the integration of strategies, environmental and social issues.[28]

The code was clearly wedded to a stakeholder approach. It saw the additional environmental and social and governance information as an integral part of financial reporting as it relates to the sustainability of the reported earnings and as such was not non-financial information. It anticipated that companies would want to provide 'forward-looking' information as that would facilitate more accurate valuation of the business. (*Note:* It needs to be recognised that forward-looking information is easier to provide in some legal environments than others depending on director liability laws and whether there are safe harbours for honest forecasts based on reasonable assumptions at that time. Hence in some countries there has been a reluctance to provide such projections.)

The code was initially aimed at companies listed on the Johannesburg Stock Exchange and large corporations. However, over time it was recognised the principles were applicable to a much wider range of organisations[29] including not-for-profit organisations.

20.6 The efforts on which integrated reporting builds

Readers should realise that integrated reporting is in its infancy and is building on the experience with previous forms of 'non-financial reporting' including triple bottom line reporting (financial, environmental and social reporting), sustainability reporting, and multiple bottom line reporting which often includes good governance as an additional item of focus. These earlier initiatives were developed by far-sighted individuals who wanted to contribute to a better world. As such, a number of organisations were founded to provide guidance and encourage companies to broaden the coverage of their reporting and, more importantly, to reflect these important issues in everyday management decision making.

A number of the organisations that created the momentum and knowledge base on which integrated reporting draws will be discussed next. They include the Global Reporting Institute, The Sustainability Accounting Standards Board (SASB), the United Nations Global Compact, CDP Worldwide, AccountAbility, The Eco-Management and Audit Scheme, The Association of British Insurers, DJSI (the Dow Jones Sustainability Index), and the FTSE4 Good index series. Whilst the list may seem long they all cover different elements of environmental, social and governance achievement and reporting. Thus they range from guidelines on the matters to be reported, databases for comparisons across companies, guidelines on responsible investment disclosure with emphasis on the management of the risks, a range of audit possibilities, identification of high-performing organisations in terms of economic, social and governance factors and scoring of such performance. Among other things, this highlights both the number of dimensions involved in improving sustainability and in its measurement and reporting. Further it shows the upsurge in focus on this, particularly over the last 25 years.

20.6.1 The Global Reporting Initiative (GRI)[30]

The GRI has a mission to develop global sustainability reporting guidelines for voluntary use by organisations reporting on the three linked elements of sustainability, namely the economic, environmental and social dimensions of their activities, products and services.

- The economic dimension recognises that performance is not just economic performance from a shareholder perspective but also covers economic impacts on all significant stakeholders. An example would be to disclose the impact on the local community as a result of the expansion of a facility or the closure of a factory. It also includes disclosures of specific expenditures such as those on research and development and training.
- The environmental dimension covers air, water, land, biodiversity, pollution, and health impacts.
- The social dimension covers human rights, corruption/anti-corruption, compliance with laws and regulations, impacts on supply chains, responsible products and marketing.

The Global Reporting Initiative means that parties contemplating a relationship such as assessing investment risk and obtaining goods or services will have available to them a clear picture of the human and ecological impacts of the business. Its influence has been growing and there are jurisdictions, such as Sweden, that require a GRI report.

How useful are the GRI disclosures?

The usefulness of the disclosures depends on their credibility. Credibility is addressed in three ways:

- firstly there is a governance requirement that the level and extent of management involvement in sustainability policy setting, reporting, and compliance with those policies, have to be clearly identified;

- principles for defining report content and principles for defining report quality have to be specified; and finally

- it encourages reports to be 'verified' for assurance[31] by an independent expert.

Its reports are based on the concept that they should disclose material factors and not be cluttered with insignificant material. The important negative messages are not to be buried in the fine print. They are based on disclosing both the areas of good performance and of bad performance.

Typical disclosures would include, for example, benefits obtained from government subsidies, tax breaks, and special privileges and, on the other side, information on fines or other sanctions for environmental and regulatory breaches. Where significant spills have occurred, the number of events, the volumes released and their impacts have to be given. If the company identifies instances of corruption these need to be reported on as well. If you want to use their framework you cannot cherry pick. Nor can you exclude information that makes management uncomfortable unless it is truly not material.

The company also has to outline its plans for the short, medium and long terms and how those will impact on sustainability.

What if a company outsources?

It also recognises that companies might outsource task which create adverse consequences if a narrow coverage is chosen. Hence the emphasis on the group of companies' impacts irrespective of whether they are internal or external. As an example of these principles, the company or group of companies is required to report on employees and supervised workers, and in addition where a substantial portion of its work is conducted by 'outsiders' such as self-employed workers or subcontractors then that has to be reported on as well. In addition it requires the company to report on the supply chains and their impacts.

It is interesting to note that GRI does not see its application restricted to large corporations but sees it as also applicable to small and even micro businesses.[32]

Increasing disclosures – Diageo plc

An interesting case study is Diageo plc in so far as it started with a Sustainability and Responsibility Report. It then decided to start the journey to integrated reporting beginning with the 2014 annual report. At the same time, they continued to support the Global Reporting Initiative and the United Nations Global Compact (see below for a discussion of this). They realised that the new report did not include all the items previously covered so they published a Sustainability and Responsibility Performance Addendum.[33]

20.6.2 The Sustainability Accounting Standards Board[34]

This is a US non-profit organisation set up in 2011 dedicated to encouraging business to undertake sustainability accounting and provide information that is material, decision-useful and cost effective. To improve the quality of reporting they have developed standards for a number of industries with particular emphasis on the need for comparability to improve investor decision making and to reduce the hurdles and costs facing analysts. As this is not a government entity its standards are not binding. However, they rely on the quality of the research and the resulting standards to attract companies to use their standards and metrics where applicable to the companies' strategies. At the time of preparing this chapter they had a 'full set of provisional standards for 79 industries in 10 sectors'.[35]

20.6.3 United Nations Global Compact

The United Nations has since 2000 been engaged in an attempt to influence society in adopting sustainability principles. As part of that initiative it has sought to get business and communities to sign up to a set of 10 principles covering human rights, labour, the environment, and anti-corruption.[36]

Signing indicates a commitment to the Global Compact and its principles and to filing an annual report on the Global Compact website with a description of practical action taken supported by quantitative and qualitative measures of outcomes. Companies which do not match commitment with adequate action can be removed from the Compact scheme

The intention is to get companies to incorporate sustainability as an integral part of their activities including strategic planning and operations. Rather than being a burden these should be viewed as significant contributors to the success of the business including providing competitive advantages and in assisting in the identification of opportunities for growth and innovation. While the Global Compact believes that the adoption of sustainability involves very fundamental values and obligations and not merely a question of risk containment, there is no doubt that if they do not become embedded in the core values and become significant drivers of the business then considerable risks are being taken.

The Global Compact endorses the GRI and < IR > approaches. In addition, it recognises the possibility of resistance by some investors who adopt a narrowly interpreted shareholder primacy view. There is, therefore, a requirement that Global Compact signatories provide their investors with metrics describing gains in terms of extra revenue, cost savings and risk reductions flowing from a sustainability approach.

20.6.4 CDP Worldwide

CDP Worldwide is a UK charity which collects environmental information including emissions, water usage and forestry data. It also collects information on companies' environmental strategies and plans and drivers of changes in environmental performance both past and planned. Where companies agree the data is publicly available. Its data collection is designed to be compatible with GRI requirements. The information is claimed to be the largest self-reporting world wide database on the issues covered.[37] Companies can use this information to self-assess how they are performing relative to their peers.

20.6.5 AccountAbility[38]

This organisation follows a stakeholder approach to corporate social reporting and, based on such an approach, spells out both reporting principles and assurance standards.

Essentially its principles require an organisation to take responsibility for its material impacts on stakeholders, which in turn implies knowledge of those impacts gained through ongoing and systematic engagement with its stakeholders.

Its approach to assurance is interesting in that it has two types of assurance, both of which evaluate the information reported and systems used in terms of adherence to the principles developed by AccountAbility. Whereas Type 1 assurance assumes that the information is reliable and reports on adherence to AccountAbility principles, Type 2 assurance verifies compliance with Accountability principles and that the reported information is reliable.

This approach reflects the desire to have some assurance that the information is not selective and has some degree of credibility. However, at the same time there is a need to reflect the different stages of development of the environmental and social reporting in corporations, and the cost of providing comprehensive assurance.

20.6.6 The Eco-Management and Audit Scheme (EMAS)[39]

The Eco-Management and Audit Scheme was adopted as a voluntary environmental management scheme by the European Union (EU) in 1993 and has been upgraded over time. As such the scheme can now be used by organisations outside the EU. This scheme incorporates ISO 14001 (revised in 2015), the non-government international standards relating to systematic assessment of environmental impacts and the audit of compliance with those.

EMAS requires registered users of this system to report on energy efficiency, material efficiency, waste, biodiversity (land use and to start considering the impact of such land use on the eco-system or on habitats), and emissions. The objectives of EMAS include acting as a catalyst for innovation which improves both environmental and financial outcomes including identifying new business opportunities related to environmental performance.

The European Union had legislation on Corporate Social Responsibility Reporting which came into effect in 2017. Those who are compliant with EMAS and GRI will also be compliant with the new legislation.

Return on investment
In regard to this system it is interesting to contemplate why we have traditionally placed emphasis on return on investment. It is suggested that one reason for placing such emphasis is a recognition that as economic resources are in scarce supply it is desirable to optimise their use, i.e. look for good returns relative to the risks taken. In a world where more resources are going to be in scarce supply (e.g. water, clean air, liveable places, rare earth metals) it is also important for stakeholders to bear in mind that increased scarcity will force up prices, which will affect profitability if production systems have not found ways of minimising their use.

20.6.7 The Association of British Insurers (ABI)

The Association of British Insurers, being an industry association which represents companies who have major investment portfolios, is well placed to establish guidelines for reporting companies. In those guidelines the stress is on limited disclosure which is focused on the significant risks and opportunities in relation to ESG (environmental, social and governance) in the context of other risk factors, the mitigation of those risks, and their future plans. Thus if companies want to attract these insurance companies to invest in their shares it would be prudent to follow The Investment Association Guidelines on Responsible Investment Disclosure.[40]

20.6.8 FTSE ESG ratings

Based on public information, summarised information is provided about ESG performance based on the three pillars (economic, social and governance). Within those three categories various themes are explored in more detail in line with the UN Sustainable Development Goals such as no poverty, zero hunger and gender equality.[41] Overall ratings are calculated not on a simple addition of the scores on the three pillars, but rather the score weights the factors according to their importance and the likely impact of performances in those areas: 'The criteria have been designed to help investors minimise ESG risks'.[42]

20.6.9   S & P Dow Jones Sustainability Index and RobcoSam Analyses

This index is designed to drive the ESG movement worldwide. Companies are analysed by RobcoSam (a company with expertise in sustainability assessment) according to the three dimensions and are compared to the industry average and the best company within the industry on the individual dimensions (economic, environmental, and social) and overall.[43] Then the S & P Dow Jones Sustainability Index is calculated plotting the performance of leading sustainability driven companies worldwide (i.e. from 'the top 10% per industry of the 2,500 largest companies in the S & P Global Broad Market Index that lead their field in terms of financially material ESG factors'[44]).

20.7   The contribution of accountants

As pointed out previously, accounting professional bodies have been early advocates of broadening reporting to encompass environmental and social and governance dimensions. Thus in 1975 The Accounting Standards Steering Committee tried to get recognition for a broader scope of accountability when it published 'The Corporate Report'.

Various accountants argued for environmental and social accounting both before and after that report where the topics were sustainability, environmental accounting, corporate social responsibility, and triple bottom line. As momentum increased the ACCA established a Sustainability Reporting Award in 2002 and since that date such awards have been established by ACCA national bodies in 20 countries. Similar to other professional accounting bodies ACCA has embedded corporate social responsibility into its educational requirements.

When in 2009 Mervyn King and the Prince of Wales ('Accounting 4 Sustainability') called a meeting to discuss the future of reporting, the accounting profession was represented by IASB and FASB, IFAC as well as the big four accounting firms. This initiative led to the formation of the International Integrated Reporting Council.

While sustainability normally involves technical, scientific, legal, and social issues there are still roles for accountants in terms of strategic planning, control systems, external reporting and auditing.

Strategic planning

As people intimately involved in all aspects of the business they should have a good overview of the business and its plans for the future. This means they are in a good position to identify what environmental, social, and human rights issues are important in the organisation, or are likely to be in the near future.[45]

As accountants are normally involved in strategic planning they can ensure that the environmental, social, human rights, ethical and governance, supply management, resource maintenance issues are adequately addressed. Whilst others may have more expertise in the technical issues it is the accountant who can relate these issues to the potential costs of not adequately addressing the issue. In project evaluations such as net present value assessments, for example, they can ask searching questions in relation to relevant costs or benefits which have not been included in the analysis.

Control systems

In relation to controls systems, accountants can have important input into the items to be collected. They should monitor what other companies are reporting in terms of disclosures in annual reports and strategic reports with a view to ensuring their own systems cover all elements which are likely to be the focus of community demands in the future.

They should also be intimately familiar with the recommended measures established by the organisations discussed previously. Having identified the critical issues, the information system can be designed to capture the relevant information. Accountants have a lot of experience in capturing information and what can go wrong in such a process. They should, therefore, be involved in identifying the most important information, the units of measure, how it is to be captured, designing the controls necessary to ensure its integrity, advising on key performance measures and how these are to be used when carrying out performance evaluations and attempting to predict any undesirable consequences from their use for evaluation.

Management accountants

Management accountants have the challenge of how to collect and present information so as to capture management attention. For example, in relation to waste, it might be possible to extract costs from a range of accounts such as the costs paid to store, process or dispose of waste internally; the costs of transporting and disposing at commercial dumps; waste management salaries and estimated costs incurred by customers to dispose of discarded products and packaging, etc.

Highlighting such costs could lead to the identification of alternative strategies such as use of alternative materials in the product itself and in packaging or the need to invest in new processes to process waste.

Taking the retail industry as an example, close attention will need to be given to the cost implication of reducing the use of plastic in packaging and the potential increases in cost of recycling.

The following is an extract from the Guardian.[46]

> Former Asda chief executive Andy Clarke said recently supermarkets should not use any plastics for packaging. "It is vital that the UK packaging industry and supermarkets work together to turn off the tap," he said.
>
> Supermarkets in the UK pay less towards collecting and recycling their plastic waste than in any other European country – leaving taxpayers to pick up 90% of the bill – in a system which is shrouded in secrecy.
>
> On average supermarkets and retailers pay £18 per tonne towards recycling, whereas in other European countries, businesses pay up to £133 per tonne for recycling, according to the figures provided to the Environmental Audit Committee. In Germany producers pay 100%.

Financial accountants

Financial accountants can focus on how to communicate the environmental and social information so as to show trends and its relation to the strategy and value proposition of the company.

They take a positive proactive role, raising questions such as:

● Are there any issues of comparability of information across an industry which may need to be addressed?

● Is any information missing which is necessary to really understand the current position of the organisation and the future prospects of the company?

- Is there a need for strategies to address different audiences with different levels of information in different reports?
- Is there a need to revise any of the figures in the draft accounts?
- Is there a need to recognise impairments of intangible assets?
- Has there been any increase in pollution that warrants the inclusion in the accounts of provisions or liabilities for rectification?
- Is there a need to recognise environmental liabilities (IAS 37) and environmental assets or to report contingent assets and liabilities?
- Will there be pressure to reduce financial accounting disclosures to reduce information overload?
- Are the disclosures limited to the key facts and communicated in a clear, easy to understand manner?
- How should any Notes to the accounts be worded?

The following example of wording is taken from the BHPBilliton 2015 Annual Report:[47]

Provision for closure and rehabilitation

The Group's accounting policy for the recognition of closure and rehabilitation provisions requires significant estimates and assumptions such as: requirements of the relevant legal and regulatory framework; the magnitude of possible contamination; and the timing, extent and costs of required closure and rehabilitation activity. These uncertainties may result in future actual expenditure differing from the amounts currently provided.

The provision recognised for each site is periodically reviewed and updated based on the facts and circumstances available at the time. Changes to the estimated future costs for operating sites are recognised in the balance sheet by adjusting both the closure and rehabilitation asset and provision. For closed sites, changes to estimated costs are recognised immediately in the income statement.

A further example taken from the Royal Dutch Shell 2016 Annual Report makes a similar statement:[48]

The amount and timing of settlement in respect of these provisions are uncertain and dependent on various factors that are not always within management's control. Additions to provisions are stated net of reversals of provisions recognised in prior periods.

Reviews of estimated decommissioning and restoration costs and the discount rate applied are carried out annually. In 2016, there was a decrease of $2,361 million in the provision resulting from changes in cost estimates reported within remeasurements and other movements (2015: an increase of $3,620 million resulting from changes in cost estimates and a decrease in the discount rate).

Of the decommissioning and restoration provision at December 31, 2016, an estimated $4,747 million is expected to be utilised within one to five years, $6,069 million within six to 10 years, and the remainder in later periods

This statement is interesting in that it highlights the subjective nature of the decisions as to the issues of timing, appropriate discount rates and estimation of future costs.

Other areas that may be monitored

There may be other areas which accountants may want to monitor and bring to the attention of management. One such is the vulnerability of the company to climate change. Again, practice questions are raised, such as:

- Are any of the assets vulnerable? For example, In filings with the Securities and Exchange Commission, several oil and pipeline companies acknowledge that climate change – which the fossil fuel industry has contributed to significantly – could undermine their bottom line and threaten their most valuable physical assets, including pipelines, oil storage "tank farms" and export terminals.[49]
- Which products and customers are sensitive to climate variability[50]?
- What are the implications for inventory levels?
- Is there a concentration of supply chains in areas which could be affected ?
- Is there a need to diversify the locations of suppliers?

Value added statements

An earlier attempt to address social accounting was the adoption of the value added statement as mentioned earlier. Of particular interest is that accountants perceived the need for this item of social accounting well before social accounting became more widely acknowledged.

Events of 2011 showed that the issue of fairness (which is one element underlying the issue of the value added statement) is perceived by many as being a major factor in whether to support the current version of the economic system. Following the crash covering 2007 and 2008, governments around the world were required to borrow to support the financial institutions (banks were supported including the British government taking an 81% interest in RBS, and the USA government supported non-bank lenders, such as General Electric and insurer AIG, to preserve the overall economic system).

This support was perceived by many as the rich being the beneficiaries in the good times prior to the crash and then getting subsidies when the investments performed badly. Irrespective of who were the ultimate beneficiaries, the perception of many was that the top 1% of society were getting excessive benefits from the system whereas the remaining 99% were being unfairly treated.

The statement of value added also illustrates how the perspectives adopted can determine the content of the social report and that social reporting is not always self-evident. Before discussing those issues, a real example is provided.

Example: Barloworld Integrated Report 2015[51]

A measure of the value created by the group is the amount of value added by its diverse trading, distribution and other activities to the cost of products and services purchased. The statement below shows the total value created and how it was distributed.

Statement of total value added for the year ended 30 September

	2017 Rm	%
Revenue from continuing operations	61,959	
Revenue from discontinued operation	4,076	
Paid to suppliers for materials and services	49,622	
Value added	16,413	
Income from investments *a*	76	

	2017 Rm	%
Total value created	16,489	
Value distribution		
Employees	9,948	62
Capital providers:	2,141	13
Finance costs	1,338	
Dividends to Barloworld Limited shareholders	755	
Dividends to non-controlling interest in subsidiaries	48	
Government	904	5
Communities (corporate social investment)	18	
Reinvested in the group to maintain and develop operations	3,479	20
Depreciation	2,589	
Retained profit	850	
Deferred taxation	40	
	16,489	100
Value added ratios		
Value created per employee (rand)	824,326	
Corporate social investment – % of profit after taxation	1	

If this report is confusing the following should help. The report views the company as a mechanism for both creating products and services out of external inputs and then deciding how the economic gain is distributed to the various stakeholders who helped generate those benefits. So the above statement says the company sold goods and services for Rm66,035. These goods and services were only possible because the company paid Rm49,622 to external suppliers. Therefore the work performed within the company generated additional economic benefits of 66,035 minus 49,622, or Rm16,413. In addition, the company earned Rm76 from investments so that is added on to the 16,413 to give total additional economic benefits generated (or the value added) of Rm16,489. That money was then divided up as follows among stakeholders as follows:

Employee benefits including wages, pensions and healthcare	9,948
	62%
Rewards to financiers in the form of interest and dividends	2,141
	13%
Payments to government departments	904
	5%
Payment to a community group	18
Reinvestment into the business	3,489
	20%
Total of the amount shared up	16,489 (which equals the amount of the value added calculated above)

How is this information actually used? Can one draw accurate conclusions regarding the fairness of the division of the benefits generated?

Note: Barloworld has followed the traditional methods of preparing the value added statement and the comments below are not in any way related to their circumstances or business activities.

However, there are questions which could be raised about such calculations in general.

What are the rewards to the financiers?

It could be argued that they get interest and dividends as shown above. But shareholders get both dividends and capital gains from the increase in the value of shares. So it could be argued that, although part of the reinvestment into the business is to cover wear and tear and obsolescence of equipment, the remaining part enhances the value of the shares.

What is the category 'payments to government departments'?

This may in some circumstances be ambiguous. For example, is a payment of a royalty by a mining company based on the sales value of the ore which was shipped a payment of a tax or is it an agreed method of pricing the ore body sold to the mining company? If it is a fair cost of the raw ore then should it be a payment for goods and services in the calculation of the value added?

Where a government department provides services such as water, electricity or use of a motorway is that a payment to suppliers or is it an allocation to the government?

Employee benefits

While the total allocation to employees is interesting it might be more informative to know payments to different categories of employees, as the rewards for top-level employees may be considerably different from those to other employees. In the USA from 1 January 2017 a pay ratio will be filed under Item 402 of Regulation S-K. The ratio compares the total compensation of the chief executive officer to the median compensation of all other employees. Note the reference to median compensation rather than average compensation, which is to avoid the possibility of averages being skewed by atypical employees. The reported ratio will tell readers the number of times greater the chief executive's remuneration is compared to the typical (median) employee. It will be interesting to see if this information will be required by other countries.

Auditors

Internal auditors and external auditors need to consider which of the environmental and social disclosures need to be certified and who has the skill to perform the certification. If they are not accountants what supervision and training is desirable to ensure they apply the appropriate audit skills (as opposed to the technical skills)?

Although the certification does not have to be performed by an accountant or an accounting firm, the skills developed in traditional audits are a possible competitive advantage as could be the reputation of an established auditor.

20.8 Integrated reporting – its impact on the future development of financial reporting and accounting

As the world becomes more aware of the need to modify industry behaviour to reflect the challenges posed by the impact of their actions on the sustainability of our lifestyle, and the social and environmental systems which make that lifestyle achievable, there is pressure to adopt different mindsets.

The implication for accounting is to encourage integrated reporting. Instead of the previous focus primarily on financial capital and its changes, the integrated approach requires reporting on six types of capital, as illustrated in Figure 20.1.

This is not to suggest companies don't have to perform well on financial dimensions but rather that good financial performance is not sufficient on its own. It is integrated in the sense that it recognises that the achievement of the organisation's strategy probably requires support from all six areas and that the interaction with the other five capitals varies across organisations and hence the reporting should reflect that.

Further to understand the reports one needs a clear idea of the linkages between the strategy which builds on a sustainable competitive advantage and the various capitals. As the range of areas on which the organisation reports grows, the need to avoid information overload becomes much more important. Thus materiality is important with the focus is on the critical factors only. There is a need to communicate a coherent story of the organisation's current achievements and what it has done to position it to take advantage of the types of opportunities which are likely to arise in the future.

By reporting on multiple capitals it is hoped that the quality of external reporting will improve due to a more comprehensive analysis and that the limitations inherent in current reporting will be partly compensated for by the additional information. This is particularly relevant in businesses where the major assets are intangible (technology breakthroughs, systems, images and brand connotations, integrity, and governance systems), and where it is difficult to assess a value.

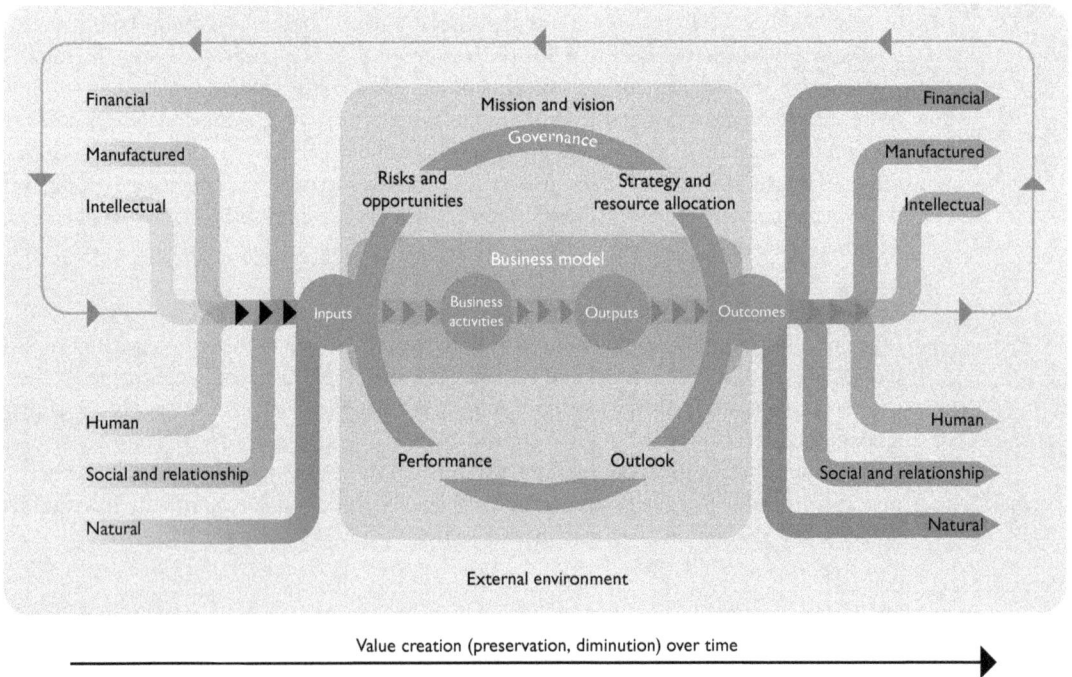

Also the looming risks associated with achieving sustainability often revolve around environmental issues and levels of social support, as well as legal frameworks and infrastructure. It is hoped that better reporting will lead to better and more reliable valuations and subsequently to better allocations of resources in society.

There is an expectation that, as reporting changes, the pressures on management to achieve on all capitals will lead to greater alignment of business decision making with the needs of society as a whole. In other words, the incorporation of corporate social responsibility into the integrated reporting system will reduce the number and size of externalities. Some companies will use integrated reports as public relations statements but it is a matter of the degree of puffery. Obviously companies like to promote their achievements. To the extent that major issues are avoided and not reported exposes the company to major risks such as litigation risks, reputational risks, and exposure of top management to career risks. Hopefully this will constrain the use of public relations to manageable proportions. Auditors have an opportunity to show their value by ensuring reporting is not misleading.

Ultimately, integrated reporting is only successful if it changes business behaviour to align more closely with what is good for society as a whole. This means reward systems must support the broader objectives. Accountants can contribute to the debate by providing feedback on practicalities and effectiveness.

REVIEW QUESTIONS

1 GRI has Principles for Defining Report Content. Included in those is the principle of stakeholder inclusiveness, which says 'The organization should identify its stakeholders, and explain how it has responded to their reasonable expectations and interest.' Using your university as the case study,

- identify its stakeholders

- decide what would constitute reasonable expectations

- discuss steps being taken to provide the information necessary to make an informed judgement.

2 GRI has Principles for Defining Report Quality, which states that 'The report should reflect positive and negative aspects of the organization's performance to enable a reasoned assessment of overall performance.' Further they go on to say 'The overall presentation of the report's content should provide an unbiased picture of the organization's performance. The report should avoid selections, omissions, or presentation formats that are reasonably likely to unduly or inappropriately influence a decision or judgement by the report reader.' Obtain either an integrated accounting report, or a sustainability report, or an annual report and examine two graphs or diagrams and explain whether or not these criteria are met.

3 Identify an organisation that undertakes corporate social reporting and has an independent party provide assurance on such reporting. Explain in your own words what the assurance covers and does not cover, who it is addressed to, whether the assurance follows any particular standard(s).

4 Obtain three Viability Statements from published financial statements and critically compare.

5 Identify a company that is registered under the EMAS and discuss its disclosures under that scheme and what it indicates in terms of progress in achieving significant improvement in environmental achievements.

6 Access https://www.frc.org.uk/getattachment/76e21dee-2be2-415f-b326-932e8a3fc1e6/Risk-and-Viability-Reporting.pdf and discuss what impact viability reporting has had on companies.

7 Linda Midgley[52] suggested that the major deficiency with current integrated reports is that they do not provide a story which shows the linkage between the reporting on the various capitals. Explain in your own words why the story is important and why you think companies are not performing better on that aspect.

8 The Prince's Accounting for Sustainability Project was responsible for bringing together the sponsors of the International Integrated Reporting Council. The project is a co-sponsor of the Finance for the Future Awards to bring to the attention of the financial community the skills required for accounting in the twenty-first century. Identify one of the latest recipients (there are multiple categories so just choose one) of the award and explain in your own words the innovation in financial applications which they have been responsible for and discuss whether it has broader applications.

9 In 2016 the UK Financial Reporting Council objected to the proposed European Union directive on integrated reporting for large companies.[53] The discussion seems to revolve around disclosure of specific items of information versus discretionary disclosure based on the perceived relevance or importance of the information in relation to the reporting company's strategy. Discuss the pros and cons of discretion in relation to the disclosures in integrated reporting.

10 Aviva plc provided in relation to 2016 three relevant reports. Those reports are the Strategic Report 2016, Corporate Social Responsibility Summary 2016, and Aviva Environmental, Social and Governance Data Sheet 2016. Read those reports and rank them in terms of usefulness to you and justify your ranking.

11 Obtain copies of three integrated accounting reports (including at least one which has been certified) and identify whether or not they have been certified. On any that has been certified review the 'statement' by the certifier and identify what they have actually done as part of the review, what guidelines (if any) they have followed, and whether they have confidence in the report. (Note: ACCA and CPA Australia have produced integrated reports.)

12 From the IIRC website identify a company producing an integrated report. Read the report from an investor perspective and then from an employee perspective. Then provide two evaluations with reasons for your comments.

13 The Integrated Reporting Framework stresses the need for linkages to the business strategy to be clear and the reporting to be restricted to significant items. However, other parties stress the need for comparability. Discuss whether or not these two views are compatible.

14 Should integrated reports address allocation of value added? Justify your conclusions.

15 Select an industry and explain the best approach to conveying to readers the state of human resources.

16 Whenever a new system of metrics is used for performance evaluation smart people try to game the system. Identify a metric in the G4 system[54] and identify how the system might be gamed.

(By to game the system we mean to beat the system by undertaking actions which are not desirable under the system but which get a good score on the evaluation system. An example might be an academic who is being evaluated on the number of publications in academic journals. The academic is going to publish a long article and then changes their mind and decides to split the research into two parts to get two publications without doing much extra work. The amount of research undertaken is not increased but the academic appears to be a better researcher.)

17 Nissan, the Japanese car company, decided that 'any environmentalism should pay for itself and for every penny you spend you must save a penny. You can spend as many pennies as you like as long as other environmental actions save an equal number.[55] Discuss the significance of this for each of the major stakeholders.

18 Consumer-oriented models are more likely to be influenced by ethical principles. Discuss.

19 Look up the S & P Dow Jones Indices and then discuss:

(a) what you think the index can be used for;

(b) the number of high-performing companies by country;

(c) the comparative performance of two of those high performers.

20 One of the questions in a survey[56] of chartered investment analysts in 2017 asked:

'Which, if any, of the following ESG (Environmental, Social, Governance) issues do you take into account in your investment analysis or decisions? Select all that apply'.

27% of analysts surveyed replied that they did not take ESG factors into consideration.

Access the survey and assess changes that might encourage all analysts to take ESG into account.

21 In a speech given for the Arthur Burns Memorial Lecture,[57] Mark Carney highlighted paradoxes in addressing the financial risk from climate change. The first paradox is that 'the future will be past'. Discuss what is meant by this.

22 Discuss two sectors where climate change could adversely affect shareholder value.[58]

23 Future of Accounting Profession: Three Major Changes and Implications for Teaching and Research

Access [https://www.ifac.org/global-knowledge-gateway/business-reporting/discussion/future-accounting-profession-three-major] [http://www.accaglobal.com/us/en/member/ab/ab-archive.html]

Discuss these three major changes and how accounting undergraduate programmes and professional bodies might prepare students for such a future.

EXERCISES

Question 1

Geoworld Enterprises plc has the following information extracted from its statement of income and payroll systems:

	£
Revenue	411,000,000
Compensation expenses	158,000,000
Raw materials used	100,000,000
Payments to subcontractors	51,000,000
Energy expenses	1,000,000
Depreciation expenses	1,000,000
Interest expenses	2,000,000
Taxation expenses	16,000,000

| Employment statistics | | Full time | | Part time |
	Number	Total payment to the group £	Number	Total payment to the group £
CEO	1x	1,000,000		
Senior executives	5x	3,000,000		
Other executives	10x	4,000,000		
Local employees	2,000x	80,000,000	1000x	10,000,000
International employees	2000x	40,000,000	4,000x	20,000,000
Subcontractors	2,000x	35,000,000	2,000x	16,000,000

Each fulltime employee works double the hours of part time staff.

Dividends paid to shareholders   3,000,000

Required:
(a) Prepare a value added statement.
(b) Prepare your version of the ratio of the chief executive salary to the median income of other employees. (Note the objective is not to get you to look up the standard form of the calculation but rather to get you to think about the complexities of the calculation and the need for standardisation of the system.) Justify your calculation(s).
(c) Would the required information be readily available in the typical information system? If not could such systems be easily modified?
(d) Look at the calculation in (b) above and consider how the CEO could improve their score in the future and whether all those possibilities would be in the interests of shareholders.

Question 2

Wonder Kid Enterprises Company has produced the following results over the last three years:

	20XX	20XY	20XZ
Profit before interest and taxes	1,000,000	1,600,000	3,000,000
Interest	160,000	320,000	900,000
Taxes	252,000	384,000	630,000
Profit after interest and taxes	588,000	896,000	1,470,000
Financing using debt	40%	40%	40%
Funds employed ($debt + equity$)	4,000,000	8,000,000	20,000,000
Shareholders' before tax required rate of return on investment	20%	20%	25%

Management has just issued its annual report for 20XZ and a fair reading of their commentary is that the company has done very well because the trend in profit after interest and taxes have shown a high level of growth. In addition it is disclosed that the development of its latest technological breakthrough is taking longer to get regulatory approval than earlier thought. A review of the financial press ascertains that interest rates have remained steady over the three years.

Required:
Discuss the results showing calculations where appropriate.

Question 3

(a) Prepare a value added statement to be included in the corporate report of Hythe plc for the year ended 31 December 20X6, including the comparatives for 20X5, using the information given below:

	20X6	20X5
	£000	£000
Non-current assets (net book value)	3,725	3,594
Trade receivables	870	769
Trade payables	530	448
14% debentures	1,200	1,080
6% preference shares	400	400
Ordinary shares (£1 each)	3,200	3,200
Sales	5,124	4,604
Materials consumed	2,934	2,482
Wages	607	598
Depreciation	155	144
Fuel consumed	290	242
Hire of plant and machinery	41	38
Salaries	203	198
Auditors' remuneration	10	8
Corporation tax provision	402	393
Ordinary share dividend	9p	8p
Number of employees	40	42

(b) Although value added statements were recommended by The Corporate Report in 1975, as yet there is no accounting standard related to them. Explain what a value added statement is and provide reasons as to why you think it has not yet become mandatory to produce such a statement as a component of current financial statements through either a Financial Reporting Standard or company law.

Question 4

The following items have been extracted from the accounts:

	2005 (€m)	2004 (€m)
Other income	844	980
Cost of materials	25,694	24,467
Financial income	−188	54
Depreciation/amortisation	4,207	3,589
Providers of finance	1,351	1,059
Retained	1,815	1,823
Revenues	46,656	44,335
Government	1,590	1,794
Other expenses	4,925	5,093
Shareholders	424	419
Employees	7,306	7,125

Required:
(a) **Prepare a value added statement showing % for each year and % change.**
(b) **Draft a note for inclusion in the annual report commenting on the statement you have prepared.**

Question 5

David Mark is a sole trader who owns and operates supermarkets in each of three villages near Ousby. He has drafted his own accounts for the year ended 31 May 20X4 for each of the branches. They are as follows:

	Arton		Blendale		Clifearn	
	£	£	£	£	£	£
Sales		910,800		673,200		382,800
Cost of sales		633,100		504,900		287,100
Gross profit		277,700		168,300		95,700
Less: Expenses:						
David Mark's salary	10,560		10,560		10,560	
Other salaries and wages	143,220		97,020		78,540	
Rent			19,800			
Rates	8,920		5,780		2,865	
Advertising	2,640		2,640		2,640	
Delivery van expenses	5,280		5,280		5,280	
General expenses	11,220		3,300		1,188	
Telephone	2,640		1,980		1,584	
Wrapping materials	7,920		3,960		2,640	
Depreciation:						
Fixtures	8,220		4,260		2,940	
Vehicle	3,000	203,620	3,000	157,580	3,000	111,237
Net profit/(loss)		74,080		10,720		(15,537)

The figures for the year ended 31 May 20X4 follow the pattern of recent years. Because of this, David Mark is proposing to close the Clifearn supermarket immediately.

David Mark employs 12 full-time and 20 part-time staff. His recruitment policy is based on employing one extra part-time assistant for every £30,000 increase in branch sales. His staff deployment at the moment is as follows:

	Arton	Blendale	Clifearn
Full-time staff (including managers)	6	4	2
Part-time staff	8	6	6

Peter Gaskin, the manager of the Clifearn supermarket, asks David to give him another year to make the supermarket profitable. Peter has calculated that he must cover £125,500 expenses out of his gross profit in the year ended 31 May 20X5 in order to move into profitability. His calculations include extra staff costs and all other extra costs.

Additional information:

(i) General advertising for the business as a whole is controlled by David Mark. This costs £3,960 per annum. Each manager spends a further £1,320 advertising his own supermarket locally.

(ii) The delivery vehicle is used for deliveries from the Arton supermarket only.

(iii) David Mark has a central telephone switchboard which costs £1,584 rental per annum. Each supermarket is charged for all calls actually made. For the year ended 31 May 20X4 these amounted to:

Arton	£2,112
Blendale	£1,452
Clifearn	£1,056

Required:

(a) A report addressed to David Mark advising him whether to close the Clifearn supermarket. Your report should include a detailed financial statement based on the results for the year ended 31 May 20X4 relating to the Clifearn branch.

(b) Calculate the increased turnover and extra staff needed if Peter's suggestion is implemented.

(c) Comment on the social implications for the residents of Clifearn if (i) David Mark closes the supermarket, (ii) Peter Gaskin's recommendation is undertaken.

Question 6

(a) The draft income statement of the Verti Group as at 30 April 2016 shows profit attributable to ordinary shareholders of the parent entity of $12 million and a loss from discontinued operations attributable to the parent entity of $8 million.

Verti has 4 million ordinary equity shares outstanding with a market value of $80 each. There are 400,000 ordinary share options outstanding with an exercise price of $60 each.

Verti has in issue 1.6 million convertible preference shares with a par value of $100 each. The preference shares are entitled to a cumulative dividend of $0.10 per share. Each preference share will convert into 2 ordinary shares.

Verti has $200 million 6% convertible bonds in issue. Each $1,000 bond is convertible into 20 ordinary shares. Interest expense is not affected by amortisation of premium or discount.

The relevant tax rate is 30%.

Required

Advise Verti of the basic and diluted earnings per share figures to be disclosed in the group income statement for the year ended 30 April 2016.

(b) Verti operates in the telecommunications industry. The entity's directors are supportive of the International Standards Board's (IASB) attempts to publish Generally Accepted Accounting Principles (GAAP) which govern how entities define their periodic earnings. They believe that GAAP helps to ensure a level of reliability and consistency across firms and over time. The directors have now become concerned about the development of non- GAAP earnings performance measures disclosed by a large number of the entity's competitors in their financial reporting and require advice on whether Verti is at a competitive disadvantage by not disclosing such information.

Required

Advise Verti's directors on whether the disclosure of non-GAAP (also known as 'pro- forma') earnings measures is likely to add valuable information to the entity's annual reporting or whether it would be seen as an example of the entity indulging in earnings management.

(c) Verti's directors are keen to develop the entity's engagement with capital providers and have been informed of a development in corporate reporting known as The International Integrated Reporting

Framework. They were previously unaware of the existence of the framework and would like advice on what impact it may have on the entity's annual reporting, which presently focusses primarily on traditional concepts of historical performance.

Required
Advise Verti's directors on the possible impact of the above 'framework' on the annual reporting of the group as far as its engagement with capital providers and its focus on historical performance are concerned.

(Association of International Accountants)

Notes

1 'BHP Billiton withdraws from Ok Tedi Copper Mine and establishes development fund for benefit of Papua New Guinea People', www.bhp/documents/investors/reports/2001/oktedimineexit-briefingpaper.pdf

2 https://www.slatergordon.co.uk/commercial-and-group-litigation/product-liability-group-litigation/volkswagen-scandal-legal-investigation/claiming-compensation-against-vw-for-the-emissions-scandal/

3 www.sustainability-indices.com/images/150929-statement-vw-exclusion_vdef.pdf

4 http://www.rightinginjustice.com/news/2017/12/08/vw-exec-gets-7-year-sentence-for-emissions-cheat-role/

5 www.theguardian.com/world/2013/june23/rana-plaza-factory-disaster-bangladesh-primark

6 Ibid.

7 https://www.cfr.org/backgrounder/understanding-libor-scandal

8 http://www.rogierholtermans.com/blog/2017/3/21/environmental-performance-and-the-cost-of-capital-evidence-from-commercial-mortgages-and-reit-bonds

9 https://www.reuters.com/article/us-usa-guns-breakingviews/breakingviews-blackrock-puts-gun-complex-boards-in-crosshairs-idUSKCN1GE2I8

10 L. Stout, *The Shareholder Value Myth*, San Francisco, Berrett-Koehler, 2012.

11 Stakeholder theory has much in common with agency theory, which views the company as a network of contracts of which shareholder contracts are essentially no different from other contracts. A residual interest is not the same as ownership. See Stout (2012), op cit.

12 Companies Act, 2006, section 172.

13 Financial Reporting Council, *Guidance on the Strategic Report*, June 2014, www.frc.org.uk/Our-Work/Publications/Accounting-and-Reporting-Policy/Guidance-on-the-Strategic-Report.pdf, p. 14.

14 *The Stern Review: The Economics of Climate Change*, 30 October, 2006, HM Treasury.

15 The strategic report is extracted from the Unilever 2015 Annual Report.

16 The International < IR > Framework, www.theiirc.org

17 These descriptions are in 2.15 of the International < IR > Framework.

18 http://www.wipo.int/sme/en/documents/ip_innovation_development_fulltext.html

19 'During the process of preparing his bank ratings, Lafferty's team went back and analysed the 2007 annual report of HBOS, a British bank which blew itself up in the financial crisis. The report showed staff gave management a rating of 76 per cent. At the time, this number surprised industry pundits because the average was 50 per cent. Later, an HBOS whistle blower Paul Moore revealed that management had bullied staff into answering questions in the staff survey in the "correct" way.' Chanticleer, 'Banking on cultural change', *The Australian Financial Review*, 12-13 March 2016, p. 56.

20 www.shell.com/investors/financial-reporting/annual-publications/andentire_shell_ar15.pdf, p. 25.

21 http://drcaroladams.net/the-international-integrated-reporting-council-a-call-to-action/

22 With the extension of the range of reporting the term multiple bottom line covering economic, governance, social, ethical, and environmental (EGSEE) performance. See Z. Rezaee, *Business*

Sustainability, Sheffield, Greenleaf Publishing, 2015, who says over 6000 public companies issue comprehensive reports compared to 50 companies ten years ago.

23 The history is outlined in J. Gleeson-White, *Six Capitals*, Sydney, Allen & Unwin, 2014.

24 'The Corporate Report', a discussion paper published by the Accounting Standards Steering Committee.

25 Based on information reported in Z. Rezaee, *Business Sustainability*, Sheffield, Greenleaf Publishing, 2015. The reference to the Brundtlund Report is to the United Nations World Commission on Environment and Development, *Our Common Future*, Oxford University Press, 1987.

26 R.G. Eccles and M.P. Krzus with S.Ribot, *The Integrated Reporting Movement*, Hoboken, NJ, Wiley, 2015.

27 www.mervynking.co.za/downloads/CD_King2.pdf

28 www.ru.ac.za/media/rhodesuniversity/content/erm/documents/xx.%20King%203%20-%20 King%20Report.pdf

29 www.prconversations.com/2009/09/difference-between-king-ii-and-king-iii-reports-on-governance/

30 www.globalreporting.org

31 https://www.globalreporting.org/resourcelibrary/GRI-Assurance.pdf

32 www.globalreporting.org/resourcelibrary/Ready-to-Report-SME-booklet-online.pdf

33 www.diageo.com/en-row/csr/building-thriving-communities/sustainable-supply-chains/Pages/default.aspx

34 For more information, go to www.sasb.org

35 A letter from Jean Rogers, SASB CEO, 6 April 2016.

36 www.unglobalcompact.org/docs/publications/UN_Global_Compact_Guide_to_Corporate_Sustainability.pdf

37 www.cdp.net/CDP%20Questionaire%20Documents/CDP-Climate-Change-Information-request-2016.pdf

38 www.accountability.com

39 http://ec.europa.eu/environment/emas/news/index_en.htm#138

40 https://www.ivis.co.uk/media/11203/Rebranded-Guidelines-on-Responsible-Investment-Disclosure-January-2007-3-June-2015-.pdf

41 https://sustainabledevelopment.un.org/

42 www.ftse.com/products/indices/f4g-esg-ratings

43 www.sustainability-indices.com/review/industry-group-leaders-2015.jsp

44 Ibid.

45 Rezaee, op. cit., suggests that 'about a third of the US GDP is sensitive to weather changes' and relies on J.K. Lazo, M. Lawson, P.H. Larsen and D.M. Waldman, 'United States economic sensitivity to weather variability', *Bulletin of the American Meteorological Society*, vol. 92, 2012, pp. 709–20.

46 https://www.theguardian.com/environment/2018/jan/17/nearly-1m-tonnes-every-year-supermarkets-shamed-for-plastic-packaging

47 www.bhpbilliton.com/~/media/bhp/documents/investors/annual-reports/2015/bhpbillitonannualreport2015_interactive.pdf?la=en

48 http://reports.shell.com/annual-report/2015/consolidated-financial-statements/notes/18-decommissioning-and-other-provisions.php

49 https://www.thedailybeast.com/big-oil-believes-in-climate-changewhen-its-talking-to-shareholders

50 http://www.hbs.edu/faculty/Publication%20Files/JiraToffel_2013_advance_3cd6388c-791b-465c-9810-11008650d1f3.pdf

51 www.barloworld-reports.co.za/integrated-reports/ir-2015/bar-value-highlights.php

52 http://pwc.blogs.com/corporatereporting/2016/03/why-does-integrated-reporting-so-often-leaves-us-dissatisfied.html

53 www.iasplus.com/en/news/2016/04/frc

54 https://www.globalreporting.org/resourcelibrary/GRIG4-Part1-Reporting-Principles-and-Standard-Disclosures.pdf

55 M. Brown, 'Greening the bottom line', *Management Today,* July, 1995, p. 73.

56 https://www.cfainstitute.org/learning/future/Documents/ESG_Survey_Report_July_2017.pdf

57 http://bruegel.org/2017/01/climate-change-and-financial-markets/

58 https://www.mckinsey.com/business-functions/strategy-and-corporate-finance/our-insights/how-climate-change-could-affect-corporate-valuations